THE TUDOR ARTE OF WARRE VOLUME 1

The Conduct of War from Henry VII to Mary I, 1485–1558

Jonathan Davies

Helion & Company

Helion & Company Limited
Unit 8 Amherst Business Centre
Budbrooke Road
Warwick
CV34 5WE
England
Tel. 01926 499 619
Email: info@helion.co.uk
Website: www.helion.co.uk
Twitter: @helionbooks
Visit our blog http://blog.helion.co.uk/

Published by Helion & Company 2021
Designed and typeset by Serena Jones
Cover designed by Paul Hewitt, Battlefield Design (www.battlefield-design.co.uk)

Text © Jonathan Davies 2021
Black and white images © as individually credited
Colour photographs by Chantal Lashmar and Jane Bennett © Helion & Company 2021
Colour figure on front cover by Patrice Courcelle © Helion & Company 2021
Flag artwork by Mats Elzinga © Helion & Company 2021
Maps by George Anderson © Helion & Company 2021

ISBN 978-1-913336-41-7

British Library Cataloguing-in-Publication Data.
A catalogue record for this book is available from the British Library.

For details of other military history titles published by Helion & Company
Limited, contact the above address, or visit our website: http://www.helion.co.uk

We always welcome receiving book proposals from prospective authors.

Contents

Preface

This book has taken a very long time to write. For almost forty years I have been reading, teaching, writing and re-enacting medieval and Tudor history and this book is the unexpected consequence. It reflects my knowledge, enthusiasms, pet loves and hates. I have always written on subjects about which I wanted to know more and to address the questions that arose. The purpose of this book is to help answer some of those questions.

In the introduction I have endeavoured to put England firmly into its place, or rather context, in Europe. England would be competing on European battlefields and would be compared by contemporary opinion with European armies for efficacy and modernity. The first part of the book provides a narrative of events to explain the context in which decisions of war and peace were made, and then analyses the campaigns and battles that were the consequence. The second part deals with how the armies were raised and supported and how their tactics developed. The third part deals with the military hardware. I try at the same time to enliven and engage in the debates surrounding these subjects. I have concluded with an assessment of England's military performance in the light of the current 'military revolution' debate.

I have tried to provide as broad a narrative and as extensive an analysis as possible, relying very heavily on the work of others. I hopefully fully acknowledge and recognise their efforts in my own analyses. I have spent considerable time on some issues that may appear of marginal importance but which were central in the conduct of campaigns and in the lives of those who participated in them. The issue of logistics and planning which are too often ignored were of vital importance. It is clear that a campaign's success depended to a great extent upon the availability of coin, bread, beef and ale. Boulogne was besieged in 1544 because it was an objective that could be achieved with the resources at hand. Pinkie was won by the brilliant management of the army's logistical support as well as by the sacrifice of the Bulleners and Gentlemen Pensioners. Campaigns collapsed in Spain in 1512 and France in 1523 because of failures of leadership and provisions. Flodden was fought, at least in part, because the English army had run out of ale.

An army is only as good as the officers and men it recruits. There were a small number of 'professional' soldiers in the realm, too few to constitute a viable force of their own. The Army Royal was recruited from gentlemen-at-arms and the 'commons-in-arms'. This was at a time when Continental armies were becoming professionalised by long periods of war and the widespread use of mercenaries; the difference between the English way of war and that of Europe should be acknowledged. I have also devoted some space to the provision of medical services. The widespread use of firearms caused new suffering, both from the injuries they caused and the treatment that was prescribed.

I have devoted considerable space to the arms and equipment but I have tried to focus on two areas of contention. Firstly the bow versus gun debate, which was both one fiercely contested among contemporaries and which even today has its protagonists. The second discussion concerns the modernity and efficacy of the 'Device forts' which have been subject to much ill-considered criticism. I have concluded with an analysis of the concept of the 'military revolution', as it relates to England in this period. In this I am pleased to say I am at least swimming with the tide, as the outright condemnation of England's backwardness, which was once common, is now tempered by more balanced opinions.

The horrors of war are often forgotten when discussing matters of strategy, tactics and equipment. This is why I have included a section on *Disease and Want*, which I hope highlights the unnecessary suffering of the English soldiers and unfortunate civilians.

I beg the reader to forgive my sins whether of omission or commission. It is a book that is both too long and too short. I have found the task of assembling the material and ideas not an easy one, especially in these plague years. I hope that the reader will find something of interest both of fact and argument and will find much to appreciate as well as to condemn in the lives and actions of our forebears.

Acknowledgements

Many people have helped me directly and indirectly in the preparation of this book. I would like to thank Jonathan Cooper and Dr Edward Fox in generously sharing their research, allowing me thereby to amend some errors and reappraise some of my conclusions. Pauline Asher and Dr Catharine Davies have contributed their helpful comments and expertise. Charles Singleton of Helion has proved an editor with a light but deft touch, who has guided me through the labyrinthine processes of publishing. I must thank Thomas Davies, whose trenchant comments on many different aspects of the subject have helped temper my own opinions. I would like to thank Dr Tobias Capwell for providing a fascinating tour of some of the key exhibits in the Wallace collection. I gratefully acknowledge the generous assistance of the Society for Army Historical Research whose grant enabled me to embellish these pages with suitable illustrations. I must mention the generous assistance of Dr Bastian Asmus in sharing his insights in the area of archaeometallurgy, and Dr Dominic Fontana, who has provided such excellent images of the Cowdray engravings. I would also like to thank Dr Edward Fox and the members of Commotion Times, who have generously provided me with the splendid photographs based on their meticulous research of Tudor soldiers. I should conclude by thanking my many, many former pupils, who in their own way taught me far more history than I taught them.

Introduction

If there is in the affairs of mortal men any one thing which it is proper uniformly to explode, and incumbent on every man by every lawful means to avoid, to deprecate, to oppose, that one thing is doubtless war.

There is nothing more unnaturally wicked, more productive of misery, more extensively destructive, more obstinate in mischief, more unworthy of man, as formed by nature, much more of man professing *Christianity*. Yet, wonderful to relate! war is undertaken, and cruelly, savagely conducted, not only by unbelievers, but by Christians.

Nor are there ever wanting men learned in the law, and even divines, who are ready to furnish firebrands for the nefarious work and to fan the latent sparks into a flame. Hence, war is considered so much a thing of course, that the wonder is how any man can disapprove of it – so much sanctioned by authority and custom that it is deemed impious to have borne testimony against a practice in its principle most profligate, and in its effects pregnant with every kind of calamity.[1]

Although many contemporaries would have agreed with Erasmus when he condemned war (between Christians), war was certainly one of the principal preoccupations of European monarchies in this period. War defined and legitimised them, especially in the eyes of their nobility. War was 'sanctioned by authority and custom', so that Henry VIII might self-consciously and publicly ape the actions if not the achievements of Henry V of Agincourt fame. Henry VIII may compare himself to his illustrious predecessors, but he would be judged against his European brethren: James IV, Ferdinand and Isabella, Francis I and Louis XII and the emperors Maximilian and Charles. He was, to use J.R. Hale's memorable phrase, a fully paid-up member of the 'College of militant monarchs'.[2] Waging war was the prerogative of princes in pursuit of their princely priorities – dynastic security, defence of their lands or 'legitimate' claims to another's and religious obligation – but above all glory and the defence of their honour.

---

1   Desiderius Erasmus, Vicesimus Knox, *The Works of Vicesimus Knox*, vol. 5 (subject matter: Personal Nobility, Spirit of Despotism, Antipolemus) (London: Mawman, 1824). Full text available online, see bibliography for URL.

2   J.R. Hale, *Renaissance War Studies* (London: Hambledon Press, 1983), p.88.

The battlefield of Marignano by Urs Graf ,1521. Graf was a colourful, or more accurately a disreputable, character. He had trained as a goldsmith and engraver and may also have served as a mercenary on the battlefield he depicted here. It portrays the violence and intensity of battle and all the horrors that the individual soldier would experience. What is surprising is that men like Graf would return to the battlefield willingly, in fact to make it their 'profession'.

This book will attempt to investigate why and how the Tudors from the reign of Henry VII to that of Elizabeth I waged war. This is a not an inconsiderable task and it is one that should be placed in a broader context. England's army found itself fighting enemies that were often trained and equipped according to the latest 'Continental' fashion.[3] England was assessed by contemporaries as to how far it matched them, and more recently historians have devoted much effort to considering how far England conformed to the concept of the 'military revolution'. This introduction is designed to explain the context in which England found itself and the ways in which war was changing.

'O, wad some Power the giftie gie us. To see oursels as others see us! It wad frae monie a blunder free us, An' foolish notion.'

Robert Burns 1786

It is first necessary to put England into its European perspective, to see her as others saw her, as an ally, an enemy, a dupe, or on occasion an irrelevance. The significant European powers were Spain, France, the Empire, the Papacy and in Italy the city states, especially Venice and Milan. Traditionally England

---

3   The author apologises to all Welshmen, especially as they played a significant part in Tudor military life, for not referring to England and Wales separately. Wales was 'shired' by Cromwell in the Acts of Union 1536–1543, effectively incorporating her into the English system of administration.

'The White King as Child Playing with Other Children': from *Der Weisskunig* by Hans Burgkmair. The 'little king' tumbles with his playmates but also learns the skills of the hunt, the challenge of the joust and the excitement of firing junior artillery. He is also stringing a longbow in such a manner as would earn a peasant boy a thick ear. Like his aristocratic playmates, any king would see war as an inevitable and essential test of his true worth. (Metropolitan Museum of Art, Open Access)

and France were the best of enemies. The more than hundred years of the Hundred Years' War had concluded in 1453. Although England's claims to French territory might remain extensive, she held on to only one tasty morsel of French property, the Pale of Calais. As England's strength diminished due to a weak monarchy and civil war, that of France increased. Spain had long been primarily concerned with the conquest of the remaining Muslim state of Granada. By 1492 that would have been concluded, and this left Ferdinand and Isabella the triumphant defenders of Christendom and in possession of a strong and experienced army.

In Italy, Venice was the most powerful of the city states on both land and sea. Milan was to become the valuable prize in the seemingly endless conflict between France and the Empire. The Papacy still possessed considerable territory in Italy, wealth, and until 1517 unquestioned authority throughout Western Christendom. The Pope sought to protect Rome's independence from other Italian states or intrusive foreign powers.

The industrial heart of Europe, where craft, materials and demand produced innovation and enormous prosperity, formed a belt stretching from the Low Countries, via the Rhineland and southern Germany to the cities of northern Italy. Europe had great agricultural wealth, an increasing

Charles VIII, King of France
c.1494–95 Attributed to
Niccolò Fiorentino. The artist
was recognised as being
one of the finest of the age,
and as can be seen here
was not prone to flattering
his subjects. Charles, with
his hare-brained scheme
to restore Naples to French
rule, was the author of the
dreadful events that were to
overtake Italy and Europe.
He died when he struck his
head on a door lintel in the
Château d'Amboise when
on his way to watch a tennis
match. Nothing so became
his life as the leaving of it.
(Metropolitan Museum of
Art, Open Access)

population and burgeoning industry that would provide enormous prosperity for its people. It also enabled its leaders to equip and conduct wars on an unprecedented scale.

It was the action of Charles VIII of France in 1494, invading Italy and seizing the throne of Naples, that would set Europe on its head. The reaction to this onslaught was the formation of the Holy League, established in 1495 by the Papacy to defend its independence. This alliance included the other Italian city states and Spain. The conflict between France and Spain (later the Empire) in Italy would come to dominate the following decades. In 1500 it would now be Louis XII who would capture Naples for France and restart the conflict. This led to a French defeat at the hands of Ferdinand I, the king not only of Spain but of Sicily and Sardinia. This was not, however, the end to French ambition.

The League of Cambrai established by Louis XII, King Ferdinand of Spain, Emperor Maximilian and the Pope in 1508, ostensibly to counter the Ottomans, now turned against the Venetians. The Pope feared the power of Venice encroaching on the Papal States. The Venetians were soundly defeated at Agnadello (1509) but the principal beneficiary had been France. Fear of France, rather than antipathy towards Venice, now led to the formation of the Holy League (1511), between erstwhile enemies Venice, Spain and the Pope. The war led to further indecisive conflict in Italy with the battles of Ravenna in 1512 (a French victory) and Novara in 1513 (a French defeat).

In England, Henry VII devoted his efforts to maintaining a tenuous grip on a throne that he had so surprisingly gained, and then only due to aristocratic treachery. His priority within the realm was ensuring the loyalty of the nobility, who had gained little and lost much in the previous reigns. His foreign policy was directed at isolating the two pretenders to his throne from the support of France, Scotland and Ireland, countries which were more than willing to discomfort any English sovereign. Once achieved he sought to establish the legitimacy of his dynasty through the marriage of first Arthur and then Henry to Catherine of Aragon. War when he engaged in it was a necessity, not a hobby. He used it only to secure his kingdom from domestic and foreign threats. His son was to pursue a different set of priorities.

Henry VIII had been part of the League since 1509. It was only in 1513, when Emperor Maximilian joined, that Henry could consider military participation. The Emperor offered logistical support from his territories in the Low Countries and suggested to Henry a suitable objective. This was the French town of Thérouanne near the Imperial border, which on its capture would naturally become Imperial property and face destruction. A French campaign by the English king led almost inevitably to Scottish intervention. This was intended to force Henry to abandon his French expedition and return to defend his kingdom. The unexpected outcome of this confrontation

Left: Francis I (1494–1547), King of France from the workshop of Joos van Cleve. This is a royal carte-de-visite, one of several portraits to be sent to other European monarchs. Francis and his court represented the height of fashion in both clothes and beards. The appearance of the King's doublet was created with a red glaze overlaying silver leaf. No expense was to be spared in these Continental fashion wars. Henry VIII was to copy some of the habits of the French court and king, including signing documents at the bottom rather than the top. Anne Boleyn's time spent in the French court provided her with social cachet and a style that made her especially attractive to Henry. (Metropolitan Museum of Art, Open Access)

Right: Portrait of Charles V by Hans Baldung Grien. It was said that he liked his uniformly dreadful portraits, as when people came face to face they were pleasantly surprised. The look on the face of this beardless youth is one of consternation rather than mere surprise. (Metropolitan Museum of Art, Open Access)

on the border was the total defeat of the Scottish army and the death of James IV at Flodden. King Louis of France had meanwhile effectively negotiated a separate peace with the Emperor. This left Henry once more alone, with the indefensible city of Tournai as the sole prize for all his efforts. In 1515 the young King Francis I had, by defeating the Imperial army at Marignano, regained control of Milan but this would soon be contested by a new and vigorous emperor.

Henry had by now exhausted his financial resources, and with the able Cardinal Wolsey attempted diplomatic initiatives. This gave England the appearance of a great power without actually being one. The Treaty of London in 1518 and the Field of the Cloth of Gold (1520) would be of little importance compared to the massive shift in power that was taking place in Europe. As part of the Holy League of 1495, the son of Emperor Maximilian had married the daughter of the King and Queen of Spain. It was Charles V, the product of this union, who would now unite Spain and the Habsburg Empire to form a European superstate. France now found herself surrounded by an Empire on both her eastern and western borders, as well as facing the continuing threat posed by England. Francis and Charles were bound to clash in Italy once more and also in the north-east of France, where Imperial territories now bordered those of France.

This new confrontation provided an opportunity for Henry to once more play a significant part in Europe, but only as the ally of the Emperor. The expedition of 1523, which should have seen an Anglo-Imperial march upon Paris assisted by a renegade French prince, came to nothing. Once again, the Empire failed to fulfil its part of the bargain and there was little enthusiasm in France for civil war. If this front was to prove a disappointment to Charles V, in Italy the victory at Pavia in 1525 appeared decisive. The French King became an Imperial captive in Madrid, and France was now at the mercy of the Empire. Henry's entreaty that his victorious ally should share some of the fruits of victory was dismissed with contempt. This should have made him aware of his true status in the 'special' Anglo-Spanish–Imperial relationship.

Henry's divorce from Catherine of Aragon now placed his relationship with Charles in jeopardy, as the Queen was the aunt of the Emperor. The capture of the Pope and the 'accidental' sack of Rome by Imperial troops in 1527, meant that any hope that Henry might have had of gaining Papal permission for the divorce was lost. Cromwell pursued the highly original but somewhat dubious policy that would divorce the Queen and make the King supreme head of the Church.

England was in no position to actively participate in European affairs. In the face of Imperial intransigence even Francis had appeared attractive as an ally for a while. France and Spain had inevitably renewed their conflict from 1536–1538, until both were so exhausted that peace was forced upon them. The Pope had excommunicated Henry VIII in 1538 and the next year coordinated an anti-Henry alliance with Francis and Charles. Henry now faced the possibility of invasion, and began the construction of the 'Device forts'. Under the tutelage of Cromwell he dallied with the possibility of an alliance with Protestant German princes and made a disastrous marriage with Anne of Cleves. Henry's latest queen was 'wafted' across the channel accompanied by 50 vessels and a 150-gun salute from the *Lion* and the *Sweepstake*, the celebrations costing about £2,000.

Franco-Imperial unity was short-lived and in 1543 war broke out once more. France had acquired a new ally, the Ottoman Turk, which it might be thought would have put France beyond the pale in Europe. Francis made no headway in Italy and Charles V sought to launch an Anglo-Imperial onslaught on Paris in 1544. The grand strategy faltered as the Emperor besieged St Dizier and Henry determined that his best option was to besiege Boulogne, while a covering force was sent to sit outside Montreuil. Henry now suffered his greatest and final humiliation, for as he entered Boulogne in triumph he learnt that his ally the Emperor had made a separate peace with Francis. The English force besieging Montreuil was forced to flee ignominiously in the face of a French relief force led by the Dauphin. Boulogne was only barely saved, through luck and bad weather, from being recaptured by a French night attack. In Piedmont the French achieved a victory over the Imperial forces at Ceresole but failed to gain the prize of Milan.

Testoon of Henry VIII (third coinage). The portrait of the King here was derived from Holbein's famous portrait of him standing in his aggressive four-square posture. What Henry considered a manly and heroic pose was considered in foreign courts as rather vulgar. David Starkey has described the Holbein portrait as one of a 'hulking tyrant with the face of a Humpty Dumpty of nightmare', and it is difficult to disagree. The testoon was a heavily debased coin and this devaluation contrasts with the impression that this portrait was intended to give. (Metropolitan Museum of Art, Open Access)

It was England, alone once more, who was now on the defensive. The French fleet, with a substantial military force and a superiority in war galleys, now descended on England. July 1545 brought the confrontation between the two navies on the Solent. This led to the accidental loss of major warships on both sides and a short-lived invasion of the Isle of Wight, before the French withdrew. In 1546 Henry had to abandon any future campaigns. He was old, diseased, and short of money and allies. Peace was agreed and it was arranged that Boulogne would be returned for cash and a recognition by the French of his spurious titles. The death of Henry VIII and Francis I in 1547 brought a temporary end to one prolonged conflict but not to Anglo-Scottish differences.

France had long been the ally of Scotland. James IV had been wooed by the French queen into declaring war in 1513 and James V had married not one but two French princesses, admittedly on separate occasions. Scotland saw an alliance with France as the only means of countering English ambitions, which included the assertion of England's sovereignty extending to the possible union of the two kingdoms. Scotland also faced deep political and religious division, something which England could exploit. Edward VI, or rather the Lord Protector his uncle, had inherited the policy of the 'Rough Wooing' which had begun in 1544. This was an attempt to force the Scots to fulfil their promise to marry their young queen to King Edward. This was an agreement forced out of them after the disastrous defeat at Solway Moss (1542). This also meant that England could concentrate her military efforts against France, for as Thomas

Cromwell had so wisely pronounced, quoting a common saying: 'Who that intendeth France to win, with Scotland let him begin.'[4]

Somerset's policy of roundly defeating the Scots in battle succeeded at Pinkie (1547) but then the creation of an English Pale proved an expensive failure. It also inevitably drew in French support to such an extent that war with France was declared in August 1549. Somerset's fall saw the final collapse of English forces in Scotland and the humiliating treaty that followed. Boulogne, the sole prize gained by Henry VIII, was returned to King Henri II, who had failed to recover it when he was the dauphin. Because of English bankruptcy and her abandonment of any aggressive ambitions towards France or Scotland, relations between England and France became far more cordial, so that the monarchs granted to each other their highest orders of chivalry.

Franco-Imperial relations remained as fraught as always, and Henri now allied France to the German Protestant princes in January 1552. He then proceeded to capture the key Imperial cities of Metz, Toul and Verdun and later Thérouanne. Charles V, exhausted by years of strain and disappointment, abdicated (1554–1556) and divided his empire. The Habsburg portion was left to Ferdinand I and the Spanish portion and the Netherlands passed to Philip II the king of Spain, who was also joint sovereign of England through his marriage to Queen Mary. The treaty of Vaucelles in February 1556 was only a pause in the conflict between France and Spain, which reopened in 1557 with the Imperial siege of St Quentin. Henri had also forced England into the war by supporting a foolish attempt to raise rebellion in England. A French attempt to relieve the siege of St Quentin led to a disastrous defeat which should have brought the war to an end: Henri, it was assumed, had no more resources to continue the fight. However in a brilliant *coup de maître*, he deceived both the English and the Spanish as to his objective and besieged and captured Calais. England's last stronghold in France was lost and so ended the more than Hundred Years War. This was a humiliation that Queen Mary suffered and in which all England and her successor Elizabeth shared.

France and Spain were both bankrupted by war and defaulted on their massive loans. France and the Empire also now faced the problem of increasing religious division. Neither Philip nor Ferdinand were willing to be involved in the conflict in Italy, which had begun the slaughter in 1494. The Treaty of Cateau-Cambrésis (1559) ended the Habsburg–Valois wars which had for over half a century poisoned Europe. Elizabeth I was a signatory, and although she felt the loss of Calais deeply, she had few resources and nothing to gain personally from further war.

In this long and bloody history England played but a small part. Matters of war and peace were decided by the big players, and England under Henry VIII was little more than a makeweight. Henry VII had never seen foreign policy as anything more than a means to furthering his principal end, the securing of his throne and dynasty. Henry VIII sought glory, and although he may have

---

4   Charles Carlton, *This Seat of Mars: War and the British Isles, 1485–1746* (Newhaven, Ct.: Yale University Press, 2011), p.11; J.S. Brewer (ed.), *Letters and Papers, Foreign and Domestic, of the Reign of Henry VIII*, vol. 3, 2598 (Vaduz: Kraus reprint, 1965), p.149.

felt his conquests justifiable it is difficult not to see him as anything more than a 'patsy', who was exploited and then abandoned by successive 'allies'. Somerset inherited the Rough Wooing and felt obliged to support his nephew's claims, however difficult that may have been. Northumberland and Mary for different religious reasons sought domestic calm and wished to avoid costly foreign involvements.

It was great pity, so it was,
That villanous saltpetre should be digg'd
Out of the bowels of the harmless earth,
Which many a good tall fellow had destroy'd
So cowardly; and but for these vile guns
He would himself have been a soldier.

William Shakespeare Henry IV Part 1

Although Shakespeare's Henry IV is set at the beginning of the fifteenth century, the sentiments expressed by Hotspur in the quotation above are those that any Tudor or Elizabethan might have felt. Gunpowder had apparently taken all the 'fun' out of war! Blaise de Monluc provided a very personal condemnation of the 'fierie weapon':

> Would to heaven that this accursed engine had never been invented, I had not received these wounds which I now languish under, neither had so many valiant men been slain for the most part by the most pitiful fellows and the greatest cowards; poltroons that had not dared look those men in the face at hand, which at distance they laid dead with their confounded bullets. But it was the devil's intention to make us murder one another.[5]

There is a reasonable assumption that gunpowder transformed or revolutionised warfare. It is a conclusion easily drawn, as for at least 400 years firearms have been employed as the principal weapon of all European armies. The chronology of this technology would suggest that the popular narrative requires reconsideration. The first useable recipes for gunpowder appeared in 1267 and the first cannon was represented in a manuscript in 1326. The first recorded appearance of cannon was on the battlefield at Crecy in 1346.[6] Although European armies adopted firearms in the fifteenth century in some numbers, the cannon had still not come to dominate the battlefield after more than a century of its presence there. The bombard in its various forms had mostly replaced the trebuchet by the end of the fourteenth century, but it was just a better 'stone-thrower'. Its impact was not as profound militarily, architecturally or psychologically as might have been expected.

---

5   Blaise de Monluc, ed. Ian Roy, *The Habsburg–Valois Wars and the French Wars of Religion* (London: Longman, 1971), p.41.
6   Jonathan Davies, J. Shumate, A. Hook, S. Walsh, *The Medieval Cannon, 1326–1494* (Oxford: Osprey, 2019), p.6.

'Storming of Moran, at the Shore', from *Der Weisskunig* by Hans Burgkmair. Amidst this scene can be found what would be called a 'plump' of pikes, with at its heart a band of halberdiers protecting the colours. It is the pikemen that also form the assault column that is assailing the town. Meanwhile the stradiots and heavy cavalry wait upon events. One can imagine that relationships between infantry and cavalry were not always easy! (Metropolitan Museum of Art, Open Access)

The appearance of gunpowder weapons was not revolutionary: they were adopted gradually and integrated into the existing forms of warfare.

In the sixteenth century it was not the arquebus that would transform warfare but the pike. The triumph of the aggressive Swiss pikemen over the ultra-modern Burgundian forces of Philip the Bold in the 1470s transformed the perception of warfare, as well as its nature. Infantry equipped with the pike were now a dominant force on the battlefield. It was in Italy that the Habsburg–Valois conflict would see almost continual warfare and military development.

It was the French who would bring Swiss pikemen to Italy, and they performed well at the Battle of Fornovo in 1495. It was the Swiss again who defeated Gonzalo de Córdoba (El Gran Capitan) and his 1,500 Spanish crossbowmen and sword and buckler men at Seminara in 1495. The defeat led to the reorganisation of the Spanish infantry, who would fight pike with pike and fire. In 1497 Spanish formations were reorganised with one third each of pikemen, swordsmen and 'shot' equipped with arquebus and crossbow. Infantry in the form of combined formations of pike and shot were to play a new and important role in warfare from now on. Italy was to become the testing and training ground for Europe's soldiers, as:

coping throughout the first twenty years of the Italian Wars the powers involved all ended up struggling to learn the extent of the offensive and defensive capabilities of their new tools and with their administrative and Strategic implications (mostly by an empirical process of trial and error, passing with disturbing ease from victory to defeat and vice versa).[7]

The main trends in warfare and the lessons learnt can be readily summarised. Firstly, the increased importance of infantry. In 1494 in the fighting in Italy there was roughly parity in the ratio of infantry to cavalry, but by 1525 it had become six to one. Infantry was now a powerful force on the battlefield and essential in the Italian wars, which were of conquest, siege and occupation. The pikemen and arquebusier were also far cheaper to pay and equip than mounted troops, especially the men-at-arms. There was at the same time a considerable addition to the cavalry arm with the increased use of light cavalry. In 1493, of the 25 Spanish cavalry companies raised, only five were the light cavalry type known as genitors but by the turn of the century there were 10 companies of heavy cavalry to 26 of genitors. Light cavalry performed many roles unsuited to men-at-arms, such as reconnaissance and convoy escort, but they were also now to be found on the battlefield as well. Other mounted formations such as those of crossbowmen, arquebusiers and pistoleers were developed, offering greater mobility and firepower to their commanders. Artillery which had long dominated siege warfare was also to appear increasingly as a force on the battlefield.

The Swiss pikemen were indomitable in attack, advancing at speed in echelon to overwhelm their enemy. This they had achieved against the Burgundians and later at the Battle of Novara in 1515, where they smashed an unprepared French army. They were defeated with heavy losses at Cerignola in 1503 and Bicocca in 1522. On both occasions their headlong attack, unaccompanied by artillery or cavalry, foundered when it smashed itself on defences too deep and broad for their long pikes and incomparable bravery to have any effect. At Marignano in 1515 they almost succeeded against the army of King Francis I. Powerful artillery, cavalry charges and determined Landsknecht formations slowed and then flung back the Swiss pike columns, but only after two days of slaughter. It was then Francis who would suffer disaster, this time at Pavia in 1525. His brave gendarmes were massacred by arquebusiers and pikemen in a confused melee, while his magnificent artillery was unable to play a significant part.

The pike, even when wielded by the Swiss, could not on its own be expected to carry all before it on every occasion. Infantry formations were undergoing a transformation as the combination of pike and shot became the norm. The pike were the assault element but could also protect from cavalry, and the shot could assist the pikemen in their assault and be protected by the pike. Sword and buckler men, halberdiers and bearers of the great *Zweihänder schlachtschwerter* (two-handed slaughter sword) would be included in the formation, to be used

---

7   Maurizio Arfaioli, *The Black Bands of Giovanni: Infantry and Diplomacy during the Italian Wars (1526–1528)* (Pisa: Edizioni Plus – Pisa University Press, 2005), p.4.

in hand-to-hand fighting. The Landsknecht formation known as the Black Band of Guelders, which fought at Marignano, was a balanced force made up of 12,000 pikemen, 2,000 arquebusiers, 2,000 swordsmen and 1,000 halberdiers. Each weapon contributed to the strength of attack or defence.

Artillery pieces cast from bronze and mounted on resilient field carriages provided a mobile source of firepower, which would remain technically unaltered in principle until the mid nineteenth century. The French artillery was overrun at Novara but the grand battery of 72 French guns at Marignano caused massive casualties to the advancing Swiss. At Ravenna in 1512 there were 84 guns engaged in a deadly two-hour bombardment, often cited as the first of its kind in war. It was this bombardment that forced the Spanish relieving force to abandon its strong positions, upon which it had hoped to lure and destroy the French army. In a sense this battle became a siege where both sides were not pounding walls of stone but flesh and blood. Jacopo Guicciardini recorded the slaughter in horror: 'It was a horrible and terrible thing to see how every shot of the artillery made a lane through those men-at-arms, and how helmets with the heads inside them, scattered limbs, halves of men, in vast quantity, were sent flying through the air.'[8] This was a scene to be repeated for centuries to come. Artillery could prove itself a powerful force as at Ravenna and Marignano, but could also prove almost completely ineffectual as at Novara and Pavia. All these battles could be used to prove the triumph or failure of one arm or another. In practice success or

---

8   Michael Mallett and Christine Shaw, *The Italian Wars 1494–1559* (London: Routledge, 2014), p.183.

failure depended on so many different factors that a simple appeal to supposed technological superiority, of one or other weapon, is unjustifiable.

The high-velocity iron shot fired by the bronze artillery would have a profound effect on the design of fortifications. Tall walls and towers were lowered and emplacements provided for artillery. Angled bastions were to be employed to provide flanking fire on an enemy assaulting the walls, and the traditional thick stone wall would give way to earthen structures better able to absorb the impact of stone shot. This would ultimately produce the *trace italienne*, the star-shaped forts which would soon spread across much of Europe and would accompany Europeans on their conquests around the world. The effectiveness of fortification in defence was as impressive as the power of the attack. The 15-year siege of Pisa by the Florentines and the nine-month siege of Siena by French and Florentine troops in 1554–5 demonstrated the strength of defences, even in the face of the most powerful weapons and sophisticated tactics. Success or failure in a siege did not by any means depend solely on the fortifications, equipment and tactics employed. Many more factors than those should be included into the complex equation that explained the outcome of a siege.

The inevitable consequence of a near perpetual state of war was the development of permanent military establishments. The campaign season from April to October would be

Landsknechts and ladies by Christoph Bockstorffer 1531. The image that the Landsknecht had of themselves was very different from that of hostile observers such as Folengo. In an age when sumptuary legislation was designed to ensure that noone dressed above their station, the extravagant and sometimes absurd clothes of the Landsknecht and his female companions cocked a snook at contemporary values and attitudes. The soldier was identifying himself as part of a different, and as he thought, a superior community. His dress and conduct scandalised conservative society but were acknowledged and permitted as he performed a role that others were unwilling to fulfil. (Metropolitan Museum of Art, Open Access)

concluded with troops either being paid off like the Swiss, to return in the spring like malignant swooping swifts, or kept in garrison towns. The wealth of Italy and the superpowers that were France, Spain and the Empire could afford to maintain and sustain very large armies and to require their use not for a season or a year but for decades. The Swiss pikemen, Italian hackbutters, Landsknechts, Gascon crossbowmen, *Schwarz Reiters* and the rest of the 'professionals', developed into a 'society of soldiers' that 'put themselves outside of the community'.[9] As J.R. Hale records, in Europe:

> There emerged, then, a mental frontier between man of peace and man of war different in kind from the observation that had watched the peasant that had become the temporary bowman, the landlord replace for a while the falcon glove for the gauntlet ... Infantrymen, wrote Claude de Seyssel, in 1515 are so 'out of key with everything that they can hardly believe themselves to be thought men of experience and courage unless they blaspheme the names of God, the Virgin and the saints'.[10]

For the soldier, the disregard or contempt felt for social norms was expressed in their language, their dress, even their hairstyles, as they flouted the ties and conventions that so bound the timorous civilian to his lot in life. The demand that mercenaries either avoided pioneer duties or were paid extra for this demeaning service was not simple bloody-mindedness on their part, but to force those in command to recognise that the 'soldier' had escaped the labouring life of the despised commons and formed a separate more honourable warrior caste. The civilian population responded to mercenaries and their pretensions with a mixture of fear and contempt, expressed in these lines by the Italian poet Teofilo Folengo (1491–1544):

> ... a terrible noise springs out among the stars
> and the tops of the highest mountains rumble.
> Could it be the Swiss? Could it be the Gascon canaille?[11]
> Could it be the Italians, with their bold words?
> Is that the German rabble fit for the tankard?
> Or could it be Spain sending her tramps?[12]

What was true of the common soldiers was true of their officers. The aristocracy, always used to obedience from their inferiors, developed a new professionalism as commanders. Whereas the tournament had been the training ground in skill at arms, now the battle ground that was Italy would educate them in the complete art of war. Successful commanders would understand not just how to use the lance and the sword but how to maintain and sustain an army in the field, to choose ground well, to manage cavalry, infantry and artillery in effective cooperation, to exploit their strengths and mask their weaknesses.

---

9   J.R. Hale, *War and Society in Renaissance Europe 1450–1620* (Stroud: Sutton, 1998), p.127.
10   Hale, *War and Society*, p.129.
11   From the French for a pack of dogs, otherwise a rabble or 'scum of the earth'.
12   Teofilo Folengo, T.H. Moschaea, w 39–44, preface to Arfaioli, *The Black Bands of Giovanni*.

This did not mean that they no longer inhabited the world of chivalry and the necessity of demonstrating personal bravery. Gaston de Foix at Ravenna and James IV at Flodden both died performing the role allotted to them, as did many more subordinate commanders. When Monluc was governor of Siena he received generous gifts of food and drink from the enemy commander, the Marquis of Marignano. His explanation for fraternisation with the enemy explained how far contemporary attitudes to an enemy were from our own times: 'Such little civilities as these are very gentle and commendable, even betwixt the greatest enemies; ... He served his master, and I served mine. He attacked me for his honour, and I defended myself for mine. He had a mind to acquire reputation, and so had I.'[13] What the gentleman-officer fought for was honour and repute, and if he achieved those then he would be rewarded with advances in both rank and wealth.

In 1505 Ferdinand I appointed the first *cabo de colunela* or commander of a column, a title shortened in 1508 to *colunela* or colonel. The 20 colonels appointed by Ferdinand in 1505 began the establishment of well-defined mixed armed units. The *bandera* was the basis of the Spanish system, equivalent to a company varying in size but ostensibly about 250 in strength. The tercio emerged in 1534 as a formal unit of approximately 3,000 men, initially drawn as its Italian name suggests from Spanish-controlled regions of Italy. Thomas Audley refers to the rank of colonel in his treatise on the art of war written at the end of Henry VIII's reign, but in practice only mercenary commanders were granted this title. In England the sole rank was that of captain, usually of a company of 100, with subordinate officers including a lieutenant and ensign to assist.

The armies that faced each other at Ceresole in 1544 demonstrated what changes had taken place in the structure and tactics of armies in the preceding half century. The armies were led by commanders who had been bred to war, men such as Blaise de Monluc, Monsieur de Taix and Ramón de Cardona. Infantry combining pike and shot actively skirmished prior to the main engagement and then fought bitterly in massive blocks of pike and shot. Artillery was brought forward on the battlefield to provide direct support. Meanwhile cavalry both light and heavy manoeuvred on the battlefield to protect the flanks of infantry, while seeking an opportunity to intervene decisively. The armies were now organised as mixed-arm formations, flexible and formidable. The armies of Europe had come a long way, but at what cost?

There is a supposition that all of Europe should have adopted new weapons, tactics and equipment at the same pace, or face the accusation of 'backwardness'. This has led to a catechism against which a nation can be tested. When were firearms widely introduced, what was the first fortification built on the principle of the *trace italienne*, what constitutes professionalism, how many volumes on martial practice were published and when? These are the questions which are asked by historians. Whether they are the best or even the right ones when considering the development of a military system, is something which hopefully this book will help to investigate.

---

13   Monluc, *The Habsburg–Valois Wars*, p.139.

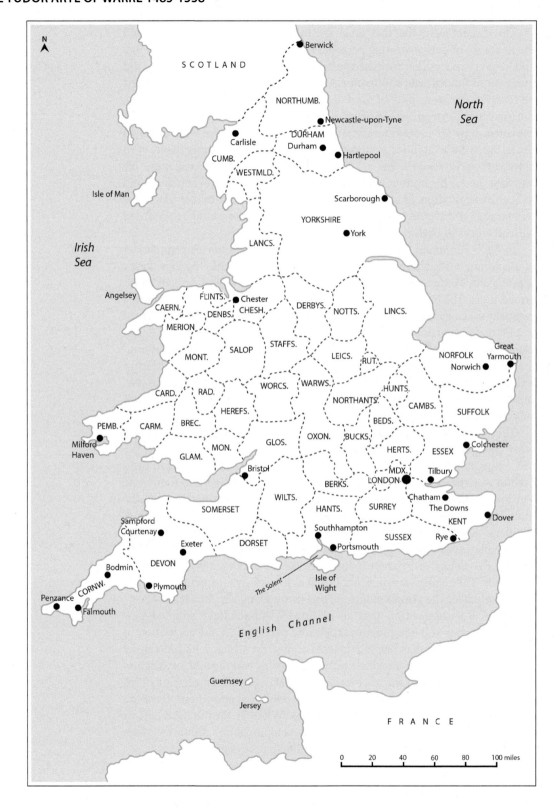

County Map of England and Wales

N

SCOTLAND
Edinburgh

North
Sea

Baltic Sea

SWEDEN

DENMARK

D. OF
PRUSSIA

Lübeck
Stettin

Hamburg

ENGLAND

Amsterdam

BRANDENBURG

Berlin

KINGDOM
OF POLAND

London

Gravelines 1588
Calais

Antwerp

Brussels

HOLY
ROMAN
EMPIRE

Breslau

SILESIA

English Channel

Luxembourg

St Quentin 1557

RHINE
PALATINATE

BOHEMIA

Prague

MORAVIA

Paris

UPPER
PALATINATE

Brest

Orléans

WÜRTTEM-
BERG

Augsburg

BAVARIA

Vienna

Pressburg

Nantes

LORRAINE

Munich

ARCHD. OF
AUSTRIA

Budapest

Besançon

Basel

FRANCE

FRANCHE
COMTÉ

SWISS
CONFEDERACY

TYROL

Mohacs 1526

Geneva

Bicocca 1522

REP. OF VENICE

Bay of
Biscay

D. OF SAVOY

Milan

Venice

D. OF MILAN

OTTOMAN
EMPIRE

Bordeaux

Genoa

REP. OF
FLORENCE

Adriatic Sea

San Sebastian

Toulouse

Marseilles

LUCCA

Burgos
Pamplona

Siena
R. OF
SIENA

PAPAL
STATES

Saragossa

Corsica

Rome

Cerignola 1503

Barcelona

ARAGON

The Garigliano 1503

Naples

CASTILE

Sardinia

KINGDOM OF
NAPLES

Murcia

Palma

Cartagena

Mediterranean Sea

Palermo

Sicily

Algiers

Bougie

Malta

0   100   200   300 miles

Sixteenth-Century Europe

Part I

Politics, Diplomacy, Strategies and Campaigns

1

Four Reigns

Henry VII – Guarding his Kingdom

Henry Tudor had been an importunate exile in Brittany and France, from the age of 14 in 1471 until his return in 1485. He was threatened with betrayal and return to certain death on several occasions. It is unsurprising that on his accession he was aware of the danger posed by pretenders and determined to establish the security of his throne and dynasty.

In 1483 the Yorkist King Edward was in an apparently unassailable position. The King was only 40 years old and had an heir and a spare and the means and thirst to make more. Edward's death, on 4 April of that year, created a crisis within the ruling family. Richard's actions in bastardising and probably murdering his nephews, in order to secure his position against what he saw as a potential Woodville coup, made him few friends and many enemies. Henry's claim to the throne was tenuous to say the least: it was Richard III's own actions which made him, for the first time, appear to be a viable candidate. Supported by the Duke of Burgundy, Henry's inept and foolhardy attempt at invasion in October fortunately failed and led to his return to the safety of exile. This was to be found first in Brittany and later in France, after Edward had suborned some Breton nobles to aid him in capturing a man who clearly now could be the king. His promise to marry Elizabeth, Edward IV's surviving heir, increased his appeal to potential supporters. It was French support which gave him the wherewithal to launch his successful claim to the throne in 1485.

Henry's victory at Bosworth was more a martial political assassination than a proper battle, as loyalties on all sides were tested and treachery determined the outcome. Henry came to the throne because of the Stanley family's betrayal of Richard and Northumberland's inaction. He was determined that he would not rely on the 'loyalty' of the nobility but on their fear of his disfavour, by execution when necessary and more worryingly by threatening to cripple their families economically. The challenge to his throne would come from two pretenders to the throne who would find support from England's natural enemies: France, Scotland and Ireland. Henry's foreign policy was first to isolate and defeat the pretenders to secure his throne and then to make alliances with neighbouring monarchies which would secure his dynasty.

In previous decades the Yorkists had had more of a free rein in matters of policy, although many of the same issues were to arise. In 1475 Edward IV had united the divided kingdom with his planned invasion of France in support of Charles the Bold of Burgundy. His strategic intention was to recover lost territory, but as the Burgundians were unable to make headway after becoming embroiled in the siege of Neuss this plan was foiled. Edward now felt obliged to reach a diplomatic and financial agreement with Louis XI. This gave him an excellent dynastic marriage, proposed between his daughter and the Dauphin, as well as some much-needed cash. In Scotland Richard Duke of Gloucester recovered Berwick in 1482 and for a time occupied Edinburgh in a war from 1481–4. Securing the border with Scotland and engaging in campaigns in France, as part of a powerful alliance, was a pattern that would be repeated under the Tudors.

Henry's return from exile in 1485 occurred when Richard III was at his weakest. Richard III had (quite literally) lost the Crown at the Battle of Bosworth; in future years it would be Henry VII's onerous responsibility to keep it, and challenges would come soon. The rebellion of the Stafford brothers had failed disastrously in 1486 but it created the opportunity for a new pretender to be promoted, under the aegis of Richard's former henchman Lovell. Lambert Simnel claimed to be the son of the Duke of Clarence, the brother of Edward IV, who was in fact a prisoner of Henry's in the Tower. The danger, posed by this most unlikely challenger to the throne, made it apparent how insecure the 'usurper' Henry VII in fact was.

Henry had made the serious error of alienating Margaret of Burgundy, the sister of Edward IV, who would quite naturally espouse and legitimise pretenders to the throne of England. Margaret recognised Simnel and provided him with a force of 2,000 Landsknechts, the core of his invasion force. From Burgundy Simnel travelled to Dublin, where he was crowned and collected around himself a substantial army of Irish, Landsknechts commanded by Schwarz, other mercenaries and English renegades. Simnel's not insubstantial force of some 8,000, far greater than Henry's in June 1485, landed in Yorkshire where support for the Yorkist Richard had been strong, but not unfortunately for Simnel. The Yorkists' advance was at first speedy and successful but was delayed by heavy skirmishing around Nottingham. On the 16th the royal forces met the pretender's army at East Stoke near Newark, where they were soundly defeated, with few allowed to live. Schwarz, who may have come from Nuremburg and whose former profession may have been shoemaking, was, like the other leaders, killed. Simnel was placed in the royal kitchens while Lovell, the principal supporter of the pretender among the English nobility, fled and was never heard of again.

Henry had been granted sanctuary and given military assistance by Brittany and France when in exile, so he knew what evil could come from abroad. France remained something of a quandary, having assisted him to the throne but remaining a potential enemy. In 1487 French troops occupied the Duchy of Brittany, to stop a marriage between the child Anne, heir to the dukedom, and Emperor Maximilian. France had provided both sanctuary and troops to the pretender Henry in his last years of exile. Whatever debt he may have owed the French crown, it was still in Henry's interest to maintain the independence of Brittany, in case of renewed French enmity. Henry attempted to act as an honest broker between the French and the Bretons. The defeat of the Breton army in 1488, the accession to the ducal throne of the 12-year-old Anne, and the likelihood of her marriage to Charles VIII of France, made it impossible for Henry to remain neutral. He gained the political and financial consent of Parliament for war and alliances with both Burgundy and Spain in 1489.

In 1489 the treaty of Medina del Campo with King Ferdinand Aragon and Queen Isabella of Castile was arranged. Although it gave Henry little material advantage and bound him to war with France, it did result in the tacit understanding that Catherine and Henry's eldest son Arthur would marry. This matrimonial alliance, with such an important European royal family, confirmed the legitimacy of the Tudor dynasty across Europe. Brittany remained an unresolved problem. In 1489 Henry sent an army of 3,000 to Brittany to aid the Duchess after receiving financial and

Half groat of Henry VII (1485–1509). Henry VII's portrait is of a medieval rather than Renaissance sovereign, it was a 'billboard for the boss'. Unlike his son he preserved the high standard of his coinage. Debasement was almost tantamount to defacement. It was Henry VII who minted the first sovereign of fine gold, further establishing his wealth, his authority and his legitimacy. (Metropolitan Museum of Art, Open Access)

territorial sureties, and a further 3,000 men were sent to assist in the siege of Dixmude. Despite his efforts, in December 1491 Anne married Charles VIII. Henry's alliance with Spain, Burgundy and the Empire had come to nothing.

If Lambert Simnel's forces had proved a serious danger, that posed by Perkin Warbeck proved of much greater longevity and even greater potential seriousness. Warbeck claimed to be Prince Richard, the younger of Edward IV's legitimate sons, who had been murdered by either Henry or Richard III. In 1491 the newly emerged claimant appeared in Ireland; intelligent and handsome, he found considerable support in Ireland and Scotland. He was soon to be chased out by Henry's men, but unsurprisingly he would find refuge in France under Charles VIII, who was more than irritated by Henry's interference in Brittany. Henry, whose Breton policy lay in tatters, led an army into France in October 1492 (very late in the campaign season), not to conquer but to force Charles to withdraw support form Warbeck. Henry besieged Boulogne and the account of the siege in Grafton's *Chronicle* makes it clear what was thought of the venture. The castle was a tough nut to crack: 'In which fortresse was such a garrison of warlike Souldiers, that valiauntly defended the towne, and the same replenished with artillery and municions, that the loss of the Englishemen assaulting the towne, should be greater damage to the realme of England, than the conquering of the same should be gaine or profit.'[1] Such sound calculation of profit against loss, would not unfortunately be found in his son's reign.

Charles of France, who now had eyes only for his Italian campaign which was planned to take place in 1494, was eager to dispose of Warbeck and agreed at the Treaty of Étaples to abandon Yorkist pretenders. He also granted Henry VII the fabulous sum of £159,000 (745,000 Crowns), in part to defray the cost of Henry's Breton expeditions. The money raised by Henry from Parliament and other sources from 1489–91 totalled £181,500, almost four times as much as the cost of the King's invasion. Henry VII was clearly keen to turn a profit, diplomatic or financial, from foreign involvements.

If Charles had lost interest in discomforting England, it would henceforth be Maximilian who would support Warbeck, in response to Henry's perceived failure as an ally. Warbeck made a pathetic attempt at invading Deal in July 1495 and subsequently fled to Ireland. Edward Poynings was sent with an expedition there and in 1495–6 re-established royal authority. Henry had done his best to undermine the Scottish crown during a period of turbulence following the death of James III in 1488, and it was hardly surprising that when the new king, James IV, came of age he would seek to undermine the position of the English king. James therefore supported Warbeck and greatly added to the credibility of the pretender by his marriage to his own cousin, Lady Catherine Gordon. For Warbeck, having been driven from France and Ireland, James was his only support. Warbeck now was put in command of an army of some 1,400. On reaching the border in September 1496 these few 'supporters' fled fled once more to Ireland.

Henry had meanwhile prepared an expedition against Scotland in 1497. This campaign was abandoned, as the taxation that was necessary for the war led to rebellion in Cornwall, which resulted in a Cornish army marching on London. Henry used the army that he was planning to use against the Scots against the rebels at Blackheath on 22 June, and after their bloody defeat he advanced to Cornwall. James of Scotland was still determined to twist the lion's tail, and in July 1497 besieged Norham castle, forcing Henry to send a force north to the relief of what was one of his principal northern fortresses. In September the truce was agreed at Ayton recognising the real desire of both sovereigns to avoid further conflict, confirmed by treaty in 1502 and the betrothal of Princess Margaret to King James.

Warbeck, having been driven from Ireland as by now the Irish had discovered that he lacked any support from his erstwhile allies, was forced to sail to Cornwall in September 1497. The recently chastened rebels in this county rejected him and a royal army chased him into sanctuary at Beaulieu Abbey and later into captivity. Warbeck had ceased to be a threat, but his fate was sealed in 1501 when the marriage between Arthur and Catherine of Aragon was imminent. No living pretender could be permitted to mar this happy union, and Warbeck and the unfortunate 'real' Earl of Warwick were despatched, as their status determined, by the rope and axe respectively.

---

1   Richard Grafton, *Grafton's Chronicle: or, History of England. To which is added his table of the bailiffs, sheriffs, and mayors, of the city of London. From the year 1189 to 1558, inclusive.* Vol. II (London: Printed for J. Johnson, 1809), p.190.

Henry VII's position now appeared secure, with the removal of actual and real potential pretenders, but his final years were to prove catastrophic for his hopes of a secure dynasty. Pedro de Ayala considered that 'his crown is … undisputed and his government strong in all respects.'[2] This happy situation would not last. In 1501 Edmund de la Pole, the Earl of Suffolk, who had a strong claim to the throne, fled to the court of Maximilian. In 1500 Henry VII's son Prince Edmund died and in 1502 so did Prince Arthur, leaving a grieving widow and little eight-year-old Prince Henry as the new Prince of Wales. In 1503 Elizabeth his wife and the daughter of Edward IV died, which was both a personal and political tragedy. Henry was very much alone and his position as a successful usurper led him to pursue enemies both real and imagined. A secret report of a conversation between 'many great personages' in Calais, concerning the succession, recorded that: 'some of them spake of my lord of Buckingham, saying that he was a noble man and would be a royal ruler. Other there were that spake in like wise of your traitor, Edmund de la Pole, but none of them spake of my lord prince [Henry].'[3] In 1506 Henry was still looking and failing to find a new queen, but he did arrange for the marriage of Princess Mary to Charles, the eldest son of Ferdinand and Isabella, and of course of Henry to Catherine their daughter. Up to the very end of his reign. it was clear that war and diplomacy were there to produce domestic and dynastic security. Polydore Vergil, writing of Henry's reign, concluded with some justice that: 'leagues and confederacies he had with all Christian princes, his mighty power was dreaded everywhere, not only within his realm but without also.'[4]

Henry VIII – Guarding His Honour

There is no doubt that Henry and his personality 'filled a room and turned heads' as tends to be the case if the 'personality' can have those self-same heads cut off. His relationships with those he admired, and even loved, could become dismissive and even murderous. His ego was expressed through his ambition, which found its greatest expression in his replacement of the Pope as head of the Church with himself. He had above all the chivalric concept of honour to uphold. In 1544 he declared of his honour, that 'we have hitherto guarded and will not have stained in our old age.'[5] This sentiment was not uncommon amongst those who were of a high enough status to possess such a precious commodity. Francis I, after having been defeated and captured at the Battle of Pavia in 1525, wrote to his mother: *'De toutes choses ne m'est demeuré que l'honneur et la vie qui est saulve'*:[6] 'Of all I had, only honour and life have been spared.'

---

2   David Loades, *The Fighting Tudors* (Kew, Richmond UK: National Archives, 2009), p.30.
3   G.R. Elton, *The Tudor Constitution* (Cambridge: Cambridge University Press, 2nd edn, 1982), pp.5–6.
4   Loades, *The Fighting Tudors*, p.36.
5   Betteridge, Thomas, Lipscomb, Suzannah (eds), *Henry VIII and the Court: Art, Politics and Performance* (Farnham: Ashgate Publishing Ltd, 2013), p.300.
6   Susan Ratcliffe, *The Concise Oxford Dictionary of Quotations* (Oxford: Oxford University Press, 2011), p.155; *Collection des Documents Inédits sur l'Histoire de France* (France, Ministère de l'éducation nationale 1847), vol. 1.

Groat of Henry VIII (first coinage). Henry VIII's first coinage used the image of his father, just as he used or rather squandered on war all the coins his father had carefully accumulated. Claiming his titles to France, England and Ireland on this coin, he would spend his reign attempting to give his French and Irish claims some reality. (Metropolitan Museum of Art, Open Access)

It is impossible to like Henry VIII. Whatever the role of the present author, it is not to pass moral or personal judgement on people who are a lot less alive and a lot more important. Historians tend to admire 'busy' bureaucrats such as Thomas Cromwell, who leave a trail of paperwork behind them, although they rather suspect Cardinal Wolsey, who they feel should have spent more time in the chapel and less time in the court. They approve of a balanced budget and large national infrastructure projects. On the other hand, it has been said that a prince is not brought up to be a bookkeeper and in fact Henry did promote massive infrastructure projects, such as the Device forts and his 'knockout' palaces such as Nonsuch. To comment on his actions, it is important to appreciate what he thought was valuable, even though his judgements may appear to a modern audience to be perverse.

His foreign policy was an expression of his ego. It was, he felt, quite reasonable that he should present himself as a candidate to the Imperial throne in 1519, he had after all been encouraged in this delusion by Emperor Maximilian himself. It was also therefore equally reasonable that he should promote his pet Cardinal for appointment to the papacy, not once but twice, in 1521 and 1523. Henry VIII was *Rex Imperator* in his combined realm of England, Ireland and occasionally Scotland and France as well. He was *Fidei Defensor*, (Defender of the Faith) a title granted by the Pope for his authorship of *Assertio Septem Sacramentorum*, a denunciation of Lutheran heresy, a nonsensical title he chose to keep after he had separated his Church of England from the Church of Rome. Henry was never a Lutheran, let alone a Protestant. Even so, the consequences of his divorce led him to contemplate alliances with such heretics. Francis I had gone much further by allying himself with the Turk! Henry was more interested in titles than territory, he wanted the appearance of greatness, despite the fact that he was not and never could be anything much more than an extra on a stage dominated by a few superstars.

England was relatively small: in area it may be over six times the size of Wales but only a quarter the size of what is currently metropolitan France or Spain. Her population even including that of Wales was certainly less than three million, roughly half what it had been under Rome and before the catastrophe of the fourteenth century. She boasted only one European-sized city, which was of course London. Henry's income at the beginning of his reign was about £90,000 per annum and his war chest, inherited form his father, amounted to £350,000. In France he controlled Calais and its environs and nothing more. The era when the king of England could boast of possessing more territory in France than the French King was long gone. The disastrous reign of Henry VI had seen the loss of Normandy in a firestorm of French artillery and Henry VII had failed even to protect the independence of Brittany.

France had a population of 16 million and the French monarch in the 1520s had a reliable income equivalent to £350,000 per annum. Spain had a population of 7.5 million and when united with the territories of Maximilian in 1519, at least double. The revenue of Charles V was an impressive £540,000, six times that of Henry VIII. Of course, their massive revenues did not save either of these super-sovereigns from becoming bankrupt. In a modern comparison, by wealth and population England would be equivalent to modern day Belgium while sixteenth-century France and Spain would be France and Germany. At the beginning of Henry's reign Ferdinand of Aragon, Louis XII of France and Emperor Maximilian commanded the armies, wealth and respect of much of Europe. Charles V would succeed to the thrones of Spain in 1516 and the Empire in 1519 and Louis XII would be replaced by the princely superstar Francis I in 1515. These were the characters who would control European affairs. The focus of the conflict would be on the borders of their territories, and even more importantly in the true cockpit of Europe, Italy.

Under these circumstances, Henry's strategy was to take advantage of whatever opportunities presented themselves, military or diplomatic. Grander strategies have been suggested. A.F. Pollard considered that Henry's intention was to pursue a strategy of conquest, completing the integration of Ireland and fulfilling his historical claims to France and Scotland. Undoubtedly, on occasion he made such claims to other thrones but only when it suited him, or in a fit of pique; both objectives were realistically quite beyond him.

1509–13 Preparation for War, and War with France and Scotland

On his accession in 1509, Henry's judicial murder of his father's most capable and loyal servants, Empson and Dudley, indicated that the son was not going to pursue the policies or style of the father. Henry VII's priority had always been the security of the kingdom from pretenders, and through treaty and marriage to secure the future of his dynasty. These objectives he had achieved, and through the careful exploitation of his resources and had amassed a large sum of cash. Henry VIII's priority was to spend what his father had so assiduously collected, on war.

Henry was a little shy of 18 years old when he came to the throne. His father had never allowed him into the tournament lists but only permitted him to run at the ring and the quintain. He first appeared at a tournament 'properly' in 1510, after the pregnancy of his queen was announced. He remained an enthusiastic participant for the next 17 years. As king he was determined and encouraged to take part in tournaments at home and far more bloody engagements abroad. War was the stage which would give him the opportunity to appear as a true Renaissance prince. Machiavelli had asserted that 'Nothing brings a prince more prestige than great campaigns and striking demonstrations of his personal abilities,[7] and although this was written in 1514 and would not be translated into English until Elizabeth's reign, it would certainly serve to explain Henry's enthusiasm for war. Henry began participation in martial events with some caution. He sent a force of 1,500 archers to join his father-in-law Ferdinand in a campaign against the Moors in Barberry and a similar force under Sir Edward Poynings to aid Margaret of Savoy, the daughter of the Emperor, against the Duke of Guelders. Neither were substantial commitments but were designed to make useful friends in a future war against the French.

Although in 1509 he had sworn to revive the war with France, he had instead, on the advice of his counsellors, renewed the Treaty of Étaples in 1510 and received the pension that his father had negotiated. The French were in an alliance with his father-in-law Ferdinand of Aragon, Maximilian, and Pope Julius II all of whom combined in the League of Cambrai against Venice. This political initiative had begun in 1505 with the marriage of Ferdinand to Louis XII's niece Germaine de Foix (Ferdinand's second wife after the death of Isabella). Henry VII was not invited to take part in this Spanish–Imperial rapprochement, and it is unlikely that he would have seen any advantage in doing so. In 1510 Louis abandoned the League, and Pope Julius allied the Papacy with the Venetians against the French. Now it was the turn of France to be the enemy of the Papacy, which had formed the Holy League, consisting of Spain, the Empire and finally England. On the coat tails of a much larger conflict, Henry could now with religious justification go to war against the French and establish his Plantagenet claim to Gascony. He began this project by sending a large force of infantry under Dorset to Spain.

The expedition by the Marquis of Dorset in 1512 should have taught him a lesson about the fickleness of allies. Acting in support of Henry's father-in-law King Ferdinand, Dorset's force of infantry wasted its limited resources drawing away the French force at Bayonne, so that Ferdinand could invade Navarre unmolested. It was not an inconsiderable force, 7,108 strong, provided primarily from noble and ecclesiastical retinues supplemented with Spanish infantry and cavalry. The invasion of Navarre may have been planned as the prelude to the English conquest of Guienne as was suggested at the time, but came to nothing. Without draught horses or cavalry, both of which were promised but not provided by Ferdinand (although 200 mules were supplied), the English force was immobile and ineffectual and collapsed through sickness and mutiny. This futile war drew France and Scotland closer together, which would have very significant implications the following year. The mobilisation of men and resources in 1511–12 was however a useful rehearsal for Henry's larger enterprise of 1513, one that would be managed far better.

Despite the fiasco in Spain and a disaster at sea, with the loss of the royal warship *Regent* in action against the French fleet, Henry was determined to commit an army to an invasion. The object of his efforts would be Thérouanne and Tournai in Artois. These had no strategic or tactical significance for

---

7   Niccolò Machiavelli, *The Prince*, transl. George Bull (London: Penguin Books, 1961), p.70.

Maximilian's alliance with Henry VIII; from *The Arch of Honour*, 1515, by Albrecht Dürer. The besieged towns and the cavalry combat in this engraving record the sieges of Thérouanne and Tournai and the Battle of the Spurs. Although apparently representing a meeting of equals, the balance of the engraving, as in life, is clearly in favour of the Emperor, placed in the foreground. It is interesting to note the close formation of the charging cavalry, with the lance point only dropped just before the strike. Using a lance effectively was a great skill, and if not initially lethal this unwieldy weapon would have to be discarded and other weapons employed. The painting of the Battle of San Romano by Paolo Uccello shows a battlefield littered with broken lances, a detail often overlooked.
(Metropolitan Museum of Art, Open Access)

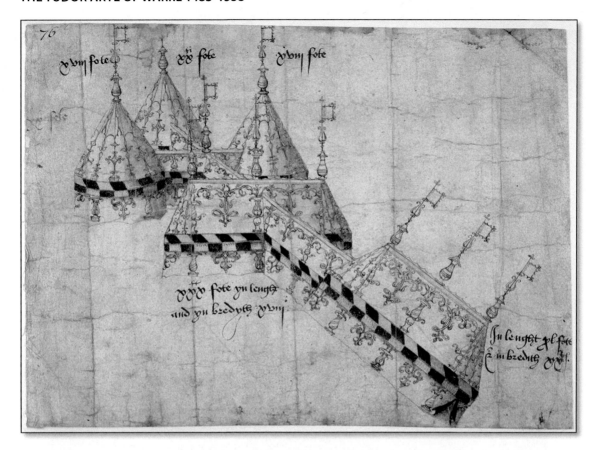

Design for tents for the Field of the Cloth of Gold. Although perhaps not adhering to the full rules of perspective, this conglomeration of tents is truly impressive. There are three large circular pavilions and two rectangular halls joined by galleries or passageways. The decoration is in the grotesque style which emerged in Italy in the late fourteenth century when the lavishly decorated rooms of Nero's Golden palace were discovered. (Courtesy of the British Library, Cotton Augustus I.ii.76)

Henry but they did for the Emperor upon whose territory they impinged. In August 1513 Maximilian and Henry met as equals, in a tent made of cloth of gold, in miserable weather. The Emperor deigned to wear the English red cross, pandering to Henry's vanity, while Henry in turn willingly spent money and lives on behalf of the Emperor. Soon after the meeting a French attempt to relieve Thérouanne was routed, in what came to be known as the Battle of the Spurs, a name that appealed to Henry's conceit but was in fact little more than a skirmish. No longer with any hope of relief, Thérouanne surrendered and Henry turned his attention to the city of Tournai. Its surrender was inevitable, as it was almost indefensible and again no relief force was available.

Two major events had occurred during this time which were of far greater significance than Henry's 'conquests'. The inevitable Scottish attack, designed to reduce the pressure on her ally France, led to the Battle of Flodden which resulted in the slaughter of the Scottish king surrounded by his nobility and thereby transformed Anglo–Scottish relations. Of greater European significance was the defeat of the French on 6 June at Novara, which meant that the French were driven from Italy, for the moment. This explained the Emperor's short-lived enthusiasm for war with France, which had prompted Henry to pursue his campaign in Artois as the gull of the Emperor rather than his equal.

Henry was more than satisfied with his accomplishments. He had been treated as an equal by the Emperor, he had fought his first battle – admittedly safely surrounded by Imperial infantry – and he had destroyed Thérouanne and kept Tournai. Abandoned now by his allies and prompted by the Pope to choose peace, even then it still required Louis to offer a generous settlement for Henry to accept. He would keep Tournai from which he gained financially and it was also agreed that his favourite sister Mary would marry the French king, bringing to an end, it was hoped, the enmity between the kingdoms. So pleased was he with the architect of this campaign, Thomas Wolsey, that he made him Bishop of Tournai. This was a post he would hold only until 1518, when the city was handed back to the French by the Treaty of London.

1513–22 Diplomatic Triumph and Defeat

Having exhausted his treasury and glutted his martial appetites, Henry found himself again without allies or enemies. If he could not gain glory through warfare, perhaps Wolsey could gain it through diplomacy? Henry did not control events in Europe, but events in Europe, along with the state of his finances, could determine what Henry could do. The death of Louis XII in January 1515, according to prurient rumour exhausted in bed by his 18-year-old bride Mary (Henry's sister), led to the return of the unhappy girl into the welcoming arms of Charles Brandon, Henry's closest friend. It also led to the appearance of a new, younger, more handsome and wealthier prince on the European stage: Francis I. Just like Henry, Francis was determined to cut a dash at home and abroad. He also had three practical objectives to achieve: the recovery of Tournai from Henry, Navarre from Spain and Milan from the Empire.

Henry felt he had to appear a significant figure in Europe, and conducted a diplomatic offensive under Cardinal Wolsey to make himself appear as the arbiter of Europe. Pope Leo X was promoting a crusade and a universal peace amongst Christian kingdoms, and Henry was willing to countenance participation in a universal peace, as well as a treaty with France. The Treaty of London in October 1518 returned Tournai to France for the fabulous sum of 600,000 gold ecus and Henry's infant daughter Mary was affianced to the Dauphin. Spain and the Empire and more than 20 minor powers now made a pact of perpetual peace with England, all agreeing to ally against any that broke it. Wolsey had put Henry triumphantly at the heart of Europe.

The death of Ferdinand of Spain in 1516 led to the accession of Charles, the son of Philip the Fair of Burgundy and Joanna the Mad (daughter of Ferdinand and Isabella). In 1519 Charles further succeeded to the throne of Emperor Maximilian, becoming Emperor Charles V at the age of 19. Francis, who had once faced two enemies in Ferdinand and Maximilian, now faced a single implacable opponent, who commanded the combined and massive resources of both. This new reality was what would determine the future of Europe. In June 1520 Francis and Henry now participated in one of the most extraordinary diplomatic initiatives of any period: the meeting at the Field of the Cloth of Gold, so called because of this massively expensive fabric being used for tentage. Held at a spot equidistant between Guînes in the English Calais Pale and the French town of Ardres, it combined a diplomatic summit with a royal sports day and provided an opportunity for ostentatious display.

In Greenwich the armourers had to rush to produce the special 'tonlet' armour which had been specified for the foot combat, in which both sovereigns were keen to take part as allies and not enemies. The logistics of this event were masterfully directed by Cardinal Wolsey and the whole show was brilliantly choreographed, except for the spontaneous wrestling match between the two monarchs which Henry lost, leaving him 'bitter and heavy hearted'. The Breton wrestlers also defeated their Cornish counterparts, and to Henry's chagrin the French court was also considered more fashionable. The Venetian ambassador tartly observed: 'these sovereigns are not at peace … they hate each other cordially.'[8] The practical results of this vast expenditure were to further strengthen the position of Wolsey and increase Henry's dislike of Francis. The extravagance of Wolsey, in having a prefabricated palace built for the King, complete with a fountain spouting three different vintages of wine, was later to be cited against him in the trial that he faced on his fall from the King's grace.

Henry now attempted to act as an honest broker between the two principal European contestants for predominance: Charles V and Francis I. It was unfortunately clear to all that England had always been an enemy of France, and had always benefited from her alliance with Spain and later the Empire against France. Events were decided for Henry when in May 1521 Francis invaded and reconquered Navarre and attacked the Duchy of Luxembourg. By doing so Francis had broken the Treaty of London, and Henry's response in May 1522 was to declare war on France.

1522–29 War, Peace and the King's 'Great Matter'

England was unable to make a significant contribution to the war at that point, as she simply lacked the resources to do so. This partly explains why in August 1522 the General Proscription was ordered, to assess the military and financial resources of the population. Wolsey had agreed in 1521 to a significantly larger invasion in 1523, but in 1522 a raid from Calais around Picardy was led by the Earl of Surrey, with a force of 7,000.

If England intended mayhem in France, it was inevitable that Scotland would choose to threaten the northern border, as the Regent Albany chose to do in 1523. The usual English response came in the form of two large raids led by Thomas Howard, who had now succeeded to his father's title as Earl of Surrey. With only enough artillery to destroy a bastle house all went well, until the siege of Cessford Castle. The castle's walls were reinforced with earth in the latest manner, which negated Surrey's artillery. The second raid led to the usual inconclusive skirmishes and opportunistic arson. In October Albany lead a Franco-Scottish army south to besiege Wark, but the Scots refused to cross the Tweed. Albany now settled before Wark and with only 3,000 men faced Surrey's 5,000. Surrey did his best to initiate the engagement by threatening to 'strike off his [Albany's] head and send it to the King of England'.[9] Albany did not take the bait and Surrey complained that it was '[a]

---

8   J.J. Scarisbrick, *Henry VIII* (Berkeley: University of California Press, 1970), p.79.
9   Edward Hall, *Chronicle*, vol. 1, p.304. Quoted from Gervase Philips, *The Anglo-Scots Wars 1513–1550* (Boydell Press, 1999), p.144.

grete pitie it were that the King is Highnes shuld spend thus moche money withoute batayle'.[10] Henry agreed, and Surrey returned to London if not in disgrace then at least in bad odour. Albany was also humiliated and fled for France. Henry supported a new Scottish regent, Archibald Angus, who offered to provide a peaceful border. Lord Dacre was relieved of his wardenships in the North as Henry felt such a powerful figure was a potential problem, especially when the threat from Scotland had significantly diminished.

In the new European situation what was lacking was a strategic plan which would combine the efforts of King Henry and the Emperor. What again decided Henry's actions were events in Europe or specifically France, with the treason of Charles de Bourbon the Constable of France. With France divided, the Constable, Charles V and Henry agreed on an invasion in July 1523. Henry would provide the majority of the manpower, and Margaret of Burgundy the artillery and supplies. Charles promised to launch an attack, as did Bourbon. The English army taken to France in 1523 was made up of some 2,000 men from Suffolk's own lordship, principally in North Wales and the Marches, 1,000 volunteers, 1,600 men from the Calais garrison and the remainder drawn from the county militias. In total Henry disposed some 16,500 men including 3,500 mercenaries.

Suffolk's forces had some success, capturing eight towns, which now acknowledged Henry as sovereign. However Bourbon's attack on Paris failed to materialise, as did the invasion of France by Charles from Spain. He provided no reinforcements for Suffolk's forces and less than half the money promised, about £16,000. Suffolk was forced to withdraw; his army, suffering from the plague and dreadfully cold weather, had effectively disintegrated. The cost of the two years of futile campaigning was about £400,000. The overall cost of England's military efforts was calculated by Wolsey to add up to some £800,000. Parliament had granted some £300,000 and a forced loan had raised a further £352,000. Patience amongst those who had to pay for these wars was running thin. The words of Thomas Cromwell best sum up what many have felt when considering Henry's regular calls for war and the money to pay for it, when he condemned the expense associated with the capture of Thérouanne, 'which cost his highness more than twenty such ungracious dogholes could be worth'.[11] Henry was deeply disillusioned by the abject failure of the Emperor to fulfil his obligations, and relations between them, like the weather, were frosty.

Steven Gunn considered the expedition of 1523 to be the 'last campaign of the Hundred Years War'.[12] He provides this analysis which puts Henry's ambition in the broader European context:

---

10 Henry Ellis, *Original Letters Illustrative of English History: Including Numerous Royal Letters; from Autographs in the British Museum, the State Paper Office, and One Or Two Other Collections*, vol. 1 (London: Richard Bentley,1846), p.231.

11 Diarmaid MacCulloch (ed.), *The Reign of Henry VIII: Politics, Policy and Piety* (Palgrave Macmillan, 1995), p.109.

12 S.J. Gunn, 'The Duke of Suffolk's March on Paris in 1523', in *English Historical Review*, vol. 101, no. 401 (Oct. 1986), p.629.

Henry VIII had pursued the traditional English offensive strategy of the previous three centuries, but he could not make: 'semblable warr against the Frenchmen'.[13] Most French peers would not now desert or stand aside, none had the military resources of a John the Fearless, and the loyal standing army and arrangement with the Swiss gave the French Crown flexible military strength. Charles V, with his commitments from Italy to Friesland and his readiness to promise what Margaret in the Netherlands could never provide, had proved both too powerful and too unreliable to be an effective ally in England's Continental ambitions.[14]

The Battle of Pavia on 14 February 1525, which saw the French army crushed and Francis captured, changed the game once more. This should have provided a golden opportunity for Henry, who was still intent on making his claim to portions of France a reality. He asked his imperial ally for Normandy, Picardy and Boulogne, in return for his help in the dismantling of France. Henry attempted to drum up support for another invasion amongst the population, providing bonfires and limitless supplies of cheap drink for Londoners. Unfortunately the 'Amicable Grant' proposed by Wolsey to pay for yet another foreign expedition was met with outright hostility, and worse, refusal to pay up. In addition the Emperor also rejected Henry's proposal, and to add insult to injury repudiated the previous marriage offer to princess Mary.

Henry and Wolsey now reversed their pro-Imperial anti-French policy, signing the Treaty of the More with France in August 1525 and encouraging the anti-Imperial League of Cognac. What determined Henry's foreign policy for the indefinite future was the 'King's matter'. This was the promotion of his divorce from Queen Catherine, who was also of course the aunt of the Emperor. Henry had begun his affair with Anne Boleyn in 1526 and the issue of the divorce was placed in Wolsey's supposedly capable hands in 1527. This was also the year in which Henry stopped participating in the joust, perhaps a recognition of his age and his own mortality. Queen Catherine naturally sought the intervention of her nephew, Emperor Charles V, with the Papacy. Charles was in a strong position to put pressure on Pope Clement VII, as Clement had become his prisoner in 1527 after the Sack of Rome. This event was not intended by Charles, but was a spontaneous and very violent act by his Protestant Landsknecht mercenaries. It was said that after this the Emperor never again smiled. The Pope unsurprisingly declared his undying support for Charles after the decisive defeat of the French by Imperial forces at Landriano in 1528, a position confirmed with the Treaty of Barcelona in 1529. The Peace of Cambrai, between France and the Empire in August of the same year, left England isolated and without a clear future course.

Divorce, Reformation and Isolation 1529–39

Henry's prime concerns were now domestic rather than foreign. Wolsey's failure to gain the impossible divorce led to his humiliation and trial and his ultimate replacement with Thomas Cromwell, whose role in Henry's

---

13   Tito Livio dei Frulovisi, ed. C L. Kingsford, *The First English Life of King Henry V* (Oxford: Clarendon Press, 1911), p.190.
14   Gunn, 'Suffolk's March', p.630.

reign has been long mulled over. The divorce process led ultimately to the Reformation in England, which again placed England in a perilous relationship with a predominantly Catholic Europe. The dissolution of the monasteries 1536–1541 and the effective submission of the Church in England to royal control did give Henry access to enormous wealth, some of which was used to effectively bribe the nobility and gentry to support him. The Dissolution also led to the Pilgrimage of Grace in 1536, a mass movement in the North determined to save what they knew and loved from further despoliation. Henry defeated it with guile and cruelty. He recognised that he did not have the military resources to crush it in the way his father had crushed the Cornish rebels in 1497.

The death of his first wife, the much-wronged Catherine of Aragon, and execution of his second wife, the unpopular Anne Boleyn, both in 1536, made Henry somewhat less of a European pariah. Those who served him, in particular the Archbishop of Canterbury Thomas Cranmer and Thomas Cromwell, may well have preferred a more radical religious settlement than Henry but remained his servants in such matters. Edward Fox was despatched on an embassy to Germany and the Schmalkaldic League in 1535–6 to consider the religious and diplomatic future of the kingdom, an initiative deeply opposed by the conservative Bishop Gardiner.

While Francis and Charles were engaged in their efforts to control Italy and defend their borders from each other, England was secure from any threat. On 18 June 1538, after the latest outbreak of fighting in Italy had come to an end, the two mortal enemies signed the Truce of Nice, which had been promoted by Pope Paul III. This settled some of their outstanding territorial disputes and was designed not to ensure peace in perpetuity but for a decade (equally unlikely). The negotiations between the two, conducted by the Pope, took place in separate rooms as the two sovereigns refused to be seated together, an indication of the real state of relations between these obstreperous rulers. Henry had hoped that Franco-Imperial hostility would ensure the safety of his realm, and in fact relations with the Empire had improved after the death of (Queen) Catherine. The recent truce brokered by the Pope, who had excommunicated Henry in December 1538, made the possibility of a combined European 'crusade' against Henry appear feasible. On 12 January Charles and Francis signed the Treaty of Toledo, whereby they agreed not to ally with England but to stand against this excommunicate monarch. Henry responded by the massive programme of defensive constructions which were known as the Device forts. Foreign ships were detained in English harbours and a chain of warning beacons prepared between March and April 1539. On 3 May a parade of 16,500 men took place before the King in London, indicative of the seriousness of the situation. However the unity between Francis I, James V and Charles V could not last, and as the London militia marched past the King the threat had receded.

The obvious allies of the embattled sovereign were Europe's Protestant princes, which of course explains the unsuccessful marriage to Anne of Cleves (January–July 1540). Henry was never attracted by Protestant beliefs, although he greatly enjoyed the power and prestige he had gained in his dominions from usurping the authority of the Pope. Cromwell's fall in 1540, in part due to the Cleves match, led to the rise of aggressive noble factions, less competent than Cromwell but determined to serve the King in peace but preferably war.

Another Scottish Interlude – the 'Rough Wooing' Begins

Henry's relations with Scotland now also presented difficulties. After Flodden Scotland had ceased to pose a serious military threat to England. Scotland would never be reconciled to a subservient position and within a decade would threaten disturbance along the border. James V succeeded to the throne on the death of his father James IV, who had been killed at Flodden, but he was of course also the son of Margaret Tudor. He was thus Henry's nephew and Henry expected him to prostrate himself before his wealthier and more powerful elder relative.

This state of affairs did not appeal to the young king, who had seized the throne from Archibald Douglas 6th Earl of Angus in 1528, at the age of 16. Between 1532 and 1534 there was low level conflict between the two nations especially in the Debatable Lands, resolved in a settlement negotiated by France. The serious diplomatic problem facing England was posed by the Scots king's clear intention of seeking a close alliance with France. His second French marriage was to Mary of Guise in 1540, a woman who had already wisely rejected Henry's advances. Francis I offered a dowry that would match that of a royal princess, which indicates the importance he gave to the match. James's failure to meet Henry at York in 1541 was considered by the King as a calculated insult: 'we be in dedes so injured, contemped and despised, as we ought not with sufferaunce to pretermitte and passe over'.[15] Henry insisted on a humiliating climbdown by James, and a declaration of amity or neutrality in case of a war with France. He threatened to attack Scotland if James did not give way. The young and seriously ill Scottish monarch, instead of submitting to renewed English claims to the overlordship of Scotland, invaded England at the end of November 1542.

His army was humiliatingly defeated at Solway Moss, as a consequence of the collapse of leadership and morale in the face of a small but aggressive and well-led English force. The Scottish losses were few, but an Earl, five barons, hundreds of gentlemen and the King's favourite were all captured. They were taken to London in December 1542, where the majority were treated as honoured guests and swore to accept Henry as his 'assured' subjects. Those who did not, remained as less honoured prisoners of the English until 1551. What Henry's intentions were in what he referred to as: 'Our greate afayre of Scotland', are difficult to fathom. Marcus Merriman suggests that he was utterly pragmatic and considered four possible solutions to the issue of Scotland: 'sovereignty itself, union by marriage, control of the area south of the Forth–Clyde line, or at least influence over whatever Scottish government emerged in 1543'.[16] The union of Prince Edward with Princess Mary of Scotland was the most attractive option. It would secure the Tudor

15   Susan Doran, *England and Europe in the Sixteenth Century* (Basingstoke: Macmillan International Higher Education, 1998), p.13.
16   Marcus Merriman, *The Rough Wooings: Mary Queen of Scots, 1542–1551* (East Linton: Tuckwell Press, 2000), p.113.

dynasty, it would gratify Henry's Imperial pretensions, it would once and for all separate Scotland from France and thereby secure England's northern border, thereby saving a fortune in defensive measures.

The unfortunate Scottish king died in despair on 15 December, leaving the infant Mary under the supervision of his wife, the French princess. In July 1543 at Greenwich the Scots lords, led by the Earl of Arran, agreed to first a peace treaty and then the betrothal of Edward and Mary. This joyful arrangement did not last. Arran, having returned to Scotland, formally repudiated the treaties in December 1543 and sided with the pro-French party led by Cardinal Beaton. Scotland was as weak as she had ever been, with political, religious and clan rivalries creating ideal conditions for English intervention. The French diplomat Jacques de la Brosse reported that:

> the whole country was under arms, not for national defence but because all the friends of one faction mistrust all those of the other faction. So much so that not merely is the nobility in arms, but churchmen, friars and the country people only travel through the countryside in large companies all armed with pikes, swords and bucklers and a half pike in their hands.[17]

Henry's response to Arran's treachery was cruel and simple; his orders to Edward Seymour Earl of Hertford in May 1543 were to:

> Put all to fire and sword, burn Edinburgh town and as many towns and villages about Edinburgh as ye may conveniently, sack Leith and burn and subvert it and all the rest, putting man, woman and child to fire and sword, without exception where any resistance shall be made against you.[18]

Thus began the Rough Wooing, intended to force the union of the two crowns in the persons of King Edward and Queen Mary. This was a phrase derived from the supposed response by the captured Earl of Huntly on the field at Pinkie after the Scottish defeat. When asked about the marriage proposal he replied: 'I wade it sud gea furth [should go forth], and haud will with the marriage, but I lyke not thys wooing.'[19]

After considerable preparation, including the collection of a large fleet to support the army, Hertford with about 15,000 men landed in Scotland on 2 May. Scottish resistance to the English invasion, at least at first, was not impressive. A force of 6,000 Scots barring the way to Edinburgh was easily thrust aside, only causing two English casualties. It was said that Cardinal Beaton was the first to seek safety in flight. On 8 May the city of Edinburgh was taken but the castle successfully resisted, mainly because of its impregnable position and the accurate fire of its artillery. Further raids

---

17 G. Dickinson (ed.), *Two Missions of Jacques de la Brosse* (Edinburgh: Scottish History Society Third Series, vol. 36, 1942), p.23.

18 Joseph Bain (ed.), *The Hamilton Papers: Letters and Papers Illustrating the Political Relations of England and Scotland in the XVIth century, formerly in the possession of the dukes of Hamilton, now in the British Museum*, vol. I (Edinburgh: H.M. General Register House, 1890), p.207.

19 Merriman, *The Rough Wooings*, p.8.

caused much damage and did nothing to make the Scots accept Henry's offer. In military terms Hertford did display remarkable originality in the use of a balanced mobile force, landed and sustained by sea wherever possible. It also established in his mind the possibility of a new strategy, the creation of an English Pale. The Scottish, outraged by the wanton destruction, discovered a degree of unity. Beaton and Arran were joined by the Earls of Moray, Huntly and Argyll acting in support of the French Dowager Queen. The Scots now turned on the English and a large raiding force was defeated with heavy loss by a much smaller Scottish force at Ancrum Moor, on 27 February 1545.

1544 The Enterprise of Paris (Boulogne)

In Europe Pope Paul III was busy dealing with domestic problems caused by heavy taxation of his flock and the promotion of his family members. The peace between Charles and Francis was very short-lived, with war breaking out yet again in 1542. Henry's concern towards the end of his reign were matrimonial, as well as martial. His disastrous marriage to Catherine Howard had ended in his humiliation and her execution in February 1542. He married Catherine Parr in July 1543, who was to prove far more politic than her flighty predecessor. Henry established her as regent in 1544 during his absence on campaign in France. War at this point for Henry was an attractive project, he now had a son by the short-lived Jane Seymour and two daughters for the succession, a new reliable and competent wife, an enthusiastic nobility, full coffers and no threat posed from Scotland; he also had a powerful ally and a worthy opponent. What he lacked was a plan.

Henry had been negotiating with Charles from 1540 but a treaty of mutual aid was not signed until February 1543. It was too late to plan a major expedition but Sir John Wallop was sent with 5,000 men, including some 400 highly valued border horse, to support the Emperor in the Low countries at the (unsuccessful) siege of Landrecies. The infantry was drawn equally from county militia and trusted gentlemen's retinues.

The 1523 French expedition was supposed to have been part of a pincer movement on Paris. With France divided and with the Emperor as a powerful ally anything seemed possible, including the capture of Paris and the coronation of Henry as King of France. In 1544, as in 1513, although there was to be an invasion it was not certain what it was for or what it could achieve. It was to be named the 'Enterprise of Paris' and agreed to in December 1543. Henry had a sizeable army made up of Englishmen and mercenaries but he could still not hope to conquer France. His alliance with the Emperor was agreed upon the basis of an attack on Paris. From the beginning the distrust between the allies was exploited by the French, which made determined coordinated action between Charles and Henry nearly impossible and both were permitted to pursue their own plans, 'as strategy, victuals and the enemy shall permit'.[20] Henry had been 'stood up' by his Imperial ally once too often and he therefore chose instead to pursue

---

20 Paul Hammer, *Elizabeth's Wars: War, Government and Society in Tudor England, 1544–1604* (Basingstoke: Palgrave Macmillan, 2003), p.17.

a more modest target. Combining realism with bombast he considered that 'it would be better to take two or three frontier places than to have burnt Paris'.[21] The Duke of Norfolk suggested the capture of Montreuil, while Sir John Russell recommended Boulogne. Henry chose both. It was Boulogne which his father had besieged in 1497 and had been the probable objective of the 1523 campaign. Henry, at the end of his reign, was attempting to achieve what he and his father had previously failed to.

The invasion was on an even more massive scale than that of 1513, and achieved its objective. Henry entered Boulogne in triumph on 18 June. It is doubtful on the other hand whether it was ever intended that Montreuil would also be seriously besieged. The army at Montreuil was there mainly to act as a diversion for the Boulogne siege, which is where Henry devoted his main efforts. The defence of Boulogne was extraordinarily stoic in the face of a bombardment of more than 100,000 cannonballs. It was not this bombardment but the failure of a relief force which forced it to surrender.

On the day that Boulogne was captured Charles and Francis signed the Treaty of Crépy. Henry had once again been betrayed by the Emperor. Meanwhile at Montreuil the army was now threatened with attack by the French army and fled with its tail between its legs. The cost of Boulogne's conquest and the additional costs of rebuilding its walls and garrisoning were immense. It was calculated at over £1,000,000, not including the unfortunate loss of many lives. Once he had captured Boulogne Henry was not going to abandon it, as he had done with Tournai.

In 1545 the King now faced a determined and aggressive France, without an ally. Francis now sought to discomfort Henry by supporting the Scots on Henry's northern border, renewing the siege of Boulogne, making large incursions into the Calais Pale and launching a seaborne attack on the south coast. The strain on England's resources was great, and for the first time England faced a strong enemy fleet in the Solent and even invasion, if only of the Isle of Wight. The outcome was neither a disaster for Francis or triumph for Henry but meant further expense and pointless bloodshed. Stephen Gardiner, the Bishop of Winchester, closely involved in the management of Henry's policy, was at his wits end:

> We are at war with France and Scotland, we have enmity with the Bishop of Rome [the Pope]; we have no assured friendship here with the Emperor and we have received from the Landgrave, chief captain of the Protestants, such displeasure that he has cause to think us angry with him … Our war is noisome to our realm and to all our merchants that traffic through the Narrow Seas … We are in a World where reason and learning prevail not and covenants are little regarded.[22]

What better critique of Henry's action could there be, coming from one of his most stalwart supporters and competent servants.

---

21 Hammer, *Elizabeth's Wars*, p.17.
22 John Julius Norwich, *Four Princes: Henry VIII, Francis I, Charles V, Suleiman the Magnificent and the Obsessions that Forged Modern Europe* (Kindle Edition, 2020), loc. 2441–2448.

Henry quite unrealistically prepared for a further French expedition in 1546. The county militias were mustered and a force of 16,000 English infantry and 14,000 mercenaries was proposed. Hertford was sent to Calais in March to prepare for this new army. The initial objective was to establish a fort at Ambleteuse, to ensure the line of communication between Calais and Boulogne. After some skirmishing around Boulogneberg both sides abandoned further aggressive action.

In practice the cost and dangers of continued conflict made a settlement essential. On 7 June 1546 Hertford found himself negotiating the Treaty of Camp (or to the French, the Treaty of Ardres), not leading an army on campaign. Henry finally agreed to the return of Boulogne to take place in 1554 after the payment of two million crowns (£600,000), the arrears of his French pension. As important to Henry as the money, if not more so, was the recognition by Francis of Henry's titles as Defender of the Faith and Supreme Head of the Church. Henry was always more interested in titles than territory.

The Costs of War

War was always expensive and never in Henry's reign profitable. The first French campaign of 1512–1514 cost the stupendous sum of £1,000,000 and the more modest excursions between 1522 and 1524 emptied the royal coffers to the tune of £400,000. In his definitive study of the Anglo-French War David Potter summarised the appalling cost of the French and Scottish wars between 1538 and 1547.[23]

Table 1. The Cost of Henry's Wars

Landrecies Campaign 1543	£36,500
Boulogne (siege) 1544	£ 586,718.2s.4d
War and fortifications at Boulogne	£ 426,306.19s.5d (of which £318,884.3s.4d in wages)
Fortification and garrison costs at Calais 1538–1547	£276,765.9s.7d
The Scottish wars 1542–1547	£350,243.2s.2d
Naval expenditure	£265,024.4s.3d
Device fortifications 1538–1547	£203,205.13s.0
Total	£2,126,763 10s 9d

The non-Parliamentary revenues that the King could call on amounted to only £90,000 per annum, about four percent of the costs of his late conflicts. New sources of revenue came from Henry's status as Supreme Governor of the Church. Hale summarised the new relationship between Church and state nicely, when he wrote 'Peter with the keys was robbed to pay Paul with the sword.'[24] The retention in England of Peter's Pence (the tithe payable to Rome) and clerical taxation

---

23 David Linley Potter, *Henry VIII and Francis I* (Leiden: Brill, 2011), pp.243–255.
24 Hale, *Renaissance War Studies*, p.71.

through the Court of First Fruits and Tenths produced £42,000 per annum in 1535. The income from property seized as a consequence of the Dissolution of the Monasteries, and administered through the Court of Augmentations added between £25,000 and £50,000 per annum. The sales of monastic land, mostly as a means of paying for the Device forts, made a substantial sum of £66,000 per annum between 1539 and 1542. The sale of monastic property accelerated as demand increased, with £900,000 raised between 1542 and 1551. The family silver, or rather in practice the lead off the monastic roofs, was up for sale, to pay for the consequences of Henry's ambition. The actual quantity of lead was phenomenal, some 12.5 million kilogrammes, an amount so great in fact that its sale would have flooded the market. The entire stock was eventually sold for £58,000 which was less than half its normal value.

Parliament had an important part to play in raising funds from what was an unenthusiastic country. Between 1543–1545 Parliamentary loans, grant subsidies and the delightfully named Benevolences raised £712,382, while clerical subsidies from the nationalised Church added a further £84,000. The money raised from the sale of stolen goods and taxation of Church and people was still not enough. Wriotheseley, a character who on this rare occasion it is difficult not to have sympathy for, wrote to the council in some despair:

> his subsidy and benevolence ministring skant thre hundrethe thousand therof as I muste sustyene where the rest being so greate a summe hathe been gotten soo the landes being consumede, the plate of the realme molten and coyned, wherof moche hathe assay, I sorowe and lament the daunger of the tyme to com.[25]

The coinage was the last victim of Henry's desperate search for more cash. The English silver coinage at 92.5 percent purity was universally acknowledged as a source of confidence and pride. The addition of base metal began in May 1544, with the silver content reduced to 50 percent and later to as low as 25 percent. Gold coins were also reduced from 23 carat to 20. The most embarrassing product of this policy was the Testoon or shilling (12d) which had a thin layer of silver over copper. The silver overlying the most prominent royal feature was soon worn off in circulation and Henry became known as 'Old Coppernose'. For a monarch deeply sensitive to a slight of any sort this must have been hurtful, but it also must have profoundly damaged the respect the people had for the image of the King in every sense. In fact it was Francis I, Henry's great rival, who was the proud owner of the monarchical mega-nose, known to his people as 'le roi grand-nez'.

The debasement of the coinage was a profound blow to the prestige of England and the King. It was however extremely profitable and a source of revenue to Henry and his immediate successors. Between 1544 and 1551 an enormous sum £1,270,000 was derived from this source, about half in Henry's reign. To further deepen royal indebtedness substantial loans of £1m were made on the Antwerp market at the ruinous rate of 12 to 14

---

25 Potter, *Henry VIII and Francis I*, p.249. Wriothesley to Council, 14 Sept. 1544, NA SP 1/207, f.172 (174); (*Letters and Papers*, XX, ii, 366).

percent per annum. The inevitable consequence of debasement and wild government expenditure was of course serious inflation. In five years landed incomes based on rents and fines halved, causing increased tensions between landlords and tenants as well as disdain for the Crown.

The Final Act

Scotland should not be forgotten during this period, although after 1542 it no longer posed a serious threat to the North. Hertford led a new raid into Scotland in August 1545, and although it achieved little he began to develop his idea of establishing garrisons in Scotland, suggesting Leith and then Kelso as potential bases. Henry seemed enthusiastic at first but numerous objections were raised and the project was abandoned. In Scotland the conflict between Catholicism and Protestantism was creating a major crisis which concluded with the murder of Cardinal Beaton (1546) who had turned Arran from an English ally into her enemy. Henry died in January 1547 and King Francis in March, and the issue of Boulogne became important again. Henri II of France immediately reneged on the treaty and intended to recapture Boulogne. England, facing a potentially difficult regency for the young King Edward, agreed to the return of Boulogne in return for less than a quarter of the agreed amount. England needed the cash; she did not need another expensive and futile war. Henry's sole territorial gain, and his son's inheritance, was abandoned in 1550.

Henry, described by Sir John Russell as 'the father of all Europe in this world',[26] was of course nothing of the sort. The big players were Ferdinand, Maximilian, Francis and Charles; Henry's actions very much depended upon what they had done or wanted to do. His policies were pragmatic and opportunistic, as he lacked the wealth and the power to match those he considered his equals. It is difficult to argue that any of his wars were in any sense necessary for England's defence. The only 'invasion' of England by the Scots in 1513 was in response to his invasion of France and was never aimed at conquest. Only twice did England face the possibility of invasion 1538–9 and 1545, and on both occasions this was as the consequence of his own actions. At ruinous expense and the loss of many lives he had no doubt maintained his 'honour' but had failed in everything he had ostensibly set out to achieve.

An Irish Interlude

Ireland was on the fringe of Henry's realm, and although he claimed sovereignty, in practice he controlled little more than the English Pale around Dublin and sometimes not even that. In 1520 Surrey was sent there with a small force to discover how to restore the people to 'obedience'. Surrey argued that only a harsh policy enforced by an army of 6,000 could achieve anything and only then if English colonists were settled as well. Henry considered Surrey's mission a vain consumption of royal treasure. Throughout his reign

---

26 Jeremiah Holmes Wiffen, *Historical Memoirs of the House of Russell*, vol. 1, part 1 (London: Longman, Rees, Orme, Brown, Green, and Longman, 1833), p.344.

his lordship of Ireland cost him £4,000 per annum. For much of this time government alternated between the families of Kildare and Ormond; on occasion Ormond might be held as a prisoner in England before returning to govern in Ireland on the King's behalf. In 1534 Sir William Skeffington was sent with a small force to prop up what was left of English authority, but this attempt to assert control ended with the invasion of the Pale in 1539.

A change in policy was needed and it proved remarkably successful. Ireland was now deemed a separate kingdom and not part of England. The rival families and clans were encouraged to 'surrender' to the Crown, on the understanding that their property and power would be regranted. Thus, O'Neill and O'Brian were now awarded the titles of the Earl of Tyrone and Thormond respectively. This splendid fiction did bring about a remarkable change, so that in 1544–5 Irish troops served in Scotland and France rather than opposing English rule in Ireland.

Ireland would continue to present an almost insuperable problem for successive English sovereigns. Catholic Ireland presented a challenge to England after the religious changes of Henry VIII and even after the accession of Philip and Mary there was little trust in the loyalty of their Irish subjects. To enforce English rule would require endless expense, and in the environment of Ireland a definitive military outcome was unlikely. The establishment of English settlements had and would in future provide a constant source of dispute and hostages to fortune.

Edward VI

Henry's death was shrouded in self-interested shenanigans. In the last months of his reign final political battles were being fought to establish whether there would be a conservative Catholic or a reformist Protestant regency. His death was first hidden and then managed brilliantly, and it was the conservatives who found themselves either in prison or in exile from the court. The Duke of Norfolk was to be found not in power but in the Tower, awaiting execution, which was suspended on the old king's death. The Council, which had been well rewarded with the 'undisclosed gifts' clause in Henry's 'will', agreed to the promotion of one of their number, the young king's uncle, Edward Seymour the Earl of Hertford and newly created Duke of Somerset, to the fine new title of Lord Protector of the Realm.

There was no question that the war with France would be reopened. The kingdom had been impoverished by wars that had resulted in heavy taxation, domestic unrest and disastrous debasement of the coinage. It was clear that the religious settlement would tend towards the Protestant, which would certainly please the young king; peace at home and abroad was desirable but the question of Scotland remained. Edward and Queen Mary had been contracted in marriage in 1543 and Edward's father had gone so far as to claim the Scottish throne. Somerset, who had devoted so much effort to the pursuit of Henry's Scottish policy, the Rough Wooing, was hardly likely to abandon what (little) had been gained at such a great cost.

Edward VI (1537–1553), When Duke of Cornwall c.1545; reworked in 1547 or later from the workshop of Hans Holbein the Younger. Edward may have been only a boy during his short reign but his person and his personality were not to be ignored. He was an intelligent and active child who wanted a more Protestant settlement than his father would have considered. Until his final illness he was a healthy youngster, and like his father enjoyed archery and other manly sports. (Metropolitan Museum of Art, Open Access)

The policy that he pursued appeared at first to be a great success. The shock and awe achieved by his victory at Pinkie on 10 September 1547 was followed up by a coherent political, diplomatic and military strategy to create an English Pale, to seduce or subdue the Scots and revive the hopes of marriage. In practice the policy fell apart as the Scots resented the English invasion, regained a degree of political unity and sought French assistance. The cost of garrisons increased and the flight of Mary to France in August 1549 made the ultimate objective unachievable. Conflict with France became inevitable with Henri II declaring war in August.

Somerset's reputation as the 'Good Duke', as a social reformer and the friend of the commons, was not well deserved. The religious and economic tensions that were building up finally exploded in the summer of 1549 with major armed rebellions in East Anglia and the South West. Somerset's response was confusing, dilatory and ineffectual. The crisis also led to any military resources available now being devoted to saving the realm from chaos. Somerset's abject failure in Scotland and the blame attributed to him for the rebellions led the Council to seek another leader. He was overthrown by consent of the Council, which put in place a new regent, the Duke of Northumberland, who had suppressed the East Anglian rebels with an admirable combination of ruthlessness and lenity.

Northumberland realised the impossibility of carrying on war of any sort on any front. His attempt to negotiate with France over the return of Boulogne and a Scottish settlement was from a very weak position. In practice Scotland was left in the French sphere of influence and Boulogne would be returned, with at least a monetary sweetener. Anglo-French relations now verged on the cordial, with Henri II made a Knight of the Garter and Edward admitted, in absentia, to the order of St Michael. Northumberland concentrated on creating religious, political and economic stability. When the question of his marriage to the Scottish Queen arose once more, Edward replied with considerable maturity and sagacity: 'they had taken too much pain and spent too many lives for her'.[27] Restoring the currency, establishing a determinedly Protestant settlement and maintaining domestic peace, meant that antagonising foreign powers and engaging in ruinously expensive war was inconceivable. Even the companies of 850 gendarmes which he had established in February 1551

---

27   W.K. Jordan, *The Chronicle and Political Papers of King Edward VI* (London: George Allen and Unwin, 1966), p.68.

to protect the King and for 'the staie of the unquiet subjectes, and for other services in all eventes',[28] were disbanded in the Autumn of 1552 to save cash. This was a mistake that he might well have rued.

Mary and Philip

King Edward died on 6 July 1553, but his death was not announced until the 8th; the Tower of London was put into a state of defence and on the 10th Lady Jane Grey was brought thence and proclaimed queen. Princess Mary was at Kenninghall Castle, supported by Sir Thomas Wharton and numerous local gentry. Northumberland had failed to secure the person of Mary but he feared that her most likely course would be to escape the kingdom rather than raise rebellion. Emperor Charles had previously planned a cloak-and-dagger escape for Mary organised by two Spanish agents posing as corn merchants. This dusty pair would take the incognito Queen aboard a boat in Maldon and rendezvous with a Spanish warship off the coast.

Mary was the daughter of Henry VIII and Catherine of Aragon, and thus in the eyes of many the legitimate claimant to the throne. Her mother's popularity, enhanced by her father's mistreatment of her, was inherited by Mary. Northumberland's machinations in putting his daughter-in-law on the throne, a girl with small claim to it, was clearly a coup that would gain little support except from those few Protestants who sought to maintain the religious settlement of Edward VI. Mary was a Tudor and would not run.

The Duke of Northumberland now set out to bring Mary to heel. He claimed the right to lead the expedition against her, as he was the 'best man of warre in the realme',[29] and in addition as had already triumphed once in Norfolk over Kett's rebellion he was 'so feared, that none durst once lift up their weapon against him'.[30] At Durham House he collected men and ordnance for the field. On 12 July in Norwich Mary was proclaimed queen, after some delay, as the Corporation ascertained that the King was truly dead. Mary had wisely avoided any association with Kett's rebels or the authors of their repression, avoiding potential hostility from the common people. Six royal ships had been sent to Yarmouth to capture Mary if she had tried to flee, but they declared their support for her instead. The reinforcements that she received in both men and ordnance from the fleet was an indicator of how the wind blew. In the Tower our anonymous observer recalled that 'Then eche man then began to pluck his hornes';[31] what came as a particularly shocking blow was that it was reported that 'the noblemen's tenants refused to serve their lords against queen Mary'.[32] On 19 July Mary was proclaimed queen in London, and on hearing this Northumberland abandoned his doomed project and proclaimed

28 Hammer, *Elizabeth's Wars*, p.45.
29 Anon., *The Chronicle of Queen Jane by a resident of the Tower of London from July 53–October 54* (London: Camden Society, 1850), p.8.
30 Anon., *The Chronicle of Queen Jane*, p.8.
31 Anon., *The Chronicle of Queen Jane*, p.9.
32 Anon., *The Chronicle of Queen Jane*, p.9.

Shilling of Philip and Mary 1554. Two sovereigns are represented here, if not cheek to cheek then face to face, in amity if not great mutual affection. Although absent from England for most of the reign, Philip was clearly presented as co-ruler. The early coins combined the titles *King and Queen of England, France and Naples, Prince and Princess of Spain*, despite Philip having been deprived of an actual coronation by Parliament. The shilling (1/20 of a pound) was a new coin, in part intended to deal with the consequences of inflation, requiring higher denomination coins, brought about by successive disastrous debasements. (Metropolitan Museum of Art, Open Access)

her queen himself. Having been arrested by the Mayor of Cambridge, he could do little more than throw himself on the new queen's mercy.

Mary succeeded not because of her military superiority. Northumberland had been abandoned by his allies and the Privy Council in London, the people rallied to her cause, as she and not the Lady Jane was obviously the legitimate heir to the throne. If Northumberland had not disbanded the gendarmes then he might have had a reliable force that would have nipped her rebellion in the bud and taken her prisoner. It was the loyalty of the local nobility and gentry and their men assembled at Framlingham castle, along with the sailors from the fleet, that gave her the appearance of strength, while Northumberland's force slowly melted away on the road from London.

Mary came to the throne amidst public jubilation. Bonfires were set throughout London to welcome her accession, other bonfires made of more than brushwood would colour the later reputation of her name. Initially she did not seek to persecute those with a Protestant leaning, nor did she ever permit the Holy Inquisition to operate in her Kingdom. She was determined to restore Catholicism in England, not an unreasonable objective, as Protestantism had hardly gained a hold on the majority, but it would take time. What had been the priority of her father was now hers, the provision of an heir and therefore for her the acquisition of a husband.

During her unhappy life after her parents' divorce, she had sought and received unquestioned support from her Spanish 'family'. It was this connection that would lead her to marriage with Philip II of Spain. Queen Catherine, the wife of Henry VIII, was Charles V's aunt and he would always side with her and her daughter in disputes with Henry VIII and Edward VI. The proposed match between Charles's son Philip II and Queen Mary of England made excellent sense for many reasons. Mary had long relied on the emotional support provided by Emperor Charles and the Imperial ambassador. This had enabled her to continue worshipping in the traditional Catholic manner. Such support was especially important during the accelerating religious changes that occurred in her brother's reign, changes she never accepted.

Mary had first considered the Emperor himself as a marriage partner, to whom she had been affianced twice already, or Edward Courtnay, a loyal Catholic courtier but an unattractive personality as she soon discovered. Imperial ambassador Simon Renard pressed strongly for the suit of King Philip. England by this marriage would now be allied with the devotedly Catholic European superpower. Spain was also an important trading partner and the traditional enemy of England's greatest enemy, France. After only a few months Mary made clear her intention of marrying her young (and handsome, for a Habsburg) cousin, Philip.

The marriage was clearly a matter of public disquiet, as it led to a rebellion that may have had strong elements of farce but was in many ways a substantial threat. Wyatt's rising, which took place from 22 January to 3 February 1555, originated in Kent but should have taken place in at least three other counties, if plans had come to fruition and the nerves of the other conspirators held. There was also the possibility of an alternative candidate to the throne, the young Princess Elizabeth, who wisely had nothing to do with the rebellion. Although the rebel forces were small and ill-equipped, the failure of the rebellion to be swiftly suppressed, the defection of loyal forces and the fact that the rebels made it to the very gates of the City of London, made it appear a very real danger to Mary. It was again only her determination and character that rallied the City and royal forces. Once the rebels realised that the regime was not about to collapse and that they faced a serious fight, they withered away.

Although the marriage suited Mary politically, diplomatically and emotionally it was by no means popular outside the court, as it was quite clear that in this match England was to be the junior partner. Philip's retainers had not helped by establishing such a reputation for being quarrelsome with their English hosts that he had to order them to go unarmed in London. The penalty for drawing a weapon was to lose a hand or even hanging. Philip was made co-ruler with Mary, both their heads appeared on the new coins and Parliament was called in both their names. While their marriage continued, Philip would share in determining the direction that England took. One provision made by Parliament, which was of great significance and importance, was that England would not be drawn into a war with France as an ally of Spain. So concerned were the English that in the marriage treaty Spanish troops were even forbidden to serve in English garrisons.

Mary naturally persevered with some success to re-establish Catholicism. Her attempt to have the monasteries restored and their property returned failed dismally, although at parish level it was easier to restore Catholic practices. The inevitable attempt to suppress Protestantism led some to choose exile, others martyrdom and many more to wait out events in hope. The persecution of Protestants that took place in her reign was on a totally different scale to the religious persecutions of earlier reigns and again did little to enamour her Anglo-Spanish regime with the population. It also led to the association of Spain with Catholicism and the burnings, which became an important feature of Elizabethan propaganda.

Her reign did contain positive achievements especially in the military field. The navy was significantly enlarged and its administration improved, after Northumberland's government had allowed it – admittedly for sound budgetary reasons – to decline. It would be this force which Elizabeth would inherit and use against the Scots in 1560. There were two key pieces of legislation in 1558 which would confirm the changes that had already been taking place, and produce, for the first time, what would become in time an efficient national militia.

War between Spain and France was a regular event and on Philip's marriage to Mary the latest war was still in progress. Although it was ended by the treaty of Vaucelles in February 1556, it soon restarted after the separation of the Habsburg Empire between Philip II and Ferdinand I. The renewed focus of the conflict would be Flanders rather than Italy. Philip naturally sought Mary's assistance in the conflict, which was not forthcoming. Neither Mary or her Council, not even such conservative stalwarts as Cardinal Pole and the Bishop of Winchester, supported any new French exploits. Domestic issues took priority and fear of the inevitable border war with Scotland as well as the ruinous cost made it unappealing. In March 1557 Philip returned to England, for the second and last time, seeking to persuade Mary to change her mind. In April the Council presented a list of reasons why England ought not and could not declare war. Mary attempted to assure Henri II of England's neutrality and to act as an honest broker in negotiations between Henri and Philip.

Henri II was convinced that Mary would support her husband, and therefore as all his predecessors had done, moved to discomfort England through diplomatic and military support for Scotland. He also reinforced the defences of Ardres on the border of the English Pale. France had undoubtedly consolidated its influence in the Scotland of Mary of Guise. This led to disquiet among the Scottish nobility, who did not want to be the cats paws of France, any more than their English counterparts wished to be seen as servants of Spain. Philip had argued that France had broken the peace in the Netherlands, against the treaties of 1542 and 1546, for which England was a guarantor. It was not this, however, that led to war but a most unlikely event: the invasion of Scarborough.

Sir Thomas Stafford had a very distant claim to the throne as a member of the Pole family. He had taken part in Wyatt's rebellion, been imprisoned and then fled to France. Stafford was one of a number of English exiles at the court of Henri. He was opposed to the marriage with Philip and promoted an English candidate to the throne. Claiming an importance for himself that he did not possess, he received support in the shape of just two ships for his 'invasion', accompanied by between 32 and 100 exiles and 'venturers'. The castle at Scarborough was in a state of disrepair, and the garrison of a dozen men surrendered on 23 April without a shot being fired. Unsurprisingly no-one rose in support of this hare-brained scheme. The Earl of Westmorland, with the militia force that he had raised for service on the border, retook the castle and captured the rebel 'army' on the 28th. Under these circumstances, that of a foreign prince encouraging an invasion of England (however risible), it was impossible for England to do anything but declare war. War had some advantages for the nobility, at least as Surian the Venetian ambassador recorded on 13 May, as: 'A great part of the nobility of the kingdom are preparing, some from a longing for novelty … some from rivalry and a desire of glory, some to obtain grace and favour with his Majesty and the Queen.'[33] The remaining family of the traitorous Duke of Northumberland – Robert, Ambrose and Henry Dudley – all joined the Army Royal.

The border with Scotland was of course in these circumstances a source of concern, but Mary had no desire for war and confirmed the treaty of

---

33   *Calendar of State Papers Relating to English Affairs in the Archives of Venice (200 Venice)*, vol. 6, 1555–1558, ed. Rawdon Brown (London: HMSO, 1877), pp.1085–7.

peace with Scotland in July 1557. The Scots were little more enthusiastic about another confrontation than the English. There was no strong French force available to act as the core of an invasion force, as the numbers of their soldiers in Scotland only increased from some 700–1,000 men. The Scots lords refused to be summoned for a large-scale invasion of their southern neighbour. Mary sought assistance from Philip in case of attack. Help, which he signally failed to offer, was fortunately not needed.

The principal area of operations was in Flanders. Philip departed England with a force of 10,000 under the Earl of Pembroke for the Siege of St Quentin, a force that proved too many to be of use. Seven hundred men from this force were sent to reinforce the Calais garrison, while some were even sent back to England as being superfluous to operations. The main battle, which was fought to defeat the relieving force, took place on 10 August before the English arrived. The English troops later did take part in the final stage of the siege, with St Quentin surrendering on 27 August. Juan de Pinedo reported on the annoying tardiness and continual complaints of the English contingent, but concluded that 'both sides fought very choicely ... and the English best of all.'[34] The job done the English force was disbanded and most men had returned to England by late October.

Mary's marriage to Philip had drawn England into a war with France that England did not want. It was caused by Henri II's failure to appreciate how unwilling England was to engage in yet another expensive and futile war. Henri expected and welcomed war, as he was determined to take Calais as he had previously recovered Boulogne. Having been defeated at St Quentin and with winter coming on, the assumption that Calais was safe was one easily made. With considerable skill Henri collected his forces together without arousing Spanish or English fears. Between 1 and 8 January the English, outnumbered, outmanoeuvred and outgunned, lost Calais, their impregnable and invaluable foothold on the Continent. Mary cannot be blamed directly and it was a national as well as a personal humiliation. Its loss may also be considered in the long term to have been a good thing, as it made further expensive invasions and expeditions impossible. What is perhaps surprising is the lack of enthusiasm in England for an expedition to recover Calais, partly due to the cost but perhaps also a deep pessimism and disenchantment with war.

What was perhaps of greater military significance in the long run were the Acts of Parliament that properly modernised the militia. It was now acknowledged that the army was to be a national force, recruited in the counties, even if still for obvious reasons officered by the gentry and commanded by the nobility. If Calais was lost, the means to fight wars, offensive and defensive, were still considerable. The Device forts and the great quantity of munitions of all sorts but especially artillery, together with an army great in number and with many soldiers rich in experience, was the inheritance of the greatest of all Tudor sovereigns: Queen Elizabeth.

---

34 *Calendar of State Papers Spain* (*CSP Spain*), vol. 13, 1554–1558, ed. Royall Tyler (London: HMSO, 1954), 27 August 1557, p.339. Available online (see bibliography for URL).

2

Conflict at Home

Bosworth

The Wars of the Roses was not a war, but a sequence of battles, campaigns and political coups that dramatically affected English history for nearly 40 years. Its causes have been long debated but in essence the conflict arose between a weak and unsuccessful monarch and powerful, passionate nobility. The collapse of the English empire in France in 1453 left the nobility equipped and talented for war, but with a monarch quite unable and unwilling to command or control them. Blame could be laid at the feet of the inadequate Henry VI and his ambitious wife Margaret, and the personalities and families that were to engage in a bloody fratricidal conflict that turned victors into victims and made treachery the cold accompaniment to hot-blooded valour. It is not a glorious part of English history but it is certainly memorable.

The course of the war in its various phases is long and complex. The first notable clash between the nobility occurred on 22 May 1455 at St Albans. Henry remained king, and due to the efforts of Margaret the Yorkists were eventually forced to flee. The Yorkists were to invade and triumph in 1461 at the Battle of Towton, certainly the bloodiest battle fought on English soil. Edward was crowned king and governed uneasily for the next eight years until in 1469 the envious Warwick, of 'Kingmaker' fame, effectively deposed him. Warwick's star was not in the ascendant for long and soon he fled to the exiled Lancastrian party. Warwick orchestrated a further coup and restored Henry to the throne for a final time in 1470–71. Edward returned in an attempt to wrest control of the kingdom from Henry and Queen Margaret. The Lancastrian cause was finally defeated with the Yorkist victories at Barnet and Tewkesbury in 1471. The murders of Henry VI and his son and the ignominious capture and imprisonment of Queen Margaret saw the end of all Lancastrian hopes. Only the insignificant child, Henry Tudor Earl of Richmond, had a distant and discredited claim to the throne. He was to spend the next 14 years in perilous and penniless exile in Brittany and France. His continued freedom was a very slender hope indeed for those who adhered to the Lancastrian cause. Kept as a pawn in diplomatic relations, he only began to appear as a realistic claimant to the throne when Edward IV died in 1483.

What occurred now was a mafia-style falling-out, with bloody and destabilising consequences. Edward IV's marriage to Elizabeth Woodville may have slaked his monumental sexual appetite and provided him with an heir and a spare (the princes Edward and Richard), as well as an apparently superfluous daughter, but it also led to inevitable conflict with his brother Richard of Gloucester. Richard was not about to allow the gains, so hard won in the bloody victories of the War of the Roses, to pass to the Woodville family and their brats. Richard had fought hard for the Yorkist cause. The Woodvilles were the cuckoos in the regal nest, a family of massive ambition but little power, who now saw the crown coming to them. Richard naturally sought to retain the crown for his family and his son; thus he first delayed Prince Edward's coronation and then abandoned it after bastardising his nephews on a legal technicality, and had himself declared king.

The Woodvilles were obviously intent on placing themselves in a dominant position in the realm and the old Yorkists were happy to see their destruction. However in Autumn 1483, after Richard's coronation, the realm once again erupted. The old Yorkist families in the Home Counties and from Dorset to Kent rose against him, under the leadership of the Duke of Buckingham. It is easy to see why those formerly loyal to Edward and his progeny might have risen against the usurper of his son's throne. Removing the Woodvilles was one thing, removing Edward's sons quite another. Buckingham, who had orchestrated Richard's triumph over the Woodvilles, was seeking merely to join what he thought would be the winning side. This disorganised rebellion was soon crushed by Richard and his Northern allies. Buckingham was captured and executed. Henry Tudor nearly fell into Richard's hands when he prepared to land on a hostile shore but returned to a further period of exile. Richard felt obliged to strengthen his position further by generous grants of southern land to those Northern Yorkists who had stood by him. His power base was further narrowed by these events and he depended more and more on a triumvirate consisting of Norfolk, Stanley and Northumberland, their energy and loyalty would determine his fate.

Richard's actions, ironically, dramatically changed the fortunes of Henry Tudor. Henry's claim was not only distant but disallowed by law, and his becoming a realistic claimant occurred because Richard disposed of the legitimate male claimants to the throne (the Princes in the Tower) and, it was rumoured, propose marriage to his own niece, Edward IV's daughter. His behaviour, despicable although explicable, was difficult even for an elite inured to bloody internecine warfare to stomach. Richard alienated his potential supporters and thereby prepared a (lukewarm) welcome for Henry. The death of Richard's wife and son in early 1485 added to the insecurity surrounding his government. Philip de Commines was clear about Henry's weak position: 'God on a sudden raised up an enemy [to King Richard], without power, without money, without right to the crown of England, and without any reputation but his person and deportment.'[1] It was only a matter of time before Henry Tudor

---

1   Philip de Commines, *The memoirs of Philip de Commines, Lord of Argenton: containing the histories of Louis XI and Charles VIII. Kings of France and of Charles the Bold, Duke of Burgundy. To which is added, The scandalous chronicle, or Secret history of Louis XI, by Jean de Troyes*, ed. Andrew R. Scoble (London: Henry G. Bohn, 1856), p.64.

would challenge him for the throne, the real question was who would rally to the two claimants and for how long would they remain loyal?

There was little enthusiasm for either party in the kingdom. Despite Richard's preparations and proclamations his potential support was in reality far less than it appeared. Northumberland was to show himself at best indifferent to Richard's cause if not an outright traitor, and Norfolk was driven much by a desire to keep what he had gained, from Oxford particularly, rather than rally in defence of Richard. The Stanleys rewarded for their loyalty could not be trusted if their own interests differed from Richard's. Although ostensibly a strong king, supreme in his realm, there was no room for complacency. Richard knew that he would have to beat Henry quickly and decisively if he was to survive.

The journey to Bosworth began on 1 August when Henry's small flotilla left the Seine estuary, and concluded three weeks later with the battle itself. Henry's expedition was the second he had made, the first, in 1483, almost ending in his landing and arrest. This was probably his last chance to affect a successful landing. The longer Richard held the throne the more likely he was to strengthen his grip on a kingdom that surveyed recent events with a mixture of horror, disbelief and fear. Richard knew that Henry would make another attempt on the throne, and soon. He chose his base well. Nottingham Castle was an old favourite of his and he was able to mobilise his forces throughout the realm in a few days. His loyal subordinates would have met a landing on the south coast, and from Nottingham he could survey his realm and coordinate his counter-attack.

Henry came ashore with a small force of French mercenaries and renegade Lancastrians including his uncle Jasper, the constant companion of his years in exile, and John de Vere the Earl of Oxford, a man with some experience and success in battle and Henry's military adviser. Where he landed requires some explanation. Milford Haven is a magnificent natural harbour but that in itself was not the most important point. Henry had not landed with an army sufficient to confront Richard's. Wales was his natural recruiting ground: his father was Welsh, although his claim to the throne came from his mother, Lady Margaret Beaufort. His name would rally Welshmen to his cause but not many Englishmen. He would spend over a week in Wales before entering England on a march towards London. The Stanleys were to join him, his stepfather Thomas, and William Stanley leaving their estates on the day Henry arrived at Shrewsbury after refusing Richard's call to arms. The treachery of William was revealed to Richard, but Thomas maintained a separation from William until the 20th and appeared to be shadowing Henry's forces, rather than coordinating with them.

Richard, benefiting from a sophisticated messenger system, learnt about Henry's landing which took place on 7 August. On the 11th he summoned the Duke of Norfolk, the earls of Surrey and Northumberland, and Sir Robert Brackenbury, Keeper of the Tower of London, to meet him at Leicester where the royal army met on the 20th.

Henry's advance was not without its difficulties. Invading with a Franco-Welsh army would not make him popular in England, and the numbers that rallied to him were few after leaving Wales. He was entirely dependent upon the Stanleys if he was to have any chance of meeting Richard with any hope of success. With staggering incompetence Henry actually lost contact with his own army on the night of the 19th. Polydore Vergil explained that Henry had to explain to his now demoralised army that, 'excusing himselfe that he was not deceavyd in the way, but had withdrawen from the camp of set purpose to receave soome goode newys of certane his secret frindes,[2] a necessary lie. He was, however, soon to meet with his potential saviours at Atherstone:

> Here Henry dyd mete with thomas and William, wher taking one an other by thand, and yealding mutuall salutation, eche man was glad for the good state of thothers, and all ther myndes wer movyd to great joy. After that, they enteryd in cownsaylle in what sort to darraigne battayll with king Rycherd, yf the matter showld coome to strokes, whom they herd to be not farre of.[3]

It seems impossible that the challenge to Henry should not end in battle. Henry must have been disappointed on the 22nd when the Stanleys held aloof from him, when they were an intrinsic part of his agreed battle plan.

Most sources agree that the King's army set out from Leicester on the day before the battle. However, the precise site of his encampment is not clear. The *Crowland Chronicle* reports that Richard encamped by the Abbey of Mirival (now Merevale). Polydore Vergil, however, places Richard's encampment in the town of Bosworth. He encamps the Stanleys in Atherton, and Henry's forces in or near Tamworth. All these locations would make sense considering that all of them are within a few miles of the battlefield. As to the conflicting locations of Richard's army, it seems more likely that Richard was encamped in Bosworth, as this would mean that he would be in place before the arrival of Henry, which fits with most sources' accounts of the battle.

Bosworth was probably the single most important battle in English history after Hastings, and yet its actual position was unknown and the subject of debate and dispute until recently. The 'Bosworth Battlefield Project' interdisciplinary team, led by Glenn Foard, unearthed the battlefield in a complex campaign between 2005 and 2010, when it was able to publicly identify the actual site. Mike Ingram provides an excellent description of the field:

> The ... battlefield [was found] at the junction of the boundaries of the medieval villages of Dadlington, Stoke Golding, Upton and Shenton. It was 2.5 miles (3.6 km) south-west of Ambion Hill, the traditional site of the battlefield and the location of the visitor centre.
>
> The area where the two sides met was centred on a flat plain, mainly comprising of fenland which was crossed by streams, with an area of peat marsh, known as Fen Hole, on the eastern side, south of the road. South of this marsh the ground gently rises 20 metres (65 ft) to a ridge, that overlooks the road. On the top of the ridge to the east is the village of Stoke Golding and approximately 650 yards (600 metres) further north east is the village of Dadlington. The ridge

---

2   Polydore Vergil, *Anglica Historia*, book 25 (London: J.B. Nichols, 1846), p.21.

3   Vergil, *Anglica Historia*, p.21.

continues north-east towards Sutton Cheney with a westerly facing spur now known as Ambion Hill creating a shallow valley enclosed on three sides, before falling 98 feet (30 metres) back into the plain and the battlefield.[4]

The numbers of the forces reported vary wildly, and a definitive answer will never be found. Diego de Valera reports that the King came to the field with 70,000 men. This is clearly very unlikely, Jean de Molinet suggests 60,000, an equally absurd number, although he more realistically numbers Henry's slender host as consisting of 2,000 French mercenaries and 3,000 renegade English and Welsh. Philippe de Commines wrote that: 'The King of France having supplied him with some money, with about three thousand Normans, the loosest and most profligate persons in all that country, he passed into Wales, where his father-in-law, the Lord Stanley, joined him with 25,000 men.'[5] It seems more likely that, as Polydore Vergil says, that the number of Henry's soldiers 'was scarce, 5000 besides the Stanleyans, whereof about 3000 were at the battle. The King's forces were twice so many and more.'[6] Mike Ingram in his account of events suggests a figure for Richard's forces from 10,000–15,000, which would be a reasonable figure. The figures he gives for Henry's force suggest 5,500–8,000 with the two Stanleys disposing up to 5,000.[7]

One aspect of the events prior to the battle is the contentious nature of what occurred in the King's camp. Shakespeare recorded the supposed events of that fatal night as Richard was haunted by his misdeeds, and although this was certainly a magnificent example of Tudor 'black' propaganda, it might have had some element of truth to it. Richard's camp was not a comfortable place to be, treachery was suspected and feared. Polydore Vergil's account recorded treachery before the battle:

> A lyttle before thevening of the same day, John Savage, Bryan Sanfoord, Symon digby, and many others, revolting from king Richard, came to Henry with a choyse bande of armyd men, which matter both augmentyd the forces of erle Henry, and greatly replenyshyd him with good hope.[8]

In the *Crowland Chronicle* it was reported that: 'At day-break, on the Monday following there were no chaplains present to perform Divine service on behalf of king Richard, nor any breakfast prepared to refresh the flagging spirits of the king.'[9] Perhaps most significantly of all the King's writ did not run even in his own camp, as again the *Crowland Chronicle* reported:

> At length, the prince and knights on the opposite side now advancing at a moderate pace against the royal army, the king gave orders that the lord Strange before-mentioned should be instantly beheaded. The persons, however, to whom

---

4   Mike Ingram, *Richard III and The Battle of Bosworth* (Warwick: Helion & Company, 2019), p.222.
5   Commines, *The Memoirs*, p.64.
6   Vergil, *Anglica Historia*, p.223.
7   Ingram, *Richard III*, pp.221–222.
8   Vergil, *Anglica Historia*, p.221.
9   Michael Bennett, *The Battle of Bosworth* (Thrupp: Sutton Publishing Ltd, 2000), p.134.

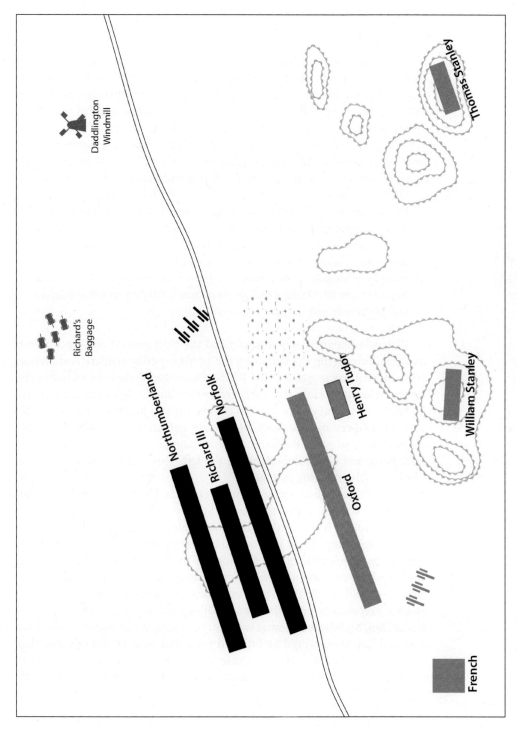

Map of the Battle of Bosworth. The key feature around which the battle was oriented was a road that lay between the two armies. The orientation of the ridge and furrow agriculture meant that the armies would be fighting along them rather than across them.

this duty was entrusted, seeing that the issue was doubtful in the extreme, and that matter of more importance than the destruction of one individual were about to be decided, delayed the performance of this cruel order of the king, leaving the man to his own disposal, returned to the thickest of the fight.[10]

It is clear from Polydore Vergil, who may have received the information directly from Henry VII, that the Earl's forces were arrayed with a vanguard made up of Oxford in the centre, John Savage on the left flank and Gilbert Talbot on the right. Following the vanguard with a larger body of troops was Henry himself. The disposition of Richard's forces is also seemingly clear. Vergil reports the army as being arrayed with the vanguard commanded by Norfolk, followed by the King in the main battle with Northumberland in the rear; his detailed account accentuates the size and strength of Richard's force:

> The next day after King Richard, furnished thoroughly with all manner of things, drew his whole host out of their tents, and arrayeth his vanward, stretching it forth of a wonderful length, so full replenished both with footmen and horsemen that to the beholders afar off it gave a terror for the multitude, and in the front were placed his archers, like a most strong trench and bulwark; of these archers he made leader John Duke of Norfolk. To the rear of this long battle-line followed the king himself, with a select force of soldiers.[11]

Richard's intention was to command the high ground and force Henry to attack him, facing the withering fire of his superior artillery and archers. Mike Ingram has suggested that Richard arranged three lines of battle: the vanguard led by Norfolk, the rearguard by Northumberland and in the centre Richard's own royal and household troops. He also places Richard's sizeable train of artillery on the flank to provide enfilading fire. The alternative disposition is to place Richard's army in a single line with Norfolk on the right flank and Northumberland on the left. This would have enabled the whole of Richard's army to engage.[12]

The position of the Stanleys is much less clear. It is reported by Vergil that (Henry) '… sending withal to Thomas Stanley … as in the midway betwixt the two battles.'[13] It seems likely that the Stanley armies would have worked together, and they would gain nothing from splitting; this provided them with an excellent view of any fighting, so the Stanleys would know when, and on whose side, to intervene. Richard would have had to assume that the Stanleys would join Henry. This was made clear by his decision to have Lord Strange executed prior to the battle. William Stanley was already attainted for treason; his brother Thomas was now his confederate. Richard must have assumed that there would be little aid from that quarter, but whether they would be committed to Henry's cause was a question that no-one, not even Henry could be certain of. The duplicity of the Stanleys was legendary; the

---

10 Bennett, *Bosworth*, p.135.
11 Bennett, *Bosworth*, p.144.
12 Ingram, *Richard III*, pp.224–27.
13 Bennett, *Bosworth*, p.144.

chilling reality of their unreliability was made clear in the communication between Thomas and Henry, recorded by Vergil:

> In this mean time Henry well early in the morning commanded the soldiers to arm themselves, sending withal, to Thomas Stanley, who was now approached the place of fight, as in the mid way betwixt the two battles, that he could come to with his forces, to set the soldiers in array. He answered that the earl should set his own folks in order, while that he should come to him with his army well appointed. With which answer, given contrary to that was looked for, and to that which th'opportunity of time and weight of cause required, though Henry were no little vexed, and began to be somewhat appalled, yet without lingering he of necessity ordered his men in this sort.[14]

Henry could have faced battle with little confidence in Stanley support, when everyone must have realised that without it, Henry was doomed. Mike Ingram has suggested a more generous interpretation, that the Stanleys were committed to Henry and their reply was an encouragement to Henry and he needed a lot of that.[15] Henry's own forces made a very poor showing in comparison to Richard's, as Vergil records:

> He made a slender vanward for the small number of his people; before the same he placed archers, of whom he made captain John Earl of Oxford; in the right wing of the vanward he placed Gilbert Talbot to defend the same; in the left verily he sat John Savage; and himself, trusting to th'aid of Thomas Stanley, with one troop of horsemen, and a few footmen did follow; for the number of all his soldiers, all manner of ways, was scarce, 5,000 besides the Stanleyans, whereof about 3,000 were at the battle, under the conduct of William. The king's forces were twice so many and more.[16]

The first, brief engagement seems to have lasted from the cannon opening fire, until Richard's front fired upon the Earl's men as they approached from the south-west, which led them to skirt marshland. The large number of lead projectiles that have been unearthed on the battlefield are an indication of its ferocity. This bombardment seems to have been one of the most significant events in the battle. Jean de Molinet recorded the event as follows:

> The King had the artillery of his army fire on the Earl of Richmond, and so the French [Henry's army], knowing by the King's shot the lie of the land and the order of his battle resolved, in order to avoid the fire, to mass their troops against the flank rather than the front of the King's battle. Thus they obtained the mastery of his vanguard.[17]

---

14 Bennett, *Bosworth*, p.144.
15 Ingram, *Richard III*, p.215.
16 Bennett, *Bosworth*, p.144.
17 Bennett, *Bosworth*, p.139.

Together with the report of Polydore Vergil this gives us a very good idea of the position of Henry's forces. 'There was a marsh betwixt both hosts, which Henry of purpose left in the right hand that it might serve his men instead of a fortress, by the doing thereof also he left the sun upon his back.'[18] Henry's line of battle now had the marsh protecting its right flank.

As to whether Henry's choice of ground was part of a plan of battle, or was serendipitous, we can only conjecture. Scouts who provided a well-defined intelligence and reconnaissance role invariably preceded armies of the period, but it seems that Henry only knew of the disposition of Richard's forces when his vanguard came under fire. Therefore, it seems most likely that his choice of position was good tactical thinking after a disastrous start. It is worth noting that the near defeat of the Tudor forces at Stoke took place because of another failure to reconnoitre. Yet again the day was won by a single decision by the leader of the vanguard, the Duke of Oxford, to stand and fight even at a disadvantage and wait for Henry's main battle to save the day.

It has been suggested that Henry's original intention was to move to join up with the Stanleys. He seems to have been fairly sure of their support, and so this may be considered to have been his original strategy. However, to do this in his current situation would have been tantamount to suicide. It would have involved moving in a vulnerable line across the field of fire in order to rendezvous with allies whose loyalty was now extremely dubious, and who could have pounced upon such an opportunity to prove their loyalty to the current King.

At first glance Norfolk's attack on Oxford seems foolhardy. Why could he have not waited for Oxford to charge at him, rather than risking the difficult terrain and charging at a prepared force? After realising that his archers were not having much success due to the terrain, Norfolk would have realised that he had to make a move for two reasons. Firstly, Richard had to be seen by the Stanleys to be winning decisively if they were to intervene on his behalf. The Stanleys may well have been naturally 'more loyal' to the Tudor cause by ties of blood, and therefore more inclined to intervene on the side of the Earl in any case. Secondly, the loyalty of the Yorkist force to the King was undoubtedly suspect: Polydore Vergil, among others, reports desertions including that of John Savage, Brian Sandford, Simon Digby, and many others. The fact that Norfolk was killed and his son seriously wounded, leading by example, reinforces the desperate lengths he was forced to resort to in order to keep his men's loyalty.

The response of Oxford to the charge is reported best by Polydore Vergil, and is similarly recorded by other sources:

> In the mean time the earl of Oxford, afraid that in the fighting his men would be surrounded by the multitude, gave out the order through the ranks that no soldier should go more than ten feet from the standards. When in response to the command all the men massed together and drew back a little from the fray, their opponents, suspecting a trick, took fright and broke off from the fighting for a

---

18 Bennett, *Bosworth*, p.144.

while. In truth many, who wished the king damned rather than saved, were not reluctant to do so, and for that reason fought less stoutly. Then the earl of Oxford on the one part, with tightly grouped units, attacked the enemy afresh, and the others in the other part pressing together in wedge formation renewed the battle.[19]

This situation should not have occurred. Oxford, by withdrawing his men into a passive and defensive formation rather than meeting Norfolk's men head on, sowed confusion and the suggestion of treachery that was always in the back of mens' minds. Norfolk's soldiers lacked the commitment to press home a charge that should have broken Oxford's vanguard with ease. The Earl's forces were now having unexpected success. In this lull in the battle Mike Ingram now introduces the French forces which he places on the left of Henry's battle. These now launched an attack on Richard's right flank, with pikes, halberds and swords causing mayhem.[20]

It has been said that Henry, accompanied by a small force of mounted men-at-arms, set out to request the aid of the Stanleys. From the source it seems unlikely that this took place at all. All that is mentioned is that, 'Richard learnt, first from spies, that Henry was some way off with a few armed men as his retinue, and then, as the latter drew nearer, recognised him more certainly from his standards. Inflamed with anger, he spurred his horse, and road against him from the other side, beyond the battle line.'[21] Henry attempting to reach the Stanleys personally would have been extremely foolhardy. Not only would it remove the leader of the army from his main forces, which would cause a crisis of morale in his army, it would also place him in danger of attack by the Stanleys and by Richard.

Mike Ingram suggests that it was Richard who was facing defeat. Norfolk's vanguard was crumbling in the face of the French intervention and Northumberland's men were beginning to slip away.[22] Richard, when he was made aware of Henry's own isolation, sought to stave off defeat by leading a final charge against his opponent. Richard took advantage of the vulnerability of Henry, detached from his main body (an assertion only made by Polydore Vergil) and chose to charge, with his knights, the leader of his adversaries. This was a fairly desperate action, as Richard must have realised the danger it placed him in from attack in the flank by the Stanleys. Richard was desperate to swing the battle his way in a single dramatic act. It was the act of a brave and desperate commander who had seen his careful plans come to naught and his chance of a quick victory disappearing.

How many accompanied him it is impossible to say. It took considerable skill and space to conduct an effective charge and it could easily leave its participants disorganised and separated. The charge had considerable momentum and almost succeeded. As Polydore Vergil recorded:

---

19   Bennett, *Bosworth*, pp.144–145.
20   Ingram, *Richard III*, p.234.
21   Bennett, *Bosworth*, p.145.
22   Ingram, *Richard III*, p.235.

King Richard at the first brunt killed certain, overthrew Henry;s standard, together with William Brandon the standard bearer, and matched also with John Cheney a man of much fortitude, far exceeding the common sort, who encountered with him as he came, but the king with great force drove him to the ground, making way with weapon on every side.[23]

William Stanley in turn attacked the now exposed King Richard. The Stanleys may have chosen to fight against the King for several reasons. Firstly the Stanleys, even if they were to throw in their lot with Richard, were unlikely to benefit for long under a king who had suffered from their treachery. Secondly, this offered an unrivalled opportunity to be rid of him and gain much favour with the new king. Thirdly, Norfolk had faltered, and the Lancastrians were fighting unexpectedly well. Their decision made them 'kingmakers' and they expected to be treated as such in the new reign. William was to be sadly disillusioned in 1495 when he was executed for considering treason with a Yorkist pretender.

Their intervention was decisive as Vergil records:

Nevertheless Henry held out against the attack longer than his troops, who now almost despaired of victory, had thought likely. Then, behold, William Stanley came in support with 3,000 men. Indeed it was at this point that, with the rest of his men taking to their heels, Richard was slain fighting in the thickest of the press.[24]

All sources agree that, whatever his faults, Richard died 'fighting manfully'. The most detailed account of his death comes from Jean de Molinet:

The king bore himself valiantly according to his destiny, and wore the crown on his head; but when he saw this discomforture and found himself alone on the field he thought to run after the others. His horse leapt into a march from which it could not retrieve itself. One of the Welshmen then came after him, and struck him dead with a halberd, and another took his body and put it before him on his horse and carried it, hair hanging as one would bear a sheep.[25]

William Stanley upon 'discovering' the crown in a thorn bush placed it on Henry's head in a political coronation. This established what the Stanleys thought would be their new role, as kingmakers.

The disposition and manoeuvres on the field were as much political as military. It seems very probable that Richard only risked himself so recklessly because of the desperate situation he was in. He was concerned about the loyalty of both his own troops and the Stanleys. He needed to end the battle decisively as it is clear that his forces were less than devoted. His direct order to execute Lord Strange was disobeyed and Norfolk's troops had expected treachery when Oxford's troops failed to engage fully, both examples show how everyone was waiting on a decisive event to decide their true loyalty.

---

23 Bennett, *Bosworth*, p.145.
24 Bennett, *Bosworth*, p.145.
25 Bennett, *Bosworth*, p.139.

As to the loyalty of Northumberland there is much debate. Certainly, his murder in an affray in 1498 appeared to be a reward for his treachery. The accounts certainly condemn his inaction as a betrayal. Jean de Molinet reported his apparent treachery:

> The earl of Northumberland, who was on the king's side with 10,000 men, ought to have charged the French, but did nothing except to flee, both he and his company, to abandon his King Richard, for he had an undertaking with the earl of Richmond, as had some others who deserted him in his need.[26]

Diego de Valera reinforced this, and the *Crowland Chronicle* reported adversely on his inaction: 'In the place where the earl of Northumberland was posted, with a large company of reasonably good men, no engagement could be discerned, and no battle blows given or received.'[27]

A more charitable interpretation would be that his forces were unable to deploy themselves to reach the fighting. It seems probable that he left the battlefield as soon as he saw the matter decided, out of a desire merely to save himself. Vergil realistically reported on the morale of many on Richard's side: 'But many more forbare to fight, who came to the field with King Richard for awe, and for no goodwill, and departed without any danger, as men who desired not the safety but destruction of that prince whom they hated.'[28]

The battle in the end was decided on by the discovery of a safe ground for Oxford's vanguard and by the loyalties of the men involved, rather than any extraordinary tactical achievement. The small losses reflected the peculiar nature of the battle, with Vergil reporting 1,000 killed although they included some executed after the battle such as Richard's henchmen, including the obnoxious Ratcliffe.

So ended one of the most important battles in English history. It was decisive but not final, the Battle of Stoke was the last battle of the Wars of the Roses, and it was a much bloodier event. Bosworth was, like so many of the battles, decided by treachery rather than military skill. Richard was the better commander with the best troops, more artillery, more men and the best position. He was braver and more experienced than his rival, but wrong-footed by Oxford's decision to turn Richard's flank, an act of desperation rather than policy, he became the victim of his own insecurity and others' treachery. Henry did not deserve to win the battle but neither did Richard.

Henry VII came to the throne as a pretender and continued to govern as one, determined to assert his kingship in a way that his predecessors had not felt obliged to. Bosworth gave him the throne; he was to spend the rest of his reign grimly hanging on to it.

---

26 Bennett, *Bosworth*, p.139.
27 Bennett, *Bosworth*, p.135.
28 Vergil, *Anglica Historia,* p.224.

3

Rebellions

It might seem somewhat perverse to consider the numerous rebellions that England faced between 1536 and 1554 in this study but all of them resulted in military preparations and some turned into bloody confrontations. It would seem unreasonable to ignore them even if, as in the case of the Pilgrimage of Grace, only one person appears to have been killed by the rebels (although many more were executed in its aftermath). There is no need to consider at length the causes espoused by the rebels or analyse the demands they made of the government. The events themselves provide a fascinating insight into the capabilities and tactics of rebel and royal forces.

The Pilgrimage of Grace

The Pilgrimage itself was a popular reaction to the dissolution of the monasteries in the North of England, where they played an important part in the social, economic and religious life of their communities. The North was also a long way from London and the court and distrusted a policy which challenged their sense of what was right. It was the North that had faced and defeated the Scots in 1513 and it was ready to do the same again, having faced an increasingly bellicose Scotland under James V. It felt itself to be militarily and politically powerful and able to challenge a policy that it felt was profoundly damaging to it.

The Pilgrimage was doomed from the start. The Pilgrims failed to recognise that in Henry VIII they faced an implacable opponent, who once challenged would use every resource to destroy those who opposed him. Whatever honeyed words or generous acts he may employ he would be ruthless in pursuing his revenge. The only way the Pilgrims could have achieved their objective would have been to replace Henry with an alternative English, and Catholic, claimant to the throne. That was clearly impossible as Henry and his father had been ruthless in removing any potential challengers.

The Pilgrimage displayed all the weaknesses of the English military system as far as Henry was concerned. Whether raised by the commissioners of array or by the nobility, the numerical power lay with the commons. The Army Royal was the commons-in-arms, and if the commons chose the cause of the Pilgrims and were assisted by the gentry, there were few other military resources that the Crown could call upon. The role of the nobility and gentry was as always somewhat ambivalent. Often sharing the opinions of the commons, they feared their wrath if they did not take their side and the King's wrath if they did. Afterwards they could always claim that it was better that they commanded the commons and avoided bloodshed than if they had let the rabble have their way.

The scale of the Pilgrimage was massive: the whole of the North either rose or sympathised with those who had. The raising of an 'army' of Pilgrims in October 1536 which marched upon and entered first Lincoln and then York, was an impressive and spontaneous response to what was seen as southern interference in their world. The response of Henry was to send north forces under the Duke of Norfolk and the Earl of Shrewsbury. They intended to set up a line of defence on the banks of the River Trent, the military dividing line of England between North and South. Henry mistakenly ordered the Earl forward towards Pontefract and Norfolk was left alone to face a Northern force of tens of thousands. With royal forces now divided and massively outnumbered and unsure of the loyalty of his own men, Norfolk was forced to temporise and then compromise. Henry, whose instinct was to act with speed and brutality, realised that the forces available to him were too few and followed a conciliatory policy that led to the rebels withdrawing. Having granted a pardon to the rebels in December, he avoided considering their demands and when in frustration in January 1537 new disturbance broke out, he chose that point to intervene.

The gentry who had led or at least participated in the first outbreak now withdrew and Henry was free to pursue the leaders of the rebellion. Around 150 were executed, including a royal servant negotiating with the rebels. This unfortunate gentleman was Thomas Miller the Lincoln Herald, his treason was to admit, when speaking to the rebels, that the forces of the King were too few, thereby encouraging them and acting as a traitor! What was surprising and terrifying was the speed with which the rebel army was mustered, its size, and its good order. It was certainly no rabble and a match for Henry's forces, many men of which were sympathetic to their cause. The rebellion pointed to the reality that the King had no army as such but was dependent on the loyalty of his subjects.

The Western Rebellion

The Western or Prayer Book rebellion of 1549 was a bloody conflict that saw the commons set against a mercenary force let loose on them by a vengeful government, with the direst consequences for thousands. The rebellion was specifically against the introduction of the new Protestant Prayer Book. It was also a general rejection of the damage done to the Church as the consequence of the English Reformation, a process that had of course begun under Henry VIII over a decade before. There was also serious discontent with the role that the gentry were playing in their communities, using their position to advance their wealth at the cost of the commons. The 'articles' of the rebels were very diverse, combining religious, social and economic grievances. One of their demands, for example, was the repealing of the legislation relating to firearms.

William Body, a fairly repellent profiteer from the Reformation, had been murdered in 1548 indicating the hostility felt towards the religious changes. The authorities responded with the usual combination of coercion and compromise. There was a general pardon but 10 of the ringleaders were hanged. The rebellion proper began as a resistance to the introduction of the Prayer Book on Whitsunday 1549 (9 June) and by 6 July a large camp of rebels led by Henry Arundell, a local gentleman, was established at Bodmin. Sir Peter Carew tried to negotiate with the rebels but his efforts only further increased the tension between the commons and the gentry. His assumption of political and social superiority and his personal arrogance had further inflamed the rebels.

The absence of gentry support meant that the rebels lacked any effective cavalry, although as a militia force they were adequately armed, especially with bows. They lacked the quantity and quality of armour employed by the mercenaries, and royal troops sent against them. The rebels had few firearms, a disadvantage when facing the mercenary forces, but they were to assemble some artillery from ships, forts, and town and parish stocks. The thousands who rallied to the cause were a formidable force, fighting on their own ground, alongside their neighbours, and inspired by their faith.

In 1497 the Cornish rebels had marched to London and been slaughtered at Small Heath; they did not intend to make the same mistake again. With their numbers swollen with recruits from Devonshire, they captured Plymouth and focused their efforts on blockading and then besieging Exeter. They focused on seizing the local 'capital', just as Kett's rebels had captured Norwich. It is difficult to establish what their intention was, even if they had captured the city. It is doubtful whether this would have improved their situation one whit with the Privy Council, or moved their cause further in the country. The rebels of 1497 had a much better idea of where power really lay.

Protector Somerset and the Privy Council were facing counties across the southern half of England in rebellion, which were motivated by very different causes and posed very different degrees of threat. Communications were poor and it was difficult to establish the extent of the danger. The other major problem that the authorities faced was the absence of a substantial standing army. With many troops already heavily engaged in Somerset's Scottish campaign, those few reliable soldiers who were available were needed to protect London and the King. It soon became apparent that the Wiltshire and Somerset militias were unenthusiastic about suppressing their neighbours. In these circumstances Lord Russell the Lord Privy Seal and a principal landowner in the West, who was sent to deal with the uprising, found himself unable to act. He was short of troops, stores and money and he was left as an impotent observer. The Council complained that it would be very hard to '[send] in a short time such a number of footmen as with

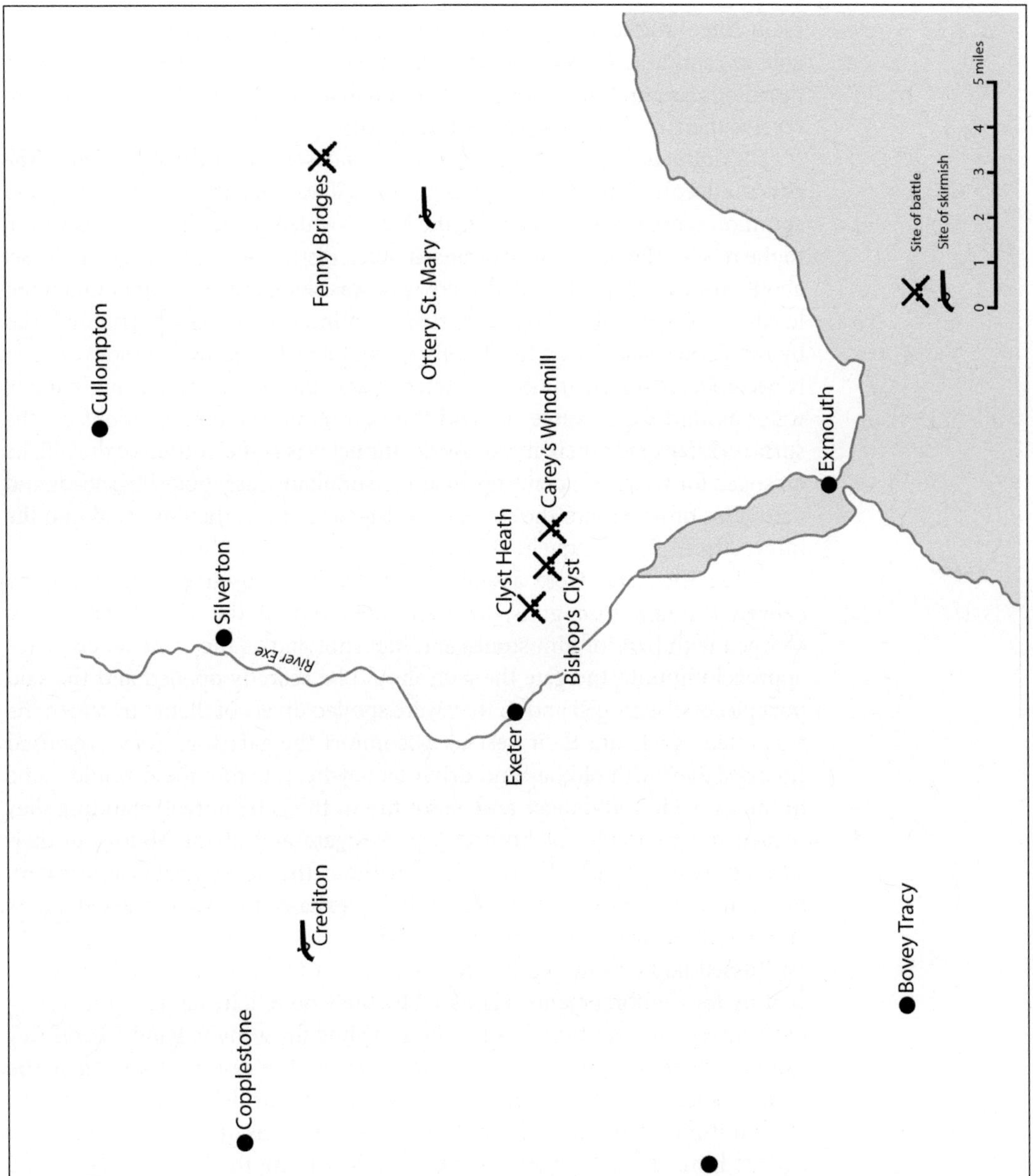

Map of the Western or Prayer Book Rebellion

Sampford Courtenay

Lapford

Copplestone

Moretonhampstead

Bovey Tracy

Crediton

Silverton

River Exe

Exeter

Cullompton

Fenny Bridges

Ottery St. Mary

Clyst Heath

Carey's Windmill

Bishop's Clyst

Exmouth

Site of battle

Site of skirmish

0 1 2 3 4 5 miles

N

plain force might be able to meet with the rebels'.[1] Even when they were able to reinforce Russell, the Landsknechts could not be sent: 'for that they be odious to our people abroad in so much as we can hardly move them to receive them without quarrel here at hand'.[2]

The dramatic history of the siege of Exeter deserves a chapter of its own. The city was deeply divided on religious grounds, it was only the determination and common sense of John Blackaller the Mayor which maintained its opposition to the rebels. The blockade had caused much distress to the poorest and he set about ensuring that what food there was, was shared fairly, maintaining their loyalty. The Cornish, whose expertise in mining had often been employed by the Crown, now used their skills to dig beneath the walls of loyal Exeter. Newcombe, a skilled miner in Exeter, found the tunnel by placing pans of water around the possible site and through observing the vibrations on the surface discovered where it was. As the tunnel was at the bottom of the hill, he arranged for all the residents upstream to simultaneously pour hogsheads and pannikins of water into the street guttering, which was then diverted into the mine, effectively flooding it.

When the gates were assaulted the defenders used port-pieces, large-calibre wrought iron guns, to blast them out of the way: '[they] were charged with bags of flint stones and hail shot and as they [the rebels] were approaching unto the gate the gate should be secretly opened and the said port pieces discharged and so they were spoiled divers of them'.[3] In return the frustrated rebels did their best to discomfort the garrison. They organised '[a] cart laden with old hay and driving the wheels before them would come to the gate without danger and so set fire in the gate: notwithstanding they scaped not scot free for both at the Westgate and at the Southgate their coming being perceived'.[4] The rebels without the heavy artillery necessary to create a breach in the walls attempted to exhaust the will of the defenders with regular alarms and sniping.

Russell had established his headquarters at Honiton on 10 July and was waiting for reinforcements. Harassed by the Council, he fell to complaining of ill-fitting ammunition: 'shot as fit as a shoe for a man's hand'.[5] The Privy Council disobligingly replied: 'As for arrows, the less he uses them the better, unless he takes greater care, for he only furnishes the enemy with ammunition, as they hear, for in a recent skirmish his own arrows were used against him'.[6] Lord Herbert was meanwhile putting the rebels to the sword in approved fashion in Buckinghamshire and Oxfordshire, where their proximity to the Privy Council had caused much distress. It was only at the end of July that Russell felt able to advance. Lord Grey had arrived with some

---

1 Frances Rose-Troup, *The Western Rebellion of 1549 an Account of the Insurections in Devonshire and Cornwall against Religious Innovations in the Reign of Edward VI* (London: Smith & Elder & Co., 1913), p.234.

2 Rose-Troup, *The Western Rebellion*, p.234.

3 John Hooker, *The ancient history and description of the city of Exeter* (Exeter: Andrews and Trewman, 1765), p.70.

4 Hooker, *Exeter*, p.69.

5 Rose-Troup, *The Western Rebellion*, p.254.

6 Rose-Troup, *The Western Rebellion*, p.254.

250 horse, while William Grey soon joined with 200 more men. A large mercenary force would eventually serve to defeat the rebels. This included 400 'horsemen strangers' made up of Stradiots, Germans and Italians under the command of Jacques Jermigny and Pietro Sanga.

The first major battle was at the crossing at Ferrybridge on 28 July where the rebels made a determined stand but were driven off by the mercenaries' greater discipline. Their victory was marred by a counter-attack which found the 'victors' enjoying the spoils and unaware of their presence: the royal troops, 'being in the middle of their game [looting the dead], and they nothing thinking of any more enemies to be coming towards'.[7] The consequence of this setback and the fear of another counter attack was Russell's withdrawal to Honiton, having suffered some 300 casualties and inflicting a similar number on the rebels. He was soon to advance again, having been substantially reinforced with Paolo Baptista Spinola's 150 or 160 mounted arquebusiers and Lord Grey's company from Gloucester.

Leaving Honiton on 3 August his augmented army camped at Cary's Windmill after marching 12 miles without interference from the rebels until that evening. Russell's force now made their way uphill from the valley of the River Otter and camped by Gregory Cary's windmill. Here they were attacked once more, and although the first attempt at surprise failed, the attacks continued but were eventually rebuffed: 'notwithstanding they were of very stout stomachs and very valiantly did stand to their tackles, yet in the end they were overthrown and the most part of them slain'.[8] Even then the battle was not over, for as the royal army was being led in prayer for its victory it was attacked once more. To stop any further advance towards Exeter the rebels now sought to rally all their local forces at Clyst Bridge, in the village of Bishop's Clyst. The rebels, with perhaps 4,000 men, organised into four companies, barred the way having dug entrenchments, and on 4 August placed a company in ambush in the hedges beside the road at Woodbury Common.

Russell's force was divided into three, each to advance into the village on one of the roads. Each road was protected by earth ramparts, and although strongly held one was breached. The 'forts' constructed by the rebels were forced, using Spinola's arquebusiers to provide suppressive fire. The weight and numbers started to force the rebels from their positions. The army advanced, only to be panicked into a retreat all the way back to Cary's Windmill. This was caused by the sound of a drum and trumpet to their rear, ostensibly passing orders to a phantom rebel force. This was the fiendish ruse of Sir Thomas Pomeroy who had hidden his small musical duo in the rear. The chaos and panic caused led to the abandonment of the artillery and wagons in the narrow lanes, and the rebels took the artillery to reinforce their positions. Pomeroy the cheeky rebel captain was captured after the relief of Exeter and very surprisingly Russell appealed for clemency on his behalf to

---

7   Rose-Troup, *The Western Rebellion*, p.259.
8   Hooker, *Exeter*, p.85.

the Privy Council. This was agreed upon as long as he now assisted Russell in the capture of ringleaders.

After rallying his humiliated forces Russell once more attacked, but while most of his forces assaulted the rebels' positions a third force under Sir William Francis advanced along a sunken lane. This was an ideal ambush site and the rebels who had been waiting for such an attack slaughtered the royal force with arrows and rocks. The unlucky Sir William had his helmet staved in so hard that it could not be removed. Fortunately for the attackers, one of the ramparts was forced by dismounted and probably armoured cavalrymen and the village was entered. The village had been fortified and the royal troops now faced bloody house-to-house fighting against a determined enemy. Russell's response was simple and brutal: the town was set ablaze, driving the rebels out.

The rebels set up a further barrier to the royal advance, using earth and tree trunks and supported by guns commanded by John Hamon, a skillful (and an alien or 'stranger') gunner. After an unsuccessful frontal assault, a small party of cavalry crossed at a ford and took the position in the rear. The fighting had lasted all day and perhaps 1,000 rebels had died, whilst only a score of fatalities were suffered by the royal forces. The road to Exeter was now open.

The royal forces, their numbers swelled by hundreds of captives, now prepared to camp on Clyst Heath about a mile away, when Lord Grey mistakenly thought he saw a rebel force to their rear. Russell responded by ordering the murder of the prisoners, an event which was especially distressing and which was later blamed upon the mercenaries. This atrocity was made remarkably little of at the time and it was indicative of the insecurity rather than the confidence of the royal forces.

On Clyst Heath on 6 August the royal forces were encamped ready for the final advance on Exeter, when they were themselves assaulted by the rebels, supported by artillery brought from the siege. Russell quickly formed his forces into three battles, and after sending pioneers to break some hedges and fill ditches, was able to send a force round to the rear of the rebels, cutting off their line of retreat. The fighting was vicious, and Hooker records that 'Thus thrown into confusion, finding themselves entrapped, attacked both in front and rear, confined much between the hedges, the rebels turned at bay.' When called upon to yield, they boldly refused:

> rather would they fight to the death. Valiantly and stoutly they [the rebels] stood to their tackle, and would not give over as long as life or limb lasted, yet in the end they were all overthrown and few or none left alive Great was the slaughter and cruel was the fight and such was the valour and stoutness of these men that the Lord Grey reported himself that 'he never in all the wars he had been did know the like'.[9]

---

9   Rose-Troup, *Western Rebellion*, p.276.

The rebels having now lost some thousands of their number and their artillery, quietly abandoned the siege of Exeter. Meanwhile the royal forces were further reinforced with men from Bristol and Wales led by Lord Herbert. The relief of Exeter took place on 6 August and the city was provided with victuals, courtesy of the relief force, who had pillaged the countryside around and now sold their loot at a good profit. Russell spent almost a fortnight rounding up and executing rebels, and distributing property that had been seized to those deemed worthy of reward. He was following the injunction sent to him by the Lord Protector that: 'So we pray you that sparing the common and mean men ye execute the head and chief stirrers of the rebellion: And that in so diverse places as ye may to the more terror of the unruly.'[10] The Privy Council added the warning that he should act decisively after his victory: 'for if you shall suffer those rebels to breathe, to catch a pride by your somewhat forebearing to follow them, and winning time so to gather strong upon you, you shall not do that with a great number that taken in time you might have done with a much fewer.'[11]

Those rebels not captured killed or fled rallied at Sampford Courtney, where the rebellion had broken out and where they were assailed on 16 August. The rebels were once again strongly entrenched outside the town, and Russell again employed his pioneers to make a route for his force in the maze of hedges. Lord Herbert led the vanguard and the rebels were displaced from their defences, again with the effective use of Spinola's arquebusiers. At this point Humphrey Arundell, the leader of the rebels, led an attack on the rear of Russell's forces which were now forced to face about to meet it. Arundell was eventually obliged to retire and those forces that were left made their last stand: 'they would not yield to no persuasions nor did, but most manfully did abide the fight: and never gave over until that both in the town and in the field they were all for the most part taken or slain.'[12] Well over 1,000 were killed on this day. Arundell and the remnants of his forces made their way to Launceston, where he was captured having failed to raise support for his cause within the town. Fleeing rebels were hunted down as they sought to escape from the county, and at King's Weston in Somerset over 100 more were killed. After the end of the main fighting the royal army continued to hunt down rebels; in total perhaps 7,000 in all were killed, in battle, massacre and lynchings.

The rebellion was doomed from the start because it was isolated and lacked a serious attainable political objective. The siege of Exeter had no value in itself and showed how little the rebels understood the national scene. The Lord Protector and the Privy Council were initially overwhelmed by the scale of the crisis but were able to manage their resources well, finally sending overwhelming force against the commons. What is surprising is how sophisticated the rebels were in their tactics, producing well-placed and well-constructed defences, launching ambushes and surprise attacks which wrong-footed their opponents again and again. The strong mercenary force is what

---

10 Rose-Troup, *Western Rebellion*, p.294.
11 Rose-Troup, *Western Rebellion*, p.296. See Pet. MSS. 453 d, Pk. p.57.
12 Hooker, *Exeter*, p.94.

finally overwhelmed the rebels, superior in equipment and discipline, able to drive the rebels from their positions with arquebuses and pikes. It was hardly surprising that Northumberland planned in the future to rely upon companies of mercenaries placed strategically around the country. If he had not disbanded them, perhaps he could have dealt with Princess Mary more successfully when the young King Edward died.

Kett's Rebellion

The Rebellion in East Anglia, known as Kett's Rebellion, was a horrible and bloody event that is too often ignored. It was brought about by the deep divisions within society between the gentry who had benefited from the enclosure of land, and the commons who had been the principal losers. Somerset, who had the undeserved reputation of being a friend of the people, had established enclosure commissions, which aroused expectations amongst the poor and fear amongst the gentry. The poor thought that the 'Good' Duke of Somerset and the young king were their allies, giving them the authority to act against those who opposed them in the King's name. On 7 and 8 July (Sunday/Monday) there was a large meeting at Wymondham, which became a demonstration against enclosure. On the 10th Sir William Windham, High Sheriff of Norfolk, arrived and ordered those assembled to disperse. He was almost dragged off his horse for his pains and forced to flee. In Norwich the Mayor Thomas Codd and the aldermen, as well as the principal citizens, assembled and sent to London and Windsor to inform the King of 'the rising of the people'.

The Rebels were now led by Robert Kett, a landowner who had taken up their cause. He decided to move the rebel camp to Mousehold Heath which overlooked the city. Attempts to conciliate the rebels by providing beer and provisions had little effect. Somerset and the Privy Council were overwhelmed by the scale of the civil dissent, not only in Norfolk, Suffolk and Cambridgeshire but closer to the capital in Oxfordshire and Buckinghamshire. There were also disturbances in the South East and of course the Prayer Book Rebellion in the South West. With too few troops and too little hard information Somerset's response was bound to be inadequate.

Mousehold Heath Camp was established by 12 July and the rebels soon numbered about 16,000. They collected food and war stores from the surrounding district, including raiding Old Paston Hall. They also still had access to the markets in the city, with the agreement, for the moment, of the city authorities. Somerset responded to the crisis by sending the York herald, one Bartholomew Butler, to Norwich on 21 July. The herald's message was as might be expected: he offered a pardon if the rebels immediately dispersed, and threatened severe consequences if they did not. Kett replied that 'Kings are wont to pardon wicked persons, not innocent and just men; they for their part had deserved nothing [in the way of punishment] and were guilty to themselves of no crime; and therefore despised such speeches as idle and unprofitable to their businesse.' It was hardly a meeting of minds: the rebels thought of themselves as defending the right order of society rather than challenging it, and were frustrated by the failure of those in authority to understand their case.

The mayor now put Norwich into a state of defence. He purchased brown paper for cartridges, slow match, lead for shot and lambskins for sponges. As the city had purchased six falconets five years earlier it seems strange that they had not already bought the necessary accoutrements. The mayor now refused the rebels access to the city, 'in order that the minds of the rebels be strooken through want, and weary of the warres, might faint at length'.[13] Ten guns were set up at the castle but the range was too great and they were moved to the hospital meadows. From the castle to the Bishop's Bridge is about 1,000 yards and to Mousehold Heath 2,500, while a falcon had an effective range of only a few hundred yards. The city artillery now engaged the rebel guns, and 'the whole night was spent in fearful shot on both sides',[14] although with little apparent effect on either. On 22 July the rebel artillery was brought down off the hill in preparation for an assault.

The rebel attack the next day was met with a vigorous response by the city archers, but the result was not what was expected: 'Their vagabond boys came among the thickest of the arrows and gathered them up, when some of the said arrows stuck fast in their legs and other parts',[15] which they drew out dripping with blood and gave them to others to shoot back; a response, which 'so dismayed the [city] archers that it took theyr hart from them'.[16] At 10:00 or 11:00 a.m. there was a massed attack on the Bishop's Bridge gate, across the river Wensum. The rebels' assault was impossible to halt: '[They] came running down the hill and took the river most desperately marvellous to the beholders, as so suddenly abashed them, that the Gunner feared to shoot there was so great a number about him: so he left his ordnance and fled. And the rest that watched, seeing themselves nothing to resist'.[17] Kett and the rebels were now in complete control of Norwich and continued to seize arms and equipment and ordered the arrest of Codd and other aldermen who were to be held in Surrey Place. They were fettered and chained and remained prisoners until the end of the rebellion.

William Parr the Marquis of Northampton, Lord Sheffield, Lord Wadsworth, Sir Thomas Paston, Sir Thomas Cornwall and numerous other knights were delegated to lead the royal forces, which numbered only 1,200–1,400 although including Italian mercenaries. On 31 July Parr entered the city by St Stephen's gate, preceded by a sword bearer, and made his way to the council chamber where he drank a cup of wine. Watch and ward were established and then Parr and his gentlemen settled in the Steward's House on cushions and pillows, although remaining in arms. The rebels were still in the city and were singularly unimpressed by the arrival of the city's 'saviours'. The Italian mercenaries skirmished with the rebels, and one in especially fine

---

13   Russell, *Kett's Rebellion*, p.75.
14   Russell, *Kett's Rebellion*, p.78.
15   Russell, *Kett's Rebellion*, p.80.
16   Russell, *Kett's Rebellion*, p.80.
17   Russell, *Kett's Rebellion*, p.81.

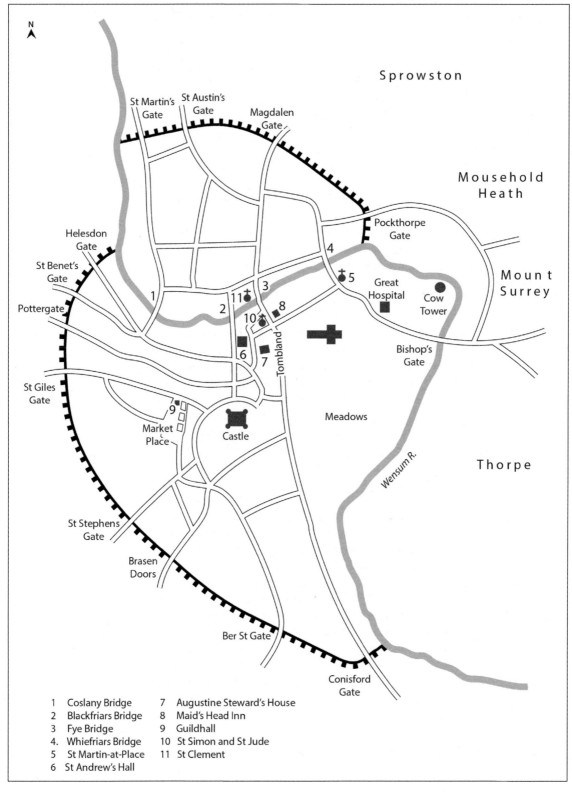

N

Sprowston

Mousehold
Heath

St Martin's
Gate

St Austin's
Gate

Magdalen
Gate

Mount
Surrey

Helesdon
Gate

Pockthorpe
Gate

4

St Benet's
Gate

1

3

5

Great
Hospital

Cow
Tower

11

Pottergate

2

10

8

Tombland

Bishop's
Gate

6

7

St Giles
Gate

9

Market
Place

Castle

Meadows

Thorpe

Wensum R.

St Stephens
Gate

Brasen
Doors

Ber St Gate

Conisford
Gate

1	Coslany Bridge	7	Augustine Steward's House
2	Blackfriars Bridge	8	Maid's Head Inn
3	Fye Bridge	9	Guildhall
4.	Whiefriars Bridge	10	St Simon and St Jude
5	St Martin-at-Place	11	St Clement
6	St Andrew's Hall		

Map of Norwich

armour was captured and then hanged on Mount Surrey, one of the very few examples of summary 'justice' by the rebels.

When the relief forces were comfortably settled for the night the rebels launched an attack preceded by artillery. The rebels' attitude is best expressed by the account reported by Nicholas Sotherton of a confrontation between a royal herald and one Flotman, who was apparently 'an outrageous and busie fellow':[18]

> With regard to the Marquis of Northampton, I think nothing of him, being as he was, a man neither of courage, counsel, nor good fortune; I despise and mortally hate him … as infamous, worthless, always standing in need of others' help, and guilty of all disloyalty and treason. We for our parts have always been earnest defenders of the king's safety and dignity. They had taken arms, not against the king, but for those things which they hoped would be hereafter for his welfare and their own. For what is it they are desirous of doing? Is it not to defend the king's name and dignity; to provide for the common safety; to defend the rights of law and liberty; to preserve themselves, their wives, children and goods, and finally to deliver the Commonwealth vexed in many ways unjustly, from the detestable pride and cruelty of their enemies? The commonwealth is now almost utterly overthrown through the insolence of the gentlemen, our intention is to restore it to its former dignity: and either we will accomplish this, by our present course of action; or else as becomes brave and high-spirited men, we will fight boldly, risk our lives, and, if it be so persists on the battlefield. Liberty may suffer much at the hands of oppressors, but never shall her sacred cause be betrayed by us.[19]

The rebels attacked with much enthusiasm but limited tactical sense, crossing the river, scaling walls and breaches, but were:

> drowned in their own and other men's blood, even to the last gasp, furiously withstood our men [the royal forces]. Yea, many also stroken through their breasts with swords, and the sinews of their legs cut asunder. I tremble to rehearse it, yet creeping on their knees, were moved with such fury, as they wounded our soldiers, lying amongst the slain almost without life.[20]

Three hundred rebels were killed and the remainder forced to withdraw. The rebels now broke into the hospital meadows while the herald, realising perhaps that his message had not been met with popular enthusiasm, left. The rebels were fighting with the Bishop's soldiers on the flat ground before the palace gate, while Northampton's main force was in the marketplace. As the attack developed, he fed men through the streets into a growing and vicious street battle across the whole eastern area of the city. Seeing things going the rebels' way, Sheffield took command of a body of cavalry and charged the rebels across the cathedral precinct, past St Martin at Place Church and into Bishopsgate Street. Outside the Great Hospital in Bishopsgate Street,

---

18 Russell, *Kett's Rebellion*, p.95.
19 Russell, *Kett's Rebellion*, p.95.
20 Russell, *Kett's Rebellion*, p.94.

Sheffield fell from his horse into a ditch. Expecting to be captured and ransomed, as was the custom, he removed his helmet, only to be hacked to death by a butcher named Fulke. The morale of the royal troops collapsed at this point and they fled the city. Norwich was once again in the hands of the rebels. In the rain, the victorious rebels camped in the cathedral church (Christ's Church).

On 10 August John Dudley, Earl of Warwick, was appointed to command the new royal forces and by the 21st this new army found itself only three miles from Norwich. Warwick was told that many in the city would seek and accept their pardon, '[so] that this flame so dangerous and dreadful might be quenched without slaughter or bloodshed.'[21] On the 24th another herald was sent to the rebels, but his message was uncompromising and the response was a disaster. A boy dropped his breeches and mooned at the herald and his escort and was promptly shot, starting a general panic. Warwick's forces had entered the city and the baggage train made its way through Tombland to Bishop's Gate. The rebels assembled in three companies in Tombland. Warwick's men advanced from the Market Place through St John's Maddermarket, where the rebel archers '[shot] a mighty force of arrows, as flakes of snow in a tempest'.[22] Captain Drury, who commanded a company of arquebusiers, 'paid them [the rebels] home again with such a terrible volley of shot, as if it had been a storm of hail, and put them all to flight, as in a moment trembling'.[23] The rebels were clearly facing a more determined and competent foe than William Parr and his gentry allies.

Warwick began to establish the security of the city. The entrance of Warwick's forces into an unknown city created some problems, as Myles, the rebels' master gunner, spotted several carriages and carts only protected by a few Welshmen. He promptly led a raiding force to seize them, driving off the few defenders and capturing the plunder. It was reported that the rebels had seized 'Campe Carts laden with gunnes, gunpowder, and all kinds of instruments of warre',[24] of which the ever-active Captain Drury recovered some. Sir John Smythe reports that of the 24 pieces of artillery, 18 were taken. The rebels then used their guns against Bishop's Gate, where they '[did] shoot down a Tower, which slew many that there guarded.'[25]

Warwick, after this bloody and confusing fracas, confirmed that unlike his predecessor he would not abandon the city to the rebels again. The royal forces garrisoned the town and were billeted with the mostly welcoming citizens, who were increasingly concerned for their safety and that of their property. On 26 August some 1,100 Landsknechts arrived as reinforcements, discharging their pieces in a noisy flourish to announce their arrival and initially causing some panic. Kett decided at this point, with Norwich now securely in the hands of a determined opponent, to leave Mousehold Heath and prepare for the final confrontation at nearby Dussindale. There is some

21   Russell, *Kett's Rebellion*, p.125.
22   Russell, *Kett's Rebellion*, p.135.
23   Russell, *Kett's Rebellion*, p.135.
24   Russell, *Kett's Rebellion*, p.134.
25   Russell, *Kett's Rebellion*, p.137.

doubt concerning the site of the final battle; Magdalen Hill, much closer to the city, has been identified but any definitive answer will depend on the emergence of further archaeological evidence.[26] There Kett made impressive preparations. The rebels 'devised trenches and stakes wherein they and theirs were intrenched, and set up great bulwarks of defence before and about, placed their ordnance all about them, dug a ditch across the highway and cut off all passage, pitching their javelins and stakes in the ground before them'.[27]

On 27 August Warwick led his 1,000 'Almains' and all his horse out of the city, leaving the English footmen and Captain Drury's badly mauled company in the town. A final envoy was sent to the rebels but to no avail. The battle started with an exchange of gunfire. Myles, the rebels' master of ordnance, opened fire and his first shot passed through the shoulder of the royal standard bearer's horse and then the thigh of its rider, bringing the standard down. Warwick's men fired a volley, despite the captured gentlemen having been chained together before the rebel line. They seem to have broken free as soon as they could and made themselves scarce as it seems that only two captive gentlemen were killed. Sotherton recorded the response of the rebels: some fled in panic whilst others were determined to make a last stand:

> instead of abiding the encounter, they like sheep confusedly ran away headlong, as quickly as they could. But others with deadly obstinacy withstood our men a little while; such however was the force of the shot and the eagerness of the Royal forces to rush open them that Kett's army being beaten down, and overthrown one every side with hot assault were with almost no labour driven from their standing. The Rebels feeling hope of pardon to be utterly taken away with obstinate courage presently recovered themselves by companies from their flight and showed plainly they intended to renew the battle, affirming that they would rather die manfully in fight, than flying, to be slain like sheep. They furnished themselves with swords and other weapons that lay upon the ground, everywhere among the heaps of the dead bodies; and so arranged their carts and carriages as to form a secure and excellent barricade; they swore either to the other, to spend in that place their lives manfully, or else at the length to get victory.[28]

Warwick sent a herald, entreating them to lay down their weapons, which if they would yet do, they should escape unpunished; if otherwise, they should all of them, even to the last man, perish. They answered that:

> they would willingly lay down their weapons, if they were persuaded that the promise of impunity would prove for their safety; but they had had already experience of their cruelty upon their companions and perceived that this pardon to be nothing else but a cask full of ropes and halters. And therefore die they would.[29]

---

26 Leo R. Jary, *Kett – 1549. Rewriting the Rebellion* (Lowestoft: Poppyland Publishing, 2018).

27 Russell, *Kett's Rebellion*, p.137.

28 Russell, *Kett's Rebellion*, p.146.

29 Russell, *Kett's Rebellion*, p.147.

Warwick went to them and had the Herald read his commission again and by this action these rebels lay down their weapons, crying 'God save King Edward'.[30]

The battle ended at about 4:00 p.m. On 28 August the hangings began, with nine hanged at the Oak of Reformation at the heart of the old rebel camp. Kett was captured at the village of Swannington the night after the battle and taken together with his brother William to the Tower of London, to await trial for treason. Found guilty, the brothers were returned to Norwich at the beginning of December. Kett was hanged from the walls of Norwich Castle on 7 December 1549; on the same day William was hanged from the west tower of Wymondham Abbey.

The gentlemen wanted condign punishment for the rebels, but Warwick had more sense. As he pointed out:

There must be measure kept, and above all things in punishment men must not exceed. He knew their wickedness to be such as deserved to be grievously punished, and with the severest judgement that might be. But how far would they go? Would they show themselves discontented and never pleased? Would they leave no place for humble petition? None for pardon and mercy? Would they be plowmen themselves, and harrow their own lands.[31]

Seymour wrote to a friend in Italy:

Kett fled, and the rest of the rebels, casting away their weapons and armour and asking pardon on their knees … were sent home without injury and pardoned … Kett, with three other chief captains, all vile persons … are still held to receive that which they have deserved … We trust, truly, that these rebellions are now at an end.[32]

They were, and he had shown himself to be the strong man of the Protectorate and one suited to be the replacement for the unfortunate Somerset. The rebels had shown remarkable bravery and discipline, they were well-organised and handled their weapons, even artillery, with impressive skill. They were defeated by a superior force of mercenaries, whose skill-at-arms and aggressiveness proved overwhelming when led by a capable commander.

Wyatt's Rising

Mary had successfully pursued her claim to the throne against the challenge of Northumberland and the unfortunate Lady Jane Grey. She was soon to face a further and potentially far more serious threat, that resulted in chaos and bloodshed. The marriage to Philip and the suppression of Protestantism was an unappealing prospect to many. In addition, there were two further

---

30 Russell, *Kett's Rebellion*, p.148.
31 Russell, *Kett's Rebellion*, p.151.
32 Russell, *Kett's Rebellion*, p.214.

claimants to the throne who together might have posed a serious alternative to the Catholic Queen Mary. One was the little-known Edward Courtenay, the Earl of Devon (who had been proposed as an acceptable English consort for Mary by Parliament); the other was his prospective bride, Princess Elizabeth, Mary's half-sister. In the rebellions of 1536 and 1549 there had been no attempt to produce a rival for the throne and Northumberland's efforts with Lady Jane had failed dismally. Devon was personally very unattractive and Elizabeth was above all loyal to her sovereign sister; they were both far more to the taste of the English people than Spanish Philip.

A group of four principal conspirators, Sir Thomas Wyatt, Sir James Croft, Sir Peter Carew and Henry Grey (Duke of Suffolk and father of Lady Jane Grey), planned to raise forces in their own counties in support of the Earl of Devon. With considerable potential support and with the assistance of the French ambassador Antoine de Noailles, whose sovereign would provide a fleet of 80 ships to keep Spain away the plotters, the plot posed a real threat to Mary. The plan was hatched in late November of 1553 and was meant to come to fruition in May 1554. Imperial ambassador Simon Renard revealed the plan to Stephen Gardiner, who upon interrogating the Earl of Devon discovered the extent of the plot.

Facing discovery, the plotters moved prematurely in January. Peter and Gawen Carew seized Exeter but failed to raise any significant force in Cornwall, which had a predominantly Catholic population which Peter Carew had fought against in 1549. Croft abandoned the plot; Grey raised a force a little over 100 strong in Leicestershire but was refused entry into Coventry and surrendered. In Kent Wyatt found much greater support from a population that had imbibed Protestantism more deeply, with Cranmer having been busy proselytizing when Archbishop of Canterbury. On 22 January Wyatt raised not so much a rebellion as an armed protest against the Spanish marriage at Allington castle, where a few local gentry and relatives rallied to the cause. On the 25th he issued a proclamation addressed to 'our neighbors, because you be our frandes, and because you be Englishmen', announcing a Spanish invasion and denouncing the marriage.

Wyatt assembled a small but well-equipped force in Maidstone, but formally raised his flag in defence of the kingdom at Rochester where his army now numbered 5,000. Even in Kent opposition to the rebels was already growing in Tonbridge, Malling and even Canterbury. In skirmishes Lord Abergavenny and Sir Robert Southwell, the Sheriff of Kent, put some of the rebels to flight. The Council at first offered a pardon to those who abandoned the rebellion and then organised a counter-attack. The ancient Duke of Norfolk was to lead a force made up of Kentish militia under the Sheriff, 500 London militia under Captain Bret and some Yeomen of the Guard. Outnumbered by the rebels, the morale of the royal forces collapsed when faced with Wyatt's army. Bret and his Londoners seem to have gone over to the rebels' cause, crying out: 'A Wyatt a Wyatt, we are all Englishmen'. Not only the Londoners but some of the yeomen went turncoat, and Norfolk fled leaving behind his baggage and eight pieces of ordnance. John Mychell, a Canterbury printer, reported the event: 'The .xxx. day of the same moneth, the duke of Norfolke came to his artillary agaynst Wyat in Rochester, but the

Londoners with Bryan Fytzwilliams & Bret, who came with the duke against Wyat fled from the duke to Wyat, and the duke hardely escaped.'[33]

Wyatt very foolishly did not take advantage of this 'triumph' and did not immediately march on London, which by now was in a state of panic. He indulged in a siege of Cowling Castle and then was further delayed at Dartford where, to gain time, royal messengers engaged him in negotiations. Meanwhile the Duke of Suffolk's rebellion had come to nothing with the traitorous Duke soon captured, found hiding in a hollow tree. The Queen now demonstrated that she was indeed a Tudor and rallied the City of London to her defence in a rousing speech in the Guildhall on 1 February. London Bridge was closed to the Rebels, a volunteer force of 20,000 was raised and Wyatt, now declared a traitor, had a bounty of £100 placed on his head.

At Southwark Wyatt's forces were welcomed by the disreputable inhabitants but bombarded from the Tower of London, although with little effect. Wyatt now faced a long march to cross the Thames with bridges systematically destroyed to delay his journey. Crossing the Thames at Kingston he hoped to take St James's Palace and enter the City at Ludgate. The roads were bad, his men were dispirited and deserting and his plan betrayed. The rain had stopped, and on a bright cold day Wyatt brought his men to Hyde Park Corner while the royal army awaited them at Charing Cross. The Earl of Pembroke in command of the loyal forces used his men to cut off the line of retreat of Wyatt's men as they advanced along Fleet Street, and then used his cavalry to break the rebel column in two. The rear was now attacked by royal archers and retreated in panic while the leading part progressed to Ludgate. Wyatt reached Ludgate and actually knocked on the gate but unsurprisingly was not admitted. The Londoners had risen in favour of the Queen. Mychell described the events, although with little drama: 'On As[h] wednisday the. vii. of Februarye, he and hys complices were overronne and taken about charing Crosse & Fletestrete, but Wyat with certayn with hym, had before knocked at Ludgate, sayinge: he hadde kept promise.'[34] Wyatt retreated with a few score men and was brought to a final fight at Temple Bar, where after an hour he and the remainder of the leaders surrendered and were taken first to the Council and then to the Tower. The captured rebel soldiers were imprisoned in the Marshalsea and then, as the numbers were too many, in London churches.

Wyatt was beheaded and quartered on 11 April. Hundreds had by that time been executed with varying degrees of barbarity, including Jane Grey and her husband. Wyatt was racked to make him confess that Princess Elizabeth had been privy to the plot but denied it and declared as much on the scaffold. The plot seems to have had little chance of real success. It was too complicated, too big and required a degree of determination and competence that all but Wyatt lacked. From the point of view of the Queen and Bishop Gardiner, the rebellion increased their sense of insecurity as they attempted to establish a Catholic sovereign on the throne of a heretical kingdom.

---

33 William H. Wiatt, 'The Lost History of Wyatt's Rebellion', in *Renaissance News*, vol. 15, no. 2 (Summer 1962), p.130.

34 Wiatt, 'The Lost History', p.130.

Conclusions

The Army Royal, either in the form of the county militia or gentry retinue, was the 'commons-in-arms': they could constitute an impressively numerous and well-armed force. In the case of the three principal rebellions they could dominate their area of operations until the arrival of 'loyal' reinforcements.

The rebels could demonstrate a remarkable degree of competence in the handling of weapons, including artillery. Both the gunner Myles in Norfolk and the 'stranger' gunner in Exeter were experts in their craft, and artillery was used extensively in both rebellions, showing that there must have been reasonably widespread knowledge of the art. Handling of bows and hand weapons also seems to have been of a high standard, causing heavy casualties even amongst professional opponents. There is nothing to suggest that the preponderance of bows in the hands of the rebels was a distinct disadvantage. The Cornish and Norfolk rebels showed a remarkable facility for, and sagacity in, the erection of extensive field fortifications. Tactically the Cornish rebels had a habit of outwitting or surprising their opponents, causing near disaster on occasion had they been in a position to exploit it. Kett's rebels also found that using their knowledge of the city that they could ambush and drive out 'foreign' troops.

The bravery of the rebels was remarked upon by their opponents and not merely to make their own successes more commendable. The rebels seem to have been willing to fight and die for their causes, which made the attempts by their opponents to blacken their name as mere criminals unsuccessful. The rebels were extraordinarily disciplined and were rarely accused of atrocities. Only one person was killed during the Pilgrimage of Grace, and during Kett's rebellion only one Italian mercenary, who was captured during a brawl, was hanged out of hand. This compares with the mass slaughter of Cornish rebel prisoners after the Battle of Clyst.

The defeat of the 1549 rebels was only achieved through the extensive use of mercenary troops, specifically Landsknechts and Spanish and Italian arquebusiers. The only comparable English formation was Captain Drury's company of 180 arquebusiers, which suffered heavy casualties in Norfolk. The strict discipline of mercenaries under fire was widely acknowledged and applauded and of course their political reliability was vital. It is notable that the royal forces committed at the Battle of Dussindale consisted almost solely of mercenaries.

The rebellions were a tragic part of England's history. They showed that the English forces that existed were formidable in number and fighting ability even when facing 'professional' troops. Their failures were the result of as much political as military miscalculations, as they faced implacable opposition from the Crown and its cohorts and stood little chance of success.

4

Wars with France

The Invasion of France 1513

The Invasion of 1513 is something of a misnomer, as of course the disembarkation was made in the English port of Calais, a possession of the English Crown since the port's capture in 1337. The objective also hardly constituted an invasion of France bent on conquest. Its intention was to defend the borders of the Holy Roman Empire by besieging and destroying the town of Thérouanne in Artois. Henry also made it clear that he was reconquering what he claimed as English territory, by capturing the cathedral town of Tournai.

Henry VII had assiduously avoided any overseas commitment that did not contribute in one way or another to increasing the security of his throne and dynasty. Henry VIII wished to make it clear that times had changed and that England was to regain its position as a European power. Opposition to the war in Council was easily swept aside, as were attempts to keep Henry from the field of battle, where death in combat or more likely disease would leave the throne without an heir. One little problem to be resolved was that of potential claimant to the throne Edmund de La Pole, who was a prisoner in the Tower. Henry had him executed, tying up that particular loose end before departing. Henry was now free to create 'such a fine opinion about his valour among all men that they may clearly understand that his ambition was not merely to equal but indeed to exceed the glorious deeds of his ancestors'.[1] This explained the real purpose of the expedition.

His actual presence would have considerable benefits for the expedition. It was essential that the King's army should be well provided for, or other heads might roll. The presence of the commander-in-chief meant that decisions could be made on site, without the delay of days or even weeks that would ensue if the King remained in England. His army was something of a hybrid formation: some 2,000 men were raised from the Royal Household, while the rest were raised through the nobility by commissions of array. The

---

1   C.G. Cruickshank, *Army Royal: Henry VIII's Invasion of France* (Oxford: Clarendon Press, 1969), p.8.

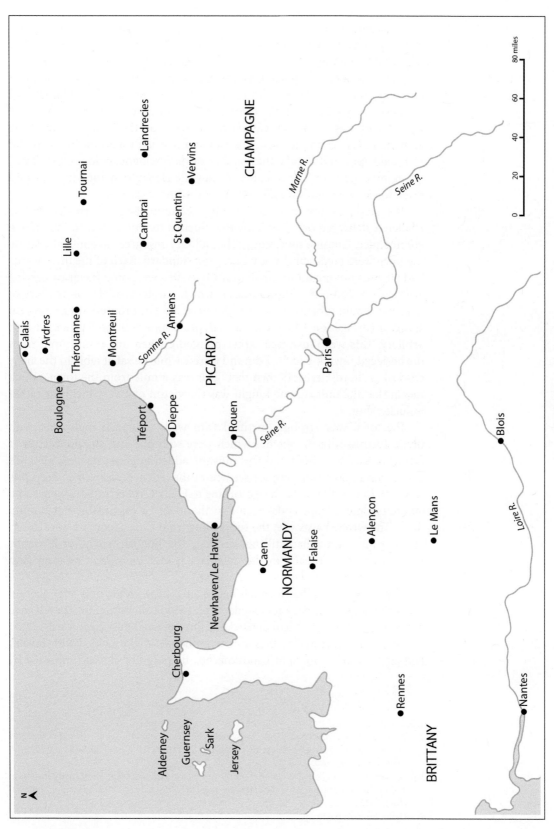

Map of Northern France

contributions of the Privy Chamber were especially valuable in quality and quantity, constituting almost an 'army- within-an-army'.[2] There were 12,000 men in the fore ward, 16,000 in the main ward and 7,500 in the rear ward.

The army was transported, as it was organised, in three waves: van, rear and main wards, all arriving in France before the King. George Talbot Earl of Shrewsbury sailed with the fore ward on 6 June and Charles Somerset 1st Earl of Worcester with the rear ward embarked on the 10th, with the King arriving in Calais on the 30th. The van and rear left Calais on the 13th and 16th, and appeared to take the route towards Boulogne, before inexplicably changing course for Thérouanne. Meanwhile Henry remained in Calais for three weeks leaving his forces divided and without direction.

The siege, as the code of chivalry required, began formally with a challenge delivered on 25 June by the Bluemantle Pursuivant to the French commander, Antoine de Crequy. The military resources assembled outside the town were creditable by any European standard. Each of the three wards had 60 guns not including small multi-barrelled weapons. The army carried a little over 500 tons of gunpowder, which would provide for 16 days of constant bombardment. However, the siege did not progress with any great speed or enthusiasm. The town was well provisioned and well provided with artillery. This was illustrated rather pointedly when one round fired from the besieged town killed Sir Edmund Carew while he sat at table in the army council, in Lord Herbert's own tent. This was a mile from the town, which meant that the unfortunate knight was the victim of a very lucky, or rather unlucky, shot.

The town was 'strongly fortified with walls, ramparts, bulwarks, with divers fortresses in the ditches which were so broad and so plumb steep it was a wonder to behold'.[3] To this must be added quickset hedges, trenches, and a wood and earth rampart set within the defences, as well as deep pits in which to trap the invaders. According to Hall's *Chronicle*, there were some 600 horse and 2,500 Landsknechts in the town,[4] a formidable but hungry force. The weather was vile, the supply line from Calais tenuous, and Henry and the main ward had still not arrived. The English had, after a month, failed to create a breach in the defences, launch an assault or even stop reinforcements arriving.

Although the siege had formally begun on 25 June, Henry only left Calais on 21 July having left the besiegers to effectively twiddle their thumbs. The advance of the main ward was well organised, the force divided into three wards, 5,000 in the van and rear and 6,700 in the main battle. Well provided with cavalry and artillery and a force of Landsknechts, its progress was accompanied by

---

2 Potter, *Henry VIII and Francis I*, p.214; D. Starkey, 'Intimacy and Innovation: the rise of the Privy Chamber 1485–1547', in Starkey et al., *The English Court from the Wars of the Roses to the English Civil War* (1990), p.90.

3 Edward Hall, *Chronicle: containing the history of England, during the reign of Henry the fourth, and the receding monarchs to the end of the reign of Henry the eighth* (etc.) (London: Johnson (etc.), 1809), p.358.

4 Hall, *Chronicle*, p.62.

The Battle of the Spurs, from *Der Weisskunig* by Hans Burgkmair. This is a somewhat more melodramatic depiction than the actual events deserved. The Landsknechts who screened Henry from any danger are well represented, as are the English archers and artillery that surprised the attempt at reinforcing Thérouanne. The heavy cavalry on both sides are fully barded, and it was this barding which slowed the French in their retreat and had to be cut free. Archers are rarely represented and the bows in use here appear to have tips that are slightly recurved. This would certainly have been more efficient but there is little evidence from the *Mary Rose* examples for its use in English longbows of the period although often represented in Continental illustrations.
(Metropolitan Museum of Art, Open Access)

an unseemly stampede by some of the horse. After considerable effort only a distance of three miles was accomplished on that day.

Attacked by a large French force, the main ward closed its ranks and increased its speed of progress. At this point one of the large guns known as the Apostles (*St John*) fell into a stream. To lose such a gun was inexcusable; the master carpenter of Calais stayed behind with 100 men to recover it. Without proper support this small party was ambushed and all men either killed or captured, an unimpressive performance. The immobile weapon was finally recovered by a larger force, the French having found it equally difficult to shift, although a second piece, 'the red gun' (probably a wrought iron bombard, as wrought iron guns seem to have had layers of red varnish or paint) was lost. Henry had finally arrived on 1 August and a proper attempt would now be made to blockade the city and reduce it by a prolonged siege.

The English siege lines were within a 'birdbolt' (about 20 yards) of the walls but even so failed to make a breach. The sallies by French stradiots (light cavalry) and Landsknechts caused few casualties but more disruption to the besiegers, even if the French losses were high. The response of the English to their slow progress was to order Sir Alexander Baynham, captain of pioneers of the rear ward, to construct a mine and lay a gunpowder charge beneath the defences. The French dug a countermine, which when exploded on 18 July destroyed the English mine and its poor miners.

The French king was also collecting his forces, and with those of the Duke of Guelders could muster 25,000 men. This force was numerous enough to seriously discomfort the English besiegers and possibly defeat them in battle. In the town, fodder and food were running short at a faster rate than expected and the date when resistance would have to end had altered from 1 November to the beginning of September. The arrival of the Emperor at the siege on 10 August brightened the scene for the moment for the English, but the foul weather spoiled the event for all concerned. On the 13th a further meeting took place, in a slightly drier tent, and Henry and the Emperor got along famously. In England matters were less rosy, as Queen Catherine had had to deal with the Scottish invasion which was an almost inevitable accompaniment to an English expedition to France.

To seal off the southern approaches to Thérouanne the English main ward crossed the River Lys, which it was hoped would be a barrier to reinforcements on its own. In one night five wooden bridges were built, to allow the passage of the English forces to complete the encirclement of the town. This was a most impressive achievement and one rarely commented upon. On 16 August, during the advance, scouts captured a prisoner who revealed that a large French force was approaching from Blangy further south, while a smaller force was advancing from the north to relieve the town. Henry insisted that if a battle was likely, he had to have all his 'rich' tents moved and set up! Taking Maximilian's advice, he set up an artillery battery on a low hill to provide covering fire and the allied cavalry advanced, supported by infantry (and Henry) about a mile behind.

The French force advancing from the south was commanded by de Piennes, carrying quantities of ham for the hungry garrison. In the face of the advancing English they discovered that this task was hopeless. The

French now came under fire from the artillery and from English archers who were hidden behind a hedge. The Albanian stradiots, who provided the light cavalry for the French, were the first to panic in the face of artillery fire. The rest of the relief force, following the example of the stradiots, was routed, with their horses galled with English arrows. The famous Chevalier de Bayard conducted a fighting retreat, while others cut the bards from their horses and fled at a gallop. It was the Burgundians who now committed themselves to the fray, in order to capture as many rich prisoners as possible. Rhys ap Thomas and his light cavalry skirmished with the small French force in the north and an attempt by the garrison to sally out was also successfully countered. The Battle of the Spurs, as it became known, because of the speed of the French retreat, was hardly more than a skirmish. De Bayard, whose heroic defence of a very small bridge was the only military highpoint, was captured for his pains. Henry on the other hand claimed a 'famous victory'. Queen Catherine wrote to her cardinal: 'the victory hath been so great and I think none such hathe been seen before. All England hath cause to thank God for it, and I specially, seeing that the king beginneth so well.'[5] This response would suggest that she was either blinded by love and admiration or had an excellent understanding of her husband's flawed character, or both. Rhys ap Thomas was also eulogised, with perhaps greater justification, by the Welsh poet Tudur Aled, in the following lines:

Next after God and the King that day,
Rhys and his ravens did bear the sway.[6]

Thérouanne, having lost all hope of relief, surrendered on 23 August and the garrison marched out with all its military equipment. Henry and Maximilian agreed to slight the town and its defences, which they did with impressive thoroughness. They agreed on this course because they could not agree on who would otherwise have control of it. The cost of rebuilding, provisioning and maintaining a garrison in such a difficult and provocative position would probably have been beyond Henry anyway.

With a successful siege and battle beneath his belt, Henry should now have directed his efforts to a worthy target that could have furthered his interests in France. Boulogne, St Quentin and Montreuil would all have usefully added to his domain, but instead he chose Tournai. The city was a target of no strategic significance to Henry but again it was of great interest to Maximilian and Margaret of Savoy, sited as it was adjacent to their territory. Tournai was effectively defenceless and was without a French garrison. By agreement it was economically tied to trade with Imperial territories, operating as something akin to a free port. With much decayed walls and an unenthusiastic population, it was bound to fall into Henry's hands should he choose to attack it. The good burghers of the city hoped to maintain their neutrality with Margaret of Savoy, but Louis XII insisted on a demonstration

---

5   Cruickshank, *Army Royal*, p.107; British Library Cottonian MS Caligula D vi, f.94.
6   Glanmor Williams, *Renewal and Reformation: Wales c.1415–1642* (Oxford: Oxford University Press, 1993), p.248.

of their loyalty. The townspeople, keen to maintain good relations with all sides, found themselves facing an attack by Henry's army and as a gesture made some efforts to burn the outlying suburbs. Margaret of Savoy now found herself in the strange position of pleading for French subjects against the martial plans of her father Maximilian and his ally the King of England. Henry considered the population to be incorrigible for lampooning him, a crime that a man of his enormous vanity could not ignore. If Queen Catherine was determined to defend the King's *amour propre*, the Tournaisiens were clearly not above cocking a snook. The town was now divided between those few who had a lot to lose (the rich) and those many who had nothing (the poor); the majority chose loyalty to Louis, thereby satisfying Henry's need for further bloodshed and glory.

The bombardment began on 16 September, while the city was unable to defend itself and faced an internal revolt as the poor and displaced forced the wealthy to provide for their needs. Henry was meanwhile personally encouraging his artillery and specifically the crew of one of the apostles, *St Bartholomew* by name, to use the towers of the Cathedral of Notre Dame as their aiming point. Amongst the many collateral casualties were a couple who were killed in their marital bed and an apothecary's maid who had her foot shattered by a cannonball. Such is the wrath and majesty of kings. By the 22nd negotiations began for the surrender of the town, but as formerly subjects of the 'false king' Louis, they would now have to change their allegiance not to the Emperor but their 'true king' Henry. Henry, specifically excluding any Imperial participation, entered the city in triumph on the 25th and remained until 13 October, indulging in a positive orgy of festivities. Tournai became part of Henry's 'French kingdom' and had the pleasure of paying him an indemnity of £2,000 per annum, as well as £10,000 towards the cost of the siege. Brian Tuke noted with satisfaction that, 'We now have the city of Thérouanne, which was called *la chamber du roi*; and Tournai, on whose walls was inscribed "'La pucelle sans reproche"* that is "the unsullied maiden". The *chamber du roi* is burned, and this maiden has lost her maidenhood.'[7] Rape and destruction had satisfied Henry's need for glory, for the moment. Cardinal Wolsey, who had managed the logistics of the campaign so well, was rewarded with the bishopric of the city. The Cardinal held this title until 1518 when the city was returned to the French by the Treaty of London.

The 1523 French Campaign of the Duke of Suffolk

This 'most ill-conceived and ill-managed war,'[8] as C.W. Oman, the great man of Renaissance warfare, described it, would have no purpose other than to place Henry in the European diplomatic spotlight to satisfy his appalling vanity. Emperor Charles on the other hand saw English participation as a useful aid in diverting the French effort from Italy, which was where the real

---

7   Cruickshank, *Army Royal*, p.133; *CSP Venice*, 1202–1603 (London: 1864–1898), ii, no. 316.
8   Charles Oman, *A History of the Art of War in the Sixteenth Century* (London: Greenhill Books, 1987), p.322.

prize was to be fought for.

The cause of this war was not to be found in England or in the Empire but in France. The Duc de Bourbon, the Constable of France, had raised the flag of revolt against the French king and his mother. who had threatened his lands and status. Bourbon, it was expected, could call on the loyalty of at least five leading nobles, although only one (Ponthièvre) responded, others such as Lautrec and Navarre were hostile to Francis but only sympathetic to the Constable. This supposed defection to the Empire by the nobility was to be exploited to the full, in what was potentially a plan to capture Paris and then to divide the kingdom. This grand strategy did not at first have the full confidence of Henry. He was still wedded to a more modest and possibly realistic strategy of gnawing away at French territory contiguous to his possession of Calais, Boulogne being the next obvious target.

Charles V may have had control of the strategy but it was Margaret of Austria, his regent in the Netherlands, who was presented with numerous practical issues. She was already faced with the problems of a war with the Duchy of Guelders, which broke out in May 1523 and rapidly absorbed both her men and money. She faced the task of browbeating the uncooperative estates into aiding her martial plans. Her objective was to force bellicose France to negotiate a realistic peace, ensuring her borders. As an ally in a grand plan of aggressive conquest she was of little use.

English efforts had begun in 1522, when the Duke of Surrey was placed in command of an army that, numbering only 7,000, was a mere shadow of the King's army of 1513. After conducting a few raids in Picardy and Artois, he attempted a siege of Hesdin which had to be abandoned due to the lack of artillery. Charles Brandon, the Duke of Suffolk and Henry's brother-in-law, succeeded to command in July 1523 and provided a large force from his own possessions in North Wales and the Marches. He demonstrated more determination and had greater resources at his disposal; he also benefited from the advice of his second in command William Lord Sandys, a respected soldier. Henry VIII had become enamoured once more with a grand vision of himself as the king of France. He ordered that his 'French subjects' were to be treated by his army with generosity and not to experience a scorched earth policy that would at least have kept his soldiers fed. In addition Henry engineered the acceptance, by the renegade Duc de Bourbon, of his title as King of France. Charles V had convinced Henry that the bulk of the Imperial army, under the treacherous duke, would combine with him on an attack on Paris itself. This pincer movement would conclude with the capture of Paris and the dismemberment of France.

The invading English army consisted of 10,668 horse and foot, which together with some men from the Calais and Guînes garrisons probably totalled some 13,000 men. Sir John Wallop led 1,000 or so 'adventurers' known as Krakers. Primarily raised and equipped according to medieval practice, the royal army lacked pikemen, arquebusiers and heavy cavalry. This lack was to be made up with mercenaries paid for by Henry, or auxiliaries from Imperial territory. He had been reinforced by 500 heavy cavalry and 3,000 Landsknecht infantry which added considerably to the strength of his force. Serious efforts had also been made to provide necessary

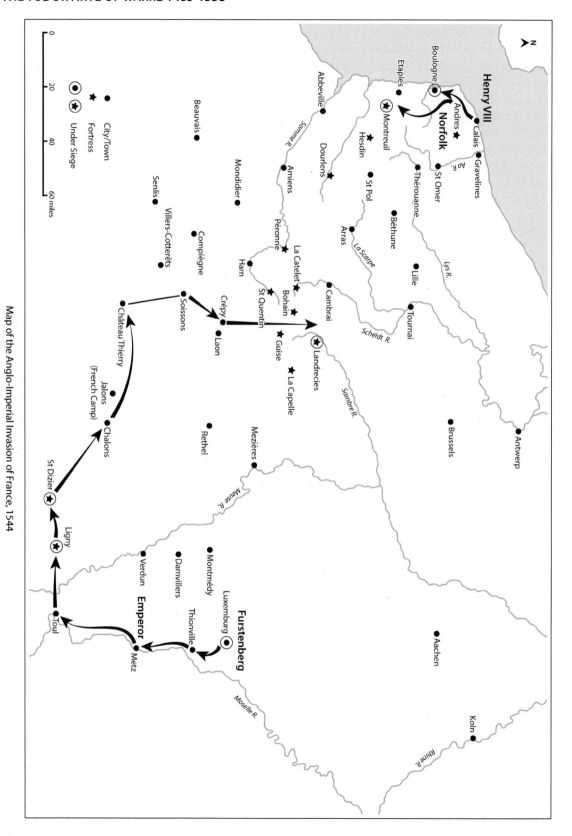

Map of the Anglo-Imperial Invasion of France, 1544

support troops and artillery, whose absence from the 1522 expedition had been sorely felt. Dutch and Italian gunners were hired and ordnance was supplied from Imperial stocks managed by John de Hesdin. In addition to this force 200 Cornish miners were recruited. The best news was probably the appointment of Floris van Egmont, the Lord of Ysselstein and Count of Buren and Leerdman, as an ally. He was as staunch a supporter of the English cause as his master was fickle.

Suffolk remained in Calais, delayed by smallpox, desertion and the usual problem of a shortage of transport, especially heavy wagons for munitions. Margaret cooperated as fully as the uncooperative Estates and unenthusiastic population permitted, but the change in objective from Boulogne to Paris seriously wrong-footed her arrangements. Thus, very late in the campaign season as October approached, the English army made its way from Calais, past first Boulogne and Abbeville, then Hesdin and Montreuil. Bray was captured and Roye surrendered. The high point of the campaign was the capture of Montdidier and the surrender of its garrison of 2,000. The expedition was now almost halfway to Paris. At this point Suffolk, who had been waiting for news of Bourbon, learnt that his Landsknechts, commanded by Graf Felix von Werdenberg, had mutinied and that the Duke himself had withdrawn. This of course meant that the fundamental premise upon which the plan depended collapsed. There would be no joint campaign or march on Paris.

Suffolk was intelligent enough to understand the futility of continuing the operation, but was unwilling to act on his own initiative. He referred the future strategy to his irascible brother-in-law, the King. As October became November, Suffolk continued making raids into Santerre and Vermandois and captured Nesle and Bourchain. With his army facing a cold winter without adequate supplies, he ordered a retreat to Valenciennes in Hainault and the security of Imperial territory. Henry, from the warmth and comfort of his court, rejected the possibility of defeat and ordered Suffolk to remain in the field. Unfortunately his army had already begun to disintegrate, seeking passage back to England from Antwerp, Sluys and Nieuport. Suffolk bowed to the inevitable and disbanded what was left of it. When he reached Calais on 15 December he received another of Henry's furious missives denouncing his conduct; fortunately, as his brother-in-law and one of his closest companions Suffolk survived with his neck and reputation intact. The military performance

Irish auxiliaries driving livestock into the English camp at the siege of Boulogne, a detail from the Cowdray engraving. This bare-legged Irish troop together with their bagpiper was a novel addition to the English forces. Although few in number, the men were hardy and well-trained in the practices of raiding and foraging, which were features of all campaigns. (Dr Dominic Fontana, with kind permission)

of the army had not been unimpressive and it had certainly seriously worried the Parisians, but tactical successes could not make up for strategic failure.

The Enterprise of Paris (Boulogne) 1544

The next great strategic plan of Henry and Charles V was not dissimilar to that of 1523. It involved the advance of an Imperial force through Champagne to Soissons and Meaux, combined with an English force advancing through Picardy, rendezvousing on the Marne with a massive army of 80,000 or more before an assault on Paris. Meanwhile in Piedmont, Del Vasto would tie down a strong force of French gendarmes and their invaluable Swiss infantry.

By 7 July when his expedition had already embarked, Henry declared himself secretly in favour of an attack on Boulogne, which he thought worth 'ten Parises'. He might have chosen other more valuable targets such as the defensible port of Étaples which was far superior to Boulogne. Montreuil was of much greater strategic significance as the chief marshalling ground of western Picardy, and its possession would have helped reduce pressure on the permanently beleaguered Calais. Boulogne was chosen as the objective, firstly because of its proximity to the bolthole of Calais, secondly because with a limited budget it was affordable, and thirdly because as a weakly defended town its capture was achievable.

Boulogne was not a very tough nut to crack. The principal defences were medieval with some additions and modernisations to take account of the importance of gunpowder weapons. Its medieval defences had been added to in the early sixteenth century with two new circular bastions and a horseshoe-shaped artillery emplacement or *éperon*. In addition, a *fausse-braye* or low wall and ditch was added to the exterior. It was still not in any sense a state-of-the-art fortification. The French Governor Jacques de Coucy, Sieur de Vervins, had a substantial force of almost 2,000 men of which approximately 800 were Italian arquebusiers. Boulogne had been unsuccessfully besieged by Henry's father in 1492; it was Henry's first thought in the campaigns of 1513 and 1523 and it was one of his demands in 1525 of the Emperor if he took part in a further French campaign. It was now certainly the last opportunity he would have to make this elusive objective his.

The Imperial advance upon which so much depended was meanwhile fatally delayed firstly at Luxemburg and then at St Dizier. The Imperial army, lacking both victuals and the means to purchase them, now engaged on ill-disciplined forays into French territory of no military significance. Henry's tardy appearance on the Continent, his natural conservatism, a shortage of transport, and the failure of his allies, made the capture of Boulogne his obsession.

Land transport, or the lack of it, was the key to his plan. The wagons were to be locally hired from Imperial territory, and despite being rated for 30 or 40 cwt could barely carry a ton. The poor quality of the transport and above all its scarcity was a constant problem for Henry when sustaining his two sieges. The *Kynges battell* included 50 wagons for brewhouses as well as wagons for bakers and cartwrights, the total for victualling alone being

Detail of the English guns at Boulogne taken from the Cowdray engraving. A hot day in the battery. One of the guns has a large wooden barrel with a 'real' barrel superimposed. The other guns all appear to be cast pieces, almost certainly of bronze. Observing the action from the 'royal box' is King Henry, while a company of horse provide his escort. As in so many illustrations there is a dog keeping watch on her human masters. (Dr Dominic Fontana, with kind permission)

724 carriages and 2,328 people. For the fore ward a total of 225 carriages were required for the carriage of artillery and war stores: one carriage carried 300,000 'Horse shewe Nailes', while 16 were required to carry 1,600 sheaves of arrows. The numbers of carriages required for the main ward must have numbered well over 1,000, or one for every 16 men in the force. It was not just the transport of stores but the ability to sustain an army some distance from its main supply base which presented problems. The convoys were inevitably liable to attacks from French cavalry.

The 'English' army numbered in total about 43,000. Of the 31,955 'English', 28,271 were foot and 3,684 horse. The remainder of the army was made up of mercenaries (2,000 mounted men-at-arms, and 8,000 foot including 1,400 Landsknechts). A further 4,000 served as Imperial auxiliaries under Egmont Count von Buren. One unique feature of this English force was the addition of 1,154 Irish Kerne together with 234 boys under the command of Lord Power. Their appearance signified the new loyalty of the Irish to the Crown as well as a desire to bulk up the numbers. The English forces were primarily equipped with bills and bows. Only seven percent were equipped with firearms and 15 percent with pikes. German pikemen, Italian and Spanish arquebusiers, German pistoleers and Burgundian heavy cavalry could fill the obvious gaps in the army's structure. The fore ward was commanded by the Duke of Norfolk, the rear by Lord Russell, both commanded about 13,000 men. The van and rearguards were made up of men provided by county landowners in the traditional semi-feudal manner, the main battle was assembled from the military resources of the Crown and his court. The recruitment of the army created organisational problems. The ideal would have been companies

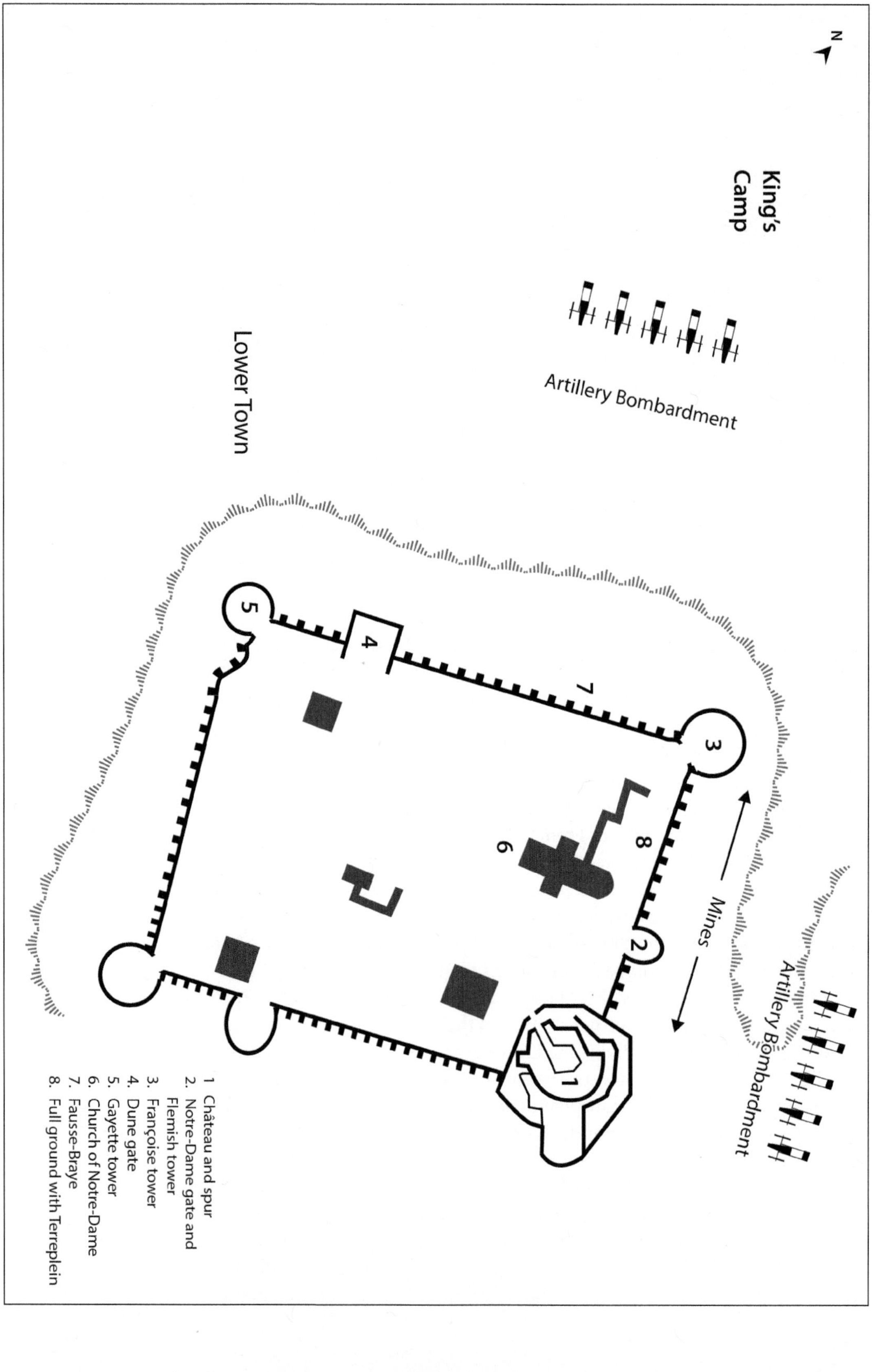

N

King's
Camp

Artillery Bombardment

Lower Town

The Siege of Boulogne

5

4

7

3

6

8

Mines

2

Artillery Bombardment

1

1 Château and spur
2. Notre-Dame gate and
   Flemish tower
3. Françoise tower
4. Dune gate
5. Gayette tower
6. Church of Notre-Dame
7. Fausse-Braye
8. Full ground with Terreplein

of horse and foot organised on the same basis as suggested by Audley. In practice there was great difference between what the magnates in the Privy Council could provide organised in companies of 100 men each, and the military resources offered by the gentlemen of Shropshire.

The siege of Boulogne demanded an additional tactical ploy or diversion. This was the investment of Montreuil, which was a means of drawing off the French field forces from interfering with the siege of Boulogne. Norfolk faced many problems, uncertain initially as to the strategic objective of the campaign and fearful because of the dangers to his extended supply lines;even so the siege of Montreuil, although arguably necessary, was badly handled. The city was not even properly encircled by an army that included the 26,000 men of Norfolk's and Russell's van and rearguard, as well as most of the mercenary and auxiliary troops. Marshal de Biez garrisoned Montreuil with a force of 7,000, making it almost impregnable, even if a serious siege had been prosecuted. The Count of Vendôme with 500 lances and 10,000 foot provided an additional field force ready to threaten the besieging forces, their lines of communication and the Calais Pale. Audley would have applauded this French strategy: he preferred 'witti skirmyshs' to dangerous main engagements for as he declared, 'the honor remaineth to him that driveth awaie the ennemyes',[9] this was clearly the French policy. Elis ap Gruffydd, the sagacious and thoughtful old soldier, recognised the true nature of this sham siege:

> To return to the camps that were laying a half siege to Montreuil for indeed sixty thousand fighting men were not enough to keep it so diligently that no one could either go out from inside to the country or come in from the country to the town, and no such diligence was shown during this siege, during which if the truth be told, there was no effort to perform one praiseworthy deed.[10]

The two commanders fell out, as Lord Russell was frustrated by the lack of serious progress made by the Duke of Norfolk. Their rivalry had blighted the siege from the start with childish bickering between them, for example who was to fire the first shot. The French commander treated the Duke of Norfolk with contempt, pointing to the futility of his task:

> let it be known to him that I will keep this town as well as I kept the castle of Hesdin against him. Therefore he can take his pleasure in hunting with hawks and hounds about the country while the weather is fine and mild and by winter, according to the old English custom, you will go home to your kinsmen.[11]

At Boulogne, a reconnaissance was made on 18 July and the town formally invested on the 19th. The Lower Town with its single inadequate wall was

---

9   Thomas Audley, 'A Treatise on the Art of War', *Journal of the Society for Army Historical Research*, vol. 6, no. 24 (April–June,1927), p.77.

10 Jonathan Davies (text transcribed by M. Bryn Davies), *Elis Gruffydd and the 1544 'Enterprises' of Paris and Boulogne* (Sunderland: Pike and Shot Society, 2006), p.20.

11 Hammer, *Elizabeth's Wars*, p.20.

captured on the 21st with little loss, although the French tried to fire it, but the Higher Town proved a much harder nut to crack. The old 12-storied Roman lighthouse, or pharos, referred to as 'the Old Man', was captured on the 22nd. The 15-strong garrison surrendered as soon as artillery was brought up, and it was garrisoned by the Duke of Suffolk with two demi-culverins and four sakers. The siege was to be won with firepower rather than taken by storm, in a demonstration of Tudor 'shock and awe', as the order was given:

> To make mountes in places without to shote from in to the town and, the housing standing thick and nere unto the walles, to bear them down and the shoote over in to the towne and with contynuall shot of his ordynance and of his mortars, the town being very little within to mak any succour or defence against the same to make … terrible frayes unto them and with the terror and trouble therof so to astonne [astonish] and torment them that they shuld be fayn to fall to composition.[12]

Henry had arrived in Calais on 15 July, three weeks after the arrival of the Duke of Norfolk and the vanguard, which had by then departed to besiege Montreuil. Henry still did not leave Calais until the 25th, arriving before

---

12 Potter, *Henry VIII and Francis I*, p.185; Paget to Suffolk, Gravesend, 12 July 1544, The National Archives (TNA) SP 1/190, ff.23–24 (289) (*Letters and Papers*, XIX, i, 903).

Above: The English battery at the siege of Boulogne referred to as the Monte. Detail from the Cowdray engraving. At Boulogne the full force of England's artillery was to be directed at what was a rather miserable and mostly medieval town. The bombardment was certainly impressive and the preparations were monumental, as suggested by this detail from the engraving. Vast quantities of powder and shot had to be transported, magazines for the storing of powder built and even the earth for the 'Monte' had to excavated and moved from elsewhere. Masons can be seen finishing stone balls for the cannon perriers and bombards. Unlike iron projectiles these could not be recovered but were inevitably smashed to pieces on impact. In addition to the war stores were the myriad items needed by the ordnance, from wheelbarrows to buckets, scythes, sickles, paper, parchment and packneedles. (Dr Dominic Fontana, with kind permission)

Overleaf: Field armour of King Henry VIII of England c.1544, Italian, from Milan or Brescia. This is probably the armour that Henry VIII wore in the French campaign of 1544. Of Italian origin it was possibly supplied by the Milanese merchant known in England as Francis Albert. It was made for Henry when his obesity and gout had made personal conflict with anyone other than his remaining wives impossible. The breast and back plates were made from overlapping plates made flexible with rivets and leather straps. The decoration is in the grotesque style, one which suited the owner as well as the armour. Weight 50 lb 8 oz (22.91 kg). (Metropolitan Museum of Art, Open Access)

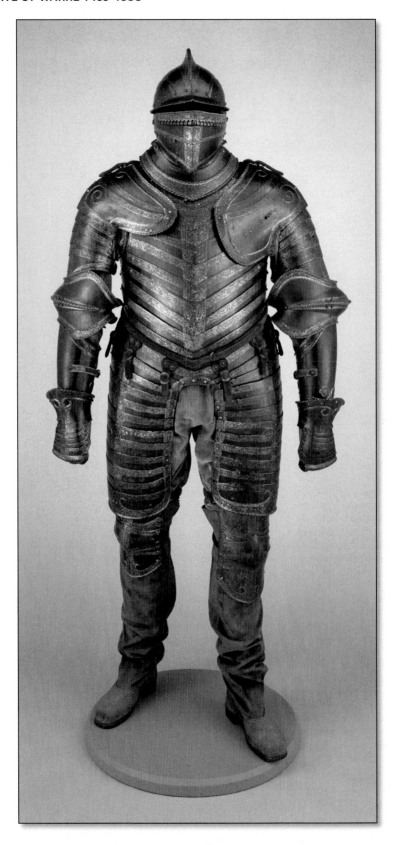

Boulogne at the camp at Marquison on the 26th. The first day of August was a night of heavy rain and thunder and there was much disarray within the camp, as illustrated in the Cowdray engraving, with several of the tents and halls being blown down. The weather throughout the campaign was noticeably foul, wet, windy and cold, causing heavy casualties amongst the besiegers.

The siege proper did not begin until the 27th after the arrival of the King, and the serious bombardment only opened on 3 August. While there was substantial damage to the town proper, there was little progress in the slow advance of the trenches towards the town walls. The English siege lines can be seen in the engraving snaking towards the High Town, barely shoulder deep and lacking the sophistication of later sieges. The ground was hard and the soil nine feet deep at the most. The first great obstacle was the *Fausse Braye* or wall and ditch placed before the remainder of the medieval defences. Audley with his usual conservative approach saw the trenches as defences against an enemy sortie rather than a form of attack. Fortunately the small French garrison concentrated on defending itself behind its stout medieval walls, sallying forth only once, on the day before the siege began.

To fully exploit the large artillery train an artificial mound called the *Monte* was constructed, which enabled gunfire to be directed into the town. Firing commenced on 3 August, the collection of enough earth having proved very difficult on such hard and thin soil. *Letters and Papers* records only three main batteries: those of the Lord Lieutenant, the Master of Ordnance and the Lord Admiral. That of the Lord Admiral consisted of three cannons, three demi-cannons, three culverins, two demi-culverins and three sakers crewed by 500 pioneers. One could assume that the battery placed in front of the *Monte* and carefully sited behind gabions also employed some of the Lord Admiral's guns. One man, presumably a pioneer, can be seen in the engraving pushing an empty wheelbarrow which was probably used for the carriage of shot as were the three 'little cartes with iii wheeles apece to carry shott',[13] to be found with each artillery train.

The demand for powder and shot was immense: it was calculated that 100,000 shot were expended in the siege in total. In the artillery train each cannon was provided with 360 rounds, requiring 12 carriages for powder and 21 for shot, and similar provision was made for the other pieces. To the right of the King in the Cowdray engraving can be seen the most substantial battery of artillery with 14 pieces and two dummy guns made of wood with two smaller barrels lashed above to provide smoke and flame. Why two such 'weapons' were necessary is not clear, although there are references to them in the Tower in 1547 which suggests that they were considered of some [perhaps novelty] value. Henry's siege train consisted of 10 cannons, 11 demi-cannons, 21 culverins, 14 demi-culverins, 20 sakers, 13 falcons, five bombards, a canon perryer and 50 mortars. The mortars fired explosive shells, used for the first time by the English. These were invented by two foreign gunmakers in royal service, Peter Baude and Peter of Cologne. Ironically the Frenchman Bernardine de Valois commanded the mortar battery of the Duke of Suffolk.

---

13 *Letters and Papers*, vol. 19, part 1, March 1544, R.O.13.

There is surprisingly little evidence of barrel cooling, commonly employing sheepskins soaked in brine or vinegar, which was essential to maintain the life of the pieces. Estimates for powder and shot expenditure were calculated based on a conservative 20 shots a day, while the maximum number referred to is 35. Twenty shots per day would still produce an impressive bombardment of over 1,000 rounds, excluding the mortar fire.

Whilst the smaller portion of the army could be sustained from Calais, most of the force besieging Montreuil had to be supported from Flanders, which was Imperial territory, with St Omer some 40 miles away, as the main supply and distribution base. The route from St Omer would be under threat from the French garrison of Thérouanne which posed a major threat to the line of supply. If the port of Étaples at the mouth of the River Canches and only some half a dozen miles away had been used to supply Montreuil, then the problem of supporting the siege would have been solved. Ellis recorded the arguments and the outcome surrounding this proposal:

> traffickers in food made a great suit … to get the King's command for one or two of the ships to raise anchor and put to sea from Beauvais in safety from the French until they entered the river of Étaples, so that they could supply the shortage and want among the soldiers before Montreuil, where there was great need. To these [they] replied 'If you wish to venture your bodies and your wealth … sail under God's protection because in truth I shall not open my mouth to order one of the ships to weigh anchor to go to guard you from here to Étaples, because I know that in the camp before Montreuil there is more victual than they can use while it is good.'[14]

At Boulogne the key defence, the *Fausse Braye,* was only captured on 1 September. This was followed by an unsuccessful assault on the walls the day after. Cornish and Devonshire miners who had been withdrawn from the siege of Montreuil dug two mines, which were exploded on the 4th and 11th, one killing Jerome de Trevisi the unfortunate (probable) artist of the sketches upon which the Cowdray engravings were based. Although the mining was not decisive it was clear that the end was near for the defenders.

The governor, short of powder but not of supplies, having experienced a bombardment of up to 140,000 shots and shells and facing certain defeat, negotiated surrender on 13 October. The mayor and corporation were opposed, an event graphically portrayed in a magnificent oil painting in the present *Mairie.* The garrison and those townspeople able and willing to leave did so, under arms and carrying whatever property they could. Henry entered the ruinous town on the 18th, at which point his part in these events had almost come to an end. Jacques de Coucy had held out for eight weeks, two more than his master King Francis had required, but his surrender and obeisance to Henry, added to the complaints of the mayor, led to his later trial and beheading. Less public were the heavy losses amongst the unfortunate citizens who succumbed to the wet and cold in their march to 'safety'.

---

14 Davies, *Enterprises*, p.24.

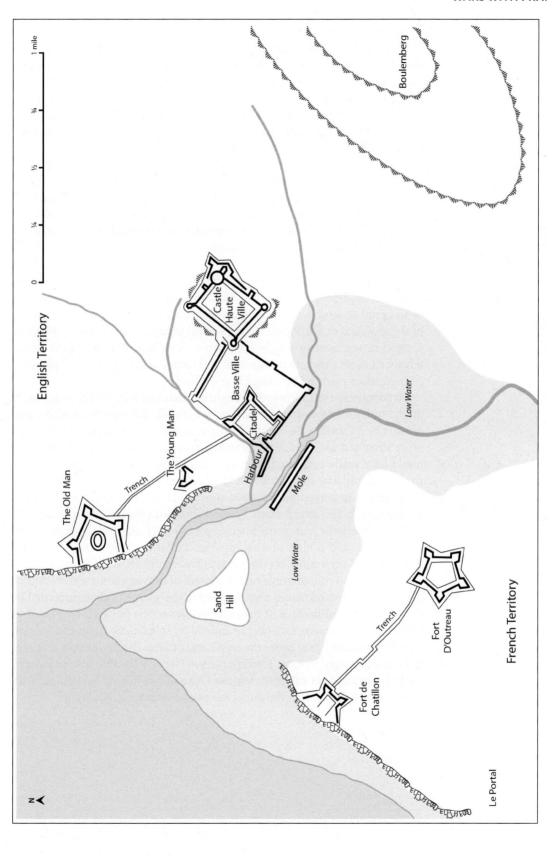

Map of Boulogne in English Hands. (© J.R. Hale, 1983, Renaissance War Studies, Hale fig. 19. Hambledon Continuum, used by permission of Bloomsbury Publishing PLC)

At almost the same time that Boulogne fell, the Emperor signed the Peace of Crépy with Francis. Henry had been aware of the negotiations and had also entered discussions concerning the possible return to the status quo ante, with some suitable sweeteners. The collapse of the alliance between Henry and the Emperor led to the urgent necessity of withdrawing the forces around Montreuil. Francis made it clear that he now had an opportunity to see off the English after the rapprochement with the Emperor had been concluded:

> Considering that the English might make some difficulty over the conditions of peace and that in this case I am determined to succour my towns of Boulogne and Montreuil, I inform you that I write presently to my son the Dauphin to march straight to Montreuil with my army … for my army is easily sufficient to dislodge the English and give them a drubbing.[15]

The commander of the Imperial auxiliary troops, Maximilian Van Buren, continued to deploy his men with Henry's, against both the spirit and letter of Imperial orders, until the English forces were in the comparative safety of the environs of Boulogne. Henry, fearful of the French advance, planned a rapid retreat first to Calais and then to England. The Dauphin's forces advanced more slowly than expected and Henry was able to leave France on 30 September escorted by a large English fleet.

At Montreuil the shortage of draught animals had led to the abandonment of quantities of stores and the sick and wounded, although the artillery was saved. On 3 October the mutinous mercenaries and the exhausted English army streamed back to Calais for evacuation or repatriation. This situation might have easily been predicted, as it was by the Flemings, who knew that the end of Imperial support would fatally compromise the English forces.

Contrary to contemporary good practice concerning order and security on the march, the retreat from Montreuil lacked either a covering force to protect its flanks or rear or any internal cohesion. Plague and dysentery allied to the wettest and coldest weather experienced for many years took its toll on the men, and even more on the poor draught animals and the cavalry. The retreat became a contemptible rout as a result of incompetence and cowardice. The complete breakdown in discipline led to the shameful chaos recorded by Gruffydd. The indifference of the commanders to the fate of their men is to be found in numerous instances of individual selfishness. Boulogne was left with a garrison of 3,300 under the command of John Dudley, but the defences remained in a ruinous state. The departure of Henry VIII, after his safe passage could be ensured on the 30th, left the Duke of Norfolk as his lieutenant in France with John Dudley Viscount Lisle as commander in Boulogne.

---

15 Potter, *Henry VIII and Francis I*, p.199; Francis I to Vendôme, 17 Sept. 1544, BnF, fr. 20521, f.75.

The Camisade of Boulogne

The Dauphin appeared with an army of 30,000 (rumoured to be 50,000) just as Henry and the English army were departing. On 6 October Monsieur de Taix with Blaise de Monluc reconnoitered the scene outside Boulogne, finding pavilions and even the artillery in place and provided with only a weak guard. On the 9th, 23 French and Italian companies, supported by 6,000 Swiss, launched a night assault or camisade (so named because the attackers would don a white shirt or *camise* to aid identification). Blaise de Monluc vividly describes the assault, which overwhelmed the unprepared pioneer companies in the Lower Town, killing some 200 as they were unarmed. They were wearing red and white and black and yellow liveries according to Monluc. We also discover the English war cry from this source: it was 'Quil, quil, quil!'

In the Italian companies, discipline collapsed after their easy entrance and 'victory': the rumour that the breaches through which they had entered were recaptured caused a panic and retreat. This allowed the English, led by Sir Thomas Poynings, to rally the English forces in the Upper Town and eject the invaders with considerable loss. The inactivity of the Swiss infantry when their intervention might have turned the tide of battle was remarked upon with disgust, and noone came out of the engagement with credit. In the French camp it ended in mutual recriminations among the captains who took part, as well as the blaming of the rest of the force which had failed to come to their aid. De Taix was free of blame as he was wounded with an arrow early on, and Blaise de Monluc played his usual heroic role, being (he claimed) the last captain to leave the lower city. The total failure of the English forces to maintain their watch and ward would have horrified Audley, who carefully detailed all the necessary security precautions that an army should take. As Gruffydd records rather sardonically:

> Well, this was a wonderful day because I did not hear either the French or the men of England make any boast of their victory and indeed each of the two parties lost many people, the Dauphin many of his cockerels and the King of England many of his sheep. Indeed had not the ways of God been greater than the works of men, the French would not have left one man of them alive, but the wetness of the night and the darkness saved the life of many an Englishman though I did not hear many giving thanks to God.[16]

The Dauphin himself was disappointed by this failure, declaring 'that the English had made capons of his gentlemen cocks and that it would be futile to send the chickens in their place'.[17]

The war in France continued with 'wittie' and 'vaine skirmyshs', involving an increasing number of mercenaries on the English side. Boulogne was invested and both sides, following the pattern of the *trace italienne*, threw

---

16 Davies, *Enterprises*, pp.39–40.
17 Hammer, *Elizabeth's Wars*, pp.19–20.

up 'modern' earthworks. The French fortress was carelessly sited beyond effective artillery range of Boulogne. The Italian architect paced out its dimensions incorrectly and produced a ridiculously small fortification, meant for 5,000 but accommodating only 500. Military incompetence or a reliance on unreliable mercenaries were not solely English characteristics.

For approximately £1,000,000, four times the original expected cost, an indefensible port had been captured which would prove a continual additional strain on the national purse and which would in any case be given back by negotiation in 1550, for the sum of 400,000 crowns. The siege of Montreuil was an especially worthless project, for as Ellis sagely noted:

> the King, indeed, could have placed the host against the town of Ardres or some such place where they would have done better service, for indeed they could not have done any less service there than they did and could have done within forty days of their arrival, namely to plunder the country and take the town by assault which, had it been done the first week or the first fortnight could have been achieved with less loss than those who died or were killed around it from all causes. But the King did not intend to capture Montreuil but only set them to lie there so that he and his host might take their ease and sleep more easily in their beds in the camp round Boulogne.[18]

It is easy to see how the minutiae of the military preparations to be found in the royal record could seduce the reader into thinking that the planning and preparation was of a 'modern' standard. There is evidence that the siege conducted outside Boulogne was well supplied; in the presence of the King the greatest efforts would be made to ensure the continuation of military operations, but outside Montreuil, where most of the army was to be found, the situation was much more hand to mouth! Individual acquisitiveness and greed were to be found amongst both officers and men as the system of supply broke down. Nothing could excuse the lack of camp discipline that led to the presence of dead beasts and offal poisoning both air and water and causing disease. Such a danger was widely understood; the failure of the master of the camp to control such indiscipline is yet another example of official failure. The only comment that could be made in defence of the English system of supply is that the French did even worse, operating over an already devastated countryside with an even longer and more difficult line of communication:

> On this march along the road from Marquise to Tavarn there were many dead bodies on the field, and if one can believe the people from Flanders who were following the French host with victuals, their bodies were lying on the face of the earth on the roads and at the edge of the roads throughout the country everywhere from the land of Picardy from Calais to Montreuil and from there to Abbeville without anybody taking the trouble to bury a single one.[19]

---

18 Davies, *Enterprises*, pp.26–27.
19 Davies, *Enterprises*, p.40.

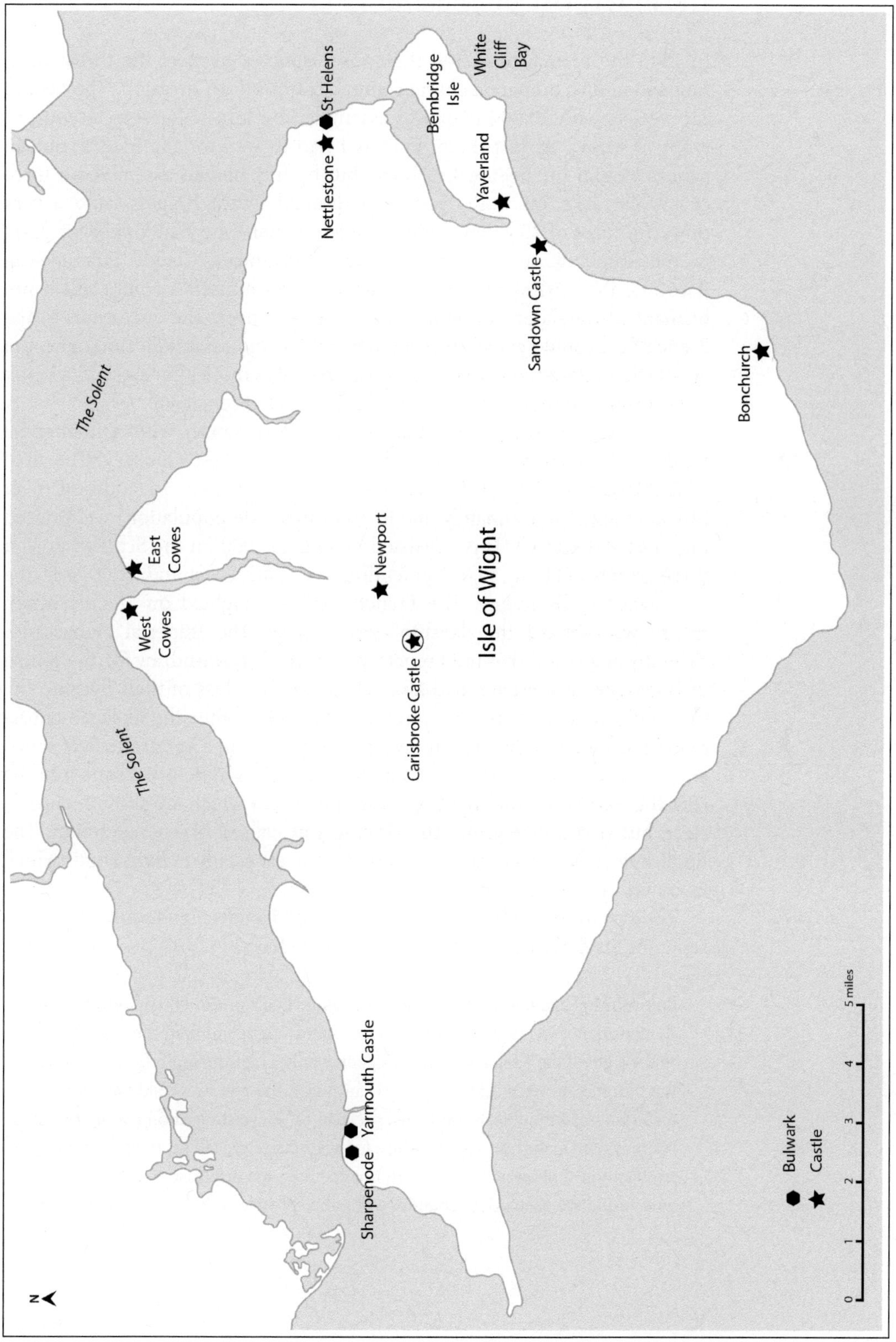

The Isle of Wight 1545

Isle of Wight

The Solent

The Solent

St Helens

Nettlestone

Bembridge Isle

White Cliff Bay

Yaverland

Sandown Castle

Bonchurch

East Cowes

West Cowes

Newport

Carisbroke Castle

Sharpenode

Yarmouth Castle

Bulwark

Castle

N

0 1 2 3 4 5 miles

The Enterprise of England 1545

In 1545 the French mustered their full resources to meet the threat from England and to prepare a counter-attack, a full-blown invasion. The fleet of 235 vessels with 30,000 men was assembled by July 1545, despite two pre-emptive strikes against them. Francis I had to wait for the Mediterranean galleys to join the fleet at Le Havre, but by July he had assembled a force of 150 carracks, 60 'fluits' – shallow-draught Dutch barges – and a very powerful force of 25 galleys, commanded by men who had fought for years in the desperate sea battles of the Mediterranean. Claude D'Annebault, Baron de Retz Admiral of France, who proved himself a competent if not brilliant commander, commanded this massive fleet. The operations of the French fleet could have been combined with a land assault on Boulogne, but an attack on Portsmouth and the south coast was more alluring, and a better opportunity for repaying Henry for his insults to French soil.

Sixty English ships were assembled at Portsmouth with a further 40 rendezvousing there from the Thames and the West Country. The final assemblage would total 104 vessels with 13,500 men. In addition, over 140,000 men (approximately one in 10 of the male population) were raised for landward service. This consisted of some 30,000 on the Scottish border, three armies of about 30,000 defending the south coast and 22,000 serving in Calais and Boulogne. The French fleet was sighted on 18 July, when Henry was aboard the flagship *Great Harry*. The Imperial ambassador helpfully suggested that the French would willingly withdraw for the return of Boulogne. The French had already suffered the loss of their flagship the *Carraquon* to a fire caused by careless royal cooks, while the replacement *La Maistresse* had been badly damaged by grounding on a bar as the fleet sailed and was run on to the shoals beside the Isle of Wight before it sank. On the 19th the *Mary Rose* was lost under circumstances which are still not entirely clear, but it is unlikely that the sinking was caused by enemy action. The English fleet were very wary of venturing out, especially in light winds which favoured the powerful force of French galleys.

The ever-resourceful D'Annebault proposed a new plan to force Henry to send out his fleet, as explained fully by Du Bellay:

Our Admiral had news that the King of England had come to Portsmouth, and he thought that if we made a landing on the isle of Wight and fired the countryside in the sight of the King and killed his people only a handsbreadth from him then the indignation he would feel at such an insult, the pity he would have for the wounding of his subjects, and the spectacle of the wasting and burning of his realm, would make him send his ships to the rescue, especially as they were barely two cannon shot away. But if he did not act, then the displeasure of his subjects, who would see themselves abandoned by their Prince, although he was present, might produce sedition and mutiny. The Admiral ordered the invasion to take place in three different areas simultaneously, so as to divide the enemy's forces.[20]

The plan, although in principle attractive, showed remarkably little understanding of the real character of Henry.

The Isle of Wight had some 50 men garrisoned in forts, 234 more working on new defences and a militia force on the Isle itself which numbered some 1,500. The French plan was initiated on the 21st with a landing at Bonchurch and St Helens where the attackers burnt a small port and captured a fort that had been engaged in firing on the French galleys. At Sandown the French landing was repelled with the loss of both captains Pierrebon and Marsay. The third attack was clearly the largest, and directed towards capturing Newport. Led by Seigneur De Taix, the colonel general of the infantry, and the commander of all the galleys the Baron de la Garde, they landed without hindrance until ambushed by archers who wounded their leader Tristan de Moneins. The French force rallied and the militia withdrew to Bonchurch. One casualty reported by Oglander, a militia officer, was Captain Fischer of the Hampshire militia: 'being a fat gentleman and not able to make his retreat up the hill (for they put our men to rout), cried out "£100 for a horse"; but in that confusion no horse could be gotten for a kingdom.'[21] No trace was later found of the poor man.

Oglander recorded Henry's order to his forces: 'Our King sent word to us that we should retreat in order, seeking to draw all their strength ashore far from their ships, hoping for a favourable opportunity to surprise their fleet.'[22] Henry did not send out his fleet but deployed militia reinforcements, including 2,700 men from Hampshire and a further 900 from Wiltshire, all under the command of Edward Bellingham. The French plan to force Henry's fleet to come out and fight had turned into Henry's plan to place the French at a disadvantage by forcing their galleys to ride offshore, in support of an army that was now bogged down in vicious and indecisive fighting.

The system of beacons established earlier provided a simple but effective form of communication between the widely dispersed English forces. The initial French force set about burning Yaverland on Bembridge and Bonchurch, while the remainder stayed on board. The sight of their comrades burning and looting was too much for some of these and they disembarked in disorder and landed, probably on Whitecliff Bay. The local militia, using their wagon horses as extemporaneous cavalry, now attacked the surprised and disorganised French raiding party. The result as reported at the time was decisive: 'We killed many, took many prisoners and drove the rest down as far as the ships, killing all the way.'[23] The French now counter-attacked but the militia conducted a fighting retreat, drawing the French further on. D'Annebault now tried to restore the chaos by ordering De Taix to Bembridge

20 Percy G. Stone, 'The French Descent on the Isle of Wight, July, 1545', in *The Antiquary*, Oct 1908, 4, 10; ProQuest, p.370.
21 Stone, 'The French Descent', p.426.
22 Stone, 'The French Descent', p.427.
23 Stone, 'The French Descent', p.426.

The castles of Calais and Newnham Bridge, a detail from the Cowdray engraving. Although there had been an attempt to update the defences of the Calais Pale, the castle of Calais was still a medieval structure. Newnham bridge, although modernised, was abandoned in haste, leading to the calamitous capture of Calais Castle. (Dr Dominic Fontana, with kind permission)

to bring some order to the forces on the ground and re-embark them.

The French galleys were now in some danger, as they could not abandon the forces that had been landed or hope to fight the English with their depleted crews. The strong winds blowing south-westerly on the 20th would have made it impossible for the galleys to return to shore. Lord Lisle's shipmasters declared that, 'If we come under sail towards them they must loose anchor … and once loosed, they could not … fetch the Wight again and would have much ado to escape the Owers [Bank].'[24] Fortunately for the French the wind had died down by the 21st but they still faced a worsening situation. Their land forces were increasingly bogged down on the Isle of Wight and the English were not to be drawn out of their anchorage. There was a proposal to sail into Portsmouth, but the pessimistic French shipmasters considered that at most four warships abreast could enter Portsmouth. The soldiers challenged their naval counterparts and insisted on sending an army captain in each of the pilot's boats sent to reconnoitre the entrance. The depressing result was that the pilots now considered that only one ship at a time could enter Portsmouth safely, and then only if wind and tide were favourable.

Henry had shown himself willing to turn the Isle of Wight into a sixteenth-century Gallipoli, where the French forces would become the besiegers rather than the aggressors. He had reinforced the Isle again and again and it now had a garrison of some 8,000 men. The French considered the possibility of establishing their own base on the Isle. To hold the Bembridge Isle, which was connected to the rest of the Island by a thin spit of land, they calculated that they would need to build three forts to protect it and the St Helen's anchorage. This would take a force of 6,000 pioneers some six months, with the necessary protection of a similar number of infantry. This would all have to be completed as the weather worsened, and no doubt under continuous attack from land and sea. The only sensible option for the French was to conduct an evacuation, always a difficult task when closely engaged with a determined opponent. During this process the unfortunate galley commander Pierre de Blacas was killed when trying to stop the retreat becoming a rout: first he was shot in the knee by an arrow, then had his brains dashed out with a brown bill wielded by

---

24 David Childs, *The Warship Mary Rose: The Life and Times of King Henry VII's Flagship.* (Havertown: Seaforth Publishing, 2014), p.170.

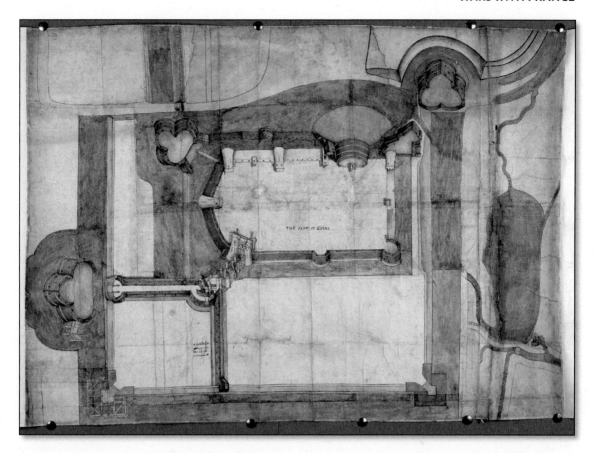

A map of Guînes castle. Only the motte of the castle survives today but this map shows a strong, recently and impressively modernised fortification. The extensive use of moats was feasible in such low-lying countryside and was fully exploited. The rectangular medieval castle with its round stone towers has been extensively extended. New circular cloverleaf gun towers built in brick, redolent of the Device forts, can be seen extending and deepening the defences and in the latest style two new angled bastions have been further added. In 1547 it was recorded that some 156 artillery pieces (mostly of small calibre) were mounted on the bulwarks, towers and walls. There were large stocks of incendiary material stored, as well as 116 arquebuses, 462 bows and 27,600 arrows. (Courtesy of the British Library. BL Cotton Augustus I.ii.52)

'some country fellow'.[25] The commander's armour was especially fine and was sent to Henry as a war trophy. It did not all go one way, and Leone Strozzi the Prior of Capua of the Order of St John (and brother of Piero) put up a stout resistance at the evacuation, killing some 30 of the militia. By 24 July, after less than a week, all the French strategies had failed and the fleet departed. It had suffered serious losses on land and a humiliating moral defeat at sea.

The losses on the Isle of Wight amongst the militia had been heavy. Oglander reported that 'there was not any family of account on the Island but lost a father, brother or uncle. Ower family lost two younger gentlemen, Hugh George and Richard Oglander.'[26] Their deaths had achieved Henry's objective,

25   Stone, 'The French Descent', p.426.
26   Percy G. Stone, 'The French Descent on the Isle of Wight, July 1545' (French Account), in *The Antiquary*, Oct 1908, p.428.

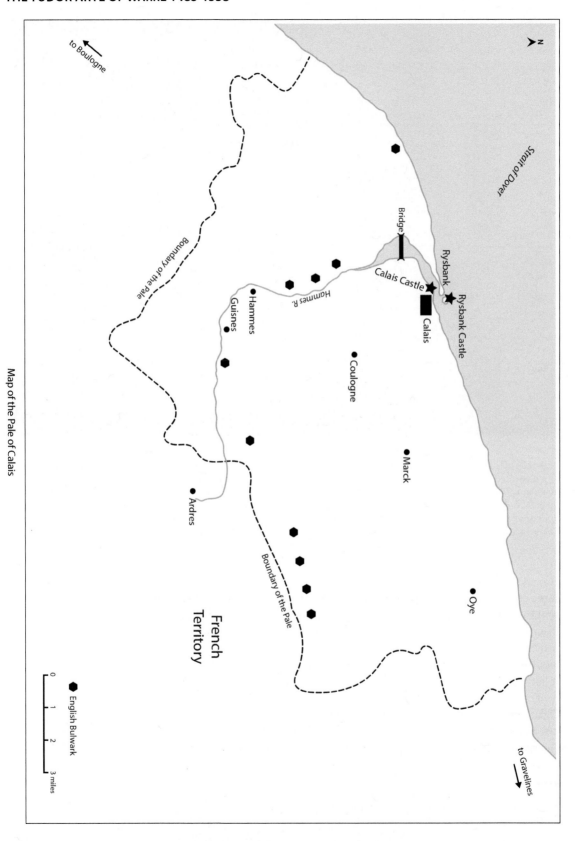

Map of the Pale of Calais

but whether he showed much pity for the wounding of his subjects, or the spectacle of the wasting and burning of his realm is doubtful. The performance of the militia, fighting in the most difficult circumstances, seems to have been exemplary; what was also noted was the effectiveness of archery, especially when in ambush or skirmish.

The Loss of Calais 1558

The loss of Calais in 1558 was as unthinkable as the fall of Singapore would be in 1942. Calais had been an English possession since its capture by Edward III in 1347. It was fully integrated into the kingdom in 1372 when it became a parliamentary borough. As a staple town it became the principal port for the English wool trade, which was itself the source of much of the wealth of the kingdom and the Crown. Although by the middle of the sixteenth century it had ceased to have the same economic importance it once had, it was still strategically central to the plans of successive monarchs, especially Henry VIII. Calais and the Pale were well defended. The walled town of Calais was rectangular in shape, oriented east to west, with the castle in the north-west corner. To the west was Newnham Bridge and to the south was Hammes Castle and then Guînes Castle. Between Hammes and Guînes were six bulwarks, in two lines of three, stretching east and west. To the east was Imperial territory and to the south and west was France. The constant rebuilding and improvement of fortifications meant that Calais and its defences were seen as impregnable and there had been no serious attempt at reconquest since 1463.

The French had been defeated decisively at the Battle of St Quentin in 1557. The English army had been disbanded giving an indication of the negligible threat perceived from France. The campaign season was over and a cold winter was now fast approaching, making further military action unlikely. The French were still determined to recover Calais. Sénarpont, the governor of Boulogne, had visited Calais incognito and assessed the strength of the defences during the short period of peace, and suggested an attempted attack, but this plan was initially put to one side. It was Henri II, who had already managed the return of Boulogne, and the Duke de Guise who were to achieve this task. The operation was a masterpiece of military deception. Guise first sent a force to the Meuse and the Ardennes, to convince the Spanish that further operations would take place there. He assembled the French fleet at Boulogne and moved troops in small numbers to Abbeville and Ardres, where an army of 25,000 had been assembled by 1 January, without apparently arousing any concerns with the English until it was too late. Piero Strozzi, the Italian mercenary colonel who had so incommoded the English in Scotland, had conducted a detailed reconnaissance of the Pale on 11 December and recognised how ill-prepared the English were.

The Governor Lord Wentworth disposed of some 500 men in Calais while the garrison of all the three main forts and the bulwarks totalled about 1,000, a fraction of what would be required to man them fully. In 1543 the garrison had numbered 4,000 men but it had been reduced by sickness as well as the need to economise. The hard frost and freezing weather discouraged the aggressive reconnaissance that could have discovered the French intent. Wentworth notified the Council of French troop and naval movements but he had no idea of either the scale, the timetable or the real purpose of the French deployments.

Guise advanced along the Boulogne road and prepared a battery to bombard the castle at Newnham Bridge, the first shot of which decapitated the gunner, one Master Horseley. On 3 January Wentworth, in the face of what was a serious attack, withdrew the garrison of 100 men to reinforce Calais itself. This was a disastrous mistake, as it gave him less time to receive reinforcements and prepare for the inevitable assault. Fort Risbank was also abandoned by its captain and garrison for similar reasons. What was worse was that the speed of the attack, or rather retreat, gave the English no time to open the dykes that would have flooded the landscape, making movement impossible. If the outlying forts had not been abandoned and the ground flooded then Calais might have stood a chance of reinforcement; as it was, the rapid retreat, although understandable as a means of consolidating the small garrison, merely aided the enemy.

On the same day as Newnham was invested a French column advanced between Calais and Guînes, thereby cutting it off, while a third force advanced along Calais Sands commanded by Piero Strozzi. With its wall battered when the sea ditch which protected it was passable, Newnham was assaulted by the French at low tide. Calais was now isolated from its outlying forts and external help.

Guise now established two batteries: one on the dunes made up of five double cannons and three culverins, to bombard the north wall of Calais town by the Water Gate, and a second larger battery of 15 double cannons to bombard the castle. The objective was to divert the garrison into preparing for an attack from the north, whereas the real attack would take the castle. The castle, although an impressive medieval structure, had received little in the way of modernisation and after only two days of constant bombardment was ready for assault. Low tide was again chosen as the time to attack, and although English preparations had been made for the use of incendiary weapons to incinerate the enemy, they failed abysmally to ignite. With the French in the castle two counter-attacks were launched and failed, with considerable loss, including the death of Sir Anthony Agar the Marshal of Calais. Wentworth had no options left and surrendered the town and castle on 6 August. On the 8th a small English fleet with a few reinforcements arrived offshore and recognised that all was lost; the French flag now flew over Calais. Wentworth was allowed to march out, with drums beating and flags flying. He was accompanied by some 4,200 Calaisiennes who were deprived of all their property except for that valued at a groat (4d) an indication of the rancour felt by Henri II for the English.

The French then turned on the castle at Guînes, which had a garrison of 1,300 men having been reinforced from Gravelines by a Spanish company of arquebusiers under Mondragon and by some Burgundians. On the 21st, after eight days of bombardment, Lord Grey surrendered, his defences in ruins. He had little choice, as his men had threatened to throw him over the battered walls of his own castle if he did not surrender. Thomas Churchyard, a poor poet and something of a soldier of misfortune, was threatened with having his throat cut by the garrison if he did not surrender; he was then thrust out of the walls where he was rudely handled by the Almains. He went on to explain the logic that lay behind the surrender. There was no hope of relief and the castle was already partly occupied by the enemy, the garrison was weakened and the casualties were the 'chiefest' soldiers. He should of course have added that the decision was made for the commander by his own men, who perhaps had a greater tactical grasp of the situation and an appreciation of the likely outcome for them if the fort was taken by storm.

Guise accepted the surrender and allowed the garrison to leave, except for Grey and his son and officers, and the castle was destroyed. Hammes remained as the sole fortification in English hands, but not for long. Its commander abandoned the castle, spiked the guns and fled with his men to Gravelines. Thus, Calais and the English Pale were lost with barely a bang and much whimpering. It could be argued that it was no great loss economically and that it meant that no more foolish foreign endeavours could be so readily undertaken. This was not how it was felt in England. Henry Machyn, a London undertaker, declared the news of the loss of Calais as 'the hevest tydyngs to London and to England that ever was hard [heard] of'.[27] Its loss was a national humiliation and Mary herself felt it to be so personally.

---

27 Hammer, *Elizabeth's Wars*, p.50.

5

Conflict with Scotland

The Battle of Flodden

The Flower of Scotland's nobility, including their heroic monarch James IV, died on Flodden Field and the memory of that slaughter still colours relations between the two nations. In many respects the battle is a fascinating example of the old coming into conflict with the new, with the Scottish army drilled and equipped with the latest weapons and the English force a traditional Northern army, equipped with bills and bows. It is also a fascinating study in the psychology of the two leaders and the two armies.

The Political Background

James IV was married to Margaret Henry VIII's sister, the marriage designed to ensure the security of the English realm from interference by Scotland. Scotland was still tied to the 'auld alliance' with France, as they shared a common enemy, England, and this was clearly the source of much potential domestic strife. James was a Renaissance sovereign in the far north, able to look at European models for his court and his country. He had come to the throne in 1488 at the age of 15 in difficult circumstances. He had succeeded in enforcing his authority throughout the kingdom after a campaign in the Highlands and Islands from 1503–5, where his use of artillery in reducing clan strongholds was notable. He was a mature and capable political and military leader, determined to stamp his authority on the kingdom and preserve its independence in the face of a more prosperous and powerful southern monarchy.

Pedro de Aloya in 1498 described James IV thus:

The King is 25 years and some months old. He is of noble stature, neither tall nor short, and as handsome in complexion and shape as a man can be. His address is very agreeable. He speaks the following foreign languages; Latin, very well; French, German, Flemish, Italian, and Spanish; Spanish as well as the Marquis, but he pronounces it more distinctly. The King speaks, besides, the language of the savages who live in some parts of Scotland and on the islands. It is as different from Scotch as Biscayan is from Castilian. His knowledge of languages is wonderful. He is well read in the Bible and in some other devout books. He is a good historian. He has read many Latin and French histories, and profited by them, as he has a very good memory. He never cuts his hair or his beard. It becomes him very well.[1]

The pen portrait and his actual portrait show him to be a figure very much in the mould of the Renaissance prince, educated and sophisticated. Aloya continues:

He gives alms liberally, but is a severe judge, especially in the case of murderers. He has a great predilection for priests, and receives advice from them, especially from the Friars Observant, with whom he confesses. Rarely, even in joking, a word escapes him that is not the truth. He prides himself much upon it, and says it does not seem to him well for Kings to swear their treaties as they do now. The oath of a King should be his royal word, as was the case in bygone ages. He is neither prodigal nor avaricious, but liberal when occasion requires … His deeds are as good as his words. For this reason, and because he is a very humane prince, he is much loved. He is active, and works hard. When he is not at war he hunts in the mountains. I tell your Highnesses the truth when I say that God has worked a miracle in him, for I have never seen a man so temperate in eating and drinking out of Spain. Indeed such a thing seems to be superhuman in these countries. He lends a willing ear to his counsellors, and decides nothing without asking them; but in great matters he acts according to his own judgment, and, in my opinion, he generally makes a right decision.[2]

The question arises as to why such a paragon would lead himself and his army to slaughter on 9 September 1513?

Scotland had threatened England's borders on many previous occasions. James had supported Lambert Simnel in his attempts to claim the crown in 1496–7, causing Henry VII no little distress and forcing him to send a sizeable force of some 9,000 to face off against the pretender. What could have been a tragic confrontation devolved into farce, but there was a lesson for both kingdoms and monarchs. Twisting the leopard's tail could become a popular diversion for the Scottish Lion King, who was now in his maturity. James was ambitious and for once, as a Scottish monarch, he was unchallenged and popular amongst all conditions of men from all parts of his diverse kingdom.

Henry's decision to launch an aggressive attack on France was almost inevitable after he came to the throne. War with France would see him appear for the first time as a significant European monarch. Despite the peace treaty signed with France in 1509, the conflict between Louis and the League of Cambrai led by the Papacy meant that Henry could now declare war on an excommunicated French monarch. He now had God, or at least the Pope, on his side. Preparations for war began in 1512 with the intention of invading France through Calais in the summer of 1513.

1   *CSP Spain*, vol. 1, 1485–1509, 25 July.
2   *CSP Spain*, vol. 1, 1485–1509, 25 July.

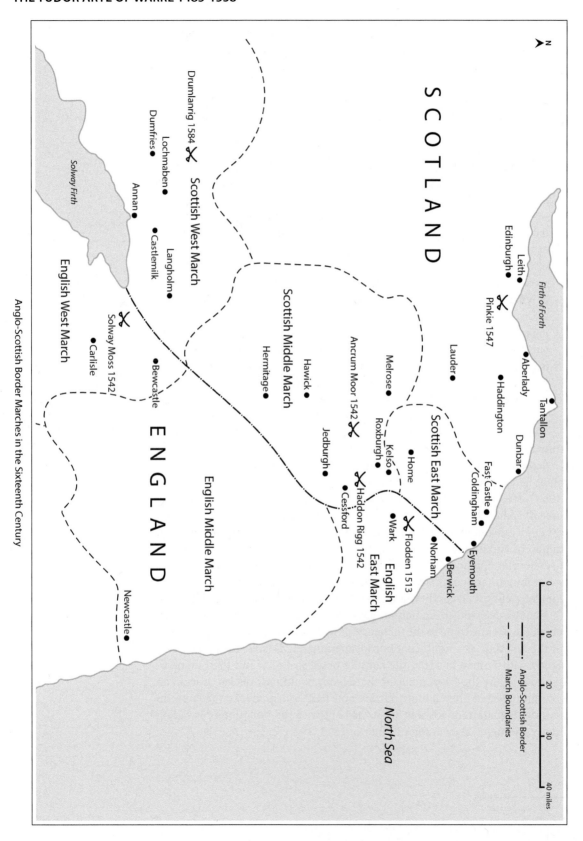

Anglo-Scottish Border Marches in the Sixteenth Century

In these circumstances James IV had to respond to English aggression against his vital strategic ally. Despite the entreaties of his English wife, it was inevitable that some action had to be taken. Polydore Vergil considered that James's aim was not to conquer England in part or whole; in fact no effort was even taken to besiege Berwick, a key point for England's defences against invasion and a worthy prize. His intention was simply to distract Henry from his campaign in France, forcing him to desist and return. Once achieved, the status quo between the three kingdoms could be restored. To achieve this, he first sent his not insubstantial fleet, including the impressively large flagship the *Great Michael* to France, via the western route. If a ship can be a white elephant, the *Great Michael* was. She was massive, with a displacement of about 1,000 tons, twice the displacement of the contemporary *Mary Rose* and possibly the largest warship in Europe. Only completed in 1512, she was sold in 1514 to the French at a knockdown price, as Scotland lacked the means or the will to maintain such a behemoth. This ship is indicative of the ambition of a Renaissance prince to achieve glory at all costs. What remained for James, having sent his fleet to support his ally, was to decide what his contribution on land should be.

Unicorn of James IV of Scotland 1488–1513. The unicorn was the largest denomination in the coinage of James IV. It was worth 18 shillings Scots. Like all gold coins it represented the wealth and power of the king; James IV gave 100 unicorns as a gift to the English ambassador Lord Dacre in 1503. On the reverse is the Latin legend EXVRGAT : DEVS T : DISIPENT : NIMICI which can be translated as *Let God arise and let His enemies be scattered* rather ironic considering the outcome of the Battle of Flodden. (Metropolitan Museum of Art, Open Access)

His army was increasingly well prepared. One requirement for any Renaissance monarch was to provide his army with a core of pikemen, the 'super-soldiers' of the sixteenth century. In Italy on 6 June 1513, Swiss pikemen had soundly defeated the French army at Novara, a testimony to their tactical flexibility, discipline and ferocity. Throughout the winter of 1512–13 James had imported pikes through Zeeland, which was Imperial territory. The Emperor could hardly intervene at a time of peace, and it was within the Scottish king's right to arm his forces as he saw fit.

The Scottish spear had, in the formation known as the schiltron, done much to diminish English haughtiness in previous centuries. As early as 1481 an attempt was made to establish a longer standard weapon at six ells or 18½ feet rather than the 12–14 feet of the Scottish spear, but little had been achieved. King James determined to make the full-length pike the standard weapon of the Scottish infantry. The pikes imported by James, known as 'Colin clouts', seem to have varied in length but what mattered was not so much the length of the pike but the discipline and training that were necessary for it to be used successfully. The pike was not a spear and its function was as much offensive as defensive, its use in battle requiring training. This was to be provided by some 50 French officers and 50 men-at-arms led by Captain or Comte d'Aussi, who divided his men into five divisions. In addition to the pikes 1,000 handguns were also delivered to his Scots allies by the French king, but they seem to have remained unused.

The other military requirement of a Renaissance prince was to possess an artillery park, well-furnished with cast bronze pieces. Robert Borthwick, the much-respected gunner and gun founder, was responsible for creating the 'new artillery' for the King's forces. Casting of guns had been going on in Scotland since 1508 but in 1511 26 French 'melters' or foundrymen came to assist at the Edinburgh foundry. Large quantities of metal were imported, in order to cast the 16 new cannon that were to constitute the King's grand battery. A German expert, Wolf of Nürnberg, was employed to manufacture gunpowder, and Dutchmen were employed to make small guns. As in England, foreign expertise was needed to man the guns as well as make them; a motley crew of Frenchmen, Germans, Flemings and a few native Scots were engaged. They manned five 'great curtalls', two 'gros culverins' known as the 'seven sisters', four culverins (sakers), and six 'culverins moyanes' (serpentines). The Scots still imported iron cannonballs, which they did not manufacture themselves, from France, together with 15,000 lb of powder. Scotland could also produce excellent blades, manufactured by Andrea de Ferrara, who was as his name suggests perhaps not that Scottish!

The nobility was well provided for with plate armour that proved proof against the English archery. For the remainder, in an Act of the Scottish Parliament of 1491, it was established that all men worth more than £10:

> shall have a helmet or salade, gorget or pisane, and mail for the limbs, a sword, spear and dagger … All other yeomen of the realm, betwixt sextie and sextene, shall have sufficient bowes and sheaves, sword, buckler, knife, speare, or any gude axe instead of bow … Every man must be accoutered in white harness or good jacks, with gloves of plate, and well-horsed 'correspondent to his lands and goods'.[3]

How far these standards were achieved is a moot point, but at least in theory all those present at the battle should have been able to fight. When it came to armour, the Lowland troops preferred a burgonet or Burgundian sallet. The Highlanders wore long bascinets fitted with nasal guards, and padded armour of linen reinforced with wax or pitch, over which was a deerskin, sometimes dyed the colour of heather. The Highland nobility wore long mail shirts, a form of bascinet, and carried two-handed swords.

James had a united kingdom and a large and loyal army, which was increasingly equipped with the most modern weapons of the age. He had the capacity to intervene decisively, at the very least to force the English King to abandon his French enterprise, and if the worst came to the worst he could take on any English force sent against him and defeat it. On 22 May James committed himself to a formal offensive and defensive alliance with France. His commitment may have been to a traditional strategic alliance; however, he had also received a gold and turquoise ring from Anne of

---

3   Informational page for Flodden available online (see bibliography for URL).

Brittany, the feisty French queen, who called upon her 'true knight' to come to the aid of her realm. Whether it was sound strategy or Renaissance courtly romanticism that determined his course of action, James prepared for an attack on England. His declaration of war was made on 16 July and was presented by Lyon King-of-Arms to Henry VIII at his camp at Thérouanne on 11 August.

In Scotland the date and place for the army to rally was 13 August, outside Edinburgh at Borough Muir. The summons to the army probably took place around the date of the declaration of war, which gave little time for the Highlanders to rally to the flag. The tradition was that every man should provide himself with 40 days of supplies, and this quantity seems to have been more than adequately supplemented by the Crown, as after the battle the Scottish encampment was found to be well stocked.

The artillery which departed from Edinburgh on three successive days from 18–20 August constituted the most powerful field and siege force ever assembled by Scotland. The size of the Scottish army is open to debate and interpretation. That it could be 100,000 strong is unlikely and the product of nationalistic hyperbole. Pitscottie, who provides a wide range of numbers over the campaign, suggests an army of 40,000, reduced after some weeks of campaigning to 28,000 which is not an unreasonable number.

The Scots crossed the Tweed at Coldstream on 22 August, and reduced Wark castle before advancing to Norham. After six days the impressive but somewhat outdated defences succumbed to the Scottish bombardment and assault, with its governor John Ainslie sent into comfortable imprisonment in Falkland. Berwick would have been the most appropriate target for a Scottish assault, but with the certainty of an English army being raised to counter the Scots incursion, a different strategy had to be followed. An advance further into England, threatening Newcastle or even York, would have led to a long and vulnerable line of communication. Any gains could not match the risks of being caught far from home. James decided to restrict himself to the siege and destruction of three small castles: Etal, Ford and Chillingham.

He then established his camp, guarded by powerful artillery on Flodden Edge and waited for the English army to arrive. The position chosen by James was admirably suited to his purpose. It constituted a steep hill some 300 feet high, with a marsh on its right flank and the River Till protecting its left: 'There was but one narrow field for any man to ascend up to the said hill, and at the foot of that lay the king's ordnance.'[4] Recent excavation of an artillery redoubt on Flodden Edge has shown a sizeable, well-constructed fortification, capable of mounting perhaps half a dozen pieces of ordnance, all mounted on wooden platforms to ensure a smooth recoil and easy reloading of the guns.[5]

At this point James could be blamed for dithering, sitting comfortably with his army in their tents, which covered a full mile along the crest of

---

4   Hall, *Chronicle*, p.560.
5   Tony Pollard and Neil Oliver, *Two Men in a Trench: Battlefield Archaeology – the Key to Unlocking the Past* (London: Michael Joseph, 2002), pp.145–151. See also TV programme, *Two Men in a Trench: Battle of Flodden*, BBC (2002–4), available online, see bibliography for URL.

the hill. He has been accused of a dalliance with Lady Heron of Ford, who was busy negotiating the release of her husband and the safety of her castle through a prisoner exchange. In fact, James need do nothing more than wait for the expected English force to arrive and either see it turn tail in the face of his impregnable position, or choose to attack him and face inevitable defeat. He was safely ensconced on English territory facing south, with a well-supplied camp which could easily return to Scotland as and when he wished.

Historians enjoy attributing blame to sovereigns. Mark Fissel roundly criticised Henry VIII for leaving his kingdom with the better part of his army, when Scotland could so easily invade from the north. Henry had left two redoubtable figures who managed the business of defending the kingdom well, his wife Catherine of Aragon and the septuagenarian commander of his northern forces the Earl of Surrey, who was contemptuously called 'a crooked old Earl in a cart',[6] by the Scots king. Henry's advice to his new lord lieutenant of the North was prescient and not neglected by its subject: 'My Lord, I trust not the Scots, therefore I pray you be not negligent.'[7]

In June 1513 it was still doubtful what part if any James would play other than perhaps a threatening one, but by mid July it was apparent to the English that James was determined to make more than an armed demonstration across the border. Surrey moved fast, leaving London on 22 July and reaching Doncaster on 1 August with his 500 men. The Scots began an aggressive campaign of raiding from the East March, led by Lord Home. Seven villages were burnt but the Scots loaded down with booty were themselves ambushed by Sir William Bulmer and soundly defeated, losing 400 killed and 200 captured in what would be called the 'Ill raid'.

Surrey ordered the mustering of the Northern forces; those traditionally in the area north of the River Trent were to assemble in Newcastle, where Sir Nicholas Appleyard the master of ordnance was to establish an artillery park. Surrey moved from Doncaster to York and then to Durham, which he reached on the 30th, assembling the county and diocesan levies. At Durham he received the banner of St Cuthbert, which gave his expedition additional religious motivation: the defence of the church against an excommunicate Scots king. By the time of Surrey's arrival in Newcastle on 1 September the North had effectively mobilised its resources in its defence. At Alnwick, the substantial contingent of the Earl of Northumberland joined the army, which included contingents from as far away as Ely. What was perhaps more surprising was the landing of a sizeable force of 1,000 men on the coast, commanded by Surrey's son Thomas, Lord Admiral of England, whose help his father had requested.

The size of the army that Surrey had at his command is unclear but could have numbered as many as 26,000, although it was probably several thousand fewer when in the field. Surrey sent a challenge to James, for what

---

6   Robert Lindsey of Pitscottie, *The Historie and Cronicles of Scotland: from the slauchter of King James the First to the ane thousande Fyve hundreith thrie scoir fyftein zeir* (Edinburgh: Blackwood and Sons, 1899), p.268.

7   Arthur Collins, *The Peerage of England … The third edition, corrected and enlarged in every family, with memoirs, not hitherto printed*, vol. 1 (London: H. Woodfall, etc., 1768), p.72.

he deemed a cowardly and unjustified assault on the peace of the realm. In a letter, informed by the conventions of chivalry, he challenged James to single combat. The Lord Admiral also sent a letter to the King via Rouge Croix herald but this time calculated to insult, offering quarter to none but the King in the future onslaught. The letters achieved the expected response: James accepted battle on the 9th. Surrey, on discovering the impeccably chosen site, in a further exchange of letters appealed to the Scots king's sense of fair play, as Flodden was not in any sense a level playing field. He proposed that: 'the king of his noble courage would descend the hill whereon he lay, for the place is no indifferent ground for the armies to fight upon'.[8] This chivalric nonsense was disregarded by James, who thought, quite rightly, that Surrey was attempting to escape from the mess that he found himself in. In the Scots camp, though, not all was confidence and bravado. The army and nobility of Scotland were now out on something of a limb, being some distance from home. In a meeting of the Council, presided over by Lord Lindsay of the Byres, they voiced their concerns. James intemperately threatened to hang this noble earl at the entrance to his own castle, but it was the English army that would slaughter the Scottish nobility.

Surrey was in a difficult position, having brought his forces far from his main supply bases at Newcastle or Berwick. He had provided carts to bring substantial supplies to his force, but these had been purloined on their way north by larcenous Englishmen. His substantial army was sitting idle, growing hungrier and thirstier by the day. Beer, normally allocated on a ration of one gallon per head per diem, had run out by 6 September, which for an army that received not only much of its courage but also its calories from that wonderful beverage was a serious concern.

Oman considers that Surrey was 'driven by sheer pride and privation to adopt the daring and risky – almost desperate – expedient of manoeuvring, which was to bring him an outstanding victory'.[9] Surrey, born in 1443, had fought his way through victory and defeat during the Wars of the Roses. Wounded and captured at Bosworth, he was determined to demonstrate loyalty to both Henry VII and now his son. His options were few and none were attractive. Firstly, he could attempt an assault on the Scots position, almost certainly disastrous. Secondly, he could attempt a withdrawal from the field, a difficult manoeuvre which would put his whole army at risk and see his personal humiliation. Thirdly, he could outflank the Scottish army and force it to face about. This would see him, short of supplies, with the Scottish army between his army and home. It would also place his army between the Scots and their way home. This third option was less risky than the first and less humiliating than the second; it would also for the first time put the Scots at a disadvantage and also put him in the good favour of the King, if he succeeded. With the appearance of the Bastard John Heron of Ford Castle, a plan was devised to outflank the Scots using Heron's local knowledge.

---

8   Oman, *A History of the Art of War*, p.306.
9   Oman, *A History of the Art of War*, p.307.

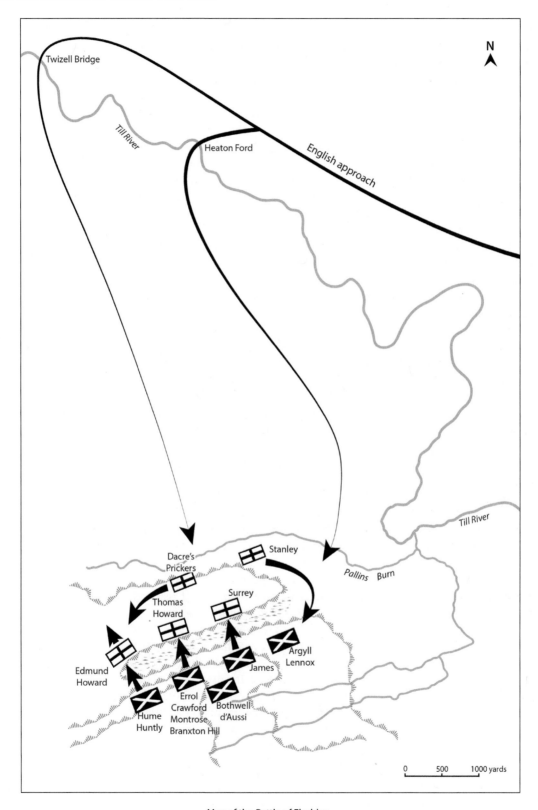

Map of the Battle of Flodden

Surrey moved his army to Barmoor Wood at the furthest extent of the Scots line on the 8th, and arranged for their future deployment. His son would lead the vanguard with all the artillery north besides the Twill, crossing at Twizel bridge; the main army would follow, crossing at Millford. The Scottish army remained inert in the face of this peculiar manoeuvre with only a little cannonading to mildly discomfort the English. James may have assumed that the English army was abandoning its confrontation and aimed to go to Berwick to resupply, or possibly engage in raiding along the Scottish border. This may explain his inactivity, but not excuse it. Gervase Philips has argued that James made a fatal error when he failed to make use of his own light horse, who could have maintained contact with the English force and provided him with essential intelligence as to their intentions.[10]

When the Lord Admiral's men crossed Twizel bridge and began to form a battle line, James had to review his own action, or rather inaction. Behind Flodden Edge rose the equally precipitous Branxton Hill; if the English were to seize it then that would place the Scots in the position that the English had been before and at a grave disadvantage. It was therefore essential that the Scots occupy Branxton Hill, as advised by the renegade Englishman Giles Musgrave. James ordered the entire army to shift its position, artillery, infantry and even the horse lines, pavilions and associated paraphernalia. What must have then occurred was an almighty shambles as heavy guns had to be withdrawn from positions, horses harnessed and tents and kitchens taken down and moved. The army and its commander had lost the initiative; psychologically they were now in a much weaker position, although in practice the balance of power had not shifted greatly. The English forces were still smaller than the Scots and now hungrier, they were still at the bottom of a hill in a marsh, and despite their best efforts the main body of the army was lagging. The vanguard now found itself in position but outflanked and outnumbered.

James IV had made few mistakes so far. His strategy and tactics had proved sound. He had drawn the English forces to him and could have held them there until they were forced to disperse. What Surrey's bold or reckless manoeuvre had done was to completely disconcert James, as his strategy appeared to unravel. Dom Pedro de Ayala, who as a Spanish emissary at James's court came to know the King well in his early years, made some trenchant comments on him which help explain his state of mind and the outcome of the battle:

> He is courageous, even more so than a king should be. I am a good witness of it. I have seen him often undertake most dangerous things in the last wars. On such occasions he does not take the least care of himself. He is not a good captain, because he begins to fight before he has given his orders. He said to me that his subjects serve him with their persons and goods, in just and unjust quarrels, exactly as he likes, and that therefore he does not think it right to begin any

10 Gervase Philips, 'England; Scotland and the European "Military Revolution", 1480–1560', paper delivered to the Richard III Foundation symposium, at the Dixie Grammar School, Market Bosworth in August 2013. Available online, see bibliography for URL.

warlike undertaking without being himself the first in danger. His deeds are as good as his words.[11]

His response to the arrival of the English army was immediate and perfectly sensible. His army would descend on the Lord Admiral's men and then destroy the remainder of the English army piecemeal. Noone would expect him to sit by and not take advantage of what appeared to be a massive blunder, and yet the alternative plan, that of doing nothing, was even more attractive. Even when the English army had assembled, their position would still be hopeless: with little food and only water to drink it would have to choose to attack or flee. James chose to lose the advantage that he had on Branxton Hill and descend on his opponents, something that he had wisely refused to do earlier from Flodden.

The Lord Admiral found the Scottish army facing him, with their artillery on Branxton Edge: 'Then the Lord Admiral perceived four great battles of the Scots, all on foot with long spears like Moorish pikes.'[12] Any hope that he might have had of surprising his enemy was lost, and finding himself in an exposed position at the bottom of the hill in a 'little valley', with little chance of immediate support. He sent his Agnus Dei medallion to his father as a parting gift and a desperate entreaty for haste. Yet James did not seek to immediately swoop down on the outnumbered vanguard. Supremely confident of victory, Pitscottie records his words: 'I am determined to have them all in front of me on one plain field and see what all of them can do against me.'[13]

The two armies clashed at 4:00 p.m, the contest beginning with an unequal cannonade. Holinshed reported that:

> Then out burst the ordnance with fire, flame, and hideous noise, and the master gunner of the English slew the master gunner of Scotland, and beat all his men from their guns, so that the Scottish ordnance did no harm to the Englishmen, but the Englishmen's artillery shot into the midst of the King's battle, and slew many persons, which seeing, the King of Scots and his brave men made the more haste to come to joining.[14]

Why it was that the English artillery performed so well and the Scots so badly is difficult to explain. It was reported by John Lesley that the Scottish shot flew over the heads of English which he attributed to the difficulty of shooting downhill. Perhaps a lack of experience with their new pieces, the confusion as to where to place them and the estimation of the enemy range, may have caused the Scots gunners problems, or it may have been the problem associated with shooting a cannon downhill. The heavier Scots pieces would have taken longer to load and re-lay than the English. They were no longer placed upon the wooden planking in their Flodden emplacements but on a

11 *CSP Spain*, vol. 1, 1485–1509, 25 July 1498.
12 Hall, *Chronicle*, p.361.
13 Pitscottie, *Cronicles*, vol. I, p. 227.
14 George Lillie Craik, Charles MacFarlane, *The Pictorial History of England: Being a History of the People, as Well as A History of the Kingdom* (New York: Harper & Brothers, 1847), p.315.

muddy and inconvenient slope. Either way, the first great advantage that the Scots possessed, their artillery, was wasted.

Lord Home's Borderers and Huntly's Highlanders launched themselves on the advance guard led by Sir Edmund Howard. Whether this was authorised or planned by any commander, or simply the response of the Scots to the sight of their victims beneath them is not known. The result was that Howard's forces were broken and he barely escaped with his life, and although badly wounded he was saved by a charge led by the Bastard Heron. The Highlanders went on to loot and the Borderers seem to have played no more part in the battle, having clearly 'done their bit'. The main force of the army, including the royal forces and those led by Montrose, Erroll and Crawford, charged down the hill, to be joined by the forces of Bothwell and Comte D'Aussi. The only force not now committed were the Highlanders of Argyll and Lennox, who remained on the right flank upon the hill. James had been strongly advised to remain in a position of command rather than take up a place of honour, in the line of battle. As one might have expected considering his personality, he chose to ignore the advice, perhaps one of his worst mistakes.

The Scots army now descended the hill; however, the ground was broken and boggy and whatever order may have been present at the beginning of the descent would have been lost by the time the pikemen arrived at the English front line. The soaking ground would have become a quagmire under the feet of the thousands of armed men. This is perhaps why it is recorded that they removed their boots in the hope of gaining some purchase on the ground with bare feet. Whether the pike was best suited for this combat is questionable; the English bill was a heavy but a handy and short weapon that was far superior to a pike when fighting at close quarters. The power and near invulnerability of the pike square was when it was in close formation; once the formation was broken the pike was a liability, not a decisive weapon. Bishop Ruthal, who had played a part in organising the defence of the border, commented that 'the bills disappointed the Scots of their long spears, on which they relied'.[15] Although the descent of the hill began in Almain fashion in silence and good order, Brian Tuke, the secretary of Henry VIII and Cardinal Wolsey, recorded that 'the English halberdiers decided the whole affair, so that in the battle the bows and ordnance were of little use'.[16]

The fighting was ferocious but indecisive for the next two hours and Home and Huntly, who might have been able to intervene on the flank, remained curiously but decisively inactive. When faced with the defeat of the Scottish army, Home was said to have declared: 'he does well that does for himself. We have fought our vanguard already, let others do as well as we.'[17] On the English side Lord Dacre protected the English right flank. He had suffered heavy losses but it was suggested that he and the Scottish Borderers under Home had reached an agreement to end the fighting.

15   Norman MacDougall, *James IV* (Edinburgh: Tuckwell, 1997), pp.274–5.
16   *Calendar of State Papers and Manuscripts, Relating to English Affairs: Existing in the Archives and Collections of Venice, and in Other Libraries of Northern Italy (CSP Italy)* vol. 2, 1509–1519, ed. Rawdon Brown (Cambridge: Cambridge University Press, 2013), p.134.
17   Oman, *A History of the Art of War*, p.312.

Sir Edward Stanley, whose late arrival in the line of battle was something of a family tradition, set his archers against the ill-protected Highlanders, outflanking them under covering fire; they fled, leaving their commanders to perish. With the Scottish left inactive and the Highlanders defeated on the right, Stanley could now reform and attack the rear of the main Scottish force. At this point the fate of James and Scotland was decided. He had an arrow shot through his jaw, his left hand was almost severed and finally he had his throat cut. Almost all the nobility other than Home and Huntly were to die alongside their sovereign; as the Lord Admiral had insisted in his letter, no quarter was given. In addition to the nobility, two abbots, a bishop and the Archbishop of St Andrews, who was the son of the King and a pupil of Erasmus, were cut down as they fought.

The King was identified by his bloodied surcoat, which was presented to Queen Catherine by Thomas Hawley, the Rouge Croix pursuivant. Catherine sent this bloodied remnant to her loving husband in his camp outside Thérouanne. She would have sent the mangled body but that 'Englishmen's hearts would not suffer it'.[18] Henry was more gentle and generous than his sweet wife, ensuring that James, although excommunicated, would be buried in consecrated ground, a process that took some time to achieve.

The consequences for Scotland were catastrophic and it would be some 30 years before the kingdom would again fully challenge the English Crown. Probably 10,000 Scots died that day and 4,000 English, and the political consequences for the Scots were dire. Surrey triumphed and regained the title of the Duke of Norfolk (lost to the family after their participation at Bosworth alongside Richard) and his son became the Earl of Surrey. Politically Norfolk was back in high favour but noticeably the 30 manors granted to him did not constitute a power base in East Anglia. He might be a hero, but he was one upon whom Henry would keep his beady eyes.

That an army equipped with bills and bows and old-fashioned artillery should defeat an army of pikemen equipped with modern bronze artillery, may come as a surprise. The Scottish army was not recruited from Landsknechts or Switzers. Its structure and ethos was Scottish and its failure cannot be attributed to its choice of weapons. James made the terrible mistake of not knowing when to stop. His sole purpose had been to draw the English army north; once that was achieved, he could have withdrawn. However, being at the height of his powers and having assembled the full force of the realm he felt obliged to use it, rather than run away. Surrey's outflanking manoeuvre turned the tables psychologically, and true to his character James then failed to effectively command his army. Victory might still have been his, if he had been able to command Home and Huntly to reform and attack the weakened English line, or if he had committed the Highlanders to the battle before the archery of the Stanley force decimated and demoralised them. Success or failure in a battle is down to a multitude of factors; on this occasion the battle could have gone either way but it was James who lost it because he should never have fought it in the first place.

---

18   Craik and MacFarlane, *The Pictorial History of England*, p.317.

The Battles of Solway Moss and Ancrum Moor

Solway Moss and Ancrum Moor were both part of an Anglo-Scottish war that could never be resolved without the unity of the crowns, something which England hoped for. The marriage of Prince Edward to Princess Mary was an outcome which the Scots would never easily or willingly accept. The Auld Alliance made perfect sense for Scotland. Mary was in many ways a French Princess, the pro-French party led by her mother, and Cardinal Beaton had a strong argument supporting their position. Henry's attitude towards King James V had started as one of condescension, developed into the hectoring of an older and more senior relative, and then finally he threatened to assert his territorial rights over Scotland.

James V had not had an easy life. His father had been killed at Flodden and the kingdom was governed first by John Stuart Earl of Albany and in 1525 by Archibald Douglas 6th Earl of Angus, who had been in exile in England. The young king finally asserted his right to rule independently in 1528 at the age of 16. With the support of the Scottish lords, Angus was forced into exile again, fleeing to Henry VIII's court. James would now devote his time in Scotland to bringing the Highlanders to heel with his artillery and realigning Scotland with France through his two marriages. The endemic border conflict had occasionally almost become open warfare, but while Henry was tied up in the King's Great Matter, peace with his northern neighbour made sense. The Pilgrimage of Grace in 1536 also gave Henry reason to wish for peace, as this domestic challenge was profoundly dangerous.

With the threat of a Franco-Imperial 'crusade' passed by 1540, Henry's policy of alliance with the Emperor against the French made the neutralisation of Scotland essential. A large English raiding force had been soundly beaten at Haddon Rig on 24 August 1542, with the Borderers fleeing with heavy casualties. Norfolk was sent north to negotiate a humiliating settlement, which demanded neutrality and the handing over of hostages for good behaviour, or he was to launch another punitive raid. Unsurprisingly, Norfolk's diplomatic initiative failed, as did his military expedition. The failure was principally logistical. Berwick was unable to provide him with bread and beer and he would have lacked the means of transporting it anyway. With only six days of provisions, the campaign collapsed after the usual practice of burning some villages. James had mustered 12,000 men at Fala Muir but the bad weather and the withdrawal of Norfolk led to its disbandment.

James raised an army of 15,000–18,000 in October from noble retinues, with the intention of launching a sizeable series of raids into the West March, and ultimately to advance on Carlisle. Although very late in the year, there was every expectation that his well-provisioned force would prove successful. James himself was seriously ill and was unable to take the prominent part that might have been expected; the absence of the sovereign proved crucial. The large Scots army crossed the border on 24 November and proceeded to cause as much destruction as it could. Sir Thomas Wharton, the English Warden of the West March, led a force of 3,000 Borderers, of which probably a third were on horseback. He knew well that he was outnumbered but he also knew the strength of his own forces and the problems of any large army advancing over difficult country. Wharton's forces shadowed the two Scots battles and carried out raids to their rear, north of the border. However, the Scots army could not be held up by a series of skirmishes. On 24 November Wharton rallied his forces on Hopesike Hill, where he was able to confer with his commanders and gather his infantry in a defensive position. He had identified the ground upon which to fight the numerically superior enemy: the Scots were advancing in a pass with the River Esk and Solway Moss to their right, and Sir William Musgrave was sent with 700 horse to hit the left flank of the Scottish force. The Scottish army was struggling with its artillery and baggage wagons in the boggy ground.

The appearance of the English infantry to their front and the attack on the flank was disconcerting, but not a disaster. Robert Lord Maxwell, the Warden of the West March, had commanded the army up to this point, when he was challenged by Oliver Sinclair, the King's favourite, who chose this moment to claim his right to command. King James may have distrusted Maxwell and secretly appointed Sinclair to take command if he saw fit, but this was definitely not the time for Sinclair to claim it. The Scots now had two leaders but no orders. Wharton recorded that the tactics of the border horse, constantly pricking the flanks of the army, proved successful: 'Our prekers ... gatt theym in a shake all the waye.'[19] The Scottish force 'in a shake' disintegrated and fled, abandoning all their heavy equipment. The final rout took place when the Scots host was attempting to cross the Esk at Sandyford, where the numbers drowned probably exceeded the numbers killed in fighting. What was left of the rabble fled north through the territory they had so recently despoiled, and where they received little mercy from the inhabitants.

The losses in the battle on both sides were farcical. The English lost seven killed and the Scots perhaps 20, as well as losing all their artillery. This included four falconets, 12 bases, three demi-bases and 20 carts of war, and well over 100 firearms. Some 1,200 Scotsmen were captured, including both Oliver and Maxwell as well as an earl, five barons, 500 gentlemen and more than 30 standards. James V died on 14 December, leaving a six-day-old Queen Mary to succeed and his nobility in the hands of the English. Of course, the political machinations came to nothing and England and Scotland continued in a futile but bloody conflict.

Ancrum Moor

The Rough Wooing did not drive the Scots into the arms of the English. After Hertford's major campaign north, which burnt the city of Edinburgh in May 1544, further raids were encouraged. A force of 5,000 was led into Teviotdale by Sir Ralph Eure, Warden of the Middle March, and Sir Brian Layton, captain of Norham Castle. Jedburgh, Kelso and Dryburgh were devastated with fire and theft. Melrose Abbey, where many of the Douglas family were buried, was desecrated, adding insult to injury. Archibald Douglas the 6th Earl of Angus, who had been in exile in England and had some sympathy for

---

19 Philips, *The Anglo-Scots Wars*, p.152.

their cause, was outraged by the insult to his family; he rallied 300 men from his retinue and rode south, adding about 1,000 more to his slender force during his progress.

The English army consisted of 700 assured Scots led by Neill McNeill of Gigha, 1,400 border horse and 3,000 German and Spanish mercenaries. After its 'successes' this force was making its way to the border, having been offered no resistance. Although there was some 'bickering' there had been nothing to halt the raiders and the appearance of Angus and his tiny numbers, although reinforced, was hardly a cause for great concern. Angus established his men on a low hill overlooking the English camped on Ancrum Moor, five miles from Jedburgh, on 27 February 1545.

Facing the Scottish force, the confident English placed their cavalry to the fore and their infantry in one battle to the rear. They also assumed that Scots morale would be low and they were already on the verge of breaking, as they had done at Leith and at Solway Moss. The English cavalry advanced confidently into the sun and chased the Scots horse over the brow of a hill, only to find themselves facing hastily dug pits as well as a determined pike block mixed with arquebusiers. The English cavalry was broken, and those who skirted the pikes found themselves in a marsh where they were easily picked off as they foundered helplessly. The Scottish horse now returned and attacked the infantry in their flanks, while the victorious pikemen fell on them from the front. The 'assured' Scots proved rather less than reliable and tore off their red cross of St George and joined in the slaughter of their very recent allies.

Another interpretation suggests that there was no cavalry charge by the English and the advance was of badly ordered footmen and driven back. The outcome remained the same. Both English commanders were killed, as were 800 of their men and a further 1,000 were captured including 80 knights and gentlemen; what happened to the thousands who fled is not recorded. Scottish casualties were few: the figure of two dead is unbelievable but they were certainly too few to be of any significance. There is one memorial named *Lilliard's Stone* dedicated to a Scottish female casualty on the battlefield. The inscription is worth repeating:

> Fair Maid Lilliard
> Lies under this stane
> Little was her stature
> But muckle was her fame
> Upon the English loons
> She laid monie thumps
> And when her legs were cuttit off
> She fought upon her stumps.

Solway Moss and Ancrum Moor show how important the quality of leadership is to success, or rather failure. The Scots at Solway Moss and the English at Ancrum Moor outnumbered their enemy by 5:1 and 4:1 respectively. The winners were well led, chose their ground carefully and fought the battle on their own terms. Underestimation of an enemy and divided leadership were the undoing of the defeated parties.

The Battle of Pinkie

Edward Seymour, Duke of Somerset, Earl of Hertford and Lord Protector of the Realm was proud, ambitious, pious and profoundly frustrated by the Scots. His rise through Henry VIII's court provided him with invaluable political, military and diplomatic experience. The marriage of his sister to Henry VIII and the production of a male heir, gave him a considerable leverage as the young King Edward's uncle after Henry's death. When it came to the management of his nephew's regency his position was secure, especially after the 'paying off' of his staunch supporters thanks to the generous nature of the old king's will. He was an experienced soldier who understood the new warfare. He had been Captain of Boulogne at the time of the camisade, achieving praise for his staunch defence of the town but not apparently opprobrium for letting it happen in the first place. Once he had established himself in power, he had to resolve the seemingly intractable problem of 'what to do about the Scots'? He had already been deeply involved in the attempt to intimidate the population through systematic destruction of towns and villages, a policy known as the Rough Wooing. This was an attempt to make the Scots accept the marriage of Mary to Edward VI agreed to in 1542, an outcome that was most acceptable to the English but quite the opposite to the Scots.

Somerset developed a more sophisticated strategy in Scotland. This was to establish an English Pale: an area that recognised England's authority and acted as a buffer to hostile Scottish incursions. Somerset offered peace and security, on England's terms, as well as a Protestant religious settlement. At the same time, he promoted anti-French and anti-Catholic sentiment in favour of the idea of a greater Britain. Such ambitious religious, ideological and territorial programmes had to be supported by military intervention. Its purpose was to demonstrate the powerlessness of the government of Scotland under Arran, who acted as Mary's regent. Scottish campaigns had always presented the greatest logistical challenges to any English commander; the hostile population, the distance from the closest English bases and the dreadful poverty of the North, required realistically a short campaign of no more than a month in duration.

Arran was aware of Somerset's plans from the reports of his London agents. He prepared his defences as far as he was able and assembled, according to William Patten the chronicler and participant in these events, a sizeable field force of 26,000 pike, 4,000 Highland archers and some 1,500 light horse. The total is more likely to have been 23,000, a figure reported by the Earl of Huntly and recorded in Edward VI's own journal. There were few arquebusiers to be found in their ranks but the infantry were well provided for. John Hayward recorded their equipment in some detail. The foot:

> were well furnished with Jacke and skull, pike, dagger, bucklers made of boorde [wood], and sliceing swords, broad, thinne and of ann excellent temper. Every man had a large Kercheife folded twice or thrice about the necke, and many of them had chaines of latten [brass] drawne three or four times along their hoses and doublet sleeves, they also had to affright the enemies horses, big rattles

covered with parchment or paper, and small stones within, put upon staves about three ells long. But doubtles the ratling of shot might have done better service.[20]

There was also a powerful artillery train, most of which was later captured on the field of battle. It consisted of one bronze demi-cannon, two culverins, three sakers, nine falconets, and a robinet as well as 17 iron guns mounted on carriages (probably of wrought iron rather than cast iron).

There were serious tensions within the Scottish army, religious as well as ethnic. The Highland troops of the Earl of Argyll were feared by Lowlanders as 'this irismen … waist and destroyis all menis gudis quharever they cum' [these Irishmen … waste and destroy all mens' goods wherever they come].[21] Arran's forces were sympathetic to the Catholic cause and contained priests within their number, while Angus commanding border and Lowland troops, found his men tending towards the Protestant cause. The Earl of Angus led the vanguard, Arran commanded the main battle and George Gordon, Earl of Huntly, the rearguard. Angus and Huntly were capable commanders but both had some sympathy for a peaceful settlement with England. The army took a long time to assemble and many men had already served for a fortnight of their 40 days military service, leaving Arran little time to bring his opponent to battle. Arran had to move against Somerset's forces as soon as he knew from which side of the border they were coming.

Somerset's main force did not follow the usual inland route, instead it progressed close to the east coast. This was to remain under the protective guns of the substantial English fleet, which could provide food as well as additional firepower. To increase the difficulties of his enemy, a smaller force of almost 3,000 was sent to Annandale under the Warden of the West March, to divert efforts and add to the confusion, which it did admirably.

The main English army entered Scotland on 4 September, with 3,000 foot under John Dudley the Earl of Warwick in the vanguard; Lord Dacre commanded the rearguard with a similar number and Somerset with 4,000 men led the mainguard. Spanish and Italian arquebusiers under Sir Peter Mewtys provided a valuable addition to missile power. The majority of the English infantry force was made up of the traditional combination of bill and bow. The artillery train was well provided for, with some 15 'great guns' as well as numerous smaller calibre weapons, all of which would play a key role in the future battle. The army was an assembly of noble retinues and county levies, many of whom had served in the successful Scots campaigns of 1544 and morale was high, especially as they were led by experienced commanders.

Accompanying the 10,000 foot was a powerful force of cavalry commanded by Lord Grey of Wilton. Sir Francis Bryan commanded 2,000 light horse, mostly northerners, and Sir Ralph Vane commanded a powerful force of 3,000 heavy cavalry, made up of men-at-arms and demi-lancers,

---

20 John Hayward, *The Life, and Raigne of King Edward the Sixt* (Kent, Ohio: Kent State University Press 1993), p.55.

21 William Patten, *The expedicion into Scotla[n]de of the most woorthely fortunate Prince Edward, Duke of Soomerset,* in introduction by A.F. Pollard, *Tudor Tracts 1532–1588* (Westminster: Archibald Constable and Co. Ltd, 1903), p.108.

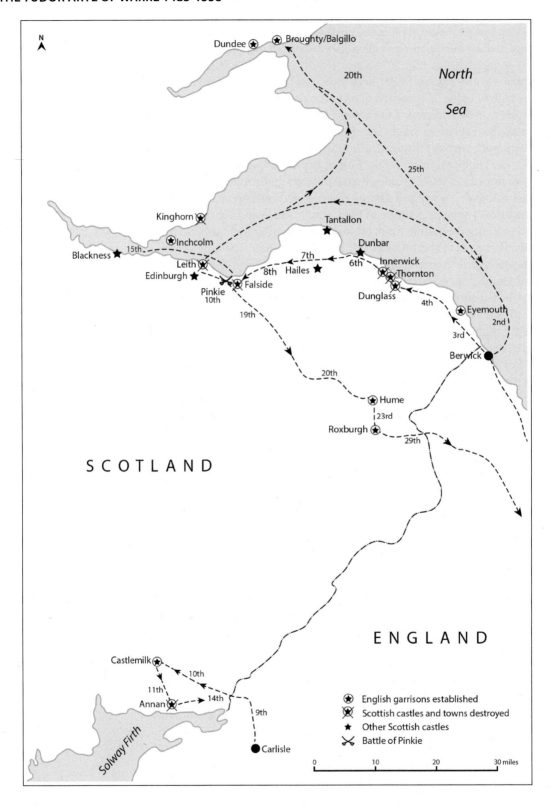

Map of the Scottish Campaign 1547

most of whom were mercenaries. The full might of England's heavy cavalry contingents, the 'Bulleners' of the Boulogne garrison under Edward Shelley and the Gentlemen Pensioners under the command of Sir Thomas Darcy, were deployed. The famous mercenary Pedro de Gamboa commanded some 200 arquebusiers on horseback. These would play an important part in the battle, combining as they did mobility and firepower. Somerset had one of the most powerful, balanced and confident forces of cavalry in Europe, and he was to use it well.

The advance of the English army continued unchecked, other than some 'bickering' with Scottish light horse. The army was preceded by 400 light horse and was flanked on the landward side about two bowshots (about a quarter mile) from the army by heavy cavalry supported by their own artillery. Discipline and order predominated in what was a very heterogeneous army. A deep ravine, difficult to pass, called the Peaths (Pease Bridge) now presented a potentially serious obstacle if it was garrisoned by a determined foe, but what few forces had been there had fled. Arran had expected an attack to take a westward route, and when he discovered the true direction of attack it was too late to deploy to the Peaths, as his army had already taken too long to assemble at Fala Muir. Pioneers in the English army filled in what little work had been done to slow progress, and the road north now lay open. Somerset's policy was not to capture fortified places but to allow the garrisons to surrender, and even showed mercy to some of those who resisted. He also spared the civilian population, as his intention was to make the creation of an English Pale feasible through popular support.

Dunbar castle was too strongly and aggressively held to be reduced quickly. It was bypassed as it posed little threat to the advancing army, as was Tantallon Castle. Time was of the essence, and little could be spared or wasted on prolonged sieges that would be unnecessary if Somerset achieved his primary objective, the destruction of the Scottish field army. The crossing of Linton Bridge on 7 September presented the Scottish light horse with the opportunity of causing confusion in the English rearguard. Discipline and organisation succeeded, but in a thick fog Warwick faced capture or even worse, when with his usual foolhardiness he chased after a party of Scots light horse who turned out to be far more numerous than he thought. Bravery was expected from noble commanders by their soldiers and even more so by their social equals, even if it deprived the army of an essential commander, as it had the Scots at Flodden.

The English fleet had not been idle and was now anchored off Leith. Its admiral, Lord Clinton, met with Somerset on the 8th and discussed future deployments. Clinton had found Arran's army at Musselburgh and reported that the Scots intended to hold a position overlooking the River Esk. The fleet bombarded Leith as well as the Scottish camp; Clinton's supply ships and smaller vessels were moored off the coast, in order to support the English army as it advanced towards the Scots' field fortifications.

Arran's choice of battlefield was excellent. Positioned on Edmonston Ridge, it was flanked by the Firth of Forth on the left and a marsh, the Shire Moss on the right. At the bottom of the valley the River Esk presented a further obstacle to an enemy. The naturally strong position was reinforced with field fortifications with a turf wall constructed on the flank to protect the camp from naval gunfire. The defences mounted artillery of all calibre including examples of the *arquebus a croc*, a large-calibre wall-mounted form of the arquebus.

Prior to the battle there took place a most significant engagement that tells us much about the armies and their commanders. For the preceding days the Scottish light horse had been attempting to goad the English cavalry into foolhardy charges. Warwick had, after all, been tempted into such an attack. Lord Grey and his troopers, frustrated by their inaction, requested permission from Warwick to accept the challenge. Somerset agreed but reinforced the English light horse with men-at-arms and demi-lancers, who together advanced towards the hill of Fawside Brae. They were ordered only to attack when the Scots cavalry had wheeled or turned and would thereby be in a state of potential disorder. The charge took place at that exact time and the Scots light horse were pursued three miles, almost to the Scots camp. Some 1,300 were killed; their commander Lord Home was seriously injured, falling from his horse and smashing his collarbone; his son, two priests and six gentlemen were captured and the remainder fled. The Scots light horse were to play no further active part in the battle.

On the top of Fawside Brae, Somerset now observed the strength of the Scottish position. A frontal assault was the only possible option if the army was not to retreat, and an attack would have carried a terrible cost. An attempt to outflank the army would have posed a threat to his line of communications and there was no feasible landing point for the soldiers in the English fleet to land and attack the Scots in the rear. In the English camp the fear of a Scottish night attack led to the laagering of the 'wagonborough', and close watch and ward kept. All this was evidence of a well-disciplined force. The embarrassment of the camisade at Boulogne was not to be repeated. The alternative strategy to a frontal assault was to treat the battle as a siege, as had been done at Ravenna. The fleet could bombard the east flank of the enemy and Fawside Brae would provide space for some batteries, other batteries could be placed on Carberry Hill on the west flank and further pieces could be mounted on the hill at Pinkie Cleugh beside St Michael's church at Inveresk. To achieve this there had to be a general advance towards Inveresk by the army to occupy these positions.

The rules of chivalry demanded a formal challenge to personal combat by Huntly to Somerset, which was naturally rejected out of hand, as was the offer of combat between 20 of the finest men-at-arms on both sides. Somerset presented a more politic and pacific suggestion, offering to withdraw the English army and pay compensation for the damage already done, in return for an agreement to the marriage of Mary and Edward. Arran could hardly agree to this, and his military position seemed unassailable but only as long as he was willing to face a vicious bombardment with equanimity.

On Saturday 10 September the English army began its movement towards the Scots. Its advance had been preceded, to its amazement, by the rapid approach of the Scottish army streaming down towards the Esk in battle formation. It has been suggested that Arran somehow mistook Somerset's advance as a retreat and that Arran sought to pursue a defeated enemy. How he might have expected to defeat or pursue an enemy so well provided with

Following page:

The Englische Victorie Agaynste the Schottes by Muskelbroghe 1547 (the Battle of Pinkie). (National Gallery of Scotland, with permission). This remarkable engraving includes many of the key moments in the battle.

1.The English camp. Any expedition into Scotland was entirely dependent for its success on the quantity and quality of its logistical support. Somerset used the merchant ships employed by the fleet to provide a 'sea-train' supplying the army. Small boats can be seen transporting stores to shore from larger vessels.

2. The Scottish camp. Although pictured during the defeat it does show the strong position of the Scottish army overlooking the River Esk, well supported with artillery of all calibres. To leave such a strong position would suggest an urgent necessity or extraordinary opportunity.

3. The English galleys provided effective gunfire support against the advancing Scottish left wing. The galleys mounted their principal armament facing the bow which required no doubt some fine management by their sailing masters and oarsmen. Galleys were powerful vessels and with their large crews made useful additions to land power, as the French demonstrated in Scotland.

4. The three Scottish battles have advanced rapidly and seriously discountenanced the English commanders. The remarkable speed with which the Scottish artillery was brought up to support their infantry is also worthy of comment. As usual the guns are seen in battery placed wheel to wheel.

5. The church at Inveresk was the first objective of the Scots, from which as can be seen useful artillery support could be given. The Scots' advance was not complete folly but a calculated risk.

6. This is the point at which the English heavy cavalry, the Pensioners and Bulleners, have stopped the further advance of the Scots pike blocks. The Scots have already halted, perhaps to consolidate their position and formation. The sacrifice of the cavalry held the Scots army long enough for the next phase of the battle to develop.

7. The Lord Protector can be seen besides the guns he has brought forward to enfilade the Scottish battles. A commander disposing of individual guns in a battle is usually the sign of a general who has lost the plot. but not in the case of the Lord Protector. Somerset acted quickly to bring his forces into line of battle and use their firepower to decimate the Scottish infantry.

8. Artillery and arquebusiers can be seen in action against the Scots. The arquebusiers are clearly deploying and skirmishing forward, not a task that could be given to inexperienced or unreliable troops. The superiority of firepower against infantry, however determined, was a feature of Pinkie as well as successive battles in the troubled year of 1549. The battery that has been brought into action, no doubt firing anti-personnel shot at the rate of two rounds per minute per gun, can be seen to be causing havoc in the flank of the Scots battle.

9. The bloody pursuit begins. The horrors that took place are vividly described by Patten and were brought to a premature conclusion after too much blood had already been spilled.

10. This scene shows the English camp on the march at the moment it was attacked by the Scots horse. This was apparently the only part played in the battle by the light horse that had been routed on the previous day. The formation above is labelled as being *Carters,* an indication that even those in the logistics train were expected to be able to fight if necessary.

11. The Scottish light horse running away.

12. The position of the English camp after the battle. The military victory preceded a political and religious initiative to create an English Pale and make Scotland subject to its neighbour. It was a project that in the light of subsequent events seems doomed to failure.

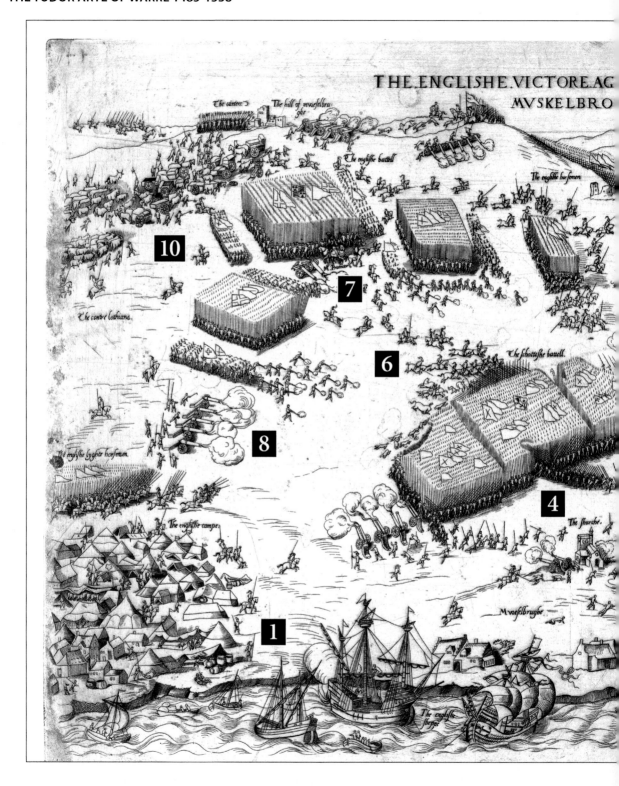

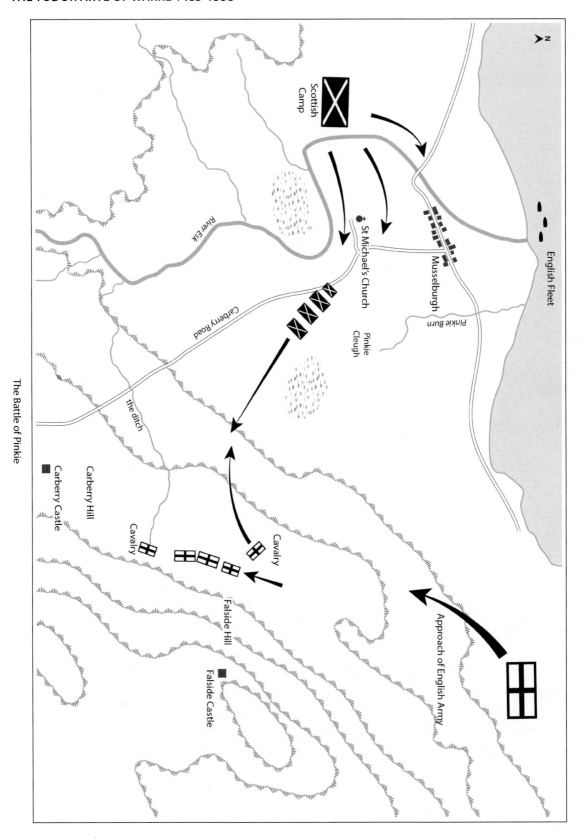

The Battle of Pinkie

cavalry while his own had been so ignominiously bested, it is difficult to say. It seems more probable that Arran had made a simple calculation. He was unwilling to face a prolonged bombardment; he was also unable to retreat without cavalry to screen his army against slaughter by the far superior English force. The only alternative was to attack his enemy unexpectedly and while it was still deployed in line of march, not in line of battle. If his pike squares could advance fast enough, they could overwhelm the English forces before they could employ the firepower necessary to stop them. It was a Scots force of infantry and artillery that reached Inveresk first. There was some confusion in the English army, as the infantry deployed and the artillery sought to bring their guns into action, as the remainder of the army sought to seize Fawside Brae. Patten's response to Arran's bold initiative, written with the advantage of hindsight, was to repeat the common proverb of the time: 'It is better to sit still, than rise up and fall.'[22]

The fleet played a crucial role by bombarding the left flank of the Scottish army as it advanced. The first shot killed the Master of Graham and more than a score of his men. The Scottish left flank was thrown into disorder and suffered heavy casualties, naturally turned inland and collided with the main battle that was also descending the hill. Importantly the 4,000 Irish archers commanded by the Earl of Argyle 'could never after be made to come forward'.[23] Somerset sought the advice of his lieutenants and realised that he could only halt the Scottish advance with his vastly superior force of cavalry. Patten describes the tactical decision made at this time:

> Their device was thus. That my Lord Grey with his band of Boulogners, with my Lord Protector's band, and my Lord Lieutenant's; all to the number of an eighteen hundred men, on the East half: and Sir Ralf Vane, with Sir Thomas Darcy captain of the Pensioners … all to the number of sixteen hundred … on the West half: and thus all these together, afore, to encounter the enemy a front: whereby either to break their array, and that way weaken their power by disorder; or, at the least, to stop them of their gate, and force them to stay, while our Foreward [infantry vanguard] might wholly have the hill's side, and our Battle and rearward be placed in grounds next that in order, and best for advantage.[24]

Somerset had at his disposal the Bulleners and the Gentlemen Pensioners but unfortunately they were not prepared for immediate action, as their horses were not provided with the barding (armoured protection) which would reduce their vulnerability. Lord Grey proposed the attack and chose to lead it, a foolhardy but expected role for him to play. Somerset meanwhile reinforced Fawside Brae with three pieces of artillery.

At this point the Scottish army stalled in its assault or at least paused. Patten records that 'the enemy were all at a sudden stay, and stood still a good while. The sight and cause hereof was marvellous to us all; but understandable

---

22 Patten, *The expedicion into Scotla[n]de*, p.105.
23 Patten, *The expedicion into Scotla[n]de*, p.108.
24 Patten, *The expedicion into Scotla[n]de*, p.109.

THE TUDOR ARTE OF WARRE 1485-1558

of none.'[25] Earlier their advance had been likened to that of cavalry rather than infantry in speed, and it appeared that they could have achieved their objective, which was to overwhelm the English army as it attempted to deploy. Perhaps Arran, aware of the likelihood of an English counter-attack, thought it necessary to restrain and reorder his forces to meet it. Some of the Scottish artillery accompanied the advance but drawn by men rather than draught horses. This was an exhausting process which placed these valuable items in jeopardy, as it would be impossible to withdraw them to safety if the battle was lost. Patten records that each of the three Scots battles had four or five pieces of ordnance placed on their flanks. The Scots infantry jeered the English, goading them to an attack, crying 'Come here lounds [rascals]! Come here, tykes [dogs]! Come here, heretics!'[26]

This pause prepared his troops for the next act in the drama but also achieved exactly what his enemy wanted: a pause long enough for the English army to deploy against him. The force available to Somerset was considerable, but the conditions that the cavalry found were hardly ideal. They faced a fallow field and a sizeable ditch, which some including Grey chose to jump, and a deeply furrowed field which made it difficult either to achieve the speed or maintain the disciplined formation that was ideal if the attack was to achieve the desired result.

The Scots infantry equipped with the pike now set themselves in a defensive position. Patten again provides a detailed description of how this was done:

> [The Scots] cloased and in a manner locked themselves together, shoulder to shoulder, so neere as possible they could, their pikes they strained in both hands and therewith their buckler in the left, the one end of the pike against the right foote, the other breast high against the enemy. The fore ranke stooped so low as they seemd to kneele, the second rank close at their backs, crossed their pikes over their shoulders, and so did the third and the rest in their order, so as they appeared like the thornie skinne of a hedgehogge, and it might be thought impossible to breake them.[27]

The Scottish pike blocks did not break. The cavalrymen that arrived found themselves hemmed in by colleagues behind and were despatched bloodily with swords and axes. Casualties were heavy, and in the face of Scottish determination the force had to withdraw. Some 'turned themselves, and made a soft retire up towards the hill … to confess the truth, some of the number made, of a sober advised retire, a hasty temerarious flight.'[28] Casualties among the leaders were heavy. Edward Shelley was killed and his body was discovered after the battle, 'pitifully disfigured and mangled';[29] Lord Grey 'with a pike through the mouth was rased a long from the tip

---

25 Patten, *The expedicion into Scotla[n]de*, p.110.
26 Patten, *The expedicion into Scotla[n]de*, p.116.
27 Hayward, *The Life, and Raigne*, p.57.
28 Patten, *The expedicion into Scotla[n]de*, p.117.
29 Patten, *The expedicion into Scotla[n]de*, p.130.

of the toong, and thrust that waie verie dangerouslie more than two inches in the necke.'[30] Sir Thomas D'Arcy was also injured, as 'a bullet from one of their field pieces … struck glancing wise on the right side … and thereby his body bruised with a bowing in of his harness, his sword hilt broken, and the forefinger of his right hand beaten flat.'[31] Sir Andrew Flammack, carrying His Majesty's standard, only just managed to keep hold of the flag itself, leaving the lower end of the staff with the Scots. As Hayward wisely remarked: 'Assuredly albeit encounters betweene horsemen on the one side, and foot on the other are seildome with the extremity of danger, because as horsemen can hardly breake a battaile on foot, so men on foot cannot possibly chase horsemen.'[32] Yet as he records, the disorder among the English cavalry was such as to promote the possibility of a rout. This was only halted by Lord Grey and the personal intervention of Hertford rallying their men.

The cannon on Fawside Brae were now unlimbered and ready to engage, and Warwick's vanguard, which was well provided with archers and men-at-arms, was ready to outflank Angus. Its deployment had been delayed by the 'indiscreet gadlings', fleeing from the field. With the mainguard and rearward also deployed, the mass of Scottish pikemen, in what was now a confused single block, was enveloped or 'encompassed' on both flanks. The Scottish artillery, which had tried to keep up with the advance, could not match the English cannonade. The Highland archers who had suffered from the naval bombardment had fled. The tattered remnants of the Scottish light cavalry force now devoted itself to heroically threatening the English baggage train, rather than attempting to take any productive part in the battle. When it faced determined resistance, organised by one Parson Keble, it also departed the battlefield. Sir Peter Mewtys brought his arquebusiers forward to play upon the close-packed Scots, as did Pedro Gamboa. He brought his 200 hackbutters on horseback forward to pour their fire into what were now defenceless formations. To this was added the archers, who 'pricked them sharply with arrows as they stood',[33] and the ordnance, which 'did gall with hail shot and other [shot] out of the great ordnance directly from the hilltop … and certain other gunners, with great puissance and vehemency.'[34]

Arran's position was critical: to advance was now impossible, and to conduct a fighting retreat when facing a committed enemy provided with superior cavalry would have been difficult. Angus led a well-drilled column and would have been able to stand against Somerset's vanguard, but his column's deployment made it appear as if they were retreating and the impact this had on Arran's force led to panic. Arran, now seeing his own column breaking and sharing in the opinion that Angus rather than coming to his aid was choosing to flee, cried 'Treason!' and took to his horse and left the army to its fate. Angus had shown little enthusiasm for the advance from

---

30 Raphael Holinshed, *Holinshed's Chronicles of England, Scotland, and Ireland*, vol 3 (London: Routledge, 2013), p.879.
31 Patten, *The expedicion into Scotla[n]de*, p.120.
32 Hayward, *The Life, and Raigne*, p.58.
33 Patten, *The expedicion into Scotla[n]de*, p.123.
34 Patten, *The expedicion into Scotla[n]de*, p.123.

the very beginning of the battle, and had to be ordered to attack 'under pain of treason'; his dubious political loyalty made Arran's interpretation of events understandable but still inexcusable.

Angus now led his men towards Huntly's rearguard, which he had managed to keep together. In the driving rain and with smoke obscuring the view, the retiring Scots were interpreted as an English force and whatever hope there might have been for a stout resistance was lost. The pikemen fled, discarding their armour and their pikes so that 'the place they stood on like a wood of staves strewed on the ground as rushes in a chamber; impassable they lay so thick, for either horse or man.'[35] Unlike many of the poorly dressed nobility and gentry, Huntly was captured, almost certainly because of the gorgeously decorated armour he wore.

The slaughter now began, as the English cavalry that had suffered at the hands of the pikes took a bloody revenge which sickened those who witnessed it. The massacre was ended by Somerset, who saw nothing to gain from such a bloody business. The slaughter included the gentry who might have expected capture or ransom, as well as the commoners who expected no mercy. This was attributed to the similarity of dress between rich and poor, with the absence of gold chains, brooches or rich garments that would have saved the lives of the wealthy for ransom.

Scots casualties amounted to between 6,000 and 16,000 with Patten recording 13,000 in his account. English casualties were far fewer, the overall figure was perhaps at most 1,000 but as earlier mentioned included some of the important captains. The monetary cost of the expedition in soldiers' wages was very precisely calculated at £26,299 7s 1d. Payments were made to Scottish guides, spies and bonuses paid to mercenaries, even the Scottish herald was rewarded with 100 shillings, a chivalric courtesy.

It is easy to explain the English victory and the Scots defeat. It could be attributed to so many factors, the indiscipline of one side compared to the discipline of the other, superiority and modernity in weapons, unity among the English commanders and disunity among the Scots. Somerset fought a much better battle than Arran, whose behaviour at the end was contemptible. Was it, as has been argued, the triumph of a 'modern' army over a 'medieval' one? This is a much more difficult question to address; after all the Scots were equipped with the puissant pike, not the spear, and their artillery was as modern, although perhaps not as numerous as that of their enemies. Where they differed most was in the matter of cavalry, where they lacked any heavy horsemen, and in infantry firepower where they had few if any handguns. Even so, the English Bulleners and Gentlemen Pensioners did not win the battle, they only stopped it being lost. It was English firepower that swept the Scots columns from the field but only because the Scots columns had paused to reorder themselves. Could the Scots have won? If Angus had responded immediately to the order to advance; if Huntly's men had taken more notice of the danger of the English fleet; if Arran had not paused to receive the English cavalry, then what might have happened? Without a doubt a superior

---

35 Patten, *The expedicion into Scotla[n]de*, p.124.

English force commanded by a better general won in the end but whether this was the triumph of the new against the old is a moot point.

Somerset did not immediately take advantage of his remarkable victory. His army was itself not undamaged, the heavy cavalry having suffered grievous casualties. Yet, for some eight days his army remained inactive in Leith which he made no effort to fortify, nor did he seek to besiege Edinburgh or Stirling. The expedition cost far more than what had been budgeted for and the campaign season was coming to an end. The expedition was posited on achieving a quick victory within the capacity of its logistical supply, which had been achieved. The strategy was not one of successive sieges and conquest but occupation through garrisons and the support of the assured Scots. Having decisively defeated and humiliated the Scots, the way now lay open for a new strategy: the establishment of an English Pale.

Somerset and the 'Rough Wooing'

The defeat at Pinkie left Scotland desperately weak and enabled Somerset, ably assisted by Grey of Wharton, to besiege and capture numerous strongholds which unsurprisingly had put up little effective resistance. The use of garrisons in the 'bowels' of the realm, to hold down territory and population, was not new. Threave, Lochmaben and Caerlaverock had been garrisoned by Thomas Wharton the Warden of the West March in 1544, and Hertford himself regretted the destruction of the blockhouse at Inchgarvy, which he felt should have been fortified and held. The system of garrisons that was established after the battle for the: 'preseruation of the countrie thereabouts to the King of England's use',[36] now controlled land containing thousands of 'assured' Scotsmen who had sworn an oath of loyalty to the English Crown. The policy that Somerset promoted, even though it might rely on a system of hostage taking and coercion, was working, and peace reigned by the year's end. The Scots benefited from English garrisons that paid them for their meat and drink, while the Scots provided information and military assistance. This process was assisted by the spread of Protestantism in the south of the country.

Even before the invasion and the Battle of Pinkie, Somerset had established a strategically placed bastioned fort at Eyemouth, only six miles north of Berwick. Built across the narrow neck of a small peninsula, it was provided with a trench 20 feet deep and a massive single bastion, well provided for with artillery, and it set the pattern for his new fortifications. Using earth and masonry, it was a strong fort that was abandoned in 1550, but extended and re-armed by the French from 1557 until the treaty of Cateau Cambrésis of 1559. Further garrisons were established at Dunglass, Fast, Fernihurst, Hailes, Saltoun and Inchkeith. Somerset chose the sites of his future garrisons carefully.

---

36 Holinshed, *Chronicles* (2013), p.552.

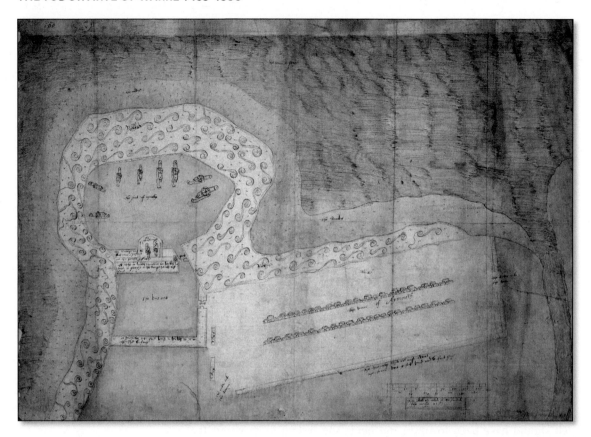

Plan of Fort Point, Eyemouth Castle. Little evidence now remains of Eyemouth castle, which was in its time a substantial fortification that had been greatly extended by the French. Set on a small spit of land with near vertical cliffs on three sides, it needed only a short earth wall to cut it off from the mainland. The positioning of artillery pieces pointing out to sea would suggest that French naval gunfire was more to be feared than any landward Scots. (Courtesy of the British Library. BL Cotton Augustus I. i. 60)

The island of Inchcolm in the Firth of Forth could control the approach to Leith some six miles away; its abbey provided first shelter and later material for a new fortification. It was provided with a heavy armament of one culverin, one demi-culverin, three iron sakers, one brass saker, two iron falcons, three brass falcons, four fowlers, two port pieces; 14 bases, 90 arquebuses, two chests of bows, 50 pikes and 40 bills. It is little more than half a mile offshore to the north and less than three miles to the nearest shore to the south; the island provided fresh water for drinking and rabbits for eating. With a garrison equipped with fast rowbarges, it held a strategically valuable position which was unassailable.

Broughty Craig, also known as 'Bragyng Trowble', was an important castle sited on the narrowest passage of the Firth of Tay, thereby controlling access to Dundee. Dundee had early on become a centre for Scottish Protestantism and therefore a potential source of allies. Broughty Craig castle was surrendered to an English fleet after only three shots had been fired and became a base for operations on the Tay. It was, however, in a poor state and could only be readily supplied by sea. It was built not on a rocky outcrop but on sand and pebbles and presented major problems for anyone seeking to provide it with strong defences. The cost of refortifying it, under the expertise of the Italian engineer Giovanni de Rossetti (John de Rosset), was over £2,000 and by May 1548 the cost of maintaining a garrison there would add almost £17,000 more. Somerset's policy clearly was not as cheap as he might have hoped.

Somerset continued to collect Scottish castles, with Home Castle first and soon after the medieval ruins of Roxburgh; Castlemilk, Cockpool and Dumfries were also garrisoned. Roxburgh was in a strong natural position but needed the modern fortifications that had been designed by Richard Lee. Somerset himself worked on the fortifications for two hours a day, acting as an inspiration to his officers, who followed his example with apparent enthusiasm. Provided with stabling and barracks, the new fortification included brewhouses, bakeries and store houses. Lord Grey of Wilton was put in command and from there he controlled the English effort in the east, while Warton was responsible for the west from Carlisle.

The euphoria and enthusiasm that had established these garrisons was now tempered by the reality of a Scottish winter, which almost inevitably began early. All suffered in the cold and wet but especially the horses, which were essential if the garrisons were to act aggressively and maintain the appearance of regional predominance. In October, of the 1,528 light horse on paper only 840 were fit, there were 100 men unfit while the remainder of the horses were described as 'evill'. Their owners were 'Yorkshire men, too poor to remount themselves'.[37] Grey wrote to Wilton in high dudgeon, because of his failure to appreciate the pressures that constant operations had on his horses and men:

> Your grace may please consider they were never at rest, but ever travelling – what with convoys from here to Haddington twice or thrice weekly – nightly scouting – sending to the country for carriages – bringing victuals from Aberlady, biscuits and faggots on horseback – and many other occasions that you know happen in war – besides their evil fare [inadequate fodder] for long. So that there be as many dead as £1000. Will not supply![38]

Grey's letter to Somerset of 27 October summarised the difficulties that he faced that made further offensives impossible. He wrote that:

> The device for invasion [A plan for an invasion by 6000 men, proposed by Lord Douglas on October 20th. Somerset doubted his loyalty and advised Lord Grey to treat him cautiously] lately sent to your grace must be given up this winter, for there has since been and still is such an abundance of rain, the waters so high, and the ground so rotten, as has not been for many years, that neither horsemen nor carriage can pass. And unless your grace give orders for beerhouses at the new erected peeces and reinforces us with horses, we cannot help them for the country carriages are so utterly decayed and tired that they cannot serve us, or even bring home their own corn, which yet lies in great quantity in the field, as they right piteously lament and bewail.[39]

---

37 *Calendar of the State Papers relating to Scotland and Mary, Queen of Scots* (*CSP Scotland*), vol. 1, 1547–1563, ed. Joseph Bain (Edinburgh: HM General Register House, 1898), p.30, 23 October, Lord Grey to Somerset.
38 *CSP Scotland*, p.122.
39 *CSP Scotland*, p.32.

The dreadful conditions did not seem to hinder the labourers and soldiers, who had deserted their posts, from leaving.

At Inchcolm the island had in effect become a prison for the garrison, as they could neither interdict the shipping entering Leith nor receive supplies by sea. At Broughty the conditions for the garrison were vile: without decent accommodation or supplies of fresh food, the troops were incapable of doing anything more than defending themselves and mutiny was feared. A letter from Sir Andrew Dudley to Somerset reveals the frustration, anger and sense of impotence faced by those facing the task of establishing a garrison far from home:

> I am in great need, in the middle of enemies, in a weak house slenderly left, my men tired with constant watch, many sick with the ague and more like to be. There is neither wood, coal, nor candle, glass for windows, scant window to shut, nor door, lock, nor bolt, latch nor nail. I have no workmen or artificers, other than Mr John de Rosset the Italian Engineere, fallen sick with overwork. I have sent for a smith's forge, but have not got it, and but three carpenters, one aged and sick and another lame. Never man had so weak a company of soldiers given to eating and drinking and slothfulness and I have not three gunners that can load or discharge his piece, and I lack nine of the twenty I should have, and sixteen other soldiers besides sick men.[40]

The dire conditions did not stop Dudley from defending his position successfully, with the aid of 100 men from the ships *Mary Hamborough* and the *Phenix*, from a Scottish force of 3,000 well supplied with ordnance. The Scots had 'trenched' to the walls and battered the tower and had driven the ships away, but even so they had been driven back and their ordnance almost taken. It was Arran who eventually abandoned the siege on 9 December. Yet Dudley had expended much of his munitions and his castle was '[but] a weak house beaten and shaken at the siege and all our work (no great matter) only rotten sandy turf and shingle, falling down daily'.[41]

It was felt that if only Dundee could be garrisoned it would have provided a suitable base for operations but it would also be a hostage to misfortune. The arrival of a small but efficient English fleet now permitted the long-sought counter-attack, seizing Dundee by using naval gunfire and a small land force. This included 70 arquebusiers as well as three mercenary captains: Tiberio, Cattlyne and Pompey. Dundee was now ostensibly 'assured'. Dudley was still facing significant logistical problems both to provide for his expanded garrison as well as for the needs of Dundee, which was now isolated from its neighbours. On Christmas day 1547 Arran received a present of 50 French captains, who brought with them enough coin to pay for an army of 10,000 for a year. This largesse was supplemented with £5,000 from the Scottish bishops. Arran now had the money and the impetus to besiege Broughty Craig, which was still far from fully prepared.

---

40   *CSP Scotland*, p.24.
41   *CSP Scotland*, p.53.

Dudley at Broughty faced many problems; a shortage of cash left his mercenary force unhappy and his relations with Wyndham, the captain of the small squadron of ships, were strained. Dudley described his men as 'idle and vicious' and fell out with the men who had brought their 'Scottes quenes' (wives) with them. Neither the sailors nor soldiers would set to the task of refortification as they said they were not sent to be labourers. His own defences were in a parlous state. Most stores, wet and dry, were transported in barrels: to save shipping space on the return journey the barrels could be broken down and fitted inside other barrels. This was possible because barrels were held together with hazel withies, not iron bands. In the absence of building materials on site, Dudley had filled the barrels with earth as a form of gabion, without which his ramparts would have collapsed. As no barrels were returned to Berwick no stores were sent and instead the supplies were left to rot.

Somerset considered fortifying Dundee but this would require a larger garrison, provided by the assured population. When Argyll approached the town the 'loyal' Scots rediscovered their original loyalty, and the English forces in the town were forced to retreat. Wyndham explained to Somerset that 'Notwithstanding the promises of the men of Dundee, when they saw the great power with Argyll, they have wholly left the town.'[42] Wyndham boasted that 'with 500 men I would have held it against all Scotland, or died in it'.[43] The latter outcome seems most likely. Despite his protestations, the English ordnance in the town was removed to the ships and the church steeple burned. Wyndham carried out raids along the shore to divert Argyll from his intended target, which was Broughty. The French brought with them the latest military equipment and what became noticeable was the large number of arquebusiers among the Scottish ranks. Argyll's bodyguard was made up of 100 arquebusiers, and a mounted force of supposedly 1,000 arquebusiers chased one of Wyndham's raiding parties back to their boats.

The second siege of Broughty, with Argyll having double the number of troops of his previous effort as well as 12 cannons, was again unsuccessful, this time lasting only 10 days. Broughty was now even more battered and more useless a base. Inchcolm was abandoned in March as it had proved a liability rather than an asset and its commander was sent to Dundee, which he soon found could not be made defensible. The effort was now made to secure Broughty with a new fortification at Balgillo some 600 yards to the north-west of the castle. This was an excellent site for what would be a new style of fort based on the principles of the *trace italienne*, designed by the Italian engineer master, John de Rosset, who on its completion was appointed master of ordnance. The outer ditch was 10 feet broad and six deep and went down to the rock; a much happier site than that of Broughty which was built on sand and shingle.

This new plan was fully supported by Lord Grey with men, money and equipment, including prefabricated dwellings for the soldiers. Despite this stronger position and Grey's support, Luttrell, the new commander first of

---

42   *CSP Scotland*, p.67.
43   *CSP Scotland*, p.67.

Balgillo and on 21 March of both fortifications, found himself isolated and ill provided for. The men's pay was some 18 months in arrears. The soldiers had been making match cord from their shirts for the past three months when Luttrell reported to Somerset on 30 April. The fortifications required continual repair, the diet of salt meat was damaging to the digestion and morale, and rather than dominating the surrounding area he found himself surrounded by a hostile population. He wrote to Somerset, in terms that would not have endeared him to his commanders, that for the failure to supply Broughty 'I cannot judge great fault in your grace's ministers and commissioners in the north parts.'[44]

Somerset wished to extend his control over Scotland before the French arrived in numbers. To achieve that, in February 1548 Wharton would advance from the west and Grey from the east. Grey's advance was unimpeded, but Wharton suffered a disaster at Drumlanrig. He was leading a mixed force of English Borderers and assured Scots, and was met by a Scottish force commanded by the wily Angus, victor of Ancrum Moor. Wharton had divided his forces, and a large raiding party commanded by his son was ambushed by Angus and betrayed by the 'assured' Maxwells who rode with them. In Wharton's force the majority of the assured Scots turned against their English allies. Wharton's footmen proved staunch and he was able to retire; with the Scots close on his heels at only a pike's length, the discipline of the infantry in a fighting retreat in close contact with the enemy was most commendable, as it could have become a rout and a rout a massacre. He was only just saved from defeat when his son Henry arrived with the remnants of his force, and surprised and broke the Scottish infantry that threatened his father. Wharton had regained his son but lost his baggage train at Dumfries as well as any confidence that he may have had in the assured Scots.

The English had lost the initiative, and although they still held numerous garrisons, their policy of creating an English Pale had collapsed. The mutual dislike that characterised Wharton and Grey's relationship now turned to loathing. Grey had also fallen out with the mercenary captain Gamboa. He concluded a letter to Somerset saying that Gamboa 'may act like a Spaniard, but I have an english heart not dreadfull of Spanish Italian, nor other bragges, will not take revenge after his country's manne.'[45] Grey now also had a personal feud with the Maxwells and any hope for a political settlement was lost.

To ensure the line of communications across the border a new and very sophisticated fort was built at Lauder, again employing soldiers rather than pioneers. The use of earth rather than stone made the use of unskilled labour possible; it also ensured that it was built quickly. The garrison consisted of a lieutenant, ensign, drummer, two clerks, a surgeon, day and night watchmen, six gunners, 10 light horse, 40 Spanish arquebusiers, 30 English billmen or archers, three bakers, two millers, one brewer, one cooper, one slater and a millwright.

---

44   *CSP Scotland*, p.112.
45   *CSP Scotland*, p.151.

Somerset was now seeking to build fortifications to defend the route back to England rather than to control Scotland, as he was aware that the spring of 1548 would bring French reinforcements and a reinvigorated Scottish army. Dunbar would have been his first choice as a base but to capture it and then refortify would have taken too long. Instead he decided on a new fortification in the small town or *burgh* of Haddington, some 18 miles from Edinburgh and supplied by sea from Aberlady five miles away. As Grey reported, the place chosen was not ideal: 'the evil site overlooked by higher ground, the infidelity of some expected friends, scarcity of victuals, and nearness of the enemy, might have feared us, yet I doubt not with constant labour to overcome these difficulties'.[46] Under the direction of Sir Thomas Palmer the project continued, with Grey remaining there for two months.

The fort encompassing the town was an impressive structure, again made of earth rather than stone, built on the latest principles with four angle bastions, a *fausse-braye* and base court (an outer courtyard that was lightly protected for the safe and secure protection of livestock) as well as what Grey refers to as a tollbooth. This was a substantial multi-storied building, not what one would normally consider a toll house to be. The fort was well provided for with artillery, with one demi-cannon, two iron and three brass culverins, one iron and four brass demi-culverins, three iron and two brass sakers, six brass falcons, three double bases and 15 single bases; it could house a garrison of 2,500. Surprisingly the work was not interrupted and in fact was assisted by local labour. In April 1548 its store contained 538 quarters of food grains, 489 quarters of grain for ale, 130 tuns of beer and 14 tuns of sack and Malmsey wines and 33 tuns of Gascony wine, 800 nolts (cows), 1,000 sheep and 38 bullocks; an impressive quantity of food and drink.[47] The Scots were waiting on the arrival of the French and were incommoded by Somerset's continued raiding. What Somerset failed to realise was that the building of Lauder and Haddington was proof of the failure of his original strategy, as the idea of collaboration gave way to coercion. James Henrisoun pointed out the contradiction in Somerset's action, asking: 'whether it were better to conquor hearts without charges [expense], or burn and build forts at great charges, which will never conquer Scotland'.[48]

Henri II of France was determined not to let Scotland fall into English hands. The loss of Boulogne was a terrible shame and the French were determined to do as much damage as possible to England's interests. The French fleet had arrived in June, undisturbed as the English fleet had been withdrawn in March for the sake of economy. The force that arrived was sizeable and well equipped with some 10,000 infantry of which 2,000 were French and the remainder German and Swiss, plus 1,200 gendarmes and 800 light horse. Just as important were the commanders of these veteran troops, highly experienced in their own right, including Piero Strozzi and 'The Rhinegrave' the Count of Salm, and the commander of the Landsknechts. The English forces were now dispersed and weakened by harsh weather and poor provisions and their pay was months in

46 *CSP Scotland*, p.111.
47 *CSP Scotland*, p.113.
48 *CSP Scotland*, p.180.

arrears; above all there was little or no chance of reinforcement or replacement and their horses were few and in a poor state. At Haddington for example the force of 400 light horse had been reduced to 120, the remainder of the men having fled. The mercenaries that were relied upon to provide the specialist skills were on the verge of mutiny and many had already deserted. Pedro de Gamboa and his mounted arquebusiers were only mollified by doubling their rate of pay to eight ducats a month, justified by 'considering our want of men and his good service'.[49]

It was not Haddington that was first attacked but Captain Luttrell at Broughty on 16 June 1548, when a French squadron of 16 galleys appeared offshore and engaged the castle, not Balgillo fort, with artillery. Philips suggests that this was because of the defensive strength of the earth defences to artillery as opposed to the tall stone walls of Broughty Castle. The fort was about a mile from the castle and some 40 metres higher up: it might simply have been the limited elevation of the main armament of the galley that determined its target. The contest between wooden ships and a stone castle was unequal and the galleys were forced to withdraw because of the accurate shooting from Balgillo and the current, which kept them from facing the castles bow-on: the heavy armament of a galley was fitted to the bow along the centreline of the craft, not as a broadside as on sailing vessels. Luttrell continued his spirited defence with aggressive patrolling and raids. In the absence of the horses and carts he had requested, he used two teams of captured oxen and 16 horses to carry the material needed to strengthen his fortifications. Whatever he achieved mattered little, as the main French and Scottish forces now descended upon Haddington.

It was felt that the siege of Haddington would be the decisive moment in the campaign, for as Thomas Palmer wrote to Somerset: 'Keeping Haddington you win Scotland.'[50] On 30 June the besieging army arrived, after some bickering with Tiberio's infantry company. In front of Haddington they were met by a confident English garrison that had been given a holiday for having completed their defences, leaving 'nothing left unperfected';[51] morale on both sides was high. The French commander, Sieur D'Ésse, began the slow business of conducting a siege. Emplacements were dug for the artillery, one cannon, four 'moyennes' and eight falcons, together with their powder magazines; trenches were dug. All was achieved with the assistance of 900 Scottish pioneers assisted later by 500 oarsmen (probably galley slaves). Piero Strozzi was wounded by an arquebus shot in the leg which disabled him for some time, much to the delight of the English who had hoped the wound fatal.

The English defence was very active, engaging in sallies to disrupt the French preparations. The earth fortifications brought down by artillery fire during the day were rebuilt at night. Inside the fortifications the remaining houses suffered heavily from French gunfire and the results were disastrous for the garrison: 'And in the ende, our enemies did so beat the towne with

---

49   *CSP Scotland*, p.122.
50   *CSP Scotland*, p.133.
51   *CSP Scotland*, p.133.

shott, that they lefte not one whole house for our men to put their heads in: Whereby they were constrained to lye vnder the walles, (for other lodging was there none).'[52] St Mary's Church was used by the French to mount small pieces of artillery called 'cuthroats' on the steeple but they were eventually driven out through accurate English fire. Disappointed with the effect of his gunnery, D'Ésse moved a six-gun battery within 60 paces of the defensive ditch and fired 200 rounds in one day to greater effect. The garrison's stout defence surprised the French, who were also suffering heavily, especially the pioneers on whom depended so much.

Haddington needed reinforcement if it was to survive, and this was soon to arrive. Sir Thomas Palmer led 400 (some sources suggest 210 Englishmen and 150 Spaniards under Pedro Negro) carrying a large supply of powder and slow match, which was escorted by a large force of horse and foot. The operation was planned and carried out with precision, speed and success and gave new heart and much-needed supplies to the garrison. The horses remained in Haddington and were killed, a terrible waste of expensive horses for perhaps 1½ tons of powder. The conditions for the besiegers worsened, however. The French mines had been destroyed with countermines, French artillery had been dismounted and their Scots allies now refused to take part in any more assaults; even Argyll had departed although promising to return.

The utter collapse of Somerset's strategy occurred on 7 July within sight of the Haddington garrison. The Scottish Parliament agreed in the Abbey of Haddington to a marriage between Queen Mary and the Dauphin and in return France would acquire permanent garrisons in Scotland. Scotland was now in effect a client state of France. Somerset's response, which was to renew the unrealistic claim of the English king to the throne of Scotland, could only be achieved with a new aggressive policy. This was at a time when England's resources were stretched to the limit and her garrisons under attack. Haddington's defences, especially Wylford's bastion, had by now suffered considerable damage. One of the bastions had been 'beaten down to flatte so that a man might ryde in and out at the breach'.[53] Flanking fire made it impossible to retain it and a further fortification was built behind it, a standard procedure. The French had managed to drive a sap into the defensive wall and the ditch was now filled with fascines; all that was required was a final assault.

Francis Talbot was now ordered to raise a royal army that would relieve Haddington, which was possible, and to then conquer Scotland, which was quite impossible. Lord Grey and Sir Thomas Palmer meanwhile brought a substantial force of horse and foot to relieve the fort. This was on the understanding that the French were about to abandon the siege and that their watch would be as bad as it had been the first time they had relieved the fort. In practice the French were waiting, and Palmer's impetuosity led to the force becoming heavily engaged and being driven from the field, with himself being captured.

52 Ulpian Fulwell, *The Flower of Fame* (London: William Hoskins, 1575) 5. From J.P. Cooper, 'Whitecoats and Rascals', p.23.
53 Fulwell, *The Flower of Fame*, 51. From J.P. Cooper, 'Whitecoats and Rascals', p.55.

When Talbot arrived in Scotland he found that the substantial cavalry force that had accompanied Grey had been almost completely lost and that the light cavalry had dispersed. In addition, the 2,000 Landsknechts which he considered essential were still to arrive. The French had their own problems. The siege of Haddington was maintained, but with little chance of success. The English army would have to be met soon and the English fleet, now substantially reinforced, threatened the French galleys. The galleys had been stripped of their soldiers for the land campaign but if they were to face the English fleet the soldiers would have to be re-embarked, leaving the land campaign dead in the water. The galleys left, without their soldiers but with the young queen. The English fleet led by Clinton could now blockade the Scottish ports, leaving the French army facing similar difficulties of supply and reinforcement as the English had suffered. Clinton fought off a small French galley attack and drove the remainder of the French fleet away; he conducted further raids and burnt 12 ships. Leith however remained in French hands and was being transformed into a defended town, using the *trace italienne* guided by the wounded but still vigorous Piero Strozzi, who was carried about the town in a chair carried by four men. In 1554 this plucky Italian was made a Marshal of France and continued to serve loyally and successfully until his death in action in 1558.

On 18 August Shrewsbury's army began its advance from Berwick, with 11,412 foot including 1,200 arquebusiers, the much-awaited Landsknechts and 1,800 horse. Organised into three battles of roughly equal size and one of Landsknechts 2,020 strong, it was a powerful force and was now probably double the size of D'Ésse's much-reduced army. Shrewsbury forced the French to withdraw and entered Haddington on the 29th. Wylford and his garrison were greatly praised for their conduct but both the commander and his men were utterly exhausted. D'Esse was strongly fortified in Musselburgh now with 15,000 Scottish reinforcements, and Shrewsbury was unwilling to risk a battle without certainty of victory. Somerset was left railing at Shrewsbury's timidity and the cost of the expedition.

After confronting the Franco-Scots army and burning Dunbar, Shrewsbury withdrew, using his men as a covering force and constructed a modern star-shaped fort at Dunglas. It was too far from Haddington to be of much use and without a port it was of little value but great cost. In the East March the warden led destructive raids in Teviotdale and Liddesdale against those assured Scots whose loyalty had lapsed, a policy not bound to restore their faith in or love for English government. Somerset had hoped for a more decisive outcome from all this effort, but as it was, very little had changed.

It was the intention of D'Ésse that the strategic situation should be drastically altered and quickly: a victory was needed. His Landsknechts had been involved in a violent riot in Edinburgh, treating their Scottish hosts as enemies and receiving as good as they got. A quick victory was needed to restore the confidence of his men and the support of his allies. If Haddington could not be taken by assault, then perhaps it could be by stealth. A camisade was launched on 7 or 9 October (there is some disagreement over the precise date). After overwhelming the few pickets, the French found themselves in the base court. Here either a renegade mercenary Frenchman serving in the garrison or Captain Tiberio fired a 'double cannon' (not a double-barrelled weapon but a cannon of the largest size) into their midst, just as they shouted 'victory, victory'. The English garrison now rallied and drove them out at the point of pike and bill killing several hundred, to the apparent satisfaction of the much-wronged Edinburgh population who cheered the victory over their loathed allies. There was also much disgust in the garrison that their Scottish assured 'allies' had not warned them of the approach of 3,000, apparently extremely stealthy, Frenchmen.

The assurance system had by now collapsed. The French were still determined to continue the war and were harassing the English lines of communication. Winter was coming and the walls of the earth forts were collapsing. Luttrell in Broughty reported that: 'thennymye shall not need to laye ony battery unto hytt for theye shall fynde hytt fallen downe redy to ther handys'.[54] Despite this he continued to skirmish with the French and drive them from his forts. He was short of money, bread and beer and there were not even coals enough in the smithy to enable his horses to be shod. Somerset offered him nothing but criticism, and 'for this tyme lie there as you were ded for the while'.[55] The conditions in Haddington were equally parlous. On 1 November Wylford, addressing Somerset, wrote that:

> The state of this town pities me both to see and to write it; but … I hope for relief. Many are sick and a great number dead, most of the plague. On my faith there are not here this day of horse, foot, and Italians, 1000 able to go to the walls, and more like to be sick, than the sick to mend, who watch the walls every 5th night, yet the walls are not manned, they lie in litter without beds, go in their single white coats, for there is small provision of clothing.[56]

The garrison was in a worse condition than when it had been besieged by the French. Supplies were spoiling through lack of transport, reinforcements had yet to arrive and the escort of convoys was exhausting what few cavalry Wylford had left. Worse still, the gallant commander was captured when escorting a convoy into Haddington, by French troops based in Dunbar.

Somerset was in no position to act aggressively in Scotland, and his order to the English forces was now to do as little as was needed. Closer to home he had been appalled by his brother's apparent treason in January 1549 and his preoccupation with domestic matters was hardly surprising. France had declared war in August and there was likely to be a renewed attempt to recover Boulogne. Grey, whose energy and sagacity had been essential for the Scottish strategy, was utterly exhausted physically and financially. He wrote to Somerset in August in a state close to despair:

> Now we have Haddington out of peril … as I am quit of my last commission of lieutenantship, I trust your grace will licence me to come home and live on my small portion, while seeking to win back what is wrongfully kept from me. I have

54 Philips, *The Anglo-Scots Wars*, p.243.
55 Philips, *The Anglo-Scots Wars*, p.244.
56 *CSP Scotland*, pp.165–166.

often showed your grace that the great charges … have brought me in debt, and now by my late great loss, I can endure no more.[57]

While the English were despondent the Scottish party was now reinvigorated by the return of Lord Huntly, who breaking his parole now joined Arran and the Dowager Queen as the Chancellor. Using spies and subtlety, first Home Castle was recovered and soon after Fast Castle, where humble carters turned out to be Scottish commandos. The capture of Ferniehurst Castle was less subtle, and involved a rapid assault that overwhelmed the English skirmishers outside and then the use of firepower to drive the defenders from the ramparts. It was only a matter of time before the doors were broken open and the unpopular garrison surrendered. Those who met with a Scot were dealt with swiftly and those who surrendered to a Frenchman were then sold to a Scot, to end the same bloody way.

With a base in Jedburgh the Scots and French took part in savage raids in England, burning farms and villages and stealing livestock from Northumberland. De Biron led a force to the gates of Newcastle and D'Esse led an attack on Ford Castle. Here the resistance was stout and his Scottish allies fickle. After glutting themselves with the plunder of 10 villages and expecting reprisals, they turned for home. D'Esse's army was now reduced to some 2,000 men, who were attempting to survive in winter in a ravaged country; their only option was to follow the Scots north, facing no interference from the equally exhausted English.

Still wedded to the idea of interdiction rather than occupation, Somerset used the fleet to establish a garrison on Inchkeith island, a scant four miles from Leith itself. D'Esse had been recently reinforced with some 300 horse and 1,000 foot, under the command of Paul de la Barthe, Sieur de Thermes. In June 1549, some 16 days after they had landed on the island, the English force including Derbyshire archers and Italian arquebusiers was defeated in a fierce battle that saw the deaths of their commanders.

The summer of 1549 was catastrophic for Somerset and his regime. In England rebellions had broken out across the southern counties, most seriously in East Anglia and the West Country. Within the regime political opposition to the campaign was becoming more and more vocal. Sir Thomas Smith informed Somerset that the coffers were empty and it would be October before more money would be available. Overseas borrowing, principally in the Antwerp money market, was also at a much higher rate of interest as it was clear that England was in serious trouble. The formal declaration of war by France at the beginning of August meant that a new front had to be opened, with Boulogne and Calais reinforced. Paget made the position clear to Somerset:

You have to mayntayne contynally during the warres great nombers of men against Scotland, great garrison against fraunce both by land and sea and no small power

---

57   *CSP Scotland*, p.163.

thorough your Realme for the reducynge of the same to the kings obedience, All which can not be furnished without great sommes of money.[58]

Aberlady, the port for Haddington, was seized by the French, and despite best efforts the supply and support of the English fortification was no longer feasible. It had long outgrown any use it might once have had, and was abandoned in September 1549. As Hayward sagely commented, it 'could not bee kept without danger, nor lost without dishonour'.[59] It had cost £1,423 in construction and £31,641 12s 4d in running repairs, cartage and munitions (but not victuals). Eyemouth had cost £3,598 9s 1d, Roxburgh £5,303 9s 10d and Lauder £6,656 15s 3d.[60] It is difficult to argue with the description of Somerset's forts as 'sumptuous endles vayne Fortificacions'.[61]

Somerset was replaced in a coup by the Earl of Warwick, who had recently vanquished Kett's rebels, in October 1549. Warwick realised that the war with France and Scotland could not be continued and that a peace, however humiliating it might be, was essential if there was to be social and political stability in the realm. In February 1550 Balgillo fort and soon after Broughty Craig fell, already in practice abandoned by England, if not by their brave garrisons and commander. Lauder was besieged by Thermes and would have been taken, except that the end of the war came about by treaty. Lauder and all the other forts still left in Scotland were abandoned. The Treaty of Boulogne, signed in March 1550, was effectively dictated by France to England. Boulogne was to be returned immediately at a fraction of the agreed price. Edward VI's claim to the Scottish throne and the hand of Queen Mary was abandoned and his new bride would be a French princess, Elizabeth de Valois. The humiliation was complete. Henri II could now write in triumph to his Ottoman ally, the Grand Sultan, 'I have brought peace to Scotland which I hold and possess with the same order and obedience that I have in France.'[62]

---

58 Merriman, *The Rough Wooings*, p.344.
59 Hayward, *The Life, and Raigne*, p.73.
60 Merriman, *The Rough Wooings*, p.316.
61 Hale, *Renaissance War Studies*, p.95; *Statutes of the Realm*, vol. iv (London, 1819), p.176.
62 Merriman, *The Rough Wooings*, p.298. From Guillaume Ribier, *Lettres Et Memoires D'Estat Des Roys, Princes, Ambassadeurs Et autres Ministres sous les Regnes de François premier, Henri II & François II* vol. 2 (Clouzier, 1666), p.188.

Part II

The Armies

6

Tactics

The Armies and Tactics at Bosworth

The armies that faced each other at Bosworth with their bills and bows, men-at-arms and a few and often 'foreign' gunners, were inheritors of a long and on the whole remarkable tradition of military success which had begun over 150 years before. The Wars of the Roses, which began in 1455, neatly dovetailed with long war with France, which had ended in almost complete defeat only two years before. The skills which had been of such use against the French would now be used against fellow countrymen.

The men were drawn from the household of their masters as a consequence of a system referred to as livery and maintenance. They wore their lord's colours and badge and served him either as professional soldiers, members of his household or his tenants or in some other binding social, familial or economic relationship. Aged from their late teens to their early forties, although some older and younger, they could be found in the camp and sometimes the grave; they were, on the basis of archaeological evidence, well grown, fit and healthy, although demonstrating the diseases of poverty and the consequences of lives of back-breaking hard work.

The principal weapons of the infantry were the bow and the bill. The war bow was capable of shooting a war shaft well over 200 yards with a velocity of about 50 m/s. A skilled archer could loose six to eight per minute. Able to penetrate plate armour at short ranges and unprotected flesh at any range, it was a fearsome weapon. The bill was a substantial polearm weapon derived from the agricultural bill. Able to catch, cut, thrust and smash, it was thought half a dozen blows would be enough to finish off any opponent.

Infantry such as these would be provided with iron caps or helmets, with the salet most popular for archers. The linen jack, made up of many layers of material, was the basic protection for the torso. This could be improved by the addition of mail and plate armour, especially for the legs. Arm defences could be improvised by the use of chains as well as plate armour, and further plate in the form of plakart or breastplate would protect the stomach and chest respectively. The heavy single-edged falchion was the soldier's sword. A man cleaver, it was devastatingly effective particularly when used with the buckler, a small shield used for deflecting and giving blows. Fighting knives and daggers of varying forms would also be an essential accompaniment in both camp and combat.

Well-equipped men-at-arms provided with full plate armour and armed with sword, axe, mace and poleaxe would provide the real strength of the formation. Strong, well trained and capable, they required the support of billmen, but like a heavy rugby pack they could be the real powerhouses of an army. Mounted men-at-arms would have made up only a small part of either army. Unlike the French, the English elite were used to fighting on foot surrounded by their own men, as Norfolk and Oxford were to demonstrate. The war horse was a valued addition to their armoury, a highly specialised and expensive addition it had been found of little use in the domestic confrontations of this period. That is not to say it was not used or of little value, it certainly played a part in the Yorkist victory at Tewkesbury. Richard's final and fatal charge saw how effective it could be; it is, however, unlikely that Richard could have mustered a large body of mounted men-at-arms, certainly not the 1,000 or so suggested by some. Henry's army was not in the business of charging anyone, it looked only for survival until something (like the Stanleys) turned up.

The English and Welsh who fought at Bosworth would have conformed to these types, but the French mercenaries may well have had different weapons. In France the crossbow was preferred to the longbow. In addition, the handgun was much more popular. Both crossbow and handgun shared similar characteristics: they were designed to be used against armoured targets, had a low rate of fire and short practical range. The other weapon they could have been employed was the pike, a long spear of about 18 feet in length, which was increasingly gaining favour in Europe as the weapon of infantry. The pike may have been present at Bosworth and it was well represented at Stoke Field two years later in the hands of Landsknecht mercenaries.

The final accompaniment to any army was its artillery, and in this Richard's forces seem to have been particularly well equipped. The guns were constructed of wrought iron using a hoop and stave system. Bronze guns were also commonly employed: the two damaged bronze barrels found on the Towton battlefield are clearly evidence of such weapons being in use. The barrels were anything from one to six inches in diameter and mounted on increasingly sophisticated carriages. They could fire stone shot or anti-personnel hail shot. The lighter pieces could be reloaded twice in a minute, perhaps more often with removable breeches, and could shoot their projectiles several hundred yards with some degree of accuracy. Artillery bombardments might be expected to precede a general engagement: at this early stage in the tactical deployment of artillery difficulties in precise aiming, ranging, consistency of powder and shot all made its operation a rather hit or miss affair.

How the individual contingents, made up as they were of a combination of different men and equipment, were organised into a fighting force is unclear. Armies were arranged in three battles or vans. The vanguard was the strongest part of the army and led it on the march and onto the field of battle. The main was commanded by the leader and was the heart of the army while the rear formed the left wing and was deemed rather less crucial to the army. At Bosworth the Duke of Norfolk, the more politically 'reliable' of the two other commanders was placed in charge of the vanguard and the less committed Northumberland in charge of the rear. Although Henry's army ostensibly conformed to the same arrangement, its numbers were so few as to make any distinction between van, main and rearguards irrelevant.

It was accepted practice that battles would begin with an exchange of gunfire followed by the archers engaging in a duel. The missile barrage of all sorts was designed to weaken the enemy and force him to attack. The choice of ground was important and especially a strong defensive position. It was assumed that an army goaded into an attack on a strong position would have the worst of it, but in practice many other factors needed to be considered, especially the morale of the troops and the possibility of betrayal.

The soldiers and commanders who faced each other at Bosworth were no strangers to conflict. Some were veterans of a lifetime's campaigning, others nervous novices, all were well equipped and able to do enormous harm to their opponents. Bosworth was a battle that was less decided by hand strokes than by treachery, and the small losses reflected the political nature of the battle; it was not a Towton.

Mid-Tudor Armies and Tactics

It is well worth beginning this section with the description of the English army provided by Barbaro the Venetian ambassador in 1551:

> Of the English soldiers, some serve on foot, others on horse-back. Those who are neither tall nor short but of agile frame, are mounted and are divided into light-horse and men-at-arms, consisting mostly of gentlemen, as they are better able to bear the expense and get good horses. Part of the light cavalry are armed in the Albanian fashion, and the rest with a shirt of mail, a sallet and a light, long spear, and use any sort of horse, as they charge only in flank: these are called demi-lances. The infantry consists of taller men, divided into four sorts. First, the archers who abound in England, and are very excellent both by nature and practice, so that the archers alone have routed armies of 30,000 men. Second, the bill-men, armed with a short, thick staff with an iron like a peasant's hedging-bill, but much thicker and heavier than the Venetians use. With this they strike so violently that they unhorse the cavalry: it is made short, as they like close quarters. Third, the harquebusiers, who are good for little, as few have had practise south of the Channel, and these, together with the fourth, the pikemen, have been but recently added to the ancient militia of England. The military commanders are first, the captain general; second, the marshal, who in the general's absence takes his place; and there is a provost of all the cavalry. There is a treasurer, a master of the militia, a master of the ordnance, a colonel, and other inferior officers. The infantry is divided into companies of a hundred men, each with its captain, lieutenant, ensign, and serjeant. The cavalry is divided into squadrons of one hundred, and similarly officered. The latter use trumpets, the infantry drums; and legitimate war is announced by a herald. When the army takes the field the

camp is fortified with wagons and barricades, if near the enemy trenches, and earthworks are made and artillery placed in suitable position. There are two sorts of watchmen, the cavalry have scouts and the infantry have sentries. On notice of the enemy's approach, the whole camp cries, "Bows! Bows!" which is the nation's last hope, and all rush to a spacious place called the camp square, to await orders.[1]

It is also worth noting that the battle cry of the English as recorded by Blaise de Monluc at Boulogne in 1544 was not something heroic and patriotic such as 'For Harry and St George' but 'quil, quil, quil'. The army that is described here was little different from that of a century before in armament and structure. Arquebusiers and pikemen were a recent and apparently not a successful introduction. This apparent 'backwardness' compared to European practice is worth considering as it was an issue both among contemporaries and historians. On the other hand, the presence of archers who were 'very excellent both by nature and practice' is considered an advantage.

The changes that occurred in the half century or so between Bosworth and Boulogne were very considerable. Bows and bills there were aplenty but pike and arquebus as well as the new artillery would seem to take pride of place. The use of mercenaries led to the appearance on a large scale of the weapons that were now dominating the Continental battlefields. The English soldier was no longer the semi-professional retained in a household but more likely a tenant or servant or even someone chosen by his parish to muster for the county commissioners. However, armies were still organised in three parts and the leadership still and inevitably lay with those of the nobility favoured by the Crown.

There are three versions of an invaluable contemporary analysis of mid-Tudor military affairs written by Thomas Audley. Audley was an experienced soldier who had been the Provost Marshal of Guînes, the largest of the 'satellite' garrisons of Calais (responsible for the discipline of the garrison), and later became the Lieutenant of the Lower Town of Boulogne after its capture in 1544. He was probably the brother of the more famous Sir Thomas Audley, Chancellor of England, and rather unhelpfully had two nephews also called Thomas. A Thomas Audley, possibly our man, was 'a gentleman usher of the chamber' in 1545. He was one of the few men in England who was in some senses a 'professional' soldier and he was to witness and participate in the last of Henry VIII's campaigns against the French. At some point during the reign of Edward VI (1547–1553) he wrote what would now be described as a 'briefing paper' on the art of war, for the benefit of the child-king.[2] As

---

1   *CSP Venice*, vol. 5, 1534–1554. May 1551, pp.338–362.
2   The transcription used here is that found in the *Journal of Army Historical Research*, vol. VI, April–June, 1927 contributed by Lieut-Colonel W. St. P.Bunbury, Royal Artillery. The BM. Add. MSS. no. 23971 is a copy of the same document which was then in the possession of Bunbury as part of the property of Barton Manor, which had previously belonged to the Audley family. This is the second version of Audley's work and according to JR Hale dates from 1547, a third copy was 'newly corrected' in the first year of the reign of Queen Mary 1553. The first copy was written at the end of the reign of Henry VIII. There is some difference of opinion as to the significance of the differences between the three copies.

such it is perhaps the first comprehensive Tudor document on warfare which describes, with some authority, the way in which the early Tudor state made war. The handwritten document was probably dictated and there were some later attempts at revision. When reading this document, it is still possible to hear the authentic, irascible and opinionated voice of the old Tudor soldier.

The document is addressed to the young king directly, and Audley assumes that the monarch will command the army personally. After conventional protestations as to his unworthiness to proffer advice, he very sensibly and honestly encourages the king to seek advice from a number of different sources, for he would: 'wishe that your Majestie should have divers mens opinions, as well strangers as Englishmen',[3] 'For I never met with no souldier but if he had knowledge in one thing or divers things yet he was ignorant in some other things.'[4] His recommendation that 'strangers' or foreigners' opinions should be sought may perhaps be a recognition of the differences between English and Continental practice, which is so often cited as English backwardness. Audley refers with some awe to the: 'Almains ... who be compted among all nations the flower of the worlde for good order of footmen and all Nacions have learned of them.'[5] Henry VIII's extensive use of German mercenaries, who made up for the English weakness in pikemen, arquebusiers and heavy cavalry, had clearly left a great impression on Audley.

Audley confidently asserts what he thinks is of greatest importance in organising an army:

> I thinke in myne opinion the division [of] weapons and placing of them is the chief strength of all batailes both on horseback and on foot for if you have to many of one kynd of weapon and too few of one other kynde of weapone when you shall come to setting out the battaile you shall fynd a great weakness by reason thereof.[6]

This concern was reflected in the list of issues to be 'ordered by the King's Majesty' in the 1544 campaign. The fifth item in the list of pressing decisions to be made was 't'appoint how many of each other weapons shall be of every hundred'.[7] Audley's ideal company would have 20 pikemen in corslets and perhaps 20 more without corslets, 20 archers and 12 arquebusiers with the remaining 28 as billmen. This was the ideal, the reality could be far different, and overall the percentage of arquebusiers was likely to be much smaller than his suggested figure. The intention to use what troop types were available, in a sophisticated mixed formation is certainly worthy of note.

The army Henry raised displayed many of the fundamental problems that Audley recognised. Although very large numerically it was made up of a great number of contingents. There are two lists of retinues of foot which

---

3   All page references are to the transcript contained in Thomas Audley, 'A Treatise on the Art of War', *Journal of the Society for Army Historical Research*, vol. 6, no. 24 (April–June, 1927), p.64.
4   Audley, 'Treatise', p.66.
5   Audley, 'Treatise', p.67.
6   Audley, 'Treatise', p.66.
7   *Letters and Papers*, 1544 No.271 R.O. 2

give a detailed analysis of the forces raised by the Privy Chamber.[8] In the first section there are 28 separate contingents and in the second 54. The largest contingent in the first list belongs to the Earl of Essex and Sir Richard Long, both with 300 men, but 14 of the smaller contingents have fewer than 50 men. The second group has even more smaller contingents: 39 have fewer than 20 men and 19 have only three or less. John Rowland and his one billman had to serve alongside Sir Richard Manours with his 20 archers and 60 billmen and the Lord Chamberlain with 80 archers and 220 billmen. The total numbers raised by the Privy Chamber were as follows:

250 assorted firearms (arquebuses, demi-hakes etc.)
1,155 archers,
410 pikemen,
1,464 billmen.

Total 3,279 men

If they were organised into 33 companies there would be seven firearms, 36 archers, 13 pike and 45 billmen in each. This would leave each company short of seven pikemen with too few firearms and too many archers. The great shortage appears to be of pikemen and arquebusiers and the equivalent superfluity of archers and billmen. What is not explained is how companies were formed, and how a multitude of retinues were formed into companies and then battles which would be able to manoeuvre with speed and flexibility.

It is quite clear that the massive forces that were raised and deployed were organised into companies of 100, for the *Calendar of State Papers* refers to the appointment and pay of 52 captains and petty captains for the 5,226 horse, and 337 captains and petty captains for the 33,693 foot.[9] The pay of a captain of foot was four shillings per diem, that for a captain of horse six shillings, with petty captains receiving half that amount. How this was achieved with a force that consisted of a myriad different, large, small and tiny contingents provided by different sources with different loyalties, no doubt containing petty jealousies and conflicting ambitions is difficult to surmise. Ian Heath points out that the distribution of captaincies was not as simple as the figures above would suggest: 'because a number served in a staff capacity (one retinue of just 60 men, for instance, included four captains), while the King's mounted Yeoman of the Guard had a captain each for their archers and arquebusiers even though neither numbered more than 50 men.'[10] It was essential for the satisfactory functioning of the army that such issues were resolved if the battles were to be successfully deployed.

---

8   *Letters and Papers,* 1544 No.275 R.O.4 i &ii
9   *Letters and Papers,* 1544 No.273 R.O. 6
10 Ian Heath, *Armies of the Sixteenth Century* (St Peter Port: Foundry Books, 1997), p.32.

Infantry

Audley insisted that each company should follow a single pattern: 'For let every standard be like appointed to so many shott so many pykes so many bylles, then shall all your army of footmen be in good order.'[11] He averred that the first act of an 'Almain' colonell and his 'expert men' was 'devysing his men to necessarie weapons which is the chiefe poynt that belongeth to a man of warre'.[12] The rank of colonel, which Audley embraced fully, was only applied to mercenary commanders in Henry's army. The ratio of shot (including bows) to pike was the key issue, for he considered that 'for many Tymes it hath bene sene that s hathe been gotten [won] by shott onlie, without pushe [of pike] or strocke stricken'.[13] He thought that the larger the force, the smaller the proportion of shot required: 'For in a small nomber you shall nede the thirde parte shott and in a bigger the iiiith part shote & in a bigger the Vth parte shott and so upward.'[14] Henry's army in the 1544 French campaign was certainly deficient in firearms, with only seven percent of English troops equipped with the arquebus whilst the proportion in France and Spain approached one third. The total numbers of shot were made up with archers but in a much higher proportion than Audley would have wished.

The shot should form several ranks surrounding the battle, the much-admired Almains 'three in a rank', while Audley suggested up to five. He recognised that the armies of the time had to 'mingle Archards and Hargabusseers',[15] and he recommend that if the ranks were even numbered there should be an equal number of the two types of projectile weapon, and if they were odd numbered then the bow should be preferred. He considered that a morion or skull was the only armour required, considering further armour an impediment to those who had to move rapidly about the battle and skirmish with the enemy.

Protection of the weak flanks of the battle was one of their key functions. Each flank should have a 'sleve' of shot, and he later recommends that a single rank of archers and one of arquebuses was sufficient. These sleeves should always remain protecting the flanks, while the shot placed before the battle would be expected to skirmish with the enemy. He explained the options available to a commander thus:

> some use to place them abrode before the forefront of the battell, and so thei do advaunce themselves, somewhat beforre the Battell, and to shote off at their enemyes as often as thei myght retyre to the sides or ever that the Battell did joyne and then to greyve their ennemyes with shot to thuttermost of their powere as long as the fight doth endure … [while] some at this daie to, sett within the first Ranke of Pykes, one Ranke of harkebusses to shotte at every joyning of the Battell

---

11 Audley, 'Treatise', p.66.
12 Audley, 'Treatise', p.67.
13 Audley, 'Treatise', p.68.
14 Audley, 'Treatise', p.68.
15 Audley, 'Treatise', p.68.

and othere, some useth it not; also some useth to place the shot, that shall assail there enymes lyke two sleves streight out at ii corners of the Battell,[16]

He added the proviso that they should not interfere with the deployment of the artillery on the flanks of the battle nor be interfered with. Audley was wary of having too many shot as he considered that the strength of the battle lay in its block of pikemen; he did however encourage the presence of a small surplus: 'to serve you for any nede or devise you might happen to have in your Iourney.'[17] If there was a great superfluity, which there might be if one considers the large reservoir of archers, then you might 'put them to other weapons in the boddie of your Battaile.'[18]

'Thalmaynes trusteth much to the push of pyke',[19] and so not unsurprisingly did Audley. He recommend that 'of every hundrede of men XX corseletes for the front of the battayle and to have them in whyte harness [polished plate armour] is by cause white harnes is a terror in sight of your Enymie from farre ... everie man that should wear a corselett should be a man of strength and of experience',[20] and should receive double pay and the respect of his officers and comrades. The corslet of white (polished) armour was quite an expensive item, which Audley recommended should be issued to the soldier from a national armoury, another one of his pet enthusiasms, as we shall see: 'Those pikemen without full corslets should armour themselves: with such armour as thei bring out of there Countrie [county] with them for somewhat is better than nothing.'[21] Audley asserted that until England could put the right proportion of men into good corslets, 'we shall never be strong in the felde. And I feare me if it not be looked to in tyme, it will one daie put us in great Danger.'[22] Under no circumstances should those with corslets be mixed with those without: 'fir if thei be, farewell the strength of footmen.'[23] The psychological importance of keeping this elite together was vital. If there were enough corslets available, those who were surplus would be placed to the rear of the battle, where they would protect the rear and keep the men from flight.

Audley recommended five or six ranks of corslets in the front rank, and then a rank of corslets equipped with bills where the ensigns would be kept. Then there should be bills, then pikes, then bills or halberds, this time encompassing the King's standard in their midst together with any other ensigns. Then the ranks behind should mimic those in front of the King's standard. The weakness of the flanks where bills or halberds were placed would be reinforced by two or three ranks of pikes. It was generally recognised that for the close-quarter fighting the double-handed sword, the bill or halberd was far superior, as the events at Flodden proved in 1513.

---

16 Audley, 'Treatise', p.130.
17 Audley, 'Treatise', p.68.
18 Audley, 'Treatise', p.68.
19 Audley, 'Treatise', p.68.
20 Audley, 'Treatise', p.69.
21 Audley, 'Treatise', p.69.
22 Audley, 'Treatise', p.69.
23 Audley, 'Treatise', p.129.

A shrympe with a clearly dejected soldier (probably after being told that he has to man it) at the siege of Boulogne, a detail from the Cowdray engraving. Shrympes accompanied Henry to France but none saw action and after his departure their guns were dismounted and allocated to fortifications. I have crewed one reconstruction of this truly terrifying vehicle. It may have proved of some use if the enemy were downhill and cooperating fully but in every other respect it was a useless burden which probably explains its disarmament and disappearance. (Dr Dominic Fontana, with kind permission)

The 'push' of pike was a very specialised form of assault and defence; once the pike wall was breached then the pike became less of a weapon and more of a liability. The Spanish used sword and buckler men to breach and then decimate the pike block. The 'shrympe' was also an attempt to achieve the same result but with firepower and mechanical intrusion. This was a two-wheeled vehicle, fitted with two small breech-loading guns mounted under a protective snout-shaped coaming. The effective use of shot could also break a pike formation, but if it did not, then the 'push of pike' had to be employed.

The company could be deployed so that the various weapons effectively complemented each other. Gervase Philips in his excellent study of Anglo-Scottish warfare provides a detailed description of an independent company of 308 men, commanded by an Italian mercenary named Tiberio. This force consisted of mercenaries and English troops which might have altered the normal proportions of weapons. The formation consisted of:[24]

> For landing from the ships:
> Skirmishers – 20 harquebusiers and 20 'bowes.'
> For the battle – 4 ranks of harquebusiers, 7 ranks of pikes, 4 ranks of bills.
> For the wings of the battle – 40 archers, 20 swords and targets for 'wyfflers'.
> The whole number of Tiberio's company is 308.[25]

These figures produce a total of 60 archers, 76 arquebusiers, 98 pikemen, 48 billmen, 20 sword and buckler men. The total is 302, presumably a

---

24 *CSP Scotland*, p.84.
25 *CSP Scotland*, p.172.

captain, petty-captain, ensign, whiffler, drummer and fifer would make up the remaining six. The unusual proportion of missile weapon-equipped soldiers (especially arquebusiers) was probably explained by the presence of mercenaries. Sword and buckler men operated on the flanks of a formation but could be used to break up formations of pikemen.

The organisation of this band was thoughtful and flexible. A score of arquebusiers and an equal number of archers were thrown forward as skirmishers. The main body consisted of seven ranks of pikemen and four ranks of billmen, preceded by four ranks of arquebusiers and flanked by 40 archers and 20 sword and target wyfflers. Philips has suggested that the 20 'wyfflers' performed the role of 'proto-NCOs',[26] or were the equivalent of the Landsknecht *Doppelsoldner* or double-pay soldier which seems more likely as they were performing the same high-risk skirmishing role.

Most intriguingly there is a reference to a document called *The Rules for Military Discipline*, undated but probably from late 1548.[27] It considers marching in two arrangements: in 'troup' when in action and when 'charge[d] on a sudden', when the formation is 'dubbling the ranks to receive the enemy' and marching in 'ordur', presumably when the more open formation is adopted. It conventionally refers to the shot marching on the wings or flanks of the pikemen and it even refers to standardised words of command such as moving to right, to left and right-about. It also contains an early reference to 'callivers' and muskets as the shot to accompany the pikes. It is all very modern and suggests the approach of a later date.

Cavalry

The English forces in the Tudor period had little in the way of heavy cavalry: the mounted man-at-arms who had flourished in France and was to evolve in Germany as the reiter was a *rara avis* in England. The 1544 expedition to France could boast only 196 fully equipped men-at-arms in two contingents, one of 121 and the other of 75. In the area of light horse, the English were well served by the northern border horse which had generations of experience in skirmishing. In the first of Henry's expeditions to France they had proved very successful against the French. Mercenary horse were to prove of great importance in this period in providing both increased numbers and new types of horsemen. In the 1544 expedition, 2,000 German and Burgundian cavalry served Henry, including in their ranks 500 reiters, the last word in modernity.

In the opinion of Audley, 'ther is no army of so great a force unlesse thei be thoroughly furnished with horsemen as with footmen'.[28] The proportion of infantry to cavalry in the 1544 expedition to France had been seven to one in the army overall, but three to one in the King's battle. The favourable ratio of three to one was achieved in the English army that defeated the Scots

26 Philips, *The Anglo-Scots War*, p.84.
27 *CSP Scotland*, p.171.
28 Audley, 'Treatise', p.67.

A mounted charge a detail from *The Arch of Honour*, 1515, by Wolf Traut. It is difficult to imagine the chaos and slaughter that accompanied the clash of heavy cavalry. The heavy spear was by no means obsolete or ineffective if the user understood their business and had the time and space to choose his target. It was after all a form of warfare practised assiduously in the joust of peace and for good reason. Once the first impact had finished, lances broken or unbroken would be discarded, as seen here, in favour of hand weapons. The horseman's hammer and mace would probably have been of more use than the sword as his opponents were likely to be other well-armoured men. Against a pike square even a mounted charge would be ineffectual, if the infantry kept their nerve as at Pinkie. (Metropolitan Museum of Art, Open Access)

at Pinkie in 1547, although only with the withdrawal of the Bulleners from France and by employing mercenaries. The cavalry probably did more than any other arm to achieve victory in that battle.

The mounted man-at-arms was the most powerful single element in the cavalry, the organisational unit was called the spear or lance. The paucity of such in England that there was only one permanent body of such men the 'King's Spears' as they were known until 1539 and then the 'King's Honourable Band of Pensioners'. They numbered originally 50 lances, but the number eventually rose to 75. The lance may consist of two, three or even five men including the man-at-arms (which was the case in France at the time). Audley recommended that if three horses made up the unit then one should be a man-at-arms the next a demi-lance and the third a 'hargabusseere' or mounted arquebusier, equipped either with a arquebus, or a 'bores spere and a Dage which is a short gonne, to hang at the Saddle bow'.[29] Strangely Audley does not mention the *reiter* (a mounted armoured pistoleer) which appeared in the 1540s in Germany, although 500 of them accompanied Henry's expedition in 1544, and their importance grew as that of the mounted men-at-arms diminished. In 1544 the lance probably numbered the man-at-arms and two 'harnessed' servants all mounted on fully barded (armoured) war horses. If there were five mounted men in a 'lance' Audley recommended that they should consist of a man-at-arms, two demi-lances, two mounted arquebusiers and finally a page to carry 'his Masteres hed pece and his staffe'.[30]

Audley argued that half of all the horse should be light cavalry capable of reconnaissance, the escort of convoys, skirmishing and the pursuit of a defeated enemy. Although some thought that a man-at-arms and his horse should be fully armoured, Audley demurred. He drew attention to the French experience where the shortage of light cavalry proved a particular weakness. The fully armoured man-at arms with his horse fully barded (armoured) was the exception, forming but a fourth part of the men-at-arms. Horse armour, as Audley explained: 'bringeth his mastere from the danger of the fight',[31] but as at the Battle of the Spurs where many bards were found abandoned upon the field, they could also act as an impediment to a prudent retreat!

It was above all essential that the men-at-arms maintained their battle and did not lose their cohesion with futile gallops in support of their light horse, as 'peradventure bothe light horsemen and men Atarrmes also might be overthrown'.[32] Audley counselled a prudent approach: he 'would never wish That a man Atarmes should follow fast in the chase But that all the men Atarmes should follow softly in a Troup together keeping their horses in breath'.[33] Without discipline in the field mutual support was impossible, and as the Battle of Pavia had proved (1525), even the best cavalry in Europe could face annihilation at the hands of determined infantry.

Artillery

This is an area where Audley has little to say. He advises against confusing or combining artillery and 'small shot' on the flanks of the battle, implying that it is best deployed on the flanks of the army. His clearest statement on the matter is a little gnomic to say the least: 'And the Artillerie to be newly charged, and set in good order for doubt of any chance that might happen.'[34]

Machiavelli gave little prominence to artillery in the field; there was a general assumption that after a short bombardment the artillery would either be overrun by the enemy or become irrelevant as friendly formations blocked fields of fire. The evidence of Ravenna, Marignano and Bicocca and elsewhere,

---

29 Audley, 'Treatise', p.71.
30 Audley, 'Treatise', p.71.
31 Audley, 'Treatise', p.70.
32 Audley, 'Treatise', p.70.
33 Audley, 'Treatise', p.70.
34 Audley, 'Treatise', p.70.

and the use by Henry VIII of his magnificent train of artillery in the field as well as during the sieges seems to have carried little weight with Audley. The preoccupation with the siege, and the grave distrust of the field battle as an attractive military option, led to the limitation of artillery to a fixed battery role.

Tactical Deployment

Thomas Audley only recommends two tactical formations for the battle, the 'just square' and the 'broad square'. These eponymous formations described either a formation where the numbers in front and flank were equal or where the frontage contained twice the numbers in the flank. The space allotted to a single foot soldier in formation was three feet by seven, thus a square formation would appear rectangular with its face half the width of the length, while the broad square would in fact appear more or less square! Audley records that 'Thalmaynes' and the French used the broad square, 'but as the bredethe of the ground will serve them'.[35] He also recommended the 'broad square' as being very good for cavalry.

Although infantry could form a single great battle, he recommended that cavalry should form 'dyvers and several bandes to thintent that if one Bande were repulsed or disordered that then the other band might be readie to reskew at hand'.[36] He considered that it was essential to place the cavalry on the flank of the main battle, as it would both protect its flank and give opportunities to attack and disrupt the enemy. This was especially true if the enemy cavalry failed to protect the flanks of its infantry battle, and then you could use your own cavalry to attack their flanks.

At this point the army still consisted of three portions, the van, main and rear battles, with the main battle often referred to simply as the battle. If they were deployed in line then they provided mutual support for their flanks, while the cavalry thrown out on their extreme flank protected the outer flanks of the infantry in the rear and van battles. Any superiority in cavalry over the opponent should be consolidated in new battles, and while the main force of cavalry contended one with the other, the enemy flanks may be attacked. Similar tactics could be employed by the cavalry against the enemy infantry, where an attack upon their front accompanied by an attack upon their flanks should overwhelm the opponent.

If the enemy were to 'demeane them selves', that is redeploy their army, then their opponent must match their redeployment, so that the two armies mirrored each other. The main blocks of infantry should face one another and then cavalry on the flanks. Victory would therefore go to the army that could muster the greatest force, especially cavalry, which would confront and then envelop its opponent.

There is only one formation that Audley recommended for a small unit action, where for example a company of a few hundred men on convoy duty

---

35 Audley, 'Treatise', p.68.
36 Audley, 'Treatise', p.68.

Detail of English infantry squares at the Battle of Pinkie. To form such massive formations was a time-consuming task at the best of times, to do so in action as at Pinkie is a testament to the competence and discipline of the army. The usual pattern was to place the halberds and bills within the ranks of pikemen, with the colours and drums in the centre. Here can be seen the 'sleeves' of shot that were being brought forward to skirmish against the Scottish battles. The combination of pike and shot was undergoing continual experimentation, as can be seen by the sophisticated organisation of Tiberio Perroni's company during the Rough Wooing.

was threatened by a superior force. He suggested that the three or more ranks which were in line of march should form a circle with the ensigns protected by billmen in the centre. The pike should form the outer carapace with a rank of shot 'within the first Ranke of Pykes', and then ranks of bills and halberds. Any shot remaining could be used for skirmishing This formation is very similar to that described by Thomas Styward in his *Pathwaie to Martiall Discipline* (1582). The alternative was to fight in line of march which gave little mutual support and could easily be outflanked or overwhelmed

The Captain and His Company

The captain was the principal field officer. 'Colonel' was a Spanish title that was gaining general favour in the rest of Europe and described a much more senior commander who would have authority over a number of companies. In England the company under its captain was the basic unit of the army. He was in turn responsible to the commander of the battle of which he was a part. Audley writes with some admiration about: 'Thalmaynes' and their professional officers and staff, his 'expert men of warres' who would: 'counsel with him [the colonel] in devysing his men to necessarie weapons … and to make certaine constitucions necessarie for the souldier.'[37]

Audley had a high opinion of the office of captain and a very low opinion of its usual incumbents. The main fault was in the appointment of captains, as 'captaynes be chosen in England by favor and not by worthynes.'[38] He considered that '[The] good Captaine will traine his souldiers and make him a mann of warre mete to serve within a fortnight though he never saw warres before with taking a little paynes.'[39] A fortnight was not an unreasonable amount of time to teach the rudiments of drill, as pike and arquebus were simple weapons compared to the bow and sword. Bert Hall writes about the proletarianisation of the 'early modern' soldier, who was undoubtedly less skilled than his late medieval counterpart. Audley attributed the poor training of many soldiers to the failure of their captain, as many were in his opinion made captains before they were fit to serve as a soldier.

Audley spoke from experience and from the heart when he wrote that 'I wyshe also that captaines would be as readie to take payns to traine their men as thei be readie at the paie daie to take paynes to tell [count] mony, for it is a grevouse payne to sett a battaill with untrayned men.'[40] The captain should have a 'leutenant' or petty captain as his second in command, a 'standardbearer' for his ensign, and '[a] Sergeant of the Band, four Vinteners, which is XXV men to every vinten [previously of 20 men], one sergeant, one drummer and a fife to call men to service.'[41] The vintener was a rank associated with the medieval archer, and its continued use has been seen as further evidence of 'backwardness'. What such critics would make of such arcane titles as fusilier, bombardier, grenadier and corporal of horse, in the current British Army, it would be interesting to discover.

The musicians were essential, as 'Drummer & Fife is always conted as the mouth of the Captaine.'[42] The drummer was a senior and experienced soldier who had to master not only all the commands for his own company but be able to recognise and sometimes simulate those of the enemy. Audley strongly recommended that the captain be given command of 200, and the 'dead pay' of the other captain would enable him to provide for his own comfort as well as little comforts for his men such as improved food, and transport for the sick and injured. 'Dead pay' was payment for 15 nonexistent soldiers in a company and was permitted as a recognised 'perk' for the captain and his company. The consequence of an underpaid captaincy was that 'no captains that hath but iiii shillings by the day can be able to furnishe him selfe to his honestie and to the help of his souldiers except he dothe both Robbe your majestie and also pole [defraud] your soldiers.'[43] As similar recommendations and complaints were being made at the end of the century it was clear that his words fell on deaf ears.

---

37 Audley, 'Treatise', p.67.
38 Audley, 'Treatise', p.69.
39 Audley, 'Treatise', p.69.
40 Audley, 'Treatise', p.69.
41 Audley, 'Treatise', p.72.
42 Audley, 'Treatise', p.72.
43 Audley, 'Treatise', p.72.

Administration

Much of the treatise concerns itself with the problems involved in raising and maintaining an army. Again 'Thalmaynes' provided him with his exemplar for the formation of units. The colonel authorised to form a band would choose his senior officers, and with their assistance he would decide on the force structure and the code of discipline which all must follow. He then concerned himself with the movement of troops to collection and embarkation points such as Newcastle and 'Callis' [Calais] where they would be inspected by 'Lieutenants generall'. He advocated that the 'Chyffest with his counsail' should be responsible for the collection and transportation of all foodstuffs and stores of war. He details minutely all the various stores that an army could require, from 'Bows arrows and stringes' to 'wheles and axeltrees'; engineers' stores such as boats and gabions are included. In addition he lists the craftsmen required to serve, such as the masons, fletchers, smiths and 'otherlyke'. His preoccupations reflect those to be found in the official letters and papers dealing with preparations for war.

He identified two key requirements for any army, '[for] above all thynges Provision ys chieflye to be forsene … for hunger overcomethe without strooke of the enemyis. Another provision unto that is mony sufficient so that your souldiers have monye, and be well pade and oftn. For mony gyve the life and courage to a souldiour.'[44] If provisions were plenty and money plentiful the army would not be leached away with desertion or racked with disorders. Again, it was the wise captain who would make provision for failures in food and transport by the main army.

March and Camp

The field army would pursue a line of march guided by scouts who possessed local knowledge. Several guides or 'a sufficient number of the said countrie', would be used: 'they must be examined severally apart every man by himself',[45] and their information collated to provide a broader and more reliable source. Several routes would be discussed with the guides, so that they might not know which was the intended one. They should be well and promptly paid but threatened with 'cruell punishments if they do not do well and trulie.'[46] The march should not be so much as to be 'over travailed and made wery for weried men if thei be assailed in tyme of his weriness is half overcome'.[47] Using the example of his illustrious predecessors, Audley declared that 'the common distance of the waie that old warriors were wount to Lead there army in a somers daie was V miles in iii hours',[48] a figure not significantly greater in the Napoleonic period.

---

44   Audley, 'Treatise', p.71.
45   Audley, 'Treatise', p.72.
46   Audley, 'Treatise', p.72.
47   Audley, 'Treatise', p.74.
48   Audley, 'Treatise', p.74.

The marshal before halting the army should choose the 'Lodgings of tharmy' on the basis of the provision of three commodities, that is 'water, wood and pasture, and in especial water nere at hand for it is a thing that may in no wise be spare, nether of man nor beaste … [the water should be] be sweete, and holesome.'[49] One camp for the whole force was preferred unless a siege was to be conducted. If possible, the camp should be set on the highest ground, 'so shall you be sure alwaies to have thadvantage of your enemyes,'[50] as it would make an enemy attack more wearisome and a counter-attack more energetic, and artillery would be able to play its part in covering the surrounding ground. The camp should have a large area set aside for the artillery and as a rallying point in an emergency. Also, '[The] artillerie of every battell [should be pointed] towards such places as you thinke be most dangerous where you thinke your enemies maie assaile you.'[51]

Field fortifications should be dug if the army intended to remain for any length of time. In line with contemporary judgement Audley deferred to 'thopinion of olde auncient warriors' and recommended a trench 12 feet deep by 15 feet broad, along which there would be bastions mounting small cannon, each no further apart than an arquebus shot. Arquebusiers were to 'flanke the trenches of the campe'.[52] Self-consciously or otherwise he was attempting to replicate the conditions that had led to the defeat and slaughter of the Swiss at Bicocca. If the threat was deemed less, a trench of nine feet by seven feet was deemed adequate. On the other hand, 'if you tarrie not in a place but remove dailie and that the power of your enemyes liethe farre of, then it shall suffice you to have your carriages about the camp'.[53] This method of defence is well illustrated in the Cowdray House engraving of the English camp outside Boulogne in 1544 and at Pinkie in 1547.

Audley goes into painstaking detail when recounting how the watch and ward (guard) and watchword of the camp be organised and distributed. He also gives prominence to the 'Scoutes' and their master. He declares that 'I would all good men of warre or other, marching towards thir ennemies or coming from their ennemyes, should appoint verye good and skilful Scoutes.'[54] In camp, scouts should seek the high ground and use that as a base for further patrolling. The scouts should form a close protective ring around the camp; 'Thalmains and the Spaniards thei use their scoutes to be V in a companie,'[55] only the leader of which would have the watchword.

49   Audley, 'Treatise', p.74.
50   Audley, 'Treatise', p.74.
51   Audley, 'Treatise', p.74.
52   Audley, 'Treatise', p.74.
53   Audley, 'Treatise', p.75.
54   Audley, 'Treatise', p.75.
55   Audley, 'Treatise', p.76.

Battle and Siege

Very much in line with contemporary opinion, Audley approached the idea of a battle with the greatest caution. He wrote that:

> Many olde and auncient men of warr be of thopinion that it is not good for a prince or leadre of an Army to be overhaste to give Battel to his enemyes, unless it be greatlie to his advantage, for it is a thing very weightie and ought very sagelye to be foreseen, And also to be dreddyd for the wealth and honor of a King and his realm liethe thereupon.[56]

James Wood, in his detailed study of 'The King's Army' in the French Wars of Religion 1562–76 summarised the situation extremely well when he wrote: 'The fact was that a battle was an extremely difficult event to arrange unless both sides simultaneously sought one. Battles were also extremely risky and chaotic events whose outcome was impossible to predict or control.'[57] The domestic and Continental examples of Flodden (1513), Pavia (1525) and Ravenna (1512) demonstrated how disastrous a major battle could be for at least one of the protagonists.

Before battle was contemplated various calculations had to be made concerning the strength of the enemy and one's own forces. Numerical strength, equipment, experience, 'and chieflie to know what good will thei have to fight'.[58] He warned that an outnumbered enemy would fight more valiantly, so that 'one man is worth two men'. On the other hand if an army was prepared for battle and the soldiers 'give the onset stronglye and manfullie and to be utterly determined to abyde the tyme of goode fortune and victorie … one of these [your own] men is worth three others.'[59] Numerical calculations based upon such opinions would be of doubtful value, and as Audley admits: 'victorie is uncertain and God giveth it where yt pleasethe him'.[60]

Audley recommended 'wittie skirmishes'[61] that would reduce the opponent's strength and sap his morale, although care should be taken to avoid unnecessary losses in 'vayne skirmishes'.[62] A good captain would 'greve his enemyes in the night by sodeyne alarmes',[63] and prepare the way for an unexpected attack when the enemy had become slothful. Even if the enemy was suffering from a shortage of food there should be no precipitate attack as they may have become desperate. His prisoners should be treated well, as in a battle the enemy might prefer to die fighting than to be captured and face torture and death. In truth Audley would prefer a war of attrition of

---

56 Audley, 'Treatise', p.76.
57 James B. Wood, *The King's Army: Warfare, Soldiers, and Society During the Wars of Religion in France, 1562–1576* (Cambridge: Cambridge University Press, 1996), p.184.
58 Audley, 'Treatise', p.77.
59 Audley, 'Treatise', p.77.
60 Audley, 'Treatise', p.77.
61 Audley, 'Treatise', p.77.
62 Audley, 'Treatise', p.77.
63 Audley, 'Treatise', p.77.

petty skirmishes and enemy desertion, for a victory could be gained without having to risk battle. He approved of the general who 'shall not be so hastie to hasard the Battell upon them [the enemy] but shall seke upon them daylie to diminishe them by skirmishes, for the ennemies having thos lackes, ye shalbe suere thei shall retyre with dishonor, and the honor remaineth to him that driveth awaie the ennemyes'.[64]

If the commander was either forced by his opponent to battle, or 'both wisdom and his honor adviseth hym to gyve battell',[65] then he must show a 'cherefull and a manful countenaunce' and animate his men with a suitable oration, also provided by Audley. The oration consisted of a conventional appeal to the sense of duty, patriotism, the memory of glorious forbears and self-interest of the soldiers, offering rewards in victory and promising an ignominious death to cowards. There is a sense of hopelessness in all this, as quite clearly Audley feared battle and could not have much confidence in these lacklustre and formulaic phrases.

Audley is much happier when dealing with the siege as an element of warfare, though even here his perspective is defensive rather than offensive. The first purpose he gives for trenches and fortification is the defence of the camp. He is more concerned that an enemy sortie should not disrupt the siege and 'peg' (spike) the guns, than he is that the wall should be breached. Even when the assault is proposed, he is concerned that the army should not be surprised by a relieving force, and that several bands be made ready for the assault if one be defeated.

Command Structure and the Organisation of the Camp

Audley provides a good description of the command structure within the battle and camp. The provost marshal was responsible for the discipline in the camp, including the market, and responsible for the 'watch' which provided camp security. He also lists the other principal officers who reported directly to the high marshal. The captain of pioneers was important in ensuring that the route identified by the 'high harbinger' was made safe for the wagons controlled by the carriage master. The forge master would ensure that the inevitable wear and tear on the wagons would be repaired, as well as refurbishing the shovels, pickaxes and scythes that the pioneers would be using for repairing roads and digging the field fortifications that defended the camp. The high comptroller was responsible for the acquisition and distribution of stores to provide the clerk of the market with something to sell. The high treasurer would (hopefully) provide funds for the comptroller and wages for the soldiery. If anyone failed in their duty, they would be responsible to the king or his deputy the high marshal.

64 Audley, 'Treatise', p.77.
65 Audley, 'Treatise', p.78.

Henry Barrett

The first handbook designed for the putative captain and his novice company was penned by Henry Barrett in 1562. Barrett was a yeoman of the guard possibly appointed as early as 1549, and was identified in 1568 as a lieutenant guarding Queen Mary of Scotland after her flight. He was part of a very small military elite and as he wrote in his preface appreciated the need for a captain's handbook:

> Consideringe how throughe mutacion of tymes and invencions of menns wittes the practises of the warres dothe daylie alter and change to the greate perill of the ignorante in suche behalfe, the zeale I beare unto my native contrie hathe moved me to write of suche experience or knowledge as I have by my few yeares travaile amongest dyvers nacions obteigned and gotten.[66]

What is unusual about Barrett's handbook is that there was 'No trace of the classical fad';[67] it appears to have been the product of experience, common sense and common knowledge. He deals with the duties of the captain, the structure of the company and then the equipment, training and tactics. Although the largest formation he refers to is 1,500 strong, his advice is meant for the captain of no more than 300. He is open in acknowledging the necessity of the novice captain learning from the most experienced soldiers; perhaps he had seen too many Ruperts (brand new officers) ignoring the advice of their experienced soldiers:

> the captayne chueseth a certayne [men] to accompany hym selfe whose experience and counsaile he will sircumspectly examyne and trie, and sometymes use accordinge to their devises. Suche be oftentymes for their experience appoynted to assiste and geve orders in arraye with the sergentes.[68]

He displays the conventional concerns for arms and equipment and he has some handy hints, such as: 'In rayne, mist or wynde, their peces charged and prymed, cary their touccholles under their harmholes, their mache lighte under or within the palme of their handes.'[69] He also suggests that the archers should carry '[a] maule of leade with a pyke of five inches longe, well stieled, sett in a staffe of fyve foote of lengthe with a hooke ... [and] mayntayne the fighte as oure elders have donn, by handye stroaks.'[70] He recognises and stresses the importance of having the slope and the wind in your favour when facing an enemy and concentrates almost exclusively on defensive tactics.

He explains and provides neatly labelled diagrams of formations, in broad and 'true' squares, with 'shott', thrown out on the flanks or skirmishing, or in triangular formation (shades of the elusive archers' hearse). Another

---

66 Hale, *Renaissance War Studies*, p.271.
67 Hale, *Renaissance War Studies*, p.259.
68 Hale, *Renaissance War Studies*, p.278.
69 Hale, *Renaissance War Studies*, p.276.
70 Hale, *Renaissance War Studies*, p.277.

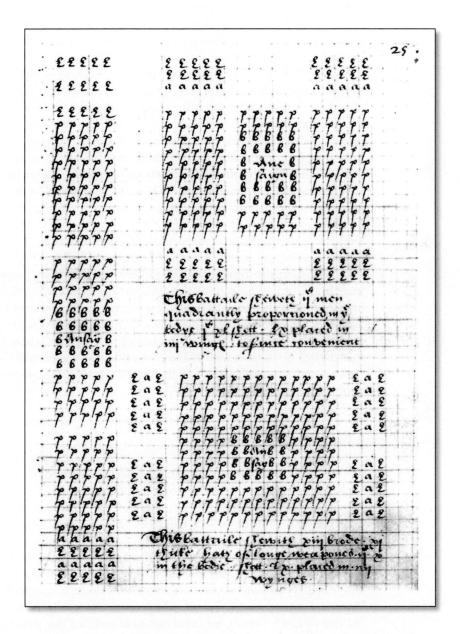

A diagram from Barrett's handbook. This clearly demonstrates the importance of the pike (*P*), which was at the heart of all the formations. The shot, arquebus and bow provided the firepower that would help protect a defensive formation and augment an offensive one. How far this neat diagram could be converted into a flexible tactical formation would depend very much on the training of the men and its officers (© J.R. Hale, 1983, Renaissance War Studies, Hambledon Continuum, used by permission of Bloomsbury Publishing PLC)

formation he included was similar to a capital S, where the arquebusiers could seek shelter. He explains how a column of three could be 'augmented' to five and then seven files. The column could form square and then move in all directions (but without half-turns). Open and close order are described as are formations for escort duties, and battle formations with 'shott' detached on the flanks or skirmishing.

Arquebusiers and archers are considered as working in pairs or squads, with one firing while the other was reloading and then 'reskewing' or relieving the other. He also writes about arquebusiers advancing or 'wading' through the formation, in order to face the greatest threat. In a defensive formation he recommended that the shot retire behind the hedge of pike points to maintain fire on the approaching foe. He considered that: 'The shott, which some call the forlorne hope, needeth not that name amongeste the Englishmen, thear is so ways provided for their safegarde.'[71] Most intriguing of all he demonstrated what Hale explained as "[a] curl-shaped" formation [which] is in fact his notation for a column of shot wheeling rank by rank after firing, in order to reload, a perfectly practical manoeuvre although one as he [Barrett] notes was "not a common practice amongest Englishmen".[72] This is but the smallest step away from the 'revolutionary' European countermarch proposed in a letter by William of Nassau in 1594. This intelligent and sophisticated use of firepower was something that might have been developing wherever a captain was willing to experiment with his tactics. One wonders if William of Nassau's eureka moment was quite as original as he may have thought. Blaise de Monluc thought that his use of a rank of arquebusiers behind the pikes at Ceresole in 1544 was unique as well as devastating until he discovered that the enemy had done the same.[73]

Conclusion

By the mid sixteenth century there was considerable and increasing sophistication in the tactical deployment of English soldiers, mercenaries and auxiliaries. Great thought had gone into the armament and structure of formations, with the bow complementing the arquebus and the bill the pike. Although there was not as yet a Tudor parade ground the belief in order, discipline and skill-at-arms, was recognised and applauded. Of course, the classical model reigned supreme and it was against this that a commander was tested. When one of the Lord Protector's officers commented that 'if Vegetius Frontinus were present, which wrote the stratigemes, Ordre and Policies of Civill Warres, he could not have mended our proceedings', no praise could have been greater.

---

71   Hale, *Renaissance War Studies*, p.257.
72   Hale, *Renaissance War Studies*, p.258.
73   Monluc, *The Habsburg–Valois Wars*, pp.110–111.

7

The Professional Soldiers

Introduction

The king required a guard of gentlemen and yeomen. Their numbers were few except in time of war as their role was primarily ceremonial, although they could be detached for civil and military service as the Crown saw fit. There were only a few large garrisons that needed to be manned. Calais with its numerous outlying forts would need a few thousand in times of peril. In the capital the Tower was the home of what was in effect a corps of gunners that would be increased by the use of mercenaries and the secondment of 'civilian' gunners. Berwick and Carlisle stood guard in the North but principally as logistical bases and their garrisons were small, numbering only about 40 at Berwick. The Device forts would have required many thousands of men if they were to be fully manned but there is little evidence that they ever were, except perhaps in 1545 when the French fleet mobilised against the south coast. As it was, their garrisons were barely enough to keep a regular watch and maintain their own security.

There were few 'professional' soldiers in England, that is men trained in arms who were paid full-time to perform their military role. The border reiver, trained from boyhood in the dubious martial and criminal skills of his forefathers, was not a 'professional' but may well have been the most competent light cavalryman in the whole of Europe. A Warwickshire yeoman who had learnt his skills with sword and bow from his father and uncles, tested at the butts and in bruising combat with his fellows with quarter staff and broadsword, was also not a 'professional' soldier. There was in England a large body of men whose life and training would enable them to take up a soldier's life but there were few actual professional soldiers, as they were not needed.

Mercenaries there were aplenty and much of Henry's pre-war and wartime correspondence deals with their recruitment, disposition and maintenance. Mercenaries were expensive to hire but their equipment and expertise were difficult if not impossible to reproduce in England. If the cost of a mercenary force was high, the expense of a standing army would have been impossible to bear. That mercenaries were cost-effective and made sound financial, political and military sense was an opinion that was widely shared across Europe.

The Commanders

Henry's commanders were not 'professionals' but nor were they 'amateurs' in the pejorative sense. They were brought up to and expected to command their family, their servants and tenants and when called upon to do so, their military retinues. Although not in continual military service they could between them boast vast experience in a great variety of roles and against all of the king's enemies foreign and domestic. If they could not rank any really great military commanders among their number, there were many who were more than up to the tasks set them.

Luke MacMahon in his convincing defence of the English military hierarchy points to the longevity and experience of many of Henry's commanders. Perhaps the best example was Thomas Howard, 3rd Duke of Norfolk, who:

> enjoyed a military career that lasted almost fifty years. Before his final command as one of the two generals entrusted with the siege of Montreuil in 1544, he had led campaigns in Ireland, Scotland and France which varied from punitive raids to full scale invasions. In Henry's wars with France he had directed sieges and led amphibious operations. Acting as a military governor he had defended the Anglo-Scottish border and sought to bring order to Ireland. He fought with his father at Flodden and ten years later directed the forces that halted the admittedly somewhat timorous Duke of Albany in his plans to lead a Franco-Scottish army into northern England.[1]

His military career stretching from Bosworth field, admittedly on the wrong side, to Wyatt's rising, was unique in longevity but many others served Henry VIII over decades. John Wallop served in Henry's wars against France in 1512, 1513, 1522, and 1523 before commanding the expedition to Landrecies in 1543. He also served in Ireland and held various posts in the Calais Pale for over a decade. Commanding at sea in 1514 he attacked shipping in the harbours of Treport and Étaples, as well as burning 21 coastal villages. Another old warrior was George Talbot, 4th Earl of Shrewsbury who had fought at Stoke in 1487 and later in the French expedition of 1492 before accompanying Henry in 1513 as lieutenant of the forward battle. He was considered by Wolsey to be '[As] active a captain as can be chosen within your realme, mete convenable and necessary to be appointed for the ledinge of an armye.'[2] It was men such as Talbot who mentored Henry's favourite, Charles Brandon the Duke of Suffolk, who was given a grand title but little responsibility in 1513 but who in 1544 would command at the siege of Boulogne.

It was the Privy Chamber which provided Henry with valued companionship and his most trusted commanders. The names of these men were to be found

---

1   Luke MacMahon, 'Military Professionalism in the early Tudor armies in Renaissance Europe: a reassessment', in D.J. Trim (ed.), *The Chivalric Ethos and the Development of Military Professionalism* (Leiden: Brill, 2003), p.186.
2   MacMahon, 'Military Professionalism', p.187.

again and again as commanders, bringing both military experience and often substantial retinues with them. John Wallop has been mentioned but there were many others, including Nicholas Carew, Francis Bryan, Anthony Browne, Richard Wingfield and Thomas Cheyne. MacMahon lists some 33 long-serving officers who took part on average in at least two or three of Henry's French campaigns,[3] although only John Wallop took part in all six. Nine of the 33 served in Scottish campaigns and two thirds had served in various senior roles in the French and Scottish garrisons. Some, such as Ralph Ellerker, spent most of their service on the Scottish border, where there was an almost continual state of undeclared war and brigandage, although he also served time as marshal of Calais and Boulogne. These men provided a wealth of experience in a variety of roles over decades.

These were also 'fighting soldiers' not content to command from the comfort of their tents. Thomas Palmer in 1523 led a force 60 strong against a stronger French force, killing three and capturing 25. The year before, Richard Whetehill was ambushed while leading his company and was wounded and captured. Most surprisingly, the master of the king's tents & revels Sir Thomas Cawarden, who might be thought of as having a 'cushy number', was

Charles Brandon, Duke of Suffolk. Brandon had been brought up with the young Prince Henry and was perhaps his best friend, even surviving his treasonous marriage to Henry's sister, Princess Mary. His failure as a military commander in the 1523 French expedition was also not held against him. He was to play an important part in the 1544 invasion. He never lost the trust and affection of the King, although at best he wasa commander of mediocre ability.

seriously wounded at the siege of Boulogne and lost his leg. He was knighted at Boulogne and continued a long and successful career, from a lowly start as an apprentice mercer to become the lieutenant of the Tower.

Experience did not necessarily mean competence. In January 1545 Surrey failed to stop the reinforcement of the key French fortification facing Boulogne at Outreau. In apparent despair he called upon his officers to end his life. A common soldier passing by, who was seriously unimpressed by his commander's histrionics, suggested that instead he should face the French who 'would finish him off quickly enough'.[4] In the aftermath of this engagement where neither army covered themselves with glory, they both first claimed victory and then sought to forget the whole sorry venture. A suitable 'whitewash' job was done by the English and the report of the Council of Boulogne found that 'ther was no defaulte in the rulers, nor lacke of courage to be geven them, but an humour that sometyme raigneth in Englisshe men.'[5]

---

3   MacMahon, 'Military Professionalism'.
4   Potter, *Henry VIII and Francis I*, p.288.
5   Potter, *Henry VIII and Francis I*, p.288.

The service of the nobility and gentry was not continuous for the simple reason that neither was war. They were professional courtiers but that does not mean that they were necessarily 'amateur' soldiers. They were expected to command and shared with the king the same enthusiasm for war as a means of displaying personal bravery and rising high in the estimation of their peers and sovereign. This was especially apparent in the enthusiasm with which they (the loyal and formerly disloyal) rallied around Queen Mary in the war with France in 1557.

A gentleman pensioner. Dressed in full armour, this gentleman is clearly 'on parade'. His breastplate has the *arret de lance* (the rest for the lance) attached but his poleaxe would suggest that he is on foot rather than mounted duty. The highly decorated cloth surcoat clearly dates this painting to the early decades of the sixteenth century. Costly decoration and the lavish use of expensive materials all indicated the importance of this servant of the king, thereby augmenting the status of his master. (Courtesy of the British Library, Cotton Augustus III, f.25)

The King's Spears and Gentlemen Pensioners

The term 'pensioner', it should be said, is derived from the French *pensionnaire*, that is someone who ate at the king's table or at his expense and (not like the present author) merely a grumpy old man. The Gentlemen Pensioners were the only really professional officers in royal service. Pitifully few in number, the King's Spears – as they were called from 1509–39 – provided a core of heavy cavalry, a royal bodyguard and a training school for those who wished to command troops in action. They accompanied the King to war and in peace were the regular participants in his tournaments. The Spears were organised as a standard Continental 'lance', with 'every of them to have an archer, a demi-lance and a costrel [a mounted page, not a water bottle], and every spear to have three great horses'.[6] In 1509 there were 50 mounted men-at-arms supported by 50 light horse and 100 mounted archers. Their expertise meant that they were of use as garrison commanders, responsible independent contingents or even acting as sea captains. In 1515–16 this body was disbanded, according to Hall because of the great cost of maintaining them. They were remodelled to number 75 men with five officers including a captain, lieutenant and standard bearer. The captain was appointed from the senior nobility while other officers rose from the ranks. The pattern of service required two thirds of them to be at court, later reduced to half, in order to allow them to conduct family and estate business. In 1540 they became the

---

6   Ingram, *Richard III*, p.53.

Gentlemen Pensioners numbering 50, with five officers of which only three were on active service. Their captain was not chosen from among their number but was a prominent figure appointed by the King in return for their loyal service. In 1548 he chose Sir Anthony Browne, master of the King's horse and principal subject of the Cowdray engravings.

They were not merely 'band box' soldiers. They took part in the Battle of the Spurs in 1513 and attended the King at the Field of the Cloth of Gold in 1520. Seventy-two pensioners accompanied Henry to war in 1544 and an enlarged force of some 200 gentlemen-at-arms formed the basis of the Boulogne garrison after its capture. Their hour of glory was of course at the Battle of Pinkie. The Gentlemen Pensioners, commanded by Sir Thomas Darcy, launched themselves without their horses' protective barding against the Scots pike columns, at considerable cost but gaining great honour. One of those injured in service was Nicholas Corothers, '"late one of our sperers". Grant[ed] for life (in reward for services in wars in Scotland and Ireland and the last wars in France, where he was maimed) with 'the office or room of weyleyship and nottleyshipp of and within our town of Penrith, Cumb[ria], which Hen[ry] Swynbur[ne] now holds at a rent of 23s. 4d.; together with the said rent.'[7]

By 1549 the numbers had been reduced to only 39, but in 1550 a further 60 were added from the disbanded Boulogne garrison. On Edward's death they divided almost evenly 29 to 25 between Mary and Northumberland. It was, however, to be a loyal band of pensioners who rallied to the Queen in 1555, as Wyatt's rebels approached the city of London.

A gentleman pensioner, probably William Palmer, attributed to Gerlach Flicke *c.*1539. This three-quarter portrait of a gentleman pensioner indicates the status of this select company. He wears a double gold chain with a large medallion and on his hat another, this time of St George on horseback. He is carrying his weapon of office, a gilded poleaxe, and at his side a basket hilted broadside, a practical weapon rather than just a decorative item. He served from 1539 until at least 1553 when he attended the coronation of Edward VI; he died in 1568. (Courtesy of the Royal Armouries)

The Yeomen of the Guard

Henry VII had founded the Yeoman of the Guard, 'the private guard of faithful followers', in 1485. It was a personal bodyguard, similar to those of other European sovereigns. The first evidence for them comes from one of the very earliest warrants in the reign of Henry VII, one of which on 18 September 1485 mentioned 'William Browne, Yeoman of the King's Guard, for good service that our humble and faithful servant hath heretofore done

---

7   *Letters and Papers*, 1544 Volume 19 Part 1 March 1544 R.O. 24.

unto us as well beyond the seas as at our late victoreuse journeye.'[8] Henry was following European custom in providing himself with a permanent bodyguard. The Scottish archers of the French monarchy, the *Compagnie Ecossaise de la garde du Corps du Roi*, was the closest European comparison and competitor. The yeomen provided for Henry's close protection and an impressive ceremonial body for state occasions; they also accompanied the King on all his major campaigns and engagements: Stoke 1487, France 1492, Blackheath 1497, Thérouanne, Tournai and the Spurs in 1513, Morlaix in 1522 and Boulogne 1544 are examples of their 'battle honours'. They also served as garrison troops in Tournai in 1513 and at Boulogne in 1544.

They were meant to impress with their bearing, dress and weapons. According to the Venetian ambassador in 1515 they achieved that end:

> we were conducted to the presence, through sundry chambers all hung with most beautiful tapestry, figured in gold and silver and in silk, passing down the ranks of the bodyguard, which consists of 300 halberdiers in silver breast-plates and pikes in their hands; and, by God, they were all as big as giants, so that the display was very grand.[9]

They were equipped with halberd, sword and buckler; plate armour replaced brigandines in later years. They were: 'bold men, chosen and tried out of every lord's house in England for their cunning and virtue.'[10] They were drawn from known loyalists and recommended for service from established households, and their local knowledge and contacts were of value in maintaining links between court and country. They came from across the country, although in the early period the Welsh were well represented. Physical appearance and athletic ability were highly prized and those chosen should be 'either good wrestlers or casters of the bar, runners or tall men of personage.'[11]

The initial number seems to have been about 100, with the normal number attending on the sovereign being 50 to 70. During the 1513 campaign its numbers, swelled by the appointment of 'extraordinary yeomen', reached 600 which was the largest number attained. It was unsurprising that in 1515 as part of an economy drive some 170 were discharged with a generous retainer of 4d a day, to be re-employed in case of need. At the Field of the Cloth of Gold there were some 200 in attendance, demonstrating their wrestling when the poor weather precluded the tournament taking place. At the King's command some 24 demonstrated their skill with the bow. At a display for the young King Edward they shot and penetrated one-inch thick seasoned oak planks with their arrows. The strength of the Guard remained at about

---

8   Reginald Hennell, 'The King's body–guard of the yeomen of the guard, 1485–1920', in *Journal of the Society for Army Historical Research*, vol. 4, no. 16 (April–June 1925), p.73.

9   *CSP Venice*, vol. 2, 1509–1519 i, p.85.

10   A.R. Myers, *The Household of Edward IV: the Black Book and the Ordinance of 1478* (Manchester: Manchester University Press, 1959), p.116.

11   Hale, *Renaissance War Studies*, p.253; Jordan, *The Chronicle and Political Papers of King Edward VI*, p.73.

Image of a yeoman of the guard. Detail from 'The New Treaty between King Philip and Henry VII', from *Der Weisskunig* by Hans Burgkmair, 1514–1516. Images of the King's yeomen carrying their bows are few and far between. His bow is a good length and appears slightly recurved; a bow should be as tall as the archer plus a few inches. The string is attached to the upper nock, most likely it was side-nocked and the lower string has a loop fitted. There is no handle to the bow and it is clearly of heavy draw weight. Under his coat the yeoman is wearing armour, including greaves and upper arm protection which would not limit his ability to draw 'full', something the present author knows from experience. His sword is fitted with downturned crossguards and a substantial pommel similar in form to that of the painting of the gentleman pensioner and probably of a similar date. (Metropolitan Museum of Art, Open Access)

180 until 1526. Then at Cardinal Wolsey's insistence as part of the Eltham Ordinances they were reduced to only 80, with the remainder pensioned off at the usual rate.

In 1540 Cromwell increased the number to 88 and then 130. The warlike preparations of 1544 led to a further increase in their number to 500. With the threat of invasion past, their number was reduced to 128 by 1546. The crises of 1549 naturally led to their numbers increasing to 300 and an extra 100 were available at Mary's coronation and to face Wyatt's Rebellion in 1554. The Yeomen could serve on land and sea as well as performing a training role with the militia. Normally they would accompany the sovereign, although individuals could be detached for service elsewhere. In 1515 a strong company of 130 reinforced the garrison of Tournai where they remained until 1519. In 1544 at Boulogne a company of 185 were sent to serve as part of the garrison, an indication of the importance of this task in the King's eyes.

In the early 1500s the majority of the yeomen were paid at 12d a day (with a quarter paid at the lower rate of 8d a day), which placed them on the same pay scale as a captain of a company. They were also provided with 40s, annually given on the feast of Saint David on 1 March, a recognition of the early preponderance of Welshmen in their ranks. Other monetary gifts and annuities were granted as well as gifts of venison and payments of pensions to widows and provision for the sick. As servants in the Royal Household they were well looked after. The Order of the Garter feast conformed the high status of the yeomen. They carried in the dishes, and 'none did service in carving, bearing of cups and sewing under the degree of a Gentleman, but the yeomen of the king's Guard'.[12]

They were provided with several sets of clothes, as were all members of the Household. In the reign of Henry VII and until 1526 their livery colours were white and green, with the Tudor rose, rather than the cross of St George, worn back and front. At the marriage of Catherine of Aragon and Arthur in 1501 the yeomen in attendance wore:

> large jackets of damask, white and green, goodly embroidered both on their breasts before and also on their backs behind, with round garlands of vine branches, beset before richly with spangles of silver and gilt, and in the middle a red rose, beaten with goldsmiths' work, with bright halberds in their hands.[13]

In May 1519 they were provided with coats of scarlet, set with spangles of silver and gilt. At the Field of the Cloth of Gold in the next year they were issued with two outfits: one was a coat with a scarlet base, guarded with cloth of gold, the other consisted of a white satin doublet, green velvet coat, with crimson velvet arrow girdles and white kersey hose, all topped off with Milan bonnets.

---

12 Anita Hewerdine, *The Yeomen of the Guard and the Early Tudors: The Formation of a Royal Bodyguard* (London: Bloomsbury Publishing, 2012), p.70; College of Arms Ms. N50, f.39v; Anstis, i, App. p.xx.

13 Francis Grose, *The Antiquarian Repertory: A Miscellany, Intended to Preserve and Illustrate Several Valuable Remains of Old Times*, vol. ii (n.p., Forgotten Books, 2018), p.258.

Their principal role was providing close security, which included checking the royal apartments and even the royal bed. To do this they had to thrust their daggers through the straw before placing the canvas and feather bed on top, to ensure the 'that there be no untruth therein'. In later years this formality was dispensed with and the fortunate yeoman now only had to 'leap upon the bed' and roll up and down, 'before smoothing it down for future royal use.'[14] They also had to ensure the provision of royal night-time snacks. They would protect the King during public events and even separated unruly participants during a tournament. On one occasion when the 'commons' threatened to come too close, 'the king's Guard came suddenly and put the people back, or else as it was supposed more inconvenience had ensued.'[15]

They had many other roles, including escorting bullion convoys to pay armies and taking inventories of property that Henry would acquire. They could act as escorts or guards for courtiers. In 1521 Sir Henry Mamey the captain of the Guard with a force of 100 yeomen arrested the Duke of Buckingham, an indication of the importance of the task. Cardinal Wolsey was accompanied by substantial numbers of yeomen when on diplomatic service and on his fall from favour he was escorted by yeomen, chosen for having been in his service in happier times and aware of his needs. The Yeomen were even responsible for catching, arresting and imprisoning civilians including a pair of larcenous Etonian schoolboys.

Gunners and Their Training

Gunners were part of a separate organisation from the rest of the army. In a camp the provost of artillery could overrule the provost marshal in matters relating to his gunners, creating something of a state within a state. This distinction must have caused some confusion and friction. Gunners reported directly to the Tower, bypassing the usual channels. The Office of Ordnance was created by Henry VIII in 1544 and became the Board of Ordnance in 1597.

The numbers of gunners employed in Henry VII's reign increased dramatically from 30 in 1497 to 200 in 1497, the majority raised from overseas and in preparation for a war with Scotland. In 1508 there were only 12 gunners at the Tower, a number that had increased to 30 by 1526 and 110 by 1552. Also appointed were 'fee'd gunners' who received a royal patent and were lodged in the gunners' room in the Tower of London, some were clearly given as sinecures for outstanding service as was John Falley after Flodden. In some cases, and more likely in garrisons other than the Tower, the title 'fee'd gunner' referred to a master gunner. Gunners were paid at the rate 10d per diem (£15-4s-2d per annum) and were also supplied with bed and board

---

14 Anita Rosamund Hewerdine, 'The Yeomen of the King's Guard 1485–1547', unpublished London School of Economics and Political Science PhD thesis 1998, p.52; British Library Add. MS. 21,116, ff. l6r and 20v; British Library Add. MS. 34,319, f.19r; British Library Harl. MS. 2210, f.20v; The Royal Society MS. 61, f.17.

15 Hewerdine, *The Yeomen of the Guard*, p.50; Hall, *Chronicle*, p.519; H. Ellis, *Original Letters Illustrative of English History*, 11 vols, series II (1827), i, p.187.

A detail from the Siege of Boulogne from the Cowdray engraving. At the far left a gunner is pricking a cartridge or more likely cleaning out the vent using a brass 'pricker'. Vents could easily become clogged with poor powder producing a 'hang fire', that is delayed ignition or even no bang at all. Another gun is being withdrawn, probably to avoid overheating. Bronze guns could be weakened by too rapid firing, endangering the piece. One gunner holds a carefully made powder scoop while two others load powder directly from a 'budge' barrel, perhaps not the safest of tasks in the heat of the action. Thirty ells of canvas were provided for each battle for the manufacture of 'cartewyches' or cartridges. These may have been used for a stock of ready-to-use ammunition, while for conducting a slow bombardment loose powder was used. Another gunner is using a linstock to set off a charge, held sensibly at arm's length, as the rush of hot gas out of the vent was very dangerous. (Dr Dominic Fontana, with kind permission)

at the rate of 6d per diem in 1509, rising to 12d by 1600, a recognition of inflationary pressures rather than a pay rise. The figures for payment often varied depending on whether it was peacetime or wartime and what 'perks' may be provided. In comparison a skilled worker such as a carpenter or plumber received 8d pd (£12 per annum) and it was considered that £15 per annum, the pay of a clerk, was sufficient for the maintenance of a single man of 'modest carriage'.

A master gunner was appointed to oversee gunners in garrisons or on board ships; his role was to oversee all the gunners, guns and equipment in a ship or garrison. Master gunners could be appointed and despatched as need arose. Gunners were paid according to their level of responsibility: in 1513 those who commanded bombards received 2s per diem, one of the Apostles 16d and falcons the standard rate of 8d. Their assistants would receive 6d (the pay of a soldier).

Whatever number of gunners may have been trained domestically, war required the recruitment of foreigners. Henry VII recruited Frenchmen and his son Dutch, Germans and Italians. Christopher Morres, when master gunner, declared that he 'had rather have one Englishman, as he is, than five strangers', although this does not seem to have had an effect on their continued employment. Some stranger gunners were granted the privilege of denisation: Bernardyn de Valois, from Piedmont, who had entered royal service in 1514, was granted this honour in 1541. As many as 38 gunners from the Low Countries served in the 1513 expedition, 20 of whom were considered 'master shooters'. Bourne, writing much later, referred to the preference that Henry VIII had for the recruitment of 'strangers' even at the end of his reign.

Although there are gunner's notes made by individuals, there is no evidence relating to the systematic training of gunners other than a requirement for Tower gunners to practise weekly. There were certainly difficulties in providing adequate numbers of trained gunners and those who served were not necessarily always competent. At Berwick in 1545 Symon Sage, in a letter to the Secretary of the Ordnance Sir William Petre, complained: 'ffirst there is in the side castell x gounners in wages and ther is butt foure that can shoite'.[16] It is uncertain how training would have taken place at this time, other than by individual instruction and practice, in the same way as all craft skills were transmitted. How and where powder and shot could be expended in the quantity needed to ensure competence is unclear; perhaps a lack of practise is the problem that Sage faced. There was an appeal to Queen Elizabeth to licence gunners, and although a programme was devised it was never pursued. There are several gunner's notebooks[17] from the last quarter of the century and one can assume that the information contained within them was common knowledge amongst them.

The only active firing range or artillery garden in this period was outside Bishopsgate in the Spital Fields, referred to as the 'teasel field'. A record from the reign of James I, employed during a dispute between the Tower gunners and the Honourable Artillery Company, claimed that the old 'Teasel Ground' had been leased by the prior of the convent of St Mary Spital in 1537 for 297 years. It was significantly leased for the practise of great and small artillery, clearly not only for archers and arquebusiers. In the Agas and Copperplate maps of c.1553–9 and 1561 there can be seen next to Spitalfields an enclosed space, where an arquebusier is practising shooting at a distant target set on what appears to be an earth butt. What became the 'Artillery Ground' was granted in 1537, under Henry VIII, for the use of 'The Fraternity or Guild of Artillery of Longbows, Crossbows and Handguns'. The Honourable Artillery Company developed from the Fraternity. There were four other artillery gardens/yards, including Finsbury Field, set aside specifically for archery.

Only Bishopsgate seems to have been used for artillery training, with clear references in 1571 to the movement of guns and shot for the 'goners and skollers [scholars]', suggesting that instruction was taking place. There is an intriguing reference in 1491 to 'costes and charges late [had] abowte the cariage and setting forth of owre great ordenaunces from owre towre of

---

16 Stephen Ashton Walton, 'The Art of Gunnery in Renaissance England', Unpublished Institute for the History and Philosophy of Science and Technology University of Toronto PhD thesis, 1999, p.225.
17 Adrian B. Caruana, *The Halberd and other European Polearms 1300–1650* (Bloomfield: Museum Restoration Service of Canada, 1998), pp.19–36.

London unto the Blak hathe and from thens unto the same towre agayne'.[18] One can only assume that the purpose was to practise. It has been suggested that gunners formed associations like the *schools of fence*, which were devoted to skill-at-arms, supervising training of their members and maintaining standards, but the evidence for this is slight. The references to artillery pieces used in training, where they exist, are only to falcons and falconets, which presumably were the only guns suitable for firing in what was a relatively small enclosed space.

The master gunner, from at least 1537, was required to ensure that practise was carried out once a month in winter and twice a month in summer. He was to satisfy himself that all fee'd gunners were fully capable in all aspects of the gunners' craft. Bourne recorded that 'Ordnance hath beene had into the field [for range practise] both in maister Bromefields time when that he was Liefetenant of the Ordnance [1558–1563], & at divers times since'.[19] This practice seems to have fallen into disuse later as Thomas Smith recorded that he 'never heard nor reade of any that hath as yet fully put the same [that is, range firing] in practice'.[20] This tardiness in the development of an artillery school is in contrast with practice overseas. The Scuola St Barbara for gunners (St Barbara was the patron saint of gunners) was set up in Venice in 1500 and other schools were established throughout her territories. Their graduates were classified under three headings: *capi* (master), *sotto capi* (under-master) and *Scolari* (student). An artillery school had also been set up in Spain in 1513 at Burgos.

Mercenaries and Auxiliaries

The military resources of the kingdom could be rapidly augmented by the use of auxiliaries (an allied soldier serving under English command) and mercenaries. Henry VII's army at Bosworth was perhaps a third French, led by the poor adventurer Philibert de Chandee. Opinion as to their numbers and quality vary. The general conclusion appears to be that they numbered 2,000–3,000 and that they were not quite the desperadoes that Philippe de Commines considered them. The army that faced Henry VII at Stoke Field was provided with a backbone of German mercenaries led by Martin Schwarz and a large number of Irish, neither receiving quarter at the end of the bloody battle. After Bosworth Henry seems to have relied on domestic forces at home and abroad, except for a small number of gunners mostly from Germany and the Low Countries, who were the acknowledged experts in their field.

The numbers of mercenaries employed by his son were prodigious and their expense ruinous. Henry VIII benefited from the presence of auxiliaries and mercenaries in almost all of his Continental exploits. It began modestly enough with some 500 German mercenaries accompanying the Marquess of

---

18 Public Records Office, E.404/80, bdle. 3, No. 69.
19 William Bourne, *The Arte of Shooting in Great Ordnaunce* (London: Thomas Woodcoke, 1587), preface p.1.
20 Smith, *The Arte of Gunnerie* (London, 1600), p.48.

Dorset's expedition in 1512. In 1513 Emperor Maximilian himself donned the Cross of St George to humour his ally, who was admittedly using his English forces to pursue Imperial strategic objectives. Out of a total of 24,000 men in the army of 1513, there were 6,000 German pikemen and 1,000 Burgundian heavy cavalry. Neither distinguished themselves, the cavalry hanging back at the Battle of the Spurs. At the confrontation at Oye on 21 September, near Calais, after the English cavalry charged the mercenary heavy cavalry refused to join them, and engaged in what might be described as 'argy-bargy' with the English infantry. Even worse was the serious riot that broke out on Assumption Day 1513 between English troops and German mercenaries which required the intervention of King Henry and the Emperor to subdue.

In the campaign of 1523, 6,000 of the 20,000 troops were foreign, again mostly pikemen and cavalry. While in the massive force of 42,000 mobilised for the 'Journey of Paris' there were 4,836 mercenary horse and 5,392 foot which were mostly pike and shot. This force contained not only the usual large bodies of Landsknechts, but 500 Dutch and Danish reiters, armoured pistoleers. These were the very latest in military fashion, but still a disappointment to Henry who preferred fully armoured lancers of which Burgundy provided 724. Elis ap Gruffydd, an old campaigner in this expedition, recorded with disgust the numerous foreign contingents:

> there were so many depraved, brutish soldiers form all nations under the sun – Welsh, English, Cornish, Irish, Manx, Scots, Spaniards, Gascons, Portingals. Albanians, Greeks, Turks, Tartars, Almains, Germans, Burgundians, Flemings, who had come there ... to have a good time under the king of England, who by nature was too hospitable to foreigners.[21]

It is interesting to note his identifications of clearly national contingents, five of which might reasonably be described as British, so much for a 'national' army! One further crisis in this expedition was that when the Emperor abandoned Henry, all those mercenaries who owed him allegiance as well as the auxiliaries were ordered to withdraw, leaving Henry in a decidedly tricky position. Some chose to remain with Henry, as English pennies bought their loyalty, but soon the appalling conditions in Boulogne led them to abandon his service. Despite this 'betrayal', mercenaries remained widely employed by Henry and later Somerset in France, Scotland and England, by reason of their availability and military competence. In 1546 Hertford's army in France intended for continuance of the war contained 16,000 Englishmen and 11,000 mercenaries, consisting of 2,000 Spanish, 2,000 Italians,, 3,000 Landsknechts and 4,000 unidentified horsemen.

In the opinion of one contemporary observer there were good reasons to employ mercenaries, for 'They render excellent service on a day of battle ... or when the camp is to be pitched near the enemy, or when the army is in

---

21 Gilbert John Millar, 'Mercenaries under Henry VIII 1544–46', in *History Today*, vol. 27, issue 3 (March 1977), p.145.

Three Soldiers with Muskets *c*.1511–15 by Hans Schäufelein. These swaggering arquebusiers are just the men to fill the gap in Henry's force structure and to start a fight with English archers in the allied camp. Their weapons are probably snap matchlocks using a push-button trigger, or perhaps without any trigger and merely touched off with match cord by hand, as shown in contemporary illustrations. The arquebusier on the far right has a round powder flask slung on his chest, but there is no evidence of the bandoliers provided with powder charges which were coming into use at this time. The stocks of their guns are very short and could have been better shot from the hip rather than the shoulder. The middle soldier wears a breastplate and a bishop's mantle of mail. All are provided with swords: probably the ubiquitous katzbalger. (Metropolitan Museum of Art, Open Access)

retreat, as they are well-disciplined and obey their officers.'[22] On the whole and despite these qualities he was against their employment:

> But such is their beastliness and arrogance that unless they are commanded by a captain of their own nation whom they know to be generous and courageous, and who holds a commission from the Emperor, they are rather a firebrand and a source of trouble than any real advantage.[23]

The relations between mercenaries and what may be described as English soldiers were always difficult, as disparities in pay and status were bound to cause friction. To avoid conflict in the 1513 expedition it was laid down that:

> no Englishman intermeddle or lodge himself within the ground assigned to the Almains for their lodging, or to give them any reproach or unfitting language or words by which the noise or debate might ensue, on pain of imprisonment and further to be punished as the case shall require … And over that, the King's highness commandeth that all Englishmen and other friendly and courteously do treat the Almains after like said manner as though they were his proper subjects.[24]

Despite the efforts of the commanders, relations between the Almains and the English descended into violence on 15 August. In the fighting many were killed and the German pikemen seized some artillery in a face-off with English archers. Although the outcome would have been interesting, officers on both sides brought the domestic war to a precipitous end but only after the arrival of Emperor Maximilian himself.

The cost of purchasing the expertise and equipment of a mercenary was considerable. A Landsknecht pikeman was paid 8d a day compared to 6d for his English counterpart. The discrepancy in the matter of horse was greater, with the 8d of an English light horseman compared to the 1s 8d of an Italian hackbutter on a horse. Two thousand German Landsknecht and 500 Burgundian horse would cost about £3,000 a month, plus a month's wages were paid for any major engagement fought. To add to this, at the beginning and end of their employment they would be paid conduct money for their journey. They were not averse to some sleight of hand when it came to demand their wages. Grey complained in March 1548 that the Spanish mercenaries in service in Scotland, to make up their numbers, would 'fill up at muster days with boys and Englishmen'.[25]

Their cost may have been considerable but their political reliability was undoubtedly useful. They played a large part in the suppression of the 1549 rebellions, where the Italian and Catholic horse and foot companies of Jacques Jermigny and Paolo Baptista Spinola crushed the Prayer Book Rebellion, while Conrad Pennink and his German mercenaries crushed

---

22 C.G. Cruickshank, *Army Royal*, p.33.
23 C.G. Cruickshank, *Army Royal*, p.33.
24 C.G. Cruickshank, *Army Royal*, p.33.
25 *CSP Scotland*, p.90.

Kett's (Protestant) Rebellion. Burnet wrote that when suppressing the Prayer Book Rebellion:

> the bulk of the people of England was still possessed with the old superstition [Catholicism] to such a degree, that it was visible they could not be depended on, in any matter that related to the alterations [of religion] that were made: whereas the Germans were full of zeal on the other side [Protestantism] so that they might well be trusted to.[26]

Although it was in the end the Italians who slaughtered their co-religionists.

The Privy Council considered, perhaps quite rightly as events proved, that the English would 'most faintly fight' against the rebels. It was noticeable that the leaders of royal forces in Cornwall and Norfolk relied heavily on the skills of their mercenaries when confronting rebels in battle. At the Battle of Dussindale Warwick left his domestic troops behind, relying on his 1,000 or so Almains and heavy horse. These blood-soaked mercenaries seem to have possessed surprisingly tender consciousnesses in matters of their own religion, and even sought absolution for fighting on the side of heretics. In Augsburg in 1551 Richard Morysine wrote that during Lent, 'Many Spaniards and Italians this Lent went to the Bishop of Rome's Nuncio to be absolved, for that they had served in the wars the King of England.'[27]

Mercenaries were not only a great expense to the Crown but the object of fear and loathing to the people. In 1516 Giustiniani spoke of the 'inhumanity of the Germans, who do not content themselves with plundering, but burn and kill, filling every place with death and slaughter'.[28] Their brutality and bloodthirstiness was only matched by the Swiss who boasted of 'irrigating and inundating the earth with human gore'.[29] Hooker, who wrote an account of the Prayer Book Rebellion from the government perspective describes the 'Burgonians' as 'abhorred of the one side and nothing favoured of the other'.[30] One other consequence of using mercenaries was to damage further the reputation of what had once been the 'Good' Duke of Somerset, who had now set the dogs of war upon the English people. Burnet made this point very clearly when he wrote: 'Howsoever, this [use of mercenaries] had an odious name put on it, and was called a ruling by strangers, so that it very much shook the Duke of Somerset's popularity'.[31] The use of mercenaries in

26 Rose-Troup, *The Western Rebellion*, p.237.
27 State Papers Foreign, Ed. VI. No. 144, 14 April, 1549.
28 Sebastian Giustiniani, 'Four years at the court of Henry VIII; selection of despatches written by the Venetian ambassador, Sebastian Giustinian, and addressed to the Signory of Venice, January 12th 1515, to July 26th 1519', transl. by Rawdon Brown (Cambridge: Cambridge University Press, 2013), p.233.
29 Giustiniani, 'Four years at the court of Henry VIII', p.233.
30 Hooker, *Exeter*, p.96.
31 Gilbert Burnet, *The third part of the History of the Reformation of the Church of England. A general index to the History … A collection of records, letters, and original papers with other instruments referred to in the former History*, ed. Edward Nares, 3 vols (Oxford: Oxford University Press, 1829), p.365.

Photographs by Chantal Lashmar and Jane Bennett © Helion & Company
See Colour Plate Commentaries for further information.

1

2

3.1

3.2

4.1

6.1

6.2

7.1

7.2

8.1

8.2

11.1

11.2

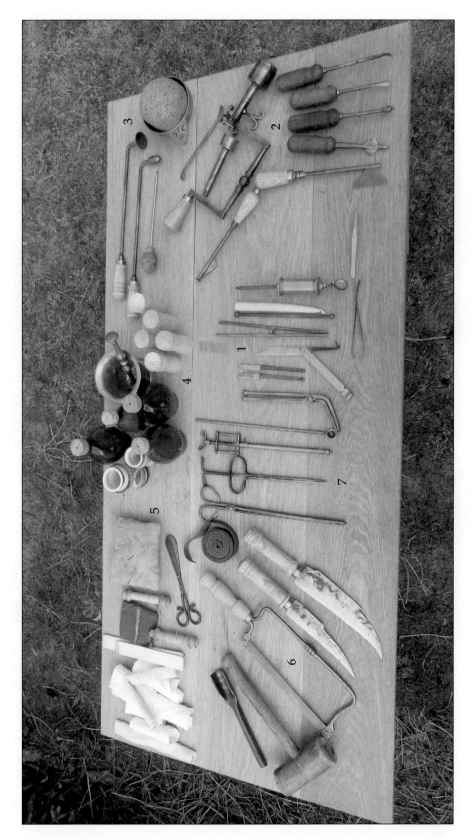

14

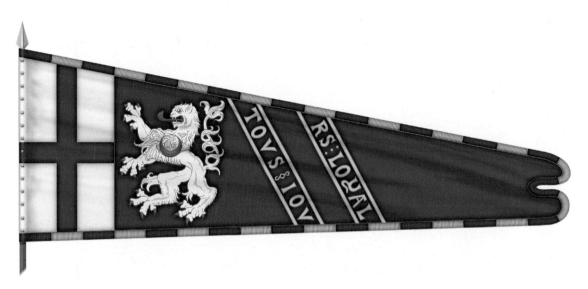

15

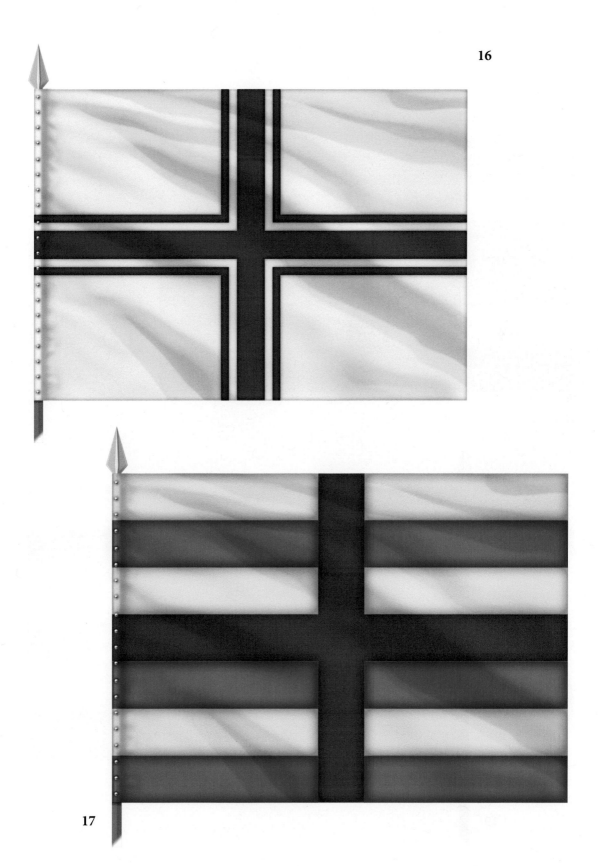

16

17

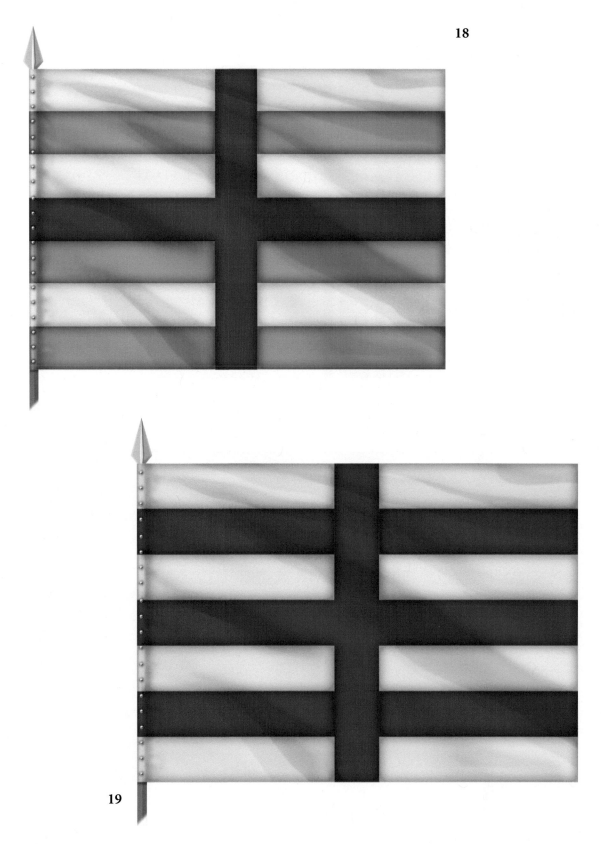

18

19

a war against the Scots or the French was one thing, using them against the commons of England quite another.

Even when they did serve, as in Scotland, they expected special treatment in terms of pay, accommodation and food. Wylford wrote to Somerset complaining about his recently arrived German mercenaries: 'Two "enseygnes" [companies] of Almayns have come here, who are hard to please, for they will only lie in houses, and "howsrome" [house room] is very scant here – yet seeing the small number of English, I must have another "enseygne" of them.'[32] Mercenaries could also refuse to carry out the essential work of building and maintaining fortifications. At the construction of the fortification at Lauder, Grey reported that the Italians boasted they were men of war not 'artificers' and refused to help. The final nail in the coffin of the Rough Wooing was the refusal of mercenaries to serve any more in Scotland, as conditions were so poor and the risks too great. Ironically not all mercenaries in Scotland were so fickle. One of the stalwart captains in French service at Haddington and Leith, and the man who was to play no small part in the loss of Calais, was the great Italian mercenary captain and later marshal of France, Piero Strozzi.

Pedro de Gamboa exemplified the advantages and problems that mercenaries could bring. He first served Henry VIII at Boulogne and then at Portsmouth, and his 200 mounted arquebusiers proved of immense help bringing the Scottish pike bocks to a halt at the Battle of Pinkie. He well knew his value to Seymour, and he and his men insisted and received double their rate of pay, now eight ducats a month, during further service in Scotland. He was clearly not the easiest of characters and Lord Grey fell out with him. Grey, purple with anger at some hurt, concluded a letter to Somerset condemning the Spanish captain: 'Gamboa may act like a Spaniard, but I have an english heart not dreadfull of Spanish Italian, nor other bragges, will not take revenge after his country's manner.'[33] Gamboa was as popular with the King as he was unpopular with Grey, being knighted and granted denisation together with the lordship of Stanmer and 276 acres. He was to die, not in action but at the hands of other Spaniards in the streets of London. He was ambushed by four disgruntled compatriots who had served with him in Scotland and took their revenge after their country's manner. They were arrested in Smithfield and would follow him to the grave by way of the hangman's rope five days later.

Tiberio Perroni was a less annoying mercenary captain than Gamboa and perhaps more representative. He hailed from Calabria and commanded, initially at least, a company of Italian arquebusiers; in April 1546 he received pay for himself and his company in Henry's service. Although he commanded Italian arquebusiers there is also a reference to a large company of over 300 men, and a sophisticated mixture of different weapons. In June 1547 during the operations around the siege of Dalkeith he received high praise from Lord Grey, who wrote: 'Tiberio, as he doth always, showed himself a valiant soldier in the enterprise.'[34] In December 1547 he was one of a number of mercenary captains reinforcing Broughty Craig and then Dundee with his arquebusiers.

---

32 *CSP Scotland*, 11 Nov. 1548, p.332.
33 *CSP Scotland*, p.103.
34 *CSP Scotland*, vol. 1, 1547–63. 236. Grey of Wilton to Somerset. [June 4. 1548.]

In March 1548 Perroni foiled a plot by some Spanish mercenaries to murder the captain of Hume Castle and surrender it to the Scots. He revealed the plan to Lord Grey and the plotters were eventually captured. Their leader was hanged by other Spaniards, disgusted by his disloyalty and perhaps because of the implications it had for their future employment, as 'This has had the effect of making them [Englishmen] less desirous than formerly of having foreigners in their service.'[35] He was later posted to the key fortification at Haddington where he, with his company of arquebusiers, skirmished and slowed the advance of the French army as it advanced on the fort at the end of June 1548. During the siege he commanded one of the bastions and may have been the man responsible for foiling the attempted camisade on 9 October by firing a cannon into the approaching enemy. After impressive service in Scotland, Perroni was sent to the garrison of Boulogne. In November 1548 together with a Flemish captain he led a sortie from the town to enable ships loaded with provisions to get to Boulogne without French interference.[36] He seems to have remained in English service until his death in around 1566, when Antonio Bruschetto wrote to Cecil because of a substantial debt of £300 'due to him by the late Captain Tiberio Perroni.'[37]

One other mercenary colonel deserves to be remembered: he was Friedrich von Reiffenberg who had had a personal interview with Henry VIII, who subsequently chose to employ him. He was authorised to raise an army of 13,000 and to use it to divert the French from their efforts to retake Boulogne. As required, he mustered his army at Koblenz and marched into France, but accepted bribes from the French to withdraw from France, achieving nothing to assist the English, having had already accepted the enormous sum of £80,000 from Henry.

A body of about 800 mounted men known as gendarmes (*gentilhomme d'armes*) were raised in February 1551 by the Duke of Northumberland. They were to provide a firefighting force against domestic disturbances in the six most troublesome counties: Essex, Sussex, Dorset, Hampshire, Kent and Suffolk. They were organised into 12 bands, each commanded by an aristocrat including 10 from the Privy Council. This force was paraded through London in December 1551 and May 1552 wearing 'ther cottes in brodery of yche [each] lord's colors'.[38] Their cost, and domestic peace, led to their premature disbandment in late 1552. This may well have been considered a false economy by Northumberland when he faced the forces rallying to Queen Mary after Edward's death.

Mary and her successor avoided employing mercenaries; the limited extent of warfare in Mary's reign and the long period of comparative peace under Elizabeth made their use far less necessary. Even so, Mary would have been better protected in 1554 with mercenaries when Wyatt's rebels turned the 'royal' forces sent against them, even including some yeomen of the guard.

---

35 *CSP Spain*, vol. 9, 1547–1549, March 22 1548.

36 *CSP Spain*, vol. 9, Nov. 1. Vienna Imp. Arch. f.28. 1549

37 *Calendar of State Papers Domestic: Edward VI, Mary and Elizabeth*, vol. 1, 1547–80, ed. Robert Lemon (London: Longman, Brown, Green, Longmans & Roberts, 1856), p.274. June 29 1566, London.

38 Hammer, *Elizabeth's Wars*, p.45.

8

Recruitment and Discipline

The Medieval System

The feudal system, introduced into England by the Normans, whereby land was held from a lord in return for specific military service, usually lasting some 40 days, had long been superseded in England by a more practical and effective method. The system of recruitment that had served England during the Hundred Years War was based on a system of retaining. It was so-called as the contract or indenture was written twice on the same document, it was then indented to separate the two records with one part being 'retained' between the king and the member of the nobility. This contract was to supply a specific number of men for a period of time or campaign. This produced what was in fact a semi-professional force, led by those who were interested in and could gain by war, whether in wealth or power. The Black Book of Edward IV had ostensibly limited the numbers that could be retained by a member of the nobility, so that a duke could retain 240 men, an earl 140 and a knight only 16, a pious hope as numbers and ambitions fluctuated. These retainers could be within the actual household or more distant properties, but still owing allegiance to their lord. Such allegiances could be multiple, so that Sir John Paston owed allegiance to the Duke of Norfolk and Lord Hastings. To serve your lord required the wearing of his livery (or heraldry and colours), as was made clear to Sir John by Norfolk in 1485, when he was instructed to:

> bring with you such company of tall men as ye may goodly make at my cost and charge, besides that ye have promised I pray you ordain them jackets of my livery, and I shall content you at your meeting with me.[1]

He did not obey this missive and avoided being on the losing side at Bosworth.

---

1   James Gairdner (ed.), *The Paston Letters, A.D. 1422–1509* (London: Chatto & Windus, 1904), vol. 6, p.85.

The king could order commissions of array to raise men for service in the shires and towns. This 'national' system of recruitment operated with the authority of commissions of array under the Great Seal. They would require a group of gentlemen to levy troops from the hundreds and parishes in their area. In the quasi-feudal system, under the authority of a signet letter (a letter from the king authenticated by his signet or seal), gentlemen were required to raise troops from their tenants, servants and dependents. The Statute of Winchester of 1285 had established the requirement of the male population to own weapons, and was still active if not well enforced. This was a time-consuming and unreliable process in terms of both numbers and equipment, and a commission of array also created problems when the authority or authenticity of such a commission was questioned.

During the Wars of the Roses a noble's regional monopoly of power meant that he could use his influence to raise troops from his household, as well as his tenants and those who would serve for favour or through fear. Mercenaries would be recruited because of their special skills, especially those skilled in handling gunpowder weapons. Mercenaries could be provided by a foreign monarch to assist a pretender, as was the case with Henry Tudor and Lambert Simnel, when domestic recruitment was clearly impossible. There was also still in operation the ancient principle, which could be traced back to the Anglo-Saxon Fyrd and *arriére ban*, that all men aged between 16 and 60 could be called on to serve in time of need.

The large numbers of skilled and experienced soldiers, hardened by their service in France, was something of a disservice to the realm when they were called upon to fight each other during the Wars of the Roses. Richard III's army at Bosworth consisted of the royal forces together with those of the Duke of Norfolk and the Duke of Northumberland. The 'third force' consisted of the army led by Lord William Stanley, whose treachery to Richard led to Henry's victory. All these forces were retinues raised by the nobility for their service, not for the Crown but in pursuit of their own interests. On his accession Henry VII was naturally concerned that the presence of what were in effect private armies would be a potential problem for him. He had inherited both quasi-feudal and national systems and these were to work together throughout this period, although the balance between them would alter over time. By the end of Mary's reign it was to be the militia drawn from the counties that would predominate, although their leaders would be drawn from the nobility and gentry, reflecting the contemporary social order.

The first Tudor used whichever system seemed more appropriate, dependent upon the degree of urgency. In 1485 he demanded an oath of loyalty from the nobility, reinforced by a legal judgement in 1486, which restricted further the established limitations to personal retinues. Henry established commissions of array in 1488 consisting of a magnate, six gentlemen and a sheriff in each county. Local gentry operating under the commissions chose the most able to serve in Norfolk, Suffolk, and Essex to counter Lincoln's rebellion. When Perkin Warbeck landed in the west and there was no time to issue commissions of array, the King ordered Sir Peter Edgecombe, sheriff of Cornwall, to simply 'raise the country'. The armies sent to Brittany in 1488 and France in 1492 were made up of indentured retinues.

The Earl of Oxford addressed the ever-loyal John Paston thus: 'Acording to the Kyng our soverayne Lordis commaundemente late to me addressid, I desire and pray you that ye will in all godely haste, upon the sighte hereof, prepare youre selfe to be in a redinesse with as many personnes as ye herfore grauntid to do the Kyng service.'[2] Henry VII was fearful of the nobility, even if he was dependent upon them to a great extent both to lead and provide his army. He relied upon the forces of Bedford, Oxford and Derby as well as some North Midlands gentry and the Royal Household in 1487 and 1489. Once the initial crises were over he was determined to impose strict limits on the numbers of men that could be retained, which was the point made in the last line of the command to Paston.

However, the militia was slow to muster. It was a bureaucratic system and there was serious disquiet about serving in another shire let alone overseas. The quasi-feudal system was therefore often preferred. Henry was able, after the execution of Warbeck and Warwick in 1499, to increase his authority. Thus in 1504 he passed the first effective control on retaining the statute of liveries (*De Retentionibus Illicitis*). This enforced retaining by placard or licence, which limited both the number and the purpose of troops 'owned' by the nobility who were now to serve only the interests of the monarch. The justification for the system was that it was politic that in time of peace there should be preparation for war, in order to provide a substantial number of captains and able men as required for royal service. The fines for granting or wearing unauthorised livery were massive, amounting to 100s or 40s per month for the granter and receiver. Under this legislation not only did the dubiously loyal Lord Abergavenny suffer, but also the eminently loyal Earl of Oxford, who had won the throne for Henry at Bosworth and retained it for him at Stoke: both were fined. Abergavenny was charged the phenomenal sum of £10,000, for going beyond the new strict limit (a sum that was never paid in full but served as a warning to others).

Henry VIII's Reign and the General Proscription of 1522

Jeremy Goring identifies 5 July 1511 as the key date in the development of the militia, as Henry VIII began to clearly define the responsibilities of all subjects. It was established 'That every man have in his house armour for kepyng of the peace accordyng to his havyour [wealth/status] and substaunce, as they have been and shal be ordered by the commyssioners after the olde assise.'[3] This was now also a very clear statement concerning where troops could be recruited by the gentry:

Forseing alweyes that ye nether prepayre ne take any personnes for the warre but oonly suche as bee your owne tenauntes or inhabitauntes within any office

---

2   John Jeremy Goring, 'The Military Obligations of the English People 1511–1558', unpublished University of London PhD thesis, 1955, p.11; Gairdner, *Paston Letters*, vol. iii, p.353.

3   Goring, 'Military Obligations', p.15; Public Record Office. C6 /615 m.7d. (L.P.1, g.833(11)).

that ye have of oure graunt or of the graunt of any other person or personnes or commynaltie, not being tenauntes or officers to any other person or personnes havyng semblable commaundment.[4]

This meant that what had been in effect mercenary bands now became contingents of household or estate servants and tenants. Although the larger part of the royal forces that served abroad were drawn from private retinues, these inevitably declined both as a proportion of the total forces and in military professionalism. The Crown could also, by the granting of stewardships of Crown estates to King's servants, create substantial contingents that could rival those of the established nobility. Thus, Lord Darcy and Charles Brandon were able to bring some of the largest contingents for service in France in 1513.

The exigencies of war put great pressure on the resources of the Tudor state. To satisfy Henry's bellicose ambitions required both cash and recruits. The campaign of 1511–13 had emptied the coffers, and the system of recruitment that had been used was deemed increasingly inadequate for its purpose. The muster rolls of 1511 were unreliable, especially after the 'great pestilence and dearth' of 1520–21. The monarch, or rather his trusted adviser Thomas Wolsey, had little idea of the numbers and national wealth that could be called upon. In the negotiations surrounding the secret Treaty of Bruges, which committed England to action, Wolsey referred to the 'Mightie power and puissant realme' of England, although neither could be accurately assessed. This issue would be addressed, at least in part, in 1522.

The General Proscription of that year was compared by some contemporaries to the Doomsday Book in its extent and aspirations, others considered it principally a military census rather than a fiscal survey. The population were to be 'sworne of what substaunce and landes thei were of'.[5] Wolsey's or the King's intention was 'not oonly to vieu [view] hys people [and] cause the same to be sett in sufficiente Arredinesse … but also to put hymself with the [aid] of hys loving subjects in such state of substance and treasour that he may be hable [to] contynew the warrys.'[6] The annual values of land, cattle and property as well as details of lordship and administration of property were all to be recorded. The numbers and status of aliens or strangers were noted, as well as all those over the age of 16 able to bear arms.

As one might have expected of the Tudor Englishman, whose attitude to governmental taxation was to say the least unenthusiastic, the original returns were, as Wolsey complained, useless because of 'favour, affeccion and other colourable driftes and practises',[7] which guided the first commissioners. The outcome was ultimately rosy, at least for Henry. Polydore Vergil wrote that: 'When the assessment had been made the King could readily see that his people were by no means poor and this greatly pleased him, since what

---

4   Goring, 'Military Obligations', p.16, Historical Manuscripts Commission. Middleton, pp.126–7.
5   Hall, *Chronicle*, p.630.
6   In Jeremy Goring, 'The General Proscription of 1522', in *The English Historical Review*, no. CCCXLI (1971), p.684; Letter to the English ambassadors from Charles V, 22 Mar. 1522, British Library Cotton, Galba B vii, fo. 280 (*L.P.* iii. 2127).
7   Goring, 'The General Proscription', p.686; TNA SP 1/25, fo. }j (*Letters and Papers* iii. 2393).

belongs to a people belongs also to their prince when there is need to use their wealth for the benefit of the realm as a whole.'[8]

The process of completing the Proscription began in March 1523, and Sir Henry Willoughby 'sat upon the muster' at Birmingham on the 29th of that month. The military returns still proved more reliable than the fiscal. That the records varied greatly, from those minutely detailed records of age, occupation, ability and armament, to those which were simply a record of numbers, makes a detailed assessment of the military condition of the realm impossible. In the 28 counties for which there is evidence, there were 128,250 able-bodied men ready to serve, of which a third were archers. There was, on occasion, an attempt to distinguish between the 'good' archers and billmen and those of lesser strength and skill but there is no indication as to how this was achieved. There was no systematic recording of tenants, or those dependent upon the gentry, which meant that the Crown had no idea about the 'power' of the gentry and nobility.

For a martial monarch the lack of military resources would have been a matter of frustration and righteous indignation, although the overall numbers appeared satisfactory. The commission provided a dismal picture of military preparedness. In Rutland, of 36 residents with the 20 marks in land that made them liable to provide military equipment, 17 had no harness (a set of armour for billman or pikeman) of any sort and six had incomplete sets. There was also very little evidence that at this time parish armouries existed or would have contributed equipment for their parishioners.

There were various rates or scales relating to the provision of military equipment. Edward Waldegrave in Sudbury provided 10 harnesses reflecting his wealth which was calculated as being £200 in goods. This rate of £20 per harness seems to have been quite common, those worth between £4 and £20 were assessed collectively. The most common problem was that able-bodied men lacked equipment, whilst the infirm often had equipment that they could not use. In March 1523 this problem was clearly being addressed by a second set of commissioners. In Hampshire John Morecoke, possessor of 'almon Ryvettes Complete', had them assigned to Robert his son. The renewed attention of commissioners in Hull 'caused every man of honesty to bye [buy] harness and weapon,'[9] though it is not recorded how many 'honest' men there were in Hull. The reassignment of armour and weapons to those able, if not necessarily willing, and the purchase of equipment to meet current expectations went some way to addressing the problem of matching men and equipment.

Recruitment in Operation

The commissions of array were well established in English public life and the commissions themselves were phrased in a standard way. The following was addressed to the county of Oxfordshire at the time of the invasion threat in 1545:

---

8   Goring, 'The General Proscription', p.700.
9   Hall, *Chronicle*, p.277.

1. There were Lettres adressyd frome the kynges highnes most honorable Counsell to the Commyssioners of … and for the mustres for to Levye the holl [whole] force and power of the Countye of Oxford to convey theym with all possible spede to Portesimowth for the repulse of enymyes than entendyng to envade in those partyes; by reason wherof … being one of the Commyssioners appoyntyd for the said Mustres and being Allottyd by Comen divysion with other gentymien to certen hundredes, Assemblyd by for them the force and power of the said hundredes to hym and other Allottyd.[10]

The commissioner would order men to be mustered at a specific place and time; in Kent in the hundred of Codsheath, this was at the Muster Oak. Parish constables were responsible for attendance and would assist the commissioners in recording the men and their equipment. They would also admonish those who failed to attend with the requisite arms and armour. In 1539 at Stanton St John (Oxfordshire) the following attended well-armed and equipped:

Kellam Rede, gentyllman, in londes [lands] – x Li.[£10] a footman furnysshed with hernes [harness], byll, sword, and dagger.

Edward ffrenche, in goodes xxti markes [£14], a fotman furnysshed with hernes, byll, sword, and dagger.[11]

Those with less wealth would be expected to share the burden of supporting a soldier: at Stanton St John in 1544, 11 men worth in total 26 marks (£17 6s 8d) were ordered to equip an archer with arms and armour. Towns and parishes were also required to find men and equipment. Thus in 1535 in Newcastle-under-Lyme, the town was required to find four able men with the harness consisting of two archers and two billmen. In 1539 this was reduced to two archers and a single billman.

Commissioners were not free of accusations of bribery and favouritism, the most glaring example of which occurred in Glamorganshire, where it was claimed that 52 people who had been selected for service had paid from 3s.4d. to 33s 4d to William Herbert, to avoid the hardship and cost of service. In 1545 one commissioner, a William Harford of Crayford, had recruited:

[not the] 'most apte and liable men' [but] 'dyvers symple and weke persones … levyng [leaving] dyvers and many of his tenauntes and of their servauntes (being apt, able, and strong men for the warres) at home, not onely at that tyme but lykewise at dyvers other tymes when men were set forth to serve the kynges majestie in his warres.'[12]

Commissioners may have considered it part of their role to ascertain the competence or level of training, but there is a lack of evidence other than an

---

10   Goring, 'Military Obligations', p.47; The National Archives, Sta. Cha. 2/2 f.162.
11   Goring, 'Military Obligations', p.31; The National Archives, E 36/28 f.21b
12   Goring, 'Military Obligations', p.83; The National Archives, Sta. Cha. 2/33/52 f.12.

occasional distinction between 'good' archers and the others. The manorial court on the other hand seems have taken a particular responsibility for archery. On 20 April 1532 in Methley (Yorkshire), all males had to bring their bow and two arrows to the butts by the parish church between Nones and Vespers on Ascension Day. Whether they were required to shoot their bows, or display any skill in their use, is not recorded. This may also have been a simple way for the manorial court to extort the 4d fines on those who failed to present the right equipment. Thomas Wyatt, the enthusiastic military reformer, recommended that commissioners should judge the quality of the archers and not simply count the equipment: they 'must see suche as shoote with there longe bowes, shoote before them one after another.'[13] How many did so is unknown.

There are few if any references to practise, whether individual or collective, being carried out either at musters or at any other time. Archery legislation required all men from the age of seven to 60 to practise at the butts, especially on holy days, and in some villages this was no doubt valued as a long-held tradition. In Bishopsteignton (Devon): 'a payre of buttes stonding upon ... Chapell grene', for 'the mayntenaunce and practyse of the feate of Artyllary' (archery in this context), had been there since 'tyme owt of mynd of man'.[14] They were maintained under the authority of the steward of the manor, rather than the commissioners. In Shipham, 2s 2d were spent on bread and ale, 'at the altering of the Butts'. At North Elmham, the 'gravyng of the flaggs' and the ditch digging cost 5s 8d, to which was added the cost of 17 loads of stone for 4s 3d. Clearly archery butts were not simply small piles of earth.

As the century progressed, more military equipment was clearly being purchased. In 1542 the Statute of Winchester was repealed and the War Horses Act began a new period of defining the military duties of the King's subjects. The situation in 1522 had been lamentable, with fewer than 100 harnesses in Oxfordshire with an able-bodied male population of over 2,000. Farnham was in a worse state, with one harness for every 30 able men. In Hertfordshire in 1557 the situation had not greatly improved, as for 3,628 able men there were only 427 harnesses.

One of the innovations in Henry's reign was the appointment of a lord lieutenant to mobilise the forces in his county, a move officially sanctioned by Parliament in 1549. In Edward's reign there were more frequent appointments of such officers, partly no doubt as a response to widespread domestic unrest. In Mary's reign they were appointed only during times of crisis, in order to speed the process of mobilisation, as commissioners could take weeks or even months to raise their forces. The rebellion led by Sir Thomas Wyatt in 1554 was one such moment. The Lord Treasurer the Marquess of Winchester was appointed to the lieutenancy of Hampshire, together with the Isle of Wight, with 'power to levie all the subjects inhabiting within any the places aforesaid, and then to arme, muster, and put in redynes and ... to leade them as well against enemies as rebelles.'[15] The new system was distrusted by some, as it

---

13 Goring, 'Military Obligations', p.78; British Library Loan 15, Wyatt 23 *r.6b*.
14 Goring, 'Military Obligations', p.42; The National Archives, C 1/1101, f.23.
15 Goring, 'Military Obligations', p.50; The National Archives, SP 15/7 f.20a.

rode roughshod over local sensibilities. The commissioners of array, who were often also commissioners of the peace, were invariably drawn from the upper ranks of society and defended their duties and rights jealously. The city of Norwich even took issue with the Duke of Norfolk being appointed to the lieutenancy in 1554, but eventually they withdrew their objections.

Recruitment and Geography

The recruitment map of England was more or less coterminous with the ecclesiastical division of the realm, between the archdioceses of Canterbury and York, the dividing line being the River Trent. Thus, the nine northernmost shires of England were invariably raised for defence against the Scots; Lancashire, Cheshire, Gloucestershire, Somerset, and Devon were found best for service in Ireland with the remaining southern counties serving against the French. There were exceptions such as Shropshire, where the Earl of Shrewsbury held sway. He was a member and sometimes president of the Council of the North, thus Shropshire found itself sending men to the border. Catherine of Aragon sent troops from Berkshire and Cambridgeshire against the Scots in 1513, so serious was the threat.

In 1545 when reinforcements were sent to Boulogne, they came from the southern inland counties in Bedfordshire, Cambridgeshire, Hertfordshire, Huntingdonshire, Leicestershire, Norfolk, and Northamptonshire. The southernmost counties on the coast were mobilised to face the threat of invasion. A similar principle was in operation when the Isle of Wight was reinforced by men from the northern hundreds of Sussex, while the coastal hundreds prepared to oppose invasion on the Sussex coast. These sound principles were sometimes ignored, again in time of crisis. In 1558 when Calais was threatened, the militia from Suffolk, Essex, Kent, and Sussex made their way to Dover for embarkation.

Problems Facing Recruitment

Sometimes the number of men requested could not be raised. The commissioners of the peace in Northamptonshire wrote to the Marquess of Winchester, lord lieutenant of several Midlands shires in 1558, that they were unable to fulfil their quota of 1,000 men. This was not because of a shortage of men, 'personages and boddyes we confesse to have in nombre', but because too many were 'stopinge [stooping] and crockyd', and therefore 'unmete to doo any servis in warres'.[16] The sweating sickness had hit hard in the late 1550s, and 'this mortality fell chiefely or rather on men, and those also of the best age, as betweene 30 and 40 yeeres'.[17] Again in 1558, although Derbyshire was expected to provide 1,500 footmen, the commissioners could only raise

---

16 Goring, 'Military Obligations', p.64.
17 Goring, 'Military Obligations', p.65.

100; the reason was that sickness had carried off many able men.

This shortage of manpower on a national scale was perceived as a major problem. One of the issues popularly associated with this problem was the increase in sheep farming and the decline in arable, which had major implications for society as a whole. The 'Doctor' in Smith's *Discourse of the Commonweal* explained what many believed: 'then you know that a few sheepmasters would serve for a whole shire; so in process of time the multitude of the King's subjects would be worn away and none left but a few shepherds, which were no number sufficient to serve the King at his need or defend this realm from enemies'.[18] In addition it was thought that sturdy yeomen were far superior, as 'shepeherdes be but yll artchers'.[19] This was undoubtedly part of the general hostility to the apparently harmless herbivore, as 'sheep that were wont to be so meek and tame, and so small eaters, now, as I heard say, be become so great devourers and so wild, that they eat up, and swallow down the very men themselves'.[20] The conversion of arable land for pasture led to depopulation and unemployment, constituting a challenge to the social order.

The apparent decline in gentry households was also perceived as a problem. In 1544 *A Supplycacion to … Henry the Eyght* pointed to the decline of households as being a serious issue, as 'Scarce a worshipful man's lands, which in times past was wont to find and maintain twenty or thirty yeomen … the same now is not sufficient and able to maintain the heir of the same lands, his wife, her gentlewoman or maid, two yeomen and one lackey'.[21] Sir William Paget advised Somerset to raise his forces from 'trusty servants', as they were both well fed and liable to be more loyal to their masters than ploughmen or shepherds.

There were also problems with the quasi-feudal system, as tenants increasingly refused to see military service as part of their duties to their landlord. In 1542 John Port had requested military service from his tenants. They had proved obstinate and refused although he claimed that his request was in line with 'ancient and laudable custom continued since and afore time of mind … throughout the whole realm of England'.[22] His tenants on the other hand thought 'it was not their duty'. It was because of such increasing opposition that the *Act Against Unlawful Assemblies* stated that tenants refusing to provide military service should lose their lands. The cost of equipping men also lay heavily on the nobility and gentry, who were not always able to meet the cost of military service in straitened times and faced

---

18 *A Discourse of the Commonweal of this Realm of England*, attr. Thomas Smith, ed. M. Dewar (Charlottesville: University Press of Virginia, 1969), p.89.

19 Steven Gunn, David Grummitt, Hans Cools, *War, State, and Society in England and the Netherlands 1477–1559* (Oxford: Ouxford University Press, 2007), p.291. Ref 184; *Certayne causes gathered together, wherin is shewed the decaye of England onely by the great multytude of shepe* (London: Hugh Syngelton, 1552),

20 Thomas Moore, *Utopia*, Book I, in Henry Craik (ed.), *English Prose* (New York: The Macmillan Company, 1916). Available online, see bibliography for URL.

21 John Jeremy Goring, 'Social change and military decline in mid–Tudor England', in *History* (June 1975), p.190.

22 Goring, 'Social Change', p.189; The National Archives, C1/1053/48.

heavy financial losses. Fixed rents and debasement added to the ills of the landed gentry at the end of this period, reducing substantially their real wealth.

The pay available to the recruit, which had served well in attracting and retaining soldiers at the beginning of Henry VIII's reign, had through inflation by the end of his reign come to seem a poor reward. The 6d a day was sometimes barely enough even to provide him with sustenance even when food was available. The opportunities for acquiring wealth from booty also diminished, especially for those serving in the North. In the 1539 musters in Lincolnshire and Nottinghamshire, it was the 'haveless, poor and needy' who were willing to serve so that they 'may have the King's wages.'[23]

Who Should Serve?

Those soldiers who were recruited should be 'able' or 'mete to serve in the warres', which were rather general requirements. Barely more specific were the requirements for the commissioners to 'have spetiall regard that … the said nombers be taken of the most apte and hable men.'[24] The Earl of Westmorland ordered the commissioners of Derbyshire to recruit only 'the most lustye, tallest, and servyceable personages … and most metest to assault and defend thenemy.'[25] The majority of soldiers were in their 20s and 30s although older men in their 60s were not unknown. Sir Thomas Wyatt thought that 'suche as be unmarried' would make better soldiers. His explanation is well worth recording in full:

> They [married men] will, when they have a while endured the contynuall travaille and perill that is to be suffered in an army, call righte lightly to remembraunce the differrence of sleepinge under an hedge and, in a bedd which there wyves weare wont to make; In somuche that they have wished themselfes to be at home in there smoky houses and because suche holowe folke cannot well keepe owne counsaille, they faile not to be the occasion that many another growe to be of the same opynion; whereupon there failethe not to followe as well daungerous perill to the Army as dyshonour and muche forlorne cost to the prynce.[26]

Married men were clearly 'lacking in moral fibre' and likely to infect others with their cowardice, to the detriment of the whole army. Wyatt's contempt for those who preferred the comfort of a warm bed and a cheerful wife in a smoky house, to the rigours and joys of the soldier's life, mirrors Gruffydd's opinion of such whingeing 'civvies'.

---

23 G.R. Elton, *Policy and Police: the Enforcement of the Reformation in the Age of Thomas Cromwell* (Cambridge: Cambridge University Press, 1972), p.330; *The Papers of George Wyatt Esquire of Boxley Abbey in the County of Kent*, ed. D.M. Loades (London: Royal Historical Society, Camden Fourth Series, vol. 5, 1968), 171.23.

24 Goring, 'Military Obligations', p.72; The National Archives, SP 11/12 f.18b. GT72

25 Goring, 'Military Obligations', p.73; H.C. Talbot, MS D I. 288a

26 Goring, 'Military Obligations', p.79; British Library Loan 15, Wyatt 23 f.3b.

There were two other categories of men who were recruited as soldiers, not because of their energy, enthusiasm and skill but because they would be better off out of the way. In 1549 commissioners were encouraged to: 'have special respect to take suche as be idle persons and will not labour'.[27] The term 'idle' included those masterless men, drunkards and petty thieves who were responsible for causing so much disquiet and fear amongst the population, especially the governing class. It could also include those who were not engaged in agriculture. In 1558 in Northamptonshire, those mustered should be 'artificers and ydle persons and not of mowers, reapers, husbondmen, and suchlike, by whose labours and travaill the common wealth of this realme ys increased'.[28] The campaign season was the busiest time of the agricultural year and to empty the fields of workers would have been disastrous. Small tradesmen on the other hand could serve with less danger to the economy as their labour was less essential for the survival of society.

The other group that it was felt would be better off in the army and under martial discipline, were those Goring describes as 'troublemakers'. One surprising example was London Alderman Richard Reed, whose refusal to pay the benevolence for the war in 1545 led to him being sent post haste to serve on the border. Kett's Rebellion provided many unwilling recruits for Henry's wars. To provide reinforcements for the Boulogne garrison, commissioners were ordered 'specially to pike out those that wer grettest doers and ringleaders in the late sedition and commotion'.[29] Lord Gray went so far as to suggest to Mary I that the garrison at Guînes should be reinforced by 'soldyars, parte of siche as were condempned to be hanged'.[30]

Recruitment of Officers

Officers could only be recruited from the ranks of the gentry, that is 'gentlemen of haviour', 'gentelmen of inheritaunce, or their heires apparaunt'.[31] The English nobility were few in number compared to their Continental counterparts and the gentry were not especially numerous. Mike Ingram considers that at the time of Bosworth there were no more than 2,300 and 2,500 gentry families in England.[32] To exclude those too old, too sick or too busy, meant that the pool of candidates was relatively small. This, it is argued, may be one of the reasons why company sizes grew from 100 in 1544 to 200–250 in 1548 or even 400. It was hoped those chosen would be 'experte', 'discreete and skilfull'. Richard Barkhede had a low opinion of the current generation of young gentlemen destined to lead raw recruits into battle:

---

27 Goring, 'Military Obligations', p.79; The National Archives, SP 10/9 f.87a.
28 Goring, 'Military Obligations', p.79; British Library, Add. MS. 25079 f.10a.
29 Goring, 'Military Obligations', p.80; The National Archives, SP 10/9 f.87a.
30 Goring, 'Military Obligations', p.81; J.G. Nichols, *The Chronicle of Queen Jane* (London: Cam. Soc. 1st ser. xlviii, 1850), p.62.
31 Goring, 'Military Obligations', p.74; The National Archives, SP 11/11 f.75a.
32 Ingram, *Richard III*, p.47.

> The moost part of gentlemen … ar and have ben of laite days brought up so deyintely [daintily] and in such vanities that they can little skill of the service of their countree … I cannot passe over with silence (for the worlde doth se) what tenderlinges the greatest part of our younge gentlemen be.[33]

On the border, where warfare was endemic, it was perhaps easier to find captains who possessed the expected martial qualities, and it is possible to see how the individual skills of a soldier such as horsemanship, marksmanship and swordsmanship could be acquired. How an officer could learn the very different role of the captain, without the opportunity to exercise his company, is difficult to understand. The plethora of instructional manuals in the second half of the century could indicate a renewed interest in martial disciplines or more likely desperation in the face of possible invasion. Thomas Audley wisely remarked in 1550 that many a man 'was made a captain before he was a soldier'.[34] Sir Richard Morison had noted with contempt that many of the gentry summoned to serve against the Pilgrimage of Grace in 1536 could not even sit on their horses properly. There was an exceptional example, a captain in the Dorset militia named Bartholomew Hussey, who had served under the Grand Master of the Knightly order of the Hospital in Rhodes, on the front line of the Crusades; he was known as 'Husey, late of the Rodes'.

Proposals for Reform 1539 and 1550

There was an attempt by Thomas Cromwell to thoroughly reform the system of recruitment, in a 1539 document entitled 'Articles for the ordering of the manred'. This seems to have suggested a single system of recruitment, similar to what was achieved by the legislation of 1558. Three Kentish gentlemen, Sir Thomas Wyatt the younger, Sir William Pickering and Sir James Wilford, put forward a scheme to 'strengthen the Kings part with a power of the choise of his most able and trusty Subjectes, which might be upon a very short warninge in a reddines (wel armed and Ordered against al suddin attemptes either at home or abrode)'.[35] Each shire would be required to provide a reserve of well-trained, well-equipped men, commanded by a paid, professional, 'chief captain'. None of the soldiers were to be married men or to have a farm or land worth more than £1. It even specified that those men 'booked for archers', had to be 'nimble shooters' and men of 'great corpulence' (presumably of great strength rather than girth). The scheme was proposed to the Lord Protector, who:

> was with greate likinge approved and alowed of, but not concluded upon – either for the newnes of the thinge, or for that it was not at that season thought so

33 Hale, *Renaissance War Studies*, p.248, Barkhede, *A brief discourse* 3i.
34 Audley, 'Treatise', p.69.
35 Goring, 'Military Obligations', p.302; British Library Loan 15, Wyatt MSS. no. 17, see Agnes Conway, 'The yatt MSS. in the Possession of the Earl of Romney' (British Institute for Historical research, 75; 1925).

convenient to have – the subjectes armed (whereof the greater numbers were evel affected to the Religion then professed), or for that (sum divition then beinge amongst thos that bore the sway) sum hindered that others liked of.[36]

Sir Thomas Audley strongly supported the establishment of a national arsenal in his guidance to King Edward in 1550. He cited European examples by Charles V and from Venice, and recommended the permanent acquisition and storage of 'harnes and weapons' for 4,000 horse and 4,000 corslets. He considered the cost too great for the individual soldiers to bear and judged it a much better investment for the Crown than plate or jewels.

Henry VIII had acquired a significant national armoury by the end of his reign. Those weapons held in store in 1547 amounted to at least 43,000 polearms, 11,000 bows and 10,000 firearms and 6,000 sets of Almain rivet.[37] The quantities held privately would have also been considerable. By 1547, therefore, England had a substantial national armoury that even Audley would have been proud of. It would, however, be in Mary's and Elizabeth's reigns that a well-equipped and well-trained national militia would emerge, as a consequence of threats from abroad rather than from a desire for conquest.

A National Militia, 1558

The demand for large numbers of men to be raised in 1544–5 had led to Henry relying upon the militia system more and more as the quasi-feudal system could not respond adequately. The attempt to raise troops to retake Calais was a fiasco and showed how little prepared the militia were; when 1,000 men were assembled at Dover and Sandwich, it was found that fewer than 200 were provided with weapons and equipment.[38] The crisis, brought about by the loss of Calais in January 1558, led to the Crown ordering the shire commissioners to levy the tenants of nobility and gentlemen, a compete break with the earlier principle of recruitment. This dramatic change was to be advanced in the legislation that followed soon after: the 'Act for the Taking of Musters' and the 'Act for the Having of Horse Armour and Weapons', both enacted in 1558, eight months before Mary's death. These extensive pieces of legislation divided the population into 10 income groups, prescribing precisely what equipment they should possess and maintain. It included all males between 16 and 60, excluding from it only nobility of baronial rank who were expected to raise their own contingents, and the clergy, who were expected to make their own monetary contribution. Parliament, always overstocked with members of the legal profession, considered including lawyers as an excluded group, a motion that produced much merriment but no action. The Acts failed to make provision for training or local armouries, which significantly reduced its effectiveness.

---

36 Goring, 'Military Obligations', p.302. British Library Loan 15, Wyatt MSS. no. 17, see Agnes Conway, 'The yatt MSS. in the Possession of the Earl of Romney' (B.I.H.R.i, 75; 1925).
37 See Appendix I for details.
38 Hammer, *Elizabeth's Wars*, p.51.

Corporate towns and cities were expected to raise their own militias and provide a well-stocked armoury. As one might expect at this time, the ancient liberties and corporate status of towns led to conflict with the commissioners. Towns preferred to obey their own military hierarchy, rather than having to muster at the command of the county, perhaps to a site some distance away, adding to the time and trouble of the whole process. The clerk of Liverpool smugly recorded that through the diligent labour of the mayor and the council the town escaped any attendance at musters at all. Both the universities of Oxford and Cambridge were exempted from the city musters and Oxford city included itself in the exemption from musters arranged by the commissioners; even the lord lieutenant could be defied, though not always successfully. The Cinque Ports refused to attend musters which were not authorised by their lord warden, and a happy fiction was therefore created by which the lord lieutenant accompanied the lord warden to musters of the Cinque Ports, saving the faces of all concerned. Less pliable were the stannaries (the ancient courts of the Cornish tin miners) which maintained a continual refusal to cooperate with the commissioners. The Privy Council might have felt themselves constantly frustrated by these petty rivalries and the counties had to provide the full number of men even if a town failed to contribute.

By the end of Mary's reign England was beginning to develop a national militia system, where although there might be local resistance, there was a clear understanding of what was expected in terms of service and equipment. The officers would be provided by the gentry and commanders almost exclusively from the nobility: the correct social order had to be maintained. What was lacking at this point was systematic training and universally accepted tactics and orders. These would only develop in Elizabeth's reign, when Continental commitments and the threat of invasion provided the impetus and the skilled personnel required to create a fully equipped and trained militia.

Discipline, Disorder and Mutiny

A distinction should be made between discipline in battle and the general issue of discipline in the camp, garrison and field, although it is easy to confuse them. Discipline in battle requires the soldier to perform the role allotted to him and not do what comes naturally when placed in danger: flight. Thomas Audley made a nice distinction between a soldier's oath to do his duty, and 'penal statutes' or regulations designed to maintain good order. There is very little evidence to suggest that the English troops, whether in France or Scotland, siege, skirmish or battle lacked courage or gave way to panic. Of course, cowardice in the face of the enemy and desertion would be included in the disciplinary codes both formal and informal but this work will deal with the more general issue of discipline, or rather indiscipline.

The Tudor soldier was in the main not a professional but a 'common man in arms' and his officer a 'gentleman in arms'. Service in the army did not preclude the Tudor soldier from displaying dissent and negotiating with his superiors over conditions, or even the future of a campaign. The social relationship that existed in civilian life was transferred to a military context. The officers were from the gentry and they could expect deference and obedience from the common soldier, but in return he might expect fairness and competence. If the officer failed in his duty, then he could expect to be challenged in what would be considered to be a mutiny, a refusal to obey orders. The complaint of Kett's rebels in 1549 was that the gentry were exploiting their position to the detriment of the commons, that the gentry were in fact failing in their duty towards them and that their rebellion was also in a sense a social mutiny! This is certainly how it appeared to the gentry. The rebels, though willing to damage and seize property, did not exact physical revenge on the gentry or their families. There were strict boundaries of acceptable conduct.

'Mutinie' would occur when the common soldier felt that he was being mistreated or mismanaged. In the Gascon expedition of 1512 the Spanish king failed to provide either the food or the transport needed by the small English force, who were dependent upon the local population for sustenance. Suffering from the hot summer weather, dysentery, an absence of accommodation and high prices, they sought an increase in their pay from 6d to 8d. This led to a mutiny that concluded with arrests and at least one execution. The failure here was of the commanders and allies, who did not fulfil their responsibilities and kept the men in idleness. Thomas Grey, the commander, deserves some blame. He was inexperienced in command, and neglected to maintain a regime of training and inspection which would have given his troops some purpose.

In February 1515 there was a mutiny in the garrison in Tournai because the soldiers were now to be paid at the end of the month rather than the beginning, as was common practice. This would have meant that they had to rely upon expensive credit from a hostile population to see them through. What was surprising was that the 'mutiny' included some of the Yeomen of the Guard, whose discipline was thought to be better. The mutineers' cry was simply 'Money! Money! Money!' They refused to allow the gates of the city to be opened but made no further threats. The garrison commander gave in, and the provost marshal Sir Sampson Norton provided a useful scapegoat and was dismissed. A second mutiny occurred in October, again about pay and service conditions. This was far more serious, as some of the men appeared in arms. This time the treatment was much harsher and five were executed and others banished. The distinction that was made between the two mutinies and the individuals involved demonstrates how the issue of military discipline was not a clear cut one at this time. All depended upon context and the role of individuals, both those demonstrating and those in authority.

The miserable conditions during the Rough Wooing on land and sea, added to by the abject failure of the logistical system to provide adequately for garrisons and crews, caused much distress. Wyndham, writing about the conditions in Broughty Craig in February 1548, stressed the need to provide the 'soldiers and mariners', with their pay in order to 'get clothing as they die every day for the lack in the extreme cold and my lord Clinton and the Admiral promised a groat a day above their wages to the men that laboured night and day at the fort, which unless paid will cause a mutiny'.[39] The dreadful conditions in November led to a further *cri de coeur* from Dudley, a capable officer. He complained that:

> I am in a weak house with a raw company, and have only got three months' victual, but such rotten biscuit and sour beer as was never had! I am in as much danger of my men as of the Scots – they cry out of the bad victuals, and have neither shirt nor hose, and many fall sick daily. There is much to do and few to do it. "Master John" the Italian is very sickly, but does what he can. I have but 2 ship-carpenters – one 'stark lame', the other sick of ague. I have not a plank, or place to store victual in but one of the ships. My men lie together like swine as wet as in the field, and I can scant lie dry myself.[40]

Despite this miserable existence there was no large-scale mutiny and many examples of remarkable resilience and collective bravery, as exemplified by the siege of Haddington. On the other hand, if large-scale collective mutiny did not take place it was common, especially for those northerners close to home, for soldiers to simply slip away.

In the French campaign of 1523 the mutiny was far more damaging to the army, as it forced its commanders to abandon operations. This was perhaps something that they would have done before, if they had not feared the wrath of the King. The campaign tool place late in the season and it was soon clear that it had little strategic purpose. At the siege of Bray there was considerable dissent among the infantry after the town was captured, as they waited not very patiently outside, as Gruffydd recalled:

> During this time the footmen of the rearward were standing in front of the town on the slope of a watery hill where many men had water in their boots, and for this reason everybody was complaining because they could see night coming and the weather wet and they likely to stand in their ranks through the greater part of the night unless they crossed the river, or so the story went among those in the field … Some Welshmen from South Wales who were under Lord Ferrers, among whom were many unruly men, heard this and these took the matter so seriously that they sent round word to cry all together 'On to the town' 'On to the town' which they all did, while beginning to turn back.[41]

The troops were cold, wet and miserable and they saw no reason why they should suffer in silence. They did not resist their officers; they did not refuse to face the enemy; they were simply fed up. This was perhaps the inevitable consequence of having an army of civilians who were unwilling to put up with what they saw as unnecessarily harsh conditions.

---

39   *CSP Scotland*, no. 173, Feb. 1548, p.85.
40   *CSP Scotland*, no. 74, Nov. 1. 1547, p.35.
41   Jonathan P. Davies (text transcribed by M. Bryn Davies), *'An ill jurney for the Englshemen': Elis Gruffydd and the 1523 French Campaign of the Duke of Suffolk* (Sunderland: Pike and Shot Society, 2006), p.9.

When news of reinforcements reached the army, the response was very varied. The news:

> was well received by the gentlemen of England and those men of the common soldiers who had set their mind on being men of war, but those who were thinking of their wives and children and husbandry and those cowardly men with base hearts who would rather go home to their mothers and fathers, some to plough and thresh, others to follow the cart and hedge and dig and live niggardly, these were unwilling and were angry with anyone who talked about staying there during the winter.[42]

The worsening of conditions also led to greater discontent:

> During this time grey bearded winter began to show his face in black cold frost wind and short days and long nights which caused the decrepit shivering soldiers to complain and groan to each other. Some said it was too much for them to be there lying on the earth under hedges and bushes dying of cold, another said that he wanted to be home, in bed with his wife which was a more comfortable place for his head than here. This complaint many of the English and the Welsh made with great weeping and wailing.[43]

Gruffydd's attitude and response was that of the old soldier who despised these lily-livered grumblers; he despised them above all as 'civvies' who were 'cowardly men with base hearts' who had chosen to 'live niggardly', they were not 'men of war' as he would have thought of himself. The discontent grew, and reached a point at which the expedition was endangered. The response of the commanders was swift and decisive: it was not to hang the 'mutineers' but to flee with their own booty.

> It is certain that the Duke and all the captains who had any sense were amazed at this shouting, not only from shame that the foreigners from Burgundy should see the: shiftlessness, the weakness and the unruliness of the English soldiers, but also for fear lest the enemy should get to know of this tumult and fall suddenly upon them. So the sensible men got up and went each to his company to pacify the unruly ones with fair words and promises that they should take their journey back to England the next morning … the Duke and his captains went into council to decide which way they should next take with their goods in safety.[44]

It was similarly the refusal of the soldiers to carry on that led to the collapse of the Gascon expedition of 1512, despite the wishes of the King for them to remain.

The contempt that Elis felt for these soldiers and their officers is palpable. However there was nothing to suggest that the troops in this expedition had failed in 'action', they wanted to return home as they could see no point in

---

42 Davies, *Ill Jurney*, pp.12–13.
43 Davies, *Ill Jurney*, p.13.
44 Davies, *Ill Jurney*, p.14.

remaining under such harsh conditions, with no clear purpose, an analysis of the situation which was objectively correct. What Elis points to is the failure of leadership and the weakness of an army that was made up of civilians, not 'warriors'.

The troops could take a lead from their officers. Captain Luttrell at Broughty Craig continued to carry on an aggressive campaign against the Scots with his loyal garrison despite the misery of their conditions. Somerset chose to dig in the trenches himself for two hours every day to encourage his officers and men to complete the important task of building defences. Other officers showed themselves concerned only with their selfish interests: for example in 1544 some captains sought to benefit from the shortage of rations at Montreuil by setting themselves up as sutlers, profiting from the shortages. The ever-eloquent Elis ap Gruffydd recorded that at Calais:

> all the captains desired wealth quite shamelessly without bothering where it came from. And as far as taking pain and trouble in the service of the king went, the only pain they took was to lie with whores in their beds at Calais until dinner time which they took at the table of the Deputy or one of the Council of Calais while the common soldiers were compelled to lie in the low country where there was great shortage of bread and drink. When they did come to Calais to fetch provisions and ask for help and advice the captains drove them out of the town with foul words.[45]

The keys to the discipline and military efficiency of a force were the system of recruitment employed and the quality of the officers who commanded. The quasi-feudal system of recruitment, although less important now than it had been, encouraged a sense of loyalty and duty among the group, partly enforced by social opprobrium or economic sanctions if the individual failed. The raising of the county militia from its parish structure also encouraged a degree of homogeneity, especially as the individuals were 'chosen' from their communities to serve. Collective loyalty was important in maintaining unit cohesion, but it could also result in collective disobedience. Tudor soldiers were not the sweepings of the gutter and the prison: that was a pattern associated with the later Elizabethan campaigns. An army of citizen soldiers does demand more careful handling by those in charge than a disparate band held together by harsh discipline. The commons expected to be treated with a degree of consideration and expected competence from those who led them, unlike in Europe, where the experience of war had produced a military caste that was separate from and often quite inimical to the civilian population. The English army was quite simply the commons-in-arms.

---

45   Davies, *Enterprises*, p.18.

Lawes and Ordinances

The Tudor equivalent of the Queen's Regulation was the 'lawes and ordinances'. There are surviving ordinances dateable to 1385,1415, 1417, 1419/21, 1513 and possibly 1475. They were proclaimed at the beginning of a campaign and should have been read by the captain to his company twice a week. This had a long historical precedence, and the ordinances proclaimed in 1513 at Calais were an enlargement of those used by Henry's predecessors, suggesting a remarkable degree of institutional continuity. Henry V had 43 clauses in his 'Lawes' of 1415, whereas Henry VIII had some 60, which perhaps reflects the increased scale of the new Tudor bureaucracy. In fundamentals both remained the same as those issued by Richard II in 1385. The significant differences occur much later in the century with the concept of conscription and allegiance to the state.

The details relating to the mustering of companies were more extensive in the 1513 Ordinances than in the previous examples. They also related to the usual supervision of the men and their equipment, including ensuring that the weapons and armour provided by soldiers was their own and not borrowed. In addition, it required that all deaths (of soldiers in the company) must be certified, to avoid fraudulent claims for pay. This should not be confused with 'dead pays' which were legitimately added as a form of bonus payment. Captains were also required to pay their soldiers' wages in full when they received them. Wages seem to have been paid at the beginning of the month; on occasion they were paid by the day, as a form of encouragement to remain, rather than desert with a month's wages!

One of the surprising inclusions in the Ordinances is the regulations relating to ransoms and booty; there are more clauses relating to prisoner-taking in the 1513 Ordinances than those of 1385. The Ordinances recognised the legitimacy of such activity and were an attempt to control individual profiteering as opposed to collective sharing, especially as the captain and the Crown might expect the lion's share. Henry VIII unsurprisingly repeated the clauses in Henry V's Ordinances relating to the protection of the French population, as both sought legitimacy as kings of France and this requirement seems to have been generally observed. The protection of non-combatants including women and children, and especially the Church, its property and personnel was also stressed. None of this protected the population from the exigencies of war, fire, siege, disease, individual cruelty and displacement. Even Elis ap Gruffydd felt sympathy for the French population driven from their homes in 1544 in desperate conditions. Every expedition involved the pillaging of villages and towns, sometimes as policy if not as an inevitable consequence of war. In 1512 in the Gascony expedition the English army went so far as to pillage Santa María, which belonged to their Spanish allies, where they 'slew and robbed the people without mercy'.[46]

---

46 Robert Hutchinson, *Young Henry: The Rise of Henry VIII* (London: Wiedenfeld & Nicholson, 2011), p.162.

Military discipline in the face of the enemy was stressed, and desertion ostensibly punished harshly. Anyone who cried 'havoc' without authority was subject to the death penalty. The cry of 'havoc' meant that the soldiers were released from discipline to pursue private booty. One example of formal discipline being applied, was that of a soldier hanged after the camisade of Boulogne for failing in his duty as sentry, although his equally unobservant commanders were free of censure let alone punishment. One prohibition which should not really surprise in an army drawn from so many nations, was that any disputes driven by national sentiment, whether French, English, Northern, Welsh or Irish would be punished severely.

The Ordinances required that 'every lord, captain, and petty captain, having any retinue great or small, see for the good rule and guiding of his people at his parcel and charge, as he will answer for them to the King'.[47] The injunction that captains should visit the lodgings of their soldiers, to ensure that they were living a 'Catholicke and Christian life', was no doubt more honoured in the breach than in the observance. There was a concern for the moral wellbeing of soldiers on campaign. In 1513 women were completely banned from the camp, a policy which, according to a Venetian observer, seems surprisingly to have been fully applied. Any woman found would, on the orders of the marshal, be branded on one cheek. The English camp in 1544 was far different and seems to have had a large number of women present, if the Cowdray engraving is accurate. This change in policy might have simply been a practical and pragmatic recognition that women in the camp could perform many useful and perfectly legitimate roles, and need not pose a great threat to camp discipline. It was not surprising that dice, cards and other games were banned (with no doubt little success), as they were a cause of dissent and distracted the men from their duty. Excessive drinking was also discouraged for the same reasons.

The administration of the Tudor army in the field included the post of treasurer, responsible for paying soldiers on the advice of commissioners, as well as supervising the sales of booty. The marshal was responsible for the supervision of prisoners and commanded a provost company to keep discipline amongst the soldiers. The provost marshal, sometimes called the under-marshal, was a regular appointment in Henry VIII's reign made for specific campaigns. His role was to suppress dissent and impose discipline. Lord Darcy appointed Henry Guilford as provost in the 1511 expedition against the Moors, and presumably he was called upon to suppress disorder when the expedition was disembarked in Cadiz, as Hall's *Chronicle* records there was trouble:

> The Englishmen which went a lande, fell to drinking of hote wynes and were scarce masters of theim selfes, some ranne to the stews, some brake hegges, and spoyled orchardes and vyneyardes, and orynges before they were ripe, and did many other outragious deedes: wherfore ye chefe of the toune of Cadys [Cadiz],

---

47 Matthew Hale, *Historia Placitorum Coronæ, The History of the Pleas of the Crown ... In Two Volumes*, vol. 1 (London: E. Rider, 1800), no. 673 pp.671–672.

came to complaine to the lorde Darcie in hys shippe, which sent forth his Provost Marshal which scarclie with peyne refrayned the yomen archers, they were so hote and wilfull, yet by comaundement and policie, they were all brought on borde on their shippes.[48]

A provost marshal was appointed for the 1513 and subsequent expeditions, and one was of course appointed in Tournai and had to face disaffected soldiery. He would hold a court three times a week, when cases and complaints could be brought to him.

Punishments were intended to match the seriousness of the crime. If a soldier sounded the general alarm without cause it would result in the death penalty, but if he left his post he would only forfeit his equipment. Keeping a woman in the camp would incur the loss of a month's wages and imprisonment. If he was caught gambling, the wagers and winnings were forfeited and he would be imprisoned for eight days. Those who served under the master of the ordnance fell under a separate disciplinary procedure, although no doubt no less demanding. This was an anomaly that lasted for centuries and which reflected Continental practice, where the guns of the ordnance could act as a place of sanctuary from army discipline.

Provosts were appointed in the wake of the 1536 and 1549 rebellions and to accompany the expeditions to Scotland and Ireland. For obvious reasons they do not seem to have been much loved, and the stories surrounding them suggest that they had a peculiar sense of humour. Sir Anthony Kingston, appointed 'provost marshal in the field' during the suppression of the Cornish rebels in 1549. Kingston, it was said, made the mayor of Bodmin erect gallows and then dined with him as the work was carried on. After what must have been a difficult lunch for one of them, the mayor was invited to first test the strength of the gallows before being hanged on them.

Conclusion

Henry VIII's army was described by Brian Downing as 'little more than a rapidly put together collection of freebooters and dregs, augmented by a few thousand Landsknecht',[49] and Neil Murphy declares that 'Poor discipline and disorder were endemic among English armies during the early sixteenth century'.[50] These views do not do justice either to the army or the men who served in it. The 'commons-in-arms' served well, often in very difficult circumstances, but they were unwilling to experience ill-treatment or incompetence that would cause pointless suffering. Warfare was a joint effort by the whole of Tudor society and this created limitations as to what could be sustained or achieved. Thomas Audley outlined the consensus that was to

---

48 Hall, *Chronicle*, p.521.
49 Brian Downing, *The Military Revolution and Political Change* (Princeton, N.J.: Princeton University Press, 1992), p.164.
50 Neil Murphy, 'Henry VIII's First Invasion of France: The Gascon Expedicion of 1512', in *English Historical Review*, vol. CXXX, no. 542 (Oxford: Oxford University Press, 2015), p.44.

be achieved between commons and gentry:

> And all the saide souldiers to be swarne to their Standarde and to obeye those constitucions which made by the colonell and worthiest expert men of warre which constitucions or ever thei be admitted as a lawe be first redd unto the Souldiers And if thei thynke them reasonable they will consent to them and hold up their hands which signifieth agreement.[51]

---

51   Audley, 'Treatise', p.67.

9

Supplying and Supporting Tudor Armies

> Above all thynges Provision ys chieflye to be forsene … for hunger overcomethe
> without strooke of the enemyis.[1]

Introduction

The logistical problems facing any military exercise or expedition are and have always been considerable. In the expedition of 1544, some 48,000 men and 20,000 horses were transported to France and sustained there for a prolonged period. The Museum of London figures suggest that the capital's population in 1500 numbered 50,000 people, therefore a population of 60,000 in 1540 is not unreasonable. The figures for the population of England and Wales suggest something over two million at the beginning of this period and a little less than three million at the end. The size of the 1544 army was therefore not much less than that of London, by far the largest city in the realm and four times the size of the population of Bristol and Norwich, two of England's other biggest cities. The scale of the equivalent effort today would be of supporting a force of almost seven million men, a truly staggering figure. With a road system that was at best slow and unsuited to mass transportation, carts of limited capacity, speed and roadworthiness, and ships that could be delayed for weeks if not months by bad weather, the problems facing the logisticians responsible for the management of any campaign were horrendous.

Small expeditions of a few thousand may have relied on their own resources, or those of the land they advanced through. Larger expeditions to Scotland and France required considerable preparation and massive expense, although in France the Imperial territories could provide some support. The individual soldier could be expected to carry a few days rations when called upon for service. When making their way to a rallying point from their home counties, the men

---

1   Jonathan Davies (text transcribed by M. Bryn Davies), *Thomas Audley and the Tudor 'Arte of Warre'* (Sunderland: Pike and Shot Society, 2002), pp.19–20.

would rely on local civilian stocks of food and drink to support them; after that, much depended on the competence and concern of their lords and masters.

When planning a sizeable incursion everything from horseshoe nails to lanterns, beer to candles and even firewood had to be provided. One other factor that loomed large was the time of year and the weather. With an army and a logistical system dependent upon horses the availability of fodder was crucial. When preparing for a Scottish campaign in 1523, the Earl of Surrey commented on 'the bad plight of their horses … the impossibility of finding forage in Northumberland, and the necessity of dispersing his horsemen … [thus] No inroad can be made into Scotland, and remain there all night, for lack of fodder.'[2] In further correspondence with Wolsey he commented on the abysmal conditions and the inadequacy of his draught stock:

> Philip Dacre, sheriff of the shire, who told him "cattle was so poor", twelve oxen could not draw one pipe[3] of beer ten miles a day; which their appearance confirmed … [I] Will send to Yorkswold to hire ninety draught horses, and proceed on the expedition as soon as possible; but the ground is so wet with rain that no great ordnance can be carried till better weather.[4]

In 1522 even King Henry had to admit defeat by the weather when considering a siege of Boulogne, as 'the wetness of the cuntre upon the rivers side shall not suffre his army to march with artillery, either grosse enough for battery or sufficient for the field'.[5]

Administration

The only institutions used to the regular employment of large numbers of people, the purchase, storage, distribution of stores and then the accounting of everything to the last penny, were of course the Royal Household and the Church. It was these organisations, mobilised and expanded for wartime service, which provided the basis for the logistical organisation that provided for the army. The expeditions of 1513 took place under the supervision of Hateyclyff, the clerk of the Green Cloth, who was responsible for organising royal journeys and the administration of the Household. The other key figure whose title did not represent his actual role was the master almoner, Thomas Wolsey. In total some 2,000 officials from the court accompanied the King to France. The 1522/23 expeditions were Wolsey's sole responsibility, assisted by Bishop Fox of Winchester, employing two royal custom officials from Southampton, John Dawtrey and Richard Palshide who supervised the provisions sent to Portsmouth.

---

2   *Letters and Papers*, vol. 3 1519–1523, British Library Cotton Calig. B. VI. 238, no. 2995, May 1523.
3   126 imp gallons as established in 1 Richard III, chapter 13 (1483–1484). Cask weight 300 lb. Total weight 1,350 lb.
4   *Letters and Papers,* vol. 3, 1523, April; British Library, Calig. B. II. 151.
5   Charles Ffoulkes, *The Gun-Founders of England* (Cambridge: Cambridge University Press, 2010), p.101.

Left: *Portrait of a Man in a Red Cap, c.*1532–35 by Hans Holbein the Younger. This young man is clearly a member of Henry VIII's court, as his red cap and coat embroidered with HR (Henricus Rex) demonstrates. Whatever office he held at court he may also have been expected to play an administrative and even martial role in war. At the siege of Boulogne, the Master of the Kings Tents & Revels fought, was wounded and then rewarded, for his service. (Metropolitan Museum of Art, Open Access)

Below: Image from the masters of virtue 1531 engraving by Hans Burgkmair. Commanders might command and soldiers fight but without the company of clerks no army could form or function. The orders to assemble, the management of purveyancing, the payment of the troops and the dispositions in the camp all had to be communicated by clerks. Each company and garrison required a clerk to manage its administration and every official whether in charge of bakehouse or brewhouse needed his skills. Ignored by military historians and no doubt the subject of either soldiery ridicule or disdain, the skills of the humble pen-pusher were essential for the conduct of any martial endeavour. (Metropolitan Museum of Art, Open Access)

The King's 'great matter' would have a profound effect on both domestic and foreign affairs. It would cause the dismissal of Wolsey and see the rise of Thomas Cromwell, pursuing a new strategy. For a decade from 1527 England lacked the resources to engage in large-scale conflict and was crippled by domestic crises. The consequences of the King's divorce from Catherine of Aragon forced Henry in the 1530s and 1540s both to defend the kingdom against the possibility of invasion and to contemplate aggressive policies abroad. It was the Privy Council and the Household which shared responsibility for organising the resources needed to meet Henry's ambitions.

The key figure in the Privy Council was the deeply unlikeable Bishop Gardiner, who together with William Paulet and Sir Robert Bowes was to supervise the victualling supplies for the army against Scotland in 1542. Paulet had long experience in administration within the Household from 1532, and Bowes was deputy warden of the East March. It would be Gardiner again, together with Paulet the lord great master and head of the Royal Household, who would organise the French expedition of 1544. They were assisted by full-time royal servants including Sir Edmund Reckham, the clerk of the Green Cloth, Anthony Harvey, an official of the Court of General Surveyors, and John Ryther, Prince Edward's cofferer. In addition 47 Royal Household officials in the victualling train accompanied the army. Gardiner complained that he was so closely associated with victualling that amongst the common soldiery he was referred to, and not with any affection, as 'Simon Stockfish'.

Table 1. Estimate of men and wagons etc. required for victualling the army, French expedition of 1544

'Surveyors and expediters of victuals'

'Vaward' – Chief masters 2, clerks 2, for sale of bread 6, for sale of drink 10, for sale of flesh and butchers 12, for conduct and watch 20, herdmen and drivers 12, carters for 145 wagons 'after 2 men to every wagon, after the rate of 30 cwt to every wagon', 290, carters for 6 wagons tocarry necessaries ('exelltres', timber, ropes, cart clowtes, nails, cartsaddles, mattokes, 'showvles', etc.) 10, coopers 2, cartwrights 2, smiths 2, labourers to lade and unlade the victuals in store 12. Total persons 382, wagons 160.

'The rerward' – The same.

'The Kynges bayttell' – Chief masters of victuals 2, clerks 2, for sale of bread 8, for sale of drink 16, for sale of flesh and butchers 16, the conduct and watch of victuals 80, herdmen and drivers of cattle 16, carters for 234 wagons 468, carters for 6 wagons of necessaries 12, coopers 3, cartwrights 3, smiths 8, labourers 20. Total persons 599, wagons 240.

Source: *Letters and Papers, Foreign and Domestic, Henry VIII*, vol. 19, Part 1. 31 March R O 4.

Bishop Gardiner was certainly subject to perhaps reasonable criticism for providing a monotonous diet, and for his incompetence, complacency and indifference to the sufferings of the men, as Gruffydd recalls apropos of the Montreuil siege of 1544:

> At this time some of the traffickers in food made a great suit to Mr. Palette [Pawlett] the King's Chamberlain and to Steven Gardiner Bishop of Winchester who controlled all the victuallers in the host and who were so learned in arithmetic and geometry and making accounts that they could show by signs and figures how many pieces of bread would suffice for all the people who were under the King on that side of the sea, to ask these two worshipful lords to get the King's command for one or two of the ships to raise anchor and put to sea from Beauvais in safety from the French until they entered the river of Étaples, so that they could supply the shortage and want among the soldiers before Montreuil, where there was great need. To these the ungodly, I mean godly bishop replied 'If you wish to venture your bodies and your wealth to get more for your victuals to your own profit and advantage, it is better for you to arrange for one or two ships to guard you while going and coming from Étaples which is not far from here, but if you intend to go by yourselves, sail under God's protection because in truth I shall not open my mouth to order one of the ships to weigh anchor to go to guard you from here to Étaples, because I know that in the camp before Montreuil there is more victual than they can use while it is good', which was perfectly true because most of it was stinking before it came to the field. This answer had to satisfy the victuallers, one of whom called Thomas Lane was living in Calais and told me the story.[6]

Purveyancing

To provide for large expeditions, the government of necessity engaged in the compulsory purchase of provisions or purveyancing. This was an inevitable source of friction and grievance between the population and the state. Purveyors were granted commissions by privy councillors or 'Great Men' for the compulsory purchase of stores on behalf of the Crown. Typical of those purveying grain in 1544 was John Reppes, a landowner in Norfolk and Cambridgeshire and subsequently a Cambridgeshire JP, while John Launde, a prominent butcher, was active in purveying beef. In some cases the quantity purchased was recorded, both by the parish constable and a magistrate at the port of embarkation, and such documents were returned to the Council. However unpopular it might have been, this system existed within an acknowledged and accepted framework and could not be equated with illegal seizure or theft.

---

6   Davies, *Enterprises*, p.30.

Table 2. 1523 French Expedition – Details of Purveyancing

Receipts from Edw. Weldon and Sir John Daunce, 7 Feb. 14 Hen.VIIL, 1,233l. 17s. 6d., spent as follows:

For corn, at 8s. 2d. a qr., 620l. 5s. 9½d. For malt, at 3s. 10d. a qr., 364l. 13s. 10d. Keelage between Reche and Lynne, at 2½d. a qr., 17l. 6s. 6d. Carriage at Lynn, from the keels to the granaries, and thence to the ships,ld, a qr., and for measuring at ½d. a qr., 9l. 6s. 8d. Hire of granaries and a boulting house at Ipswich, at 4d. and 8d. a week, and wages of men for keeping the granaries, &c., 6d. a day, 7l. 15s. 10d. Carriage of corn from Ipswich to Haxsted, Haxston and Nacton mills, and grinding at 6d. a qr., 15l. 13s. 10d. Necessaries for the mills: "filles," 4d.; shovels, 16d.; pitch for marking the sacks, 3d. 2,100 "hoping" nails, 21d.; 3 pieces boulting cloth, 15s.; 80 quarter sacks, 52s. 4d. 8 ells hempen cloth at 6d.; for making a boulting house, &c. 37l. 18s. 1d. Wages of bakers, 8d. and 7d. a day, 21l. 15s. Freightage from Lynne to Calais at 10d, a qr. by various ships. John Smith, for 62 doz, mats for putting over the corn, 10d. a doz., 121l. 5s. 11½d. Car¬riage of corn from the ships to the granaries at Calais, 2½d. a qr.; malt 1d. a qr., and flour at ½d. a barrel, 15l. 16s. 0½d.

Delivered to Bryswood by the masters of the said ships, in all, corn, 836 qrs. 2 bushels; malt, 1,833 qrs. 2 barrels ; flour, 985 barrels.

Source: *Letters and Papers, Foreign and Domestic, Henry VIII*, vol. 3 1523, 7 Feb.

There were inevitably complaints that the prices paid were well below the market. It was ironically the shortages created by purveyancing on a large scale that were responsible in themselves for the rise in prices. That purveyancing could lead to higher prices was a cause of complaint, from both those forced to buy at the 'new' price and those who had been forced to sell at the 'old'. The inevitable rise in prices as a result of purveyancing caused the Crown to issue proclamations to control prices of foodstuffs, which meant that the authorities at least appreciated the problem and attempted to mitigate it. The purchase price of goods offered by the purveyors seems to have been not wildly out of kilter with market prices, despite complaints. When faced with the refusal of Sir Humphrey Browne to sell wainscot (planks of wood) at the price offered by the purveyors, the Council went so far as to offer to have the goods valued by 'indifferent men', at what they considered a fair price. The principal objection to purveyancing was not so much the prices paid but the delay in payment. In 1548–9 the Harwich purser purchased some £2,547 worth of provisions and paid just £1,129, the remainder only finally being paid in 1552. Sharp practice was not unknown amongst those selling to the Crown as well. Checks were also made on the goods that had been supplied, to make sure that the contract was fulfilled properly. Sometimes sharp practice was reported as in this case:

> the King has been deceived; for the surveyor of victuals, Mr. Nevile, declares that, after the rate delivered to him, every pipe of beef should contain 400 pieces of 2lb. each, whereas every pipe contains from 40 to 140 pieces short of that number, and none of the pieces weigh over 1 lb, and some not 1lb.[7]

Selling off the surplus at the end of a campaign was an area where profits could be made by the purveyor buying cheap and selling dear, and the council were careful to see that any profits made were reasonable. This did not preclude the government itself from making a profit. It was calculated that it should make £500 profit out of the food sold off during the 1544 Scottish expedition. There was some recognition in Mary's reign of 'the greate deceypte' of the purveyors, which would be addressed by precise accounting. Gruffydd recorded the indifference and cupidity of the purveyors during the Enterprise of Boulogne:

> During this time there was a great shortage of bread and drink among the three hosts who were waiting for the people who had gone to get victuals from St. Omer. The lack of bread was very unnecessary because a large amount of wheat had been found in many houses in the country since the host had crossed the river … indeed, if the wheat had been ground and baked, there would have been no shortage of bread and also there would have been no lack of wheat to grind, if the King's Purveyors had given sixpence and eight-pence for every peck [A unit of dry capacity equal to eight quarts] of wheat that the soldiers who were scouring the country brought to them. But they refused to do this because they set more store by their own advantage than by doing a haporth [a half penny] of good to the common soldiers.[8]

Living off the country, which may have seemed an attractive choice, was vexatious to the local population and unreliable as a source of sustained supply. Gruffydd records in both his expeditions examples of both regular and irregular troops (the Krakers) engaging in looting and mayhem. Troops that engaged in this form of warfare could expect no mercy from the peasants if caught. The English garrison at Haddington, near Edinburgh, was forced to seize supplies from the local population which led to inevitable bitterness at a time when the policy was to try to ensure a contented and compliant population.

---

7   Bain, *The Hamilton Papers*; British Library Add. MS.32,654, f.141; British Library Hamilton Papers, ii. no. 220.
8   Davies, *Enterprises*, p.22.

The camp of Charles V at Lauingen, 1546, by Mathis Gerung, 1551. Bread and ale are for sale in the market. Plentiful provisions at a reasonable price would result in a contented soldiery. Supplies for even a small force of a few thousand was equivalent to that required in peacetime for a small town. As urgent as food for the troops was the provision of forage for horses. Each horse required fresh grass or 10–20 lb of hay per day as well as a plentiful supply of good water. The supply of fodder for men and beasts was the principle priority of any competent commander. (Heimathaus der Stadt Lauingen (Donau). Photo: Hermann Müller. With kind permission of the owner, Stadt Lauingen)

Rations

The English soldier and sailor were, at least in theory, provided with copious quantities of victuals of all sorts. Figures vary, and much depended on what was actually available, but a week's ration for a soldier could include 7–10 gallons of ale, a pound of biscuit, four pounds of beef, two pounds of pork, three quarters of a pound of salt fish, two pints of peas, 12 ounces of cheese, and six ounces of butter. The rations for a sailor varied, but they usually amounted to (in theory) a pound of biscuit or bread, one gallon of beer and a pound of fresh beef or half a pound of salt beef or bacon each day. This diet provided the 4,000–6,000 calories required to keep a soldier or sailor fit, for the cold and often arduous duties he would be expected to perform. The large quantities of salt fish provided on land and at sea was not only intended to vary the diet: the eating of fish was prescribed by the Catholic Church on three days a week, Wednesdays, Fridays and Saturdays. This practice encouraged the sustaining of a healthy fishing industry and therefore provided sailors for the fleet; unsurprisingly it was therefore continued and reinforced during England's Protestant years.

The soldier was expected to pay for his own food and drink from his pay, which was some 6d a day for the majority of the foot soldiers who made up the bulk of any army. This would work satisfactorily only in times of peace and relative plenty. The demands of war inevitably led to food shortages and higher prices. In the Berwick garrison the cost of rations absorbed almost all the soldier's pay, with 1d allocated for breakfast and 4d for lunch and supper. On rare occasions supplies were provided free, as once at Boulogne where the hard-pressed pioneers were issued with free beer, and in 1545 when the

Council provided £100 11s 4d of victuals for those engaged in fighting the French on the Isle of Wight.

The captain of the company was responsible to his men for their provisions, which would have been dispensed and accounted for by the company victuallers. These men, often small merchants, yeomen or even minor gentry, were appointed by the captains, which created an unhealthy and potentially profitable relationship between them at a cost to the soldiery. The clerk of the market was an important official in the garrison or on an expedition, as it was his role to set 'fair' prices for both buyer and seller. There was some attempt to control the profits of victuallers: some checks can be seen in the regulations issued in Boulogne in 1547. Victuallers were reminded that they were servants to the Crown and not private traders; they were only permitted a fee or profit of 2d on a shilling's worth of bread and similar profit on beer, otherwise they were to sell at cost price, and the captain was to study the accounts.

Private victuallers could be English or be subjects of an ally, as in the case of the Flemish victuallers and waggoners supporting Henry's campaigns in France. In France it was also possible to encourage local merchants to sell their stock in the English camp. In Calais, merchants who were 'protected' from prosecution for debt were expected as their part of the bargain to provide victuals for the royal forces. Government victualling could be delivered through contracts with large merchants, as it would be in Elizabeth's reign.

Sources of Food and Drink

For campaigns in France, armies could be supplied from England and from the nearby Imperial territories, and even on occasion from French merchants as well. For French expeditions, provisions passed almost exclusively through Calais. Grain came again from Norfolk and Hampshire, and Suffolk provided most of the dairy products supplemented by supplies from Essex. Fish was provided from stocks supplied from Norfolk and Hampshire.

Provisioning of the Scottish garrisons in the period 1548–50 created a particular set of problems. On the whole they had to be sustained with English money and provisions, for both food security and because it would be difficult and unpopular to draw on very limited local resources. Food came from quite specific localities, thus grain, almost exclusively wheat but with some barley for brewing, came primarily from East Anglia, with butter and cheese provided by Suffolk. The grain was shipped down the Ouse from Huntingdon, Cambridge and Bedford to Bishop's Lynn; almost all the stores were transported in barrels by ship, to Scotland. The thriving East Coast ports such as Boston and Bishop's Lynn (from 1537 known as King's Lynn) were well provided with storage, wharves and cranes to move large quantities of cargo. The principal supply of beef was from the Midlands, whose drovers had on occasion to drive their cattle to slaughter all the way to Berwick.

Cooking and Brewing

It is difficult to establish how such large quantities of food were cooked. Ovens had a multitude of purposes other than bread making: meat could be roasted, the bread baked and pies and custards would be warmed in the oven, with the residual heat used to dry the faggots for the next day's cooking. Using this system, no heat or precious firewood would have been wasted. Ovens could be requisitioned from the civilian population, or in the case of the Field of the Cloth of Gold, transported and built on site. Berwick, Portsmouth, Boulogne and Calais were all provided with bakeries, mills and brewhouses, although they were not always in good order. For the 1542 raid on Scotland only two of the three bakeries in Berwick were in operation and this was one of the reasons for its abject failure. For the 1544 French invasion, more than adequate provision was made in this area by the simple expedient of building ovens and mills on site. The extraordinary attention to necessary detail, as found in contemporary documentation, indicates an efficient bureaucracy that was able to organise and sustain a prodigious logistical effort.

Table 3. Baking and brewing company establishment for the siege of Boulogne

Sir Clement Hurleston charge for baking. Wagons for ovens 33, carters for them 66, wagons for 100 mills 50, carters for them 100, wagons for tents and hales 10, carters for them 20, bakers 100, millers 100, millwrights 10, cartwrights 10, bricklayers 6, pioneers to them 6, mortar makers 2, Mr. Harleston's soldiers 30, clerks 2, one priest, one surgeon, three drums, petty captains 3, captains 3.

Total persons 463, wagons 93. 'Necessaries for the same' – Axes 200, crows of iron 100, mattocks 12, shovels 20, wedges 20, sacks 200, bags for iron pins 100.'

'For the brewers' – Wagons for 50 brewhouses 50, carters for the same 100, master brewers to every house 50, underbrewers to them 50, labourers to them 100, petty captains 3, drums 3, surgeon 1, captains 3. Total persons 310, wagons 50. 'Necessaries' – Axes 50, wedges of iron 20, mattocks 50, shovels 100, sacks 100

Source: *Letters and Papers, Foreign and Domestic, Henry VIII*, vol. 19, Part 1, March 31 1544.

London played an important part, as with a large domestic population it had developed a large brewing industry which could be mobilised to support an army overseas. For the 1544 expedition the London brewers offered a five month guarantee on the 1,000 tons of beer they were contracted to brew, and

The camp of Charles V at Lauingen 1546, by Mathis Gerun, 1551. Everyday life in the camp would have been pretty similar across Europe. Women play their essential roles and food; drink and good cheer are in full flow. The extemporised nature of the tents indicates that this is not an 'official' part of the camp. (Heimathaus der Stadt Lauingen (Donau). Photo: Hermann Müller. With kind permission of the owner, Stadt Lauingen).

the London coopers provided 1,000 costrels (a costrel was a measure of two quarts or four pints, which equates to half a gallon) for carrying wine. Even so, the Lord Mayor sought even more casks, to contain the mountains of food and drink needed for the princely quantity of provisions ordered. The beer provided in such copious quantities was probably 'small beer' with about two percent alcohol. It would last in the cask from 12–15 weeks, which was the maximum time that a ship might be expected to remain at sea without revictualling. Hops had only recently been introduced for beer making, and one of the alternatives, nettles, could not ensure the longevity of the brew.

On campaign the companies must often have had to make their own preparations and the sight of iron and brass cookware hanging over the campfire, as found in contemporary European illustrations, must have been common. At sea, cooking took place in a large brass cauldron which was set with lead into a substantial brick oven. The royal vessel *Sovereign* required 6,500 bricks and 600 paving stones for its kitchen. The floor appears to have been salted to insulate it from heat, and arrangements were made for a chimney. For large ships the oven would be sited midships for the sake of stability. It is worth noting that careless French royal cooks were probably responsible for the loss of their flagship the *Carraquon* in 1545 to fire. The practical tests of the *Mary Rose* kitchen have proved that a wide range of meals in considerable quantities could be produced in a single large cauldron. Meals for the crew were probably taken on deck with the crew messing together, as they would on shore, in groups of four. There are a few references to trestle tables, but none to benches

or stools for the crew. Each man might be expected to have his own knife and spoon, again current practice on land. Much valuable pewter ware has been found with the *Mary Rose*; its quality and value made it the prerogative of the high-ranking officers, and the crew would have relied on turned wooden bowls for both eating and drinking. Wooden bowls are far superior to pewter for everyday use as they retain the heat of the food, and can be held more easily in the hand when eating, which was common practice.

Preservation and Storage

Food could be preserved by salting, air-drying and smoking. The butchering and salting of beef was a well-practised art and could, if properly carried out, preserve food for a great length of time. When salting food, the ratio of salt to herring was 1:3 by weight; two ounces of saltpetre and the same amount of salt was used to preserve a pound of beef. Meat pies in a heavily salted crust or 'coffin' could

Quite complicated and delicious meals can be provided in relatively simple facilities. In this case under a small damp awning on a cold Dutch day. This Sunday dinner consisted of goose pie, boiled capon in white sauce, roast beef, quaking pudding and sausages in red wine, and bread, cheeses and fruits. It was delicious, especially the beef, but obviously a captain's fare. (Historic Dining Group. Grolle 2019)

remain perfectly edible for several weeks. The crust acted as a barrier to bacteria, furthermore some spices, especially cinnamon, have anti-bacterial properties.

As well as food and drink, salted butter, pitch, soap, gunpowder, small cannon shot and even bowstrings were stored in barrels, usually made with oak staves and bound with split coppiced hazel. These universal containers were stored longitudinally bow to stern aboard ship and could be broken down and stored in pieces to conserve space. The Lord Mayor of London was required to collect casks, and the citizens were required to offer their casks to the King's purveyors for purchase. London coopers were conscripted for service in Berwick, to make and remake casks. Barrels were essential for transport but they were easily damaged on the poor roads of the North, and a surprising quantity of beer was lost from barrels in transit apparently due to 'leakage'. Such wastage was included in logistical calculations but clearly depended upon the roughness of the roads and the thirst of the carter. The Duke of Suffolk recommended that to deal with the problem of insufficient transport in a Scottish campaign, mounted troops should carry two small beer barrels on their steeds, an idea that was treated with unseemly levity.

Transport

The problems of transporting food and drink over even a short distance were highlighted by Gruffydd during the siege of Montreuil:

> bread and drink … had all to be fetched from St. Omer which indeed was a terrific amount, nevertheless the men who went to fetch it consumed the third part of the food and drink, and a lot was lost on the way through the leaking of the barrels in the carts. Sometimes the wagons overturned and beer and barrels were lost so that it did not last four whole days in the camp.[9]

The condition of the roads was crucial if anything other than a raiding force needed to be sustained. In the Boulogne expedition of 1544, there was one wagon provided for every 16 soldiers; the provision of horses and wagons was key to the success of any operation and bad weather could even then make transport impossible. This point was made very clear by Lord Grey to Somerset in October 1547:

> The device for invasion lately sent to your grace must be given up this winter, for there has since been and still is such abundance of rain, the waters so high, and the ground so rotten, as has not been for many years, that neither horseman nor carriage can pass. And unless your grace give orders for beerhouses at the new erected 'peeces', and reenforce us with horses, we cannot help them, for the country carriages are 'so utterly decayed and tyred' that they cannot serve us, or even bring home their corn, which yet lies in great quantity in the field, as 'right pytiously lament and bewayle'.[10]

In the Gascon expedition of 1512 the English ambassador to Spain provided 200 mules for the army, but they were unable to provide the necessary transport capacity.

Seven horses or 10 oxen were required to draw a wagon, but in Flanders the wagons were usually drawn by three mares, or four if in Imperial service, drawing 2,500 lb or 3,000 lb respectively. In 1544 confusion over whether seven-horse or four-horse carriages were to be provided from Flanders was a cause of both friction between the countries and supply problems for the army. The cost of a carriage complete with harnesses etc. was £10 in 1513 and the price of a limner (horse) £2. The demand for these vehicles could be massive: in the case of the 1544 expedition 392 carriages were required each for the van and rear battles and a further 598 for the main battle. In 1544 a request was made for Imperial resources in Flanders for 2,556 horses to draw artillery, and 2,260 four-horse waggons with their horses for the munitions and baggage of the King's army and pioneer stores. It was reported that the most that could be provided without making it impossible for farming to continue was only some 4,000 of the 11,596 horses. Frantic calculations were

---

9   Davies, *Enterprise*, p.24.
10 *CSP Scotland*, no. 70, Oct. 27 1547, p.32.

Right: Waggoner, from the Dance of Death after Hans Holbein the Younger. The disaster that has overtaken this waggoner would have been well understood at the time. Spare axletrees as well as carpenters and wheelwrights accompanied the Tudor army for a good reason. A skeleton is loosening the stick that tightens the withies that hold the staves of the barrel together. It is hardly surprising that much liquid was lost during travel and not only to the thievery of thirsty carters. (Metropolitan Museum of Art, Open Access)

Below: An 'ale' wagon, a detail fom the Cowdray engraving. The simple bow sided four-wheeled wagon was as essential for the Tudor army as the 'deuce and a half' trucks for the Allied armies in 1944–5. Carrying everything from gunpowder to horseshoes, ale and arrows, their wooden construction required constant attention and they needed a good supply of strong horses to draw them. These splendid animals needed to be fed even when not in harness. (Dr Dominic Fontana, with kind permission)

made in 1544 to establish the cost effectiveness of using carriages taken from England:

> Seven horses at 33s. 4d. for each carriage, with 33s. 4d. for harness, collars and other necessaries, make for 600 carriages 8,000l. (sic). Ten oxen at 23s. for each carriage, and yokes, chains, etc, 30s, make for 600 carriages 7,800l. And 1,200 wagons at 4l. cost 4,800l. Total 20,600l.
>
> Whereas 1,200 wagons hired in Flanders at 3s. 4d. the day, counting 30 days in a month, cost in five months 30,000l. Wages of 2,400 carters to attend upon the said carriages at 6d. a day, are in five months 9,000l, so that ultimately 400l. less is spent and all remain to the King's use.[11]

Wagons and their teams would be requisitioned from the English counties for military service. In the 1544 Enterprise of Boulogne for example, Buckinghamshire had to provide 43 carriages, Cambridgeshire 26, Huntingdonshire 30 and Essex 42. A standardised form was used to request each county to provide 'horses, mares, geldings and oxen, meet for draught and carriage, to be employed in our service of the wars against France'.[12] Horses and carriages were to be provided with all the necessary harness and equipment. There was an important caveat that the number taken should only be 'as might be conveniently spared without disfurniture of necessary tillage and husbandry of any man'.[13]

Horses, men and their equipment had to be carried overseas using the standard commercial transport: 'playtes' (small vessels used for river and coastal trade) and 'hoyes' (small single-masted vessels of 25–80 tons, originating in Flanders and also used for coastal trade). Transport was mostly provided by vessels from the Low Countries. There was great concern that the horse transports should not damage their precious cargo. In the Duke of Norfolk's own hand, indicating the importance of these apparently small details, it was stated:

> That the hoyes be so chosen that they may carry horses on both sides. Item, to get as many playtes as may be, for they be better to convey horses than hoyes. Item, to have a sure regard that when the ships be ballasted they may have their beams so high that the horses may stand under them; for if they be too low the horses' backs shall be marred.[14]

One other issue arose, this time from those ships taken up from the fishing fleet which were found to be unacceptable, because '[They] stynke so sore of the saied fisshe that no man being not used to the same can endure it.'[15]

---

11 *Letters and Papers*, 1544, R.O. 12 31 March.
12 *Letters and Papers*, 1544, R.O. 9 31 March.
13 *Letters and Papers*, 1544 R.O. 9 31 March.
14 *Letters and Papers*, 1544 R.O. 9 31 March.
15 Potter, *Henry VIII and Francis I*, p.220; Norfolk to the Council, 7 Sept. 1542, Bain, *Hamilton Papers*, I, no. 151, p.186.

The Soldiers' 'Cote'

There was little that was uniform about the uniform of the Tudor soldier. The civilian clothes of the time were more than adequate for the vigorous outdoor life that was required of him. Tudor clothing was well-designed, comfortable and suitable for all weathers when in good condition and well-fitting. What was required of 'uniform' was not that it gave protection from the elements, but it distinguished friend from enemy and was an adornment to the commander. Throughout this period the only item that might be considered uniform of any sort, was the 'sodyers cote' or coat. This item was issued to the soldier when he was mustered and paid for with coat and conduct money. The soldier was paid conduct money at the rate of 1/2 d a mile from his mustering point to the assembly point for the army. This was the sum necessary to provide the soldier with his coat and the amount needed to pay for his needs on the way to the muster.

The soldiers' coats were traditionally white, and made from kersey. In 1558 it was insisted that they should be of white 'after the old manner'; in earlier periods they had sometimes been made of different colours. The Duke of Somerset, when preparing for the invasion of Scotland that concluded with the Battle of Pinkie Clough, had noted and disliked this confusion of different coloured coats, 'beycause much diversitie in the cotes of suche men as shal be sent at such present [time] wolde appeare verie unseemly we have resolved to have all their cotes all of redde'.[16]

Henry VIII's invasion of France in 1544 was a most colourful expedition. The main guard wore coats of red guarded with yellow, the vanguard wore coats of blue, welted or guarded with red, whilst the rearguard wore blue coats guarded with yellow. To add to the general gaiety, the men of the vanguard word red and blue caps with red hose on the right foot and blue on the left. The main ward wore blue and yellow caps and hose of a similar hue and similar order. An Essex gentleman whose company was in the vanguard was ordered to ensure that his soldiers had their coats 'after suche ffashion as all footemens cotes be made here at London'.[17] The left sleeve could be trimmed using the captain's own colours but no badge was permitted; the men were expected to provide their own parti-coloured hose with a wide stripe of red on the left leg. They were also to have a cap which would be worn under their helmets, of a pattern made by William the Capper of Ludgate, which cost the not inconsiderable sum of 8d each. Somerset in his cruel suppression of Kett's rebels in 1549 had his men wearing coats of yellow, while the royal infantry putting down the Prayer Book Rebellion wore coats of blue 'guarded' with red, the right leg of their hose was red and the left blue. One may assume that these were coats and hose left over from the 1545 campaign.

Whatever the colour of the coat, it was accompanied front and rear with the red cross of St George. This was not the only device to be found: Henry VIII when ordering coats for his army demanded that they be provided with

---

16   Jeremy Goring, 'The Dress of the English Soldier in the Early Tudor Period', *Journal of the Society for Army Historical Research*, vol. 33, no. 135 (Autumn,1955), p.136; PRO, 11/12, f.113a.

17   Potter, *Henry VIII and Francis I*, pp.262–263.

'A jaquet of our colours with our cognisance and yours.'[18] In the case of the city of Canterbury in 1513, for men in sea service, these were sea choughs and for the horsemen from Coventry in 1542 this meant 'conysaunces of the elifant'.[19] In 1545 the Lord Mayor of London ordered the livery companies not to put the City arms on their coats. In 1549 the troops serving the Carews, in the suppression of the Prayer Book Rebellion, wore their livery colours of black and yellow.

The style or 'fasyon' of soldiers' coats is unknown and it is difficult to draw conclusions as to their structure, even on what purport to be contemporary images. In 1544 George Smyth did provide the Cambridge University tailors with a pattern garment but unfortunately this has not survived. On occasion coats were not issued because of haste or a shortage of cloth. This proved to be the case in 1558, during the crisis caused by the siege and then loss of Calais. Kentish levies were ordered to 'Departe furthewith in what garmentes they have',[20] and in January 1558 soldiers were sent without coats because of the absence of the white kersey from which they were traditionally made. The coat was not an inexpensive item: in the 1523 French campaigns thousands were purchased at either 2s 4d or 3s 4d. each, for a total cost of £1,349 12s 4d. Unsurprisingly, of the thousands issued only 93 were eventually returned to the King's use.

One other item of clothing was issued to the Yeomen in 1513, when the King was accompanied from Greenwich by 600 yeomen: they were provided with 'white gabberdines and cappes'. The gaberdine was a long, loose gown fitted with sleeves and ideal for wet weather. It had been a high-status item in earlier generations but was clearly now appreciated for its practicality.

Accommodation

Accommodation for the army in the field would never be provided for the vast majority of the soldiery. Transport was always limited, especially in Scottish campaigns, and could only be provided for essential logistical support, principally food and munitions. The only exceptions would be for senior officers and especially the King, where lavish provision for their housing was made. In the 1513 French invasion Henry was provided with an entire prefabricated wooden building, with an exterior painted like brickwork. One room was 27 feet by 14 feet, with eight-foot high walls, and windows made of lantern horn. The fireplace was fitted with an iron chimney and the interior was hung with cloth of gold.

If this was not enough, he also had large gaudily painted canvas pavilions surmounted by royal beasts. These magnificent buildings were called the *Lion*, *Dragon*, *Greyhound*, *Antelope*, and the *Dun Cow*. Other pavilions were

---

18   Goring, 'The Dress of the English Soldier', p.136; The National Archives, E 101/59/5.
19   Goring, 'The Dress of the English Soldier', pp.136–137; Coventry City Muniments A.9. p.8.
20   Goring, 'The Dress of the English Soldier', p.137; F. Grose, *Military Antiquities Respecting a History of the English Army, from the Conquest to the Present Time*, vol. I (London: L. Stockdale, 1801), pp.310–311.

Design for a royal pavilion. There could be no doubt as to who the owner of this magnificent pavilion was. The rich colour and grotesque decoration spoke of wealth and good taste and the heraldry identified royalty. The imposing beasts were the White Greyhound of Richmond and the Red Dragon of Cadwaladr, which were both associated with Henry VII. The strange creature, the Beaufort yale, referenced Henry VIII's grandmother the Lady Margaret. The Lion of England in Gold was easily identifiable but the antelope or stag is something of a mystery (to me at least). The small flags appear to have the fleur-de-lys, the Beaufort portcullis, a Tudor Rose and the arms of England painted on them and above them all a crown.(Courtesy of the British Library. BL Cotton Augustus III, f.18)

named after colours, or given the names normally associated with inns, such as the *Wheat Sheaf* and were provided with the equivalent of inn signs to help identify them. The tent allocated to the carpenters was called the *Hammer* and the armoury tent was the *Gauntlet*. Wolsey's tent was given the impressive name of the *Inflamed House* and covered 1,700 square feet, while that of Lord Lisle the second in command only covered two thirds of that area, an indication of their relative political importance. Of course, all this tentage paled into insignificance before the Great Tent made of cloth of gold. This was illustrated in the painting of the meeting between Henry and Maximilian during the siege of Thérouanne. The Great Tent was connected to his wooden house by a gallery. Less impressive but no doubt very welcome was a small canvas room, 25 feet square, for his close stool, true luxury in a crowded and insanitary encampment. These tents were under the supervision of Master of the King's Tents Sir Thomas Cawarden, who was paid at the phenomenal rate of 20s a day. He was responsible for the refurbishment of the 1513 tents in 1523, when a detailed account of the tents and their condition was made.

In 1544 the provision for Henry was as extravagant as it had ever been. The 'Officers, artificers and soldiers appertaining to the King's Majesty's tents, hales and pavilions' numbered 574, including three surgeons and two chaplains, one assumes for the physical and spiritual wellbeing of the others. There were all the associated craftsmen including 89 tailors, 30 carpenters, 26 joiners, 12 painters and a single mat maker. These skilled men were recruited from the Office of the Revels, where their skills in creating sumptuous sets

The Cowdray engraving shows 'The Kinges lodging of Tymber for the warres', which had been under construction since 1543. It was 'all of ffyrre paynted and gylded' with a tower at each corner and 'covered with whyte plate (bullnose tiles of steel or tin) … sylyd withyn with paste worke [plaster], paynted, wyndowes of horne.' Potter, *Henry VIII and Francis I*, p.261; Surrey History Centre, 2 Folger SL, Loseley MSS, Lb. 3). On the roof were seven heraldic beasts fitted with small painted metal flags and the coats of arms of Henry and Edward the Prince of Wales, were set over the main entrance. All was in the antique or Italianate style, very *à la mode*. In all there was Crown provision made for 2,696 men in 'ronde howses' and 'ruffes' as well as 'hales' which were apparently awnings, mostly used for the stabling of horses. (Dr Dominic Fontana, with kind permission)

for the royal masques could be put to more martial use. Sir Thomas was a fighting soldier as well as an erector of tents and halls, and was to lose his leg in the siege of Boulogne when commanding a company of light horse. He was appointed master of the revels in 1545.

The most common type of tents were bell tents, 18–20 feet in diameter, and pavilions of a similar size but square, supported at each corner and with a central pole supporting the roof. There were larger 'hales' or marquees with walls six feet high, provided with either square or round ends and numerous central poles to support the ceiling. Tents seem to have been made to standard sizes: 24x12 feet, 30x15 feet and 50x20 feet. These larger tents could sometimes be fitted with an inner tent to provide a degree of insulation. To connect large pavilions, 'tressans' or galleries were used. Guy ropes were sewn into the canvas in threes, in what was known as 'crowfoot tackling', and held in the ground with pins of iron. The finest tents could be made from damask and say cloth, but were usually of linen or canvas. England was principally dependent upon Brittany and southwestern France for her best canvas.

Of course, for the common soldiers no provision was made. During the Gascon expedition of 1512 the soldiers were forced to 'lie nightly under the

Detail from *The Camp of Charles V at Lauingen 1546*, by Mathis Gerung, 1551. This is the heart of the camp, carefully encircled for security and privacy. The royal court was peripatetic in peace and its transformation to a court at war was not traumatic. The commander's comfort could be ensured, as he was insulated from the misery that the commoners would often suffer. On the far right can be seen a messenger about to set off with his scrip and staff. (Heimathaus der Stadt Lauingen (Donau). Photo: Hermann Müller. With kind permission of the owner, the City of Lauingen)

bushes'.[21] In 1544 it was agreed formally in Council that: 'No man [captain] shall carry tents or hales for his soldiers footmen, who shall make their lodgings as men of war of other nations do.'[22] The captain of a company of 100 men was allowed a single carriage, although this would hardly be sufficient for the day-to-day needs of himself and his company, let alone tentage for all. Audley listed what the captain should take with him: 'Tents, Cofers [coffers or chests], & bedding besides other necessaries for his kitchine'; he hoped that 'Also all good Captaines will make provision of carriage for some Victualles for his men And also for the carriage of sicke & hurt men.'[23]

The expectation that a good soldier could take care of himself was made clear by one of Henry's old sweats, Elis ap Gruffydd, when he castigated those unable to look after themselves in the disastrous campaign of 1523:

> For there was no lack of food or drink or wood for fire or making huts, and plenty of straw to roof them and to lie on if they had only fetched it. But there was many a man weak in body who preferred from sheer laziness to lie under the hedge rather than take the trouble to make a snug warm hut to keep him from the frost wind and the snow, and they preferred to shiver with cold rather than take the trouble to light a fire, which was all very well known to me.[24]

---

21 Grafton, *Grafton's Chronicle*, p.245.
22 *Letters and Papers,* 1544 31st March.
23 Audley, 'Treatise', p.72.
24 Davies, *Ill journey*, pp.5–6.

A good soldier should be able to scrounge straw or gather ferns, as well as cut branches to support a canvas tilt; forests were far better managed than they are nowadays and coppicing and pollarding would provide ideal material for the camp. There is a detailed description of soldiers' tents provided by Patten, when he investigated the Scottish camp, after the Battle of Pinkie:

> These white ridges, as I called them, that, as we stood on Fauxside Bray, did make so great a muster towards us, which I did take then to be a number of tents: when we came, we found them to be a linen drapery, of the coarser camerick [cambric] indeed, for it was all of canvas sheets. They were the tentacles or rather the cabins and couches of their soldiers: which much after the common building of their country besides they had framed of four sticks, about an ell long a piece; whereof two fastened at one end together aloft, and the two ends beneath stuck in the ground an ell asunder, standing in fashion like the bow of a sow's yoke. Over two such bow, one, as it were, at the head, the other at their feet, they stretched a sheet down on both sides whereby their cabins became roofed like a ridge, but scant shut at both ends; and not very close beneath, on the sides, unless their sticks were the shorter, or their wives the more liberal to lend them larger napery. Howbeit within they had lined them, and stuffed them so thick with straw, that as the weather was not very cold, when they were couched, they were as warm as [if] they had been wrapped in horsedung.[25]

During the Scottish campaign under Somerset (1547–1550) the provision for the soldiers in the newly built forts was often poor, as the priority was to build the defences first. The abysmal weather and poor diet were at least in part responsible for the high rates of sickness and desertion. The mercenaries refused to live in the primitive huts made from branches and turves that provided the accommodation for so many. At Broughty Craig prefabricated huts were eventually provided, but for the majority it seems they had to simply make do with whatever shelter was available.

Medical Provision

There were three principal ranks in the medical 'profession': physicians, barber-surgeons and apothecaries. Physicians were university educated and dealt with the 'internals' or illnesses. The barber-surgeons – who were craftsmen, having undergone an apprenticeship – dealt with the 'externals' or bodily injuries. Apothecaries provided the medicaments used by the physicians and surgeons as well as providing remedies for patients. There was a degree of crossover between these roles, so that the surgeon might apply and prescribe post-operative treatment and the apothecary would often be the first port of call for most accidents and illnesses. The principal provider of medical care was still, of course, the housewife, with the contents of kitchen and still room at her command and lifetimes of shared experience.

---

25 Patten, *The expedicion into Scotla[n]de*, p.129.

There were some female surgeons or surgeresses and apothecaries but they were increasingly facing the hostility of what was a predominantly male profession, and there is no record of them serving in a military capacity. There were specialist practitioners such as bonesetters, often again female, and surgeons who specialised in the couching of cataracts and cutting for the stone (lithotomy).

Surgeons were provided for the army but there are no references to other medical personnel. The Act of 1540 amalgamated the Fellowship of Surgeons and the United Company of Barbers. Their new status was granted by Henry VIII himself and memorialised in a painting by Holbein. Apprentices were admitted to the craft after assurance of their health, literacy and the possession of a smattering of Latin. A female surgeon could have three apprentices, but the usual number was four. When apprenticed to a qualified surgeon, where their education would be primarily practical, they were also expected to attend lectures and dissections at Surgeon's Hall. The large number of apprentices would mean that if managed well, the surgeon would always have at least one competent assistant and others able to carry out the necessary business of dressing wounds, preparing poultices and pledgets etc. The apprentices would be examined at Barber-Surgeons' Hall after seven years; if successful they would be granted the First Preferment which was a licence to practice. Further examination and years of experience would lead to the title of master of anatomy and surgery and finally the grant of a Bishop of London's Licence or Great Diploma. Training was highly practical and demanded an excellent knowledge of human anatomy. The Fellowship of Surgeons in London was clearly considered to be the crème de la crème. According to the statute of 1540 which created the Barber-Surgeons' Company, their members were exempted from 'Bearing arms or being called up for watches and inquests'.[26] It was agreed with the City authorities in 1556 that in return for the Company providing medical services, no member of the Company would be conscripted as a private soldier. There were 26 other towns and cities in England that also had barber-surgeons' companies, but none were as prestigious as that of the capital.

Surgical provision for his armed forces was clearly a matter of importance to Henry VII, who granted a cognizance to the fellowship of surgeons, as a reward for organising the medical services for the French expedition of 1492. In the French expedition of 1513 Henry provided himself with 31 physicians, surgeons, apothecaries and their assistants. The navy was perhaps best provided for in that year, with the Barber-Surgeons' Company having sole and special responsibility for their appointment. This might be because of the relatively small number of 'capital' ships which required the services of a surgeon and because of the high status of the officers on board. There are even hints at some form of rank structure in naval service. In 1513 there are accounts for payments to a chief surgeon, 'other surgions being most expert' and junior surgeons,[27] for service with the fleet. The naval surgeons in that

---

26   Rory W. McCreadie, *The Barber Surgeon's Mate of the 17th Century* (Upton: Gosling Press, 1997).

27   James Watt, 'Surgeons of the Mary Rose: The practice of surgery in Tudor England', in *The Mariner's Mirror*, 69:1, (1983), p.5.; British Library, Cotton MSS, Galba, B, III, f.1 54 (formerly

campaign served under four masters and a chief surgeon. Robert Sympson appears to have been the surgeon in the *Mary Rose*, assisted by Henry Yonge.[28]

The problems faced in providing medical staff when a large force was sent on campaign was well illustrated by the problems in the French campaign of 1544. Thomas Gale, author of *Certain works of Chirugerie*, served at Montreuil in 1544 and later with Philip II at St Quentin in 1557. He was an able and well-respected surgeon. The Duke of Norfolk at Montreuil asked Gale to assess the quality of the other medical staff; he was empowered to drive those he thought 'dogge leeches' out of the camp. Gale judged most of those who claimed any medical expertise as a 'great rabblement',[29] little better than sowgelders, tinkers and cobblers, whose favourite potion was a mixture of grease for horses' feet, shoemaker's wax and rust. It was reported that soldiers with even minor wounds were succumbing to infection because of the abysmal quality of their treatment. 1547 Lord Grey complained that the only surgeon in Berwick was 'base and symple' and requested that a more capable man should be sent. The senior nobility might be expected to provide their own medical men to ensure competent and timely treatment. Sir Andrew Dudley was accompanied by Dr Derham when he first landed at Broughty Craig in September 1547, the good doctor would be presented with many problems in the future. In 1557 the army sent to assist the Spanish at St Quentin was well provided for: the City of London Barber-Surgeons provided 57 surgeons, seven were allocated to the senior officers and the remainder to the infantry at the rate of one per company.

The status of the ordinary army surgeon was not high, something which was reflected in his pay. Two surgeons attended Norfolk at Flodden, at the miserly rate of 8d a day. In the 1523 French campaign in the ducal contingent the master surgeon received the rate of 2s a day, the same as that of a petty captain, while the eight additional surgeons were paid at the rate of 12d. In other contingents the ordinary surgeon was paid at 10d a day with a master surgeon receiving 12d. The daily rate for a carpenter was 8d, masons 6d and servants and chaplains 8d. Master craftsmen were all paid at the rate of 12d a day. Therefore the surgeons were considered superior craftsmen , in pay and status, although in the case of those attached to the principal commanders they were seen as gentlemen, of sorts. In 1544 two surgeons in Henry's army were paid the same daily rate as the drummers and chaplains at 1s 6d. The rewards from treating the wounded could be considerable: Captain Drury, who commanded the professional English arquebusiers during the bitter fighting in Norwich, paid local surgeon John Porter 33s 4d for treating his wounded; a third of his company of 180 were killed during the rebellion.

Civilian surgeons could be of great use when treating English casualties. Those hurt when bringing supplies to the siege of Montreuil were treated by Imperial citizens, as Gruffydd reported: 'There I saw Dutch doctors taking a great deal of trouble over attending the wounded, most of whom had their wounds in

136), British Library, 1 512 or 1 513.

28   Watt, 'Surgeons of the Mary Rose', p.5, *Exchequer Accounts*, 5 6 (10), 1 5 13.

29   Watt, 'Surgeons of the Mary Rose', p.5; T. Gale, *The Office of a Chirurgion* (London, 1586).

their heads, where those men who died got their death wounds.'[30] It would be a fortunate soldier indeed who found himself in the hands of a well-qualified London surgeon. Care at the hands of camp followers or other soldiers was all that might be expected for many. Paré recalls a 'shee friend' in 'boyes apparell' who solicited his assistance for her companion. The bandaging of wounds and the provision of herbal remedies would be the best that might be expected in such cases, and which might be sufficient in most. There was no formal provision for hospitals, and at Montreuil in 1544 the wounded were abandoned in the camp, left to fend for themselves when the army retreated to Calais.

Distribution of Wounds

The majority of wounds on the battlefield could be categorised under three headings. Sharp-force, caused by bladed weapons, blunt-force crushing injuries, and penetrative wounds caused by swords, daggers, arrows, bolts and – increasingly – gunpowder weapons. It is difficult to analyse the distribution and nature of wounding in this period. The much-copied illustration of a 'wound-man' displays a wide range of injuries across his anatomy from a variety of weapons and projectiles. The analysis of mass graves from Towton 1461[31] and Lützen 1632 shows which wounds were not survivable. At Towton, the sharp force injuries were considerably greater in number than blunt force and the head and arms suffered most, with fewer injuries to the lower limbs. At Lützen fatal pistol wounds to the face were frequent and reflected current cavalry tactics against infantry. These poor souls were clearly killed in a specific context and may not reflect the distribution on a different battlefield or even a different place on the same battlefield. Sieges would also produce a different distribution. In an analysis of wounds received by the surviving members of a French infantry company in 1567 there were 224 recorded injuries. Of these, some 43 percent were to the head face and neck, 27 percent to the upper limbs and hands, six percent to the trunk and 14 percent to the lower limbs.[32] These results may reflect the proportion of injuries received or perhaps, as in the case of wounds to the trunk, few would have survived those.

Treatment of Gunshot Wounds

Bullet wounds were penetrating wounds and could be treated similarly to those caused by arrows, with the wound being irrigated and searched before closing. They did present additional problems for the surgeon, as the large diameter, high velocity spherical projectile, produced a ragged wound with severe contusion. The wounds would be trumpet shaped as the spherical projectile quickly lost energy in the body and the wound track would close

---

30 Davies, *Enterprise*, p.28.
31 Veronica Fiorato, Anthea Boylston, Christopher Knusel (eds), *Blood Red Roses: The Archaeology of a Mass Grave from the Battle of Towton AD 1461* (Oxford: Oxbow Books, 2000)
32 Wood, *The King's Army*, p.114.

rapidly. The ball could exit the body easily at short range, or if it was travelling at 100 m/s or less it might even 'rebound' inside the body, making it especially difficult to find. Clothing could be carried into the wound and would need to be removed with care. Splinters from bone, armour and fragments of the ball might also be driven deep into the body.

The appearance of the handgun on the battlefields was reflected in the increasing preoccupation of the surgeon in the treatment of the wounds they inflicted. In 1460 Heinrich von Pfolspeundt, a Bavarian surgeon, described in full the treatment of arrow wounds, while only referring in passing to the recent novelty of bullet wounds. By 1497 Jerome of Brunswick in his manual dealt with both in detail, and Hans von Gersdorff produced a further surgical manual dealing with the problems provided by both projectiles in 1517. Ambroise Paré, who had to deal with both the gunshot and arrow wounds caused by Henry VIII's invasion of France, produced his brilliant treatise on military surgery in 1545.

The wound would first be cleaned with oxycrate (vinegar diluted with water) and then probed to find the extent of the injury. If this was not possible then a metal probe or 'sound' would be used, preferably made from 2–3 mm silver wire and preferably round headed, as this shape passed more easily down the wound track and caused less pain. The probe could also be dipped into oil of roses, which had some antiseptic qualities and which would also lubricate the probe's passage into the wound. Wounds could contain not only the filth of the battlefield but clothing and fragments of armour.

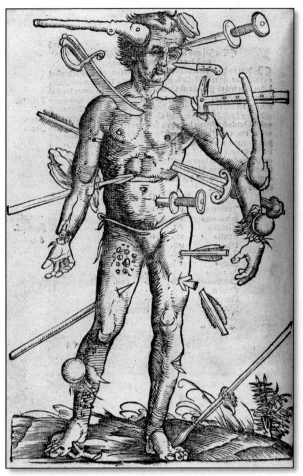

Wound-man from Hans von Gersdorff's *Feldtbuch der Wundartzney* (Strasburg, 1519). Clearly this is a very unlucky man. It does illustrate something of the range of weapons and consequent injuries that could be expected on the battlefield as well as the rough and tumble of everyday life! Often copied, it is interesting to note that it does not seem to show small-calibre bullet wounds. Many but not all of these wounds would be potentially survivable.

At the attack on Boulogneberg, for example, 'Captain Warren … received two shots in his corselet and one of them drove two or three links of his chaine into his necke.'[33] A dilator could be inserted to open the wound further and the ball removed, either with the fingers or one of a range of beaked tools. Fingers were preferred for this operation as they were far superior in finding and grasping the ball. If the ball was embedded in the bone a *terebra* was used. This was a corkscrew device within a *cannula*, that could be screwed into the

---

33 Raphael Holinshed, *Holinshed's Chronicles of England, Scotland, and Ireland*, vol. 3 (London, 1808), p.908.

Portrait of Ambroise Paré, the King's surgeon, 1582, by Etienne Delaune. Paré was a most remarkable man as well as an expert surgeon, and he understood the importance of treating the patient as well as his injury. He was prepared to learn both from the knowledge of other surgeons and the wisdom of peasants. Military surgeons could expect to gain much practical experience in a short time; in addition, their patients would not prove as litigious as those in civilian practice. (Metropolitan Museum of Art, Open Access)

ball. Paré pioneered the technique of placing the victim in the position he was shot, and then plotting the path of the projectile from its point of entry. At Perpignan in 1542 the master of the artillery, de Brissac, was wounded by a musket ball which the surgeons were unable to find. Paré placed him in the position he was shot and with his sensitive touch found the ball nestling beneath the scapula.

The treatment of gunshot wounds was until the early sixteenth century the same as that used for other penetrative wounds, with the necessity of cleaning the wound before closure being stressed. John of Vigo, surgeon to Pope Julius II, changed the management of such wounds dramatically and for the worse. He established what rapidly became current orthodoxy in the treatment of gunshot wounds; his textbook of surgery was printed in 1514 and soon went through 40 editions in five languages.

He assumed that gunshot wounds were particularly life threatening, as the wounds were 'envenomed' by the gunpowder. The venom would be dealt with by the dilation (opening) of the wound and the introduction or injection into it of 'burnyng' (scalding hot) oil (oil of elders mixed with treacle), or by the application of red-hot cauterising irons. Sometimes a rag would be soaked in the boiling liquid and then drawn through the wound. The wound would then be 'cured' using melted butter, or if the wound was in the sinews with a mixture of melted butter, barley water with earthworms, hollyhock, and red sugar. It would be then bandaged with a 'digestive' made of egg yolks, oil of roses and turpentine in the form of a plaster. Although the bullet should be removed there was no attempt to remove the other fragments that might well be present!

Ambroise Paré, the most famous surgeon of the age, used this conventional method proposed by John of Vigo when serving at the siege of Turin in 1536, until he ran out of oil. Now, after searching for and removing the ball, he applied a harmless mixture which consisted of yolks of eggs, oil of roses and turpentine, the 'digestive' suggested by Vigo. After a sleepless night worrying about his patients, he found that the wounds which he had treated in this way were 'without inflammation and tumour'. Those unfortunates who were treated using the conventional approach were feverish, in great pain and showing signs of inflammation. Paré went on to acquire an even more efficacious ointment made of 4 lb of violet oil, a pound of earthworms and two new-born puppies boiled until their bones dissolved! One assumes that this somehow worked, as he had an enviable reputation in assisting his patients to recovery, but as he modestly said of his own work 'I dressed him, and God healed him.' Paré's other major contribution to military surgery was the use of ligatures to tie off the main blood vessels when carrying out an amputation, rather than using cauterising irons.

How widely the enlightened techniques of Paré were employed it is impossible to say, with cauterisation remaining a common practice. What is apparent was the failure to adequately search and clean wounds. In 1578 Don Juan de Silva, a Toledan nobleman, was shot in the left arm by an arquebus. He reported that:

> I have seven wounds that the surgeons have had to make in my arm because each one festered as a result of the problems and bad treatment I had in the first 40 days. Four of these wounds have now been covered with cloth and balm and have almost healed over; three are in the very joint of my elbow and are so stubborn, and the two very small ones, so resistant to the medicine that for two months nothing has been able to heal.[34]

He was in considerable pain and feared that the wounds would have to cauterised. Some six and a half months after the original injury nature fortunately took its own course:

> When I was about to leave at 8 o'clock … they found a bone that was sticking out of that small wound they had tried to close. There wasn't room even for a lentil to fit, and the bone was so big that it looked as though it would not fit through anything but a big hole. When the surgeon tried the next day to widen the wound with sponges and other devices, it was so difficult, but he started to pull the bone out with his hand and made room for it till it came out. The bone is an inch thick, and the length of three fingers; it was God's great favour to reveal it and remove it with so little damage though with a lot of pain. That same day, from another wound that I have on the inside of my elbow, another bone came out without any pain, though it left a large wound in my elbow that has now closed up these last few days, and seems to be healing. I was doubtful and very unconcerned about finding the shot, and when one day I went to take my pulse, I found it in that very spot, on the inside of my arm between the muscles, about a finger's length from where my hand joint is. It is amazing that it had travelled from alongside my shoulder to reach this spot, without me having felt it set off, move or stop.[35]

This injury highlighted the importance of thorough searching and cleansing of the wound. If a Spanish nobleman and an ambassador of Phillip II to the Portuguese court suffered such abysmal treatment, then what hope for the common soldier?

---

34 Lorraine White, 'The Experience of Spain's Early Modern Soldiers: Combat, Welfare and Violence', in *War In History*, vol. 9, issue 1 (January 2002), p.23; Colección de documentos in éditos para la historia de Espanã (CODOIN), 113 vols (Madrid, 1845–95). *CODOIN* xl, pp.99–100, cited in Bouza Alvarez, 'Corte es decepción', p.473.

35 White, 'Combat, Welfare and Violence', p.24; letter written on 16 Feb. 1579, CODOIN xl, pp.99–100, cited in Bouza Alvarez, 'Corte es decepcio'n', p.474.

Serratura.

x 3

Amputation scene, woodcut, sixteenth century. The patient is sitting up, the usual position then for an operation, as to lie the patient down would be to simulate death. With the patient upright, he may also faint due to blood loss, which would be a mercy. He is remarkably stoic and only a team of two rather than the usual four or five seems necessary on this occasion. The surgeon has used the tourniquets as suggested by von Gersdorff and the sharp knife in the picture has separated the flesh from the bone. The saw only cuts in one direction and would take some time. His assistant is holding the leg to ensure that the bone will be cleanly sawn. Severed limbs are surprisingly heavy, I have been told. The onlooker has lost his left hand and the stump has been provided with careful protection from further damage. This is not an image of horror but of competent craftsmen saving a life. (Wellcome Collection. Attribution 4.0 International (CC BY 4.0))

One can only wonder at the resilience of the human body, exemplified by the history of Gabriele Tadino di Martinengo, the brilliant military engineer responsible for the defence of Rhodes in 1522. While peering out at the enemy he was shot through the right eye, the ball exiting the side of his head by the ear. In only six weeks he returned to the fray, this time leading a raid against the Turkish sappers. This time he suffered a bad wound from a scimitar on his knee. He survived until 1543, after two decades of service as military engineer and captain of artillery.

Amputation

Amputation was not the operation of first resort, it was only considered when either the limb was so badly damaged as to be irrecoverable, it had already been partially amputated, or when the development of gangrene made removal of the limb essential to save the life. It was an operation that was well understood and was conducted as soon as the injury was suffered, when the patient was full of adrenaline. The operation was conducted as quickly as possible to reduce blood loss, which with infection would be the most likely cause of post-operative death.

Hans von Gersdorff provided an excellent description of an operation that he must have conducted frequently. Although various forms of analgesic and anaesthetic may have been available and were referred to, their use was considered very dangerous and they do not seem to have been employed.

Before you operate you should have all your instruments and preparations in order, such as razor, saw tourniquet, bandages, lint, eggs, and whatever else is needed. Arrange them in the order you will need them after the incision is made. When you are about to cut have someone draw the skin firmly back, and tightly bind the skin with a constricting band, and then tie a cord near the constricting band, leaving a space about a fingers breadth between the two, in which the incision can be made, so that the cut will be correct and even and make a good stump, when you have made the incision (through the flesh) take a saw and cut the bone. Afterwards remove the constriction and have someone draw the skin and flesh down over the bone and pull firmly forward. Then take a bandage, which has been thoroughly moistened until wet, and bind the limb down to the incision to keep the flesh over the wound and bind it so, afterwards apply the haemostyptic over it and a good thick compress. Afterwards take the bladder of a hog, bull or ox cut so that it will go over the stump and dressing and moistened, draw it over and bind it with a cord and you will not have to worry that the stump will bleed.'[36]

There is no reliable contemporary data relating to survival rates, but if the limb was not amputated then the mortality rate would have been 100 percent! In the Peninsular War in the British Army where conditions on the battlefield, the sharpness of the knives and the skills of the surgeon were little different from those 250 years before, survival rates were surprisingly high. One man in 20 died after the amputation of a forearm but over one third died from the amputation above the thigh.

Disease and Want

It was not battle casualties that would seriously diminish an army but disease and desertion. It was generally considered that an army would lose half its strength within six months of being raised.[37] The situation could be far worse, as it was amongst the 1,200 pioneers who were rebuilding the harbour defences of Boulogne in January 1545: by June their numbers had been reduced to 300 by death and sickness and to only 100 by the next month. Diseases, whether 'sweating sickness' (a fatal disease with flu-like symptoms), 'bloody flux' (dysentery), or typhus (spread by human lice, and generally known as 'camp' or 'gaol' fever or plague), would thrive in the insanitary conditions associated with a military camp, especially in warm weather. Their impact would be far worse if the soldiery had already been weakened by poor diet and inadequate clothing and shelter, allied to the exhausting business of everyday soldiering. When the campaign was short or when provisioning was adequate, then the army could be protected from its worst ravages.

In theory the quantity of provisions provided by the system of purveyancing should have been more than adequate in calories to sustain the health and strength of any man, with generous amounts of beer, bread and beef. A Tudor soldier's clothes and issue coat would have been adequate in most conditions for the duration of a short campaign. In Scotland, however, where conditions were especially harsh, there were frequent complaints about the abysmal state of the soldiers' clothing, caused by the lack of any new issues. This was hardly assisted by the shortage of match cord, the soldiers being forced to use their own shirts to make a substitute.

Common soldiers were not provided with tents as a matter of principle. They were 'expected to make their lodgings as men of war of other nations do,'[38] that

---

36 Julie Gardiner with Michael J. Allen (eds), *Before the mast: life and death aboard the Mary Rose* (Portsmouth: Mary Rose Trust, 2005), p.179; from I. Zimmerman and L.M. Veith, *Great Ideas in the History of Surgery* (Baltimore: The Williams & Wilkins Company, 1961), pp.215–17.

37 Hammer, *Elizabeth's Wars*, p.26.

38 *Letters and Papers,* 1544 31 March.

The Four Horsemen of the Apocalypse *c.*1497/1498, by Albrecht Dürer. A vision from the Book of Revelations, the four horsemen represented war, famine, pestilence and death. It was an image that was both well known and oft experienced. It was war that so often brought the other three to pass, not only to the armies but the civilians caught up in conflict. Again and again Tudor armies were laid low not by an enemy force but by sickness and want, which was partly the inevitable consequence of large numbers congregating together in unhygienic conditions and partly the systemic failure of commanders and bureaucracies, unable or unwilling to adequately support their own army. (Metropolitan Museum of Art, Open Access)

is to bivouac using what materials they could glean from the countryside. Most campaigning would take place during a fairly well-defined season from spring to autumn, the precise date very dependent upon latitude. In good weather and with soldierly ingenuity it may have been possible to establish a degree of comfort; the greatest hardship was probably experienced by those troops garrisoning Scottish forts in autumn and winter.

When provision was inadequate conditions could rapidly worsen, and even bring the expedition to a disastrous conclusion. The Guienne campaign of 1512 suffered through the failure of King Ferdinand to provide adequate food supplies or the means of transporting them. The indiscipline of the men, the failure of their officers, poor hygiene, the climate and the unusual diet led to the physical collapse of the army, succumbing to the inevitable combinations of dysentery and typhus. If heat and bad diet was to bring disaster in 1512, it was cold and incompetence which led to the collapse of the French expedition of 1523. Food there was aplenty, if Elis ap Gruffydd is to be believed, but once again the failures of command led to empty bellies. The combination of cold, inadequate clothing and poor accommodation produced a sick and mutinous army that eventually forced the commanders to admit failure and return home. The severely cold weather in 1523 caused great suffering:

This day if people can be believed many men on horse and on foot died from sheer cold. Others said that some had lost the use of their limbs from the force of the frost wind. And others said that they had lost the use of their waterpipes and could not pass any water that way until they had got fire and warm water to thaw them.[39]

Sir John Wallop, reporting on the condition of his troops during the siege of Landrecies at the end of the campaign season in October 1543, said the men were 'veray poore and few or none of theym have any greate store of money, victualz be dere, clothes wax thyn, and cold wether encreseath'.[40] In

39   Davies, *Ill Jurney*, pp.5–6.
40   Potter, *Henry VIII and Francis I*, p.148; Wallop et al. to Council, 10 Oct. 1543, National Archives, SP 1/182, ff.11–13 (*Letters and Papers*, XVIII, ii, 267)

1522 a similar extension of the campaign season into October had brought misery and death as Surrey reported to Wolsey from France:

> Since writing the above last night, at midnight, the weather has been so wet and cold that there are a great many men dead, and so many sick that he must lead them to some good town to refresh them. The Spaniards and Almains have departed in great numbers without licence.[41]

Those serving at sea was no less prone to hardship, as John Lisle, commander of the *Harry*, reported on 28 August 1545: 'You shall understand that the men in this army [Navy] decay very sore, and those that be whole be very unsightly having not a rag to hang on their backs.'[42]

Lisle reported to the Duke of Suffolk that:

> There is a great disease fallen amongst the soldiers and mariners almost in every ship, in such sort that if the same should continue, which God forbid, we should have need to be newly refreshed with men. The disease is swelling in their heads and faces and in their legs, and divers of them with the bloody flux.

The explanation was simple, it was caused by 'the heat and the corruption of their victual by reason of the disorder in the provision, and the straight and warm lying in the ships'.[43]

If provisions and discipline had been adequate at Thérouanne in 1513 and Boulogne in 1544 it was because of the presence of the King. At Montreuil, the diversionary siege, provisioning was poor, worsened by the cupidity of captains who saw the possibility of profiting from the desperate condition of their men. As Gruffydd reported: 'Then there was the stink of the carrion of the mares and horses that died among the host, which were left to rot on the ground for want of anyone to bury them as the discipline of a host demands.'[44] The location of the 'shambles', or area designated for butchering and disposal of offal, should have been strictly laid down in the standing orders of the camp master. The failure to apply such rules, which were commonplace in this period, reflects badly on the leadership of the army. Gruffydd recalled how 'this stench struck within and filled the vital senses and spirits with rotten air which made great havoc with the heart and the mind and for all these reasons as well as the displeasure of God there fell a great pestilence'.[45]

An outbreak of dysentery in the crowded camp meant that morale and discipline was at its lowest when the order came to retreat. The sick, and those drunk on the stocks of wine, were abandoned and the French 'killed all, both sick and sound, whom they could find there, among whom there were many feeble men pining from lack of warm food to heat their bowels which were full of the cold phlegm which bred in the vessels of their bodies from

---

41 *Letters and Papers*, vol. 3, 1522 4 Oct. R. O. 2952.
42 Gardiner and Allen, *Before the Mast*, p.174.
43 Gardiner and Allen, *Before the Mast*, p.174.
44 Davies, *Enterprises*, p.18.
45 Davies, *Enterprises*, p.20.

the diseased food which they had during the Summer'.[46] Those who made the journey from Montreuil to Calais found little comfort there. Gruffydd, who was an experienced and hardy soldier, reported that:

> The dwelling houses, which were not enough to lodge half the people who were inside the town, were full, so the warehouses for skins and wool were thrown open and also the two churches, one of which, that of St. Nicholas was full of wool. But as soon as the sick men came to have a little warmth and ease they fell sicker than ever. Those who were sound also fell sick, some from the filthiness of the smell of the skins and wool, some from heart disease, some from ague and some from the pestilence … Others had fallen ill of hot fevers which were so fierce that they took away people's memory and senses. I myself suffered from this disease and I lay ill for more than three months and would have died or lost my senses if I had not had the advice of my physician and the help of the doctor to let blood'.[47]

Those troops who returned to England from France in 1544 were not hale and hearty and brought their diseases with them:

> the soldiers coming from Calais and Boulogne were dying along the road from Dover to London, and along the roads from London to every quarter of the kingdom, while trying to go home. After they had come home those who were well fell sick and those who were sick got worse, and from this sickness and feebleness and pest they died in every part of England.[48]

Sometimes it was the quality of the food and drink that was provided which was the root of the problem. The ever-watchful Gruffydd analysed the issue thus:

> they brought much victual especially sour bread made from wheat which had never been put through a mill but was beaten in a mortar with pestles and slipped through the fundaments of the people who ate it like filthy excrement, which with the coldness of the water [water was seen as an inferior drink to ale as it provoked cold humours, being of its nature moist and wet] which was the greatest part of the drink of the common soldiers, and the damp which chilled the bodies and hearts of the people, threw them into the sickness called by physicians *Lienttria* [diarrhoea], which means sluggishness and cold in the temper and lack of heat in the liver to effervesce the bowels so as to function naturally.[49]

The English garrisons in Scotland during the Rough Wooing seem to have been places of particular hardship. Poor diet, inadequate clothing and shelter and a dreadful climate all added to the misery that reduced the men and their animals to a pitiable condition. The English fleet supporting the army was in a poor state as well. In February 1548 Wyndham reported that

---

46 Davies, *Enterprises*, p.34.
47 Davies, *Enterprises*, pp.36–37.
48 Hammer, *Elizabeth's wars*, p.27.
49 Davies, *Enterprises*, p.25.

the manning of the fleet required 610 men and boys but were some 140 short, and of those on board 120 or almost a quarter were sick.[50] Wylford, commanding at Haddington, faced similar problems as he recounted when informing Somerset about the dreadful state of his men:

> Many are sick and a great number dead, most of the plague. On my faith there are not here this day of horse, foot, and Italians, 1000 able to go to the walls, and more like to be sick, than the sick to mend, who watch the walls every 5th night, yet the walls are not manned, they lie in litter without beds, go in their single white coats, for there is small provision of clothing.[51]

Rutland pleaded with London to prioritise supply to Scotland, where the English soldiers now fled their posts in droves and where it was impossible to persuade mercenaries to take their places.

Conclusion

There are two very conflicting views of logistical competence. Mark Fissel writes that, 'The English mastered logistics well, fielded large numbers of men in spite of a hybrid recruitment system.'[52] However, Clifford Davies in his article on the provisions for armies in the period 1509–1550 declares that:

> the failures of the period point to something more than [the general absence of professionalism and continuity], to a fundamental lack of seriousness and concern for their people on the part of their rulers. On the one hand, war was a readily used instrument of policy, in many cases pandering to nothing more than the vanity, the desire for glory on the part of the monarch. On the other hand, little thought was taken for the fates of those who suffered, whether the king's own soldiers or the enemy peasantry … The provisioning of armies was no easy task, but it could have been done more successfully. Had the sufferings of the [common soldiers] seriously disturbed the lives of those at Greenwich and Hampton Court it would have been.'[53]

There is little evidence to suggest that much if any 'thought was taken for the fates of those who suffered'; there is, however, often a great deal of evidence of thought when it came to the provision for armies. In practice the bureaucracy and technology available to the Tudor state was simply not up to the job if, as always seemed the case, what is often referred to as 'friction' entered the system. The point that Davies makes so well is that war pandered to the vanity and the desire for glory on the part of the monarch: the sufferings of the soldiers did not therefore enter into his calculations.

---

50 *CSP Scotland*, no.172, p.84.
51 *CSP Scotland*, no 329, pp.165–166.
52 Mark Charles Fissell, *English Warfare 1511–1642* (London: Routledge, 2001), p.47.
53 C.S.L. Davies, 'Provisions for Armies, 1509–50; A Study in the Effectiveness of Early Tudor Government', in *The Economic History Review*, New Series, vol. 17, no. 2 (1964), p.248.

Perhaps the last word in bureaucratic arrogance and indifference to the humble soldier was the boastful report of the Council of Boulogne recording its management, or rather mismanagement, of its stocks and the dire consequences:

> ill meals [grains, probably wheat] sent hither in hering barelles and lost by ill packing and taking of wete in the carriage … and also the corrupt lothesomeness of a great quantetie of bareld beif [beef in barrels] happening by myxture of the filthyness of a great nombre of coles [coal] laded in the vesselles upon the same … never the lesse we vsed soche pollice in mingling that ill wheate and meals with other corne of better sorts and by washing and clensing the beife after soche a facion, That asmoche as may in any wise serve of every kinds of those victuales are put in dayly vse to the victualing of this garison …[54] we thinks surely that meny people have dide amongst vs in their sikeines for lacks of socour of freshe meates being driven to take vnely [only] of the provision or the store by the Want of money to bye other victuales withall.[55]

---

54 Davies, *Provisions for Armies*, p.242; National Archives, SP 1/203, f.105r (L.P.xx 1 1123).
55 Davies, *Provisions for Armies*, p.242; National Archives, SP 1/203, f.106r (L.P.xx 1 1123).

Part III

The Equipment

10

Infantry Weapons

The Puissant Pike

For anyone who has had the misfortune to handle the pike, or morris pike, as it was usually called in England, what is apparent is that it is ill-balanced and cumbersome. The appellation 'morris' or 'Moorish' was ostensibly used because it was an Ottoman weapon, which no doubt added to its attraction as something exotic. On his own, a pikeman is incapable of either defence or offence, it is only when he is working alongside others that the purpose of the pike becomes clear. As a weapon of defence against cavalry its length will keep horses away from the formation, and as a weapon of offence, used at a brisk pace it will face a less well provided for opponent with an overwhelming hedge of steel points.

The pike was far more than just a long spear. The spear was not to be despised: it was an ancient and most efficient weapon; it was the preferred weapon of the medieval soldiers of North Wales and of course the Scots. Light, flexible and lethal it gave considerable punch while keeping an enemy at a distance. It was also cheap, an important factor amongst the impoverished Celtic fringe. In the hands of the Scots en masse it composed the schiltron (or moving thicket) which laid waste the chivalry of England at Bannockburn in 1314.

The pike was developed not in Scotland but in Switzerland. This was a similarly mountainous and impoverished region and was also facing the imposition of an alien feudal host. The Battle of Sempach in 1386 saw the triumph of the infantry forces of the confederation over a Habsburg army dominated by men-at-arms. Fought on foot, the battle saw the defeat of the Habsburgs not with the pike but the halberd, effectively a long-handled axe, with their opponents using cut-down lances. The battle demonstrated the power of determined infantry who could come close to a hated and despised foe. The pike emerged principally to keep the armoured knight on horseback at a safe distance from the ill-armoured or unarmoured infantry that faced him. The gradual addition of the pike to the Swiss infantry formations was a recognition of its principal purpose; the halberd remained a weapon for closer-quarter combat. The Swiss genius was to transform the pike from a weapon of defence into one of offence. This could only be achieved if a large formation could move with discipline and speed towards its objective, as was

'The Battle Near Naples', from *Der Weisskunig* by Hans Burgkmair. All the pikes are being held overarm and not at their full extent, which would make them more manageable as well as providing the opportunity if need be to extend them further, thrusting into the faces and upper body of an unwary foe. The vicious and highly effective halberd is also brought forward in close-quarter fighting. Accompanying the advancing Imperial forces a drummer and fifer provide encouragement as well as orders. On the ground can be seen an unfortunate arquebusier and a wounded swordsman. It is surprising how few appear to be wearing armour, especially helmets, although simple metal 'skulls' may have been worn beneath their flamboyant headgear.
(Metropolitan Museum of Art, Open Access)

achieved so successfully against the Burgundians in successive battles. Such tactics were only possible if those in the formation were well trained and committed to their collective action.

Elsewhere in Christendom there were significant differences in military commitment and equipment. South Wales, specifically Glamorgan, produced excellent archers, however North Wales, economically and politically different from the south, provided agile spearmen. Poverty and social homogeneity explain the equipment of the Scots and the Swiss and their effectiveness on the battlefield. Neither Scottish nor Swiss society could afford to produce cavalry in any numbers; the hardship and communal nature of their lives created physical strength and social homogeneity and the absence of expensive body armour led to a necessary aggressiveness to overcome their vulnerability in the face of archers or mounted attacks.

The weapon of the poor, the spear or pike gave them the ability to defend themselves against cavalry. The bow and crossbow provided the wherewithal to defend the pikemen. If to this was added the choice of a naturally defensible position, then as long as they maintained discipline they would triumph. This was nothing new: the army of Frederick Barbarossa was held by determined Milanese pikemen in a phalanx formation at Legnano in 1176. Although Frederick's forces were finally defeated by a desperate cavalry attack, it was the resilience of the infantry in the face of constant assaults which was most impressive. Where discipline failed or where the formations were weakened, then infantry would succumb to aggressive mounted forces as the Flemings did at Mons-en-Pévèl in 1304 and Cassel in 1328. The pike was suitable equipment for a Swiss, just as it had, in the form of the *sarissa*, suited the hoplite in the ranks of Alexander the Great. The Renaissance with its admiration for all things classical, not merely the aesthetic but the moral and military, saw in the Swiss pikemen the shade of the Macedonian phalanx. This made the adoption of this otherwise outlandish weapon acceptable. It was not so much its modernity as its antiquity that made it the weapon of the age.

The battles that brought the pike to general notice were the three grand defeats of the Burgundian armies led by Charles the Bold: Grandson and Murten in 1476 and finally and fatally for the Duke, Nancy in 1477. Burgundy, although territorially small, was enormously wealthy and much of that wealth had been devoted to war. Charles the Bold had created what was in many ways the most 'modern' army in Christendom, based around the professional Compagnies d'Ordonnance which provided a 'lance' consisting of mounted men-at-arms, light cavalry and mounted infantry. To this powerful force were added crossbowmen, pikemen and hand gunners, and English archers added to this comprehensive 'force mix'. Charles also possessed perhaps the most extensive and sophisticated artillery park of both field and siege artillery. This was a force subject to strict rules relating to attendance and training.

The three defeats he suffered at the hands of the pike-wielding Swiss can be readily explained. At Grandson in 1476 he lost after his army's feigned retreat turned into a rout. At Murten in the same year the failure of the Swiss to attack when expected led him to allow his army to return to its tents, and when the Swiss appeared, despite a brave attempt by English archers to hold

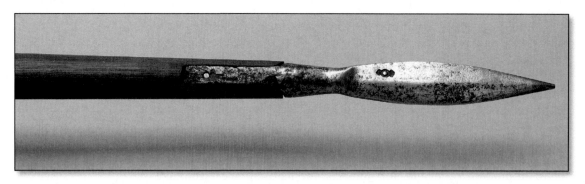

Pike head *c*.1500 from Germany. The pike had a lethal thrusting point; its target was the face and limbs of an enemy against which it could cause horrible injuries. As a defence against cavalry it provided a veritable hedge of steel. Varying in length and weight the pike was always heavy and unwieldy, though it could be carried on wagons if available and if the enemy was not near. This example has protective strips of metal known as langets (possibly in this case broken off short), to protect the shaft from being shattered. With such a weapon a peasant could defy a prince. The point itself weighs only two ounces (57 g). (Courtesy of the Royal Armouries)

the line, the gun line was overwhelmed. At Nancy in 1477 he lost his life as well as his army, when his opponents outflanked his carefully prepared positions. It was the relentless advance of the Swiss rather than what they were carrying which mattered. The Duke made serious tactical errors on all three occasions, as well as underestimating his enemy and overestimating the quality and capabilities of his own forces.

The impact of the defeat of the most modern army in Europe by simple mountain folk could not easily be attributed to the people themselves but rather to the pike they shouldered. For almost half a century the Swiss would remain the mercenaries of choice for European rulers, leading to the expression 'pas de monnaie, pas de Suisse' (no money, no Swiss) and of course the continuing presence of the Swiss Guard in the Vatican. If the Swiss could not be bought or were not available, then surely the addition of the pike to the burden of the poor infantry would somehow make him the Renaissance super-soldier? This was certainly the hope of James IV when he purchased pikes to equip his soldiers in the struggle against their 'backward' foes. In 1523 the English were equally convinced of the value of this weapon and those who wielded it. When Surrey faced the possibility of another struggle with the Scots, he sought to hire 4,000 Landsknechts to train his men, for 'the English are not accustomed, but will easily learn when they see the order of the Almaynes'.[1]

The assumption that the new pike formations were the strength of an army gave to the weapon a social and political significance which changed the status of the soldiers who carried it. Emperor Maximilian I chose to march in the front rank of the pike-carrying infantry into Cologne in 1505, symbolising the new importance of the infantry. Blaise de Monluc at the Battle of Ceresole dismounted and joined his men with a pike, assuring them

---

1 *Letters and Papers*, vol. 3 1519–1523, British Library 1 Calig. B. VI. 238, no. 2995, May 1st, p.1265.

that 'I could not die in a more honourable place than in their company, with my pike in my hand.'[2] In the English Civil War the front rank of the pike was a post of honour for officers, not the front rank of musketeers. The pike was to be the dominant arm of the infantry, socially and militarily, whilst the arquebus was to be its servant.

Patten described the manner in which the Scottish pikemen managed their weapons at the Battle of Pinkie in 1547:

> Hereto every man his pike; and a great kercher wrapped twice or thrice about his neck; not for cold but for cutting. In their army towards the joining with the enemy, they cling and thrust so near in the fore rank, shoulder to shoulder together, with their pikes in both hands straight afore them; and their followers in that order so hard at their backs, laying their pikes over their forgoers' shoulders; that if they do assail undissevered, no force can well withstand them.
>
> Standing at defence, they thrust shoulders likewise so nigh together, the fore rank, well nigh to kneeling, stoop low before their fellows behind holding their pikes in both hands and therewith on their left[arm] their bucklers; the one end of the pike against their foot, the other against the enemy breast high; their followers crossing their pike points with them foreward; and thus, each with the other, so nigh as place and space will suffer, through the whole Ward so thick, that as easily shall a bare finger pierce through the skin of an angry hedgehog, as any encounter the front of their pikes.[3]

Much later Humphrey Barrett described the manner in which pikemen should be arranged in battle:

> Five ranks will couch, cross and defend as followeth. Two ranks crosseth by the mid pike, the third rank coucheth forth right betwixt the two aforesaid, holding their pikes fast with both hands, stay the same against their left knee, kneel on the same with right knee firmly. The other two ranks beareth their pikes above hand, ready to push with the right hand at the whole length of the pike.[4]

Pikemen always formed the outer carapace of the block of bills and pikes. They were the core of any formation, for as Barnabe Rich asserted, 'the very strength and bulwarke in the field, is the stand of pykes, which being impald and trouped with shot orderly, are defensible against both against horse and shot.'[5] The great reach of their weapons (up to 18 or even 20 feet rather than the 6–8 feet of the bill) enabled them to keep cavalry and infantry a 'safe' distance away. The pikemen in his corslet of armour, his morion, cabasset or burgonet upon his head and short sword and dagger, provided the storm troops of the band. Barnabe Rich, in line with current thinking, asserted that 'the stronger your pikes are together in number, the battaile is accounted to

---

2   Monluc, *Memoirs*, p.109.

3   Patten, *The expedicion into Scotla[n]de*, p.112.

4   Henry Barrett, *Handbook*, ff.10r–10v.

5   Barnabe Rich, *A Pathway to Military Practise* (London, 1587). Available online (see bibliography for URL).

be the most forceable, but the shot to be devided into manie troupes, are the better to maintain fight, and the apter for service'.[6] The pike could be held overarm and at about their point of balance or at full length. The former method achieved greater offensive potential and avoided the pike naturally rising up uselessly in the press of battle, while the latter exploited the length of the weapon to the full.

Training in handling the pike for an individual was relatively simple (in the present author's case it took about 15 minutes); what took longer was to drill a block of pikemen so that they responded as one to the commands of their officer. These would be passed on usually by the drummer, a senior and respected soldier or by 'signs' or arm gestures. Barrett describes such training later in the century:

> Such must instruct soldiers as well by signs … as by words and deeds how to train, march and use themselves in all points … laying the [pike]staff on his shoulder [the sergeant] march[es] forth, the company doing the like, sometimes he traileth the same on the ground, sometimes coucheth the same as it were to encounter enemies, sometimes retireth so couched, still his face toward the enemies, sometimes standeth still advancing his staff on high, the company standing still giveth silence, and according to every sign by him framed they do the like.[7]

The assumption that putting a pike into the hands of a foot soldier somehow made him unbeatable led to the tragedy of Flodden, and the failures that attended the Italians when seeking to mimic the achievements of what they called the Swiss or *montani besdales* (bestial mountaineers),[8] with what they called the *regina dell'a'rme* (queen of arms). The reason for this failure was explained by Arfaioli Maurizio:

> pike fighting required a very specific and taxing type of training: one that could only be effectively exploited by homogeneous ensembles of troops already united by a sense of cohesion – a cohesion that found in battle its proof of worth, not its origin, and whose need increased more than proportionately with the growth in size of the square one wished to array.[9]
>
> In Italy the introduction of a mechanism similar to that of the Swiss, which permitted a large number of good infantrymen to be gathered from a relatively small population like that of the Helvetic Confederation, was impossible. The Italian socioeconomic structure was too different from that of the areas where the new tactic of pike fighting was first practised successfully en masse, and the Italian powers could not count on a successful incorporation of the new tactics.[10]

6   Rich, *A Pathway to Military Practise.*
7   Barrett, *Handbook*, f. 5r.
8   Arfaioli, *The Black Bands of Giovanni*, p.5.
9   Arfaioli, *The Black Bands of Giovanni*, pp.6–7.
10 Arfaioli, *The Black Bands of Giovanni*, p.7.

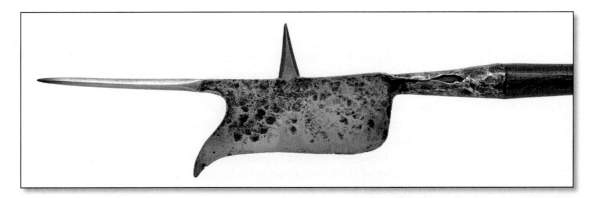

Above: English bill, early sixteenth century. Not a sophisticated or elegant weapon, the English bill is similar to the halberd in that it has a thrusting spear point, a heavy curved blade and a sharp beak or fluke for penetrating armour. The finish is rough and the socket is not a work of art but good enough. The billman was a poor substitute for a trained man-at-arms but fought well when facing foreign mercenaries in the dreadful year of 1549. Heavier and less handy than a halberd, the bill was still lethal in the hands of a sturdy countryman. Overall length 2.763 m (108 3/4 in.), head length 683 mm (26 7/8 in). (Courtesy of the Royal Armouries)

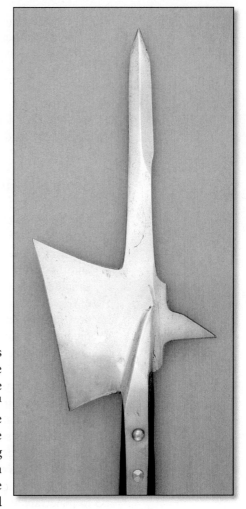

Right: Halberd from the late fifteenth or perhaps early sixteenth century, of German origin. The name halberd was derived from the German word for axe (*barte*) and long shaft (*halm*). Unlike the pike this weapon could be wielded effectively by a soldier on his own and could be devastating against even a man in armour. It is thought that Richard III was killed by a Welsh halberdier. Length 81 3/8 in (206.6 cm), length of head 16 in (40.6 cm), width 8 3/4 in (22.2 cm), weight 4 lb 12 oz (2,154.6 g). (Metropolitan Museum of Art, Open Access)

The Humble Bill

The halberd and the bill, or black or brown bill as it was sometime known, still had their uses, but not as frontline weapons, as '[the] ranks of Billmen in order of Battle are always environed and compassed about with pikemen'.[11] A mixture of pikes and bills was disliked because of the 'unseemely shew' they made, although such practice appeared common in the 1540s as is apparent when studying the Cowdray House engravings. The purpose of the billmen was to 'serve specially for execution if the Enemy in Battle be overthrown … and there must be reserved a few armed billmen or armed halberds to guard the ranks wherein the ensigns and drums etc, are placed in the order of battle'.[12] It

---

11   Robert Barret, *The Theorike and Practike of Moderne Warres* (London, 1598), p.47.
12   British Library, Harl. MSS 168, f.110, November 1587.

was felt important not to have them facing any of the flanks, as the short reach of their weapons would create a weak spot that the enemy could exploit.[13]

The halberd was similar to the bill, although lacking the curved beak of the latter. Of Swiss/German origin, it was often rather finer than its more 'agricultural' English equivalent. It could perform a more ceremonial role because of its appearance and eventually became a more decorative and symbolic weapon. Similar to the halberd were the Jedburgh stave and Lochaber axe, used south and north of the Scottish border respectively.

One other staff weapon requires notice, if only because it loomed large in the report of the Venetian ambassador in 1557, and that is the 'holly water sprinkle'. He noted that:

> among their offensive weapons in those parts they use certain long poles of the height of a man, thick, and armed with certain iron spikes at the head, three inches in length, issuing from all parts, which are very perilous weapons, calculated to smash and break the hardest substances.[14]

The relative importance of bill, halberd and sprinkle can be gauged by the stocks of each held in the Tower. There were 610 sprinkles, 306 halberds, 6,700 'Blake Billes', and 20,100 'morrispickes', counted in the inventory of 1547.

Swords, Shields and Daggers

The armies that fought for Henry VII at Stoke Field and accompanied his son Henry VIII to France in 1513 and 1545 were equipped with broadswords and bucklers, as the contemporary illustrations in the Cowdray House engravings and the Field of the Cloth of Gold painting attest. The swords shown were simple broadswords, sometimes with a plain crossguard, although this could develop into a characteristic L or horizontal S-shaped guard that acted to protect the knuckle. The fully developed guards which are associated with the rapier could also be applied to cut and thrust sword blades in the form of what has been described as the 'sword-rapier'. In the North the basket hilt associated with Scottish swords (but referred to as an Irish hilt) was used with a broadsword blade.

The term 'broadsword' refers to the blade and not the guard. This weapon possessed a relatively heavy and short blade of no more than a yard in length (and usually less) designed principally for cutting strokes. The broadsword remained the primary weapon of almost all soldiers throughout the period. Natural conservatism allied to common sense and practical experience meant that it would reign supreme on the battlefield if not at court. The need to penetrate armoured opponents and to counter pike and halberd meant that the narrow thrusting blade of the rapier was worse than useless. The mace, war hammer and poleaxe were designed specifically to deal with

---

13 Rich, *A Pathway to Military Practise.*
14 *CSP Venice*, vol. 6, 1555–1558. May 13. MS. penes me. May 1557.

Basket-hilted sword, English, about 1560, blade possibly German. This is a very workmanlike sword. The large pommel is hollow and the guard is made from rectangular section iron, the grip is made from wood bound with copper wire. The blade is single edged with a ricasso and a rather narrow central fuller. A very similar weapon was found on the *Mary Rose*. Overall length 1,028 mm (40 1/2 in), blade length 888 mm (35 in), weight 1,195 g (2 lb 9 1/2 oz). (Courtesy of the Royal Armouries)

armour which would resist a simple sword cut. Only the estoc or tuck (as it was known in its anglicised form) was designed to perforate plate. The press of men caused by two formations of polearms coming together made it difficult to wield any sort of weapon. Robert Barret considered that even short swords 'will hardly have rome at that instant either to thrust or to strike',[15] and recommended daggers. Sir John Smythe preferred daggers without hilts or with little crosshilts, and of 9–10 inches in blade length, and short arming swords with blades less than 27 inches.

In the early years of the sixteenth century it was the Spanish sword and buckler men who reigned supreme on the battlefield, able as they were to break Landsknecht pike blocks by closing with their opponents by rolling beneath their points. Machiavelli records how at Cerignola (1503) Spanish sword and buckler men swooped beneath their enemy's pikes:

---

15 Barret, *The Theorike and Practike*, p.47.

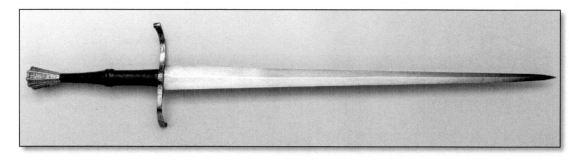

Hand-and-a-half sword, possibly British, c.1500. The hand and a half sword was a very elegant and sophisticated weapon capable of inflicting a heavy cut and a devastating thrust. Such a sword was and still is used as a training weapon for anyone wishing to learn the skills of the swordsman. The blade is diamond shaped and has no fuller; it looks wonderfully well balanced. The simple S-shaped crossguard would clearly require the user to wear a glove or more likely gauntlet if he was to spare his hand from dissection.Overall length 43 3/4 in. (116.2 cm), blade length 34 1/16 in (86.5 cm), width 8 1/2 in. (21.6 cm), weight 2 lb 10 oz. (1,190.7 g). (Metropolitan Museum of Art, Open Access)

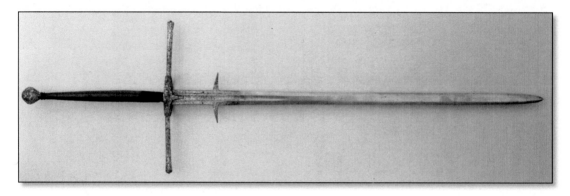

Two-handed sword c.1570 Italian, Venice. Although appearing clumsy and heavy such swords were well-balanced and lethal in the hands of a competent swordsman. Capable of inflicting devastating cuts at speed, they could also be used as thrusting weapons, especially if a gauntleted hand was placed between the crossguard and the flukes. The present author has handled a similar weapon and the blade although strong was light and flexed visibly when lifted. Overall length 63 in (160 cm), blade length 45⅛ in (114.6 cm), width 17¾ in (45.1 cm), weight 6 lb 5 oz (2,863 g). (Metropolitan Museum of Art, Open Access)

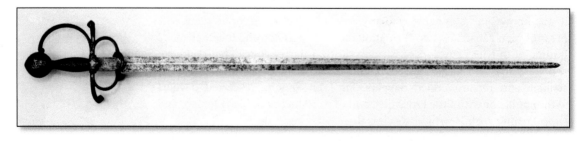

Rapier of Emperor Charles V, c.1540, handle by Francesco Negroli. The Milanese Negroli were one of the most famous families of Renaissance armourers. The hilt is not as complex as the English basket-hilted broadsword but the arms of the hilt and lower side ring beneath the quillons would protect a finger placed around the ricasso to enable it to be used better for thrusting. The large pommel would help counterbalance the long blade. The blade is probably a German import, as bladesmithing is a very different craft from hiltmaking. Overall length 42¼ in (107.3 cm), blade length 36⅝ in (93 cm), width 6½ in (16.5 cm), weight 2 lb 11 oz (1,219 g). (Metropolitan Museum of Art, Open Access)

With their pikes low, [the Swiss] opened up the Spanish infantries. But the latter, helped by their bucklers and by the agility of their bodies, so mixed themselves with the [Swiss] that they were able to join them with their swords. From this arose the death of almost all and the victory of the Spanish.'[16]

The heavy single-edged falchion also continued in use throughout the period. The weight of the blade was at the tip which could also be provided with a curved point. Short and well balanced, it was the military equivalent of the butcher's cleaver. In the late fifteenth century it gained the patronage of the nobility who prettified it for parade wear. Its guard remained limited to a crossguard and knuckle guard of the L or horizontal S form, although there were slight variations to this.

The hand-and-a-half, or bastard sword was widely used throughout this period and was probably a development of the 'sword of war' that was so popular with mounted men-at-arms. With a long sturdy blade and extended handle, it gave the horseman extra length and the dismounted man greater leverage and striking power. It is interesting to note that it was one of the weapons that the Tudor swordsman training in the art had to offer when presenting himself for his prize. As the century progressed the blade tended to narrow, producing a finely balanced weapon suitable for thrusting. The present author has used an interpretation of Wallace Collection A1492 which is both sturdy and swift. The development of the guard followed the accepted pattern of increasing complexity, although up to 1520 a simple crossguard seems to have been universal. Popular throughout most of Europe except for Italy, it seems to have developed stylistically at the hands of the German, Swiss and Spanish.

The double-handed sword was used as an assault weapon in the destruction of pike blocks and as a 'ceremonial' one in English companies for protecting the ensign, where it was known as a 'slaughter sword': a term derived from the German *Schlachtschwerter* or battle sword, or *Zweihander*. It was sparingly issued, 'because its weight and bigness require great strength, therefore these only are allotted to the handling thereof which are mighty and big to behold, great and strong in body and of stout and valiant courage'.[17]

As with most battle swords, blades, quillons and pommel could all be used offensively and defensively. The cross guard or quillons in German swords often seem to have taken the form of an enlarged S shape similar to the *Katzbalger* or cat-gutter. Hans Holbein illustrates one in action in the midst of a press of pikes in *Schweizerschlacht*, although a plain crossguard was also common. The scalloped or flambard blade is particularly associated with the double-handed sword. The edge of the scallop increased the cutting angle and length of blade in the same way as a bread knife, which achieves a similar but rather more pacific slicing action.

16 Niccolò Machiavelli, *The Art of War*, in *Machiavelli: The Chief Works and Others*, vol. II, ed. Allan Gilbert (Durham, N.C.:Duke University Press, 1989), book 2, 64–6, p.39.
17 Ewart R. Oakeshott, *European Weapons and Armour: From the Renaissance to the Industrial Revolution* (Woodbridge: Boydell Press, 2000), p.148.

The estoc was another very specialised weapon, derived from similar late medieval weapons with the same proportions as the hand-and-a-half sword, with a triangular cross-sectioned blade only suitable for thrusting. The blade underwent small changes from triangular to square section during the century. It remained a short-bladed weapon (about a yard in length) with a short hilt designed for the difficult task of thrusting through plate armour. It emerged at the end of the century as a specialist weapon of central European cavalry. The tuck as a thrusting weapon is sometimes confusingly seen as the progenitor of the rapier. There seems little doubt that the rapier came from very different stock.

The rapier was the real innovation in this period, as development in other areas was entirely evolutionary. Its name almost certainly derives from the Spanish words *espada ropera* or sword of the robe, that is a weapon for civilian use; this in turn became the French *rapiére*. The Spanish, it appears, adopted the custom of the wearing of swords by civilians much earlier and more widely than the rest of Europe, where it was the custom to carry a dagger. These were themselves formidable weapons, some over a foot in length, carried by all men, prudent travellers and even women and clerics in such lawless lands as the Scottish borders. In Germany the *Baselard*, a sword with a short blade of about 24 inches, was popular, but this was really an enlarged version of the Holbein dagger, using the same design of grip and an elongated blade.

The broadsword was heavy and a military weapon not worn with civilian dress, but in Spain in the latter part of the fifteenth century they developed a lighter version, with a narrower blade suited for thrusting rather than for cutting. The wearing of swords with a developed hilt by a civilian in Continental Europe is first illustrated in 1506 and appears commonly in the 1520s. By the 1530s the practice had become almost universal. The earliest references to the rapier are dated to 1468 in Spain, 1474 in France while in England in 1532 there is found a reference to 'the spannyshe sword', possibly a rapier. Henry VIII certainly owned a rapier, referred to in the inventory of 1547. The arrival in England in 1554 of King Philip, the husband of Queen Mary, and his entourage would have seen the appearance of the rapier in London streets on a large scale. The rumour was that one Spaniard a week was killed in London during his visit. It has been argued that only in 1570 did the rapier supersede the broadsword as the most popular weapon amongst the highest ranks in society, but legislation controlling the rapier had been put in place as early as 1557.

The blades of swords were manufactured across Europe, but the best blades were made in Spain (Toledo and Valencia), France (Bordeaux), Italy (Milan and Brescia), and Germany (Solingen, Cologne and Passau). Blades were exported throughout Europe and the hilts fitted locally, although these could also be made to 'foreign patterns'. The name of individual bladesmiths could become a byword for high quality and could be used by other (often German) bladesmiths to denote quality as well as to gull the unwary. Some of the most famous were Antonio Piccinino of Milan or Alonso de Sahagun. The name of Toledo bladesmith Tomas de Ayala became in effect a trade

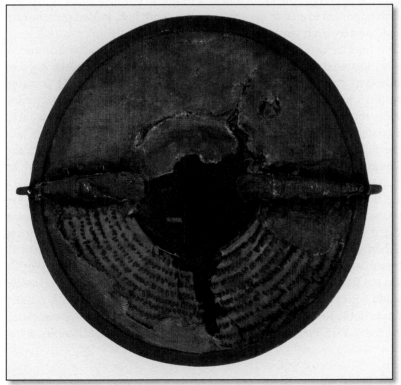

Buckler Shield *c.*1500, British. An invaluable weapon, the buckler shield's purpose was not solely defensive although it could deflect an attack and put an opponent off balance. Sword and buckler work had been a feature of warfare for centuries and was a popular exercise among the Tudor young and foolhardy. Iron, pigskin, brass, wood, fibre (flax), linen. Diameter 141/4 in (36.2 cm), weight 5 lb (2.27 kg). (Metropolitan Museum of Art, Open Access).

name, and was used into the eighteenth century. One swordsmith, Diego de Cayas, served both Francis I and Henry VIII.

It was essential that the rapier guard was more complex to protect the hand from blows. It was quite common for mail or plate gauntlets to be used in combat with the rapier but only of course if preparations could be made beforehand. One of the complaints that led to the legislation of 1557 was the wearing of gauntlets, vambraces, and bucklers with long pikes in them, contrary to the ancient use of the realm. The wearing or carrying of such items was clearly preparatory to a Tudor 'rumble'.

The hilt of the rapier was very distinctive, but it was the product of a process of evolution, and even sword blades could have developed hilts. One feature of a thrusting blade is the ricasso or blunted squared-off section immediately below the grip which would be encircled by the thumb and forefinger to better direct the blade. The cross hilt of the broadsword gave little protection to the hand. A ring was placed in front of the blade to protect the forefinger placed over the crossguard or quillon (c.1400), while a second ring appeared on the other side later (c.1450); a side ring joined these two at the blade (c.1450). Developing from the S-shaped crossguard was the knuckle guard which appeared about 1530. Counterguards would complement the knuckle guards to give complete protection to the hand.

The major accompaniments to the sword were the dagger, the buckler and the target. The cloak was an essential civil accompaniment and the limited cutting power of the rapier made the cloak a valuable addition. It could be as useful as, if not more useful, than the dagger: it could envelop a thrust and could be snapped (in the same way as a towel) to entrap a blade or thrown over an opponent to enable the fighter to close with him. Furled over the arm it could protect from cut or blow in the manner of a shield.

The buckler was the traditional accompaniment to the sword and is widely illustrated in contemporary engravings. It could be made of wood or iron, and its small size led to it being carried alongside the sword. It varied from 8–15 inches in diameter, and could take a large number of profiles: convex, concave rimmed or flat with a raised boss. It was sometimes fitted with a spike several inches in length; the normal length of these was four to five inches, but by the late 1550s they had grown to 10 or 12 (which the legislation of 1557/1562 reduced to 2 inches). Alternatively it could be equipped with a horizontal bar with which to catch and perhaps break a blade. It was carried with the sword and because it 'swashed' or rattled it gave the name 'swash buckler' to its (disreputable) owner. It was not a defensive shield: it was too small for that purpose. It was used to deflect a thrust or cut, and then to react with a punch with the boss, or a cut with its edge. Like all successful weapons it could play an effective offensive as well as defensive role. It was not just a weapon for the common man: a splendid concave example of wood with gilded brass decoration, similar to an early–sixteenth-century example in the Royal Armouries[18] (known as a Wrexham type) is associated with Henry VIII. Found in the armoury of the Château de Chantilly, it has

---

18   Royal Armouries V108 & 109, illustrated in Fiorato et al., *Blood Red Roses*, p.146.

a pomegranate-shaped centrepiece topped by a flattened spike, and has the usual portcullis and Tudor Rose decoration. It is thought that it was given by Henry to Anne de Montmorency. the Constable of France, at the Field of the Cloth of Gold in 1520.

The 'target', sometimes known as the targe or rondash, was a distinctive form of shield much larger than the well-known buckler. The target was a large shield of between 20 and 30 inches in diameter. There were clearly three different types of target: the 'parade' target of metal, splendidly inlaid and etched and of little military use; a heavy iron 'target of proof' used by engineers and assault troops when conducting sieges; and a swordsman's target to be found in the schools of fence and on the battlefield. In the Cowdray House engraving of the Boulogne expedition (1545) it is also illustrated as part of the equipment of pikemen. Wooden targets for obvious reason are far less commonly found these days, and it is surprising to see them so well and frequently illustrated in contemporary engravings of military engagements. The swordsman's target was of necessity lighter than the target of proof, although it was sometimes of such a weight that it (together with other items of armour), was often 'lost' by those deputed to bear it. Roger Williams in 1590 complained that such shields, weighing probably about eight pounds, were very cumbersome and so heavy that few men would be prepared to carry them for an hour. The target of proof was very heavy, the heaviest example in the Wallace Collection weighs 12 lb 4 oz and is s 22.25 inches in diameter.

The target was popular equipment in the Elizabethan 'schools of fence', both with native and Italian fencing masters. In the textbook of swordsmanship by De Grassi (1560) a target is well illustrated in use, and it appears in fencing manuals from 1530. It is often referred to, with the buckler, as a useful piece of sparring equipment. Though its size precluded it from being carried by civilians, unlike the dagger and cloak, it was prized by some soldiers. Targeteers were a regular addition to most bands or companies throughout the period, and they can be seen in contemporary illustrations usually preceding the assault by pike and arquebus formations. This enthusiasm for the targeteer was perhaps fuelled by a dedication to all things Roman, best expressed by Niccolò Machiavelli in *The Art of War*.

Wooden target	17–21 in	3 lb 6 oz
Steel targets	21–24 in	7¼ lb–91/4 lb
Leather targets (parade)	22 in	5½ lb
Wooden pageant shield	18–22 in	3 lb 10 oz–4 lb 6 oz
Pageant shields	21–24 in	7–9 lb

Table 4. Examples of Targets from the Mid to Late Sixteenth Century, Held in the Wallace Collection

Above: Bollock dagger excavated from the Thames, dateable to the sixteenth century. The wooden hilt is characteristic of the type and quite modest and unassuming compared to others which are more anatomically correct or boastful! It is a very effective weapon and practical working tool. It is very similar to some 65 *Mary Rose* examples but of course with its blade intact. The blade is really very long and is single edged with the back edge having a shallow central ridge. All but one of the *Mary Rose* examples was single edged. It is worth noting the damaged blade, indicating that it was probably used in action, most likely in a tavern brawl than some great triumph of arms. Overall length 429 mm (16.9 in), blade length 305mm (12 in), overall weight 284 g (10 oz). (Courtesy of the Royal Armouries, RA X.1479)

Right: A rondel dagger *c.*1400–1499. This weapon has a thrusting lozenge-shaped blade long enough to easily cause a fatal injury, and well-suited to finding a gap in armour or to thrust through mail. It would have no purpose in the civilian world, although the present author has seen one museum example labelled as a hunting weapon. This example is very modest in its lack of decoration. Overall length 351 mm (12.4 in), blade length 211 mm (8.4 in), overall weight 240 g (8.47 oz). (Courtesy of the Royal Armouries).

The dagger was a weapon that could be worn by all English adult males throughout this period, if we disregard such European specialities and oddities as the Cinqueda, the knuckle-guard dagger and eared dagger as well as Landsknecht and Holbein daggers. The eared dagger had a handle that divided into two arms to which were affixed a circular plate at an angle of 45 degrees; it gained some popularity among the wealthy and stylish in the mid century and is the dagger seen in some of the portraits of Edward VI. Its appeal was aesthetic rather than functional. There are examples of near identical daggers from the pre-classical civilizations of the Near East on display in the British Museum. One can only presume that an ancient example awakened the imagination of Renaissance Italy.

An Englishman may be expected to carry the following types. Throughout the early period the bollock and rondel daggers would have remained common. Similar in design to their medieval predecessors, during the early sixteenth century the bollock daggers tended to become longer in the handle, while the rondels became finer in profile, tending to lose the lower rondel. The quillon dagger is especially associated with this period in the form of the *main gauche* or left-handed dagger, the invaluable accompaniment to sword or rapier. The cross-guard or quillon as it may now be called was essential to protect the hand, but the addition of a thumb ring gave the knuckle some degree of protection. The *main-gauche* became widespread in about 1550, although earlier examples have been identified. The first reference to a duel using sword and dagger is dated to 1512, and illustrations of it are contained in the *Opera Nova di Achille Marozzo* of 1536. The quillons were of necessity stout and often downturned in order to entrap an opponent's sword blade. The side ring appears on quillon daggers after 1560 in increasing numbers. A quillon dagger with side-ring dated to about 1550 is displayed in the Fitzwilliam Museum. The present author uses a copy of it with a companion rapier; it is remarkably effective in its role as well as being exceptionally elegant. The blades were mostly straight and double edged. The finer blades had fullers that were ridged, grooved and pierced, as some rapier blades were. The quillon daggers referred to as Saxon daggers had three short quillons, usually turning down towards the blade, with spherical or plate finials for decoration.

The bollock and rondel dagger could be worn vertically over the right thigh (preferred in the period up to the mid century), but the quillon dagger was usually worn behind the back. The handle was logically pointing to the left if it was to be drawn by the left hand (while the right drew the sword), however illustrations of soldiers invariably show them being worn to the right, no doubt for first and emergency use, in preference to the slower draw of the more cumbersome sword.

Sword Training

In early Tudor England the sword and buckler were the preferred weapons of gallants and apprentices alike. These 'swashbucklers' mostly fought in well specified areas such as West Smithfield (known as *Ruffian Hall*), sometimes in gangs of up to 40. There were few fatalities, it was thought cowardly to strike below the belt and cutting wounds were less fatal than thrusting ones. The acquisition of some scars was apparently essential to prove manhood amongst the swashbuckling community. There were well established places of practise including Hampton Court, Bridewell, the Artillery Gardens, the Clink, Grey Friars within Newgate, and Blackfriars (which was excluded from London's jurisdiction and was therefore a popular resort of the duellist and brawler). Inns such as the Bull in Bishopsgate Street, the Bell Savage on Ludgate Hill and the Curtain in Holywell were also used for more legitimate bouts which could be well observed and the participants rewarded with public approbation.

In 1540 Henry VIII established in London a company of 'Professors in the Noble Science of Defence' which was part of his general encouragement of the English to martial practice. The title lapsed in 1547 with the death of the King and was not renewed, but the guild remained in being. The ranks and titles of those who joined the guild were scholars, free scholars, provosts and masters. The fencing schools that proliferated were described as 'the Third University in England', and they attracted a similar and probably more attentive clientele. By 1545 the famous toxophilite Roger Ascham reckoned that every town had its school of fence.

The scholar who wished to rise through the ranks had first to defeat six of his brethren with long-sword and back-sword, and then to fight all 'free scholars' who chose to attend a formal prize to claim the title of 'free scholar'.

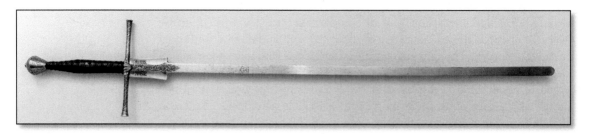

Practise sword *c.*1575 by Ulrich Diefstetter. Much more rarely found than live blades, with flat edges and neatly rounded point, the practise sword would save the scholar from injury and a sharp sword from unnecessary damage. The ability to use such a sword was a matter of both necessity and status for some classes. This is obviously a weapon for training the gentry or nobility. Overall length 50⅝ in. (128.5 cm); length of blade 40¾ in (103.5 cm); width 8⅞ in (22.5 cm), weight 2 lb. 15 oz (1,332.4 g). (Metropolitan Museum of Art, Open Access)

Seven years of training were required to prepare for the transition to the ranks of provost and seven more to become a master. The tests involved in 'fighting a prize' were exhaustive, involving the candidate matching in skill any number of his superiors who chose to attend, using a range of weapons over a two- to three-day period. The weapons used for practise and for tests were staff, sword, sword and buckler, sword and dagger, bastard and great sword, battle axe, halberd and pike.

Wearing a Sword

In England the sword belt was little modified from its medieval origins until 1560. A.V.B. Norman provides an excellent succinct explanation when he explains that the sword was suspended from a waist belt by three narrow slings:

> Two of the slings were attached to the scabbard at the mouth and the third about a foot below the mouth. This last, and one of those attached at the mouth, were then carried round to join at the waist-belt at the centre of the back. The remaining sling was carried forward and attached to the waist belt at a point some four to six inches to the left of the centre of the wearer's waist.[19]

The rapier had to hang at an angle of 45° because of its great length, whilst in the painting of the *Field of the Cloth of Gold* (the painting is dated to 1545, the event itself 1520) the swords hang almost vertically. In Northern Europe after 1540 the diagonal front sling or side piece attached to the waist belt was moved to the right hip. In addition, it was attached with a hook which applied to the other straps, allowed the sword to be removed completely. In this period four separate slings could be buckled around the scabbard, possibly grouped in pairs.

---

19 A.V.B. Norman, *The Rapier and Small-sword: 1460–1820* (London: Arms & Armour Press, 1980), pp.293–303. All the information in this section is derived from this excellent source.

Scabbards were invariably made from beech wood covered with leather, which could be decorated, or in turn covered with linen or velvet. Scabbards could be decorated to match a particular suit of clothes, so that for example in 1547 there is a record of a new rapier for Prince Edward provided with three scabbards. A chape was fitted to the end of the scabbard, while in Germany from the 1540s the mouth could be protected by a metal 'locket'. Dagger scabbards were of a similar construction and were attached to the belt either by a D-ring, or with cords or chains to two rings each side of the scabbard. The ricasso could also be covered with a metal sleeve to protect it from rust. Most swords and daggers up to the last quarter of the sixteenth century had byknives (eating knives) and bodkins (probably for making holes in fabric) fitted in their scabbards. To avoid losing the sword in action a sword knot or long thin cord was used to attach the sword to the wrist. It appears first in a painting in 1530 attached to the pommel, but it was more usually attached to the grip.

Armour

The introduction of firearms did not make armour obsolete. The Graz firearm experiments have proved that armour could provide a fair degree of protection from contemporary weapons. Arrows, swords, war hammers, daggers and pikes there were aplenty on the battlefield and armour was invaluable in protecting from, and mitigating the impact, of such weapons. Although London boasted a guild of armourers, England was never a major producer either in quantity or quality; she did not possess a great store of armour prior to the reign of Henry VIII and as recorded in the chapter on recruitment, there was no great store held by individuals. Henry's reign was to see very significant changes, brought about by purchase and by the establishment, for Henry VIII and his court, of an armoury for making supreme examples of the craft.

The role of the soldier and his personal wealth would determine what protection he might have. Padded armour was almost universal, either in the form of the jack or the arming doublet worn under plate. Its layers of linen were designed to absorb the impact of a blow that would otherwise break limbs, even if the weapon did not penetrate. The simple jack could be reinforced with plates of metal, mail or horn to add to its strength. The brigandine, made of large numbers of small metal plates riveted to a fabric doublet, gave considerable protection while not compromising flexibility and movement, as plate armour might. One peculiar item was the eyelet doublet, where a short fustian jacket was sewn with round holes in button stitch. It was a defence considered suitable for archers and it was thought rather optimistically that it should resist a sword thrust. Mail was used extensively, either as full shirts or in sections sewn on to padded clothing. The *Mary Rose* was equipped with 200 mail standards or collars, useful for protecting the neck.

The introduction of the pikeman in large numbers required the development of armour that was practical and inexpensive: Almain rivet. This consisted of a metal collar, to which was attached riveted metal arm

Brigandine c.1540–1550 from the Old Tower Collection, III.47. A sleeveless brigandine with an upstanding collar but missing the tassets that would cover the thighs. The base is canvas and it is covered in crimson velvet, the rivets would have been gilded to add to the luxurious appearance. The great advantages of the brigandine were comfort and appearance as well as an excellent degree of protection. The flexibility of the large number of plates was enough to diminish the impact of blows. The jack of plates was a much inferior equivalent designed to protect the poor billman or archer. Plate armour worn thin through cleaning could be cut up and used in brigandines and jacks. Height 635 mm (25 in), width 1.025 m (40.5 in), waist circumference 990 mm (39 in). (Courtesy of the Royal Armouries)

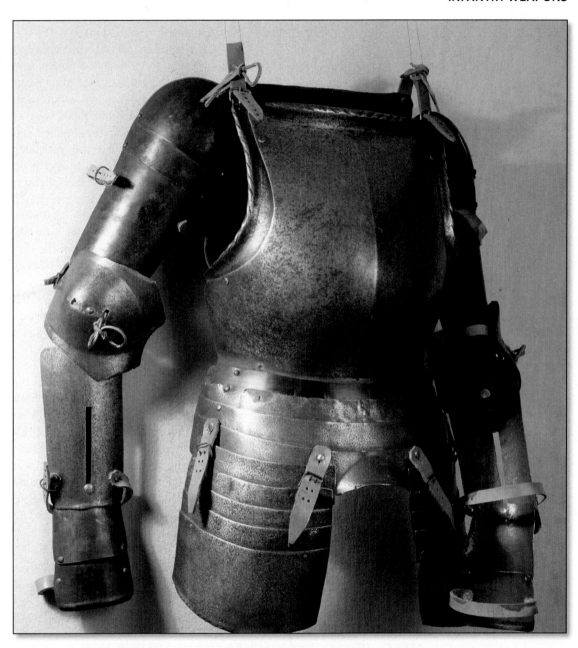

Almain rivet armour, *c*.1520. It comprises a globose (rounded) breastplate with lamed fauld (layered flexible plates), a backplate with two lower slotted splints (flexible metal plates attached to back of back plate), two couters (elbow protectors), two five lame tassets (hip and thigh protectors), spaudlers (laminated shoulder protectors) and hand lames. This example may have belonged to the Winchester town guard. One can assume that such armour came like most military issued items in two sizes: too large and too small. Armour which does not fit is not only uncomfortable but dangerous to the user, impeding his freedom of movement. One of the purposes of armour is to increase the confidence of the poor infantryman. Whether this armour would have done so is questionable. (Photo © Winchester City Council. Provided by the Hampshire Cultural Trust)

Gun shield. The present author once owned what was at least in part an original gun shield, which had a matchlock pistol refitted in the nineteenth century. The short-barrelled breech-loaded gun could be sighted through the grille provided but in practice it would have been easier and more practical to have thrown the thing at an enemy. They appear to have been a uniquely English product, for obvious reasons! (Courtesy of the Royal Armouries)

defences that almost reached the elbow. To this simple defence could be added breastplates and backplates, tassets to protect the thighs and splints protecting the arms, using sliding rivets and internal leathers to achieve articulation. In 1512 Guido Portinari sold 2,000 sets of Almain rivets, consisting of breastplates and backplates, gorget, salet and a pair of splints at 16s a pair. Richard Jerningham, acting on behalf of Henry, purchased a further 5,000 sets in Milan in 1513. In 1539 Henry purchased 1,200 complete harnesses (with additional leg armour) at Cologne for £454 (7s 6d a set) and a further 2,700 from Antwerp for the very low cost of £630 (4s 8d). The Duke of Norfolk complained that gentlemen seeking to purchase corselets in East Anglia were being charged the much higher price of 20s a set.[20] In comparison to this 'bog-standard' armour the price of a foot armour from the royal armoury at Greenwich was £8 and a full garniture some £10–12.

The usual type of helmet referred to was the salet, which was the form that would have been worn at Bosworth. The morion appears almost exclusively in the Cowdray engraving but this may have been for artistic simplicity rather than veracity. The burgonet was beginning to appear, providing additional protection to descending blows that would remove the nose and chin of a man wearing a salet. A simple 'skull' or metal cap could be worn hidden beneath headgear and no doubt the kettle hat was also in use.

One other type of hybrid gun/armour deserves something more than a footnote and that is the gun-shield. This was a simple wooden shield with a thin sheathing of iron plate. A breech-loading matchlock pistol was then fitted either on or just above the centre of the boss. Some decorated, others left plain, they were ill-balanced, clumsy and utterly impractical. They may have been used for close protection of the sovereign but as some were discovered on the *Mary Rose* they may have actually been intended for use in battle.

Henry VIII and the Woolwich Armoury

Henry VIII's particular enthusiasm was for war and the apogee of the craftsman's art in this field was in the manufacture of armour. In neither field did England excel, the magnificent gift of armour to Henry from

20   Potter, *Henry VIII and Francis I*, p.217.

Emperor Maximilian in 1511 only highlighted England's backwardness. Henry privately commissioned further armour from Konrad Seusenhofer, Maximilian's court armourer, but in the future he was determined to match the quality with semi-domestic manufacture. Henry recognised that English armourers lacked the skill of their Continental counterparts and he began by employing two Italian armourers from Milan in 1511, at a combined and very considerable cost of £80.

Established in Southwark, they were soon joined in England by two armourers from Brussels, this time at Greenwich where the royal armoury finally settled, in the Tiltyard, in 1515. By then Henry had 11 German and Flemish armourers working as part of the Royal Household, in what was now called the 'Almain Armoury', under the management of Martin van Royne. It was this armoury that produced the magnificent armour for the foot combat at the Field of the Cloth of Gold in 1520. As one might expect, the style of armour tended towards the German and Italian but was more highly decorated in the French fashion, benefiting from the designs of the court artist Hans Holbein. The Greenwich armoury was never a large organisation: in 1544 it consisted of five armourers, a gilder and two locksmiths, a millman and an apprentice, although a proposal was made to double it in size. The armoury continued to maintain the highest standards of workmanship even after it had been completely staffed by English craftsmen, finally closing in 1649. Henry also employed a Spanish swordsmith, Diego de Cayas, from 1540–1547, who made a wide range of blades, including one celebrating the capture of Boulogne with the inscription: 'Rejoice Boulogne in the reign of Henry VIII'.[21]

Continental Europe produced armour and arms in staggering quantity and some in exquisite quality. Milan was at the heart of Italian armour production, with such famous armourers as the Missaglia dynasty and later the famous Filippo Negroli. Brescia was also a centre of production for armour and firearms. In northern Germany production was concentrated in the Imperial cities: in Augsburg the Helmschmieds family was the most famous maker, in Landshut the armourer Wolfgang Grosschedel was patronised by Philip II, and in Nuremberg Kunz Lochner made the armour for Charles V. The court workshop of the Holy Roman Emperors was in Innsbruck under the management of the Seusenhofer family. France was a significant importer of Italian and German armour, although it had armourers' guilds in Paris, Beauvais and Chartres as well as Tours and Lyon which also employed Italian craftsmen. The Low Countries and Spain also had busy armourers' guilds. European production was the consequence of generations of development with continuous and considerable demand. The armourers' guild of London, on the other hand, could not hope to match either the quality of Innsbruck or the quantity production of Milan.

The manufacture of high-quality blades was a special and separate skill, as already mentioned, with Toledo and Passau perhaps producing the finest blades which were highly sought after across Europe. The 'running wolf'

---

21 Thom Richardson, *The Armour and Arms of Henry VIII* (Leeds: Royal Armouries, 2019), p.61.

THE TUDOR ARTE OF WARRE 1485-1558

trademark of Passau was copied by Solingen bladesmiths and seems to have been used by even less scrupulous producers. Nuremburg was the centre of fine clock manufacture and used the same techniques and material for wheel lock mechanisms. England could not hope to match European standards or quantity, although domestic manufacture seems to have sufficed, possibly with the use of imported blades fitted with English handles. Both Henry VIII and James IV employed European bladesmiths, for their skill exceeded that of domestic producers.

11

The Bow and the Gun

Introduction

> From its meagre beginnings in the fourteenth and fifteenth centuries developed
> a force so effective that almost all other mediaeval military technological
> innovations disappeared from use. Arms such as the bow, sword, spear, and lance,
> were quickly replaced. Armour, even the heavy plate armour of the fifteenth
> century, provided little protection.[1]

It is easy to see how historians have been seduced by the appeal of
gunpowder weapons and to assume that their development led to the rapid
obsolescence of 'medieval weapons'. The assumed superiority of firearms
made the retention of obsolete weapons explicable only in terms of poverty
or perversity. Gervase Phillips has written with his usual sagacity that:

> Less attention has been paid [by historians] to the complex interplay of factors
> beyond technical performance that have governed the choices surrounding
> the adoption of particular weapons. A people's chosen tools of war can be
> a manifestation of economic, political, cultural, and social circumstances,
> circumstances that defy the simple logic of a new technology displacing an old.[2]

When considering the history of the longbow and the arquebus in English
military service, it is vital to appreciate the whole picture and not rely solely
on a technical comparison of the two weapons, although that in itself can be
very revealing. In England throughout this period the bow was far more than
simply a weapon. Archery was the chief defence of the realm, a gift from God
to the English, a source of collective pride and a regular recourse for recreation
and competition.

---

1   Kelly De Vries, and Robert D. Smith, *Medieval Military Technology* (Toronto: University of
    Toronto Press, 2nd Revised ed. edition (30 April 2012)), p.163.
2   Gervase Phillips, 'Longbow and Hackbutt: Weapons Technology and Technology Transfer in
    Early Modern England,' *Technology and Culture*, vol. 40, no. 3 (July 1999), p.576.

A yew longbow being drawn up full. Drawing a heavy bow is as much a matter of technique as strength. This archer stands strong and in control of the bow using both arms to draw, unlike the modern technique. The string arm rotates in the shoulder coming to a natural anchor point. The three-fingered draw on the string was widely used at the time, as reported by Ascham, the royal tutor and ardent toxophilite. The longbow drawn properly is both a joy to behold and to loose. It is likely that most Tudor men employed (as their skeletons attest) to very hard physical labour on a daily basis, would have found shooting their bows a pleasant not a painful pastime. (Photograph courtesy of Commotion Times)

The Importance of the Bow in English Society

The retention of the bow was not a matter of sentiment but of success. The English triumph over the Scots at the Battle of Flodden (1513) was, in part, due to the longbow. The bow's performance in a very different Continental context, at the Battle of the Spurs was also impressive. In subsequent expeditions in 1522/3 the presence of longbows was not seen as a handicap. There was certainly no shortage of seasoned archers to use their bows: in 1530 there had been a very impressive demonstration of 3,000 archers in London, who after marching from Merchant Taylors' Hall assembled at Smithfield to shoot, a demonstration of personal and civic pride. Archery received official, nay, Royal encouragement: in 1537 Henry VIII founded the Guild of St George for the encouragement of shooting of all sorts. In 1545 towards the end of Henry VIII's reign, in the final great expedition to France, the archers remained the most prominent feature of his army, with only seven percent of the English forces equipped with firearms. As late as 1588, of the 79,798 men of the Trained Bands 42 percent were equipped with firearms and 18 percent were still equipped with bows.[3] The retention and enthusiasm for the bow, especially under a sovereign obsessed with modernity in all matters military, deserves explanation.

Bishop Latimer provides us with a valuable insight into the significance of the bow, when in 1549 he castigated the Justices before the King and his Council in a public sermon, with the following words on archery:

> I desire you, my lordes, even as you love honoure, and glorye of God ... let there be sent fourth some proclimacion, to the Justices of Peace, for they do not thyr dutie. Justices be now no Justices; ther be many good actes made for thys matter already. Charge them upon their allegiance, that this singular benefit of God [archery] may be practised; and that it be not turned into bollyng, and glossing, and horing, within the townes; for they be negligente in executying these lawes of shutynge.[4]

---

3   J. Tincey, *The Armada Campaign, 1588* (London: Osprey, 1996), p.47.

4   A.E. Hodgkin, *The Archer's Craft* (Felifach: Llanerch, 1995), p.55.

The classical scholar Ascham, tutor to Edward VI and Princess Elizabeth and keen toxophilite, waxed lyrical on the dangers of gambling and the benefits of archery, as:

> gaming [was] … a vain present pleasure; but there followeth loss of name, loss of goods, and winning of an hundred gouty, dropsy, diseases, as every man can tell. Shooting is a painful pastime, whereof followeth health of body, quickness of wit, and ability to defend our country, as our enemies can bear record.[5]

He continued on the same theme, saying that: 'The art of shutynge hath been in tymes past much esteemed in this realme, it is a gyft of God, that he hath given us to excel all other nacions wythall. It hath bene Goddes instrumente, whereby he hath given us manye victories against oure enemyes.'[6]

To practise archery was to follow God's will, to protect the kingdom and to avoid vice. In *The Boke For A Justyce of Peace* of 1534 there were clear instructions relating to who should practice the art and who, a very few, need not:

> Item whether the kynges subjectes, not lame nor havynge no lawfull impedment, and beinge within the age of sixty yeres, except spirituall men, Justices, &c. and barons of the escheker, use shotyng in longe bowes, and have a bowe continually in his house, to use himself. And that fathers and governours of children teche them to shote, and that bowes and arrows be bought for children under seventeene and above seven yere, by hym that hath such a child in his howse, and the mayster may stoppe it ageyne of his wages, and after that age he to provide them hymselfe: and who that is founde in defaute, in not having bowes and arrows, by the space of a moneth, to forfait twelve pence.[7]

This legislation is a repetition of a 1512 Act and is perhaps the best-known injunction to fathers and 'governors' for the practising and teaching of archery. The skill of the archer was passed from father to son, in the same way that religious observance or a craft skill would be passed down. Latimer described how he himself was taught:

> In my tyme, my poore father was as diligent to teach me to shute, as to learn any other thynge; and so I think did other menne dyd thyr children. He taught me how to draw, howe to lay my bodye in my Bowe, and not to drawe with strength of armes, as other nacions do, but with strength of bodye. I had my Bowes brought me according to my age and strength, as I increased in them so my Bowes were made bigger and bigger, for men shall never shute well, except they be brought up in it.[8]

---

5   Roger Ascham, *Toxophilus: The School of Schooting* (Manchester: The Simon Archery Foundation, 1985), p.39.
6   Hodgkin, *The Archer's Craft*, p.54.
7   Anon., *The Boke For A Justyce of Peace* (London, 1534), p.33.
8   Hodgkin, *The Archer's Craft*, p.54.

These are wise words still relevant today in the present author's experience, when teaching young people. Roger Ascham records a more homely and touching episode, that highlighted the importance of adult supervision and encouragement, in a reminiscence of his own patron Sir Humphrey Wingfield:

> This worshipful man hathe ever loved and used to have many children brought up in learninge in his house, amongst whom I myself was one. For whom at terme time he would bring down from London both bowe and shaftes, and when they should playe, he would go with the himselfe into the fielde, and see them shoote, and he that shotte fairest, should have the best bowe and shaftes, and he that shotte ill favouredly, should be mocked of his fellows, til he shot better.[9]

The government specifically made 'fathers and governors' responsible for providing both the equipment and the necessary coaching in the demanding skill. Archery was socially inclusive and encouraged the participation of both young and old. It formed a bond that tied society together. The central role of archery in the lives of the English was noted by Giovanni Michiel of the Venetian Embassy. He reported in 1557 that:

> But above all, their proper and natural weapons are the bow and arrow, of which so great is the number, owing to the general use made of them by all sorts of persons, without distinction of grade, age, or profession, that it exceeds all belief … and such is their opinion of archery and their esteem for it, that they doubtless prefer it to all sorts of arms, and to harquebuses, in which they trust less, feeling more sure of their bows and arrows; contrary, however, to the judgment of the captains and soldiers of other nations. They draw the bow with such force and dexterity at the same time, that some are said to pierce corslets and body-armour; and there are few among them, even those that are moderately practised, who will not undertake at a convenient distance, either aiming point-blank, or in the air (as they generally do, that the arrow may fly farther), to hit within an inch and a half of the mark.[10]

One may question the degree of precision that was achieved but not the clear enthusiasm for the bow shared by all. It is also worth noting that the Venetians continued to include bows in the equipment of the warships well into the seventeenth century.

England and the Gun

The encouragement of archery and the discouragement of 'glossing, and horing' were opposite sides of the same coin, but accompanying this was an active discouragement of the general use of firearms. In England there

---

9   Ascham, *Toxophilus*, p.135.
10   *CSP Venice*, no. 13. 1557 MS. penes me.

was systematic legislation passed in the reign of Henry VIII in 1515, 1524 and 1542. On each occasion, possession of firearms was limited to the wealthy, the final legislation making it clear why only those with an income of £100 per annum should possess such weapons. For the Act asserted that crossbows, handguns and the little arquebus had been responsible for murders, robberies, felonies, riots and routs which had imperilled the King's subjects; whereas the longbow was the legitimate weapon of all honest Englishmen, the firearm was the tool of the criminal. The dangers posed by the careless use of firearms also led to a statute issued in Westminster in 1540, limiting the use of handguns and chastising arquebusiers for discharging their weapons:

> in cities, boroughs and towns, and other unmeet places, without having any regard or respect where their pellets do fall … whereby sundry his grace's officers and subjects, being in the high way, in the open street, or in their own houses, chambers or gardens, have been put in great jeopardy of their lives.[11]

England was not the only country where firearms in the hands of the general population was something to be feared. In 1517 Emperor Maximilian I banned the manufacture of wheel lock guns and in 1523 the City of Ferrara banned the carrying of such weapons. The wheel lock was deemed especially odious, as unlike the matchlock which required a smelly and very hot match cord to be kept lit, the wheel lock could be concealed and fired instantly and without further preparation. It was therefore the ideal weapon for the assassin or criminal. In 1542 the Venetian authorities objected to any weapon small enough to be hidden in a sleeve.

In similar legislation in England in 1537, all handguns had to have a stock of at least two and a half feet in length, making them difficult to conceal. Even in 1572 the possession of pistols was prohibited except for gentlemen and their servants, and then they were to be carried openly on their saddle bow of their horses for their public protection. Guns were purchased in large numbers for military service as we shall see but they did not need to be in the houses and hands of the people. Training to use a firearm took little time and they did not have to be readily available for that purpose, unlike the bow which requires constant practise. Guns were considered socially dangerous and were never perceived as possessing the legitimacy and moral value that the bow had in the hands of the sturdy English yeoman.

The European Perspective

It is important to consider the pattern of European employment of weapons, against which Tudor practice is often compared and condemned. In Europe, although the longbow was widely used and employed, it was never exploited

---

11 P.L. Hughes and J. Larkin (eds), Tudor Royal Proclamations (New Haven: Yale University Press, 1964), 1:194. From Gervase Phillips, 'Longbow and Hackbutt', p.584.

Detail of a crossbowman from the painting *The Martyrdom of Saint Sebastian* by Hans Holbein the elder, *c.*1516. The crossbow is a frighteningly powerful and accurate weapon. This short-stocked example has a steel prod or bow and is spanned using a German cranequin. One example of a contemporary cranequin provided a mechanical advantage of 145:1, enabling a 1,092 lb draw weight prod to be spanned easily. The cranequin allowed for a short stock, which permitted the use of this design of crossbow from horseback. The crossbow was not as subject to the weather or liable to misfire as an arquebus and would take about the same time to load. The steel prod and cranequin were however more expensive to produce. The crossbowman is holding a bolt between his teeth, a posture the present author often finds himself in when using these weapons. Clearly Holbein had observed crossbowmen in action.

as the principal provider of missile power. The crossbow was preferred for its range, accuracy and penetrative power, which by the end of the sixteenth century clearly could match or exceed even the most powerful longbow.

The crossbow was an expensive and sophisticated weapon, especially when using a windlass or cranequin to load, and with a steel prod (bow or lath) slow to load. It will take about 45 seconds when using a windlass, although quicker with a gaffle or goats-foot lever. It was suited to the siege rather than the field. The firearms of the early fifteenth century were similar in their slow rate of fire; the present author's Tannenberg handgonne takes about 45 seconds to load, but it would have been cheaper to make and superior in armour penetration to a crossbow. It was relatively easy to first supplement and then replace the crossbow, without significant changes to tactics. The famed Genoese crossbowman could be re-equipped with the handgun without disturbing the social order or altering his role or tactics. Both were urban weapons, slow in reloading and best used behind some form of protection.

Small arms appeared in quite large numbers in the early fifteenth century. Although employed in increasing numbers it was not until the early decades of the sixteenth century that they were recognised as superior to the crossbow. In 1411 John the Fearless, Duke of Burgundy, had some 4,000 handgunners in his service; in 1430 in Nuremburg, a centre of firearm production, handguns almost gained numerical parity with crossbows in the City council's inventory of weapons. Even so, crossbows were still used in large numbers in the sixteenth century. The sculptural celebration of the Battle of Marignano 1515 shows French crossbows being used and not arquebuses. Blaise de Monluc began his illustrious career in 1523 with an infantry company which was exclusively equipped with crossbows and he retained a loathing for the arquebus to the end of his life. It was only with the slaughter of the French gendarmes, by pike- and arquebus-wielding infantry in 1525 at Pavia, that the superiority of the firearm became generally acknowledged. As late as 1570 a Spanish army to be raised in Aragon of 32,724 soldiers, one in 10 was still to be equipped with the crossbow although two thirds had firearms and the remainder the pike.[12] In Venice the crossbow was replaced by the arquebus in 1518 on land but the bow remained as part of the armament of galleys. Its reliability in wet weather and rate of fire were particularly valued. In 1617 the Venetian Senate complained about the continuing use of bows which they, but not their sea captains saw as obsolete and superfluous.

The gun replaced the crossbow because it had better armour piercing qualities, it was easier to use, it was cheaper to manufacture, and above all it was better suited to pike warfare as the weapon itself was far handier in a close formation than the crossbow. In addition, the gun gradually replaced the crossbow, not because it was so different to the crossbow but because it was so similar.

The Performance of Bow and Gun

There is a broad historical debate that rests very much on the perceived performance of longbow and firearms. Michael Roberts In his 1955 Belfast lecture which began the current 'military revolution' debate, suggested that 'on the battlefield firearms represented a big step backward.'[13] He argued that, 'by a curious paradox, the coming of the hand-gun brought a steep decline in firepower: the superiority of the longbow in speed, accuracy and mobility were so marked that even in the late seventeenth century, military writers were pleading for its reintroduction.'[14] David Eltis, in his recent reappraisal of the Roberts thesis, argues conversely that the introduction of the firearm actually increased the firepower of an army. This was probably true if the arquebus replaced the crossbow, but in comparison to the bow it was woefully inadequate.

David Eltis asserts that: 'The weakness of the crossbow and even more of the longbow lay in their inability to perforate plate armour,'[15] but he does not help his case by citing a bow with a draw weight of 50 pounds, the sort of bow that a sturdy adolescent girl can handle and perhaps half of the average figure for a war bow. The *Mary Rose* bows varied in draw weight from 65–180 lb. David Eltis also claims a much greater armour piercing capability for firearms: 'The arquebus and later the musket changed all that. Able to penetrate even the best plate armour they dramatically increased the firepower of the infantryman.'[16]

The firearm shooting a lead ball would always achieve a much higher velocity from its projectile than that produced by the bow. Armour penetration by early modern firearms has been tested using original weapons from the collection held in the Landzeughaus Graz. The 123 joules of energy achieved

---

12   Lorraine White, 'The Experience of Spain's Early Modern Soldiers', p.8.
13   Michael Roberts, *The Military Revolution, 1560–1660: an Inaugural Lecture Delivered Before the Queen's University of Belfast* (Belfast: Queen's University of Belfast, 1955), p.5.
14   Geoffrey Parker, *The Military Revolution: Military Innovation & the Rise of the West, 1500–1800* (Cambridge: Cambridge University Press, 1996), p.7.
15   David Eltis, *The Military Revolution in Sixteenth Century Europe* (London: I.B. Tauris, 1998), p.11.
16   Eltis, *The Military Revolution*, p.13.

by the bow is a small fraction of the energy produced by the firearms used in the trials. The muzzle velocities of the guns averaged 452 metres per second, almost nine times as fast, and the energy produced was between eight and 57 times greater.

Table 5. Muzzle Energy Figures from the Graz Trials[17]

Doppelhaken G 358	6,980J
Wheellock RG 33	3,125J
Wheellock RG 117	988J

Even with soft lead balls these velocities could achieve penetration of at least two millimetres of steel plate at short range (30 m). These figures show clearly the advantage that guns had over bows. The *Mary Rose* reconstruction of an arquebus with a 12.7 mm ball and a 5.8 g charge achieved a velocity of 520 metres per second and easily penetrated four millimetres of steel plate, at short range.[18] Another *Mary Rose*-style arquebus with a 15.6 mm ball and a 3.2 g charge achieved an average muzzle velocity of 180 metres per second (an exceptionally low figure).[19]

Shooting at fixed plates of modern steel is one means of establishing the capability of early modern weapons, but a far better test is to use contemporary armour. The Styrian State Armoury in Graz has a unique and extraordinary collection of armour and was prepared to use some examples for what have proved to be definitive trials. In these experiments, a musket was fired at a breastplate manufactured in Augsburg in about 1570, made of cold-worked mild steel of 2.8–3.0 mm. The weapon was fired at the very short range of eight and a half metres and penetrated the armour, potentially causing a serious wound. However, the inherent inefficiency of a spherical projectile had implications for longer-range shooting. Approximately half its kinetic energy was lost after 100 metres of flight, this would make the penetration of a three millimetre breastplate at anything over 100 metres by a musket firing a 27 g ball an unlikely feat.

What was especially significant was that when fired against a piece of contemporary armour the results were far poorer than when fired against a fixed flat plate. The careful shaping of contemporary armour would provide much better protection than a simple assessment of thickness would suggest. In the opinion of the authors of the Graz study: 'Good-quality body armour would offer significant protection to anyone who could afford it.'[20] Hall in

---

17　RG 33 was made in Augsburg *c.*1595, and RG 117 was manufactured in Suhl in 1593. They were the equivalent of a light and a heavy arquebus. G 358 was a 'doppelhacken', a heavy or 'Spanish' musket made in Styria in the 1580s. There were unfortunately no earlier weapons available for testing.

18　Alexzandra Hildred, *Weapons of Warre: the armaments of the Mary Rose*, vol. 3 (Exeter: Short Run Press Ltd, 2011), p.553.

19　Thom Richardson, 'Ballistic Testing of Historical Weapons', in *Royal Armouries Yearbook*, vol. 3 (1998), pp.50–51.

20　P. Krenn, P. Kalaus, B. Hall (1995). 'Material Culture and Military History: Test-Firing Early Modern Small Arms', in *Material Culture Review*, 42(1), 1995. Available online, see bibliography..

his analysis of the trials concluded that: 'Unlike modern small arms, early modern weapons have a very shallow zone generally measuring 100–120 metres in which gunfire is likely to be lethal to the target.'[21] He continues that in the sixteenth century, 'when the opposing forces wore some sort of body armour [this] might reduce the zone of lethal fire to as little as 25–30 metres.'[22] Bert Hall acknowledged the danger posed by early firearms, but concluded that 'it was possible to purchase body armour that offered a reasonable degree of protection from most, if not all, gunshot wounds.'[23] Munition armour undoubtedly fell below the standard of the armour tested at Graz: German steel was identified as being of outstanding quality. The Marquis of Winchester ordered his officers not to buy English armour but arranged for a contract with a Hamburg merchant. Sir Henry Lee's conclusion based upon his experience is therefore not surprising, he considered that in future: 'the worlde … is lykelye to use more [armour] hereafter than in tyme past.'[24]

The armour penetration capability of the long bow has been the subject of much, often ill-informed, debate. The long bodkin point could certainly penetrate mail at almost any distance but penetration of plate armour was quite another matter. In an appendix to the book *Longbow* by Robert Hardy, Peter Jones considers in some detail the penetrative qualities of a bodkin point against 1.5 mm of mild-steel sheet. Penetration is all of course dependent on the thickness and hardness of the armour and the angle of strike of the arrow, its energy and the design of the head. Penetration was achieved at up to 45 degrees, partial penetration at 60 degrees accompanied by fracturing of the tip, while the arrow ricocheted at 70 degrees and above. It seems probable that thin plate could be penetrated at 50 yards. Whether this would cause a significant injury is another issue. Recent trials using a good war bow archer and bow, representative arrows and a breastplate from the era of Agincourt, proved that the armour was excellent protection.[25] In addition, armour was invariably worn over padded protection of some sort and 'soft' armour consisting of multiple layers of fabric was commonly used.

Turning from modern experiments to actual practice, the record of the bow is undoubtedly a mixed one. At Flodden, long-range arrow shooting was clearly little more than an annoyance to those in full armour at the forefront of the battle line, who 'abode the most dangerous shot of arrowes, which sore them noyed, and yet [unless] it hit them in some bare place it dyd them no hurt'.[26] On the other hand its use against the unarmoured Highlanders proved most effective. In France in the same year Hall recorded that outside Thérouanne, 'the Frenchmen issued out of the toun and skirmished with the Englishemen, but the archers shot so fast that they drove the Frenchmen

21 Bert S. Hall, *Weapons and Warfare in Renaissance Europe* (Baltimore: The Johns Hopkins University Press, 1997), p.138.
22 Hall, *Weapons and Warfare*, p.138.
23 Hall, *Weapons and Warfare*, p.147.
24 Hall, *Weapons and Warfare*, p.147.
25 Available as an online video, 'ARROWS vs ARMOUR – Medieval Myth Busting'. See bibliography for URL.
26 Hall, *Chronicle*, p.562.

into the citie, and slew and tooke diverse of them'.[27] An English participant in the siege, an anonymous steward from Lydingetone, wrote about the use of arquebuses and bows that put the French to flight: 'but our hagbussheres and archeres shoyte so holy to gether that thei made them of the towen to go backe and so persued them to the gates of bullayne and slue and toke dyueres pesantes of the ffrencemen at the wyche Skyrmesse was slayen of our men hagbussheres iii'.[28] The use of arquebus and bow together seems to have combined the strengths of both weapons.

Blaise de Monluc who faced English archery at Boulogne was somewhat contemptuous of the longbow: 'They [the English] all carried arms of little reach and therefore were necessitated to come up close to us to loose their arrows, which otherwise would do no execution',[29] which suggests that at the very least they could cause casualties at short range. The tactic employed by the archers was to approach the French pikemen at a trot, running on until two or three pike lengths from their target and then loosing a 'cloud' of arrows, before rapidly retreating in the face of a counter-attack.[30] It is worth noting that in the camisade on Boulogne the French were driven out by English archers and whereas the heavy downpour negated the French arquebusiers, it had no effect on the longbows. Furthermore, the French leader of the attack was wounded by an arrow, and Monluc had three arrows shot into his target and one shot through his mail sleeve.

Sir John Smythe, reporting on the basis of eyewitness testimony from the 1549 rebellions, asserted the value of the longbow in clashes with arquebusiers and mercenaries.

> And whereas the Duke [of Somerset] at his first assembling and forming of his Armie, had chaunged many Archers into Harquebuziers (because he had no opinion of the Long Bowe) he after that victorie [Dussindale] and suppression of the Rebels, upon the experience that he in those actions had of the daunger and the terror of arrowes, (his own horse being wounded under him at the battaile with three or foure arrowes, whereof he died) did both then & many times after openlie protest his error before Count *Malatesta Baglion* (an auncient and noble soldier Italian) and other great Captaines *Italians* and *Almans*, saying, that from that time forward he would hold the Bowe to be the onelie weapon of the World, and so did all the notable Captaines both English and strangers affirme the same. And this I have set downe almost *verbatim*, from the report of the aforesaid *Ambrose* Earle of *Warwicke* that now is, who was present at that action and had his horse also wounded under him with two or three arrowes.[31]

27 Hall, *Chronicle* (London, 1904), vol. 1, p.62.
28 W.A.J. Archbold, 'A Diary of the Expedicion of 1544', *The English Historical Review*, vol. 16, no. 63 (July 1901), p.504.
29 Monluc, *The Habsburg–Valois Wars*, p.129.
30 Monluc, *The Habsburg–Valois Wars*, pp.129–30.
31 Sir John Smythe, *Certain discourses … Concerning the force and effects of divers sorts of weapons 1590*, reprinted in *Bow versus Gun* (East Ardsley, Wakefield: E.P. Publishing Ltd, 1973), unpaginated.

Smythe reports further that mercenary captains facing the Prayer Book rebels were similarly discomforted and impressed.

French light horse, during an ambush of an English convoy making its way to Montreuil in 1544, came off decidedly worse when facing English arrows. They had been led on to attack by the English light horse that had feigned flight:

> so as to lead the French within range of the bows and hand-guns which the English host let fly as soon as they saw the French, who, as soon as they heard the sound of arrows flying like a shower of snow, crippling some horses and killing others, turned their horses heads towards the side of a hill and a large stream to the west of the place where the host and the baggage train were standing.[32]

In practice the longbow appears to have been a successful weapon as long as it did not face very well-armoured opponents.

Accuracy of Firearms

If the impact of firearms was as impressive as discovered in the Graz trials, their accuracy was not. With ill-bored barrels, uncertain ignition, ill-fitting balls, poor powder, and careless loading it is surprising that even the one round in 500 that was fired would hit its target, as suggested by Moritz Thierbach.[33] He concluded from his research in 1886 on eighteenth-century musketry, that: 'One could assume on average that only one bullet in 500 struck home,'[34] and this on a battlefield with mass formations firing at close range to each other.

The Graz trials used a wide range of weapons covering 1571–1750 and discovered no discernible improvement in performance across this period. Charles Carlton in his analysis of the effectiveness of firearms in the English Civil War drew some sobering conclusions:

> One estimate for musket fire assumes a 10–15 per cent chance of a hit at 100 yards, and at that range envisages no more than one man in 15 being hit. [This is] assuming an equal number of men on both sides, a 50:50 ratio of musketeers to pikemen, and a 33% misfire rate from each round of volley fire. With an equal number of men on both sides Carlton envisages the same number of men on each side being hit.[35]

Sir Henry Radecliff in his inspection of the hundred strong Portsmouth garrison in 1571, found their preparedness and marksmanship poor. He reported that they were 'untrained and unredi, for amonghtes three and

---

32 Davies, *Enterprises*, p.27.
33 Hall, *Chronicle*, pp.138–9.
34 Hall, *Chronicle*, p.139.
35 Charles Carlton, *Going to the Wars: The Experience of the British Civil Wars 1638–1651* (London: Routledge, 1994), p.134, in White, 'Combat, Welfare and Violence', p.18.

twenty which were alowed serviceable, not fyve of them shott within fyve foot of a marke being sett within four score yards of them'. At that distance a good archer may still be expected to hit a man-sized target. Sir John Smythe, drawing from his own experience, recorded that:

> When horses and men that have been in three or foure skirmishes, do see that they receive no hurt neither by the fire, smoke, nor noise, and that in manie thousands of Harquebuze and mosquuet shot, there are not twentie en slaine nor hurt; they grow after to be farre lesse in doubt of those weapons of fire, than of Piques, Halberds, Launces & swords … Howbeit the volees of Archers arrowes flying together in the ayre as thick as haile, do not only terrifie and amaze in most terrible sort the eares, eyes and harts of both horses and men.[36]

The precision achievable, or lack thereof, of the arquebus was highlighted by the size of the target that was thought suitable for its use. In Northamptonshire, instructions for the range needed for the training of arquebusiers (1586) was quite explicit:

> That for every corporall [commanding 25 men] theyr maye be a butt: of xxtie [20] foote broade and sixteene foote highe erected in some convenient place remote from the highe waye or other common frequented place and in the middest therof to sett a rundell [roundel] of horde [planks] of a yard and a halfe [4.5 feet] broade with certaine blacke rundells and a white in the middest against which the soldior is to level his peece for his better ayme and reddye discha[r]ginge.[37]

The distance from the target was to be when the arquebus was 'level', that is when the point of impact of the ball was the same as the point of aim, that is without any ballistic drop. As it was described by contemporary experts: 'Any peece is saide to lye *Pointe blanke* with any marke, when the Axis of her Soule [that is, bore] directeth perfectly to the very middel or Center of that marke.'[38] This would only be possible at short range, as was explained by Sir John Smythe: 'a skillfull soldiour with a good harquebuze or with a currier may from a steadye rest discharge his piece from sighte pointe, at blanke or obiecte marke above 30 or 40 paces distant'.[39] He does go on to suggest that the 'skillfull soldiour' would 'hit the said blanke being not above the bredthe of a Dollar, with great contentment and perfection of hittinge so small a marke'.[40] A Utrechtse Leicester-rijksdaalder of 1596 has a diameter of 1.7 inches.[41] This degree of accuracy at approximately 30 yards is comparable to what a trained

---

36 Smythe, *Certain Discourses*, unnumbered.
37 Hale, *Renaissance War Studies*, p.423; J. Wake, ed, *Papers relating to musters … in the country of Northampton, 1586–1623* (Kettering: Northamptonshire Record Society, 1926), p.7.
38 Hale, *Renaissance War Studies*, p.424; Leonard and Thomas Digges, *A Geometricall Practise, Named Pantometria*, 2nd (extended) edition (1591), p.177.
39 Hale, *Renaissance War Studies*, p.425; Sir John Smythe, *An Answer to Contrary Opinions Military* (British Museum, Harl. MS 135, f.19; the date is probably 1591)
40 Hale, *Renaissance War Studies*, p.425. Sir John Smythe, *An Answer to Contrary Opinions Military* (British Museum, MS. Harleian 135, f.19; the date is probably 1591)
41 Examples can be viewed online – see bibliography for URL.

soldier can achieve with a modern high-velocity rifle. A modern expert marksman using a reproduction late eighteenth-century musket achieved a rectangular 'group' of five shots of 15.2 inches by 25.5 inches at 82 yards, which would equate to a group size of 6.2 inches by 10.4 inches at 100 feet, rather more than the 1.7 inches claimed by Smythe.[42] The present author does not believe the claims of Sir John for the precision of the arquebus any more than those made by the Venetian Ambassador for the bow.

Whilst the maximum range of a musket against an unarmoured target might have been 600 yards, as Sir Humfrey Barwick averred, Sir John Smythe recommended an engagement range against cavalry of: 'eight, tenne or twelve paces ... and in that sort they may work verie good effect.'[43] Such a short range was not unusual. During the English Civil war, Colonel Anthony Thelwall's Royalists opened fire at a pike's length[44] at the Second Battle of Newbury, while at Cheriton the Royalist musketeers extended their range to two.[45] François La Noue in his contemporary military textbook considered the optimum range of the reiter's pistol to be only three paces, or just outside the reach of a pike.[46]

One of the reasons for this miserable performance had little to do with the competence of the soldier. For ease of loading lead balls were hardly ever tightly fitting, although providing a greased patch around the ball would help. As the ball travels down the barrel it bounces from one side to the other, the larger the windage or gap between the shot and the barrel, the greater the bounce and the induced spin. This results in differentials in pressure around the ball which then operates like an aerofoil, in what is known as the Magnus effect, best exemplified by the sliced golf ball. So great is the effect that in a trial where a musket barrel was bent four degrees to the left, the ball after 100 yards had travelled not 17 feet to the left but 22 feet to the right! The effect is most pronounced with light projectiles; artillery, especially when a small windage is permitted, was far less affected.

The Performance of the Bow

It is almost impossible to determine the accuracy of the English war bow, although as we have seen, the Venetian ambassador suggested a phenomenal degree of precision. James Raymond in his study *Henry VIII's Military Revolution* said that: 'An archer could confidently expect to hit a single man at a range of 180 to 220 yards, and was expected capable of releasing as many as six arrows per minute.'[47] Modern war bow archers cannot achieve that

---

42 The trial is available as a video online, 'Practical accuracy of an original military flintlock rifle vs the musket', see bibliography for URL.

43 Smythe, *Certain Discourses*.

44 B. Hall, *Weapons and Warfare*, p.195.

45 Stuart Peachey, *The Mechanics of Infantry Combat in the First English Civil War* (Bristol: Stuart Press, 1992)

46 B. Hall, *Weapons and Warfare*, p.193.

47 James Raymond, *Henry VIII's Military Revolution – The Armies of Sixteenth-Century Britain and Europe* (London: Tauris Academic Studies, 2007), p.51.

accuracy but many would match the rate of shooting. Accuracy is dependent upon three factors, the weapon, its ammunition and the person using it. In the case of the weapon, bows of yew and wych elm, are of course subject to the vagaries of temperature and humidity, as well as those of age. It is not a consistent performer. The bow was the product of a craftsman and not a production line, and like bows and bowyers today they have their individual character. The 'sheaf' arrow, mass-produced from poplar or ash, fletched with goose feather and with hand-forged arrowheads was a magnificent if imprecise missile.

If the main material components were not consistent, the third component, the archer, is an even more imponderable quantity. Ascham, writing in 1544, was highly critical of the various 'styles' employed by his fellow archers, weaknesses that would not enable them to 'shoting straight and keeping of a length':[48]

> Some men draw too far, some draw too short, some too slowly, some too quickly; some hold over-long, some let go over-soon. Some stamp forward, some leap backward. All these faults being either in the drawing, or at the loose; with many other mo[re], which you may easily perceive, and so go about to avoid them.[49]

The same faults or habits can still be seen among longbow archers these days.

Evidence for the accuracy of longbows comes from various sources. Unfortunately, few are reliable. Pictorial sources invariably lack realistic perspective, or if they are accurate then the archers in the Luttrell Psalter could not hit a barn door at 50 paces! Where there are realistic representations of archery ranges they are about 30 or 40 yards in length, although usually depicted with crossbows being used. The one Flemish illustration of a longbow practise, in the midst of a village street scene, *The Fair at Hoboken*, has the targets placed about 30 yards apart. The targets appear not dissimilar in size to those used today by archers at this range: roundels of 60–80 cm in diameter.

There is a tremendous irony that the best account of medieval target archery is from France. The *Tir au Bersault* was an archery practice established in France in the late Middle Ages and still shot today. It was designed to encourage the *Francs Archers* to match the achievements of their English counterparts. The grounds, practise and target were very well defined. The range was 50 yards and the target was 48 cm in diameter, possibly meant to represent the chest of a man. The bull was 14.5 cm in diameter with an inner bull of 4.2 cm. My conclusion is that if a medieval war bow archer could hit a man in the face at 20 yards and the chest at 50, he could, at 100 yards, seriously discomfort an individual.

The potential accuracy of the crossbow was impressive. In a shooting competition held in Bavaria in 1467 the target was 12 inches in diameter, the

48 Ascham, *Toxophilus*, p.87.
49 Ascham, *Toxophilus*, p.142.

distance 260 feet. In another competition the target was less than half of that but probably at a shorter distance, some targets were placed at about 30 yards, when the normal distance for competitions was between 80 and 100 yards. This would suggest that the crossbow was rather more accurate than the war bow in the hands of a capable arbalastier. Both were far more accurate than any contemporary firearm.

An accurate assessment of the performance of the war bow has been determined recently using beautifully made recreations of the bow, arrow and string. The wonderful collection of archery equipment from the *Mary Rose* has proved invaluable in inspiring bowyers, fletchers and archers to reproduce the equipment and assess its performance. The members of the English War Bow Society have been in the forefront of this work and the results have been both illuminating and impressive. The numbers of bows and draw weights investigated by the Mary Rose Trust are 12 of 65–80 lb, 11 of 90 lb, 24 of 100–140 lb and 1 of 160 lb.[50] The *Mary Rose* bow number 4 (a close approximation to the original) achieved velocities from 55–64 m/s and ranges from 226–244 m with a variety of representative arrows. The Oregon yew used for the bow had far fewer growth rings than the *Mary Rose* bows, which would suggest that a heavier draw weight would have been achieved with the original high alpine yew bows, although recent practical tests by Joe Gibbs suggest that this might not be the case:[51] in recent trials Gibbs, using a 160 lb (at a draw length of 30 inches) bow of Italian yew, achieved a velocity of 55.3 m/sec at 10 metres.[52] With an arrow weighing 80 g fitted with a case-hardened arrowhead (25 g) it produced 123 joules of energy; at 25 metres the velocity was 52.1m/sec producing 109 joules. The impact of the arrow would in itself be enough to knock a man over.

Engagement Range

One of the critical issues that is hardly ever discussed is the effective engagement range of a missile weapon. This is an important issue which needs to take into consideration several key factors. These are the range at which the chosen target can be hit with any certainty, the rate of reloading and the speed at which the enemy force is advancing. If we consider that the target for missile weapons in the line of battle will be either a pike block or the equivalent cavalry formation, rather than an individual, then the importance of precision declines. Based upon the present author's experience when facing a large formation, it is difficult to identify an individual target in a group of similarly dressed and equipped troops; aiming at a large flag or the most ostentatiously dressed individual is the likely point of aim.

The speed with which a weapon can be reloaded is a critical factor. Based upon the present author's personal observation, experience and conversation with Mark Stretton, a war bow archer and founder of the English War Bow

---

50   Hildred, *Weapons of Warre*, p.617.
51   Joe Gibbs, 'Speed test of *Mary Rose* replica bows', online video, see bibiography for URL.
52   Video, 'ARROWS vs ARMOUR – Medieval Myth Busting', see bibliography for URL.

Society, a heavy bow can be shot six to eight times in one minute. It is generally agreed from both contemporary opinion and current practice that a matchlock arquebus can be loaded in approximately 40 seconds and fire three rounds in two minutes. The evidence from the *Mary Rose* arquebuses and similar weapons is that they used a snap matchlock. The spring-powered serpentine was released using a trigger or button. In other matchlocks, the spring resists the movement of the trigger holding the serpentine away from the pan. Both serpentines use a match cord to ignite the priming powder in the pan.

Using the conclusions drawn by the Graz tests, the work of Bert Hall and numerous experiments using smoothbore weapons, the effective range of an arquebus would be at most 100 metres (109 yards); the range at which English archers were trained and expected to shoot is a 'bowshot' of one eighth of a mile or 220 yards.

The rate at which an enemy could advance towards your formation is dependent upon many factors: determination and discipline, the condition of the ground and the slope, whether rising or falling are all important, as was apparent at Flodden and Pinkie. If we assume flat and good ground, then we may also rely upon some later but still relevant data. British Napoleonic infantry marched at 75 paces or 57 metres (62 yards) per minute, unless deploying into different formations. If we assume that close formations of infantry in the earlier period would advance at no better rate, then if you were to open fire at 100 yards then the enemy would cover the ground in front of you in one and a half minutes, allowing your arquebusiers to fire at most three rounds. If you wished to maximise the damage to the enemy, then it would make sense to delay the final volley to the last possible moment, which would mean opening fire with one round at 100 metres (109 yards) and the second at perhaps 15 metres (16.5 yards). Whereas archers could engage a target at 220 yards and in the three and a half minutes taken by the enemy cover the ground, shoot almost a sheaf of 24 arrows.

Again, relying on Napoleonic statistics, a cavalry gallop was conducted at 18 kilometres an hour or five metres per second (which is a similar to the speed these days achieved by horses in cross-country competitions across the sport).[53] Thus the 200-yard gallop would be completed in 40 seconds; if the arquebusiers fired at extreme range they may just have reloaded in time as long as they kept their nerve. It would make far more sense for them to wait and fire only when they saw the whites of the horses' eyes! Archers on the other hand could still have usefully sent perhaps four or even six arrows into the galloping host and a horse makes a very large target. If shooting at an individual target, then as mark Stretton has demonstrated, the rate would be much lower. Fire control would have been vital for the effective use of the arquebus, as would be the ability to reload instinctively while under considerable pressure. It is easy to see that these two weapons could be considered as being complementary on the battlefield, with the bow

---

53 'Ordonnance provisoire sur l'exercice e les manoeuvres de la cavallerie rédigée par order du ministre de la guerre du 1er Vendémiaire an XIII.'

producing a volume of fire over a longer range and the firearm providing penetrative power over a short one.

One final factor is the provision of ammunition. Powder was initially contained in large flasks or horns. The leather bandolier from which individual capped charges were strung appeared around 1500. The earliest extant example has only eight tinned-iron flasks and a match-hider. The best evidence for ammunition stocks for England comes from the fleet, where it is clear that resupply at sea would be impossible. Information in the Anthony Roll records that the *Mary Rose* carried only 20 lead shot for each of its 50 firearms. This is pretty much the case for the rest of the fleet, which averaged 20–25.[54] Lorraine White in her analysis of combat conducted by Spain in the sixteenth and seventeenth centuries also points to the small issue of powder and shot, which varied from 20 rounds per man to a mere handful.[55]

Such a paucity of shot, and the means of loading, would suggest that the rapid rate of fire necessary to win a firefight would have been not only discouraged but impossible. The archer would have been provided with a sheaf of 24 arrows with a further sheaf in reserve, not a generous supply, but one which was far more readily employed. Taking an arrow from the belt, nocking and loosing become instinctive after years of practise.

One factor that would dog the matchlock and later the flintlock was the rate of misfires. Misfires can be caused by many things: damp powder, poor match cord, failure to keep the pan clear of fouling and failing to clean the weapon. Lorraine White drew the following conclusion considering the rates suggested by historians:

> … the performance of muskets and arquebuses deteriorated and the rate of misfires increased as their barrels fouled up with combustion residues. Even with regular cleaning, misfires might average between one in eight and one in six; they increased to one in two as conditions deteriorated. In wet weather, as both the match and the gunpowder were affected, small arms could not be fired, and strong winds also impeded their use.[56]

The present author has a very low misfire rate from his 'lightly oiled' arquebus but that is when using modern powder and match in invariably ideal conditions. Contemporary match cord was made from flax or hemp, and in the Haddington garrison when besieged, the soldiers made cord from their linen shirts. This would have added to the problems of the poor arquebusier.

A reasonable conclusion would be that the firearms in the mid sixteenth century would have been very effective at short range at armoured targets, and at longer range at unarmoured targets. The longbow would be effective at a much longer range at unarmoured targets and at very short range at lightly armoured targets, and only if the archer achieved a lucky hit. Neither bow nor firearm could assure penetration of contemporary armour at

---

54 Hildred, *Weapons of Warre*, p.543.
55 White, 'Combat, Welfare and Violence', pp.11–12.
56 White, 'Combat, Welfare and Violence', p.17.

anything other than very short distances, certainly under 100 metres (109 yards). Bert Hall considers that the musket ball would unhorse an opponent at 100 metres, but not necessarily penetrate his armour. The conclusion of the Graz trials is simple and radical and that is that:

> The twin characteristics of musket fire … inaccuracy and lack of penetrating power … helps explain why the European battlefield saw a shift in the balance of power between traditional heavy cavalry (*gens d'armes*, 'knights in armour') and infantry only late in the 16th century, long after the introduction of muskets. Early guns simply were very ineffective weapons against properly armoured knights.[57]

Manufacture, Cost and Storage

Bows and arrows were manufactured and stored in very large quantities.[58] In 1523 there appear to have been over 16,000 sheaves of livery arrows and 4,000 sheaves of nine-inch fletched arrows in the Tower (480,000 in total), whilst at the end of Elizabeth's reign there were still 393,000 arrows (14,125 sheaves) held there.[59] Henry VIII's inventory of 1547 records the vast quantity of archery equipment in the King's army and navy: the ships of the fleet carried 3,441 bows and 5,191 sheaves of livery arrows (a sheaf contains 24 arrows). On land in the castles, armouries and bulwarks in England, France and Scotland were stored a further 15,072 bows and 50,260 sheaves. This would produce a total of 18,513 bows and 1,330,824 arrows, an investment of not only money but in the future utility of the bow.

Bows and arrows were stored in chests and strings in barrels; Anne Boleyn was buried in an elm arrow chest. Its use for this purpose does at least suggest that the chest was fairly deep. The four bow chests found in the *Mary Rose* were on average 2.235 m by .381 m by .357 m made of boards simply nailed together and fitted with rope handles.[60] Bows and shafts packed closely, and often in damp conditions, must have had a very limited storage life. In an armoury in Ireland in 1578, after only two years' storage most of the bows broke when drawn and strings and arrows had been badly affected by damp. There are numerous references to 'badde' or 'decaied' archery equipment, although equipment could be refurbished and returned to service. There is no evidence for a decline in the quality or quantity of archery equipment in this period, although the best-quality yew wood imported from the Alps was becoming scarcer and more expensive. Nor was there a significant decline in the numbers of archers able to handle the war bow. The bow and the archer were primarily a domestic product that could be relied upon.

---

57 P. Krenn, et al., 'Material Culture and Military History'.

58 J.P. Davies, ' "We do fynde in our countre great lack of bowes and arrows": Tudor military archery and the Inventory of King Henry VIII, in *Journal of the Society of Army Historical Research*, vol. 83, no. 333, Spring 2005.

59 John Waller in Fiorato, *Blood Red Roses*, p.134.

60 Hildred, *Weapons of Warre*, pp.641–642.

Firearms could, if properly cared for, be stored for an indefinite period for later use and used regularly for practise without being damaged. This care was not always apparent. In the example of the Irish armoury in 1578, after only two years' storage all the arquebuses were found to be unserviceable, whilst many of the calivers and muskets were badly rusted. The Earl of Essex, in correspondence with the Council, argued that privately held weapons were more likely to be maintained properly,[61] although for a rapidly developing bureaucratic system, the storage of guns that could be counted regularly and maintained if necessary was a great attraction. One arquebus which had been stored in the Tower after the Boulogne campaign (1544) was discovered to be still loaded in 1584 when it was being refurbished (at the cost of four shillings). The armourer, unable to unload the weapon conventionally, placed the dismounted breech in a fire and rested the muzzle against his thigh: the consequences were dire![62] It was not uncommon for old barrels to be re-stocked or fitted with new ignition systems, making the life of the present-day collector difficult. In the Graz Landzeughaus one expert has discovered that late Gothic barrels from 1490–1530 had been treated in such a manner for reuse in the 1630s, a testimony to the quality of the barrelmaker.[63]

One factor in the replacement of bows by guns was their costs. Good yew bows were increasingly difficult to procure and their cost reflected it.[64] In the previous century the cost of imported bow staves rose from £2 to £12 per hundred (from 5d to 2s 6d each). In 1566 the best foreign yew bows were priced at 6s 8d, and English at 2s. The cost of the bow was also regulated, so that in 1542 a bow suitable for a 14-year-old boy should cost no more than a shilling, still a not inconsiderable amount. The cost of the best bow was set at 3s 4d; a bow of the 'second sort' 2s 6d; a sheaf of livery arrows 2s; a gross of bowstrings 3s 4d; a leather case at 6d and a girdle at 2d. The total cost of two bows, spare strings and three or four sheaves of arrows could not have been less than 12 shillings. All these items were subject to wear and decay and could not be expected to survive prolonged storage or practise. The caliver cost from 6–8s: John de Castro sold 80 handguns with powder flasks at 6s each in 1513. Four stolen in 1573 from a church in Essex, together with powder flasks and touch-boxes (containers of fine powder for priming the pan) were valued at 13s 4d each. Thus, the cost of firearms was at least comparable and possibly less than the equipment needed for an archer; what is more, it had a much longer 'armoury life'.

61 Cruickshank, *Elizabeth's Army*, p.111.
62 William Clowes, *A profitable and necessarie Booke of observations for all those that are burned with gun-powder, &c. and also for the curing of wounds made with musket and caliver shot, and other weapons of warre* (London 1596)
63 Online forum discussion, 'Ca. 1520: One of the World's Oldest and Finest Matchlock Landsknecht Arquebuses', see bibliography for URL.
64 Cruickshank, *Elizabeth's Army*, p.104.

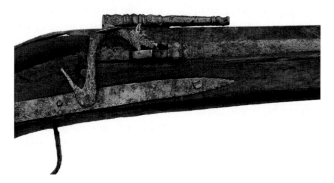

Snap matchlock manufactured in Gardone, Italy, c.1540. This weapon is very similar to those found on the *Mary Rose*. The stock is clearly designed to rest in the shoulder and the tube rear sight and blade foresight clearly expect the individual to demonstrate a degree of marksmanship. Ramrods were also provided, sometimes fitted with a wrought iron sleeve to which a scourer or worm could be attached for cleaning the bore or unloading a lead ball. The cock or serpentine is highly decorated, which is perhaps surprising for a mass-produced item. The pan cover is missing from this example. Dimensions: overall length 51.2 in (1.3 m), barrel length 38 in (974 mm), weight 7.7 lb (3.5 kg). (Courtesy of the Royal Armouries)

Manufacture

One of the problems facing those seeking to promote the adoption of the arquebus was the lack of a domestic manufacturing base. There was a King's handgun maker, one Alex Bandson, appointed in 1543 and Cornelius Johnson the King's smith provided 100 weapons for service in Ireland. The vast majority were purchased from the Continent, some from German but mostly from Italian merchants,[65] including Peter Corse of Florence, Leonardo Frescobaldi and Alexander della Fava. In 1513 Sigesmund Foyte was paid £99 for 260 handguns (at 6s each), nine great arquebuses (at 23s 4d) and six smaller arquebuses (at 15s). Peter Corsy was paid 9s each for 420 handguns with a bottle and mould. There was a massive royal purchase of 9,000 arquebuses in 1545 from Cristopher Carcano, an order that fell foul of Imperial officials and may only have been completed in 1546. The Emperor once assisted (although not personally) in a grand smuggling operation; as the Netherlands was ostensibly neutral, the weapons were brought through the city of Antwerp packed in barrels which should have been filled with sugar.

This number of weapons might seem excessive for a preindustrial world but the quantities and quality of the weapons produced using craft manufacturing were extraordinary. In the *Mary Rose* and the Royal Armouries collections are two very similar arquebuses, both barrels have a maker's crest with the letters GARDO. This indicates that they were made in Gardone, a city under Venetian control, some 11 miles from Brescia in the

65   O.F.G. Hogg, *The Royal Arsenal* (Oxford: Oxford University Press, 1963), p.37.

Trompia valley. In 1544 Captain Marino Cavalli reported that 'a mountain of guns are produced in Gardone, and they do it so easily that in two or three workshops they make 400 barrels a day.'[66] In 1562 it was reported by Paolo Paruta that from the Trompia valley, 'every year the said Valley produces XXV thousand guns that are fetched off by merchants into foreign lands.'[67] The arquebuses on the *Mary Rose* may well have been part of a contract agreed by the Doge of Venice in June 1544 to supply some 1,500 arquebuses to Henry. In addition to the guns themselves were the ancillary items: bullet moulds, flasks or horns for powder and pouches for bullets.

In the inventory of Henry's possessions in the Tower in 1547 there were 6,500 'Handgonnes complete',[68] as well as a further 475 of various types. There were 2,000 arquebuses held in the royal bulwarks, castles and armouries. There were 357 in store in Portsmouth, almost half of which were 'broken' and on the isle of Wight there were a further 218. Newcastle had a stock of some 200, some to be refurbished, and Blakeness Fort had 87. The remainder were distributed in very small numbers to 87 forts and bulwarks, with fewer than 1,000 between them. The navy disposed of but 99 in only seven warships. The vast majority of serviceable weapons were therefore held as part of a substantial national armoury.

Training

There are conflicting opinions and assumptions concerning the training in the bow and the gun. To train someone in the use of a matchlock musket takes a few minutes; to train someone to stand, load and shoot his weapon at the enemy, who one assumes would be shooting back, requires a very different sort of training. As Barwicke commented, training would be necessary to avoid the potential accidents that were so common: 'the fierie shot ... being not in the hands of the skilfull, may do unto themselves more hurt than good: wherefore the same is often to be practised, that men may grow perfect and skilfull therein.'[69] The 'shot', a term used to describe all those using the 'fierie weapon' at the time of the Armada, took six days to be trained. For the first three days 'false fire' would be used, that is only using powder to prime the pan. This was to train the embryonic marksmen to keep their eyes open: 'Without Winking, the courage thereof being once gained, he will soon shoot off his piece charge orderly Without Winking, and then he is half a good harquebussier.'[70] That this was the key skill needed for an arquebusier speaks volumes for the low expectations that officers had of their men and their equipment.

---

66 Hildred, *Weapons of Warre*, p.540.
67 Hildred, *Weapons of Warre*, p.540.
68 David Starkey, *The Inventory of King Henry VIII ... the transcript* (London: Harvey Miller Publishers, 1998) p.103.
69 Barret, *The Theorike and Practike*, p.3.
70 John Tincey, *Elizabeth's Army & the Armada* (Leigh-on-Sea: Partizan Press, 1988), p.16; British Library, Lansdown MSS 56 f.50.

To avoid the unpleasantness of firing from the shoulder it was not unusual to shoot from the hip while touching off the powder with the match cord, rather than placing it in the serpentine and using a trigger. This is to be seen in numerous contemporary illustrations. One of the best descriptions of poor weapon handling was of Spanish troops under training in 1568: they were unlikely to have been any better or worse than their English counterparts:

> To fire their arquebuses they charge them to the mouth [of the gun] with powder; they take hold of them half way along the barrel with their left hand and move their arm as far away as they can, to prevent the fire from touching them (as they are so afraid of it); and when they light it with the wick in their other hand they turn their face away, just like those who are waiting for the bloodletter to open a vein; and even when they fire they close their eyes and go pale, and shake like an old house.[71]

The loading procedure for a matchlock musket was not that complicated.

- Hold the arquebus in you left hand, at the point of balance, with the glowing slow match held there as well.
- Open the priming pan, fill it, close the cover and blow and shake off any loose powder.
- Cast the arquebus about and pour a charge of powder down the barrel followed by a ball, and ram down. Replace ramrod (a mistake often made was to shoot the ramrod towards the enemy, making the weapon useless).
- Place match in the jaws of the serpentine and adjust it so that it will touch the pan when depressed.
- Open the pan and operate the trigger (the trigger is never pulled).

The business is straightforward and logical. The crucial thing is to remember to keep your glowing match cord well separated from the powder during the loading procedure! In the late sixteenth century, the military reforms of Maurice and John of Nassau led to the production of formal drill manuals. The most famous was Jacob de Gheyn's *Manual for the exercise of Musket and Pike*, the *Wapenhandelinghe van Roers Musquetten ende Spiessen*, published by Robbert de Baudous in 1608 in Amsterdam. It contained 177 detailed illustrations, with 42 postures specifically for the musketeer.

That author has often wondered why it was felt necessary to analyse so minutely what is a very simple process, and one which should rely primarily on the common sense of the individual. This level of detailed training would be necessary if you assumed that the individual concerned had no experience, knowledge or perhaps interest in the business. It was also clearly a way of

---

71 White, 'Combat, Welfare and Violence', p.18; from E. de Salazar, *Carta al capitan Mon dragon*, BAE cxi i, p.289, cited by A. Rodriguez Sanchez, 'Guerra, Miseria y corrupcion en Extremadura, 1640–1668', in *Estudios dedicados a Carlos Callejo Serrano* (Caceres: Servicios culturales de la Excma: Diputacion Prov. de Caceres, 1979), p.607.

ensuring obedience to commands and focussing the mind of the soldier on the performance of his duty. This was important when he might otherwise have been considering the possibility of running away.

Lindsay Boynton has argued that:

> One of the reasons that firearms superseded bows, it is suggested, is that they could be mastered in a shorter time. Such an argument runs wholly counter to the growing professionalisation of military affairs [Elizabethan militia]. Training, in particular, was becoming ever more comprehensive and the specious argument that firearms required less, not more, training, bears all the marks of a propagandist's sophistry.[72]

The present author has taught archery and what used to be called 'musketry'. The principles and safe practise of both these weapons can be taught quite quickly, certainly in days. Considering the inaccuracy of the weapon and the cost of powder and shot, as long as the arquebusier could load and fire safely at a reasonable rate, that is all that would be expected. More training with such an inaccurate weapon would be pointless.

There is a vast difference between the use of a low draw weight longbow and a heavy draw weight war bow. The 'average' *Mary Rose* bow was 6 feet 5½ inches long, with a draw weight of 120–130 lb at 30 inches.[73] The physical effort required to shoot a war bow is very great, with a draw weight at least twice what is expected from today's strongest civilian archers. That does not mean it would have been beyond a male population brought up to its use, often engaging in hard manual work, as the bones of those found on the *Mary Rose* have demonstrated.

There is also a great difference between the style used by modern archers and war bow archers. Modern archery which has its origins in Victorian 'garden' archery, has concentrated on shooting for precision against a target, consisting of a series of concentric rings that can be scored, set at a fixed distance. A light draw weight bow provided with a light, thin arrow fitted with small fletchings, could achieve great accuracy. The string would be drawn to the side or front of the face to provide a fixed point to assist aiming, and the tip of the arrow then used to aim in the same way that the foresight of a rifle is used. Competition bows today can be fitted with mechanical sight systems, spirit levels, stabilisers, clickers and all sorts of worthless gewgaws that devalue the true art of archery.

The war bow uses a very different style. The string is drawn to the ear or even lower to the collar bone and aiming is instinctive, in the same way that throwing a stone is instinctive. The extra draw length produces a higher velocity, as the string pushes the arrow over a longer distance. It is possible to draw a heavier bow than one might expect, as the shoulder rotates and finds rest in a comfortable position rather than being held next to the face. It is a very efficient style that works with the archer's anatomy. It is a technique

---

72 Lindsay Boynton, *The Elizabethan Militia* (London: Routledge & Kegan Paul, 1967), p.113.
73 Hildred, *Weapons of Warre*, p.629.

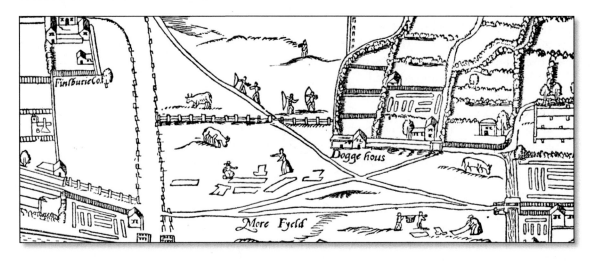

Archery practice at Moor fields from the Agas map. Although clearly a danger to washerwomen and livestock, archery was enthusiastically pursued on the edge of urban London. One accident happened to Master Wishpole, a serving man shot in the thigh, to whom William Clowes acted as surgeon and provided a very useful description of the contemporary Tudor arrowhead. Roving practice was ideal preparation for any military-minded archer and was good sport, as it still is today. (By kind permission of the City of London, London Metropolitan Archives)

that can be taught quickly but the development of the strength required to draw the bow and the skill to shoot with any degree of fluency and precision will take years. It is possible to teach a basic style of archery in a single day; it takes years of dedication to master the heavy war bow.

If the technique was difficult to master, the practises were very different from those used by the arquebusier. His target was, as we have seen, the 'bullseye', a black dot on a white circle, set at a fixed and relatively short distance, effectively flat shooting. The archer would practise at the butts, two large mounds of earth set opposite one another. The archer could also flat shoot at short range targets, such as a willow wand, to test his ability to shoot with precision. In the archery legislation of 33 Henry VIII c. 9 archers were strongly discouraged from practising at fixed distances as it would be a poor preparation for war. Roving, that is shooting to a series of marks, set at different distances and directions was very popular and enjoyed, most notably at Finsbury Fields in London. This practise, used in archery fields and informally in the countryside, was the real test of the archer. This was where he learned to judge distance, to shoot up and down hill and where he had to consider wind and weather.

Clout shooting, at a small ground target made of white linen or similar set at the effective maximum distance of the bow was excellent practice for the archery that would be used against the Scottish army at Flodden and the French cavalry at the Battle of the Spurs. None of this training would be required of the arquebusier, whose job it was to simply level his piece at the enemy, perhaps a few score yards away, and to keep reloading and firing. The archer was a craftsman, the arquebusier a labourer.

Conclusion

Hopefully it is evident that the continued use of the bow by the English was not simply sentiment or perversity. To return to the statement by Gervase Phillips: 'A people's chosen tools of war can be a manifestation of economic, political, cultural, and social circumstances, circumstances that defy the simple logic of a new technology displacing an old.'[74] The bow was clearly still an effective weapon and complemented the qualities of contemporary firearms. It was part of the fabric of English society and could be made, maintained and used on a large scale, with success and pride. The archer with regular practise could knock, draw and loose his arrows, judging distance and wind with the skill that was the product of years of practise. The arquebusier was a man who had been given a gun, the archer was a man who had grown with his bow.

---

74 Phillips, 'Longbow and Hackbutt', p.576.

12

Cavalry

The other exploits ordered by your grace cannot be done so easily … the horses are so travailed, through the extremity of cold, frost, hail, rain and snow, that they can bear no journey.

Grey to Somerset 6 April, 1548[1]

Introduction

Military historians have tended to either exaggerate or denigrate the role of cavalry. The much vaunted 'infantry revolution' of the fourteenth and possibly fifteenth century was supposed to see them tumbling down, and yet cavalry in its various forms continued to roam around the battlefield unaware of its obsolescence or fatuity. Firearms in the hands of the infantry, it is often thought, should have seen their disappearance, as seemed likely after the drubbing the French *gentilhomme d'armes* suffered at Pavia in 1525. Yet they continued to gallop around the battlefield, not for a few years but for over 400. There is also the argument proposed by Michael Roberts that the addition of firearms to the equipment of the cavalry trooper led to his neglect of or outright rejection of the lance, making cavalry impotent on the battlefield; a peculiar conclusion that gives little credit to the self-interest of the soldiers and intelligence of their commanders.

The adherence of the French to the mounted man-at-arms as their most valued single unit has sometimes been criticised, as has their lack of light cavalry. The man-at-arms proved his worth at Fornovo, Ravenna, Pinkie and Marignano although in the particular circumstances of Pavia he was the victim rather than the vanquisher. Henry VIII certainly thought he was at a disadvantage when facing the French gendarmes and paid for mercenary men-at-arms to match them. It was also the French who came to employ extensively the Balkan light cavalry, having discovered their mettle as enemies when in the service of the Venetians. All the various forms of cavalry continued to prove that for speed, surprise, shock and awe they were

---

1   *CSP Scotland*, p.108.

invaluable if used well. As always, the way in which a nation waged war reflected the way it lived in peace.

The advantages that a man on horseback has over the poor infantryman are obvious. First there is the view he has over the battlefield, placing himself in a superior position to judge the action. Secondly, he possesses the speed to manoeuvre on the battlefield which is unmatched by infantry. Thirdly, if he chooses to use it, he can convert that speed into devastating power when charging into an enemy formation. Finally, his social origins, whether high or low, as a Stradiot, border horseman or gentleman pensioner, added to the advantages of height and speed, gave him a sense of superiority over the infantry. Cavalry in all its various forms emerged from a particular portion of society at a specific time. You could no more make a cavalry trooper by simply putting a man on a horse, than you could make a man an archer by putting a war bow in his hand.

Men-at-Arms

The mounted man-at-arms was the most important and expensive single item in European warfare. Drawn from a social elite and equipped with full plate armour, *cap-a-pie*, together with lance, sword, mace or war hammer, he was set well apart from others. He was as it were, the tip of the 'lance', a group of three to five other men, less well-equipped, sometimes all on horse and sometimes on foot. The French 'lance' in the Compagnies d'Ordonance established in 1445 was made up of the man-at-arms, a squire, a page and two mounted infantrymen. This lance would be combined with 100 more to constitute a company, a powerful mobile force, able to commit to the battlefield or when dismounted as an assault group in a siege. The Burgundian companies created after 1470 added a crossbowman, handgunner and a pikeman, all dismounted, to the lance. The number of lances in the French army under Louis XII was a little over 2,000 in peace, with the addition of a further 1,000 in war. In 1523 France could mobilise some 3,752 lances, a force that was without equal in Europe. The Burgundians under Charles the Bold raised an impressive number of 1,200 lances which were, despite the quality of their equipment and training, decimated in the battles against the Swiss (1476–77).

The lance was a powerful force but it relied upon the availability of expensive war horses known as destriers, as well as other breeds, and the money to equip a fully armoured man-at-arms. It also required a large number of individuals, drawn exclusively from the nobility and gentry, who were willing and able to devote themselves to acquiring the skills required to handle such horses and weapons. France and Burgundy possessed the horseflesh, the nobility and wealth to support such a large force of gendarmes; England did not. Spain, with its hotter and drier climate, produced a finer breed of horse and the Spanish faced not heavily armed men-at-arms but a fast opponent equipped with a light lance, bow and sword. It was not therefore surprising that Spain produced an equivalent lightly equipped but lethal cavalry in the form of the genitor.

The Two Armies at the Battle of Ravenna, probably *c*.1512/1513 by Master with the mousetrap. If you discount the field gun, the mouse trap and the halberdier in the foreground the clear impression intended by the artist is that the real power of an army was to be found in a mass of mounted men-at-arms. Most of the horses are unbarded except for the Frenchman on the far left foreground. Ravenna was an example of cavalry suffering heavily from artillery fire and failing to be the decisive arm that would be suggested in this portrayal. (National Gallery of America, with permission)

The man-at-arms required full plate armour for himself and barding for his horse, in the form of plate or *cuir bouilli* (hardened leather), to which mail could be added. His principal weapon was a heavy lance that could be mounted on the *arrêt de lance* (a bracket), which would take the weight and absorb some of the impact of a strike. The holes, often seen on the left of the breastplate, are where the *arrêt* would be mounted. The armour was complex and heavy and would reduce the speed and mobility of the horse: the example in the Wallace Collection, dated to 1480, weighs a little over 30 kg, rather more than the armour worn by the rider of a similar date and weighing 27.6 kg. Barding was also time-consuming to fit, which explains why the Bulleners and Gentlemen Pensioners who charged the advancing Scots pike formation at Pinkie were without their barding. The French cavalry at the Battle of the Spurs discarded their barding so that they could escape more quickly. Francis I and his gendarmes at Pavia in 1525 were delayed in their response to the camisade or night attack, by the time it took to put on their armour for horse and rider.

Although the pasture to be found in England was excellent, the nobility were few and the gentry less enthusiastic about participating in war and the preparations for war than perhaps they had been, inured as they were to long periods of domestic peace. This was especially true after the loss of France in 1453 and the internecine conflict of the Wars of the Roses. France had a much larger population and a nobility on a much grander scale. The Tudors still took the breeding of horses for war very seriously. Even with the encouragement of the King there was a grave shortage of horses suited to war in the kingdom. It was therefore unsurprising that Henry VIII employed large numbers of mercenary men-at-arms for his overseas expeditions, especially Burgundians and Germans. Some 500 served in the expedition of 1512 and perhaps 6,000 in 1513. At the Battle of the Spurs the well-paid 1,000 Burgundians still only committed themselves to the chase rather than to the battle.

In England the numbers of men-at-arms available on 'great horses' were pitifully few. In 1519 the Venetian ambassador claimed that England could not raise 100 in the whole kingdom. This hardly seems much of an exaggeration: at Flodden the Earl of Surrey's contingent contained but one man-at-arms and even the 'master of horse' brought a pitiful six and the army in total had only 196. Although the numbers varied over time, the Gentlemen Pensioners provided a body of well-trained and equipped heavy cavalry numbering between 100–150. England could never match the mounted might of Continental Europe.

Pistoleers

There was one force of cavalry that was quite new and presaged great things. These were the *Schwartz Reiters* (black riders), equipped with three-quarter armour, swords, boar spears and most importantly handguns. In 1544 Henry VIII hired some 500 such men: Cleviots (from Cleves), Dutchmen, Westphalians and Danes under Captain Lightmaker. They served before Boulogne where they acted as part of the King's bodyguard. Wheel lock firearms were a relatively recent innovation. A manuscript of 1505 from Nuremberg has a drawing of a wheel lock mechanism, and Caspar or Gaspar the Bohemian was sent by the Archbishop of Zagreb to buy a gun fired 'by a stone' (iron pyrites) in 1507. The supposedly definitive and cruelly amusing story that dates the wheel lock to 1515, comes from an account of how one Lax Pfister shot a prostitute in Constance, a negligent discharge for which he had to pay through the nose as the woman had been shot through the chin. The cost added up to over 80 florins together with a pension of 20 florins for life.

The wheel lock did not require a lit match cord but employed a simple clockwork mechanism that turned a serrated wheel against iron pyrites to produce a spark, igniting the powder in the pan. The mechanism was expensive to make and tended to clog and misfire, while the loss of the key to wind up the mechanism would be disastrous. By the middle years of the sixteenth century the use of pistols from horseback had become quite common, although still found worth commenting upon. In 1547 the Tower armoury contained some 275 'short gonnes for horsemen with cases of lether

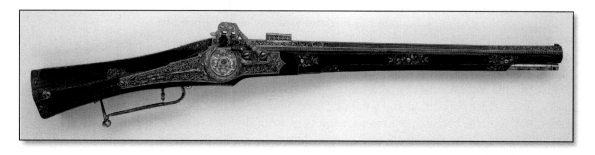

Wheel lock carbine, c.1540–50, German. The earliest depiction of firearm-equipped cavalry is to be found in the 1549 *Conversion of Paul* by Lucas Cranach. The weapons depicted appear to vary in length from pistol to short carbine and are clearly wheel locks with very similar butts. Only one weapon, attached to the pommel, is carried by each horseman. Sophisticated, expensive and lethal, the 'short gonne' for horsemen was an important addition to their armament. This is a superbly decorated example in chiselled steel, silver and gold, using high renaissance designs. Length 775 mm (30.5 in).
(Metropolitan Museum of Art, Open Access).

furnished with hornes and purse [powder horns and purses for shot]',[2] so clearly Henry was beginning to adopt the latest fashion in cavalry. In 1548 Christopher Ellerkar was shot in the neck by a French pistoleer at the siege of Haddington. Ellerkar killed the unfortunate Frenchman with his lance 'under the harness',[3] before his opponent had time to reload. No doubt traditionalists would see this as a vindication!

The procedure for loading a matchlock was much more difficult to carry out on horseback, although not impossible. Jean Jacques Wallhausen, in *The Military Art Mounted* of 1616, illustrated and explained how it should be done:

When mounted, he holds the burning match and reins in his left hand with the lighted end of the match between his fingers.

He has the smallest and cheapest horse possible so that if it is a question of dismounting and abandoning it, the loss is not too great.

Let the musketeer accustom himself to fire his musket on horseback from every side and in every way.

He will not be equipped with boots and spurs for they would do more harm than good if he has to dismount.[4]

Mounted arquebusiers who may have fired their first round from horseback, would almost certainly have had to dismount to continue the battle. They would have operated far more like mounted infantry, bringing their firepower to bear at short range. This was the role that they performed at Pinkie against the Scots pike squares.

---

2   Starkey, *Inventory*, p.104. no. 3822.
3   *CSP Scotland*, 257, p.125.
4   Richard Pearse, 'The use of the matchlock when mounted', *Journal of the Society for Army Historical Research*, vol. 44, no. 180 (December 1966), p.203.

The Demi-Lancer

The demi-lancer may be considered the poor man's man-at-arms, and was certainly being employed in the second rank behind men-at-arms by the reign of Henry VII. In 1489 during the Breton expedition there were 19 demi-lancers in the retinue of Sir Walter Herbert. Their horses were ridden without barding and the riders wore three-quarter or half armour (see photo overleaf), which meant that the weight carried by the horse would be significantly less. A far more readily available and cheaper type of horse, such as a courser, would therefore be a suitable mount. Equipped with a lighter lance, the demi-lancer was still a potent weapon on the battlefield, especially against light cavalry and infantry, as it proved before Pinkie. The 'master of the horse' at Flodden could call upon 147 demi-lancers compared to his six men-at-arms. In the Militia Act of 1558 there was no requirement to provide the equipment for men-at-arms but horses and equipment for demi-lancers were required from those with land of value over 1,000 marks. It was the demi-lancer who would provide the 'heavy' cavalry of the future.

Light Horse

Light horse had to skirmish against similar cavalry to carry out reconnaissance, in order to find the strength and dispositions of the enemy as well as gauging their morale and establish their intentions. They would counter enemy scouts, as well as taking prisoners for interrogation. In 1513, as Hall records, the border horse played an invaluable role:

> The Kyng continually sent forth his light horse to seke the country and to see yf anye appearance wer, and they ever brought tidings of such things as they saw, so that always it was forsene that the Kyng nor his people should be taken unprepared, nor the Frenchmen shoulde come on them sodainly.[5]

It was the light horse which apprised Henry of the movements of the French cavalry before Thérouanne, which culminated in the Battle of the Spurs.

Light cavalry performed picket or guard duty, some distance from the camp, as they could provide a timely warning of attack. They were also essential for escorting convoys, always a tedious but necessary duty, as well as attempting to maintain some discipline amongst the carters. At the siege of Haddington, a convoy of only two or three carts required an escort of 30 or 40 light horse. Demands on their service were great. The light horse could be combined with arquebusiers and archers to provide a combined force of some flexibility and considerable power, especially in Ireland and on the Scottish borders, as was demonstrated convincingly at Solway Moss.

In England the border horse were recognised as the finest representatives of their type but they were not unique. In Spain the horses, terrain and Muslim enemy led to the development of their own light horse the genitors or

---

5   Hall, *Chronicle* (London: 1904), vol. 1, p.83.

Half armour of William Herbert 1st Earl of Pembroke. Northern Italian, modified in England, about 1550. A fine imported half armour under which a mail shirt would have been worn. This armour would have given considerable protection but also provided ease of movement. It uses sliding rivets but the overall quality and detail is far superior to that of the Winchester Almain rivet. Suitable for a demi-lancer, or if wished, easily and comfortably worn on foot. A full set of field plate armour would have weighed over 23.5kg (52 lb) without the helmet, over three times the weight of this armour. This may have been worn by the noble Earl when fighting the Prayer Book rebels at Sampford Courtenay. Weight: Collar 1.050 kg (2.3 lb); breastplate 3.320 kg (7.3 lb); back 2.156 kg (4.75 lb); vambraces 1.135 kg each (2.5 lb); total 7.661 kg (16.85 lb). (Courtesy of the Royal Armouries)

Above: Border horse entering the King's camp at Boulogne, a detail from the Cowdray engraving. Inured to the harsh conditions of the North they can be seen protected by their short cloaks and brimmed hats. They carry their short light spears suitable for spearing infantry and keeping enemy light horse at a distance. Although lacking the sartorial spectacle of the stradiot they bested them in combat. (Dr Dominic Fontana, with kind permission)

Right: Detail of stradiots and Landsknechts from 'The Skill of the White King Dealing with Different Nations in Wartime', from *Der Weisskunig* by Hans Burgkmair *c.*1515. The Balkan stradiots were a useful addition to those countries lacking a tradition of light cavalry. Like the Northern horse they had learnt their skills in surprise attacks and raiding. They were armed with curved swords, double-headed lances and maces. Known and feared for their brutality, when in Venetian service they received one ducat for each enemy head they brought back from battle. No doubt their 'outlandish' appearance added to their appeal and mystique. The two Landsknechts standing beside them seem distinctly unimpressed. (Metropolitan Museum of Art, Open Access)

jinetes. The most exotic light cavalry were the Stradiots or Albanians. These were recruited from the Balkans and were first employed by the Venetians and later the French. They were present with the French at the Battle of the Spurs. They were noted for their short stirrups, beaver hats, curved 'Turkish' swords and small spears or javelins. Stradiots employed by the French were roundly defeated by the border horse, when they attempted to infiltrate the supply convoys in 1513. In February 1545 a large number came to offer their service to Henry VIII, fleeing from French service. This led to the formation of several companies and eventually the appointment of their own colonel, 'Cavalier' Thomaso Bua or Thomas of Argos. Although commended for his loyal service by Hertford, when he left English service in 1546 Bua was executed in Turin, for the desertion of his French employers.

Light horse could play a part in battle, as did Dacre's English border lances which tackled Home's pikemen at Flodden after they had almost overwhelmed Edmund Howard's forces. It was also a group of border horse led by John (the Bastard) Heron that came to the rescue of Howard as he was surrounded and faced capture or more likely death at the same battle. After disengaging from the Scots, Dacre played no further part in the battle, in which his men had suffered heavily with 160 men lost, which gave the impression that they had come to a tacit agreement with Home's Borderers to end this fratricidal conflict.

The reliability and trustworthiness of the Northern horse was sometimes doubted. In a 1538 muster there were recorded some 391 reivers 'able with horse and harness', they were called the 'Northe Tyndell Theiffs'.[6] Thieffs or thieves they certainly were but they were good at their job. Henry was informed of their prowess by Sir Henry Wotton, who declared that 'the light horssemen of the North were with the foremost and best skyrmysshers … puttyng theym in ordre of skrmysche, after the maner used upon your Majesties were there.'[7] In 1543 at the siege of Landrecies Sir John Wallop offered 200 light horse for Imperial service. Emperor Charles V 'saw them hoorle up the hill so lightly, he said, Par ma foy, voyla de gens qui vont de grand courraige, et ilz semblent tresbien les Alarbes d' Affrice'.[8] There were also two companies of 'border horse' employed by Henry in his French campaign in 1544. These were 'picked and chosen men', from Redesdale and Tynedale and they performed their roles well.

Light horse could not face men-at-arms or demi-lancers in battle. This was proved by the effective destruction of the Scottish light horse by the English cavalry the day before the Battle of Pinkie. After suffering heavy losses, the Scots paid no further part in the contest. Light cavalry had to stay out of range of their heavier opponents and 'bicker' with the enemy, wearing him down and causing him to make mistakes. Perhaps the greatest success

6 Professor Anthony Tuck (ed.), *War and Border Societies in the Middle Ages* (London: Routledge, 1985), p.51.
7 Henry Howard, Earl of Surrey, *The Works of Henry Howard, Earl of Surrey, and of Sir Thomas Wyatt* (London: Longman, MDCCCXV), vol. 1, Appendix xliv.
8 *Letters and Papers*, vol. 18, part 2, August–December 1543, 21 Oct. R. O. St. P, IX. 522, 291.

of light horse was at Solway Moss in 1542, where a force outnumbered many times by its enemy destroyed that enemy's cohesion and its will to fight.

The horses required for such duties were small and hardy, able to live and thrive in conditions that their heavier and more expensive stable mates could not. The principal weapon was a light thrusting lance. So skillful were the Borderers with this that it was said they could stand their horses in a fast-flowing river or stream and use their lance as a fishing spear. The other weapons were those that might be expected, such as swords, war hammers or maces. Small crossbows known as latchets were popular on the border but from mid century onward, they would be replaced by a wheel lock pistol known as a dagg. Armour was minimal and light, jacks of plate, brigandines, mail and simple helms, skulls or morions were popular. A shield could be carried on the back to protect them from the rear; on the border this was made from wood and leather and known as a targe. Estienne Perlin observed the border reivers' horse and equipment critically: '[They are] bold and gallant enough, but are not so well armed as the French, for they have very little well made, clean and polished armour, but used jackets of mail … and have the custom of using little ambling nags and small horses; their lances are small and narrow.'[9] It is doubtful whether in the conditions on the border the task of keeping armour 'clean and polished' would have been appreciated by a reiver, whose tactics and success often depended on concealment rather than appearance.

The Supply of Horses

Although there is a tendency these days to assume that one horse is very much like another, this view of the noble quadruped is not one which would have been shared at the time. The horses that were available were as varied as the motor vehicles we now use. Destriers were stallions, solely used as mounts for men-at-arms and trained for war, they would not usually be used for everyday riding. The courser or charger was a horse suitable for war and the hunt; as it was valued for its endurance and speed, it would suit the squire, or as a mount for the demi-lancer. The ambler was much valued as comfortable riding horse because of its gait which was faster than a walk but slower than a canter. The hobelar was a rugged and hardy pony, useful for campaigning when fodder may be difficult to find. It was the mount of the hobelars, the mounted archers of the Hundred Years War. The rouncey was a horse used for riding and as a pack animal, while the sumpter was only used as a beast of burden.

William Harrison in his *Description of England* of 1577, summarised the horseflesh available in the British Isles as follows:

> Our horses, moreover, are high, and, although not commonly of such huge greatness as in other places of the main, yet, if you respect the easiness of their

9   Peter Hume Brown (ed.), *Early Travellers in Scotland* (Edinburgh, David Douglas,1891), p.74. Full text available online, see bibliography for URL.

pace, it is hard to say where their like are to be had. Such as serve for the saddle are commonly gelded, and now grew to be very dear among us, especially if they be well coloured, justly limbed, and have thereto an easy ambling pace … [In an ambling gait, three of the feet are always on the ground, this produces a very smooth ride and a nice sound] it is moreover very pleasant and delectable in his ears, in that the noise of their well-proportioned pace doth yield comfortable sound as he travelleth by the way. Of such outlandish horses as are daily brought over unto us I speak not, as the jennet of Spain, the courser of Naples, the hobby of Ireland, the Flemish roile and the Scottish nag, because that further speech of them cometh not within the compass of this treatise.[10]

Henry VII blamed the shortage of horses in England on their sale abroad, and in 1495 prohibited their export. His son was as concerned as his father with the availability of good horseflesh and was responsible for extensive legislation to encourage their breeding, as well as possessing his own stud farms. James V of Scotland also felt the want of decent horseflesh in his realm and purchased suitable beasts from Denmark. The Breed of Horses Act 1535 (27 Henry VIII, c. 6) aimed to redress 'the great decay of the generation and breeding of good … strong Horses which heretofore have been bred in this realm', as 'in most places of this Realm little horses and nags of small stature and value be suffered to depasture and also to cover mares and fillies of very small stature'.[11] In the autumn, within 15 days of Michaelmas, the stock should be rounded up and 'unprofitable beastes' culled. In wild and harsh areas where large animals could not survive, small hardy ponies were at risk from Henry's ire but sense seems to have prevailed despite Henry's strictures, which explains the survival of hardy local breeds. The 1535 Act also required every owner of an enclosed park to keep at least two breeding mares over 13 hands to be bred with stallions no less than 14 hands. The Venetian ambassador was somewhat dismissive of the horses bred in England: '[they] being weak and of bad wind, fed merely on grass, being like sheep and all other cattle kept in the field or pasture at all seasons … they cannot stand much work, nor are they held in much account.'[12]

In the Horses Act 1540 (32 Henry VIII, c.13) it was required that in 30 shires and districts where mares were kept, that the stallions should be no less than 15 hands high and run with mares no less than 13 hands. This is where the term 'shire horse' derives, although the modern shire horse is of a very different breed and not a riding horse at all but much closer to the Flanders mare, suited to heavy drawing work. One further Act of 1541–2 required 'trotting horses' to be kept, the numbers dependent upon wealth and position. An archbishop or duke should keep seven horses, a marquess five and anyone with an income of £100 per annum, or whose wife wore clothes of silk or a French hood or bonnet of velvet, should keep one. The

10 William Harrison, *Elizabethan England: From 'A Description of England', by William Harrison 1577*, Book III, chapter 8; 1587, Book III, chapter I.
11 William Ridgeway, *The Origin and Influence of the Thoroughbred Horse* (Cambridge University Press, 2015), p.360.
12 *CSP Venice*, May 1557.

Gentlemen Pensioners were expected to rear horses, and Sir Francis Knollys was granted Caversham Manor and Caversham Park in Oxfordshire (now in Berkshire), formerly in possession of Reading Abbey, for this use.

The greatest demand for war horses came from Italy, and here the best examples were to be found. Henry VIII received horses as a gift from the Dukes of Mantua and Ferrara as well as 25 beautiful Spanish horses from Charles V. At the Field of the Cloth of Gold in 1520 he rode a Neapolitan horse and Francis I a Mantuan one. Henry also employed Italians in his stables: Alexander de Bologna in 1526 and Matthew de Mantua as a studman in 1545, as well as employing one Master Hannibal, the farrier.

13

Artillery

Artillery in Action

By the end of the fourteenth century artillery had become essential in siege warfare, first supplementing and then replacing that magnificent wooden beast, the trebuchet. Guns had appeared on the battlefield in the mid fourteenth century but it was only in the mid fifteenth century that they began to play a significant part, as at Formigny (1450) and Castillon (1453). By the beginning of the sixteenth century, artillery in all its varieties had achieved the forms that, with some incremental improvements, it would retain for the next 350 years. Artillery became a major source of pride, as well as expense, to European monarchs. Henry VIII acquired a vast stock of artillery during his reign, enough according to the Venetian ambassador to conquer Hell itself, a bold if slightly blasphemous claim.

At Bosworth, Richard III's clear numerical superiority in artillery played a crucial role not in defeating Henry but in forcing his enemy to alter his line of advance, beginning the confusion that would eventually end in Richard's death. Unfortunately is known of the use of artillery at the crucial Battle of Stoke. Henry VII certainly employed mercenary gunners, as was common practice, and Henry Walker cast guns for the Crown, as well as calculating the quantity of metal required for the King's magnificent renaissance tomb, the work of Torrigiano. It was his son who would dramatically increase the royal commitment to the acquisition and use of ordnance. Henry VIII would play the part of a Renaissance prince, with palaces, ships and cannon aplenty. The artillery park was as much a display of royal pretensions as of military might. Great efforts were made to ensure that artillery pieces were not only highly effective in their roles but that they also full conformed to the contemporary aesthetic. This demonstrated their value not only as weapons but as what Luke Syson and Dora Thornton refer to as 'objects of virtue'.[1]

Henry's ambitions were shared by his Scottish brother-in-law James IV, who also hired foreign craftsmen to manufacture artillery and crew them.

---

1   Luke Syson and Dora Thornton, *Objects of Virtue: Art in Renaissance Italy* (Getty Trust Publications: J. Paul Getty Museum, 2002).

Detail from *The Triumphal Arch of Maximilian I*, 1517–18 by Albrecht Altdorfer. The early sixteenth century saw the emergence of artillery as a major force in the field as well as being a necessity in the siege. This was a period of experimentation in materials, design and methods, although older ordnance such as the bombard remained in use. This engraving shows some of the innovations that would increase the efficiency and lethality of ordnance, including trunnions, a mortar and quadrant. (Metropolitan Museum of Art, Open Access)

In his case, the new powerful and mobile artillery first played an important part in bringing the Scottish nobility to heel. The confrontation between England and Scotland at Flodden should have seen the triumph of modern Scottish artillery, as the English army should have advanced uphill against his well-emplaced cannons. The formidable strength of Scottish artillery was to force the English commander to choose another strategy, and the Scots to abandon their well-prepared gun emplacements.[2] The poor performance of the Scots artillery in the battle could be attributed to many factors: inadequate preparation, poor gunnery, tactical misuse and the lie of the land. Whatever the cause, the English artillery seem to have performed better. Flodden was of course a success for English gunners over their Scots counterparts but it cannot be said that they determined the course of the battle.

---

2   Video, 'Two Men in a Trench: Battle of Flodden', see bibliography for URL.

At the Battle of the Spurs artillery was used, as well as archery, to 'ambush' the French cavalry, in a role not often commented on but clear from contemporary illustrations. Henry's 1513 French campaign was well supplied with artillery and special mention has been made of his 'Apostles'. It was a gun of this type that Henry himself served, aiming *Bartholomew* at the towers of the cathedral of Notre Dame in Tournai, hitting the bell tower with the first shot. In the expedition of 1523, the artillery was handled with professionalism and performed its limited role well, in what was also a limited campaign. The Duke of Suffolk first assaulted Bray, where he 'planted certain great guns which gave the fortress such a good day as to shatter gaps in the wall so that men could scale them and assault the town, which the English soldiers did very gallantly'.[3] At the siege of Montdidier the artillery was also handled aggressively and succesfully:

> And at vj. of the clocke in the nyght our gonners gave them a peall [volley] of gonnes at rovers, and after that they had no more joy to shote. And by ij. of the clocke in the mornyng our great ordynaunce was layd within xl.[40] foote of the walles, and gave them iiij. goodly pealles [volleys] and brake downe the walles a great bredith, hard by the myghtie stronge bolwerke, the strongist that evyr I saw, and marvelowsly mad[e] with iiij. Flowers [floors]. And at vij. of the clocke in the mornyng they were so ferde [afeard] of the sawte, [assault] ther trompet came to the walles and blew a peace, and so our gonners shott no more.[4]

In the 1544 campaign Henry could boast a substantial siege train which matched any in Europe. The success it achieved was only after a prolonged and expensive bombardment but it was still an impressive demonstration of royal firepower.

By the end of his reign Henry had an imposing collection of artillery stored at the Tower, as well as hundreds of pieces in castles and fortifications in England and France. There were also 2,071 pieces of all types and sizes aboard royal ships.[5] Although there was a very large stock of ordnance in the numerous defences of the kingdom, in 1547 only the Tower of London held a small ready reserve available for land and sea service. If one includes the captured French and Scottish ordnance kept there, for use as well as for trophies, then there were six cannons, two demi-cannons, 10 culverins, five demi-culverins, 12 sakers, and 12 minions and falcons. Although this included a substantial number of heavy pieces, they were far fewer than the numbers employed at the siege of Boulogne three years earlier. There were also 20 falconets and robinets at the Tower, the smallest pieces of bronze ordnance, almost all of which were trophy pieces. There were also 30 wrought

---

3   Davies, *Ill Jurney*, p.9.

4   Davies, *Ill Jurney*, p.37; Charles Trice Martin (ed.), 'Sir John Daunce's Accounts of Money received from the Treasurer of the King's Chamber temp. Henry VIII', in *Archaeologia*, vol. XLVII, p.25. Transcribed from British Library Add. MS. 10, 110, f.236.

5   R.D. Smith, *Ships and guns of the Tudor Navy 1495–1603*, pp.109–112, in Carlo Beltrame and Renato Ridella, *Ships and Guns: The Sea Ordnance in Venice and Europe Between the 15th and the 17th Centuries* (Oxford: Oxbow Books, 2011).

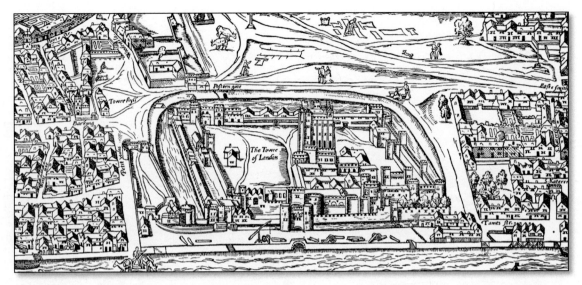

The Tower of London from the Agas map. On the gun wharf of the tower can be seen dismounted barrels as well as field pieces on their carriages. River and sea transport were obviously preferable to land transport for heavy ordnance, considering the quality of contemporary roads. No doubt it was artillery pieces on the gun wharf that fired on Wyatt's rebels on the other side of the Thames in 1554, to little apparent effect. The present author has fired artillery on the west moat of the Tower, and harbours the ambition of firing from the gun wharf itself. (By kind permission of the City of London, London Metropolitan Archives)

iron port-pieces, suitable only for sea and fortress service, and 317 smaller wrought iron pieces, most of which were breech-loading types.

In 1551 there was a programme to disarm and abandon those Henrician fortifications which were considered unnecessary and to provide a sizeable reserve, as 'the Kinges ordonance was so dispersed for the furnyture of them that presently he hathe no ordonance for the felde'.[6] The provision of artillery for field operations must therefore have been on an ad hoc basis, using the Tower stocks and removing from garrisons additional guns, such as the two sakers and four falcons 'mounted upon their Cariages',[7] stored in the citadel of Carlisle Castle.

The artillery that Somerset took to Scotland in 1547 indicates how far this branch of the armed forces had come since Bosworth. The large battery of 15 pieces accompanied the army at a good pace and was designed to play an important part in the battle to come. This powerful battery was enough to convince Arran that his first plan, to allow the English to attack his strong defensive position, was unworkable. During the Scottish advance, naval gunfire, which had been of enough concern for the Scots to have built a turf wall protecting its camp, played upon their left flank causing casualties and confusion. Both sides rapidly advanced their artillery, the Scots having to manhandle their pieces. Under the personal direction of Hertford a few guns, aided by the heavy cavalry, brought the advance of the Scots to a halt and then assisted in their destruction. It was clear that field artillery could

6   Hale, *Renaissance War Studies*, p.96.
7   Starkey, *Inventory*, p.133. 6258/6259.

be employed flexibly and effectively if under a commander who appreciated their capabilities and their limitations.

One of the features of artillery highlighted by these engagements is the role it played in changing the tactics of an enemy. The threat of the strong Scottish artillery position at Flodden Edge forced the English to abandon a frontal attack, just as the threat of the strong English artillery forced the Scots to abandon their position at Pinkie. Artillery was clearly seen as a powerful force on the battlefield and could determine how battles would be fought, but might not dictate the outcome.

Ownership and Administration

Artillery was not a royal monopoly during this period. Of course the monarch had both the means and the need to possess a sizeable stock of weapons, but he did not have a monopoly. Artillery pieces could be in private hands, as was clear from the seizure by Kett's rebels of artillery pieces from domestic armouries, including that of the Pastons. They could also be held by towns and cities for their own defence. In 1518 John Marshem the Mayor of Norwich purchased at least one robinet from Flanders, and in 1544 the city purchased six falconets from John Owen. These guns probably constituted part of the city artillery used against Kett's rebels in 1549. One early bronze gun of about the earlier date survives, in excellent condition, in the Great Hospital in Norwich. Carisbrooke parish had a falcon cast specifically in preparation for the defence of the island; made by the Owen brothers in

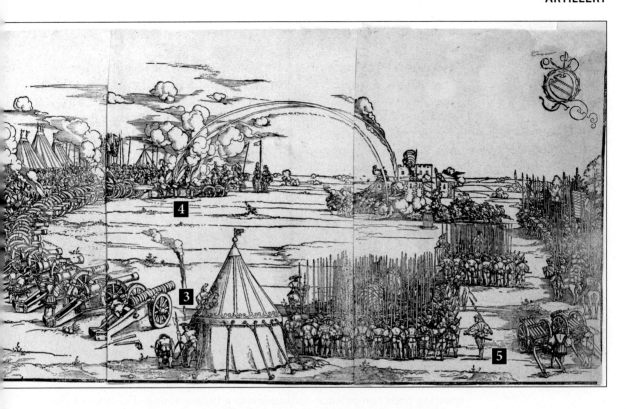

Entry of Charles V into Munich, June 10, 1530, by Sebald Beham.

This splendid testimony to Imperial power and contemporary firepower shows almost the full range of artillery and accompanying technology of the time. (Metropolitan Museum of Art, Open Access)

1. The limber first appeared at the end of the fifteenth century and was crucial in developing the mobility of artillery. By adding an additional pair of wheels joined to the trail with an iron pin, the unwieldy gun carriage became a handy four-wheeled cart.

2. These large carts were used for carrying ammunition and also the essential ancillary equipment, including the large three- or four-legged hoists which were indispensable if the gun barrel was to be dismounted. Carrying the barrel separately in a cart would significantly reduce the wear and tear on the carriage.

3. These guns are firing a ceremonial salute from left to right. They are large siege pieces mounted on very similar carriages. The closest gun appears to be unique in this battery as it is probably of wrought iron rather than cast bronze construction.

4. Mortars are providing supporting fire for an assault on a fortress as part of a military demonstration. Mortars were able to provide the high angle fire that the flat-shooting field pieces could not, and were therefore essential accompaniments to a siege as was the case at Boulogne in 1544. In this capacity they replaced the trebuchet, which had previously supplied high-angle fire.

5. Two small multi-barrel guns are not taking part in the performance. Quite large in calibre, their individual barrels could be fired, or a train of powder could fire them all simultaneously. The trail is designed to allow one or two horses to draw them swiftly about the battlefield. The author is always surprised that more use was not made of these weapons. Loading a number of closely placed barrels today is a health and safety nightmare, for obvious reasons.

1549, it is at present in Carisbrooke Castle. There was also a large quantity of 'private' ordnance carried aboard civilian ships.

Prior to the establishment in 1415 of the Board of Ordnance, the purchase of ordnance and powder was undertaken by the Privy Wardrobe. After this date all royal artillery came under the control of the Board of Ordnance, which had its headquarters at the Tower of London. The board was responsible for all artillery and supplies. Initially this included all edged weapons, armour, bows and sheaves of arrows etc. The Tower operated as a storehouse rather than a manufactory, although maintenance and refurbishment was part of its remit.

In 1509 the staff consisted of the master, clerk and yeoman. The role of master of ordnance was not a sinecure or merely being a bookkeeper: he was expected to be a master of his craft in war as well. He would accompany the army on all its major campaigns as well as understand the requirements of the varied garrisons. In 1513 the master, Sir Sampson Norton, served with the army in France, while the yeoman of ordnance, one William Huxley, served with the fleet. The master of ordnance had overall responsibility for the artillery on campaign and was supported by a lieutenant who was responsible for ensuring the serviceability of equipment and the supervision of gunners. He was assisted by the surveyor (first appointed in 1538, responsible for materials) while the roles of yeoman and clerk became sinecures. The master gunner had the responsibility of supervising and appointing gunners, ensuring their competence and supervising their training. The titles of the master gunner included such variations as master gunner of the ordnance, master gunner of the Tower and even master gunner of England.

Sir Christopher Morres was master from 1537–1544, succeeding Bernardin de Valois; his first appointment was to command a culverin in the French invasion of 1513. He was gunner-quartermaster in Tournai in 1514 and again in the French expedition of 1522, where he was responsible for using his guns to blow off the gates of Morlaix. In 1527 he was appointed chief gunner, having been appointed lieutenant in 1523. From 1531–32 he travelled to Calais and then Carlisle, inspecting fortifications. In 1535 he recruited gunners in Denmark and Germany, while at the same time he conducted some mild intelligence gathering. It was clear that his appointment as master of ordnance in 1547 could be explained by his wealth of varied experience, competence and loyalty. He continued in active service, venturing to Scotland with Somerset as master gunner of England during the Rough Wooing in 1542, and commanded the artillery at Leith and Edinburgh but with mixed results.

In 1544 he was replaced as master by Sir Thomas Seymour, brother-in-law to the King; clearly the status of the master had risen dramatically. Although Seymour did on occasion play a practical role as master, the day-to-day business devolved upon Morres who was made lieutenant general of the ordnance for life. He was appointed at twice his previous salary, a demotion to be welcomed! Morres's last campaign was in 1544, when he commanded the artillery at the siege of Boulogne. His luck had run out and he was 'Hurt on the Brest' by a handgun and later died of his wounds, ending what had been a long and varied career. On his death Henry VIII seized all his goods, using the excuse that he had the use of significant (undefined) funds during his life which were not accounted for. It is clear that Henry would not nowadays be considered a 'considerate employer'.

Manufacture

Although the period is principally associated with the development of cast bronze artillery, wrought iron pieces of traditional hoop and stave construction were numerically far more important (as the work of Kay Smith has clearly demonstrated). In addition, cast iron guns were beginning to make an appearance in small but significant quantities. Wrought iron guns were used and manufactured on a very large scale throughout this period. The Ordnance Office in 1553–8 spent £3,707 53s 6d on 'fforged pieces',[8] a remarkable figure over 20 times the amount spent on cast iron pieces and over twice as much as that spent on bronze. In the 1546 inventory of ships known as the Anthony Roll, wrought iron guns provided more than half of the 'heavy' ordnance and made up almost all of the light guns.[9]

Table 6. Distribution of numbers of guns by material and type from warships recorded in the Anthony Roll of 1546.

	Bronze	Cast Iron	Wrought Iron
Heavy	139*	20 demi-culverin	197 port-piece
Medium	110	14 saker	78 fowler
Light	7**	1 falconet	1,505***
Total	256	35	1,780

* Demi-culverin and above

** Falconet and lesser

***Bases, Hailshot pieces etc.

The King's smith, Cornelius Johnson, provided wrought iron guns in August and September 1512 and 75 more in February 1513. The cost per gun was between 1½d and 2d a pound or £15 to £18 13s 8d a ton.[10] In 1510 Humphrey Walker was paid for 50 pieces of ordnance at 12s per 100 lb (less than 1½d per lb). That the value of wrought iron guns was calculated by the pound rather than tons and hundredweight, would suggest that only small guns were being bought. The cost was still almost twice that of cast guns.

There is no doubt that for field and siege service bronze came to predominate, and that the qualities of power, accuracy and reliability that bronze guns demonstrated led to their widespread use. This was

8   Ordnance Office records E351/2614.
9   R.D. Smith, *Ships and guns of the Tudor Navy 1495–1603*, pp.109–112, in Beltrame and Ridella, *Ships and Guns*.
10 Hogg, *The Royal Arsenal*, p.37.

accompanied by a gradual replacement of wrought iron pieces. There were however still some 32 port pieces in service in 1592, three on land and 29 at sea. In England there was a long tradition of casting bronze guns. In 1414, William Woodward and Gerard Sprong cast guns from the pots and pans in the King's own kitchens. Henry VI purchased 64 small artillery pieces in 1428 from two citizens and metal founders of London, Thomas Coston and Robert Warner. This tradition was continued into the Tudor period. Master Humphrey Walker, who made the railings for Henry VII's magnificent tomb, also cast guns for Henry VIII and in 1509 was appointed his master gunner. Humphrey Walker, Richard Shokledge and Harbard de la Pole were certainly casting bronze falcons in 1513. Walker also cast a gun called *Basilicus*, which might well have been the type of very long bronze gun, known as a basilisk. Guns of a similar name associated with the siege of Rhodes were over five metres in length with a bore of 20–25 cm, shooting a projectile of 45 kg.[11] In 1517 George Brown was paid for providing 475 iron shot for this gun, confirming the *Basilicus* as a bronze piece.[12] Walker may have cast guns in the Tower, where a foundry is recorded as being active in 1514, but this business seems to have been abandoned there, possibly because a bronze foundry and a large powder store were unhappy neighbours.

Whatever the skills of Humphrey Walker, who had died in 1516, it was quite clear that English manufacture was inadequate to provide the quantity and possibly the quality of guns demanded by Henry VIII. Henry purchased very large numbers of guns from Hans Poppenruyter of Malines in Flanders. In 1509 Poppenruyter made an agreement with Spinelli, Wolsey's agent in Flanders, to purchase 24 courtaulx and 24 serpentines. In 1512 he was given a contract for 48 guns for ships, this time the weight of metal used was an impressive 108,231 lb. Each gun would average a little over one ton and would equate to a saker or small demi-culverin. In 1513 he was tasked with removing damaged guns from Thérouanne for recasting. Working for Henry was not unfortunately as profitable as might have been expected: in 1515 Poppenruyter sought urgent payment from the Crown as he was 'in great despair and danger'. Despite his protestations of poverty, he was still appointed royal gunfounder by Charles V in 1520. On his death in 1534, his wife, a formidable woman by the name of Hedwige van den Nieuwenhuisen, chose Remigy de Halu to succeed Hans in his foundry, the office and her bed.

His most famous guns were the magnificent '12 Apostles' of 1512; they weighed in total 67,225 pounds and were paid for by the Exchequer at the rate of £2 per 100 lb. The apostles formed two separate classes: Cruickshank records that there were apostles of the 'greater' and 'smaller' sort, the greater for 'battery of towns and fortresses' and the smaller 'for closing of the field'.[13] He also records that 30 horses were supplied to draw the greater and 21 the smaller. Cruickshank considers that these were to pull their ancillary equipment and stores, but they would also be an appropriate number for

---

11 Robert Douglas Smith and Kelly De Vries, *Rhodes Besieged: A New History* (Stroud: The History Press, 2011), pp 101–105.

12 Ffoulkes, *The Gun-Founders of England*, p.108.

13 Cruickshank, *Henry VIII and Francis I*, p.67.

New Inventions of Modern Times [*Nova Reperta*], *The Invention of Gunpowder*, Plate 3 *c*.1600, Jan Collaert I Netherlandish. This illustration is of a cannon foundry with, inset above the furnace hearth, a rather melodramatic and inaccurate interpretation of the manufacture of gunpowder. The furnace is being charged with broken pieces of guns, and the molten metal poured into a vertical mould buried in the ground. The pour should be continuous and the temperature maintained throughout if the cast is to be perfect. Gas, air and impurities should rise to the surface, although this was clearly not always the case. The gun was cast breech down to ensure that the quality of the cast there should be of the highest. Originally guns were cast like bells, with their muzzle downwards. The change from muzzle down to muzzle up casting took place around 1500. There should be about 10 percent more metal than required for the gun, to allow the process of shrinkage as the metal cools in the mould. A breech portion of the mould can be seen on the ground near the feet of the well-dressed man. Two workmen are clearing up the castings with cold chisels. The present author has used chisels and files to clean up a falconet, producing identical marks to those on original guns. On the left can be seen a man in a wheel, probably turning a drill to clean the bore of a cannon.
(Metropolitan Museum of Art, Open Access)

drawing the guns themselves, in line with current practice. If we conclude that the numbers of horses reflected the weight of the pieces, then the heavier would weigh 6,722 lb and the lighter 4,481 lb, not unreasonable figures for the heavier culverins. Both types of guns were provided with the same carriages, costing £12 apiece.

It has been known for some time that the large apostles fired a ball of 20 lb, with a charge of 20 lb of powder, and with a firing restriction of 30 times a day. Another reference to the apostles refers to '4 appostres [apostles] 2 of which shoot stones of 20 lb and 2 of 14 lb', and also refers to 'une visse, equal in power to the apostle'.[14] A visse appears to be another word for a culverin, as in the 1514 inventory of the Tower there is a reference to 'vice' pieces otherwise called culverins. It seems therefore that the smaller apostle fired a 14 lb shot and weighed something over 4,000 lb. This would put it in the same class as a culverin, with a barrel of perhaps 14 feet. Each of the apostles in the middle ward (*Peter, Bartholomew, Simon,* and *James the Less*) had its own gunner paid at the rate of 16d a day. *Simon* and *James* required nine and 10 carters respectively, while the other two only required eight. It seems reasonable to assume that *Simon* and *James* were of the greater sort. The high pay for their gunners, when less exalted masters of the craft were paid 8d–10d, would suggest that they were the crème de la crème of their trade. However, all the apostles seem to have been scrapped, as there is no reference to them in the inventory of 1547.

Cast iron might seem an ideal choice for the production of guns, but this was far from the case. It was difficult to find and process the right quality ore and the finished product was more likely to shatter than bronze. The first recorded blast furnace in England was probably built with royal patronage in 1496: a London goldsmith, Henry Fyner, built it at Newbridge in Ashdown forest, where cannonballs but not cannon were cast. In England the first reference to a gun cast from iron is in 1506, when three large chambered guns were cast. In 1508 Pauncelett Symart of Newbridge ironworks manufactured an iron gun, but it burst on firing, but in 1509–10 he successfully manufactured three cast iron guns with seven iron chambers, which were sent to equip the royal ship the *Sovereign*. This small-scale manufacture, dependent it seems upon French expertise, does not seem to have resulted in the 'take-off' of the Wealden gun industry.

It appears likely that cast iron gun founding began again in 1543 at Buxted. This was in response to the desperate demand for guns caused by increasing hostility to Henry VIII from Europe, culminating in the threat of invasion in 1545. Parson William Levett, his 'man' Ralph Hogge, who succeeded his master as gunmaker to the Crown, and Peter Baude the famed gunfounder, worked together to produce the first successful cast iron ordnance. In the 1547 inventory there are a number of references to cast iron guns including three in the South Castle of Portsmouth:

---

14 *Letters and Papers*, vol. 1, 1509–1514. British Library, Cotton Calig. E. I, 15 [151]. 1530. [3615.] ARTILLERY.

4428 Demi Culveryne of yrone of petir bondes [Baude?] makinge oone
4429 Sacre of yron of parsone levettes making ij
4430 Fawcon of yron of parsone levettes making oone[15]

One of Parson's products, a demi-culverin, was sent to Pevensey castle in 1547 where it remains, mounted on an impressive reconstruction of a field carriage. Levett produced substantial numbers of guns, cast shot and carriages between 1547 and 1550. Some 288 cast iron guns were manufactured, the majority by Levett but this compares with 596 wrought iron pieces in the same period.[16] Three quarters of expenditure on ordnance was for bronze pieces, a recognition of their superiority. Ralph Hogge became a stalwart of the Wealden gunfounding industry until his death in 1585, becoming 'gonnestone maker' for the Tower in 1559 and later the Queen's gunfounder of iron. These titles did not signify a great increase in demand, as bronze ordnance was strongly preferred for the reasons related above. In 1574 620 bronze guns were sent to arm ships as opposed to only 46 cast iron pieces, and even these were smaller pieces.

Varieties of Gun

Manufactured from three very different materials, the variety of pieces available for use was mystifyingly large. William Bourne's list in Appendix II includes eight principal types of cast cannon in 21 varieties; even so he fails to include the smallest classified type, the robinet. In 1547 there were in addition to the cast guns, five principal types of wrought iron gun, again in nine varieties, excluding the smallest anti-personnel types such as the *haile shotte* and *toppe pieces*.

The most numerous weapons were those made from wrought iron, almost all of which were breech-loading. The largest were the port-pieces sometimes rather confusingly referred to as 'bumbardes' and in descending size: fowlers, bases (double, single and demi), slings (hoole, double, demi and quarter). Some more ancient types remained in use in 1547 such as the 'single serpentine' in the Dover defences, the six serpentines at Sandgate Castle and the jerfawcon (gyrfalcon) in the bulwark at Higham. At the Tower there were a useful number of trophy guns, six French and 17 Scottish, unfortunately there is no indication as to when or where they were captured. The massive wrought iron bombard, of which the best extant example in Britain is Mons Meg, was still in use. They were part of Henry VIII's siege battery in 1513 although by 1547 the three remaining were relegated to storage in the Tower. One novelty that still resides in the Tower is the 'Brode Fawcon shoting iij shotte': the only remaining example of Peter Baude's work and a novelty both then and now. Perhaps the greatest oddities were two wooden barrels,

---

15 Starkey, *Inventory*, p.112. Numerical references are numbers from the inventory.
16 Sarah Barter Bailey, 'Information relating to the operation of the early cast-iron gun industry from a manuscript account in the collection of the Royal Armouries', *Journal of the Ordnance Society*, vol. 3 (1991), pp.11–17.

which were mounted and fitted with a smaller piece to give the impression of heavier guns, which can be seen in the Cowdray engravings.

The single most impressive piece in 1547 would have been the 'Basillischos of brasse' at Dover. This was almost certainly the basilisk once known as *Queen Elizabeth's Pocket Pistol*, still to be found on display in Dover Castle. It is a magnificent culverin manufactured in 1544 in Utrecht as a gift for Henry VIII, from Maximilian van Egmont the Count of Buren. It has a calibre of 4¾ inches and fired a ball of 20 lb with a charge of 18 lb. It is a monumental 23½ feet in length and is beautifully cast with flamboyant decoration. In 1644 it was used to breach the walls of the Royalist stronghold of Sheffield Castle, an impressive performance for a centenarian. In *The Gunners Glasse*, published in 1646, Eldred records that when fired in trials it hurled its projectile 1,200 yards at an elevation of two degrees.

The pieces held in garrisons were provided with their own supplies of ammunition which would mean that the great variation in weapons did not cause a major supply problem. However the wide variety of types, all with different dimensions, could cause problems for anyone on campaign seeking to be resupplied. This was a problem for Russell when facing the Prayer Book rebels in 1549. He complained that the ammunition sent to him would 'fit as a shoe for a man's hand'.[17] The use of wooden patterns to ensure the correct size of shot, well illustrated and surviving intact in large numbers with the *Mary Rose*, was essential if a catastrophe was to be avoided for the gunners. The solution to the problem was to standardise the types and designs of guns. Pattern models for cannon, demi-cannon and culverin were brought from Westminster Palace to the Tower of London as recorded in a survey of 1547. In the inventory of the Tower there are several references to 'little gonnes of brasse ... being patrons [patterns] for Cannons', with other patterns for a demi-cannon and a culverin.[18] Adrian Caruana concluded that the calibres for new royal artillery were established either in 1537 with the issue of the Artillery Charter, or possibly in 1543 with the foundation of the Ordnance Office.[19] This movement towards standardisation was taking place across Europe. Charles V established five patterns for artillery in 1544, while in France Henri II established the calibres for his artillery in 1552.

Stranger Melters and English Apprentices

In the light of acknowledged foreign expertise in all matters relating to artillery, it was not surprising that Henry should in 1514 employ a 'stranger', the Frenchman Peter Baude, to cast cannon in England. Baude was to work as a gunfounder in Salisbury Court off Fleet Street, and by 1528 he was so well established that he was granted a daily pension of 16d as a Tower gunner. He was especially active in the 1530s, receiving a contract in 1538 for £210 for guns and acquired metal and broken guns for recasting, and was so much

---

17 Troup, *The Western Rebellion*, p.254.
18 Starkey, *Inventory*, p.104. No. 3829.
19 Caruana, *Tudor Artillery*, p.7.

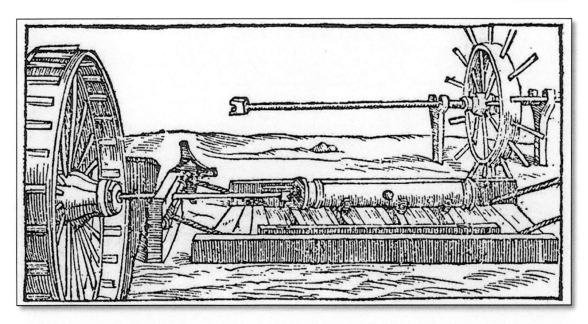

Machines for boring guns. Vanoccio Biringuccio from De La Pirotecnica (1540). Guns were not cast solid but with an integral bore produced by a core bar. The removal of the core bar did not necessarily produce a perfect finish. This required the use of the machines illustrated above. One of the first responsibilities of a gunner when examining a piece was to establish the trueness of the bore both for safety and for the purpose of aiming. It was not unusual for the core to slip, as it did with the first casting of the author's gun, which is both infuriating and expensive. The core bar should be held in place by two iron chaplets or collars, the lower of which would be incorporated into the cast. The upper would be above the muzzle and would be removed with the surplus head of the casting, by being sawn off. Additional metal was allowed to the gunfounder to take account of this necessary surplus when they were paid by the weight of the gun produced.

in favour that in 1542 he was rewarded with the granting of the status of a denizen or full citizenship. The next year he was sent to Buxted to teach Ralph Hogge the ironworker how to cast guns. In the same year he and a German, Peter van Collen (Peter of Cologne), cast two shell-firing mortars of 11 inches and 19 inches diameter, which would be used in the siege of Boulogne.

Baude was joined before 1523 by Francesco Degli Archani from Cesena with his two sons, Archangelo and (probably later) Rafaello. Francesco first appears as the 'master of the Mynes' in the French expedition of 1523. Francesco went on to build a gun foundry in Salisbury Place on the south side of Fleet Street, and combined his skill at casting cannon with a knowledge of fortifications. In 1532 he was sent to survey the defences of Calais and in 1544 went to assess the defences on the Scottish border. His career, combining expertise in so many related areas, was not unusual. His son Archangelo received a valuable pension of 16d a day in 1536 and was granted denizen status four years later. Francesco had died the year before in 1535, and Rafaello returned to Italy by 1543.

With the creation of a strong domestic manufacturing base, even if using the skills of 'strangers', very little ordnance seems to have been purchased from abroad after 1523. The exception to this was the purchase by Henry of 19 guns from Italian gunfounder Alessandro Gioardi. These were cast in Sicily in 1528 for the Knights of St John and include a fine couleuvrine moyenne

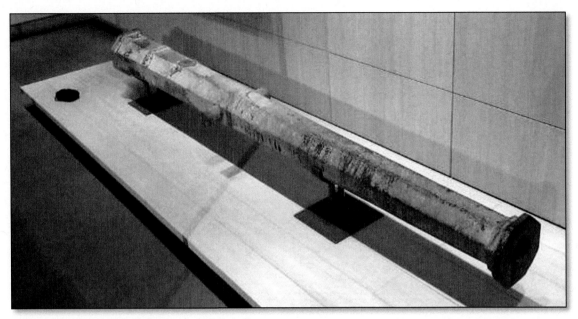

The couleuvrine moyenne, probably cast by Alessandro Gioardi in Italy for the Order of St John, on the orders of King Henry VIII. It is a fine long-barrelled piece useful on land or at sea. It bears the arms of Phillipe Villiers de l'Isle Adam, Grand Master 1521–34, and the coat of arms of England. The vent became enlarged from use, then reamed and screwed to fit a replacement bronze or possibly iron pierced screw bolt, known as a *dado*. The French expression 'Faire les quatre cents coups' was thought to be a reference to the numbers of rounds that piece could be fired before wearing out the vent and barrel. It now means to raise hell or sow one's wild oats! Overall length 108 1.25 in (2.775 m), length of muzzle to touch hole 100 in (2.55m), diameter of bore 3.15 in (80mm), diameter of projectile 3 in (76 mm; the normal windage for Italian pieces was 1/20 of the bore diameter). Weight of projectile 3¾ lb (1.7 kg); calibre 31.75. (Author's photograph)

now to be found in the museum of the Order in London, mistakenly, the present author believes, attributed to Francesco Arcano.

Peter Baude did not establish a dynasty of gunfounders but he did train the four Owen brothers (Robert and John, and John (junior) and Thomas) in the craft, in the Houndsditch foundry. They may have started working with him by the late 1520s and were certainly casting large-calibre guns by 1531. The Owens were sent to Calais in 1536 to cast great cannons, where they fell out with Master Gunner Johnson of Calais. He seems to have gone out of his way to be obstructive, even going so far as to sabotage their guns' proofing. They were, however, royal favourites: in 1540 they were granted the tenement known as the Bellfounders House in Houndsditch, and in 1546 succeeded to the role of master gunner after death of Peter Baude. In 1551 they cast a most extraordinary and beautiful piece with a polygonal barley-twist barrel. In 1553 John (junior) drowned when a wherry attempting to pass though the arches of London bridge capsized, the wherrymen being saved by their oars. His companion was Ninion Saunders, another gunner from the Tower, and the master of Gilbert Pot who for seditious and treasonous words against Queen Jane had on the same day had his ears nailed and cropped.

Loading and aiming guns from the *Pirotechnica* of Vannocio Biringuccio (*c*.1480–*c*.1539). Powder barrels can be seen at the far left in front of the guns, not perhaps the best place for them! The loading tools are long; they have to be to permit easy handling. On the move they appear to have been tied over the barrel, a practical method that modern reenactors use. The gunner on the rear piece is aiming along the line of the metal using his thumbs. A foresight would be fixed to the muzzle in line with the bore of the barrel which might not be itself in line with the metal. Over the barrel can be seen a quadrant for measuring angles and a gunsight with several peepholes drilled for different elevations. Steven Walton, when considering the attitude of gunners to their powder, thinks that far from being a science, the gunners in the sixteenth and into the seventeenth century and later cared not so much for the science of their ingredients but for the art of their mixture. Gunnery was something of a mystery. (Walton, '*Proto-scientific Revolution or Cookbook Science? Early Gunnery Manuals in the Craft Treatise Tradition*', in Ricardo Córdoba (ed.), *Craft Treatises and Handbooks: the Dissemination of Technical Knowledge in the Middle Ages* (Turnhout: Brepols, 2014, *De Diversis Artibus* series, tome 91, (N.S. 54)), p.235)

Gunpowder

The manufacture of gunpowder relied on the 'incorporation' of its three constituents: sulphur, charcoal and saltpetre. Sulphur was found naturally occurring in volcanic regions in Italy and Iceland. Charcoal was already widely manufactured but saltpetre in a reasonably pure form could only be found outside England; it was imported from India and was purchased alongside other 'spices' from the East at a high price. As early as 1347, Thomas de Rolleston purchased saltpetre for the King's Privy Wardrobe at 18 pence a pound, and sulphur at eight.

The 'incorporation' of the materials was a long, demanding and potentially very dangerous process requiring the use of a rotary or stamping mill to grind them. The final product was a very fine powder known as serpentine. Gunpowder was not prone to the separation of its three constituents if properly made, as some suggest, but was like all salts prone to absorbing water; dampening the fine powder and forming it into cakes, which were then dried, reduced the problem. When dampened cakes were pushed through parchment sieves, granules of a specific size could be produced. It was found that these granules of 'corned' powder produced a more powerful propellant but one primarily suited to small arms. Finer 'corned' powder was even easier to ignite and was used as a priming powder. However, serpentine remained the powder for artillery throughout this period. As a light, loose, dry powdery material it had to be loaded with care: if it was too lightly or heavily compressed it would not burn properly and the shot would fall short.

Saltpetre was sometimes referred to as the 'master', as it was recognised as the key ingredient. Sulphur reduced the temperature of ignition and charcoal was universally available, although some wood such as willow was thought of as preferable to others. Imported saltpetre was preferred, but the quantity needed and the desire to reduce reliance on overseas purchase led to the encouragement of domestic manufacture, with little success. Saltpetre could be derived from the efflorescences or 'brushes' of nitrate crystals, which was the product of the chemical decomposition of waste, either human or animal. This valuable but unattractive material was to be found in dovecotes, stables, latrines and cellars, and would have to be purified by reducing in copper boilers. The 'Holy Grail' was to manufacture saltpetre in 'plantations' which simulated and accelerated the natural process. This was a business that had been mastered in Germany and Italy in the last quarter of the fourteenth century, so that in France between 1380 and 1420 the price of saltpetre halved. In 1545 von Haschenperg offered Henry VIII 'a way of making saltpetre, otherwise called black vitriol, in one place without going about the realm searching for it';[20] it was only in 1561 that there was an attempt to build a plantation, this time using a method purchased from the German Gerard Honricke, but it seems to have been a failure.

Henry was desperate to increase domestic manufacture of saltpetre. There is a reference to what may have been saltpetre production in England by John Stanget of Ipswich, who 'for making saltpeter' was paid £20 in 1511. A furnace 'for makyng of Salt peter in the Towne of wynborne mynster',[21] was used by the Mayor of Poole, and Oliver Russell was described on one occasion as a 'saltpetermaker'. It is more likely that these men were 'ffynyng Salt Pietyr in meell', a process designed to produce a purer product. The saltpetre was washed through with a mixture of potash (wood ashes) and quicklime which removed most of the remaining calcium and magnesium nitrates. Or it could mean the refining of naturally occurring saltpetre harvested from domestic sources. There were efforts by Hans Van Colen (Hans Wolf) in 1515, commissioned by the Crown, to find a naturally occurring deposits and 'to go from shire to shire to find a place where there is stuff to make saltpetre of'.[22] He was also required to make restitution for any damage that occurred when digging for the rare black earth that was so eagerly sought. This was a commission on similar terms as that granted to Thomas Lee in 1531. Antonio de Napoli set about finding sources rich in saltpetre in Shrewsbury at St. Mary's Abbey, however the defilement of sacred ground so outraged the local population that they ambushed his men on the roads and forced them to abandon their efforts.

---

20 David Cressy, *Saltpeter: The Mother of Gunpowder* (Oxford: Oxford University Press, 2013), p.45.
21 Goring, 'Military Obligations', p.47.
22 Cressy, *Saltpeter*, p.43.

Henry VII had no great need of large stocks of gunpowder; his son, on the other hand, required a mountain of saltpetre to fulfil his martial ambitions. David Cressy refers to 'Henry VIII's gunpowder kingship', stressing the young sovereign's need for that substance. For his sieges of Thérouanne and Tournai in 1513 he employed 250 guns supplied with 510 tons of gunpowder.[23] In preparation for the war 707 lb gunpowder and 2,906 lb of saltpetre was bought at 3½d a pound and saltpetre at 4d a pound from a Spanish merchant Francis de Errona. Large quantities were also bought from the Italian merchants Thomas and John Cavalcanti and the German Edmond Frende of the Steelyard, who imported a large quantity of other war materials for the King. Some was purchased directly from merchants in Germany, Spain and Italy, including from the merchants France de Bara and Benedict Morovell from Lucca. Although mixed gunpowder was purchased, the Ordnance officials preferred to buy the separate ingredients, so that in 15143 46,218 lb of saltpetre was bought at 6d a pound.

The royal gunpowder makers in this period were mostly again foreign born, including Robert Fisher from 1521, who lost his post when he was found guilty of murder in 1534. He was succeeded by Luke de la Arche and Geoffrey Hughes, who were followed in turn by Antonio de Napoli and William Parker. From 1543 the manufacturer of gunpowder remained solely in the hands of Englishmen, although foreign workmen were still employed.

The quantity of gunpowder used was enormous. During the siege of Boulogne in 1544 the battery of the lord admiral would have used almost five tons of gunpowder every day, even at the conservative rate of 36 rounds per day per gun. The full siege train would require well over 20 tons per day. The reserve stockpile of powder, as well as its constituents, was held in the Tower. The standard weight of powder was a barrel of 100 lb with the barrel weighing an additional 12 lb (totalling one hundredweight or 112 lb). Twenty barrels weighed one ton and contained a 'last', or 2,000 lb of powder. There were only 13 lasts of gunpowder in the Tower in 1523 after eight had been sent to the North, although by 1536 there were 39 lasts and 11 barrels of gunpowder and four lasts of saltpetre in store. In the inventory of 1547 there was a healthy stock of 40 lasts of gunpowder, 46 lasts of corned powder and 140,000 lb of saltpetre and 20,000 lb of sulphur: an investment of around £8,000 but only amounting to 150 tons of gunpowder, far less than a third of the quantity taken to France in 1513. On Henry's death the demand for gunpowder declined but still had to be met by foreign purchase. In Edward VI's reign saltpetre was bought from the Netherlands at £3 a hundredweight, while in Mary's reign Spanish sources were made more readily available, as a consequence of her marriage to Phillip.

---

23 Cressy, *Saltpeter*, p.39.

14

Fortifying this Realm

An Era of Change

The impact of gunpowder artillery on the development of fortifications has been the subject of prolonged debate. The only effective pre-gunpowder heavy 'artillery' was the trebuchet. This could hurl a projectile weighing several hundred pounds at over 120 mph with considerable precision. This weapon appeared in England at the siege of Dover in 1217, and would only slowly be replaced by gunpowder artillery in the last quarter of the fourteenth century.

Medieval fortifications were remarkably resilient in the face of both the trebuchet and the bombard. At the siege of Harfleur in 1415 some 7,466 gunstones were shot, at the rate of 286 per day, yet the town surrendered because of the failure to relieve it rather than because of the damage caused by prolonged bombardment.

Large bronze artillery pieces had a significant impact on the development of fortifications. Although the projectiles shot from even the heaviest bronze cannon would be much lighter than those fired from a wrought iron bombard, their velocity was much greater. As the kinetic energy of a projectile is calculated using the formula K.E.= ½ MV² (Kinetic Energy equals half Mass multiplied by the Velocity squared), the key to increasing the energy of a projectile is to increase its velocity. Thus, a culverin shooting a 30 lb iron projectile at 1,500 feet a second could match in energy a wrought iron bombard shooting a stone ball of around 100 lb. Bronze guns had a much greater rate of fire than the bombard: cast iron was three times the density of stone and was much less likely to shatter on impact, and projectiles could also be recovered after or even during the siege. The accuracy of the bronze gun, with a much smaller windage than the bombard, was also much greater.

Under these new conditions medieval fortifications, which were reliant on tall masonry walls and towers, proved vulnerable. The response to improvements in artillery had already included a new strategy designed to negate the impact of projectiles by absorbing rather than repelling it. This was already well understood in personal defence, where all 'hard' armour also relied on padded protection to absorb the blow. At the siege of Harfleur a circular exterior fortification was built from large tree trunks, reinforced on the inside with earth and wood which proved easy to maintain in the face of

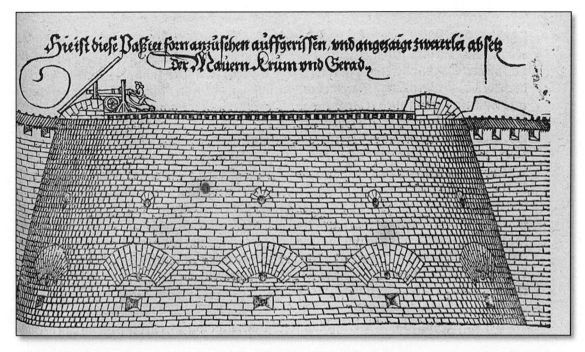

Dürer proposed strong semi-circular and horseshoe-shaped stone fortifications of great strength. This vast stone-built circular bastion was well-designed and the gun emplacements were provided with ventilation shafts, essential if the crews were not to be rendered useless by the smoke and noise. Although not invulnerable, it was an infinitely better form of defence than the flimsy earth-filled gabions the besiegers would be cowering behind. (Deutsche Fotothek, Saxon State Library)

bombardment. Inside the town the streets were covered with earth, clay and dung to in order to absorb some of the impact of the English bombardment. It was clear that earth defences could absorb the impact of high velocity projectiles as long as they were deep enough; furthermore, they were readily repairable using the displaced material.

The idea of an artillery tower designed to mount gunpowder weapons was not new. In Norwich, Cow Tower had walls built with a brick facing on a mortared flint rubble interior. Fifteen metres high and fitted with splayed gunports as well as arrow loops, it was built in 1398–9 to defend the approach to Bishop's Gate over the River Wensum. The Château de Castelnaud has a most impressive late medieval gun tower integrated into its fortifications, as well as several horseshoe-shaped blockhouses. The castle at Fougères has a magnificent horseshoe-shaped tower built in 1480, provided with six tiers of guns, and the last gun tower in Italy was constructed in Assisi in 1535. Albrecht Dürer produced a design for a massive gun tower with two lower gun decks and a massive ditch, an illustration of which was published in 1527. It has been assumed, with very little evidence, that Dürer was influential in the English Device forts. Eltis goes so far as to say: 'It is clear, however, that their [Device forts] inspiration was continental, reflecting design popularised by

The Tower of Italy at Rhodes: the Cornish castle of St Mawes in miniature? Only one of the six embrasures in the main battery point directly outwards, the others provide flanking or seaward fire. The super-firing tower was a small fortress in its own right. There were also embrasures set at ground level to sweep the deep moat, while the two upper gun levels could fire over the counterscarp. It is easy to see how this example could have acted as an inspiration for military architects seeking to modernise their defences across Christendom. (Courtesy of Travel Architecture)

Albrecht Dürer.'[1] Gun towers had always been more popular in Germany and Poland, and Dürer's drawings were showing what was becoming an obsolescent form of defence. O'Neil in his study of early fortifications has asserted that: 'The conclusion seems to be inescapable that the English works are a product of English adaptation of Continental models.'[2]

Dürer's book *Etliche Underricht zu Befestigung der Stett, Schloss und Flecken* (Treatise on the Fortification of City, Castle, and Places) was reprinted in 1530 and 1538 and was influential, especially in Eastern Europe. Dürer wrote at a time when the threat to Christendom from Ottoman Turkey was at its height. Rhodes had been lost in 1523,[3] and the disaster of Mohacs horrified Christendom in 1526. His designs were intended to provide an eastern wall against the Turk. His proposals involved massive stone-built circular or horseshoe-shaped towers and low semi-circular earthen bastions.

One other unexpected source of inspiration may have been the Hospitaller fortifications in Rhodes, which underwent considerable modernisation in the decades between the siege of 1480 and the final siege of 1522. The stories surrounding these epic sieges kept Christendom enthralled. The improvements in Rhodes were designed to counter and take advantage of the

---

1   Eltis, *The Military Revolution*, p.115.
2   B.H.J. St J. O'Neil, *Castles and Cannon: A Study of Early Artillery Fortifications in England* (Westport, Conn.: Greenwood Press, 1975), p.61.
3   The Knights departed on 1 January 1523, but the year traditionally started on 25 March.

new trend in powerful bronze artillery. Moats were broadened and a second wall or *tenaille* of earth and stone was built, often using the existing glacis and its counterscarp (which formed the inner face).[4] Fortifications were heightened and walls thickened, making a *terreplein* or wide platform upon which large-calibre guns could be mounted and moved.

The existing towers were often transformed in both scale and purpose, with a stress on the use of gunpowder weapons providing flanking fire along the moat, as well as providing counter battery fire. Both the towers of Saint George and the tower of Spain were reinforced with complex angular multi-faced bastions, for example. Most intriguing is the Tower of Italy, designed by Basilio dalla Scuola di Vicenza, Emperor Maximilian's personal military engineer, and constructed between 1515–17 at the order of the Grand Master Fabrizio del Carretta.[5] It was not an angular but a semi-circular fortification 50 metres in diameter, which was integrated with an existing tower, over 20 metres in diameter, which was heightened and strengthened. The Hospitallers also built two semi-circular bastions in the two fortresses at Antimacheia and Nerantzia on the nearby island of Kos.

Henry VIII had close connections with the Hospitaller Order, and especially their Prior of England Thomas Docwra. The Prior was a trusted servant of the Order and the Crown, acting regularly in England's interests as an ambassador and attending the Field of the Cloth of Gold. On his death in 1527 he was succeeded as prior by William Weston, who served until 1540. He had been a senior commander in the Order, being appointed the admiral of the fleet of the Knights in 1520 and wounded during the siege of Rhodes in 1522. Henry was granted the title of 'Protector of the Order' and although his relationship was often testy and exploitative he eventually purchased 19 bronze cannon and 1,023 cannonballs on the Order's behalf; one cannon is now on display at St John's Clerkenwell. Henry's connections with the Order were clearly close and he would have had the expertise of its prior to call upon. The present author would not suggest that Henry's Device forts were based on a Hospitaller or Rhodesian model, only that experimentation in military architecture was rife at the time and that there were many more possible sources of inspiration than Dürer's book.

Cathcart King, when considering the origin of Henry's Device forts, declares that: 'it appears that the answer may be disappointing to those who wish to trace a well-founded pedigree through every period; in fact, these castles seem to have been evolved in the brains of Henry VIII and his officers.'[6] It is worth mentioning that the Tudor Rose, the best example of a monarchical logo, shows some obvious similarities to Henry VIII's stone castles.

---

4   Smith and De Vries, *Rhodes Besieged*.
5   Smith and De Vries, *Rhodes Besieged*, p.176.
6   David James Cathcart King, *The Castle in England and Wales: An Interpretative History* (London: Routledge, 1991), p.186.

The Trace Italienne

The shape of fortifications also underwent a transformation in order to protect the wall with flanking fire. In the 1440s the architect Leon Battista Alberti had suggested that 'The wall should be flanked by towers acting as buttresses every 50 cubits. They should be round, standing out from the wall, and somewhat taller, so that anyone venturing too close would expose his flank to missiles and be hit; thus the wall is protected by the towers and the towers by each other.'[7] In addition, the towers were to be 'filled with a mixture of clay and straw, and packed down. Thus, the softness of the clay will deaden the force and impact of the engines.'[8] Using these ideas medieval castles could be 'modernised' by adopting some relatively simple measures. The medieval castle at Tantallon was transformed by the building of a gun tower fitted with wide-mouthed horizontal gun ports, towers and chambers in the curtain wall were filled with rubble to help absorb the impact of shot, the remaining towers were strengthened, and forward earthworks were constructed to keep enemy artillery at a distance.[9] The importance of flanking fire, the mounting of artillery and the use of material to absorb the impact of shot was clearly appreciated quite early on.

It was in the late fifteenth and early sixteenth centuries in Italy that the full effect of the new artillery would be felt and a process of refortification began. The initial response to the new dangers posed by artillery was to bury the high walls of the castle in an even deeper moat and to simplify and modify the corner towers to provide better fields of fire. The best example is Fort Sarzanello, that was completed between 1493–1502 by Francesco Giamberti. It was made up of two massive triangles, one of which had towers set into each corner and set inside a deep ditch. The problem of providing fully integrated flanking fire was being addressed in a number of Italian fortifications, the Pogio Imperiale (1495–1513) and the fortress of Nettuno (1501–1503), where the gun chambers were carefully arranged to provide both crossfire and flanking fire. The castle walls were still high, although the lower level had a pronounced scarp which meant that the guns had to fire down on their attackers. This had two disadvantages: firstly, that plunging fire meant that you would normally have a lower point of aim and secondly that the balls were less likely to ricochet, instead burying themselves in the ground.

These Italian developments ultimately produced the angled bastion, a diamond-.shaped defence that replaced the round tower as it provided a better mounting for artillery and a wider field of fire. It would provide flanking fire along the walls between the bastions, from gun chambers or casemates that were well protected from offensive fire. The tall stone walls still presented an excellent target and would be replaced by much lower structures. Stone as a material was excellent, but the cost of building massive stone-built structures was enormous. The alternative material was of course earth, which would absorb the impact of artillery projectiles rather than trying to resist them.

---

7   Leon Battista Alberti, *On the Art of Building in Ten Books* (MIT Press, 1988), p.104.
8   Alberti, *On the Art of Building*, p.104.
9   Statement of Significance. Tantallon Castle. Historic Environment Scotland. pp.15–16.

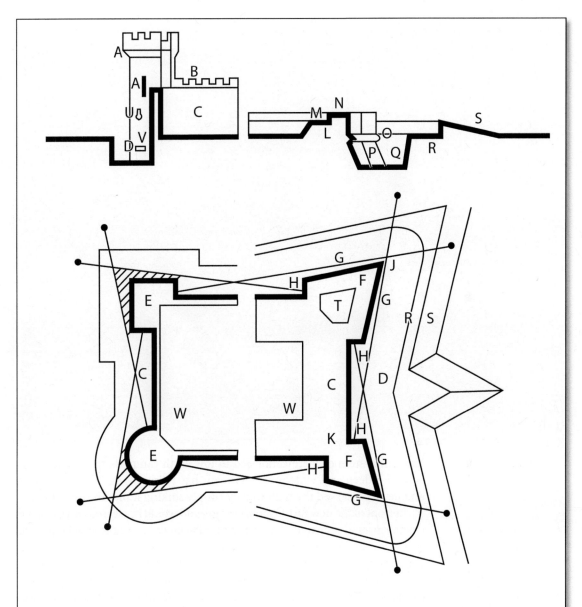

Medieval and Early Modern fortificatons

A: Machicolations from which defenders could drop objects on attackers at the base of the wall.

B: Crenels and Merlons. The gap between could be provided with moveable wooden shutters.

C: Curtain wall.

D: Ditch.

E: Towers, hatching indicated dead ground, where defensive fire could not reach attackers.

F: Bastion.

G: Face of the bastion.

H: Flank of the bastion. From which flanking fire could sweep the curtain wall between bastions.

J: Salient, the point of the bastion.

K: Gorge or throat of the bastion.

L: Rampart.

M: Terreplein, gun platform.

N: Parapet.

O: Cordon, moulding dividing vertical and battered portions of the rampart or bastion.

P: Scarp, battered section of rampart or bastion.

Q: Counterscarp.

R: Covered way, for movement of infantry.

S: Glacis, gentle slope concealing all but the upper most defensive works, providing no cover for an attacking force.

T: Cavalier, raised gun platform in bastion.

U: Keyhole, early style of gunport.

V: Letterbox gunport, usually found at low level.

W: Enceinte, the area enclosed by fortifications.

Speculum Romanae Magnificentiae (The Mirror of Roman Magnificence): Castello Sant' Angelo 1557 by Giulio de Musi. The Papal fortress demonstrates the steps taken towards the full *trace italienne*. Round towers were added to Hadrian's circular mausoleum in 1447. These were encased by octagonal gun towers in 1492–5 and all were enclosed by Francesco Laparelli's bastions between 1561–5. (Metropolitan Museum of Art, Open Access)

The new system of fortification led to low earth ramparts that could be set behind a deep and wide moat. As Lynn has pointed out: 'Thus in a sense, architects preserved the high wall by simply sinking it into the ground.'[10]

In front of the new fortifications the ground would be cleared and a glacis or sloping ground prepared, that would provide no cover for the attacking forces and a clear field of fire for the defenders. As this system developed first in Italy, where civic rivalries and the Habsburg–Valois contest made war endemic, it was called the *trace italienne*. The labour required to build and maintain earth fortifications on a scale large enough to encircle a town was still enormous and the cost horrendous, as Somerset found when building Haddington and his other forts. The introduction of the 'new artillery' did not make medieval fortifications obsolete, especially as with little effort they could be reinforced to deal with the new threat. Thérouanne and Boulogne were primarily medieval fortifications and resisted prolonged sieges, as did Metz, which held out successfully against an army of 60,000–80,000 for over two months in 1552.[11]

---

10   John A. Lynn, 'The trace italienne and the Growth of Armies: The French Case', *The Journal of Military History*, vol. 55, no. 3 (July 1991), p.302.

11   Lynn, 'The trace italienne', p.308.

The English Experience

On Henry VII's accession England was still a country of castles and defended towns and cities, but it was also a country pretty much at peace with itself. Although subject to the occasional French raid on the south coast, the only area subject to endemic warfare was the Scottish border. The War of the Roses (1455–1487) did not involve prolonged sieges but skirmishes and battles. There was therefore very little necessity for the maintenance let alone the growth of defences. The establishment of domestic peace by Henry VII was enforced by financial penalties for ill-disposed nobility, rather than by artillery. However this does not mean that walls and moats became irrelevant. Of 249 charter towns, 109 still had substantial walls in the late Middle Ages and walls could prove of use, as both Norwich and Exeter were besieged and in the case of Norwich successfully assaulted in 1549. Even London was threatened in 1554. In the north of England, the defences of castles and towns were maintained and improved in the face of probable invasion. The Calais Pale, the remaining English territory in France, also had to be secured against the threat of attack.

Guns could be incorporated in existing defences. This required the addition of small gunports to augment or replace arrow slits, such as at Kirby Muxloe and the Canterbury City walls. The weapons employed would still be comparatively small, as their purpose was to provide counter-battery fire and target the wooden and earth defences of an attacker. The most significant innovation in the history of the development of late medieval fortification in England was the building of Dartmouth Castle, begun in 1481. The Tower structure was provided with a basement-level gun room with large openings providing a wider field of fire for the seven large-calibre weapons that could have been fired from them. The recognition of the power of offensive and defensive fire led to the addition of similar gun ports and gun rooms at Norham, Carlisle and Berwick castles. In the case of Norham substantial work began as early as 1509, with three heavy guns mounted in the curtain wall while the round towers were modified into a semi-hexagonal pattern and provided with ports for firearms and light guns. At Wark Castle on the River Tweed, a polygonal four-storey tower fully equipped for artillery of all sizes was constructed. In Berwick was built the 'Lord's Mount', a massive round tower 105 feet in diameter, with walls 16 feet thick, equipped with six gunports with a large internal and external splay, permitting a wide field of fire. It must have been a most impressive structure and could have been the starting point for the later Device forts.

Earth Fortifications

Fortifications built of earth were far more extensively used than is generally thought. Field fortifications were used successfully by the Cornish rebels on several occasions, and were prepared at Dussindale by Kett's rebels in their last stand. They played an important part in the King's 'Device' and were central to Somerset's policy of establishing garrisons in Scotland.

Field fortifications could be constructed quickly and easily by a population well supplied with spades, mattocks, barrows and baskets, scythes and axes. A trench would provide the material for the rampart on the other side, and stakes, brushwood and thorns placed in the bottom of the trench would further discommode attackers. If a larger and more permanent structure was required, then a very different task presented itself.

To resist the impact of a cannonball required a great thickness of earth, and if the rampart was to have artillery mounted on top it had to be able to bear a considerable weight as well. The impact of heavy artillery on any structure was fearsome. In 1652 during trials at Woolwich, a 32 lb ball with a 12 lb charge went through 19 inches of solid oak, flew 14 yards, then through a further 19 inches of oak before finally embedding itself in an earth backstop.[12] In trials reported in 1861 a 6-pdr gun penetrated up to seven feet and a 12-pdr up to 10 feet of earth.[13] The velocities achieved by artillery in the early sixteenth century approximate those achieved centuries later. Surprisingly, there was little difference found between loose and packed earth. It was calculated that a well-packed earth wall, some 11 feet in height and 23 feet in depth would be needed to resist serious siege artillery,[14] while one foot of well-packed earth was considered necessary to stop a musket ball. There is a unique type of stone that has similar properties to earth when struck by a cannonball. This is a sedimentary stone, formed from shells with a loosely connected internal structure known as coquina. The Castillo de San Marcos, a Spanish fortification in Florida, was constructed from coquina. When bombarded by the English the cannonballs were 'swallowed', as the material was compressed and displaced and did not shatter or crack.

To attempt to construct such a fortification with earth alone was likely to end in disaster. The angle of repose, the steepest angle at which earth can be stable, varies from 30–45 degrees. Water can play a crucial part in the stability of a slope by significantly reducing the shear resistance of the material, causing it to slide or slump. At Balgillo, an earthen castle which protected Broughty Craig, the ramparts were collapsing under their own sodden weight and Sir John Luttrell, the garrison commander, ordered loads of lime to 'cement' his earthen walls. Scotland can be very wet! To construct an earth fortification of any great size required considerable labour, a range of tools and materials and engineering skill.

Giovanni Battista Beluzzi described in some detail the materials and methods of making a strong earth structure. Firstly, it required substantial foundations formed by piles driven deep into the ground and the gaps between them filled with rubble. Heavy timber uprights would then be positioned on a five-foot grid. A chain of lateral timber reinforcements would then form a carpet every three or six feet. This would be filled with 2–3 inch layers of earth and twigs well rammed. All stones or pebbles had to

---

12 Stephen Bull, *The Furie of the Ordnance: Artillery in the English Civil Wars* (Woodbridge: The Boydell Press, 2008), p.26.
13 E.L. Viele, *Hand-book of field fortifications and artillery* (Richmond, Va: J.W. Randolph, 1861), p.5.
14 Bull, *The Furie of the Ordnance*, p.87.

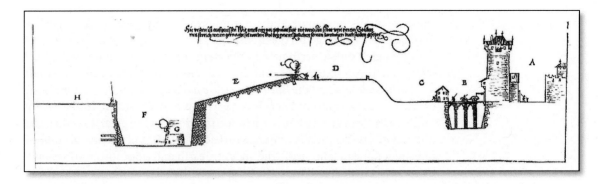

This illustration in Dürer's *Treatise* demonstrates how a feeble medieval town wall might be fronted with a massive earthwork fortification. The earth is protected by a stone skin to secure it in place. The glacis is well sloped and would provide a glancing surface against incoming fire. The wide rampart would permit guns to be withdrawn into dead ground to avoid unnecessary exposure or moved easily to a better position. The moat has a small circular pillbox which would develop into the *caponier* at a later date. What is impressive and daunting is the sheer volume of material that would need to be excavated. Such a fortification was neither cheap nor quick to construct, as Siena discovered to its cost. (Courtesy of the Library of Congress)

be removed as they might create shrapnel if hit by a cannonball. The exterior of the wall would be contained by fascines (bundles of twigs), which would be tied to the internal timber structure. The outside could then be provided with a turf wall laid horizontally, secured with vertical pegs. The deck could be made from rammed clay and if necessary additional layers of clay could be used to act as damp-proof courses. The parapet and gun emplacement would then be provided for, using gabions (large wicker baskets), which would be filled with well-rammed earth.

The equipment required was considerable and although the individual skills themselves would have been well understood and often practised, building such a large structure required men inured to hard work in the field in all weathers and having the right tools for the job. It also required an individual who had the civil engineering skills of a military architect to manage the project. Embarrassing mistakes could be made, as was in the case of the key fortification of Outreau outside Boulogne, which was intended by the French to intimidate the English garrison. Antonio Mellone, the Italian engineer, planned a fine pentagonal fort with grand bastions. He failed to consider the slopes of the bastions and made them too small to mount artillery. He also provided an internal space suitable for only 500–600 men, not the 5,000 planned. In addition the water supply was problematic and to add to his misery one of the bastions collapsed soon after construction.

With good design, some imagination and considerable labour an obsolete fortification could become a tough nut to crack. The castle at Cessford was 'vawmewred with earth of the best sort',[15] and the barmkin or defensive enclosure outside the castle also had an earthwork revetment added to it. The consequence was that it easily coped with the bombardment by the Earl of Surrey's troops when besieged in 1523. The castle was only taken by storm,

15 *Letters and Papers*, vol. 3, p.1276, 21 May.

after which Surrey remarked that: 'It might never have been taken had the assailed been able to go on defending.'[16]

Although a simple earth field fortification consisting of a ditch with a wall constructed from the spoil would be both cheap and quick to build, a full-scale fortification along the lines of the *trace italienne* could prove enormously expensive as it was meant to enclose a garrison or even a town. In the case of the Republic Siena the cost of her new fortifications was so great that when war was declared she lacked the resources to defend herself, and the city succumbed to Florence after a long siege. The 'modern' earth and stone fortifications built by Somerset in Scotland were often impressive but also ruinously expensive.

The Design of the Device Forts

The short-lived rapprochement between Francis I and Charles V in 1538 led to Henry fearing the threat of invasion.[17] This seemed an unlikely rapprochement: the relationship between the Empire and France had been one of near unremitting hostility, focused on their rivalry over Italy (some eight wars were fought in Italy during this period) not on hostility to England. Even so Henry's response was extraordinary. Perhaps the vigour and extent of Henry's building programme can be explained simply because he could now afford to do it. Access to the wealth of the dissolved monasteries provided Henry with the resources to fulfil his grandiose scheme, and grand it was. Brian O'Neil described it as 'the only scheme of comprehensive coastal defence ever attempted in England before modern times',[18] while Paul Hammer considered it 'the most elaborate and expensive system of coastal defences constructed in England since Roman times'.

The description of these fortifications as the 'Device forts' comes from the 'Device by the King for three new bulwarks to be made in the Downs and in other places frontiers to the sea', of 1539.[19] It was a scheme or 'device' designed to protect the principal harbours and important anchorages that would have been essential for an invading force. England had few problems when invading France because it had access to the secure and well-defended port of Calais. A raiding force, even one some thousands strong, could easily land on the English coast, as one did on the Isle of Wight in 1545; however to land an army and sustain it necessitated the control of a good ports and a safe anchorages, and Henry was to deny these with his Device forts.

The defences were concentrated on a few key areas. The most extensive and expensive fortifications defended the important anchorage known as the Downs, where a long line of three massive stone and four turf bulwarks were constructed. There were strong defences around Dover, where three new bulwarks were completed. The Thames estuary was protected by

---

16   Francis Groome, *Ordnance Gazetteer of Scotland: A Survey of Scottish Topography – Statistical, Biographical and Historical*, vol. 1 (Bristol: Thoemmes, 1882), p.258.

17   Hammer, *Elizabeth's Wars*, p.13.

18   O'Neil, *Castles and Cannon*, p.43.

19   Peter Harrington, *The Castles of Henry VIII* (London: Osprey Publishing, 2007), p.11.

Artillery fort on the Kent coast. Part fairytale, part architect's drawing this gives an excellent impression as to what the Device castles were intended to be, well fortified and ferocious. They never mounted the numbers of guns shown but those that they did have would have had the impressive fields of fire as represented here. The way in which the moat would have been swept with gunfire is also highlighted. The wooden walkway would have been removed if it faced a landward siege; the portcullises also added to its protection from assault. (Courtesy of the British Library. BL Cotton Augustus I. i. 20)

five blockhouses, including what would become the great fort at Tilbury. Portsmouth, the Solent, Southampton Water and Cowes were provided with eight castles. Plymouth and Falmouth were well defended and many other ports including Poole, Fowey and Yarmouth also had castles built. Anchorages other than the Downs were also defended including Camber anchorage, Weymouth Bay and the Portland Roads. Harwich and Hull received strong defences and three smaller earth forts were built to protect the River Colne and the estuary. It is worth considering how well their sites were chosen, which is why so many of these defences were modified, modernised and found useful for over four centuries, until coastal defence as a concept was abandoned.

There have been critics of the design of the Device forts, especially of the stone castles that have been considered as obsolescent if not obsolete at the time of their construction. Colin Platt has described them simply as

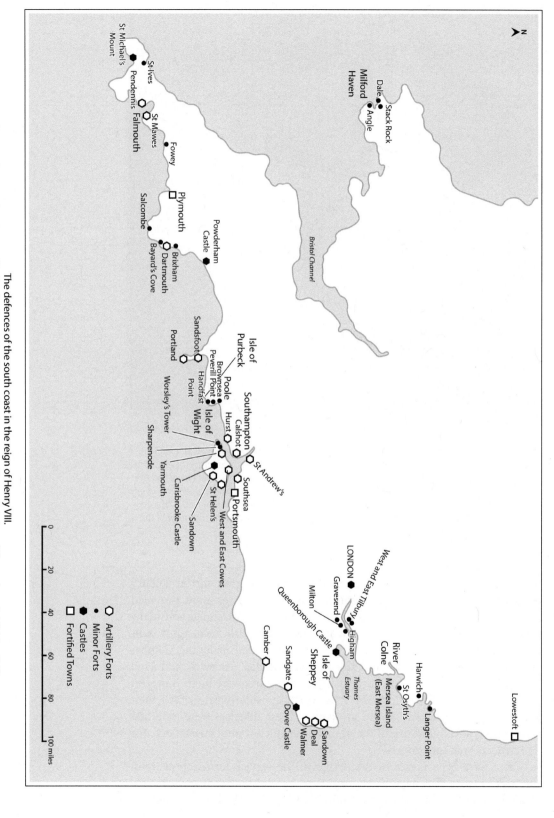

The defences of the south coast in the reign of Henry VIII.

(© J R Hale, 1983, *Renaissance War Studies* fig. 26, Hambledon Continuum, used by permission of Bloomsbury Publishing PLC)

an 'upstanding fortification' and Dr Duffy as a form of 'reinforced-castle fortification,' suggesting that they are hybrid structures and an evolutionary dead-end, combining the medieval stone structures with artillery firepower. Eltis goes further in his criticism: 'Though England was rapid enough in appreciating the importance of artillery in defence, it was far too slow in adapting the angle-bastion, which made the best possible use of defensive guns within a fortification … [the Device forts] did not use the angle-bastion but merely provided numerous openings for cannon in a relatively unsophisticated medieval design.'[20] Eltis quite rightly quotes William Bourne, who had served in the Gravesend bulwark and later as the master gunner at Upnor Castle in 1574, who pointed out that Henry's castles 'were rounds, or part of rounds, which are of no force for that they cannot flancke the ditches.'[21]

Gun towers, of which the Device forts might be considered an example, could therefore be considered somewhat passé, as it was generally recognised that the future of fortification was to be found in the geometry and resilience of the *trace italienne*. This criticism is perhaps supported by the enthusiasm with which this new style was adopted for many of the new fortifications built by Somerset in Scotland, less than a decade later. Even some of the Device forts such as Mersea, St Osyth and Brightlingsea which were simple 'bulwarkes of earth and board', were built on the new design. On the other hand, the new Italian system of fortification was only just emerging from Italy into more northern climes the 1530s, a point that both Hale and Parker make.

The present author thinks that the criticisms that the stone Device forts were obsolete and inadequate are unfair. These forts were designed to protect anchorages from an enemy fleet and this they would have achieved. Their design was outstandingly good. Only the firing platforms were visible and the forts were set in deep forbidding moats. The numerous turrets provided overlapping arcs of fire behind secure thick walls. The severe design and round form would cause projectiles to ricochet and wherever possible 'shot traps' such as machicolations were avoided. Their magazines were safe beneath a mass of masonry, and their gun positions well aired and spacious enough for the guns to be worked with efficiency. They satisfactorily performed the role of stone battleships. They were well able to defend themselves from the landward side and their entrances contained all the items of defence. These include such features as a portcullis, drawbridge, murder holes and numerous gunports to cover the entrance and sometimes a fighting gallery at ditch level, to bring arquebus fire to bear on any intruders in their substantial moats. It is important to stress their purpose, which was to sink enemy vessels seeking to anchor off the coast or to seize a harbour. It was never their purpose to host large garrisons, nor were they expected to undergo a prolonged siege. It is unsurprising that 250 years later the Martello tower was adopted to perform a similar role, in brick. An inexperienced observer might easily have assumed that the Aldeburgh Martello in its quatrefoil form (1808–1812) was a later addition to the Device forts.

---

20 Eltis, *The Military Revolution*, p.120.
21 William Bourne, *Inventions or devises very necessary for all Generalles and Captaines*, STC 3421 (1578), p.56.

Hale recognised the strengths of these impressive structures: 'The Device fortresses were massively beautiful machines designed for the maximum emission of balls and bullets.'[22] He also pointed to:

> the structural weakness of bastions, however thick their walls, that were fenestrated with artillery apertures; the progressive masking of fire from platforms, tier by tier, as an assault edged forwards; the unflanked dead ground presented by any rounded surface that allowed miners to nestle against its snout and burrow down and explode their barrels of gunpowder.[23]

Although, he also pointed out that 'close' sieges were unlikely to occur:

> Coastal fortresses did not expect to be subjected to a formal siege and to the laborious sap-work of miners. Why should an invading army bother about taking places whose garrisons were too small to provide any serious harassment to their advance? The fortresses' job was to make anchorages untenable and beat off raiding parties.[24]

Which is precisely what they would have achieved.

Deal Castle is an excellent example of its type, with much of it buried in a deep moat. The central circular keep is surrounded by six bastions forming the outer structure with six smaller bastions superimposed upon those, to produce the equivalent of the A and B turrets on a warship. In total there are 66 firing positions for artillery. Only the gun decks would be visible to an attacker. These gun positions, strong and stable, would have very little trouble hitting large wooden ships at a considerable range, the accuracy of their guns could be fully exploited as well as their hitting power. Enemy ships on the other hand would have to approach close inshore to have any hope of hitting what little of the forts that could be seen.

The criticism that can justifiably be made of the castles and bulwarks is that they were underarmed. If we consider the three principal castles on the Downs (in 1547) they had only some 20 pieces of artillery capable of doing serious damage to an enemy vessel and 12 of those were older wrought iron port-pieces. Although these could still do considerable damage to a wooden hull, as the recent trials have shown, they were by no means as accurate as a heavy bronze cannon. Their effective range would be measured in but a few hundreds of metres. The analysis of artillery by Alexzandra Hildred classifies the port-piece as being a medium range weapon with a point-blank range of 200 m: approximately half that of the heavier bronze guns.[25] The distance between St Mawes and Pendennis castles, protecting the Falmouth anchorage, is about 2,000 yards which would suggest a minimum effective range of 1,000 yards if the entrance was to be covered. John Sheriffe in his

---

22   Hale, *Renaissance War Studies*, p.73.
23   Hale, *Renaissance War Studies*, p.73.
24   Hale, *Renaissance War Studies*, p.77.
25   Hildred, *Weapons of Warre*, p.923.

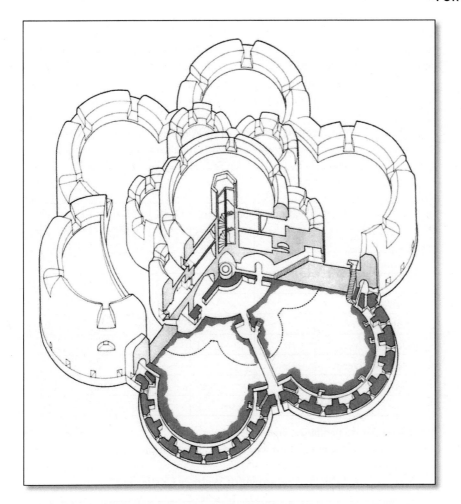

Deal Castle perspective. This image gives an excellent impression of the sophistication and strength of a Device fort. They owed little if anything to a 'medieval' tradition. It should be compared to Fort d'Ambleteuse on the Channel coast, designed by the greatest military architect of over a century later, the Marquis de Vauban. Thick-walled artillery towers with a good field of fire were more than a match for wooden ships that could be smashed to splinters. (© J.R. Hale, 1983, *Renaissance War Studies*, Fig. 34. Hambledon Continuum, used by permission of Bloomsbury Publishing PLC)

list of ordnance of 1590 suggests a point-blank range for heavy artillery of between 300 and 400 yards and a maximum range of about a mile (1,760 yards). It was also common practice to 'skip' cannonballs towards a target, in the same way that a flat spinning stone be skipped across the surface of the water. This technique would be more likely to hit the enemy vessel than direct fire. The recent trials of a recreated Vasa gun demonstrate that the point of aim at 1,000 metres would have been well above the highest topmast of any vessel. To achieve a hit would mean that either the rounds were 'skipped' at the target or that ranges were carefully marked.

The allocation of ammunition to the heavier bronze pieces was significantly greater than that for port-pieces. I would assume that the port-piece would only be shot at short range where it would have been effective, while bronze pieces would be expected to engage at a much greater distance, and probably therefore over a longer period of time and would require more ammunition. The allocation of iron shot to heavy bronze guns in six castles was 65 rounds per gun while the port-piece had only 27. The figures for ammunition allocation aboard the *Mary Rose* are not dissimilar.

Table 7. Comparative Armament of Warships and Device Forts

*There were 14 smaller bronze and iron guns as well as 14 arquebuses.

† There were 39 firing positions for artillery. It was also equipped with 14 smaller pieces.

‡ Cannon Perrier firing stone shot.

	Walmer*	Sandown†	Deal	Matthew Henry	Lesser Bark
Cannon of Brass	1		1		2‡
Demi-cannon			3	2	2
Culverin			1		1
Culverin					1
Demi-Culverin	1	1		7	
Demi-Culverin				2	
Port Pieces	5§	2‖	7	16	14
Total	7	2	12	27	20

§ There were also four port-pieces, 'broken alle in peices'.

‖ One of which lacked its breech. There were also four unserviceable port-pieces.

Table 8. Armament of Walmer Castle, 1547

Cannon of Brasse i
Demi-Culverin of brasse i
Falconets of brasse i
Sacres of Brasse i
Port pieces of yron v
Slynges of Yron vi
Serpentynes viii
Hagbusshes and Half-hakes[arquebuses] xiv
Bowes liii [53]

[Not all of the above were serviceable at the time of the survey]

If the armament of the Device forts seems surprisingly sparse, so does the size of their permanent garrisons. Walmer castle in 1540 had a garrison of one captain with two lieutenants, two porters, 10 gunners and three soldiers, which cost in one year £174. This number was clearly inadequate to man even a fraction of its armament. The full equipment of the garrison would be seven pieces of heavy artillery, 14 lighter crewed pieces, 14 firearms and over 50 bows. In the 1998 trials of a reconstructed port-piece by the Royal Armouries a crew of at least five or six was needed; the crew for a large bronze gun would have been similar in number, and these figures do not take account of the additional crew members required to bring ammunition to the gun etc. The garrison available in 1540 could on its own man only two large pieces of artillery! To man all the guns and have some infantry able to use the firearms would have required well over 100 men. The permanent garrison would therefore have to be considerably reinforced if the castle was to perform its duties fully. The preponderance of gunners in the permanent garrison would suggest that they were assigned to captain individual guns, which would have been crewed by the local militia. Walmer was not alone in being badly undermanned. Camber Castle had a garrison of only 29 and West Tilbury blockhouse only nine. Portland Castle, which had four large pieces of artillery and four smaller, was provided with a captain, four gunners and 'two others'.

There is little to suggest that other critically important defences, such as those at Berwick, were fully manned and equipped. Symon Sage complained to the Office of the Ordnance in March 1545 that of the 10 gunners there only four were competent and that the captain was in serious dereliction of his duty with but 30 men in the garrison. There were three 'portingall' bases (probably breech-loading bronze pieces of small calibre), one brass falconet, three falcons, three sakers, one demi-culverin, and seven 'hagebuthes that standeth in a hause'.[26] The store of shot was satisfactory and there were three lasts of powder (6,000 lb). The small garrison could clearly not even man these weapons and only the three sakers and the single demi-culverin could be considered powerful guns.

The stone forts, magnificent in themselves, were only part of a defensive system that included small independent blockhouses, as well as massive earth forts and ramparts. There were many more modest structures, some of which were of an earlier date. One such was the horseshoe-shaped gun tower of St Catherine's Castle, which was built with two stories, the lower gun deck of which had six gunports. It may have been constructed as early as the 1520s, as was Little Dennis Fort, although that has only a single gun deck. For many years there was also a system of signal beacons on the south coast, similar to the one that had been in use in the North of England, to warn of invasion. This would be revived at the time of the Armada.

---

26 Walton, 'The Art of Gunnery', p.225.

Construction of the Device Forts

Henry initiated the first phase in the programme to meet the Franco-Imperial invasion, and the second in 1544 to meet the expected French counter-attack for the Boulogne expedition. The 1539 programme was the fullest, consisting of major stone castles, small blockhouses and large earthworks. The castles were unique to their sites but followed a generally concentric plan, with a central tower surrounded by a series of semi-circular bastions, upon which further semi-circular bastions could be mounted. The earth forts on the Downs also seem to have been large circular constructions. Where only one area needs to be covered by gunfire, as at Portland, the central keep is only partly girdled with a round bastion.

The King undoubtedly took a considerable interest in the designs, as he did in all military activity. Sir Edmund Knyvet declared that Southsea Castle was 'of his Majesty's own device', and this may have some truth in it, though the description of him as 'a perfect builder as well of fortresses as of pleasant palaces'[27] was probably a politic exaggeration. The majority of those involved in the design seem to have been English, including James Nedeham and Sir Christopher Morris. Stefan von Haschenperg, an Almain or German, was certainly involved in the construction of the circular earth bulwarks on the Downs and supervised work at Sandgate and Camber. He was qualified as a surveyor, but his suggestion that Camber should be provided with a timber roof covered with canvas, pitch and tar, would suggest a poor understanding of military affairs or else that he was working for the enemy. Camber was eventually roofed with lead and his services were dispensed with, for at the very least incompetence. He was certainly not the European genius behind these new fortifications as has sometimes been thought. The building programme continued after the threat had evaporated, with the extensive defences at Hull continuing into 1542.

The second programme of 1544 was on a much smaller scale and was designed to fill the gaps left by the earlier work. Southsea Castle was built to complement the existing fortification on the Solent; its purpose was to protect the deep-water entry into Portsmouth that ran close to the shore. Sandown Castle was built to protect Sandown Bay on the south coast of the Isle of Wight and Yarmouth Castle on the north coast. Brownsea Castle, a simple rectangular blockhouse, was built to protect Poole harbour and Sharpenrode bulwark would defend the important Needles passage. Three of the castles are significantly different from the earlier designs, as they are far more angular structures, showing elements of the new Italianate style, without actually fully embracing it or apparently necessarily understanding it. Southsea, set into a deep ditch, had two triangular bastions and two rectangular bastions around a central keep. The tall, thin, flat-faced walls of Yarmouth Castle were built in a rectangular design, to which was attached a small arrow-shaped tower. This would be far less effective than the concentric and circular structures of the earlier period. The only example of what might

---

27 Harrington, *The Castles of Henry VIII*, p.15.

be described as a properly Italianate fortification is Mersea earth fort and presumably her two sister forts, now destroyed, which was triangular in form with round towers at each apex, providing flanking fire as well as crossfire.

Some, but not all of this money came from the dissolution of the monasteries, as did some of the material. Stone and lead was provided by Beaulieu Abbey for Calshot Castle and East Cowes and West Cowes castles, while St Margaret's Chantry was used to build East Tilbury Blockhouse. Milton Chantry provided the land but not the materials for Milton Blockhouse. The pace of construction at least in part explains the cost. Sandown Castle for example had a veritable army of 630 men all working on it at once in 1540. More than half of these were skilled men, carpenters and stonemasons who were paid at 7d–8d per day, with the labourers at 4d. In June nine men were jailed for their part in a strike to raise their rates of pay.

In the case of Sandown the local ragstone was used extensively, but for the facing Caen stone – a much stronger material robbed from the dissolved monastery – was used. Bricks and tiles were made in a dozen kilns, some as distant as Rye and Canterbury, and lime kilns were built nearby to manufacture the large amounts of mortar needed. The coal for the kilns came from the North of England by ship, timber came from the Weald and lead from the monasteries. The construction of these forts was an impressive example of administrative competence.

It seems that fortifications operated on a care and maintenance basis, rather than being expected to be fully operational at all times. Even so, with such a large number of fortifications the total number of men receiving pay was over 2,000. The cost of building the Device forts was enormous and has been calculated at £376,000, a sum that was a significant portion of the total costs of war in the last eight years of Henry's reign. The castles and bulwarks on the Downs cost some £27,092. Portland Castle cost £4,964, which considering its modest size made it enormously expensive for the time.

Some of Henry's defensive works were abandoned soon after construction. The earth bulwarks on the Downs were 'defaced' and their armament removed to the Tower in 1547; the bulwarks themselves were formally decommissioned in 1550. The majority of the large stone forts remained in commission, on and off, for centuries, sometimes remaining as armed fortifications and others falling into decay or for civilian use. The reigns of Mary and Elizabeth saw the completion of three magnificent fortifications in the *trace italienne* fashion at Berwick, Pendennis and Carisbrooke castles.

If the building of fortifications was an expensive and labour-intensive business, then maintenance was also a drain on resources. The failure to provide regular maintenance could negate the considerable investment made during a time of crisis. Berwick should have been a well-maintained fortification, as it was the centre for offensive and defensive operations with Scotland, however its captains still complained bitterly about the collapsing walls and the refuse and middens set against them. In 1533, only 11 years after a major construction programme, the defences of Berwick were in a parlous state, even after £7,226 had been spent on repairs. Her gunners were even wary of firing their pieces in fear of the towers in which they were emplaced collapsing. Although £1,800 was spent on refortifying Wark

Castle in 1543, in the following year the Italian surveyor describes it as 'a marvelouse greate ruyne … it rayneth almost into everie parte.'[28] Works amounting to £3,000 had been spent but by 1550, 10 years later, the defences were yet considered completely useless. Carlisle was in little better condition, even after modernisation for firearm use between 1540–1543. By the end of the century it was considered only fit for warfare 'in the Saxone manner of the Pictys and Vandalls against spear and sheelds'.[29]

England was still not a 'soft' target as was made clear in a conversation reported by Lord Grey and Sir Thomas Palmer with a French officer in 1547:

> We assure you that England is one of the most difficult realms to set foot on land for a foreign prince … for he cannot come to the shore without likelihood of great loss in the landing, and when he is landed, he must come as to the sault the first day; and after that, if he pass it, he must yet look to fight every day, and to have battles offered to him without end. And as our fortifications are not so easy to be beaten as you think, so though they were never so strong, it is not England's profession to trust in lime and stone. And if there were want of anything when you were there, be you assured, it hath been seen and redressed since; for your sudden attempt in England, to be plain with you, warned us in some things; and therefore we say to you as to our friend, England needeth at this day as little to care as any other realm.[30]

George Rainsford in his *Ritratto d'Inghtlterra*, produced for Phillip II in 1556, pointed to England's natural and man-made defences:

> They fear no foreign power because the places where ships can land are well fortified and guarded, and those that are not guarded are protected by high and strong cliffs. In addition the kingdom is strong because of the provisions it makes against unexpected attacks … so in time of danger the whole country can quickly take up arms.[31]

Fortifications in Scotland

The border had two principal bases for English operations: Carlisle and Berwick. In addition, the great castle at Norham held a strategic position overlooking the Tweed and the road into England. There were a large number of smaller castles, of little sophistication, such as Ford, Chillingham and Etal, unable to withstand a prolonged siege being little more than Pele towers (the equivalent of defended manor houses). The new policy of Somerset towards Scotland required a new strategy that was dependent upon fortification.

---

28 Merriman, *Rough Wooing*, p.68; H.M. Colvin, *The History of the Kings Works*, vol. Plans (HMSO 1963), iv. 614–6.
29 Merriman, *Rough Wooing*, p.68; Colvin, *Kings Works*, iv. 664.
30 Hale, *Renaissance War Studies*, p.91; *Calendar of State Papers Foreign: Edward VI 1547–1553, Calais Papers,* April 18th1547, pp.333–5.
31 Hale, *Renaissance War Studies*, p.91; *Camden Miscellany* xxvii (1979), pp.104–5.

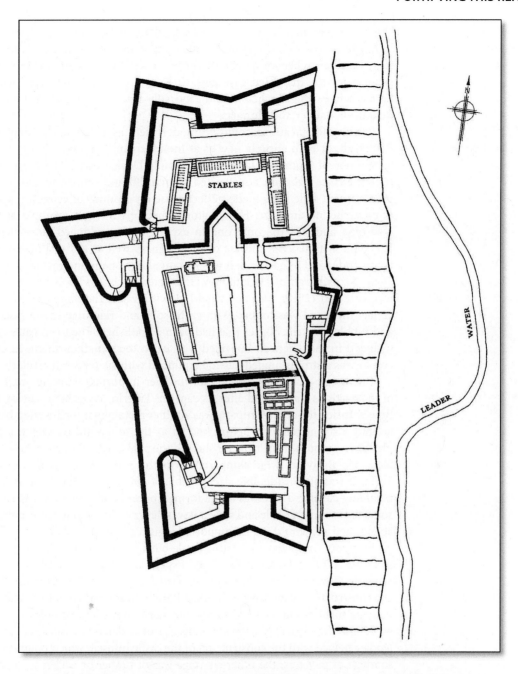

Lauder Castle was a technical success but a strategic failure. Very different in form from the Device forts, it differed also in function: it was a supply base and barracks, not a sea fort. It demonstrated all the aspects of the *trace italienne*, including the angled bastions and the provision for flanking fire to protect the walls. It also took advantage of an inherently strong position. It indicates that England was in no sense backward in matters military. (© J.R. Hale, 1983, *Renaissance War Studies* Fig. 66. Hambledon Continuum, used by permission of Bloomsbury Publishing PLC)

There were specifically two roles to be fulfilled: firstly, to provide garrisons to intimidate or to encourage the local population to declare their loyalty to England or to become 'assured'. The second role was to provide logistical support for the dispersed garrisons. The examples of the first type would be Broughty Craig, Inchcolm and especially Haddington and of the latter Roxburgh, Lauder and Dunglas.

Existing fortifications could be modernised, as at Broughty Craig and Roxburgh, or built entirely new as at Inchcolm and Balgillo. The style was very different from the famous stone-built Device forts, as for the first time the *trace italienne*, constructed from earth and timber, would be the predominant style. This made perfect sense on grounds of economy, speed of construction and size. Haddington is perhaps the best example of this new type and was the only one to experience a prolonged close siege.[32] This demonstrated the success of its design as well as the qualities of the commander and its garrison. It was rectangular in shape and included much of the Scots burgh of Haddington. The outer ditch was probably some 30 feet wide and 12 feet deep and would fill with water. The rampart was some 12 feet high and was topped with earth sods and reinforced with fascines and rubble from the houses that had been demolished. The town gates were included in the defences, but filled with earth to strengthen them. At each corner was a strong, angled bastion equipped with six pieces of artillery.

The design included provision for the ever-important flanking fire. Each of the bastions was named after its captain: Tiberio, Wyndham, Taylor and Bowes. Inside the outer ramparts was another rectangular fortification based around a strong stone structure known as the tollbooth, on which a gun platform was built. The Protector showed the plans to the French ambassador, Sieur De Bertville, who compared it to the impressive fortifications of Turin. It was of considerable size, capable of containing a garrison of 2,500 including cavalry. There was also a form of outer bailey, providing space for some thousands of cattle and sheep. It was never captured but was eventually abandoned as it could not be supported logistically or politically.

Broughty Craig was an existing castle but was in a poor state, and it cost some £2,000 to refortify it using the expertise of the Italian architect and artillerist Giovanni de Rossetti: some four times the cost of a Device blockhouse. The construction of an earth bulwark at Bargillo was an attempt to provide an outlying fortification to shield Broughty Craig, a decision that pointed to the weakness of the strategy, having to build a castle to defend a castle. Sir Andrew Dudley helped with the construction of the castle himself, which points to the shortage of pioneers; the other shortage was of timber or wicker to support the earth structures, which led to the use of earth-filled barrels. This meant that these barrels were not returned to Berwick, exacerbating the supply issues. Supply by sea was problematic at both Broughty and Haddington, as both the weather and French ships could disrupt essential supplies. The state of the earth defences became so parlous that the new commander at Broughty,

---

32 I am most grateful to Jonathan Paul Cooper for making available to me his dissertation on the defences of Haddington, 'Whitecoats and Rascals: In Search of the Fortifications and Siege Works from the Siege of Haddington 1548–1549'.

one Captain Luttrell, reported that no bombardment would be necessary to capture it, 'for theye shall fynde hytt fallen downe redy to ther handys.'[33] He reported his parlous condition to Somerset:

> What commodity is found in raising and turfing bulwarks here when for lack of masons they daily fall down and fill the dykes again-as even now the eastern part of the North East bulwark is fallen with so much earth as 100 cannon could not make a more perilous breach, yea or rather appeareth a thing utterly raised [collapsed]![34]

On the other hand, earth was surprisingly effective in negating the effect of artillery fire. The French account of the siege of Haddington by Beaugué reported that even the six cannons firing some 340 shot in one day failed to make much of an impression on a part of the wall, as the balls were 'deadened and drowned' in the earth.[35]

Lauder required a considerable work force to construct made up of some 350 labourers, six carpenters including one sent from Calais, and 20 'wallers'. Also required were 12 carts for tools and materials. The skilled workmen were paid the rather miserly rate of 7d per day and the labourers 6d, the cost was still a hefty £296 4s 8d. a month. The Spanish mercenaries characteristically refused to help in the work or live in the 'cabons' (huts built from whatever wood and earth sods were available).

The failure of Somerset's strategy and his own downfall led to the abandonment of the fortification, of which little if anything survived. What was built is of interest as it does show that England was abreast of the latest trends in military architecture. The use of Italian engineers to direct the construction was widespread, but even the French, who built new Italianate fortifications at Edinburgh, Dunbar and Leith, employed Italian engineers including Migliorino Ubaldini, known to the Scots as Captain Mellerin.

33   Annie I. Cameron (ed.), *Scottish Correspondence of Mary of Lorraine*, SHS (Edinburgh: Constable, 1927), 275–278, Luttrell to Somerset, November 1548.
34   *CSP Scotland*, April 30 p.112.
35   Cooper, 'Whitecoats and Rascals', p.43 (Miller 1884: 37).

15

The English Army – An Assessment

The Nature of War

The bullets, pellets and arrows flying each where so thick, and so uncertainly lighting, that nowhere was there any surety of safety. Every man stricken with a dreadful fear, not so much perchance of death as of hurt; which things though but certain to some yet were doubted of all. Assured cruelty at the enemy's hands, without hope of mercy. Death to fly, and danger to fight.[1]

Soon after this notable strewing of their footmen's weapons, began a pitiful sight of the dead corpses lying dispersed abroad, some their legs off, some but houghed [hamstrung], and left lying half-dead, some thrust quite through the body, others the arms cut off, diverse their necks half asunder, many their heads cloven, of sundry the brains pasht out, some others again their heads quite off, with a thousand other kinds of killing. [2]

Some others lay flat in a furrow as though they were dead, and thereby they were passed by our men untouched; as I heard say, the Earl of Angus confessed he couched till his horse happed to be brought to him. Other some, to stay in the river, cowering down his body, his head under a root of a willow tree, with scant his nose above the water for breath. A shift but no succour, it was to many that had their skulls [helmets] on, at the stroke of the follower, to shrink their head into their shoulders, like tortoise into its shell. Others again for their more lightness, cast away shoes and doublets; and ran in their shirts. And some were also seen in this race, to fall flat down all breathless, and to have run themselves to death.[3]

Thus, does Patten record the battle and slaughter on the field of Pinkie Cleugh. It is very rare to find a detailed description of the horrors of war from a contemporary observer. There are similar but shorter descriptions of the bloodshed in Norwich and Cornwall but it is not something which is ever

---

1   Patten, *The expedicion into Scotla[n]de*, p.112.
2   Patten, *The expedicion into Scotla[n]de*, pp.124–6.
3   Patten, *The expedicion into Scotla[n]de*, pp.124–6.

dwelt upon. The horrors of war, the fear and brutality of it are easily forgotten when considering the courses of campaigns, the diplomatic background and the logistical preparations. The misery of campaigning, whether in the heat of Spain, the bitter cold at Valenciennes or the constant mist and rain of Broughty Craig and Balgillo, are too easily ignored, when the perspective of the historian is from the court and the commander's comforting campfire. War was and is expensive in both money and lives, for those that fight and for those civilians unfortunate enough to have it forced upon them. When considering the criticism of the military capabilities of the Tudors it is worth remembering that war is never a 'good thing'. If we compare the history of England to that of France, Spain, the Empire and what may be called Italy, then England was extraordinarily fortunate.

The true horrors of war in Europe were exemplified in the south by the sack of Rome in 1527 and in the north by the sack of Antwerp in 1576. Neither event was planned; both were in practice the consequence of a continent that had devoted itself for decades to the creation of armies and the conduct of war. Italy, which was the cockpit of Europe during this period, experienced 19 years of 'not war' and 46 years of bloody conflict between 1494–1559. In the second half of the century France would nearly destroy itself in the Wars of Religion, while Spain became involved in the Eighty Years' War in an attempt to bring the Netherlands to obedience, as well as having to fulfil its role as a world power and defender of Christendom. War in Continental Europe was endemic and a dreadful curse.

Military 'progress' tends to be lauded by historians. Large, successful professional armies skilled in war come at a tremendous cost. The Allied armies that emerged from conflict in 1945 were vastly superior in scale, equipment and competence to those maintained in 1939; does this somehow make the Second World War a 'good' thing? When looking at war it is worth arguing that less war is a good thing and that the few potential 'advantages' that war brings are far less important to society at large than the misery that accompanies it. Thomas Cromwell may have been unwise but was perfectly correct when he said that Thérouanne, bought at such cost, was a worthless 'doghole'. His contempt for war and its petty victories was perhaps the product of his own experience as a mercenary in Italy. This was unfortunately not an opinion shared by many of those who 'mattered' in Tudor England and certainly not by Henry VIII.

Winning, or, Not Losing!

The important question when considering the military establishment of any country is whether it fulfilled its purpose by, if not winning, then at least not losing? If this is the test of the English military system, then it passed with flying colours. There were pretenders and rebellions, incursions by the Scots, quarrelsome Irishmen (in Ireland) and an attempt to continue the Hundred Years' War (in France) but England was never trampled over by foreign armies and although the Isle of Wight was invaded, it was only for four days.

If we consider the main campaigns and battles during this period, then the balance sheet seems to be decidedly in the black. Henry VII won the two battles that mattered, Bosworth and Stoke and committed himself as little as possible to further military expeditions. His son, intent on cutting a dash in Europe, captured Thérouanne and Tournai and later Boulogne, which however one may decry the costs of his achievement, were after all his objectives. He 'won' the Battle of the Spurs and he (Surrey) definitely won the Battle of Flodden. If the expeditions of 1512, 1522 and 1523 were not triumphs, nor were they disasters. They had few implications for the realm, although their cost was considerable.

To argue that Henry VIII's strategy or objectives were flawed seems unreasonable. He was a Renaissance prince and he was simply attempting to fulfil the roles that the age, fate and God gave him. Somerset in 1547 had already hammered the Scots and his political and military objective, the union of the Crowns, was inherited from his predecessor and appeared achievable. He began with the victory at Pinkie and then pursued a credible military strategy that inevitably ran into a refusal by the Scots to accept subjection, and forced them into the arms of France. Mary was forced into a war not of her choosing, and the loss of Calais could not be attributed to her but to the determination and skulduggery of the French (who attacked when the English were not ready). Arguably the loss of Calais stopped any more English rulers considering the possibility of restoring their lost French possessions. Whatever criticisms might be made in detail, the military institutions of the Tudors in this period hardly ever failed, even if the strategy that lay behind them was flawed.

The blindingly obvious is still occasionally worth stating. England is an island. It was throughout this period effectively secure from the threat of invasion and conquest. England on the other hand could chose when and to a certain extent where to intervene. This was highlighted by the Venetian ambassador's report in 1557. Calais provided her with a remarkable opportunity to play a significant part in the politics of Christendom, as the ambassador observed:

> ... by way of Calais ... [they might] ... carry over either troops or anything else for warfare, offensive and defensive, besides causing jealousy and suspicion, as Calais not being more than [ten] miles from Ardres, the frontier of the French, and the same distance from Gravelines, the frontier of the Imperialists, they can promise to join either the one or the other as they please, and to unite their forces to those of him with whom they are at amity, in prejudice of the enemy.[4]

Other nations may have wars forced upon them, England did not. This was except for the inevitable intervention of the Scots whose 'invasions' were never more than incursions. These were also invariably as a response to their belligerent neighbour's actions and never intended to occupy but merely cause a nuisance.

---

4   *CSP Venice*, May 1557.

What successive sovereigns realised was that what England needed above all, was not a standing army but a professional navy. It was this force that Henry VIII did much to create and his daughters to sustain. It was the navy, not the army, that was to be managed with such efficiency, both in its creation, maintenance and employment. Warships could not, unlike the county militia, be raised in a few days in order to be sent to war. The real administrative and long-term financial commitment of the Tudors was naturally devoted to the Navy, by which the country could be protected and force projected. England's defences lay in wooden walls, not stone walls, despite the Device forts, and least of all in a professional army.

England and the 'Military Revolution'

Tudor England has become embroiled in the military revolution debate. It is therefore important to understand the dispute, how it emerged and developed in relation to England. Professor Roberts in his brilliant 1955 Belfast lecture posited the existence of the 'military revolution' in the late sixteenth and early seventeenth centuries. His primary assumption was that the introduction of gunpowder weapons actually reduced the missile power of infantry and the shock power of cavalry. Conflicts were to be decided by 'a form of close action dependent upon the impact and mass of heavy infantry. The line of charging knights was smashed by the massed pikes of the Swiss column.'[5] He assumed, contrary to popular belief, that although firearms battered down castles, 'on the battlefield firearms for long represented a big step backward'.[6]

How was this possible? His analysis considered that:

> the effective combination of archers and men-at-arms, not uncommon in the Middle Ages, reached its climax, perhaps at Agincourt: the following generations, turning increasingly to firearms, and abandoning the bow, groped in vain for a tactical form that should take its place. For by a curious paradox the coming of the hand-gun brought with it a steep decline in firepower: the superiority of the longbow, in speed, accuracy and mobility, was so marked that even in the late seventeenth century military writers were pleading for its reintroduction.[7]

Roberts argued that: 'The training of a bowman, schooled to be a dead shot at a distance, would be wasted on so imperfect an instrument as an arquebus or a wheel-lock pistol.'[8] One reason why firearms drove out the bow and the lance 'was ... that they economised on training. Moreover deep formations, whether of horse or foot, dispensed with the need for a large trained corps of officers, and required a less high morale, since it is difficult to run away with fifteen ranks behind you.'[9] The military skills required of

---

5   Roberts, *The Military Revolution*, pp.4–5.
6   Roberts, *The Military Revolution*, p.7.
7   Roberts, *The Military Revolution*, p.5.
8   Roberts, *The Military Revolution*, p.9.
9   Roberts, *The Military Revolution*, p.9.

the sixteenth-century soldier were few, for 'if he inclined his pike in correct alignment and leaned heavily on the man in front of him, he had done almost all that could be required of him'.[10]

Many of these assumptions are questionable. The argument that the soldier became de-skilled would require careful qualification. The Swiss and Landsknecht mercenaries possessed skill-at-arms, ferocity in battle, loyalty to his comrades and the ability of a seasoned soldier to scrounge and survive. The willingness to stand and fight outweighed the ability to handle a specific weapon. The role of the non-commissioned officer, the vintener in English service or the Landsknecht Rottmeister should not be underestimated as all officers know that effective discipline and leadership in battle is dependent upon their NCOs.

If infantry had become impotent, cavalry were emasculated by the abandonment of the lance in favour of the pistol. What made this even worse was the 'intricate but futile manoeuvre the caracole', which was an equine version of firing by introduction. Cavalry, which had ruled the battlefield, was now limited to popping away pathetically at unbreakable infantry formations: there was no shock and certainly no awe to be found in these tactics. Artillery which had at least had an important role in the destruction of city and castle stone walls soon proved ineffectual against the *trace italienne*, a system of earthen star-shaped fortifications developed to perfection by Dutch in the Eighty Years' War. The consequences of failed tactics led to catastrophic consequences, as 'strategic thinking withered away; war eternalized itself'.[11] Thus by the middle of the sixteenth century the tactics associated with pike and shot working in collaboration had resulted in unwieldy formations bumbling around the battlefield, whilst the cavalry and artillery failed to make an impact, quite literally, on the enemy.

Robert's analysis here does not readily survive contact with the reality of warfare. Cavalry could be very effective on the battlefield whether with lance, sword or pistol. Infantry could be a dynamic force on the battlefield, cooperating with cavalry and artillery as at Pinkie. Campaigns, even if unsuccessful, could be based on grand strategy, and sieges and battles were conducted with vigour and success. A cursory study of the Franco-Imperial conflict in Italy gives the lie to Robert's simplistic assumptions.

The transformation of warfare was in Roberts's opinion the work of two military revolutionaries, Maurice of Orange and Gustavus Adolphus. Their revolution involved the use of linear tactics by the infantry, rather than the mass blocks of the tercio. It was drawn from the examples provided by classical authors such as Vegetius and Aelian and the muscular Christian Pope Leo VI. It was inspired by the Roman examples of standard unit size and an order of battle. What was now required was above all drill and discipline. It was Aelian's description of Roman drill which inspired William Louis of Nassau to describe the countermarch to his cousin Maurice, in a letter dated 8 December 1594. This was the drill manoeuvre whereby successive ranks

---

10   Roberts, *The Military Revolution*, p.9.
11   Roberts, *The Military Revolution*, p.7.

could fire upon the enemy and then retire through the ranks and reload, providing thereby a continuous curtain of fire.

To support this new discipline, systematised drill manuals were produced, providing 32 distinct positions or postures for pikemen and 42 for musketeers. The new formations were far more flexible and able to fully exploit their firepower, with the salvo replacing the countermarch. 'The essential contribution of Gustavus Adolphus was, to demonstrate the ability of linear formations to defeat mass, not only in defence, but in attack.'[12] Gustavus restored to cavalry its role as a shock force, substituting the sabre for the pistol and the charge for the caracole. Speed and mobility were restored not only to the infantry and cavalry but the artillery, with the introduction of lightweight field artillery that could accompany and support the other arms. The light regimental pieces and above all the legendary 'leather' guns, exemplified this commitment to mobility and firepower.

With this new 'modern' army available, it was possible to pursue grand strategic ideas with the development of strategic supply centres where arms, food and equipment would be held ready for use. The border would become the scene of conflict with both sides employing scorched earth policies. To sustain this new effort the state grew further and took over the provision and conduct of war, which had once been in the hands of the elite and the merchant class. War now became a government monopoly, although of necessity employing the ranks of society that had always fought and wished to fight. Thus, the aristocracy and gentry continued to perform their principal role but in the service of the state and often trained by it in specialist military academies. The monarch was now portrayed as the commanding officer in the uniform of his army. The seeds of the 1914 catastrophe were sown in the late sixteenth and early seventeenth centuries, by a Swede and a Dutchman. Geoffrey Parker developed the Roberts thesis by attributing its cause to the new system of fortification which would have a profound implication for warfare. Other historians have further developed the concept of the military revolution with reference to its course and chronology.

The principal critic of Professor Roberts is David Eltis. He makes some telling points. Firstly he argues, quite correctly, that the tactical combination of bow and man-at-arms which Roberts so lauded was a uniquely English phenomenon. Eltis goes on to argue that Roberts is quite wrong in his fundamental assumption that firearms reduced firepower. He argues that the key to understanding the effectiveness of the new weapons is to appreciate that the effectiveness of firepower was judged by the ability to penetrate armour. He argued that firearms could achieve this far better than either crossbow or longbow.

Eltis does point to the successful combination of pike and shot on the battlefield which together with increasingly effective field artillery and a cavalry force augmented by the use of firearms, made battles frequent and bloody. Eltis argues that battles did not take place because they were too dangerous and Roberts argued that they did not take place because they became indecisive.

---

12 Roberts, *The Military Revolution*, p.8.

A musketeer in a red doublet. Surely Elis Gruffydd would have approved of this fine, manly, soldierly arquebusier. Carrying a short-stocked 'brasse' barrelled matchlock, he is provided with a powder flask at his hip. The match cord is looped around his right arm and is aflame; match burns with an intense slow burn that gives off an unmistakeable smell and glow, which would alert an enemy to its presence. It also invariably leaves scorch marks on clothing due to careless handling. His sword, which is slung inconveniently low, is rather too fine bladed for a soldier and has a simple hilt with crossguard and knuckle bow. His coat has been slashed in the best style, displaying the underlying and contrasting mail shirt, which has short dagged or jagged sleeves, finished off with brass links to add to the decorative effect. His shoes are also slashed and he is displaying snow-white hose. How long his finery would survive contact with the outdoors, let alone the enemy, is another question. (Courtesy of the Royal Armouries RA Cotton Augustus III, f.21)

Even a cursory study of Renaissance battles will show that the reason for battles taking place, or not, is subject to so many variables as to not be understood by any such simplistic analysis. Battles had always been seen as 'high risk' and sometimes that risk was taken, sometimes not. The strategic conditions that appertained in the Italian wars were utterly different from those of the French wars of religion or the Dutch wars and these can best explain commitment to battle or otherwise. Battles were very sensibly, on the whole, to be avoided unless victory was assured. Neither Flodden or Pinkie need have taken place and in both cases it is reasonable to suggest that the other side could have won.

Commentators on the Roberts–Parker thesis have gradually modified, extended and chipped away at the individual features of the thesis, arguing strongly for an evolutionary theory. Maurice and Gustavus, although influential with contemporaries, have been placed in a more balanced perspective, where their 'innovations' can be seen as forming a logical development of tactical experience, and as a result in some cases of simple expediency.

The underlying irony is that Professor Roberts, author of the military revolution debate, argued strongly that firearms led to stagnation in warfare, whereas those supporting the concept have argued that it was the adoption of firearms which was revolutionary. In chapter 5 of *The Military Revolution in Sixteenth Century Europe* David Eltis advances his critique of England's military backwardness. While acknowledging that prolonged periods of peace before 1585 had inevitably led to a slower rate of progress towards the European model, 'England fell far behind the leading powers of the Continent, in both training and experience, until the last decades of the century.'[13] He asserts the importance of skill transference, whether by mercenaries, Englishmen serving under foreign colours or the increasing use of military literature. What particularly upsets him is the prolongation of the life of the archer in the military order of battle.

---

13   Eltis, *The Military Revolution*, p.100.

English Backwardness?

In his great survey of sixteenth-century warfare Oman wrote unenthusiastically about England's place in military history. Henry VIII's record 'is not an inspiring one ... He left his realm in a dire sate of exhaustion – the direct result of his wilfully personal ambition.'[14] He is even less complimentary about the period 1547–1603 where: 'The whole period is singularly dull from the point of view of the historian of the [English] art of war.'[15] Gilbert John Millar, writing about Henry VIII's army in 1543, asserts that: 'In organization and armament the Tudor army had scarcely progressed beyond the era of Agincourt. English field forces were unprofessional, while on the Continent, the foundations of the first permanent armies had already been laid.'[16] Millar considered that the Tudor soldiers were 'as unskilled as they were inexperienced in the arts of war ... the conclusion that English armies were inferior to their counterparts on the Continent can hardly be escaped.'[17] Helen Miller is no less scathing, concluding that: 'Fundamentally the "army royal" was an old fashioned force, raised by quasi-feudal methods, fighting with out-of-date weapons for an anachronistic cause.'[18] In Sheppard's *A Short History of the British Army* the author declares that 'Apart from certain isolated military episodes such as Flodden, the period of close on 200 years, from 1485 to 1642, must from the point of view of military history be regarded as a fallow one.'[19] Clifford Davies is no more complimentary when considering the state of the English army in 1557:

> The English army was a somewhat archaic force compared with the highly professional troops of France and Spain, hardened as they were by years of service and stiffened with the large contingents of German mercenaries. Foreign observers and English patriots alike lamented the shortage of the arquebus and pike, the reliance on bill and bow, the lack of discipline in the English levies and their reluctance to undergo hardship; above all their endemic amateurishness.'[20]

David Trim summarises the historiographical position as follows:

> Historians have traditionally seen the English and Welsh kingdom of the Tudors as militarily stagnant, exempt from trends in early modern Europe as a whole,

---

14 Oman, *Art of War*, pp.287–288.
15 Oman, *Art of War*, p.368.
16 Millar, 'Mercenaries', p.173.
17 Luke MacMahon, 'Military Professionalism in the early Tudor armies in Renaissance Europe: a reassessment', in D.J. Trim (ed.) *The Chivalric Ethos and the Development of Military Professionalism* (Leiden: Brill 2003), p.183; J.G. Millar, *Tudor Mercenaries and Auxiliaries, 1485–1547* (Charlottesville, Virginia: 1980), pp.4–5.
18 MacMahon, 'Military Professionalism', p.183; H. Miller, *Henry VIII and the English Nobility* (Oxford: Basil Blackwell, 1986), p.142.
19 E.W. Sheppard, *A Short History of the British Army* (London: Constable 1950), p.7.
20 C.S.L. Davies, 'England and the French War, 1557–9', in J. Loach and R. Tittler (eds), *The Mid-Tudor Polity, c.1540–1560* (London: Macmillan, 1980), pp.163–164.

where developments in the theory and practice of the art of war were unparalleled, perhaps even revolutionary.[21]

The most gnomic critique for the period 1485–1558 comes from Charles Carlton who declared that: 'Early Tudor warfare was a little bit like the *Mary Rose,* whenever a wind blew up, particularly a French one, it tended to capsize.'[22]

Criticism of England's backwardness was shared by well-informed foreign observers. As early as 1512 King Ferdinand had provided an assessment of the strengths and weaknesses of the force sent to assist him:

> The English are strong, stout hearted, stand firm in battle and never think of taking flight … They are very excellent men and only want experience. England has had no wars … The English do not know how to behave in a campaign. Unaccustomed as they are to warfare, they show a marked dislike to perform such labours as are inevitably entailed on soldiers. They are inclined to self-indulgence and idleness … But their greatest fault is that in a combined action, they will never assist the [allied] troops, or act in concert with the commander of another nation … It would be as well to practice a portion of the men in the evolutions of regular warfare.[23]

The Bishop of Arras, the Imperial ambassador in conversation with Thomas Chaloner, courtier, poet and diplomat, made the following trenchant criticisms in 1559:

> But is it not strange, quoth he, that ye believe the world knoweth not nor seeth not your weakness? I demand what present store either of expert captains or good men of war ye have? What treasure? What other furniture for defence? Is there one fortress or hold in all England that is able one day to endure the breath of a cannon? Your men I confess are hardy and valiant; but what discipline have they had this many years? Namely, where the art of war is now come to that issue that men be fain to learn of new well nigh at every two years' end. But admit ye had discipline, what should it avail in division, where one draweth one way, another another?[24]

Perhaps most damning of all were the supposed comments of a foreign ambassador that English warlike action 'is nothinge so nowe. I se neyther harneyes, ne weapons, of manhood amonges them, they haue ben of good hartes, coragyouse, bolde, valiant in marciall feates: But those Englyshe men are deade.'[25] Even English commanders could recognise English

---

21   David J.B. Trim, 'The Context of War and Violence in Sixteenth-Century English Society', in *Journal of Early Modern History*, vol. 3: issue 3 (1999), p.233.

22   Carlton, *This Seat of Mars,* p.18.

23   Hutchinson, *Young Henry,* p.165.

24   *Calendar of State Papers Foreign: Elizabeth,* vol. 2, December 1559, R.O. 8.

25   Potter, *Henry VIII and Francis I,* p.207; Richard Morison, *An Exhortation to styrre all Englyshe men to the defence of theyr countrye* (London, 1539).

'backwardness'. Sir John Wallop commented on the 'learning experiences' offered by service with Imperial troops at the siege of Landrecies in 1543:

> In all the warres I have ben in, I have not sene suche another tyme for youghe [youth] to lerne, first for our being before Landersey, and especyally sithen [since] thEmperours commyng, who brought wyth Hym horssemen and footemen of all nations, as Your Majesties men here might lerne and choose what faschyon they lyeked best.[26]

There we have it: England's soldiery were boisterous, violent naughty children, arrogant, ill-disciplined and backward in learning the lessons of modern war.

There has been much work done recently by historians to restore the reputation of the Tudors in arms. John Hale, David Potter, James Raymond, Gervase Phillips, Paul Hammer, David Grummitt and Mark Charles Fissell have done much to challenge the idea that England was a medieval military backwater. This is a view that the present author has tried to represent here, and reflects the balance of modern scholarship.

What were the principal charges laid against the English military establishment and its failure to participate in the European 'military revolution'? Firstly, as a consequence of the parochialism caused by the loss of her French possessions and the internecine Wars of the Roses, England adhered to a 'medieval' military tradition, of bowmen and dismounted men-at-arms. England thus failed to adopt modern weapons, such as the pike and especially firearms. This failure to 'modernise' her armament, or to develop a sizeable permanent military establishment, led to the employment of a large number of mercenaries. England also failed to develop a manufacturing base to support a 'modern' army. Another criticism of English soldiers or rather their officers is that they did not 'read', and the absence of military textbooks or handbooks demonstrated a serious lack of professionalism. Finally, England was nearly defenceless in face of invasion. The Device forts were obsolete and she did not possess a single truly defensible city with fortifications based upon the principles of the *trace italienne*.

To answer each point in turn. England was a medieval nation and employed bowmen, billmen and men-at-arms in her armies displaying an unsurprising high degree of continuity. This was a system that seemed to work rather well at Flodden and in France and was slowly undergoing a process of 'modernisation' throughout this period. England was not in a constant state of conflict but its participation was regular and often on a very large scale. European societies' conduct of warfare reflected their social structure, economic strength and strategic situation. England was no different in this but was vastly more fortunate in not being the victim of powerful neighbours forcing war upon it. Britain was unlike her neighbours in many respects and it hardly surprising that was true in war as well as peace.

---

26   Potter, *Henry VIII and Francis I*, p.120, Wallop to Henry VIII, 14 Nov. 1543, St. P, IX, pp.550–552 (*Letters and Papers*, XVIII, ii, 384).

Eltis pronounces a guilty verdict on England for he argues that 'the first signs of the military revolution in England was the appearance of the firearms,'[27] and that conversely: 'The chief reason for this backwardness was continuing faith in the merits of the longbow.'[28] England's retention of archery he sees as an act of faith in the traditional defence of the realm, explained by the: 'romanticism of the bow.'[29]The failure to adopt modern weapons is a criticism amply justified if you were to simply to take the low percentage of English arquebusiers in the army of 1544 as your measuring point. As this work has attempted to explain, the adoption or retention of a weapon depends far more than a simple analysis of its technical performance, even if that is well understood, which it often is not. England's retention of the bow made sense. The massive purchases of firearms by Henry VIII, together with the widespread employment of mercenaries did recognise that, especially in the European context, firearms together with pike-equipped infantry were increasingly becoming the norm. England in this matter was not as backward as Eltis suggests.

England's lack of a large and permanent military establishment, in effect a standing army, was Millar's principal criticism. There are several good reasons why she should and did not possess such a force. Firstly, a permanent military establishment required a permanent or near permanent state of war, which England fortunately avoided as she chose when to go to war rather than having war thrust upon her. Secondly a military establishment of any size was ruinously expensive. Even the 800 or so gendarmes employed by Northumberland as domestic security had to be abandoned for reasons of expense. It was calculated that an army of 38,865 men would cost £44,843 per month to maintain at the rate of 9d per person a day. At this rate, a standing army of only 6,500 men would completely swallow all of the £90,000 of royal income raised each year.

War in the reign of Henry VIII was only sustained by exploiting the wealth of the Church, selling monastic property, by levying heavy taxation, borrowing at an exorbitant rate, and even worse, debasing the coinage. Quite simply England could not afford to maintain even the most modest permanent military force. The Yeomen, Gentlemen Pensioners and professional gunners provided all the military establishment that the kingdom needed in time of peace, and in time of war they could be quickly supplemented. If England could not afford a small 'regular' army, she certainly could afford a sizeable army when the commons were raised in arms.

England did, however, develop a large and permanent naval establishment, which reflected her real priorities. Henry VIII was the real 'founder' of the Navy Royal, not simply because of the number and type of ships built but the essential infrastructure that underlay its existence. If anything, the military establishment mirrored the development of the naval and certainly developed significantly through Henry VIII's reign.

If England lacked a standing army she had a small but efficient permanent military establishment. There was continuity in personnel, especially within the Ordnance at the Tower of London, as well as in the Yeomen

---

27 Eltis, *The Military Revolution*, p.101.
28 Eltis, *The Military Revolution*, p.101.
29 Eltis, *The Military Revolution*, p.102.

and the Gentlemen Pensioners, who were far more than merely parade ground soldiers. The court and county elites provided the Tudors with the captains and the commanders that successive monarchs employed for their expeditions, whether at home or abroad. There was considerable experience in military affairs to be found in the court and the counties. Elis ap Gruffydd was highly critical of some (both captains and generals), although he also recognised the professionalism of others. The Tudor officer and his soldiers could on occasion demonstrate military competence, remarkable stoicism and personal bravery. There were other occasions when they were what might be described as a 'complete bloody shower'. They were, after all, the commons and gentry in arms and they reflected the strengths and weaknesses of such an arrangement.

England's lack of a standing army led, it is argued, to the employment of mercenaries. This has been cited as evidence of English 'backwardness', although Gervase Phillips has argued that mercenary forces provided principally Henry with the sheer numbers of men to match his enemies. Mercenary forces were used across Europe, often in larger numbers and as a higher proportion of national troops than in England. If the use of large numbers is indicative of backwardness, then perhaps France was more guilty than England. At the siege of Pavia in 1524/5 the French infantry, according to Guicciardini, consisted of 10,000 Swiss, 4,000 Germans, 7,000 Italians and only 5,000 Frenchmen, fewer than 20 percent of the total. In the French army commanded by Montmorency in the Piedmont in 1537, there were some 14,500 German and 6,597 Italian mercenaries and only 9,263 French and Gascon troops. The last figure is important not only for the small percentage of native troops but the separate identification of Gascons from the French. Why did such a populous nation as France employ so many mercenaries? The French monarchy did not respect or trust the French people. Michele Suriano, the Venetian ambassador, explained the situation in France thus:

> If the common people were armed they would rebel against the nobility and rulers (partly out of envy and partly for revenge for the oppression they suffer). The judges would not be able to hold them back, and they would leave their jobs, stop working the land, become robbers, throw the kingdom into wild confusion.[30]

Claude de Seyssel summarised the position of the French crown, that the people should not be granted 'too much freedom' and should be 'neither excessively rich nor generally experienced in arms'.[31] In England and Wales, of course, the Crown required the commons to bear arms and train in their use: an interesting contrast with the insecurity of their French cousins. The

---

30 David Potter, *Renaissance France at War: Armies, Culture and Society, c.1480–1560* (Woodbridge: Boydell Press 2008), p.98; Suriano, in J.C. Davis, *Pursuit of Power: the Venetian ambassadors' reports to Spain, Turkey and France in the Age of Phillip II 1560–1600* (New York: Harper & Row, 1970), p.186.

31 Potter, *Renaissance France at War*, p.98; Claude de Seysell, *La Monarchie de France*, ed. J. Poujol (Paris: Société des textes français modernes, 1961), part 1, chapter 6, p.124.

difference between France and England was that whilst both nations employed mercenaries, the French had to use them whilst the English chose to.

If one looks for weakness in a national military establishment then France, rather than England, provides some good examples. The *franc archers*, the much lauded 'professional' infantry force, were abolished by Louis XI as 'expensive to the people and worthless to the public good'.[32] The French attempt to establish legions of infantry as a national force in the mid 1530s failed, as they seem to have taken on the worst features of a mercenary force, insubordinate, hostile to the civilian population and quarrelsome to all. The system was abandoned after 1547 and what was left was a territorial force of little practical worth. This inability of the French to produce a 'national' infantry force is in great contrast to what was achieved in England. The system of recruitment in England was imperfect, training was often poor but very large numbers of troops were mobilised. When they saw action, in most if not all cases, they acquitted themselves well. When they were unsuccessful as in 1512 in Spain and 1523 in France, it was due to their leaders' many mistakes. They failed to provide the logistical support that was needed, or infected their own men with their fear, as demonstrated by the chaotic retreat from Montreuil in 1544.

England has also been criticised for the lack of a military–industrial base. It is true that she was in many respects backwards when it came to the supply of military equipment. It is important, yet again, to put this into its European perspective. The current assumption that 'great powers' have adhered to for centuries, which is that the state should have a monopoly of, or a controlling hand over, the manufacture of military equipment, is not one that would have been recognised in the early modern period. Other than large naval facilities such as the Venetian Arsenale or Portsmouth dockyard which were under the direct control of the state, production of military equipment was undertaken by private manufacturers. Military equipment both now and then was like any technology, dependent upon the availability of the raw material, the skills, and the geopolitical condition of a region. England did not possess a large and sophisticated industrial manufacturing base, unlike Italy, Flanders and Germany. Cornwall was important for the manufacture of tin and lead and the Wealden iron industry would grow significantly later in the century but there was little else. There was historically no major arms industry, other than the manufacture of war bows in England throughout the Middle Ages, and even then the best bows would have been made with imported yew.

Gervase Phillips refers to 'the complex interplay of factors beyond technical performance that have governed the choices surrounding the adoption of particular weapons. A people's chosen tools of war can be a manifestation of economic, political, cultural, and social circumstances.'[33] This was clearly apparent across Europe although European manufacturing in this period was 'localised, artisanal and small scale';[34] this did not preclude mass manufacture to a high standard. The Low Countries were at the heart of the copper, brass and

---

32   Potter, *Renaissance France at War*, p.105.

33   Phillips, 'Longbow and Hackbutt', p.576.

34   Frank Tallett, *War and Society in Early Modern Europe, 1495–1715* (London: Routledge, 2016), p.223.

bronze industries; Italy was also famous for the production of cast bronze objects including of course statuary. It was hardly surprising that these would become the centres for cast bronze cannon production as they had access to the materials, possessed the skills and responded to the demand for wartime and peacetime products. Iron and steel manufacture as well as armour production was concentrated in northern Italy and southern Germany. It was also in Germany that the skills needed for the manufacture of the wheel lock mechanism were to be found. In the manufacture of weapons and armour England clearly lagged behind but like every other European power she could buy what she needed on the open market as and when necessary.

England had always purchased what it had needed from European sources and from limited domestic manufacture. Henry VIII had established the Greenwich armoury, although this was principally a vanity project to provide for himself and a few favoured courtiers. Purchase of enormous quantities of cheap armour from Germany and Italy using existing sources and trusted merchants made far more sense than attempting to manufacture such products in England. Of greater strategic significance in the long-term, was the replacement of large-scale orders for cast bronze artillery with domestic manufacture, using foreign craftsmen. These were working under very generous terms and had established, by the middle of the sixteenth century, domestic production that could meet royal demands. Domestic gunpowder manufacture was never adequate to meet demand but foreign purchases sufficed and a shortage of powder was never a significant issue.

England had always imported bow staves for war bows. Spanish and Alpine yew grew very slowly and straight in its steep-sided valleys and produced, in about 500 years, high quality staves suitable for the best war bows. English conditions could not match the quality of foreign yew, with ash and wych elm producing reliable but not first-rate bows. This dependence on foreign production continued with the importation of firearms, purchased at very short notice in very large numbers and at very low prices, to meet a specific perceived need. It made far more sense to do this than to attempt to establish a large-scale domestic manufacturing programme. England lacked the materials and a skilled workforce; she could

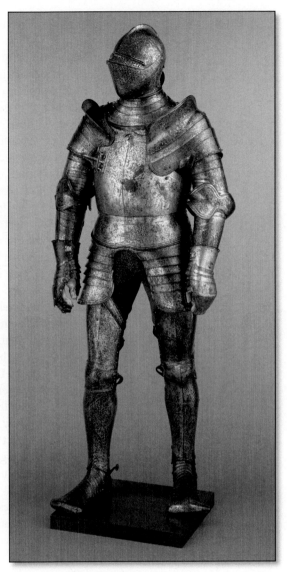

Armour garniture, probably of King Henry VIII of England dated 1527. This was produced in the Greenwich armoury with the design of the decoration attributed to Hans Holbein the Younger. It was intended for King Henry, who then presented it as a gift to the French ambassador François de La Tour d'Auvergne in 1527. It was made with exchange and reinforcing pieces and could therefore be used for battle and the different forms of the tournament. It matched the standards of the best European armours of the time although of course a product of Continental rather than English craftsmen. Henry abandoned the joust in this year as his age, weight and injuries made his participation less appealing or practical. (Metropolitan Museum of Art, Open Access)

also not look forward to a substantial domestic or foreign market to sustain such an industry.

Henry's approach to the problem that faced him when trying to equip his armies was essentially pragmatic and in practice entirely successful. He solved his problems by systematically recruiting expertise and when necessary making massive purchases from overseas. The Scottish faced similar problems and 'solved' them in a similar way. James IV employed French 'melters' to cast his cannon and 'stranger' gunners to man them. He purchased thousands of imported ash pikes and according to legend personally tested each one, discarding not a few. England did not have a domestic Nuremburg or a Brescia but it did not need one as long as the European marketplace for weaponry was open to her.

As to the absence of military publications then the case is proven by the evidence or absence of such, although there certainly were versions of the military classics, such as Vegetius and Aelian in circulation. Between 1490 and 1560 only nine military books were printed, while between then and 1600 a further 64 were added.[35] Of course, after 1585 and with the interminable war with Spain and the development of the militia force, there was an increase in domestic interest in such publications. The printing of military texts in Europe, although greater in total number, more or less matched the rate of growth in England. The real growth in the number of foreign texts also occurred after the middle of the century.[36] Does this mean that European armies were 'backward' in the early part of the century? It is unclear as to who was reading these books and whether they actually helped. The shiny new captain drilling his company, accompanied by his boy trotting alongside, holding his textbook open on the right page, was an object of Elizabethan derision. Colin Martin presents a very different perspective, arguing that in 1588 English gunners actually benefited from a lack of printed gunnery manuals:

> Most of this theoretical knowledge, however, we now know to have been unnecessarily complicated, usually inaccurate, often spurious, and generally of little practical help. Not to have easy access to or interest in such information may have been one of the English gunners' greatest strengths.[37]

Stephen Walton in his study of early modern gunnery manuals develops an important idea that is somewhat alien to those trained in an academic world, which at best ignores practical skills and at worst derides them.

> First, in the past, technical knowledge was more an art (*techne*) than a science (*scientia*); that is, it was about doing rather than necessarily knowing for knowing's sake. To put it another way, it was decidedly not *philosophia naturalis* with its emphasis on causes but rather *ars practica*, with an emphasis on doing

---

35 *English Military Books, 1480–1660* (compiled from M.J.D. Cockle [1957]) in Walton, 'The Art of Gunnery', fig. 3.1 p.117

36 *English Military Books*, in Walton, 'The Art of Gunnery', fig. 3.2 p.118.

37 Colin John Mackenzie Martin, *The Equipment and Fighting Potential of the Spanish Armada*. A Thesis Submitted for the Degree of PhD at the University of St Andrews, 1984, p.376.

and making. Second, practitioners of these arts tended to disseminate knowledge from one generation to the next more or less directly through the apprenticeship system rather than through written texts. What this means, on both counts, is that in the Middle Ages and early modern period textbooks in the modern sense were generally unavailable, irrelevant, and simply not needed.[38]

It was the Elizabethan Mathew Baker who was the first to put down the design of a ship on paper: does this mean that before then no ships of any worth were built? Crafts or mysteries were passed on through practical apprenticeships, not by book learning. In our world where all education is based upon textbooks and written tests, it is difficult to appreciate that this is not how most skills were passed on. There is also only so much that can be learnt from a book. It is understandable that historians should dwell on the number and date of military publications; but I would suggest that an increase in the readership of such volumes is not indicative of an increase of professionalism but the absence of experience.

The argument that England was backward in adopting modern fortifications and therefore slow to adopt the *trace italienne* does not bear close examination either. The Device forts were performing a very specific coastal defensive role for which they were admirably suited. England was, thank goodness, not a country at war and did not need to fortify its towns and cities as was the case in Italy, France and the Netherlands. The Venetian ambassador may mock England's preparedness by asking the rhetorical question: 'Is there one fortress or hold in all England that is able one day to endure the breath of a cannon?'[39] In practice the likelihood of such an event made preparations of that sort mostly irrelevant. Where fortifications needed to be updated to incorporate or to resist firearms, as with Calais, Berwick and Carlisle, they were. The Scottish garrisons built as a consequence of Somerset's new policies, such as Eyemouth and Lauder, were constructed according to the most up-to-date Italian principles.

The structure of the early Tudor army was unsurprisingly medieval at the end of what is now identified as the Middle Ages. As outlined in previous chapters, it underwent a transformation over the next 60 years in terms of recruitment, equipment and tactics. The army with which Somerset defeated the Scots at Pinkie was dramatically different from the one that had fought at Bosworth. The changes that took place were incremental and reflected the changing nature of warfare and the ambitions of the monarch. England was fortunate in being able to effectively choose when and who to fight. Like all armies it reflected the state and its people. To expect it to be anything other than that, is the same as criticising the tiny 'contemptible' British Expeditionary Force of King George VI in 1914 for not being the massive pickelhaube-wearing, goose-stepping Imperial German Army of Kaiser Bill.

---

38 Steven A Walton, 'Proto-scientific Revolution or Cookbook Science? Early Gunnery Manuals in the Craft Treatise Tradition', in Ricardo Córdoba (ed.), *Craft Treatises and Handbooks: the Dissemination of Technical Knowledge in the Middle Ages* (Turnhout: Brepols, 2014, *De Diversis Artibus* series, tome 91, (N.S. 54)), p.222.

39 *Calendar of State Papers Foreign: Elizabeth*, vol. 2, December 1559 R.O. 8.

Appendix I

Stocks of Weapons Held in Royal Armouries and Castles from the 1547 Inventory.[1]

This does not include 'parade' weapons, those held for garrison use, or weapons and armour held by individuals or corporate bodies as required by law.

Table 9. Staff Weapons Held in Stores

Store	Type	Quantities
Tower	Black Bills	6,700
Tower	Halberds	306
Tower	Pikes	20,100
Tower	Sprinkles 'great'	218
Tower	Sprinkles 'little'	392
Portsmouth	Black Bills	1,864
Portsmouth	Pikes	920
Carisbrooke	Pikes	500
Carisbrooke	Bills	750
Yarmouth	Bills	223
Berwick	Bills	4,600
Calais	Pikes	1,600
Boulogne	Pikes	3,550
Boulogne	Bills	1,260
Total pikes		26,670
Total halberds		306
Total bills		15,397
Total sprinkles		610

---

1   Starkey, *Inventory*.

Table 10. Bows and Sheaves of Arrows Held in Stores

Location	Bows	Sheaves
Towre of London	3,060	13,050
Calice Castell	1,500	4,720
Bulloigne-Towne	900	2,500
Guysnes (armoury)	450	1,138
Portesmouth-Towne	1,296	2,970
Carysbrooke	1,008	2,655
Hurst Castell	24	1,620
Pountfrait castell	1	535
Carleslie-Towne	200	2,000
Newcastell uppon Tyne	2,000	5,000
Berwicke within the storehouse	380	4,480
Berwicke- in the Nesse	400	2,700
Total	11,219	43,368

Table 11. Almain Rivet Armour Held in Stores

Store	Quantity
Dover Castle	One drie fatte*
Portsmouth town	326
Portsmout South Castle	20
Portsmouth Armoury	526
High Boulogne	200
The Old Man Boulogne	100
Boulogne Bargh	100
Pontefract Castle	191
Alnwick Castle	200
Kingston upon Hull	20
Westminster	544
Windsor	380
Bridewell	160
Deptford**	848
Hampton Court	433
Issued from Hampton Court	200
St Johns	419
Total	4667

* Armour kept in a cask or vat? ** Deptford stored 'Refuse harness little worthe' including breasts and backs for Almain rivets 2,000, sallets 4,000 and splints 2,000 pairs.

Appendix II

List of Ordnance Compiled by William Bourne[1]

Note: Powder weights are calculated for serpentine not corned powder.

Name	Cal. Inches	Length. of piece in feet	Weight of piece lb	Diam. of shot inches	Wt. of shot lb	Wt. of Powder lb
Old Double cannon	8¼	12	8,000	8	70	46
Ordinary Double cannon	8	11/12	7,500	7¾	64	42
French Double cannon	7¾	11/12	7,000	7½	58	40
Old Demi-cannon	6¾	11/12	6,000	6½	38	26
Ordinary Demi-cannon	6½	10/11	5,500	6¼	33	24
Small Demi-cannon	6¼	10/11	5,000–5,400	6	30	24
Foreign Demi-cannon	6	10/11	5,000	5¾	26 ½	22–23
Old or Nuremburg Culverin	5½	12/13	4,800	5¼	20	20
Ordinary Nuremburg Culverin	5¼	12	4,500	5	17	18
Small Nuremburg Culverin	5	var	4,300	4¾	15	16
Old Demi-culverin	4¾	12	3,200	4½	12½	12

---

1   William Bourne, *The Arte of shooting in great Ordnaunce* (London, 1587), pp. 65–71

Ordinary Demi-culverin	4½	10	2,700	4¼	10¾	11–12
Small Demi-culverin	4½	9-10	2,200	4	9	10–10½
Old Saker	4	10	1,800	3¾	7½	7 ½
Ordinary Saker	3¾	8/9	1,500	3½	6	6
Small Saker	3½	8	1,300–1,400	3¼	4 ¾–5	5–5½
Minion	3¼	8	1,000	3	3¾	3¾–4
Ordinary Minion	3	8	900	2¾	3	3
Falcon	2¾	7	700–750	2½	2 1/8	2½
Foreign Falcon	2½	7	600–650	2¼	1¾	2
Falconet	2¼	5–6	360–400	2	1 1/8	1¼

Appendix III

Graz Firearms Trials Statistical Summary

Firearm	Barrel Length	Weight	Calibre	Bullet diameter	Bullet weight	Charge	Muzzle Velocity m/s	Velocity at 7.5/8.5 m	Velocity at 30 m	Velocity at 100 m
G358	1.665 m	18 kg	20.6 mm	20.2 mm	49.14 g	20 g	533	514	470	349
RG 33	1 m	5.48 kg	17.8 mm	17.2 mm	30.06 g	11 g	456	435	394	287
RG 117	645 mm	2.9 kg	13.2 mm	12.3 mm	10.84 g	5 g	427	406	349	238
Glock 80*	114 mm	.66 kg	8.82 mm	9.3 mm	8 g	.4 g	360	-	342	-

		Penetration					Scatter	Scatter	Scatter	
	Muzzle energy†	Steel 30m	Wood 30m‡	Steel 100m	Wood 100m	Maximum Range 60⁰	Height	Width	Area	Percentage hits§
G358	6,980 J	-	-	4 mm	189 mm	1,279 m	53.5 cm	58.5 cm	3,130 cm²	51.5
RG33	3,125 J	3 mm	190 mm	2 mm	80 mm	1,095 m	46 cm	50.5 cm	2,323 cm²	54.5
RG117	988 J	2 mm	132 mm	1 mm	84 mm	834 m	29 cm	50.5 cm	1,465 cm²	54.5
Glock 80	516 J	2mm	126 mm	-	-	1,650 m	13.5 cm	15.2 cm	205 cm2	99.5

* The standard Austrian army 9mm pistol, included for comparison
† Joule
‡ Wooden target made from spruce
§ The target was 167 cm by 30 cm set at 100 m
Definition of scatter. These numbers represent the dimensions of the smallest rectangle that could be drawn on a larger secondary paper target that would enclose all the bullet holes.

Appendix IV

The Army of 1523[1]

Diets and wages of the army royal beyond sea, under Charles duke of Suffolk, 15 Hen. VIII.

The Duke, 100s. a day; 14 captains, at 4s. each a day; 14 petty captains, at 2s.; 1,006 footmen, at 6d.; 116 archers on horseback, at 8d.; a standard bearer, 12d.; 200 demi-lances, at 9d.; a herald, 4s.; 2 pursuivants, 2s. each.; 8 trumpets, at 16d.; 8 drumslads and fifers, at 12d.; a master surgeon, 2s.; 8 other surgeons, at 12d.

Total of the army, 10,688. Captains, 4s. a day; petty captains, 2s.; 21 spears of Calais, 19d.;[2] demi-lances, 9d.; marshal of the rearward, 6s. 8d.; marshal of the spears of Calais, 6s. 8d.; the High Marshal, 20s.; 2 surgeons in his retinue, 12d. each; clerks, 12d.; a chief clerk, 2s.; a clerk of the market, 16d.;[3] 4 tipstaves, 8d.; 2 gaolers, 12d.; 6 harbigers, 9d.;[4] 6 master scouts, 3s.; in 'executor of justice,' 4s.;[5] paymaster of the wagoners, 3s.; purveyors, 3s. 4d.; man-at-arms, 18d.; servants, 8d.; master mason, 12d.; masons, 6d.; 6 guides, 8d.; the secretary of Calais, 5s.; the two providers of guides, 3s.; Sir Ric. Wyngfeld, lords Leonard Gray, Mountagelie, and Ferrers, Sir A. Wyndesore, Sir R. Cornewale and Clarencius, 6s. 8d. each; a messenger, 12d.; Symson, Stoble and Brooke, 3s.; Cokeson, 18d.; trenchmaker, 2s.;[6] his two servants, 8d.; Humph. Hille, 'corrector of the ways', 12d.[7]

Wages of the ordnance. – Retinue of Isaac Sibles, provost of the ordnance: himself, 2s.; 10 foot-soldiers. Retinue of Sir Wm. Skevyngton, master of the same: himself, 10s.; 2 captains, two petty captains; 2 clerks, 12d, each; a master surgeon, 12d.; 2 other surgeons, 10d. each; 3 demi-lances; 14 archers,

---

1   *Letters and Papers,* vol. 3, 1523. Aug. R. O. 3288.
2   Mounted men-at-arms in full armour, demi-lances wore half-armour.
3   The camp contained a well-regulated market place in which prices as well as hygiene were closely controlled.
4   Harbingers.
5   Hangman?
6   Engineer responsible for the difficult task of planning and constructing siege lines.
7   Responsible for the maintenance of the roads used by the army.

horsemen; 197 foot soldiers. Retinue of the gunners: Th. Harte, master gunner, 4*s.*; Christ. Morres, lieutenant, 3*s.* 4*d.* ; Simon Savage, 2*s.*; Godfrey Horne, 16*d.*; 7 servants, 8*d.*

Pioneers and artificers in Skevyngton's retinue. – 7 captains of the pioneers, 12*d.* each; 28 headmen of 700 pioneers, 8*d.*;[8] 577 soldiers, pioneers, 6*d.*; Rob. Bates, master carpenter, 12*d.*; 19 other carpenters, 8*d.*; Rauf Wilde, master smith, 8*d.*; 19 other smiths, 8*d.*; James Nedham, master carpenter, 12*d.*; 19 other carpenters, 8*d.*; 71 pioneers and hurdlemakers, 6*d.*; 13 wheelers, 8*d.*; Geo. Fawsett, master stringer[9], 12*d.*; 3 other stringers, 8*d.*; John Halle, master fletcher, 12*d.*;[10] 4 other fletchers, 8*d.*; Th. Fortune and Hugh Kendale, masters of the engines, 12*d.*;[11] 7 servants thereabout, 8*d.*; Ric. Rowley, master smith for the engines, 12*d.*; 8 other smiths therefor, 8*d.*

The miners of Cornwall. – 1 captain, 12*d.*; 4 headmen, 8*d.*; 95 'mynour footmen', 6*d.*

Retinue of lord Curson. – Himself, 10*s.*; a captain, a petty captain, 4 archers and 87 foot soldiers. Pioneers, &c. in his retinue: 3 captains, 11 headmen, 196 pioneers, a clerk; Th. Sampson, master carpenter, and 11 others; John Somer, master smith, and 5 others; Wm. Wrenne, Master ferrour, 12*d*, and 10 others, 8*d.*; Gilbert Alman, master wheeler, and 4 others; Th. Godfray, master horse-harness maker, 12*d.*; and 9 others, 8*d.*

Retinue of Hans van Andwarpe, gunner. – Himself, 4*s.*; a chaplain, 8*d.*; 4 gunners that shoot double 'curtalles', 2*s.* 8*d*, each; 2 gunners that shoot double slinges, 22*d.*; 8 gunners that shoot 'sacrez', [sakers]18*d.*; 2 that shoot 'facons', [falcons] 14*d.*

Retinue of gunners with Th. Herte. – 11 master gunners, 16*d.*; 2 master gunners, 12*d.*; 24 gunners, 8*d.*; 6 gunners, 6*d.*[12]

Retinue of Philip Barnard, master provider of guides. – Himself, 4*s.* 6 foot soldiers.

Total of the ordnance, 1,648.

---

8 At a ratio of 20:1 they would correspond with the medieval rank of vintener.
9 Bow strings. Linen strings tend to be very thick and stretch a lot. Strings made from stinging nettle were much finer and less prone to stretch and break. Two bows were provided for each archer; in 1545 almost 10 bowstrings were provided for each bow, the strings were carried in barrels.
10 Fletchers not only made but also remade or refurbished arrows, replacing fletchings and refixing points.
11 Gins, cranes and other forms of lifting equipment that was so necessary to any army encumbered with a siege train.
12 Assistant gunners were referred to as matrosses in 1545. Master gunners were responsible for the larger pieces. Supernumerary gunners were drawn from the common soldiers.

Royal Houses of Europe

Valois Kings of France

1483–1498 Charles VIII b.1470
1498–1515 Louis XII b.1462
1515–1547 Francis I b.1494
1547–1559 Henry II b.1519
1559–1560 Francis II b.1544 – *King consort of Scotland 1558–1560 with Queen Mary I*

Holy Roman Emperors

1440–1493 Frederick III b. 1415 *King of Germany, Archduke of Austria*
1493–1519 Maximilian I b.1459 *King of Germany, Archduke of Austria*
1519–1556 Charles V b.1500 *King of GermanyArchduke of Austria King of Spain, Lord Of Netherlands and Duke of Burgundy*
1556–1564 Ferdinand I b.1503 *King of Germany King of Bohemia King of Hungary King of Croatia Archduke of Austria*

Spanish Monarchs

House of Trastámara
Ferdinand V of Aragon / II of Castile b.1452
King consort of Castile 1475–1504
King of Aragon 1475–1516

Isabella I Queen of Castile b. 1451
Queen of Castile 1474–1504
Queen consort of Aragon 1479–1504

Joanna (the Mad) b. 1479
Queen of Castile 1504
Queen of Castile 1516

Phillip I of Burgundy b 1478
King of Castile 1506

House of Habsburg

Emperor Charles V and King Carlos I of Spain b.1500 King of Spain 1516–1556
Phillip II b.1527 King of Spain 1556–1598 *King of England 1554–1558 with Mary I*

The House of Tudor

Henry VII 1485–1509 b. 1457
Henry VIII 1509–1547 b. 1491
Edward VI 1547–1553 b. 1537
Mary I 1553 Phillip I and Mary 1554–1558 b. 1516

Scottish Monarchy

James IV 1488–1513 b. 1473
James V 1513–1542 b. 1512
Mary I 1542–1567 b.1542

The Habsburg Succession

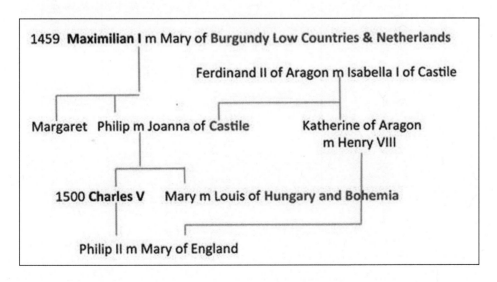

The Tudor Succession

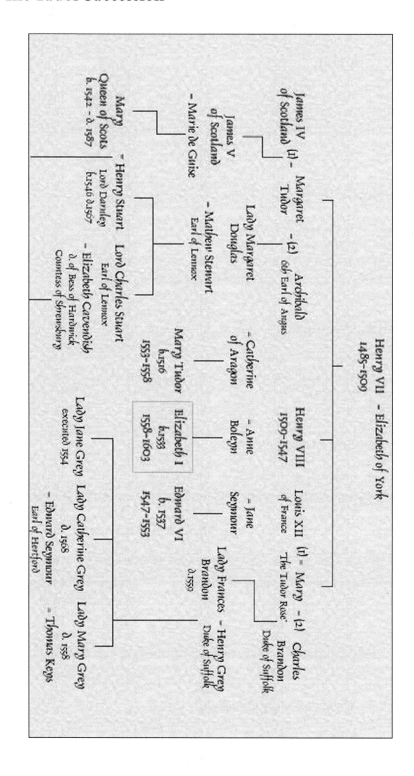

Appendix VII

Commentary on the Cowdray House Engravings

The Cowdray House engravings are to the Tudor military historian what the Bayeux tapestry is to a medievalist. The three engravings cover the events surrounding the *Enterprise of Boulogne* of 1544. The first depicts Henry's departure from Calais to the camp outside Boulogne, the second depicts scenes in the camp and the third the siege itself. The final painting is of less importance to the military historian as it records the accession procession into London of King Edward VI. Unfortunately, unlike the Bayeux tapestry the original paintings no longer exist, having been destroyed by fire on 24 September 1793. However, they were recorded in a series of engravings and paintings made by Sir Samuel Hieronymus Grimm in 1785 and James Basire in 1788. In addition, there is a detailed description by Sir Joseph Aylosse, Bart. which was published in *Archaeologia* vol. iii 1786.

Sir John considers that the paintings were possibly the work of Theodore Bernardi, an inhabitant of Chichester, painted in oils onto stucco in the dining parlour from sketches produced by Jerome de Trevisi [referred to as Geronimo by the English] an engineer and painter who was killed during the siege of Boulogne. Bernardi worked for Sir Anthony Browne. who lived at Cowdray from 1542 until his death in 1548. Browne had been made master of horse in 1539 and later was appointed lieutenant of the Gentlemen Pensioners He was a major participant in the events of the last years of Henry's reign. The picture that these illustrations give of Tudor military organisation and life is unique in its coverage and detail. The accuracy of the drawings seems excellent as when they can be tested against other sources they never seem to be found wanting.

The Departure of King Henry VIII from Calais, 25 July 1544

Henry had arrived in Calais on 15 July, three weeks after the arrival of the Duke of Norfolk and the vanguard, which had then departed to besiege Montreuil. Even so, Henry did not leave Calais until the 25th, arriving before Boulogne at the camp at Marquison on the 26th. In the left foreground can

The Departure of King Henry VIII from Calais, 25 July 1544. (Copyright Dominic Fontana)

be seen the Castle of Rise Bank, sometimes known as Risebane or Rysbrook built by John Duke of Lancaster and known previously as the New Tower or Lancaster's New Tower. The Town of Calais or Callis is well represented, as is the castle still in its mostly medieval form. Above can be seen the Castle of New Name Bridge, which is incorrect and should read Newhame or Newham Castle. The bridge itself, over which the army is crossing corresponds with written descriptions of it and crosses the River Hames.

The troop types represented are billmen, pikemen, archers and harquebusiers. The archers interestingly carry their weapons strung, which would shorten the life of the bow and the string. It is so often represented that one might assume that this was common, if bad, practice. Outside the Castle of Callis can be seen men engaged in weapons practice, a billman charging his weapon, and an interesting fight between a sword and buckler and a sword and target man. The target is well represented in these engravings and appears to have been much more frequently employed than is normally considered the case. The proportion of weapon types is however misleading. There were very few English harquebusiers and pikemen, with bill and bow predominant. Mercenary harquebusiers provide four independent companies, but these were probably involved in the investment of Montreuil with the majority of the mercenary and auxiliary forces.

Advancing up the hill is the extensive baggage train of the Middle Ward. The vehicles were locally hired from Imperial territory, and despite being rated for 30 or 40 cwt could barely carry a ton. The poor quality of the transport and above all its scarcity was a constant problem for Henry when both transporting and then sustaining his two sieges. Some of the wagons are covered, while others contain stores in barrels. The artillery appears to be drawn with limbers, or in the case of the heavier weapons out of battery on carriages. There is only evidence of one body of formed men, while there is much evidence of light horse.

The principal subject of the painting is to be found in the top right-hand corner 'The meetinge of the Kinge by Sir Antoni Browne upon the Hill Betwene Callis and Marquison', somewhere between Escales and Penplinque. Sir Anthony can be seen before a large force of mounted men-at-arms.

The Encampment of King Henry VIII at Marquison, [26] July 1544

Henry camped eight miles from Calais at Marquison, the modern town of Marquis, which was well beyond the range of the enemy guns in Boulogne. Holinshed reported: 'The King arrived that night at Marquison, being a very great tempestuous night of rain and thunder'. There is much disarray within the camp with several of the tents and halls in the process of being blown away. The King's prefabricated wooden palace, with its glass windows and metal roof, is well represented and will reappear in the next engraving. In the background the town of Marquison can be seen on fire, apparently as the result of lightning strikes. The weather throughout the campaign was noticeably foul, wet, windy and cold, causing heavy casualties amongst the besiegers.

The Encampment of King Henry VIII at Marquison, [26] July 1544. (Copyright Dominic Fontana)

In the foreground can be seen a female sutler dispensing bread unloaded from the wagon behind. Other wagons carry stores in casks and baskets. Above these scenes can be seen a small artillery park of four pieces. Throughout the camp are to be found 'shrympes' (war carts).

There is a remarkable degree of uniformity in the clothing represented during the expedition. There are examples of civilian dress to be found, but almost all men wear a uniform coat. Civilian headgear can sometimes be seen, but in action every man appears to be wearing a narrow brimmed morion irrespective of his primary weapon. The coats are cut to the thigh and all show the cross of St George before and behind. The illustrations seem to suggest that hooks and eyes were used to tie them together at the front rather than buttons, tapes or buckles. With low collars and short sleeves, they seem eminently practical garments.

The Siege of Boulogne by King Henry VIII

This is by far the largest and most complex of the engravings. In the bottom right hand corner can be seen a couple embracing. One of the features of all the engravings is the number of entwined couples. This indicated a change in discipline from his first French expedition where camp followers were strongly discouraged. Above them can be seen a group of light horsemen, some of the 2,000 javelins, staves, or Northern horse raised for this campaign. Above them can be seen a group of mercenary Irish or Scots as they were generically referred to, led by a bagpiper and escorting cattle 'liberated' from the surrounding countryside. It is thought that at least a company of such men served in the army. Further up the page can be seen details of camp life including a hanged man, a victim of the army's provost general.

At the top of the page can be seen Sir Arthur Browne's camp, with Sir Arthur himself probably, emerging from the camp going towards Montreuil with a retinue of horsemen. Above them flies an ensign described by Sir Joseph as bearing the Dragon of Cadwallader in the centre with near to the extremities the cross of St George. Also emerging from the camp is a company of foot preceded by fifer and drummer and an ensign. Below that is another body of foot, this time formed up and bearing pikes, while a similar body is formed up further right. It was felt important for all pikes to be of the same length for aesthetic as well as martial reasons. Beneath this group is one of the best illustrations of a company of foot in order of march.

Beneath this company can be seen the Lord Admiral's Camp, to the right of which can be seen a substantial powder store carefully protected from counter-battery fire in an earth revetment. The Monte was an artificially constructed mound that enabled fire to be directed inside the town itself. This battery was lauded for the martial triumph of destroying the steeple of the church of Notre Dame.

Below this can be seen the King's and the Duke of Alberkinny's (Albuquerque's) camp, the Duke was Don *Beltrán*de la Cueva the imperial representative. The camps contain conventional tents and halls as well as the King's lodging. The camp is encircled by wagons with shrympes and field pieces providing additional firepower. What is lacking is the defensive ditch which Audley recommends for any substantial stay, reflecting Henry's confidence that the investment of Montreuil would absorb the martial efforts of the available French forces. To the right of the encampment can be seen the figure of the King surrounded by his men-at-arms.

To the right of the battery is the old 12-storied Roman lighthouse or pharos referred to as the 'old man', captured on 22 July. The Lower Town with its single inadequate wall was captured on the 21st with little loss, although the French tried to fire it, but the Higher Town proved a much harder nut to crack. The English siege lines can be seen snaking towards the High Town, barely shoulder deep and lacking the sophistication of later sieges. The ground was hard and the soil thin. The first great obstacle was the *Fausse Braye* or wall and ditch placed before the remainder of the medieval defences.

The main gate on the right has been modified to meet some of the new demands of Renaissance warfare, a circular bastion or gun tower has been built at the base of one tower which has been given additional strength with wooden buttressing. A barbican pierced with gunports is also engaging arquebusiers and archers who have foolishly, for two of their number, chosen to skirmish in the open.

The main action is taking place to the left, where arquebusiers and archers are maintaining a hot fire to protect their comrades who are making the dangerous ascent into the breach. Meanwhile the Castle of Boulogne remains untouched by the siege pouring fire onto the defenders. Below this action is another well-gabioned battery and below that a company of foot is making its way through the trenches with archers preceding. As an unfortunate soldier is carried away on a stretcher, the mortars in their simple mounts carry on a lively bombardment. The mortars fired explosive shells, used for the first time by the English. Ironically the Frenchman Bernardine de Valois commanded the mortar battery of the Duke of Suffolk.

While all this mayhem is in progress beyond the city light horse can be seen fulfilling its duty of reconnaissance and in the harbour transports unload horses. In the bottom right hand corner three demi-lances patrol while a cantiniere and a few soldiers stroll towards the encampment.

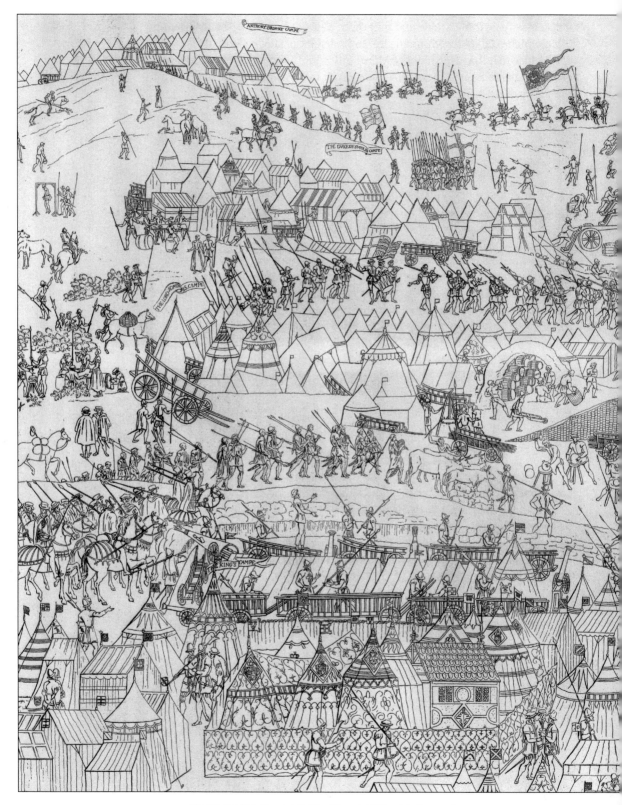

The Siege of Boulogne: left side. (Copyright Dominic Fontana)

THE CASTEL

THE MONTE

THE DVKE OF AL
BERKNAL[...] [...]MES

The Siege of Boulogne: right side. (Copyright Dominic Fontana)

Colour Plate Commentaries[1]

Photographs

1. There is only one way to string a bow properly and this is it. With the lower nock placed in the instep and by pulling with the right hand and pushing the tip down simultaneously, the string can be slipped comfortably into the upper nock. This does not strain the bow at any point and it is safe, quick, simple and elegant. If you cannot string a bow this way then the bow is too powerful for you. This yew bow is a thing of beauty with a near perfect delineation between heart and sap wood, and the bowyer has worked well with the wood. Provided with a sheaf of arrows, bollock dagger and broadsword he is a sight to please any captain. Note how the arrows can be drawn by the head through the arrow bag to be nocked quickly and efficiently onto the bowstring.

2. An archer of the better sort equipped with a lesser yew bow, probably a bough bow but still very serviceable and far superior to an ash bow. His sword has a knuckle and ring guards to protect his hand and he has a simple skull helmet to protect his head. Beneath his 'cote' he is wearing mail, just extending below the sleeve, as well as one of the simplest form of arm defences made of small plates linked together. Despite the simple and slightly archaic nature of his equipment, defence for the head, torso and arms constituted 'whole harness', the complete set of equipment theoretically required of a militia soldier. He does not possess an arrow bag, but has stuffed a sheaf of arrows into his belt. In 1545 Roger Ascham repeated an old Scottish proverb, that 'every Englysihe Archer beareth vnder his gyrdle xxiiii. Scottes'.[2]

3.1 The archers seen here are stationed behind a row of stakes, essential as a defence against cavalry. The Tudor archer's stake was quite a sophisticated item. Richard Rowley provided 5,000 archers' stakes, 'ready garnished with head, socket, ring and staple of iron', to Sir William Skevington in 1529. In 1547 there was a stock of 7,000 in Calais and 3,000 in Berwick as well as thousands of caltrops. Clearly with limited stocks of arrows, it was important to control the rate of shooting. Archers shoot to a rhythm, the result of decades of practice, to interrupt this by volley shooting would seem

---

1   With many thanks to Dr Edward Fox and Commotion Times for their generous assistance in the preparation of the text and the provision of the photographs.

2   Ascham, *Toxophilus* (London, 1545), p.38.

unnecessary. Also, once fully drawn the bow must be loosed and not held for too long, without it being endangered. To order the start and finish of shooting would make sense, but shooting by volley would not. In realistic trials an experienced war bow archer found that he could only shoot three aimed arrows in the time it took for a horseman to reach his position. Strong nerves and well-placed stakes would be needed.[3]

3.2 The bow is an ideal weapon for skirmishing through woodland and over rough ground. It can be drawn and loosed in one action and nocked with another arrow in seconds. Archers can work in pairs, ensuring their safety by always having an arrow on the bow and able to shoot with great accuracy at short range. Battles were very infrequent compared to the business of day-to-day soldiering. The bloody fighting on the Isle of Wight in 1545 and in the rebellions of 1549 mostly involved ambushes and skirmishing through woodland and hedgerows, where the bow often proved of inestimable value against 'better' armed adversaries.

4.1 Archers and billmen are here working together, one protecting the other. Such formations are often perceived as static and defensive, but in practice they are highly flexible aggressive formations, if trained well and led with confidence. This was the uncomfortable experience of the incorrigible Gascon Blaise de Monluc when he was chased out of Boulogne by the English during the camisade.

4.2 Billmen learning their trade. Maintaining formation when advancing over rough ground takes discipline and practice. The front rank have charged their arms low, aiming at the chests and faces of their enemy. The second rank have their arms charged high and fill the gaps in the front rank. Speed and determination would be the key to sweeping away the enemy, often even before they had come to 'handstrokes'. Intimidation of an enemy was an important factor in battles. The Scottish use of 'big rattles' at Pinkie did not produce the desired effect for as Hayward reported, '[the] ratling of shot might have done better service'.

5. Four worthy commoners practising with their different staff weapons. From left to right we have a halberd with next an English bill. The halberd was always deemed a higher status and worthier weapon, it was usually lighter and of superior workmanship and would ultimately become a parade weapon unsuited to battle. The third man wields a kriegsgertel, effectively a heavy bill but without the spear point. He is wearing a 'bright' armour consisting of breastplate, fauld and tassets. Thomas Audley was greatly in favour of having the front rank of any formation equipped thus, in order to make a manly show and scare the enemy. The last soldier carries an English bill of later date with a more slender spear and beak but not yet matching the elegance of the Italian bill or Roncone, which was like a rapier compared to

---

3   Author's conversation with Mark Stratton.

a broadsword. All four men are wearing the white coat which distinguished English soldiers, so much that the phrase 'whitecoat' was synonymous with 'soldier' in the same way as 'redcoat' would be in later centuries. White coats with red crosses were often issued by commanders, but in 1545 Lord Russell reported that the whole militias of Cornwall, Devon, Dorset and Somerset had equipped themselves with white coats at their own expense.

6.1 This billman wears a bishop's mantle of mail, a form of protection often associated with the Landsknechts. He may have copied the practice after serving alongside German mercenaries, as well as having acquired the German katzbalger sword he carries at his waist. The bollock dagger is characteristically English, as is his large-brimmed helmet. He would serve well on guard duty but might be expected to wear more armour when in the line of battle.

6.2 A well-armoured billmen guarding the entrance to Pendennis Castle. His Almain rivet is not bright and shiny, as it was often treated with mutton fat which darkened its colour and gave an unmistakable smell. Cleaning armour with sand and vinegar would eventually wear it away, making it thin and useless, and medieval armour so treated was sometimes cut up to provide small plates for jacks and brigandines. This man's pot helmet has been blued in the forge. Along with his bill he carries a falchion, heavy bladed and ideal for close-quarter work.

7.1 Crossbows were not unknown in English service and they were used widely for sport. In the Calais garrison there were 110 crossbows in store with 20,000 ready-to-use bolts and more ready if needed. The drawings by the Landsknecht Paul Dolnstein, show bolts driven into the faces and through the thighs of his fellows by Swedish crossbowmen. The crossbow was a very effective weapon and far handier than the longbow when in the confines of a castle. Whilst white was the most common coat colour for most of Henry VIII's reign, some troops employed directly by the Crown, such as full-time garrisons, were issued coats in the royal livery colours of green and white.

7.2 This billman has a soldier's 'cote' in blue guarded with yellow and slashed. Slashing was stylish but it also allowed freedom of movement around the shoulder, this is the case with the author's leather jerkin suited to an archer, but they can also be a terrible nuisance! Shields were not common in English armies of the period, but they were not unknown. Several billmen were recorded owning shields in the 1522 military survey, such as William Peke of Talland, Cornwall, who mustered with his 'bill and pavise'. They are also depicted in the Cowdray engravings. This one is painted with the Tudor Rose and embellished with the initials HIS which is the Latinised version of the Greek ιησους, the name of Jesus. This was used widely as a sign of devotion and appeal for divine assistance.

8.1 This arquebusier is in the process of fitting the match cord into the serpentine, which can be a fiddly business. He has two powder flasks, one for priming or 'fyne' powder the other 'grossecorne' for the main charge. Corned powder revolutionised hand-held firearms, using a long barrel to produce high velocity projectiles which were much more likely to penetrate armour. He has a leather bag for his lead shot which he might well have made himself to ensure a good fit, and thereby greater precision and consistent performance. His riding boots would suggest that he was mounted. The powerful combination of firepower and mobility was first exploited by Italian mercenaries who served in Henry and Edward's reigns. This was a period when there was experimentation in tactical forms combining the firepower of the arquebus and the flexibility of the bow.

8.2 This arquebusier has closed his eyes on firing, just as the author does. The flash from the priming is always unnerving especially when close to the face. He is also firing from the hip, which was again a common practice, especially when engaging a target en masse. To speed reloading, it was not unknown to 'touch-off' the powder with match cord held in the hand, rather than fitting it into the serpentine. He has also avoided the common novice's error of shooting his scouring stick (ramrod) at the enemy.

9. The sword was perhaps the most common and popular weapon and not to be despised, especially in the hands of the skilful. The English preferred the use of the sword and buckler together as demonstrated by the soldier on the left, it was an aggressive style that was favoured by young swashbucklers. The sword and target used by the gentleman on the right was favoured by the Spanish, who used it with devastating effects against pikemen. The combination of 'sword and shield' appealed to those enamoured with the Roman ideal, but it was also wholly practical and very effective in the hands of trained men, especially when skirmishing. A decorated target was sometimes seen being carried by the captain's boy, when it acted as a badge of office. The hand-and-a-half and double-handed sword were also still practised with and used, both requiring great skill, training and stamina. Aggressiveness and confidence were important when wielding a blade.

10. The pioneer is sometimes overlooked, considered rustic and expendable. These men were also part of the fighting order of the army, as were the carters, when occasion demanded. He is well provided for with a stout leather cap, more practical and useful than a steel helmet, a leather cape, warm and waterproof clothing. He is carrying the three tools which he was expected to bear from the store issued to his company. The essential jobs that the pioneers were expected to perform were myriad; they included the preparation of roads and mending and making of bridges, digging mines and ditches, recovering bogged down carriages and guns and constructing field fortifications, including the making and filling of gabions. Devon and Cornwall provided specialist miners who would prove essential at sieges where artillery on its own proved ineffectual. Boulogne was won by mining, not bombardment, in 1544.

11.1 The euphoniously named whiffler stands like his monarch, codpiece to the fore and afeared of no man! His double-handed sword with flambard blade was a symbol of his status but a lethal and flexible weapon. His finely polished morion would be accompanied by equally well-polished Almain rivet armour. Then, as now, the aggressive self-confidence and display of the soldier was an essential part of his public face whether to a civilian or an enemy. He may not display the extravagant clothing of the Landsknecht or the outlandish garb of the Stradiot, but he was a professional soldier of which that 'old contemptible' Elis ap Gruffydd would have approved.

11.2 The ensign and whiffler. This relatively modest silk flag combines the red cross of St George with the green and white colours of the Tudors. The short staff enabled it to be flourished and thrown in a style still used by Italian *sbandieratori* or flag wavers. Thomas Styward, writing in Elizabeth's reign, established the impressive qualities expected from this gentleman:

> The Ensigne bearer must be a man skilfull, hardie, and couragious, of able courage to advance &beare up the Ensigne, in all extremities secret, silent & zelous, able often to comfort, animate, & encourage the companie to take in hand and mainteine such enterprises as they are appointed vnto, never to retire … in time of approch, assault, or entering, imbrech he with his ensigne aduaunceth with the formost, giuing occasion that souldiers the rather follow the same.[4]

12. An archer's kit:

1. A falchion. Swords were a desirable addition to any archer's kit. This archer, evidently not a wealthy man, has equipped himself with a cheap but sturdy blade, more useful for unskilled hacking at the enemy than any fancy fencing.

2. A woollen jerkin, worn between the doublet and coat for warmth. Soldiers experienced all weathers on campaign.

3. Doublet and hose, the basic clothing of any Tudor man.

4. This archer is evidently in the pay of the King himself, demonstrated by his green and white livery.

5. Linen breeches (underpants)

6 & 7. A mug, bowl, knife, and spoon remind us of the love of all soldiers for food and drink.

8. A simple 'skull' helmet. Skulls like this were common, largely because they were cheap, but also because they provide a good amount of protection without affecting the archer's vision or movement.

9. A linen shirt.

10. A stout pair of turned boots. Not particularly fashionable, but very well suited to the rigours of campaign.

11. A pair of woollen tapes. They were intended for use as garters around the archer's knees, but could also be used for many other purposes such as

---

4   Thomas Styward, *The pathwaie to martiall discipline* (London, 1582), pp.37–38.

bundling up his blanket, or replacing a broken belt.

12. A flint, steel, and tinderbox.

13. A wooden rosary. Although the use of prayer beads was discouraged from the 1530s, several were recovered from the Mary Rose, and as late as 1549 they were still in widespread use among religious conservatives.

14. Knitted woollen cap. The woollen cap was the ubiquitous head gear of the lower orders, and not only provided protection against the cold, but was also waterproof up to a point.

15. Spare bow string. Records suggest that as well as arrows archers were issued several spare strings for their bow, and string-makers accompanied Tudor armies on campaign. Eight to 10 strings and two sheaves of arrows (48) were provided for archers on campaign.[5] Bow strings have a limited lifespan, and a bow without a string is a stick.

16. Apart from his helmet the mail standard, covering the neck and shoulders, is this archer's only form of defence.

17. Woollen blanket. Although tents were provided for a number of the major campaigns, in the smaller campaigns against domestic revolt or invasion soldiers had no more shelter at night than the blanket they huddled in.

18. Contrary to popular myth, Tudor men and women did not live in filth. This archer carries a linen rubbing cloth to remove dirt and sweat from his skin, and a cake of soap which could be used to clean his linen underclothes.

19. A relatively 'modest' bollock dagger and pouch.

20. Archers' bracers were often made of leather, such as those recovered from the Mary Rose, but horn or ivory bracers were also known. This horn bracer served partly to protect the archer's left forearm from any unfortunate strike from his bow string, and partly to keep any loose fabric out of the path of the string.

21. Roger Ascham mentioned shooting gloves to protect the archers' fingers from the abrasive action of the bow string, but no gloves or tabs have survived from the Tudor period, suggesting that experienced archers relied on the callouses they must have developed. This finger tab is copied from a late-medieval example, possibly belonging to a child, excavated in Coventry.

22. Beeswax. Both a lubricant and a waterproofing agent, beeswax was ubiquitous and had myriad uses on campaign.

23. Sheaf of livery arrows bound up in a girdle. The arrows are self-nocked with slivers of horn used for reinforcement. The fletchings are hand cut, long and low, fixed with bluebell glue and protected with verdigris. The shafts are probably poplar rather than ash.

24. Yew bow. Henry VIII introduced a statute in 1542 requiring bowyers to make four 'mean' wood bows of ash, elm, hazel or wychelm for every yew bow, in order to ensure a supply of affordable bows. The cost of the

---

5   J.P. Davies, "'We do fynde in our countre great lack of bowes and arrows", Tudor Military archery and the Inventory of King Henry VIII', *Journal of the Society of Army Historical Research* , vol. 83, no. 333, Spring 2005.

bow was also regulated so that in 1542 a bow suitable for a 14-year-old boy should cost no more than a shilling, still a considerable amount. The cost of the best bow was set at 3s 4d, a bow of the 'second sort' 2s 6d, a sheaf of livery arrows 2s, a gross of bowstrings 3s 4d a leather case at 6d and a girdle at 2d.6 The bows issued from royal armouries, however, appear to have been the better yew bows.

13. A surgeon's equipment. By the mid sixteenth century the well-trained and well-equipped military surgeon could treat many of the wounded that were brought to him and often with some success.

1. These instruments were used to search and clean the wound the first part of any treatment. Wine or vinegar, and urine if desperate, could be used to irrigate the wound. Fresh urine, even if not completely sterile, has the advantage of at least being at blood temperature.
2. Fractures and especially depressed fractures of the skull were common. Wounds that penetrated to the brain were inevitably fatal. Removal of bone fragments and drilling a hole to relieve pressure from bleeding in the brain were practical and effective treatments.
3. Cauterising irons were used to stop bleeding and reduce infection. Their application was painful and could lead to delayed healing.
4. Every surgeon would have his special preparation for the treatment of wounds involving herbs, gums and oils, as well as mineral and plant-based treatments.
5. Brass needles, suture material, scissors, splints and a variety of different bandages were essential for the closure and protection of wounds. Such practical treatment was well understood and practised with skill.
6. Amputation was rarely employed, as the dangers of further blood loss and infection were appreciated. The equipment necessary changed little over the centuries. Sharp instruments, a strong and steady hard and speed were of the essence.
7. Instruments for the removal of lead balls came in a variety of forms, and the number of different types shown here attests to the wealth and hopefully the skill of the surgeon.

Tudor Flags up to 1558

Heraldry was of great importance to the Tudors in establishing their new dynasty. Their colours and devices appeared everywhere, on garments and guns, castles and chapels. The great aristocratic families could not and would not abandon their own displays but this had to be within the bounds of common sense. Henry Howard displayed his pretensions to royal blood in his coat of arms and was executed because of it in 1547. The aristocracy who

---

6   Jonathan Davies, 'Painful pastime versus present pleasure': Tudor Archery and the Law', *Journal of the Society for Army Historical Research*, vol. 85, no. 343 (Autumn 2007), pp.224–236.

had dominated the political and military life of the kingdom until Bosworth now found themselves again subjects to powerful kings. The balance of recruitment in this period tipped from the aristocratic towards a national system, this was reflected in the heraldry or lack of it on military flags and standards. Much though was still made of aristocratic heraldry, so that the Bear and Ragged Staff were well displayed in Norwich when the Earl of Warwick suppressed Kett's rebels.

The green and white Tudor livery replaced murrey and blue the livery colours of the house of York. This is most apparent in the painting of *The Embarkation of Henry VIII at Dover c.1520–40* (Hampton Court Palace; painter unknown). The multitude of painted shields that decorate the ships are either green and white with the rose and portcullis, or white with the cross of St George. The rectangular flags in this scene, flourished gallantly from boat and bulwark, display the cross of St George and alternating green and white stripes.

Flags and banners were subject to legislation similar to the sumptuary laws applied to dress. A royal standard would be eight or nine yards in length, a duke's seven and a knight a mere four. Banners containing a full coat of arms were five feet for a king, four for a duke and but three feet for a baron.

14. This was the standard of Edmund Howard. Never as favoured at Henry VIII's court as his brothers Thomas and Edward, he still played his part in tournament and battle. He was marshal of horse at Flodden and attended Henry at The Field of the Cloth of Gold. His career, unlike his beard was inglorious and he was considered a spendthrift and rather ineffectual. His greatest disaster was his daughter, Catherine Howard. The personal rather than family motto reads 'Tous Jours Loyal' (Always Loyal). The predominant colour in Howard heraldry was red, the white lion with blue claws and tongue may have been a reference to the Scottish lion, tamed at Flodden. After the battle Henry VIII added an inescutcheon to the Howard heraldry. This was in the form of the lion of Scotland with an arrow through its mouth, recording rather tastelessly, one of the injuries suffered by James IV. To use the Scottish lion in English heraldry added insult to injury.

15. Henry 7th Baron Scrope of Boulton also fought at Flodden in 1513 and continued to serve in the North as a loyal supporter of King Henry until his death in 1533. He succeeded to the livery on the death of his father in 1506 and was made a knight banneret in 1509. As with all such flags there is a cross of St George at the hoist. The Cornish chough has a red beak and feet and is associated with Thomas Becket. The closest translation of the motto the author has found is, 'In hope of joy awaiting grace'.

16. A rectangular infantry flag from the Cowdray engravings. The red cross of St George was at the centre of the new 'colours', so called because of the variety of different colours used in their designs. Although the green and white predominated in Tudor heraldry the colour of the soldiers' coats could vary, as it did in the French expedition of 1544.

17. The rearguard in the Boulogne expedition was commanded by Lord Russell and wore blue coats guarded with yellow. They were committed to the futile siege of Montreuil, until retreating in disgraceful disorder to Calais. Unfortunately, it is likely that few acts of heroism were performed beneath this flag.

18. The addition of the Tudor livery colours to the cross of St George was a simple means of combining national and Tudor heraldry. A flag such as the one illustrated above was issued to a company of German mercenaries, hired with the intention of recovering Calais in 1558.

19. Taken from the Cowdray engraving, this flag would have been associated with the main guard or battle which accompanied the King to Boulogne in 1544 and wore coats of red guarded with yellow.

Bibliography

Official Documents

Calendar of State Papers Domestic: Edward VI, Mary and Elizabeth, vol. 1, 1547–80, ed. Robert
    Lemon (London: Longman, Brown, Green, Longman's & Roberts, 1856)

*Calendar of State Papers and Manuscripts, Relating to English Affairs: Existing in the Archives and
    Collections of Venice, and in Other Libraries of Northern Italy*, vol. 2

Calendar of State Papers Relating to English Affairs in the Archives of Venice, vols 2, 5, 6, 1509–1519,
    1534–1554 and 1555–1558

Calendar of State Papers Spain, vols 1, 2, 13, for 1485–1509, 1509–1525 and 1554–1558

Calendar of State Papers Foreign: Elizabeth, vol. 2, December 1559–1560

Calendar of State Papers, Scotland: Volume 1, 1547–63

State Papers Foreign. Ed. VI. 1549

Letters and Papers, Foreign and Domestic, Henry VIII, vols 19 and 20, 1544 and 1545

Statutes of the Realm, vol. iv (London, 1819)

Theses and Dissertations

Cooper, Jonathan Paul, 'Whitecoats and Rascals: In Search of the Fortifications and Siege Works
    from the Siege of Haddington 1548–1549'. Submitted as part of the MLitt in Battlefield and
    Conflict Archaeology (8V7S) Department of Archaeology Faculty of Arts of the University of
    Glasgow Submitted September 2008

Davies, C.S.L, 'Supply service of English Armed Force 1509–1550. Unpublished University of
    Oxford Phd. thesis, 1963

Goring, John Jeremy, 'The Military Obligations of the English People 1511–1558'. Unpublished
    University of London Phd. thesis, 1955

Hodgkins, Alexander James, 'Rebellion and Warfare in the Tudor State: Military Organisation,
    Weaponry, and Field Tactics in Mid-Sixteenth Century England.'

Unpublished University of Leeds Institute for Medieval Studies Phd. thesis, 2013

Hewerdine, Anita Rosamund, 'The Yeomen of the King's Guard 1485–1547'. Unpublished ondon
    School of Economics and Political Science Phd. thesis, 1998

Martin, Colin John Mackenzie, 'The Equipment and Fighting Potential of the Spanish Armada'. A
    Thesis Submitted for the Degree of PhD at the University of St Andrews, 1984

Spencer, Daniel, 'The Development of Gunpowder Weapons in Late Medieval England'.
    Unpublished University of Southampton Phd. thesis, 2016

Walton, Stephen Ashton, 'The Art of Gunnery in Renaissance England'. Unpublished Institute for
    the History and Philosophy of Science and Technology University of Toronto Phd. thesis, 1999

Printed Primary Sources

Alberti, Leon Battista, *On the Art of Building in Ten Books* (MIT Press, 1988)

Anon., *Certayne causes gathered together, wherin is shewed the decaye of England onely by the great multytude of shepe* (London: Hugh Syngelton, 1552)

Anon., *The Boke For A Justyce of Peace* (London, 1534)

Anon., *The Compleat Gunner* (London, 1672)

Anon., *Worke for Cutlers; or a merry dialogue betweene sword, rapier and dagger – Acted in a shew in the famous Universitie of Cambridge* (London, 1615)

Ascham, Roger, *Toxophilus: The School of Shooting* (Manchester: The Simon Archery Foundation, 1985)

Ayloffe, Joseph, *A Description of some ancient historical paintings preserved at Cowdray in Sussex, the seat of the Right Honourable Viscount Montague: representing, I. The March of King Henry VIII from Calais towards Boulogne: II. The encampment of the English Forces at Marquison: and III. A view of the siege of Boulogne, in the year 1544* (London, 1787) (ECCO Print Edition, 2020)

Bain, Joseph (ed.), *The Hamilton Papers: Letters and Papers Illustrating the Political Relations of England and Scotland in the XVIth Century*, vol. I (Edinburgh: H.M. General Register House, 1890) <https://archive.org/details/cu31924091786032/page/n5/mode/2up>

Barret, Robert, *The Theorike and Practike of Moderne Warres* (London:1598)1

Biringuccio, Vannoccio, *The Pirotechnia* (New York: Dover Publications Inc., 1990)

Bourne, William, *The Arte of Shooting in Great Ordnaunce* (London: Thomas Woodcoke, 1587)

Brown, Peter Hume (ed.), *Early Travellers in Scotland* (Edinburgh: David Douglas, 1891) <https://archive.org/stream/earlytravellersi00browuoft/earlytravellersi00browuoft_djvu.txt>

Brown, Rawdon Lubbock (ed.), *Calendar of State Papers and Manuscripts, Relating to English Affairs: Existing in the Archives and Collections of Venice, and in Other Libraries of Northern Italy* (Cambridge: Cambridge University Press, 2013)

Burnet, Gilbert, *The third part of the History of the Reformation of the Church of England. A general index to the History … A collection of records, letters, and original papers with other instruments referred to in the former History*, ed. Edward Nares, 3 vols (Oxford: Oxford University Press, 1829)

Bynnerman, Henrie, *An arithmetical treatise, named Stratioticos* (London, 1579)

Cameron, Annie I. (ed.), *Scottish Correspondence of Mary of Lorraine*, SHS (Edinburgh: Constable, 1927)

Clowes, William, *A profitable and necessarie Booke of observations for all those that are burned with gun-powder, &c. and also for the curing of wounds made with musket and caliver shot, and other weapons of warre* (London, 1596)

Clowes, William, *Selected writings of William Clowes 1544–1604*, F.N.L. Poynter (ed.) (London: Harvey & Blythe Ltd, 1958)

Commines, Phillipe, *The memoirs of Philip de Commines, Lord of Argenton: containing the histories of Louis XI and Charles VIII. Kings of France and of Charles the Bold, Duke of Burgundy. To which is added, The scandalous chronicle, or Secret history of Louis XI*, by Jean de Troyes, ed. Andrew R. Scoble (London: Henry G. Bohn, 1856)

Corneweyle, Robert, *The Maner of fortifications of cities, townes, castelles and other places* (1559)

Daunce, John, 'Sir John Daunce's Accounts of Money received from the Treasurer of the King's Chamber temp. Henry VIII', Charles Trice Martin (ed.), *Archaeologia*, vol. XLVII, pp.1–42.

Davies, M.B. (ed.), 'The "enterprises" of Paris and Boulogne', *Bulletin of the Faculty of Arts, Fouad I University*, 11 (1949)

Dickinson, G. (ed.), *Two Missions of Jacques de la Brosse* (Edinburgh: Scottish History Society Third Series, vol. 36, 1942)

Digges, Leonard and Thomas, *A Geometricall Practise, Named Pantometria*, 2nd (extended) edition (1591)

Ellis, Henry, *Original Letters Illustrative of English History: Including Numerous Royal Letters; from Autographs in the British Museum, the State Paper Office, and One Or Two Other Collections*, Volume 1 (London: Richard Bentley, 1846)

Erasmus, Desiderius, and Vicesimus Knox, *The Works of Vicesimus Knox*, vol. 5 (Personal Nobility, Spirit of Despotism, Antipolemus) (London: Mawman, 1824) <https://oll.libertyfund.org/titles/knox-the-works-of-vicesimus-knox-vol-5#Knox_0254-05_1198>

Frulovisi, Tito Livio dei, ed. C.L. Kingsford, *The First English Life of King Henry V* (Oxford: Clarendon Press, 1911)

Fulwell, Ulpian, *The Flower of Fame: Containing the bright renowne, & moste fortunate raigne of King Henry the viii. Wherein is mentioned of matters, by therest of our cronographers ouerpassed. Compyled by Vlpian Fulwell. Hereunto is annexed (by the aucthor) a short treatice of iii. noble and virtuous queenes. And a discourse of the worthie seruice that was done at Hadington in Scotlande, the seconde yere of the raigne of king Edward the sixt.* (London: In Fleete streate, at the Temple gate by William Hoskins, 1575)

Gairdner, James (ed.), *The Paston Letters, A.D. 1422–1509* (London: Chatto & Windus, 1904)

Gale, T., *The Office of a Chirurgion* (London, 1586)

Giustiniani, Sebastian, '*Four years at the court of Henry VIII; selection of despatches written by the Venetian ambassador, Sebastian Giustinian, and addressed to the Signory of Venice, January 12th 1515, to July 26th 1519*', translated by Rawdon Brown (Cambridge: Cambridge University Press, 2013)

Grafton, Richard, *Grafton's Chronicle: or, History of England. To which is added his table of the bailiffs, sheriffs, and mayors, of the city of London. From the year 1189 to 1558, inclusive.* vol. II (London: Printed for J. Johnson, 1809) <https://archive.org/stream/graftonschronicl02grafuoft/graftonschronicl02grafuoft_djvu.txt>

Grose, Francis, *Military Antiquities Respecting a History of the English Army, from the Conquest to the Present Time*, vol. I (London: L. Stockdale, 1801)

Grose, Francis, *The Antiquarian Repertory: A Miscellany, Intended to Preserve and Illustrate Several Valuable Remains of Old Times*, vol. ii, (n.p., Forgotten Books, 2018)

Hall, Edward, *Chronicle: containing the history of England, during the reign of Henry the fourth, and the preceding monarchs to the end of the reign of Henry the eighth* (etc). (London: Johnson, (etc.), 1809)

Harrison, William, *Elizabethan England: From 'A Description of England', by William Harrison* (Good Press, 2019)

Hooker, John, *The Ancient History and Description of the City of Exeter* (Exeter: Andrews and Trewman, 1765)

Holinshed, Raphael, *Holinshed's Chronicles of England, Scotland, and Ireland*, vol. 3 (London: J. Johnson, 1807)

Holinshed, Raphael, *Holinshed's Chronicles of England, Scotland, and Ireland*, 6 vols (London: Routledge, 2013)

Howard, Henry, Earl of Surrey, *The Works of Henry Howard, Earl of Surrey, and of Sir Thomas Wyatt* (London: Longman, MDCCCXV), vol. 1

Hughes, P.L. and J. Larkin, *Tudor Royal Proclamations* (New Haven: Yale University Press, 1964)

Jordan, W.K., *The Chronicle and Political Papers of King Edward VI* (London: George Allen and Unwin, 1966)

Lindsey, Robert of Pitscottie, *The Historie and Cronicles of Scotland* (Edinburgh: Blackwood & Sons, 1899)

Lindsay, Robert of Pitscottie and Freebairn, Robert, (eds), *The history of Scotland; from 21 February, 1436. to March,1565. In which are contained accounts of many remarkable passages altogether differing from our other historians; and many facts are related, either concealed by some, or omitted by others.* (Edinburgh: Baskett and Company, 1728)

Machiavelli, Niccolò, transl. Allan Gilbert, *The Art of War*, in *Machiavelli: The Chief Works and Others*, vol. II (Durham, N.C.: Duke University Press, 1989)

Machiavelli, Niccolò, *The Art of War* (New York: Da Capo Press, 2001)

Machiavelli, Niccolò, *The Prince*, transl. George Bull (London: Penguin Books, 1961)

Monluc, Blaise, Seigneur de, ed. Ian Roy, *The Habsburg–Valois Wars and the French Wars of Religion* (London: Longman, 1971)

Monluc, Blaise, Paul Courteault (ed.), *Commentaires de Blaise de Monluc, maréchal de France.* Edition critique, publiée et annotée par Paul Courteault. T. III: *1563–1576.* (Paris: Picard, 1925)

Moore, Thomas, *Utopia*, Book I, in Henry Craik (ed.), *English Prose* (New York: The Macmillan Company, 1916), <https://www.bartleby.com/209/55.html>

Morison, Richard, *An Exhortation to styrre all Englyshe men to the defence of theyr countrye* (London, 1539)

Nichols, J.G. (ed.), *The Chronicle of Calais: In the Reigns of Henry VII. and Henry VIII. to the Year 1540*, vol. 35 (London: Camden Society, 1846)

Nichols, J.G. (ed.), *The chronicle of Queen Jane, and of two years of Queen Mary, and especially of the rebellion of Thomas Wyat written by a resident in the Tower of London* (London: Camden Society, 1850)

Patten, William, *The expedicion into Scotla[n]de of the most woorthely fortunate Prince Edward, Duke of Soomerset*, in introduction by A.F. Pollard, *Tudor Tracts 1532–1588* (Westminster: Archibald Constable and Co. Ltd, 1903), pp.53–157

Paré, Ambroise, *Life and times of Ambroise Paré 1510–1590. With a new translation of his Apology and an account of his journeys in divers places* (Memphis: General Books, 2010)

Paré, Ambroise, *Ten Books of Surgery* (Athens: University of Georgia Press, 2010)

Parker, Geoffrey, *The Military Revolution: Military Innovation & the Rise of the West, 1500–1800* (Cambridge: Cambridge University Press, 1996)

Rich, Barnabe, *A path-way to military practise Containinge offices, lawes, disciplines and orders to be observed in an army, with sundry stratagems very beneficiall for young gentlemen, or any other that is desirous to have knowledge in martiall exercises. Whereunto is annexed a kalender of the imbatteling of men: newlie written by Barnabe Rich souldiour, seruaunt to the right honorable Sir Christopher Hatton Knight. Perused and allowed.* (John Charlewood, for Robert Walley, 1587). Available online at the Oxford Text Archive <ota.ox.ac.uk>

Russell, Frederic William, *Kett's rebellion in Norfolk: being a history of the great civil commotion that occurred at the time of the reformation, in the reign of Edward VI. founded on the "Commoyson in Norfolk, 1549," by Nicholas Sotherton; and the "De furoribus Norfolciensium" of Nevylle: and corroborated by extracts from the privy council register; documents preserved in the state paper and other record offices; the Harleian and other mss.; and corporation, town and church records* (London: Longmans, Brown, Green, Longmans and Roberts (etc.), 1859). Available online at Internet Archive <https://www.archive.org>

Seysell, Claude de, *La Monarchie de France*, ed. J. Poujol (Paris: Société des Textes Français Modernes, 1961)

Smith, Thomas (attrib.), *A Discourse of the Commonweal of this Realm of England*, ed. M. Dewar (Charlottesville: University Press of Virginia, 1969)

Smythe, John, *Certain discourses… Concerning the force and effects of divers sorts of weapons 1590*, reprinted in: *Bow versus Gun* (East Ardsley Wakefield: E.P. Publishing Ltd, 1973)

Stone, Percy G., *The French Descent on the Isle of Wight, July, 1545* (English Account), in *The Antiquary*, Nov 1908, 4, 11; ProQuest pp.425–428.

Stone, Percy G, *The French Descent on the Isle of Wight, July,1545 (French Account)*. The Antiquary; Oct 1908; 4, 10; ProQuest pp.368–373.

Starkey, David, *The Inventory of King Henry VIII … the transcript* (London: Harvey Miller Publishers, 1998)

Styward, Thomas, *Pathwaie to Martiall Discipline* (London: 1582)

Talhoffer, Hans, *Medieval Combat,* transl. and ed. Mark Rector (London: Greenhill Books, 2000)

Vergil, Polydore, *Anglica Historia*, book 25 (London: J.B. Nichols, 1846)

Vigo, Joannes de, *The most excellent workes of chirurgerye* (Amsterdam: Theatrum Orbis Terrarum; New York : Da Capo Press, 1968)

Wyatt, George, *The papers of George Wyatt Esquire of Boxley Abbey in the county of Kent*, ed. D.M. Loades (London: Royal Historical Society, Camden Fourth Series, vol. 5, 1968)

Printed Sources

[No author] *Collection des Documents Inédits sur l'Histoire de France* (France: France, Ministère de l'éducation nationale, 1847)

Abulafia, David, *The French Descent into Renaissance Italy, 1494–95: Antecedents and Effects* (London: Routledge, 2016)

Adams, Nicholas and Pepper, Simon, *Firearms & fortifications: military architecture and siege warfare in sixteenth-century Siena* (Chicago: University of Chicago Press, 1986)

Anglo, Sydney, *The Martial Arts of Renaissance Europe* (New Haven: Yale University Press, 2000)

Arfaioli, Maurizio, *The Black Bands of Giovanni: Infantry and Diplomacy During the Italian Wars (1526–1528)* (Pisa: Edizioni Plus – Pisa University Press, 2005)

Arnold, Thomas, *The Renaissance at War* (London: Cassell and Co., 2001)

Aylward, J.D., *The English Master of Arms* (London: Routledge Kegan Paul, 1956)

Barr, Niall, *Flodden* (Stroud: Tempus Publishing Ltd, 2003)

Beer, Barrett, *Rebellions and Riot: Popular Disorder in England During the Reign of Edward VI* (Kent, Ohio: Kent State University Press, 1982)

Beltrame, Carlo and Renato Gianni Ridella, *Ships and Guns: The Sea Ordnance in Venice and Europe Between the 15th and the 17th Centuries* (Oxford: Oxbow Books, 2011)

Bennett, Jim and Johnson, Stephen, *The Geometry of War 1500–1750* (Oxford: Ashmolean Museum, 1995)

Bennett, Michael, *The Battle of Bosworth* (Thrupp: Sutton Publishing Ltd, 2000)

Betteridge, Thomas and Suzannah Lipscomb (eds), *Henry VIII and the Court: Art, Politics and Performance* (Farnham: Ashgate Publishing Ltd, 2013)

Black, Jeremy, *A Military Revolution? Military Change and European Society 1550–1800* (Basingstoke: Macmillan, 1991)

Black, Jeremy (ed.), *European Warfare 1453–1815* (Basingstoke: Macmillan, 1999)

Black, Jeremy, *The Cambridge Illustrated Atlas of Warfare: Renaissance to Revolution, 1492–1792* (Cambridge: Cambridge University Press, 1996)

Black, Jeremy, *The Origins of War in Early Modern Europe* (Edinburgh: John Donald, 1987)

Blackmore, H.L., *The Armouries of the Tower of London*. volume 1, *Ordnance* (London: HMSO, 1976)

Boynton, Lindsay, *The Elizabethan Militia* (London: Routledge & Kegan Paul, 1967)

Braun, Anne, *Historical Targets* (London: Roydon Publishing Co, 1983)

Brewer, J.S. (ed.), *Letters and Papers, Foreign and Domestic, of the Reign of Henry VIII*, vol. 3 (Vaduz: Kraus reprint, 1965)

Brown, R.R. and R.D. Smith, *Bombards – Mons Meg and Her Sisters* (Leeds: Royal Armouries, 1989)

Bull, Stephen, *The Furie of the Ordnance: Artillery in the English Civil Wars* (Woodbridge: The Boydell Press, 2008)

Bush, Michael, *The Pilgrimage of Grace: A Study the Rebel Armies of October 1536* (Manchester: Manchester University Press, 1996)

Caraman, Philip, *The Western Rising 1549: The Prayer Book Rebellion* (Tiverton: Westcountry Books, 1994)

Carpenter, Austin C., *Cannon: the Conservation, Reconstruction and Presentation of Historic Artillery* (Tiverton: Halsgrove Press, 1993)

Carlton, Charles, *Going to the Wars: The Experience of the British Civil Wars 1638–1651* (London: Routledge, 1994)

Carlton, Charles, *This Seat of Mars: War and the British Isles, 1485–1746* (New Haven: Yale University Press, 2011)

Caruana, Adrian B., *The Halberd and other European Polearms 1300–1650* (Bloomfield: Museum Restoration Service of Canada, 1998)

Caruana, Adrian B., *Tudor Artillery 1485–1603* (Bloomfield: Museum Restoration Service of Canada, 1992)

Cathcart King, D.J., *The Castle in England and Wales: An Interpretative History* (London: Routledge Press, 1991)

Champion, Matthew, *Kett's Rebellion 1549* (Reepham: Timescape Publishing, 1999)

Childs, David, *The Warship Mary Rose: The Life and Times of King Henry VII's Flagship* (Havertown: Seaforth Publishing, 2014)

Clements, John, *Renaissance Swordsmanship* (Boulder: Paladin Press, 1997)

Collins, Arthur, *The Peerage of England … The third edition, corrected and enlarged in every family, with memoirs, not hitherto printed*, vol.1 (London: H. Woodfall, etc., 1768)

Collinson, Patrick (ed.), *The Sixteenth Century: 1485–1603* (Oxford: Oxford University Press, 1998)

Colvin, H.M., *The History of the Kings Works*, vol. Plans (London: HMSO, 1963)

Cornish, Paul, *Henry VIII's Army* (London: Osprey, 1996)

Craik, George Lillie, MacFarlane, Charles, *The Pictorial History of England: Being a History of the People, as Well as A History of the Kingdom* (New York: Harper & Brothers, 1847)

Cressy, David, *Saltpeter: The Mother of Gunpowder* (Oxford: Oxford University Press, 2013)

Cruickshank, C.G., *Army Royal: Henry VIII's Invasion of France* (Oxford: Clarendon Press, 1969)

Cruickshank, C.G., *Elizabeth's Army* (Wotton-under-Edge: Clarendon Press, 1966)

Davies, Jonathan P. (text transcribed by M. Bryn Davies), *'An ill jurney for the Englshemen': Elis Gruffydd and the 1523 French Campaign of the Duke of Suffolk* (Sunderland: Pike and Shot Society, 2006)

Davies, Jonathan P. (text transcribed by M. Bryn Davies), *Elis Gruffydd and the 1544 'Enterprises' of Paris and Boulogne* (Sunderland: Pike and Shot Society, 2006)

Davies, Jonathan P. , *The King's Ships: Henry VIII and the Birth of the Royal Navy* (Leigh-on-Sea: Caliver Press, 2005)

Davies, Jonathan P., J. Shumate, A. Hook, S. Walsh, *The Medieval Cannon, 1326–1494* (Oxford: Osprey, 2019)

Davies, Jonathan P. (text transcribed by M. Bryn Davies), *Thomas Audley and the Tudor 'Arte of Warre'* (Sunderland: Pike and Shot Society, 2002)

Davis, J.C., *Pursuit of Power: the Venetian ambassadors' reports to Spain, Turkey and France in the Age of Phillip II 1560–1600* (New York: Harper & Row, 1970)

Davis, R.H.C., *The Medieval Warhorse* (London: Thames and Hudson, 1989)

De Vries, Kelly and Robert Douglas Smith, *The Artillery of the Dukes of Burgundy* (Woodbridge: The Boydell Press, 2005)

De Vries, Kelly, and Robert D. Smith, *Medieval Military Technology* (Toronto: University of Toronto Press, 2nd Revised edition (30 April 2012))

Dickinson, G. (ed.), *Two Missions of Jacques de la Brosse* (Edinburgh, Scottish History Society Third Series vol. 36, 1942)

Doran, Susan, *England and Europe in the Sixteenth Century* (Basingstoke: Macmillan International Higher Education, 1998)

Doran, Susan, *Elizabeth I and Foreign Policy, 1558–1603* (London: Routledge,2002)

Downing, Brian, *The Military Revolution and Political Change* (Princeton, N.J.: Princeton University Press, 1992)

Duffy, Christopher, *Siege Warfare* (London: Routledge Kegan Paul, 1979)

Dufty, Arthur Richard, *European Swords and daggers in the Tower of London* (HMSO, 1974)

Edge, David and John Miles Paddock, *Arms and Armour of the Medieval Knight* (London: Saturn Books Ltd, 1996)

Eltis, David, *The Military Revolution in Sixteenth Century Europe* (London: I.B. Tauris, 1998)

Elton, *Policy and Police: the Enforcement of the Reformation in the Age of Thomas Cromwell* (Cambridge: Cambridge University Press, 1972)

Elton, G.R., *The Tudor Constitution* (Cambridge: Cambridge University Press, 2nd edn. 1982)

Embleton, G., and D. Miller, *The Landsknechts* (London: Osprey, 1976)

Featherstone, Donald, *Armies and Warfare in the Pike and Shot Era 1422–1700* (London: Constable, 1998)

Ffoulkes, Charles, *The Gun-Founders of England* (Cambridge: Cambridge University Press, 2010)

Fiorato, Veronica, Anthea Boylston and Christopher Knusel (eds), *Blood Red Roses: The Archaeology of a Mass Grave from the Battle of Towton AD 1461*: (Oxford: Oxbow Books, 2000)

Firth, Charles Harding, *Cromwell's army : A History of the English soldier During the Civil Wars, the Commonwealth and the Protectorate* (London: Methuen and Co., 1902)

Fissell, Mark Charles, *English Warfare 1511–1642* (London: Routledge, 2001)

Fletcher, Anthony and Diarmaid MacCulloch, *Tudor Rebellions* (London: Routledge, 2004)

Fox, Edward, *The Commotion Time: Tudor Rebellions of 1549* (Warwick: Helion & Company, 2020)

Gardiner, Julie with Michael J. Allen (eds), *Before the mast: life and death aboard the Mary Rose* (Portsmouth: Mary Rose Trust, 2005)

Graves, M.A.R., *Henry VIII* (Harlow: Pearson Education Limited. 2003)

Groome, Francis, *Ordnance Gazetteer of Scotland: A Survey of Scottish Topography – Statistical, Biographical and Historical*, vol. 1 (Bristol: Thoemmes, 1882)

Grummitt, David, *The Calais Garrison. War and Military Service in England, 1436–1558* (Woodbridge: Boydell & Brewer, 2008)

Guilmartin, J.F., *Galleons and Galleys* (London: Cassell and Co., 2002)

Guilmartin, J.F., *Gunpowder and Galley* (Cambridge: Cambridge University Press, 1974)

Gunn, S.J., *Charles Brandon: Henry VIII's closest friend* (Stroud: Amberley Publishing, 2016)

Gunn, S.J., *Early Tudor Government,1485–1558* (Basingstoke: Macmillan Press Ltd, 1995)

Gunn, S.J., David Grummitt and Hans Cools, *War, State, and Society in England and the Netherlands 1477–1559* (Oxford: Oxford University Press, 2007)

Hale, J.R., *Artists and Warfare in the Renaissance* (New Haven: Yale University Press, 1990)

Hale, J.R., *Renaissance Fortification. Art or Engineering?* (London: Thames & Hudson, 1977)

Hale, J.R., *Renaissance War Studies* (London: Hambledon Press, 1983)

Hale, J.R., *War and Society in Renaissance Europe 1450–1620* (Stroud: Sutton, 1998)

Hale, Matthew, *Historia Placitorum Coronæ, The History of the Pleas of the Crown ... In Two Volumes ... In Two Volumes*, vol. 1 (London: E. Rider, 1800)

Hall, A.R., *Ballistics in the Seventeenth Century* (Cambridge: Cambridge University Press, 1965)

Hall, Bert S., *Weapons and Warfare in Renaissance Europe* (Baltimore: The Johns Hopkins University Press, 1997)

Hammer, Paul E.J., *Elizabeth's Wars: War, Government and Society in Tudor England, 1544–1604* (Basingstoke: Palgrave Macmillan, 2003)

Hardy, Robert and Matthew Strickland, *The Great Warbow* (Thrupp: Sutton Publishing Ltd, 2005)

Harrington, Peter, *The Castles of Henry VIII* (London: Osprey Publishing, 2007)

Hayward, John, *The Life, and Raigne of King Edward the Sixt* (Kent, Ohio: Kent State University Press, 1993)

Heath, Ian, *Armies of the Sixteenth Century* (St Peter Port: Foundry Books, 1997)

Heath, Ian, *The Irish Wars 1485–1603* (London: Osprey, 1993)

Hewerdine, Anita, *The Yeomen of the Guard and the Early Tudors: The Formation of a Royal Bodyguard* (London: Bloomsbury Publishing, 2012)

Hildred, Alexzandra, *Weapons of Warre: The Armaments of the Mary Rose*, vol. 3 (Exeter: Short Run Press Ltd, 2011)

Hodgkin, A.E., *The Archer's Craft* (Felifach: Llanerch, 1995)

Hogg, O.F.G, *Artillery: its origins, heyday and decline* (London: C. Hurst and Co., 1970)

Hogg, O.F.G, *Clubs to Cannon* (London: Gerald Duckworth & Co. Ltd, 1968)

Hogg, O.F.G, *English Artillery* (Woolwich: Royal Artillery Institution, 1963)

Hogg, O.F.G., *The Royal Arsenal* (Oxford: Oxford University Press, 1963)

Hutchinson, Robert, *Young Henry: The Rise of Henry VIII* (London: Weidenfeld & Nicholson, 2011)

Ingram, Mike, *Richard III and the Battle of Bosworth* (Warwick: Helion & Company, 2019)

Jary, Leo R., *Kett – 1549. Rewriting the Rebellion* (Lowestoft: Poppyland Publishing, 2018)

Jordan, W.K., *The Chronicle and Political papers of King Edward VI* (London: George Allen and Unwin, 1966)

Kelly, Jack, *Gunpowder* (London: Atlantic Books, 2004)

Land, Stephen K., *Kett's Rebellion* (Woodbridge: Boydell Press Ltd, 1977)

Litwin, J (ed.), *Baltic and beyond: Change and continuity in shipbuilding Gdańsk* 2015. Proceedings of the 14th International Symposium on Boat and Ship Archaeology, pp.221–228. (Gdańsk, 2017)

Loach, J., and R. Tittler (eds), *The Mid-Tudor Polity, c.1540–1560* (London: Macmillan, 1980)

Loades, David, *The Fighting Tudors* (Kew: The National Archives, 2009)

Lockyer, Roger and Andrew Thrush, *Henry VII* (London: Routledge, 2014)

McCreadie, Rory W, *The Barber Surgeon's Mate of the 17th Century* (Upton: Gosling Press, 1997)

MacCulloch, Diarmaid (ed.), *The Reign of Henry VIII: Politics, Policy and Piety* (Basingstoke: Palgrave Macmillan, 1995)

MacCulloch, Diarmaid (ed.), *The Reign of Henry VIII: Politics, Policy and Piety* (Palgrave Macmillan, 1995)

MacDougall, Norman, *James IV* (Edinburgh: Tuckwell, 1997)

Macivor, Iain, *The Fortifications of Berwick-upon-Tweed* (London: English Heritage, 1998)

Mallett, Michael, and Christine Shaw, *The Italian Wars 1494–1559* (London: Routledge, 2014)

Martines, Lauro, *Furies, War in Europe 1450–1700* (New York: Bloomsbury, 2013)

Merriman, Marcus, *The Rough Wooings: Mary Queen of Scots, 1542–1551* (East Linton: Tuckwell Press, 2000)

Millar, Gilbert John, *Tudor Mercenaries and Auxiliaries, 1485–1547* (Charlottesville: University of Virginia Press, 1980)

Miller, Douglas and Gerry Embleton, *The Landsknechts*, Men-at-Arms 58 (London: Osprey, 1976)

Miller, H., *Henry VIII and the English Nobility* (Oxford: Basil Blackwell, 1986)

Morley, B.M., *Henry VIII and the Development of Coastal Defence* (London: HMSO, 1976)

Myers, A.R., *The Household of Edward IV: the Black Book and the Ordinance of 1478* (Manchester: Manchester University Press, 1959)

Norman, A.V.B., *The Rapier and Small-sword: 1460–1820* (London: Arms & Armour Press, 1980)

Norwich, John Julius, *Four Princes: Henry VIII, Francis I, Charles V, Suleiman the Magnificent and the Obsessions that Forged Modern Europe* (Kindle Edition, 2020)

Nosworthy, Brent, *The Stradiots* (Venture Miniatures, 2020)

Oman, Charles, *A History of the Art of War in the Sixteenth Century* (London: Greenhill Books, 1987; Methuen and Co. 1937)

Oakeshott, Ewart R., *European Weapons and Armour: From the Renaissance to the Industrial Revolution* (Woodbridge: Boydell Press, 2000)

Oakeshott, Ewart R., *The Sword in the age of chivalry* (London: Arms & Armour Press, 1981)

O'Neil, Brian Hugh St. John, *Castles and Cannon: A Study of Early Artillery Fortifications in England* (Westport, Conn.: Greenwood Press, 1975)

O'Sullivan, Daniel, *The Reluctant Ambassador: the life and Times of Sir Thomas Chaloner, Tudor Diplomat* (Stroud: Amberley Publishing, 2016)

Padfield, Peter, *Guns at Sea* (London: Hugh Evelyn, 1979)

Partington, J.R.A., *History of Greek Fire and Gunpowder* (Cambridge: W. Heffer & Sons, 1966)

Payne-Gallwey, Ralph, *The Book of the Crossbow* (London: Holland Press, 1995)

Peachey, Stuart, *The Mechanics of Infantry Combat in the First English Civil War* (Bristol: Stuart Press, 1992)

Pegler, Martin, *Powder and Ball Small Arms* (Ramsbury: Crowood Press, 1998)

Phillips, Gervase, *The Anglo-Scots Wars 1513–1550: A Military History* (Woodbridge: Boydell Press, 1999)

Pivka, Otto von, *Armies of the Napoleonic Era* (Newton Abbot: David & Charles, 1979)

Pollard, T. and N. Oliver, *Two Men in a Trench: Battlefield Archaeology – the Key to Unlocking the Past* (London: Michael Joseph, 2002)

Ponting, Clive, *Gunpowder* (London: Chatto & Windus, 2005)

Potter, David Linley, *Henry VIII and Francis I: The Final Conflict, 1540–47* (Leiden: Brill Academic Publishers, 2011)

Potter, David, *Renaissance France at War: Armies, Culture and Society, c.1480–1560* (Boydell Press, 2008)

Prestwich, Michael, *Armies and Warfare in the Middle Ages* (New Haven: Yale University Press, 1996)

Randall, David, *English Military news Pamphlets, 1513–1637* (Tempe: Arizona Center for Medieval and Renaissance Studies, 2011)

Ratcliffe, Susan, *The Concise Oxford Dictionary of Quotations* (Oxford: Oxford University Press, 2011)

Raymond, James, *Henry VIII's Military Revolution – The Armies of Sixteenth-Century Britain and Europe* (London: Tauris Academic Studies, 2007)

Richardson, Thom, *The Armour and Arms of Henry VIII* (Leeds: Royal Armouries, 2019)

Ridgeway, William, *The Origin and Influence of the Thoroughbred Horse* (Cambridge: Cambridge University Press, 2015)

Roberts, Michael, *The Military Revolution, 1560–1660: An Inaugural Lecture Delivered Before the Queens University of Belfast* (Queen's University of Belfast, 1955)

Rogers, H.C.B., *Artillery Through the Ages* (London: Seeley Service and Co, 1971)

Rönnby, Johan (ed.), *On war on board; Archaeological and historical perspectives on early modern maritime violence and warfare* (Stockholm: Södertörns högskola, 2019)

Rose-Troup, Frances, *The Western Rebellion of 1549: An Account of the Insurrections in Devonshire and Cornwall against Religious Innovations in the Reign of Edward VI* (London: Smith & Elder

& Co., 1913)

<https://archive.org/stream/westernrebellion00rose/westernrebellion00rose_djvu.txt>

Ruff, J.R., *Violence in Early Modern Europe 1500–1800* (Cambridge: Cambridge University Press, 2001)

Russell, Frederic William, *Kett's Rebellion in Norfolk* (London: Longmans, Brown, Green, Longmans and Roberts, 1859)

Saunders, Andrew D., *Fortress Britain: Artillery Fortifications in the British Isles and Ireland* (Liphook: Beaufort Publishing Ltd, 1989)

Scarisbrick, J.J., *Henry VIII* (Berkeley: University of California Press, 1970)

Shaw, Christine (ed.), *Italy and the European Powers: The Impact of War, 1500–1530* (Leiden: Brill, 2006)

Sheppard, E.W., *A Short History of the British Army* (London: Constable 1950)

Smith, Robert Douglas and Kelly De Vries, *The Artillery of the Dukes of Burgundy* (Woodbridge: Boydell Press, 2005)

Smith, Robert Douglas and Kelly De Vries, *Rhodes Besieged: A New History* (Stroud: The History Press, 2011)

Snook, George, *The Halberd and other European Polearms 1300–1650* (Alexandria Bay, NY: Museum Restoration Service, 1988)

Soar, Hugh D.H., *The Secrets of the English war Bow* (Yardley: Westholme Publishing LLC, 2006)

Stewart, R.W., *The English Ordnance Office* (Woodbridge: Boydell Press, 1996)

Starkey, David, *The Reign of Henry VIII* (London: Collins & Brown, 1991)

Syson, Luke and Thornton, Dora, *Objects of Virtue: Art in Renaissance Italy* (Getty Trust Publications: J. Paul Getty Museum, 2002)

Tallett, Frank, *War and Society in Early Modern Europe, 1495–1715* (London: Routledge, 2016)

Taylor, F.L., *The Art of War in Italy 1494–1529: Prince Consort Prize Essay 1920* (Cambridge: Cambridge University Press, 1921)

Teesdale, Edmund B., *Gunfounding in the Weald in the Sixteenth Century* (Leeds: Royal Armouries, 1991)

Tincey, John, *Elizabeth's Army & the Armada* (Leigh-on-Sea: Partizan Press, 1988)

Tincey, John, *The Armada Campaign, 1588* (London: Osprey, 1996)

Tuck, Anthony (ed.), *War and Border Societies in the Middle Ages* (London: Routledge, 1985)

Turnbull, Stephen, *The Art of Renaissance Warfare* (London: Greenhill Books, 2006)

Tyacke, S (ed.), *English Map-Making 1500–1650: Historical Essays* (London: British Library, 1983)

Valentine, Eric, *Rapiers* (London: Arms & Armour Press, 1968)

Viele, E.L., *Hand-book of Field Fortifications and Artillery* (Richmond, Va: J.W. Randolph, 1861)

Watts, John, *The End of the Middle Ages? England in the Fifteenth and Sixteenth centuries* (Thrupp: Sutton Publishing, 1998)

Webb, Henry J., *Elizabethan Science: the Books and the Practice* (Madison: University of Wisconsin Press, 1965)

Wiffen, Jeremiah Holmes, *Historical Memoirs of the House of Russell*, vol. 1, part 1 (London: Longman, Rees, Orme, Brown, Green, and Longman, 1833)

Williams, Glanmor, *Renewal and Reformation: Wales c.1415–1642* (Oxford: Oxford University Press, 1993)

Wood, James B., *The King's Army: Warfare, Soldiers, and Society During the Wars of Religion in France, 1562–1576* (Cambridge: Cambridge University Press, 1996)

Wood, Robin, *The Wooden Bowl* (Trowbridge: Stobart Davies Ltd, 2005)

Young, Alan, *Tudor and Jacobean Tournaments* (London: George Philip, 1987)

Wallace Collection Catalogue (William Clowes and Sons, 1962)

Zimmerman, I and L.M. Veith, *Great Ideas in the History of Surgery* (Baltimore: The Williams & Wilkins Company, 1961)

Articles

Archbold, W.A.J., 'A Diary of the Expedition of 1544', *The English Historical Review*, vol. 16, no. 63 (July 1901), pp.503–507

Atkinson, C.T., 'The Art of war in the sixteenth century', *Journal of the Society for Army Historical Research*, vol. 16, no. 63 (Autumn,1937), pp.152–157

Audley, Thomas, 'A Treatise on the Art of War', *Journal of the Society for Army Historical Research*, vol. 6, no. 24 (April–June,1927), pp.65–78

Awty, Brian G., 'The breakthrough of the 1540s in the casting of iron ordnance', *Journal of the Ordnance Society*, vol. 15 (2003), pp.19–28

Bailey, Sarah Barter, 'Information relating to the operation of the early cast-iron gun industry from a manuscript account in the collection of the Royal Armouries', *Journal of the Ordnance Society*, vol. 3 (1991), pp.11–17

Blair, Claud, 'King Henry VIII's chamber-pieces', *Royal Armouries Yearbook*, vol. 5 (2002), pp.22–39

Brown, Ruth Rhynas, 'Troncks, rockets and fiery balls: Military fireworks of the early modern period', *Journal of the Ordnance Society*, vol. 17 (2005), pp.25–38

Boynton, Lindsay, 'The Tudor Provost-Marshal', *The English Historical Review*, vol. 77, no. 304 (1962), pp.437–455

Caldwell, D.H., 'The Battle of Pinkie', in N. MacDougall (ed.), *Scotland and War A.D. 79–1918* (Edinburgh: John Donald, 1991), pp.61–94

Cassidy, Ben, 'Machiavelli and the Ideology of the Offensive: Gunpowder Weapons in "The Art of War"', *The Journal of Military History*, vol. 67, no. 2 (April 2003), pp.381–404

Cressy, David, 'Saltpetre, state security and vexation in early modern England', *Past and Present*, no. 212 (August 2011), pp.73–111

Cruickshank, C.G., 'King Henry VIII'S Army, Part One: Camp', *History Today* (December 1968), pp.852–857

Cruickshank, C.G., 'King Henry VIII's Army, Part Two: Munitions', *History Today* (January 1969), pp.40–46

Currin, John M., 'The King's Army into the Partes of Bretaigne': Henry VII and the Breton Wars, 1489–1491', *War in History*, vol. 7, no. 4 (2000), pp.379–412

Davies, C.S.L., 'England and the French War, 1557–9', in J. Loach and R. Tittler (eds), *The Mid-Tudor Polity c.1540–1560* (London: Macmillan, 1980), pp.159–185

Davies, C.S.L.,"Henry VIII and Henry V: the Wars in France," in J.L.Watts (ed.), *The End of the Middle Ages? England in the Fifteenth and Sixteenth centuries* (Thrupp: Sutton Publishing, 1998), pp.247–8

Davies, C.S.L., 'Provisions for Armies, 1509–50; A Study in the Effectiveness of Early Tudor Government', *The Economic History Review*, New Series, vol. 17, no. 2 (1964), pp.234–248

Davies, Jonathan, "A combersome tying weapon in a throng of men" The decline of the longbow in Elizabethan England', *Journal of the Society for Army Historical Research*, vol. 80, no. 321 (Spring 2002), pp.16–31

Davies, Jonathan, "Henry VIII and his Twelve Apostles", *Journal of the Ordnance Society*, vol. 27 (2020), pp.67–68

Davies, Jonathan, "Painful pastime versus present pleasure": Tudor Archery and the Law',*Journal of the Society for Army Historical Research*, vol. 85, no. 343 (Autumn 2007), pp.224–236

Davies, Jonathan, 'Some thoughts on Tudor military arrowheads', *Journal of the Society of Archer Antiquaries Symposium* (2002), pp.38–39

Davies, Jonathan, "'We do fynde in our countre great lack of bowes and arrows": Tudor military archery and the Inventory of King Henry VIII', *Journal of the Society for Army Historical Research*, vol. 83, no. 333 (Spring 2005), pp.11–29

Davies, M. Bryn, 'The Enterprises' of Paris and Boulogne', *Bulletin of the Faculty of Arts of Fouad I University*, vol. XI, part 1 (Cairo, May 1949), pp.1–59

De Vries, Kelly, 'Catapults Are Not Atomic Bombs: Towards a Redefinition of "Effectiveness" in Premodern Military Technology', *War in History*, vol. 4, no. 4 (1997), pp.454–70

De Vries, Kelly, 'Gunpowder weaponry and the rise of the Early Modern State', *War in History*, vol. 5 no. 4 (1998), pp.127–45

De Vries, Kelly, 'Military Surgical Practice and the advent of gunpowder weaponry', *Canadian Bulletin of Medical History*, l vol. 7 (1990), pp.131–146

Esper, Thomas, 'The Replacement of the Longbow by Firearms in the English Army', *Technology and Culture*, vol. 6, no. 3 (Summer, 1965), pp.382–393

Goring, John Jeremy, 'Social change and military decline in mid–Tudor England', *History* (June 1975), pp.85–197

Goring, J.J., 'The Dress of the English Soldier in the Early Tudor Period', *Journal of the Society for Army Historical Research*, vol. 33, no. 135 (Autumn, 1955), pp.136–138

Goring, Jeremy, 'The General Proscription of 1522', *The English Historical Review*, no. CCCXLI (1971), pp.681–705

Grummitt, David, 'The Defence of Calais and the Development of Gunpowder Weaponry in England in the Late Fifteenth Century', *War in History*, vol. 4, no. 3 (2000), pp.253–272

Gunn, S.J., 'The Duke of Suffolk's March on Paris in 1523', *English Historical Review*, vol. 101, no. 401 (Oct. 1986), pp.596–634

Gunn, S.J., 'The French Wars of Henry VIII', in *The Origins of War in Early Modern Europe*, ed. Jeremy Black (Edinburgh: John Donald, 1987), pp.28–51

Hale, J.R., 'Men and Weapons: The Fighting Potential of Sixteenth-Century Venetian Galleys', *War in History*, vol. 5, no. 2 (1998), pp.309–334

Hall, Nicholas, 'Building and firing a replica *Mary Rose* port piece', *Royal Armouries Yearbook*, vol. 3 (1998), pp.57–66

Hall, Nicholas, 'Casting and Firing a Mary Rose Culverin', *Royal Armouries Yearbook*, vol. 6 (2001)

.Harris, Valentine P., 'The Decline of the Longbow', *Journal of the Society of Archer–Antiquaries*, vol. 19 (1976)

Hennell, Reginald, 'The King's bodyguard of the yeomen of the guard, 1485–1920', *Journal of the Society for Army Historical Research*, vol. 4, no. 16 (April–June 1925), pp.71–80

Heuser, Beatrice, 'Denial of Change: The Military Revolution as seen by Contemporaries', *International Bibliography of Military History*, vol. 32 (2012), pp.3–27

Hildred, Alexzandra and David Starley, 'Technological examination of a *Mary Rose* hailshot piece; new evidence for early iron gun casting', *Royal Armouries Yearbook*, vol. 5 (2002), pp.139–146

Hocker, Fred, 'Ships, shot and splinters: the effect of 17th-century naval ordnance on ship structure', in J. Litwin (ed.), 'Baltic and beyond: Change and continuity in shipbuilding Gdańsk 2015', Proceedings of the 14th International Symposium on Boat and Ship Archaeology, pp.221–228. (Gdańsk, 2017)

Hocker, Fred, 'Understanding the Gundeck Experience', in Johan Rönnby (ed.), *On war on board; Archaeological and historical perspectives on early modern maritime violence and warfare* (Stockholm: Södertörns högskola, 2019)

Hodgkinson. Jeremy S., 'Gunfounding in the Weald', *Journal of the Ordnance Society*, vol. 9 (1997), pp.31–48

Hooker, James R., 'Notes on the Organization and Supply of the Tudor Military under Henry VII', *Huntington Library Quarterly*, vol. 23, no. 1 (November 1959), pp.19–31

Kahanov, Tresman, Me-Bar, Cvikel, Hillman (eds), 'Akko 1 shipwreck: the effect of cannon fire on the wooden hull', *Journal of Archaeological Science* 39 (2012), pp.1993–2002

Krenn, P., P. Kalaus and B. Hall, 'Material Culture and Military History: Test-Firing Early Modern Small Arms', in *Material Culture Review*, 42(1), 1995.
Retrieved from <https://journals.lib.unb.ca/index.php/MCR/article/view/17669>

Lankester, Philip J., 'A note on some partizans with the Tudor royal arms in the Royal Armouries', *Royal Armouries Yearbook*, vol. 5 (2002), pp.40–45

Lankester, Philip J., 'Two Maces from Henry VIII's Arsenal?', *Royal Armouries Yearbook*, vol. 5 (2000), pp.27–43

Leslie, J.H., 'The Honorable the Board of the Ordnance 1299–1855', *Journal of Army Historical Research,* vol. 4, no. 17 (1925), pp.100–104

Lynn, John A., 'The trace italienne and the Growth of Armies: The French Case', *The Journal of Military History*, vol. 55, no. 3 (July 1991), pp.297–330

McKee, Alexander, 'Henry VIII as military commander', *History Today* (June 1991), pp.22–36

MacMahon, Luke, 'Military Professionalism in the early Tudor armies in Renaissance Europe: a reassessment', in D.J. Trim (ed.), *The Chivalric Ethos and the Development of Military Professionalism* (Leiden: Brill 2003), pp.183–212

Martinez, Andrew, 'Disciplinary Ordinances for English Armies and Military Change, 1385–1513', *History* (2017), pp.362–385

Merriman, M., 'Italian Military Engineers in Britain in the 1540s', in S. Tyacke (ed.), *English Map-Making 1500–1650: Historical Essays* (London: The British Library, 1983), pp.57–67

Millar, Gilbert John, 'The Albanians: Sixteenth Century Mercenaries', *History Today*, vol. 26, issue 7 (July 1976) pp.468–472

Millar, Gilbert John, 'Henry VIII's Colonels', *Journal of the Society for Army Historical Research,* vol. 57, no. 231 (Autumn 1979), pp.129–136

Miller, David P., Derek Allsop and Debra J. Carr, 'The Ballistics of Seventeenth Century Musket Balls', *Journal of Conflict Archaeology*, 14:1 (2019), pp.25–36

Millar, Gilbert John, 'Henry VIII's preliminary letter of retainer to Colonel Frederick Von Reiffenberg for the raising of 1500 men–at–arms', *Journal of the Society for Army Historical Research,* vol. 67, no. 272 (Winter 1989), pp.220–225

Millar, Gilbert John, 'Mercenaries under Henry VIII 1544–46', *History Today*, vol. 27, issue 3 (March 1977), pp.173–182

Millar, Gilbert John, 'The Landsknecht: His Recruitment and Organization, With Some Reference to the Reign of Henry VIII', *Military Affairs,* vol. 35, no. 3. (Oct. 1971), pp.95–99

Murphy, Neil, 'Henry VIII's First Invasion of France: The Gascon Expedition of 1512', *English Historical Review,* vol. CXXX no. 542 (2015), pp.25–56

Pearse, Richard, 'The Use of the Matchlock When Mounted', *Journal of the Society for Army Historical Research*, vol. 44, no. 180 (December 1966), pp.201–204

Pepper, Simon, 'Castles and Cannons in the Naples campaign 1494–5', in David Abulafia, *The French Descent into Renaissance Italy, 1494–95: Antecedents and Effects* (London: Routledge, 2016)

Pepper, Simon, 'The Face of the Siege: Fortification, Tactics and Strategy in the Early Italian Wars', in Christine Shaw (ed.), *Italy and the European Powers: The Impact of War, 1500–1530* (Leiden: Brill, 2006)

Phillips, Gervase, 'England, Scotland and the European "Military Revolution", 1480–1560', delivered to the Richard III Foundation symposium, at the Dixie Grammar School, Market Bosworth in August 2013.
<https://www.academia.edu/10405187/England_Scotland_and_the_European_Military_Revolution_1480–1560>

Phillips, Gervase, 'Henry VIII and Scotland', *History Review* (September 2006), pp.15–20

Phillips, Gervase, 'In the shadow of Flodden: Tactics, Technology and Scottish Military Effectiveness, 1513–1550', *The Scottish Historical Review*, vol. LXXVII, 2: no. 204 (October 1998), pp.162–182

Phillips, Gervase, 'Longbow and Hackbutt: Weapons Technology and Technology Transfer in Early Modern England', *Technology and Culture,* vol. 40, no. 3 (July 1999), pp.576–593

Phillips, Gervase, 'Strategy and Its Limitations: The Anglo–Scots Wars, 1480–1550', *War in History,* vol. 6 No. 4 (1999), pp.396–416

Philips, Gervase, 'The Army of Henry VIII: a reassessment', *Journal for the Society of Army Historical Research*, 75 (1997), pp.8–22

Phillips, Gervase, 'To cry "Home! Home!": Mutiny, morale, and indiscipline in Tudor armies', *The Journal of Military History*, 65 (2001), pp.313–32

Phillips, Gervase, 'Weapons Technology and Technology Transfer in Early Modern England', *Technology and Culture*, vol. 40, no. 3 (July 1999), pp.576–593

Potter, David, 'Sir John Gage, Tudor Courtier and Soldier 1479–1556', *English Historical Review,* cxvii. 474 (November 2002), pp.1109–1146

Raudzens, George, 'Firepower limitations in modern military history', *Journal of the Society for Army Historical Research*, vol. 67, no. 271 (Autumn 1989), pp.130–153

Raudzens, George, 'War–Winning Weapons: The Measurement of Technological Determinism in Military History', *The Journal of Military History*, vol. 54, no. 4 (October 1990), pp.403–434

Richardson, Thom, 'Ballistic testing of Historical Weapons', *Royal Armouries Yearbook*, vol. 3 (1998), pp.50–52

Rogers, Clifford J., 'The development of the longbow in late medieval England and "technological determinism"', *Journal of Medieval History*, 37:3 (2011), pp.321–341

Rogers, Clifford J., 'The Efficacy of the English Longbow: A Reply to Kelly De Vries', *War in History,* vol. 5, no. 2 (1998), pp.233–42

Rogers, Clifford J., 'The Military Revolution: Origins and First Tests Abroad', in Clifford J. Rogers (ed.) *Readings on the Military Transformation of Early Modern Europe* (Boulder: Westview Press (1995), pp.299–333

Roland, Alex, 'Science, Technology, and War', *Technology and Culture*, vol. 36, no. 2 (April 1995), pp.S83–S100

Scott, Douglas D., Joel Bohy, Nathan Boor, Charles Haecker, William Rose, and Patrick Severts, Daniel M. Sivilich, Daniel T. Elliott, Colonial Era Firearm Bullet Performance: A Live Fire Experimental Study for Archaeological Interpretation © 2017 <https://www.academia.edu/32411984/Colonial_Era_Firearm_Bullet_Performance_A_Live_Fire_Experimental_Study_for_Archaeological_Interpretation?email_work_card=title>

Smart, W.R.E., 'On the medical services of the navy and the Army from the accession of Henry VIII to the Restoration', *The British medical Journal* (1874), pp.168–169

Smith, Robert D., 'All Manner of Peeces: Artillery in the Late Medieval Period', *Royal Armouries Yearbook*, vol. 5 (2002), pp.130–138

Smith, Robert D., 'The reconstruction and firing trials of a replica of a 14th-century cannon', *Royal Armouries Yearbook*, vol. 4 (1999), pp.86–94

Smith, Robert D, 'The technology of wrought–iron artillery', *Royal Armouries Yearbook*, vol. 5 (2000), pp.68–79

Sousa, Luís Costa, 'Between Castles and Bastions: Dürer, Luther and the (Circular) Fortification', in 'Martin Luther and Portugal, Dialogues, Tensions and Impacts', ed. Alberto Martins (Lisbon, Edições Húmus, CHAM & Universidade dos Açores, 2019), pp.335–351

Starkey, D., 'Intimacy and Innovation: the Rise of the Privy Chamber 1485–1547', Starkey et al., *The English Court from the Wars of the Roses to the English Civil War* (London: Longman, 1990), p.90

Stewart, David, 'Military Surgeons in the Sixteenth and Seventeenth Centuries', *Journal of the Society for Army Historical Research*, vol. 26, no. 108 (Winter 1948), pp.151–157

Stone, Percy G., 'The French Descent on the Isle of Wight, July1545.' (French Account). *The Antiquary*, Oct 1908; 4, 10; ProQuest pp.368–373

Stone, Percy G., 'The French Descent on the Isle of Wight, July 1545.'(English Account) *The Antiquary*,Nov 1908; 4, 11; ProQuest pp.425–428

Storr, Dr J., 'The Real Role of Small Arms in Combat', *RUSI Defence Systems* (June 2009), pp.44–46

Trim, David J.B., 'The Context of War and Violence in Sixteenth-Century English Society', *Journal of Early Modern History*, vol. 3: issue 3 (1999), pp.233–255

Walton, Stephen J., 'The Bishopsgate Artillery Garden and the First English Ordnance School,' *Journal of the Ordnance Society*, vol. 15 (2003), pp.41–51

Ward, J.P., 'Prices of Weapons and Munitions in Early Sixteenth Century Holland During the Guelders War', *The Journal of European Economic History*, 33 [3] (2004) 585–619 <http://james.wardware.com/J-Europ-Econ-Hist.pdf>

Waterhouse, Robert, 'Tudor bronze guns of the Channel Islands' (2015), pp.82–109 <http://www.christopherlong.co.uk/aanna/papers/WaterhouseR/ TudorBronzeGunsOfTheChannelIslands.pdf>

Watt, James, 'Surgeons of the Mary Rose: The practice of surgery in Tudor England', *The Mariner's Mirror*, 69:1 (1983), pp.3–19

Webb, Henry J., 'Elizabethan Field Artillery', *Military Affairs,* vol. 19, no. 4 (1955), pp.197–202

Webb, Henry J., 'The Science of Gunnery in Elizabethan England', *Isis, The History of Science Society*, vol. 45, no. 1 (May 1954), pp.10–21

White, Lorraine, 'The Experience of Spain's Early Modern Soldiers: Combat, Welfare and Violence', *War In History*, vol. 9, issue 1 (January 2002), pp.1–38

Wiatt, William H., 'The Lost History of Wyatt's Rebellion', in *Renaissance News*, vol. 15, no. 2 (Summer 1962), pp.129–133

Wyman, A.L, 'The Surgeoness: the Female Practitioner of Surgery', *Medical History*, no. 28. (1984) pp.22–41

Online Videos (URLS as June 2021)

ARROWS vs ARMOUR - Medieval Myth Busting
<https://www.youtube.com/watch?v=DBxdTkddHaE&t=27s>

Practical accuracy of an original military flintlock rifle vs the musket
<https://www.youtube.com/watch?v=ZSjvBvCaO00>

Speed test of Mary Rose replica bows
<https://www.youtube.com/watch?v=OyEc8tkGBJc>

Two Men in a Trench: Battle of Flodden
<https://www.youtube.com/watch?v=1WwjO77zht8>

Other Web Pages (URLS as June 2021)

The Battle of Flodden – informational page
<https://www.britishbattles.com/anglo-scottish-war/battle-of-flodden/>

A Utrechtse Leicester-rijksdaalder of 1596
<https://www.centraalmuseum.nl/en/collection/5355-utrechtse-leicester-rijksdaalder>

Forum discussion: 'Ca. 1520: One of the World's Oldest and Finest Matchlock Landsknecht Arquebuses'
<http://www.vikingsword.com/vb/showthread.php?t=18532&highlight=arquebus>

The Commotion Times, Living History Group

Commotion Times is a living history group based in the South of England dedicated to high-quality portrayal of low-quality people. They specialise in portraying rural militia, c.1544–1554, with a slight focus on the Western Rebellion of 1549. As militia Commotion Times has a strong civilian element and welcomes men, women, and families as members.